750 Engaging Illustrations

FOR

preachers, teachers, & writers

750 Engaging Illustrations

FOR

preachers, teachers, & writers

FROM Craig Brian Larson
& *Leadership Journal*

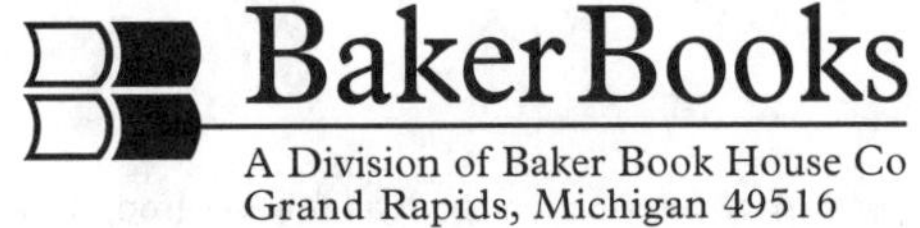

Published by Baker Books
a division of Baker Book House Company
P.O. Box 6287, Grand Rapids, MI 49516-6287

One volume edition published 2002

Previously published in 3 separate volumes: *Illustrations for Preaching and Teaching* (1993), *Contemporary Illustrations for Preachers, Teachers, and Writers* (1996), and *Choice Contemporary Stories and Illustrations* (1998).

Printed in the United States of America

Library of Congress Cataloging-in-Publication Data

Larson, Craig Brian.
[Illustrations for preaching and teaching]
750 engaging illustrations for preachers, teachers & writers / Craig Brian Larson.
p. cm.
First work originally published: Illustrations for preaching and teaching. Grand Rapids, Mich.: Baker Books, 1993. 2nd work originally published: Contemporary illustrations for preachers, teachers, and writers. Grand Rapids, Mich.: Baker Books, 1996. 3rd work originally published: Choice contemporary stories and illustrations. Grand Rapids, Mich.: Baker Books, 1998. Includes bibliographical references and index.
ISBN 0-8010-9155-1 (pbk.)
1. Homiletical illustrations. I. Title: Seven hundred and fifty engaging illustrations for preachers, teachers & writers. II. Larson, Craig Brian. Contemporary illustrations for preachers, teachers, and writers. III. Larson, Craig Brian. Choice contemporary stories and illustrations, IV. Title.
BV4225.3 .L37 2002
251′.08—dc21 2002011735

For current information about all releases from Baker Book House, visit our web site:
http://www.bakerbooks.com

Contents

Introduction

I am a pastor who preaches weekly, and I have molded this book to meet the needs I myself sense.

I need contemporary illustrations from the world we live in. While I illustrate from my own life, I also want to illustrate from the world at large, from our common culture. Contemporary illustrations are relevant and interesting to our media-engaged listeners.

I need an illustration book to have an extensive index. I put the bulk of my work and time into studying the biblical text, so I need to be able to access illustrations quickly. Therefore, if anything, I have gone overboard with the alternative subjects that accompany each illustration and are indexed in the endnotes. I have done that for several reasons. First because we all use different handles to lay hold of the same idea. One person might look for an illustration with the word *faith* and another with the word *belief;* or you might look for the opposite, *doubt.* So the alternative subjects often cover the waterfront of synonyms to make it easier to find what you need through the index. In addition, illustrations can be applied in numerous ways, and so the major heading at the top of each illustration indicates how I have applied each one, while alternative subjects at the end of the illustration give other slants that you could take with the same story. For example, a story of an argument between husband and wife could be used to illustrate marriage or anger or conflict or reconciliation or the power of the tongue. Therefore, although this book has 750 illustrations, it in effect has many times that.

I need believable illustrations that have specific places, dates, and people's names, as well as documented sources. In this book, sources are usually mentioned in the illustration itself, and the endnotes typically contain full references that not only allow you to quote the date that an article appeared if you desire but also to research the story for further details at the library or online.

I need variety and balance. In my selection of material I used an editorial grid that calls for a roughly equal number of illustrations that are positive or negative, figurative or literal, and from Christian or secular sources.

The copyright law of the United States allows for the "fair use" of a limited number of words from other sources, and I have made frequent use of that liberty. Hence my thanks for the talented writers who have contributed unawares. For longer excerpts I have secured the permission of authors and publishers, and for their gracious permission I am deeply grateful.

This book is not intended to make a pastor's life easier; its purpose is to make your sermons more effective. May the Lord Jesus Christ use these illustrations to advance his truth, bring his lost sheep into the fold, strengthen his precious people, and build his glorious church.

Craig Brian Larson

Abundant Life 1

Many men would love to lead the life of Sean Connery. Tall, handsome, and dashing, Connery played the glamorous part of 007 in six James Bond movies. Connery travels the world to shoot movies in places as exotic as equatorial Africa or the Orient. In addition to acting, Connery works as the executive producer of films, a position of considerable power.

Yet when asked in an interview why, at age sixty-two, he continues to act, Connery gave a surprising reply: "Because I get the opportunity to be somebody better and more interesting than I am."

Many people feel like Connery. Their lives aren't all that they could be. They aren't as good as they should be. Something is missing that even glamorous acting roles cannot fulfill.

Only Christ makes a person's life what it can be, should be, and must be.

Christlikeness, Salvation
John 10:10

Date used __________ Place ____________________

Acceptance 2

In the *Atlanta Journal-Constitution*, Doug Cumming writes:

> Lonnie J. Edwards, a physical-education instructor . . . was explaining square-dancing to his fifth-grade class at Hooper Alexander Elementary School in DeKalb County, Georgia. As he called the children to their places, boy-girl, boy-girl, Nancy, a little redheaded girl, said she was not coming. She started to cry and walked away, carrying a towel over her hands.
>
> Edwards approached the twelve-year-old child cautiously. With her back to the other students, Nancy privately revealed why she couldn't possibly hold hands with boys: she had been born with only her pinkies and two partial fingers. Amazingly, she had hidden her deformity from teachers—she was able to hold a pencil—but the students knew about it and were cruel to her.
>
> Gathering himself, Edwards said, "Nancy, we can't do anything about this problem, but I can help you overcome it and become the best you can be. Now I want you to hold your head up. From this moment on, you will no longer use this as a limitation."
>
> Slowly, Nancy gave him the towel, which he never returned. Four days later Edwards began the square dance as Nancy's partner. Soon all the children seemed willing—even eager—to touch Nancy's hands.
>
> That was in 1971. Over the next two years, Edwards continued to encourage her.
>
> Today, Nancy Miller, thirty-eight, can do almost anything she sets her mind to, including play the piano and type about sixty-five words a minute. Married, she lives in Orlando with her husband and four children. . . .
>
> "I grew up because of one man," Miller says.

Do you know someone crippled by shame? In the presence of others, be the first to show you accept that person. Acceptance is a precious gift we all can give others.

Community, Love, Shame
Matt. 8:1–4; Rom. 15:7

Date used __________ Place ____________________

Acceptance 3

According to the *Chicago Tribune,* on Monday, August 26, 1996, tragedy struck a Fort Lauderdale, Florida, family. Two boys found their twelve-year-old brother Samuel dead in their yard. He had hanged himself from a tree. Beneath the tree were a step stool and a flashlight.

There was little mystery about what had provoked Samuel to end his life. Samuel had a weight problem, and this would have been his first day at a new school. He had told his family that he was nervous about going to school because he was afraid of the teasing that would likely come from the other children.

There are few things more painful than shame. One of the great kindnesses we can do for others is to take away their false shame through acceptance and affirmation.

Affirmation, Appearance, Cruelty, Fear, Humiliation, Insults, Mocking, Peer Pressure, Shame, Suicide, Youth
Ps. 34:4–5; Rom. 15:1–7; 1 Thess. 5:11; Heb. 12:2

Date used __________ Place ____________________

Accountability 4

On February 26, 1995, Barings, the oldest bank in Britain, announced it was seeking bankruptcy protection after losing nearly one billion dollars in a stock gamble. At the time Barings went under, the bank held assets for Queen Elizabeth, some $100 million according to *Time* magazine.

In late 1994, the chief trader at Barings's Singapore office began betting big on Japan's Nikkei market. Then disaster struck. An earthquake hit Kobe, Japan, and on January 23, 1995, the Nikkei plunged more than one thousand points.

Barings Bank lost big money. But instead of cutting his losses, Barings's Singapore trader doubled his investment, apparently hoping that the Nikkei would rebound. It didn't. As the Nikkei continued to plummet, Barings's London office put up nearly $900 million to support its falling position on the Singapore investments. Finally Barings ran out of capital and declared bankruptcy.

How could one twenty-eight-year-old trader in Singapore lose nearly a billion dollars and ruin a 233-year-old British bank? According to *Time*, the problem was lack of supervision.

> London allowed [the Singapore trader] to take control of both the trading desk and the backroom settlement operation in Singapore. It is a mix that can be—and in this case was—toxic. . . . For a trader to keep his own books is like a schoolboy getting to grade his own tests; the temptation to cheat can be overwhelming, particularly if the stakes are high enough.

Without accountability, temptation becomes all the more tempting. Accountability protects us from ourselves.

Deception, Integrity, Management, Risk, Temptation

Prov. 4:26; 10:9; 14:8; 2 Cor. 8:21; Eph. 5:21

Date used __________ Place ____________________

Acknowledging God 5

In *World Christian,* John Huffman describes one unforgettable moment with his daughter. He had been away from home for several weeks on an overseas missions trip. When his airplane landed, he could hardly wait to see his wife and four children, but he and the other passengers were detained in customs for two hours. Finally the customs officials allowed Huffman to proceed to the lobby, where hundreds of people were anxiously waiting for family and friends. Huffman writes:

> There was such a press of bodies, I knew I would not be able to pick my children out until I walked up the ramp, past security, and got out into the open. But my three-year-old daughter, who had managed to squeeze her way to the front of the crowd, began screaming at the top of her lungs, "Daddy! Daddy! That's my daddy!" She must have shouted that at least five times, when suddenly she broke free from the crowd, and bolted past the security guards, still yelling, "Daddy! Daddy! That's my daddy!" She literally flew into my arms and began kissing and hugging me. What a welcome! I have never felt so loved and acknowledged in my life. It was a wonderful, fulfilling moment that even today brings a warm and happy feeling.

That, says John Huffman, is what God feels like when we acknowledge him in worship.

Children, God the Father, Worship
John 4:23–24

Date used __________ Place ____________________

Admonishment 6

On Monday, February 6, 1995, according to the *Chicago Tribune,* a Detroit bus driver finished his shift on the Route 21 bus and headed for the terminal. But somehow he took a wrong turn. He didn't arrive at the terminal at the scheduled time of 7:19 P.M., and a short time later his supervisors started looking for him. Meanwhile the driver's wife called the terminal and reported her husband might be disoriented from medication he was taking.

For six hours, the forty-foot city bus and its driver could not be found. Finally the state police found the bus and driver—two hundred miles northwest of Detroit. The bus was motoring slowly down a rural two-lane road, weaving slightly from side to side. The police pulled the bus over, and the driver said he was lost.

A police news release later stated, "The driver had no idea where he was and agreed he had made a wrong turn somewhere. Apparently this had not occurred to him during the four hours he drove without finding the bus depot."

Unless we confront those who have taken a wrong turn in life, they may never regain their orientation.

Backsliding, Confrontation, Confusion,
Intervention, Lostness, Shepherding
Gal. 6:1–2; James 5:19–20

Date used __________ Place ____________________

Adoption 7

In *Reader's Digest,* a contributor told of an Aunt Ruby and Uncle Arnie who had adopted a baby boy after five years of trying unsuccessfully to conceive. To their surprise, a short time after the adoption, Aunt Ruby discovered she was pregnant, and she later gave birth to a boy.

One day when the two boys were eight and nine years old, the teller of the story was visiting Aunt Ruby, and a woman in the neighborhood came to visit.

Observing the children at play, the woman asked, "Which boy is yours, Ruby?"

"Both of them," Aunt Ruby replied.

The caller persisted. "But I mean, which one is adopted?"

Aunt Ruby did not hesitate. In her finest hour, she looked straight at her guest and replied, "I've forgotten."

When we are adopted as God's children, we quickly come to cherish our heavenly Father's forgetfulness. For he chooses to forget our sins, to forget our wayward past, and to give us the full rights of sons or daughters. He treats us as if we had never sinned.

Forgetting Sin, Forgiveness, God the Father, Salvation
Rom. 8:1–17; Eph. 1:5; Heb. 8:12

Date used __________ Place ____________________

Adultery 8

A study published in the *Journal of the National Cancer Institute* confirmed what God has always known. Adultery is bad for you. One of the many ways it harms people is by increasing a woman's risk of cervical cancer.

According to the Associated Press, the study found that women are five to eleven times more likely to develop cervical cancer if they or their husbands have numerous sexual partners. Cervical cancer is directly linked to HPV, a virus commonly spread by sexual intercourse.

"Male behavior is the important thing in this cancer," said Dr. Keerti Shah, a professor at Johns Hopkins University School of Medicine and the coauthor of the study. "In effect, the husband takes cancer home to his wife." Dr. Shah explains that men who have many sexual partners are very likely to carry HPV home and that up to 97 percent of cervical cancers are infected with that virus.

In the study group, wives whose husbands had twenty-one or more sexual partners were eleven times more likely to develop cervical cancer. Wives whose husbands frequented prostitutes were eight times more likely to develop cervical cancer.

As always, God commands what is moral because he is looking out for our welfare. Nothing is more healthful than righteousness.

Health, Immorality, Righteousness, Sex,
Ten Commandments, Unfaithfulness
Exod. 20:14

Date used __________ Place ____________________

Adversity 9

Farmers in southern Alabama were accustomed to planting one crop every year—cotton. They would plow as much ground as they could and plant their crop. Year after year they lived by cotton.

Then one year the dreaded boll weevil devastated the whole area. So the next year the farmers mortgaged their homes and planted cotton again, hoping for a good harvest. But as the cotton began to grow, the insect came back and destroyed the crop, wiping out most of the farms.

The few who survived those two years of the boll weevil decided to experiment the third year, so they planted something they'd never planted before—peanuts. And peanuts proved so hardy and the market proved so ravenous for that product that the farmers who survived the first two years reaped profits that third year that enabled them to pay off all their debts. They planted peanuts from then on and prospered greatly.

Then you know what those farmers did? They spent some of their new wealth to erect in the town square a monument—to the boll weevil. If it hadn't been for the boll weevil, they never would have discovered peanuts. They learned that even out of disaster there can be great delight.

Change, God's Goodness

Date used __________ Place ______________________

Advice 10

Former President Richard Nixon gave and took a lot of advice. In his presidential campaign against John F. Kennedy, however, he paid the price for not listening to the wise counsel of Dwight Eisenhower. Otto Friedrich in *Time* magazine writes:

> Eisenhower and others warned Nixon not to accept Kennedy's challenge to a televised debate—Nixon was the Vice President, after all, and far better known than the junior Senator from Massachusetts—but Nixon took pride in his long experience as a debater. He also ignored advice to rest up for the debate and went on campaigning strenuously until the last minute. So, what a record 80 million Americans saw on their TV screens was a devastating contrast. Kennedy looked fresh, tanned, vibrant; Nixon looked unshaven, baggy-eyed, surly. The era of the politics of TV imagery had begun, and the debates were a major victory for Kennedy.

Kennedy, of course, went on to win the presidency with 50.4 percent of the popular vote and Nixon a hairwidth behind at 49.6 percent. Most analysts say if it hadn't been for the debacle at the televised debate, Nixon would have won the election.

Counsel, Decisions, Pride, Teachability
Prov. 15:22

Date used __________ Place ____________________

Anger 11

In *Wishful Thinking,* Frederick Buechner writes:

Of the seven deadly sins, anger is possibly the most fun. To lick your wounds, to smack your lips over grievances long past, to roll over your tongue the prospect of bitter confrontations still to come, to savor to the last toothsome morsel both the pain you are given and the pain you are giving back—in many ways it is a feast fit for a king. The chief drawback is that what you are wolfing down is yourself. The skeleton at the feast is you.

Forgiveness, Grievances, Revenge
1 Cor. 13:5; 1 Tim. 2:8

Date used __________ Place ____________________

Anger 12

Eric Zorn writes in the *Chicago Tribune* of a tragic accident that shows the terrible power of anger.

According to Zorn, a man and woman were driving a van in the far left lane of Chicago's Northwest Tollway in April 1994. In back were their two children. A white Cadillac driven by an ex-convict suddenly pulled up behind them, tailgating mere inches from their bumper. The man driving the van slowed down. The Cadillac driver pulled into the right lane, passed the van, and then swerved suddenly back in front of the van, so suddenly that the van driver felt he had to swerve to avoid a collision.

The white Cadillac sped away.

The van driver accelerated and gave chase. He eventually pulled alongside the white Cadillac and reportedly began yelling and screaming. According to a witness, the two men gestured angrily at each other.

The driver of the Cadillac then pulled a handgun and fired at the van. The bullet entered the side of the van and hit the baby girl, entering under her left ear and exiting above her right ear. The little girl lived, but she is blind in one eye, half-blind in the other, partially deaf, and suffers severe mental and physical disabilities.

The man who fired the bullet is in jail.

The parents of the little girl must now live with the terrible pain of regret.

Anger usually escalates—often in tragic, tragic ways.

Forgiveness, Regret, Self-Control, Temper
Matt. 5:21–22, 38–42; Eph. 4:26–31; James 1:19–20

Date used __________ Place ____________________

Anger 13

Anger is hazardous to your health.

In a study conducted by the Gallup Organization and reported in 1994, Philadelphia ranked first among U.S. cities on what was called the "hostility index." The hostility index was based on a nine-question scale that asked people how they felt about such things as loud rock music, supermarket checkout lines, and traffic jams. Other cities on the hostility top five were New York, Cleveland, Chicago, and Detroit. At the bottom of the hostility index were Des Moines, Minneapolis, Denver, Seattle, and Honolulu.

Medical experts looking at the results felt it was no coincidence that the cities that rated high on the hostility index also had higher death rates. Commenting on the study, Dr. Redford Williams of Duke University Medical School said, "Anger kills. There is a strong correlation between hostility and death rates. The angrier people are and the more cynical they are, the shorter their life span."

Emotions, Health, Hostility
Rom. 8:5–7; Gal. 5:19–23

Date used __________ Place ____________________

Anger 14

What does it take to turn a person into a Judas? What motivates someone to betray deep-seated loyalties?

Unresolved anger and resentment, for one thing. Consider the story of Earl Pitts, FBI agent turned Soviet spy.

According to Evan Thomas in *Newsweek,* Pitts was raised on a farm in Missouri and was recognized as a Future Farmer of America. His parents said they disciplined him firmly but fairly. He was a captain in the army who regarded himself as a patriot. Even today he is described by his wife as a "good man." So what happened?

After getting his law degree and serving as a military policeman for six years, in 1983 Pitts realized a lifelong ambition by going to work for the FBI. In 1987 he was assigned to the New York office, and there his troubles began. He did not see how he could afford to live in the Big Apple on his $25,000 salary.

Thomas writes, "Morale in the office was poor, and petty cheating on expense accounts was rampant. Burdened with debt from student loans, Pitts had to ask his father . . . for a loan. He felt humiliated. Pitts later told a psychiatrist that he was 'overwhelmed' by a sense of rage at the FBI."

One morning he came up with the idea of spying for the KGB. That way he could kill two birds with one stone: he could solve his money problems and get back at his bosses. He later told a psychiatrist, "I was shoved by the bureaucracy, and I shoved back."

Over the next seven years Pitts worked as a Soviet spy and for his services received $224,000. When he was finally caught and convicted, the judge sentenced him to twenty-seven years in prison. At his sentencing the judge asked him point-blank why he had become a traitor. Earl Pitts replied, "I gave in to an unreasonable anger."

Never allow anger to fester. Deal with anger as God prescribes.

Betrayal, Greed, Malice, Resentment
Jonah 4; Matt. 5:21–22; Mark 14:3–11;
John 12:4–8; Eph. 4:26–27

Date used __________ Place ____________________

Anger 15

In *Scope* Shirley Belleranti shows the negative impact of anger on our most important relationships:

> I remember one summer day when my ten-year-old son and a friend were getting a pitcher of lemonade from the refrigerator. I'd spent hours that morning scrubbing, waxing, and polishing the kitchen floor, so I warned the boys not to spill anything. They tried so hard to be careful that they innocently bumped a tray of eggs on the door shelf. Of course, it fell, splattering eggs all over my clean floor.
>
> The boys' eyes widened with alarm as I exploded angrily. "Get out of here—now!" I shouted, while they headed for the door.
>
> By the time I'd finished cleaning up the mess, I had calmed down. To make amends, I set a tray of cookies on the table, along with the pitcher of lemonade and some glasses. But when I called the boys, there was no answer—they'd gone somewhere else to play, somewhere where my angry voice wouldn't reach them.

Anger separates us from those we want to be near. Anger shatters intimacy.

Child Rearing, Family, Home,
Perfectionism, Self-Control, Temper
Eph. 6:4; Col. 3:8; James 1:19–20

Date used __________ Place ____________________

Anxiety 16

How can we quiet our fears and worries?

The answer is something like the new technology being developed to quiet noise in the workplace. Several companies now market headphones that emit what is called antinoise.

"The principle behind all antinoise devices is the same," writes Philip Elmer-Dewitt in *Time*. "Noise is basically a pressure wave traveling through the air. Antinoise is the mirror image of that wave, an equal and opposite vibration exactly 180 degrees out of phase with the noise to be blocked. When noise and antinoise collide, they interact with what is called destructive interference, canceling each other out."

Airport baggage handlers can now wear headphones equipped with a tiny microphone that "samples sound waves at the wearer's ear, processes them through special circuitry, and broadcasts countertones that cancel the offending sounds in midair. Result: silence, or something close to it."

In the same way, we can cancel worries and fears with the antinoise of God's truth.

Devotional Life, Faith, Fear, Peace, Promises, Trust, Truth
Eph. 6:16–17

Date used __________ Place ____________________

Apathy 17

In *Youthworker Journal,* Will Eisenhower recalls one night as a counselor at a Bible camp:

It had been an exhausting day; the guys in my cabin were asleep; and I was dead to the world. Then there came a dim awareness: Ants were crawling all over my body. I was so tired, and sleep felt so good, that I actually resisted rousing myself. I knew that if I were roused even a little bit, I would have to acknowledge that my sleeping bag had become an ant freeway. I didn't want to know the awful truth, so for at least several seconds I tried to fight it. At some deep level, I told myself that sleep was the reality and the ants were a dream.

Apathy is sort of like sleeping through an ant attack. Waking up means I have to recognize that although foxes have safe places to hide, the Son of Man doesn't, and his followers don't either. This world is fundamentally opposed to me, and wants to attack me when I am least prepared for it. No wonder some of us would rather stay asleep.

Watchfulness, World

Date used __________ Place ____________________

Apology 18

Thomas "Hollywood" Henderson played football for the Dallas Cowboys from 1975 to 1979. On the field the first-round draft pick starred at middle linebacker. Off the field, according to the *New York Times,* he led a life of which he is now ashamed, the life of a crack cocaine addict. Coach Tom Landry eventually found out about Henderson's habit, and a few days before Thanksgiving 1979 he fired him.

Unfortunately, Henderson didn't learn his lesson. He moved to California to pursue an acting career and continued his drug habit. Finally in November 1983 the law caught up with him, and he went to prison for more than two years.

That was a turning point for Thomas "Hollywood" Henderson. He overcame his cocaine addiction and eventually moved back to Austin, Texas, where he began working as a drug and alcohol counselor. He was clean of drugs and helping others get clean, but something deep within his conscience still troubled him. He was haunted by what the fans of the Dallas Cowboys remembered of him.

He knew he had to do one more difficult thing, and thirteen years after being arrested he finally mustered the courage. He wrote an open letter to Cowboy fans and sent it to the *Dallas Morning News,* where it was published on Sunday, January 5, 1997.

"I had arrived in Dallas," he wrote, "as a 21-year-old, wide-eyed, bigmouth rookie from Langston University as the Cowboys' No. 1 draft choice. I had a covert life in the fast lane of stardom, cocaine and sex. . . . I want to apologize to Dallas, the Cowboys, fans of football, fans of Thomas Henderson, and the kids then and now for what I did thirteen years ago. I take full responsibility and have paid the dues. . . . I wanted to commit suicide on many, many occasions. What you thought of me haunted me."

Time cannot heal the conscience. Only a sincere apology can do that.

Community, Confession, Conscience, Guilt, Repentance
Luke 18:9–14; 1 John 1:8–10

Date used __________ Place ____________________

Appearance 19

In the *Pentecostal Evangel,* church leader T. Ray Rachels writes:

Most of the famous people photographed by Yousuf Karsh and included in his book, *The Faces of Greatness,* were not physically attractive. Somebody studied the faces of the 90 people in the book and determined that 35 had moles or warts; 13 had noticeable freckles or liver spots; 20 had obvious traces of acne or other pimples; and 2 had highly visible scars.

But the blemishes did not deter these people. Thornton Wilder, the playwright; Richard Rodgers, the composer; Picasso, the painter; and many others had obvious imperfections. But what might have embarrassed some just added character when they posed before the truthful lens of the great photographer.

Weaknesses do not deter those whom God has gifted.

Blemishes, Character, Faults, Gifts, Greatness,
Ministry, Talents, Weakness
1 Sam. 16:7; 2 Cor. 12:7–10

Date used __________ Place ____________________

Appearance 20

Jeff Pierce was the 1994 captain of the Chevrolet-L.A. Sheriff professional cycling team and a top competitor. In 1987 he won one stage of the Tour de France.

But in 1994, according to *USA Today,* he accepted an interesting and potentially dangerous assignment. To prepare for an article he planned to write for a magazine called *Bicycle Guide,* Pierce worked for a month as a bike messenger in downtown New York. On the streets for eleven hours a day, he dodged taxis and buses, sometimes reaching a speed of thirty-nine miles an hour on his custom-made, $2,500 racing bike. Was he worried about this expensive bike being stolen as he dashed into buildings to deliver his packages?

You bet he was. To thwart thieves, Pierce wrapped duct tape around the frame of his bike and spray-painted it black. His bike looked like a piece of junk, and his plan worked. No one touched it.

We cannot always judge value by appearance.

Character, Externals, Judgment, Ministry
1 Sam. 16:7; John 7:24; 1 Cor. 1:18–31

Date used __________ Place ____________________

Appetites 21

Frenchman Michel Lotito has an iron gut.

For some reason Lotito likes to eat metal. In the past twenty-five years, says writer Rosie Mestel, Lotito has eaten eleven bicycles, seven shopping carts, a metal coffin, a cash register, a washing machine, a television, and 660 feet of fine chain.

Lotito says it wasn't easy eating his first bicycle: "I started with the metal and moved on to the tires," he recalls. "It was really difficult to stay that extra day to finish off the rubber. Metal's tasteless, but rubber is horrible." Now Lotito swallows pieces of tire and frame together.

But none of that can compare with his biggest meal: a Cessna. That's right, Lotito has eaten an entire light airplane, 2,500 pounds of aluminum, steel, vinyl, Plexiglas, and rubber.

With a meal like that he cuts the metal into pieces about the size of his fingernail and consumes about two pounds a day.

Most people would agree that Michel Lotito has an unhealthy appetite.

When we first come to Christ, we have appetites just as unhealthy. New believers need to change their appetites from what is not food at all to what is true food for the soul.

Devotional Life, Entertainment, Thoughts
Rom. 16:18; Phil. 4:8; 1 Peter 2:1–3

Date used __________ Place ____________________

Arguing 22

According to the *Chicago Tribune,* one husband and wife from London, England, had more than their share of arguments. One day in 1994 they argued so sharply that the wife got in their car and ran over him. The husband, who was fifty-five years old, lived, but he suffered forty-five leg fractures and a skull fracture. He was hospitalized for five months, and his wife was thrown into jail for grievous bodily harm.

Then the husband did a remarkable—and some might say dubious—thing. He asked the court to set her free. "I can't live without her," said the man, now wheelchair-bound. In response to his request, the Newcastle court suspended his wife's sentence.

The husband told the *Daily Telegraph* (London), "We are back together and happy," but he added, "She's very argumentative."

Although this man displayed some remarkable forgiveness, that marriage is clearly not made in heaven. An argumentative attitude is stubborn, ugly, and destructive.

Fights, Forgiveness, Marriage, Peacemakers
Matt. 5:9; Phil. 2:14; 2 Tim. 2:23–24

Date used __________ Place ____________________

Assumptions 23

A traveler, between flights at an airport, went to a lounge and bought a small package of cookies. Then she sat down and began reading a newspaper. Gradually, she became aware of a rustling noise. From behind her paper, she was flabbergasted to see a neatly dressed man helping himself to her cookies. Not wanting to make a scene, she leaned over and took a cookie herself.

A minute or two passed, and then came more rustling. He was helping himself to another cookie! By this time, they had come to the end of the package, but she was so angry she didn't dare allow herself to say anything. Then, as if to add insult to injury, the man broke the remaining cookie in two, pushed half across to her, and ate the other half and left.

Still fuming some time later when her flight was announced, the woman opened her handbag to get her ticket. To her shock and embarrassment, there she found her pack of unopened cookies!

How wrong our assumptions can be.

Misunderstandings, Kindness

Date used __________ Place ____________________

Assumptions 24

Colin Rizzio, a seventeen-year-old high school senior—and a member of the school math club—from Peterborough, New Hampshire, took the SAT in October 1996 in preparation for college. As he took the test, one math question caught his attention. He blackened the circle for answer "D," but he thought it just might be that the testmakers viewed the problem differently, and that as a result they would mark his answer wrong. So he made a mental note of the problem and afterward went to his math teacher for his opinion. The math teacher agreed with Colin.

Colin then sent an e-mail letter to the Educational Testing Service. The ETS receives numerous letters of this sort, but no one had found an error in the SAT since 1982. Proposed questions for the test are tried out on a battery of thousands of students and dozens of math teachers before they ever make it to the actual SAT. Nevertheless, to their embarrassment, this time the testmakers were wrong, and Colin was right.

The error was based on an assumption. Those who had written the question assumed the numerical value for the letter "a" in one equation was positive. Colin saw that the equation was such that the numerical value for "a" could be positive or negative, which would affect the answer.

False assumptions on an SAT can lead to error. False assumptions about life and reality are far more harmful. They are especially dangerous because they are rarely questioned.

False assumptions are what keep many people from believing in Christ.

Beliefs, Creation, Evolution, Knowledge, Theology, Truth, Unbelievers
Matt. 11:2–6; John 7:45–52; 9:1–41; 1 Cor. 1:18–25; 2 Cor. 10–11

Date used __________ Place ____________________

Assurance 25

General Ron Griffith served in the U.S. Army during the Desert Storm War in Iraq. As the battle neared, Griffith was apprehensive about how many casualties the 24,000 troops he commanded would suffer. In *New Man* magazine, Gene Bradley and Wes Pippert write:

> Griffith had estimated between 1,000 and 2,000 casualties during a war that might last between four and six months. After all, the Iraqis—on paper—probably outnumbered the American forces 2- or even 3-to-1. Worse, the intelligence showed the Iraqis had moved chemical weapons into position and Hussein had given his commanders authority to use them.
>
> A Christian, Griffith spoke about his concerns with chaplain Dan Davis. "Let me tell you something," Davis said. "Before we left Germany, we had a prayer group that met every morning in Stuttgart as the war drew near. We prayed there would be no war. But once it became certain there would be war, we prayed that the air war might be successful and that we would not have to put our ground forces into this potential cauldron.
>
> "We prayed that God's will be done, whatever it was.
>
> "Now, I want to tell you something that is not an instinct. This is not intuition. It is a full assurance from God. I can tell you the attack will be hugely successful, more successful than anybody has envisioned. The war will be short, very short, and the casualties will be few, very, very few."
>
> Until this conversation, Griffith had not finished his work before 1:30 A.M. each night. Even when he went to bed, he couldn't sleep.
>
> "I kept thinking about casualties," he recalls. "Am I doing everything I can to assure they have the best chance possible to get through this thing? Have we thought of everything? I thought about the number of people I would have to send back in body bags to their mothers and fathers and spouses."
>
> But after his talk with Davis, Griffith went back to his van, zipped up his sleeping bag and slept for five hours—the best night's sleep he had in six weeks. A great sense of calm fell over him.
>
> "I felt God's presence with me. I took Dan's words as absolute truth. More important, that great calm stayed with me."
>
> Gen. Norman Schwarzkopf wanted the Iraqis to believe that the Americans would attack straight ahead into Kuwait. So, the decision was made for Griffith's 1st Armored Division, as part of the U.S. 7th

Corps, to move far to the west, then sweep north and then east in a big "hooking" movement that would catch the Republican Guard from the rear.

The Americans attacked on February 24, 1991. The war was over in four days. Thousands were not killed, nor were hundreds. Only four soldiers were killed. Was it a miracle? Griffith says yes.

Assurance, even in the most trying circumstances, is one of God's great gifts to his children.

Confidence, Faith, Leading, Peace, Prayer,
Revelation, Word of Knowledge, Worry
Heb. 11:1; 1 Peter 5:7

Date used __________ Place ____________________

Atonement 26

Ron Rand writes in *For Fathers Who Aren't in Heaven:*

Michael usually takes his family out each week to see a movie or sports event. When they come home, they make a fire in the fireplace and pop popcorn.

During one of these evenings, little Billy made a real pest of himself in the car on the drive home, so he was punished by being sent to sit in his bedroom while the rest of the family had popcorn. After the family had the fire going and the popcorn ready, Michael went back to Billy's room and said, "You go out with the others. I'll stay here and take your punishment."

Through Michael's action, the entire family experienced a vivid example of what Jesus did for everyone.

Love, Fathers

Date used __________ Place ____________________

Atonement 27

One winter's night in 1935, it is told, Fiorello LaGuardia, the irrepressible mayor of New York, showed up at a night court in the poorest ward of the city. He dismissed the judge for the evening and took over the bench. That night a tattered old woman, charged with stealing a loaf of bread, was brought before him. She defended herself by saying, "My daughter's husband has deserted her. She is sick, and her children are starving."

The shopkeeper refused to drop the charges, saying, "It's a bad neighborhood, your honor, and she's got to be punished to teach other people a lesson."

LaGuardia sighed. He turned to the old woman and said, "I've got to punish you; the law makes no exceptions. Ten dollars or ten days in jail." However, even while pronouncing sentence, La Guardia reached into his pocket, took out a ten-dollar bill, and threw it into his hat with these famous words: "Here's the ten-dollar fine, which I now remit, and furthermore, I'm going to fine everyone in the courtroom fifty cents for living in a town where a person has to steal bread so that her grandchildren can eat. Mr. Bailiff, collect the fines and give them to the defendant."

The following day, a New York newspaper reported: "Forty-seven dollars and fifty cents was turned over to a bewildered old grandmother who had stolen a loaf of bread to feed her starving grandchildren. Making forced donations were a red-faced storekeeper, seventy petty criminals, and a few New York policemen."

Law, Mercy

Date used __________ Place ____________________

Atonement 28

How can we atone for our sins?

A Canadian Press photo shows how one man from Havana, Cuba, tried to appease God's wrath. The man is lying on his back on a dirt road. Attached to his ankle is a chain several feet long. The other end of the chain is wrapped around a rock. The caption explains that the bearded man is inch by inch pulling the rock on a pilgrimage to a sanctuary dedicated to St. Lazarus.

This man's devotion is misguided, for we can do nothing—absolutely nothing—to atone for our sins. God has provided instead the free gift of forgiveness through faith in Jesus Christ.

Cross, Redemption, Salvation
Rom. 3–4; Eph. 2:8–9; 1 John 1:8–2:2

Date used __________ Place ____________________

Attitude 29

The March 1988 *Rotarian* tells the story of a certain organization offering a bounty of $5,000 for wolves captured alive. It turned Sam and Jed into fortune hunters. Day and night they scoured the mountains and forests looking for their valuable prey.

Exhausted one night, they fell asleep dreaming of their potential fortune. Suddenly, Sam awoke to see that they were surrounded by about fifty wolves with flaming eyes and bared teeth. He nudged his friend and said, "Jed, wake up! We're rich!"

Faith, Trials

Date used __________ Place ____________________

Attitude 30

On January 13, 1997, reports Richard Conniff in *National Geographic,* adventurer Steve Fossett climbed into the cockpit of a hot-air balloon in St. Louis, Missouri, and rose into the sky with the ambition of being the first to circle the globe in a balloon. After three days he had crossed the Atlantic and was flying at 24,500 feet eastward over Africa.

The prevailing wind carried him on a direct course for the country of Libya, and that was a problem. Libya had refused him permission to fly in its air space, which meant he could be shot down. Of course, hot-air balloons cannot turn. When a change of direction is called for, what they must do is change altitude. At a higher or lower altitude a balloonist can usually find a crosswind blowing in a different direction.

Fossett vented helium, and the balloon dropped 6,300 feet, where it came under the control of a wind blowing southeast. Fossett skirted safely south of Libya, then heated the balloon, rose almost 10,000 feet and caught an easterly wind, which carried him back on course.

Although Fossett got only as far as India, he set dual records for the longest distance (10,360 miles) and duration (6 days, 2 hours, 44 minutes) in balloon flight.

Bertrand Piccard, another man seeking to sail around the world in a balloon, sees a similarity between balloon flight and daily life. "In the balloon," says Piccard, "you are prisoners of the wind, and you go only in the direction of the wind. In life people think they are prisoners of circumstance. But in the balloon, as in life, you can change altitude, and when you change altitude, you change direction. You are not a prisoner anymore."

A person changes altitude by changing attitude.

Faith, Humility, Praise, Submission, Thanksgiving, Trust
Eph. 4:23–24; Phil. 2:5; 1 Thess. 5:16–18;
James 4:1–10; 1 Peter 5:5–7

Date used __________ Place ____________________

Authority 31

In *Christian Reader* Erma Landis writes:

For decades, anyone living within five or six miles of the hat factory in Denver, Pennsylvania, set their clocks and watches by the sirens the factory set off five days a week. At 5:30 A.M., the wake-up siren would begin the day followed by the starting, lunchtime, and quitting sirens at the designated times.

When the siren system was eventually disbanded, a friend of mine was reminiscing with the timekeeper about his job. "What did you use to determine the exact time?"

With a twinkle in his eye, the man reached in his pocket and pulled out a child's Mickey Mouse watch.

Some experts are not as authoritative as they seem.

Evolution, False Prophets, False Teachers, Inspiration, Truth
Mark 13:22; 1 Cor. 4:20; 2 Cor. 11:4–6; 2 Tim. 3:16–17

Date used __________ Place ____________________

Balance 32

You may want to have a fire extinguisher handy when you eat horseradish made by Ellen LaBombard of Fairmont, New York. LaBombard horseradish comes in four varieties: Regular Hot, X Hot, XXX Hot, and Too Darn Hot. One of the ingredients in her hottest horseradish used to be a secret ingredient: allyl isothiocyanate. That spice is no longer a secret.

According to the *Chicago Tribune,* on February 13, 1995, Ellen accidentally spilled a one-and-a-half-quart bottle of the spice in her basement. She plugged in a fan to try to air out the room, but the overwhelming vapors forced her out. She called 911, but when the Fairmont firefighters came, they too were overwhelmed—and they were wearing masks! So they called in none other than the Onondaga County Hazardous Materials Unit! They evidently were able to clean up the spill.

The fire chief later explained to the media that the liquid spice is dangerous if inhaled in large amounts.

Even the finest spice can be overwhelming when we get too much of it. In the same way, the doctrines and disciplines of the Christian life must be kept in balance.

Church, Doctrine, Extremes, Knowledge, Preaching, Spirituality, Zeal
Eccles. 7:16–18; Phil. 1:9–11

Date used __________ Place ____________________

Beginnings 33

On a plaque marking Abraham Lincoln's birthplace near Hodgenville, Kentucky, is recorded this scrap of conversation:

"Any news down t' the village, Ezry?"

"Well, Squire McLains's gone t' Washington t' see Madison swore in, and ol' Spellman tells me this Bonaparte fella has captured most o' Spain. What's new out here, neighbor?"

"Nuthin', nuthin' a'tall, 'cept fer a new baby born t' Tom Lincoln's. Nothin' ever happens out here."

Some events, whether birthdays in Hodgenville (or Bethlehem) or spiritual rebirth in a person's life, may not create much earthly splash, but those of lasting importance will eventually get the notice they deserve.

Children, News

Date used __________ Place ____________________

Belief 34

Robert Chesebrough believed in his product. He's the fellow who invented Vaseline, a petroleum jelly refined from rod wax, the ooze that forms on shafts of oil rigs. He so believed in the healing properties of his product that he became his own guinea pig. He burned himself with acid and flame; he cut and scratched himself so often and so deeply that he bore the scars of his tests the rest of his life. But he proved his product worked. People had only to look at his wounds, now healed, to see the value of his work— and the extent of his belief.

Commitment, Evidence

Date used __________ Place ____________________

35

Actor Cary Grant once told how he was walking along a street and met a fellow whose eyes locked onto him with excitement. The man said, "Wait a minute, you're . . . you're—I know who you are; don't tell me—uh, Rock Hud . . . No, you're . . ."

Grant thought he'd help him, so he finished the man's sentence: "Cary Grant."

And the fellow said, "No, that's not it! You're . . ."

There was Cary Grant identifying himself with his own name, but the fellow had someone else in mind.

John says of Jesus, "He was in the world, and though the world was made through him, the world did not recognize him" (John 1:10). And even when Jesus identified who he was—the Son of God—the response was not a welcome recognition, but rather the Crucifixion.

Spiritual Perception, Christ

Date used __________ Place ____________________

Belief 36

Athletes illustrate what it means to truly believe in a person in authority.

A high school basketball player, for example, who believes in his coach because that coach is a former NBA champion, will do whatever that coach says. He believes the coach is right. If the coach says to change his technique in his shooting motion, he will do it even if it feels awkward and initially causes him to shoot worse. If the coach says to run four miles a day or lift weights thirty minutes each day, he will do it even though it hurts. If the coach says to pass the ball more and shoot less for the sake of the team, he will accept that role.

Why? Because the athlete believes the coach knows better than he does what makes a winner. When you truly believe in a person in authority, you follow that person in complete obedience.

The athlete who does not truly believe *in* the coach will not fully follow. He may believe things *about* the coach—that he is a former NBA champion, that he is honest, that his name is Michael—but believing certain information and believing in someone's authority are two different things.

Those who believe in Jesus not only believe the facts about his deity, atoning death, and resurrection, they believe in his right to direct their lives. True believers follow.

Faith, Lordship of Christ, Obedience,
Repentance, Submission, Surrender
John 3:16; 6:29; Rom. 1:5

Date used __________ Place ____________________

Beliefs 37

Lynette Holloway writes in the *New York Times* of a woman who unknowingly moved into a "sick building." Randi Armstrong moved from California to Staten Island in 1996 with her two daughters. Soon she and her girls began suffering recurring itching, fatigue, headaches, and cold and flu symptoms. Family members would spend days at a time in bed, missing school and work. Randi talked to the landlord and her doctor, but no one could help her or identify the problem.

After suffering for months, one day she saw a television news program describing maladies caused by a noxious mold called *Stachybotrys atra* (pronounced stock-e-BAH-trus AH-tra) that grows in dark, warm, moist conditions. It had become a problem in some buildings on Staten Island because of the borough's high water table. A library and a day-care center had been closed because of the mold. Instantly Armstrong recognized the streaky patches of black, slimy mold on some of the walls and ceilings of her apartment. As quickly as she could, she moved out of the apartment.

Sick buildings make a person physically ill. Like sick buildings there are belief systems and worldviews and religions that make a person spiritually and emotionally sick. If you live in that belief system, you cannot help but be hurt by it.

Error, Existentialism, Ideas, Myths, Naturalism, New Age, Nihilism, Pantheism, Philosophy, Postmodernism, Religion, Values, Worldview

Acts 17:16–34; 1 Cor. 1:20–21; Col. 2:8; 1 Tim. 1:4; 4:7; 6:20–21; 2 Tim. 3:7

Date used __________ Place ____________________

Beliefs 38

According to the *Chicago Tribune,* a British psychiatrist named Giles Croft, of the University of Leeds, did an experiment to find out whether people who believe in the reality of the Monday blues are more likely to feel bad on Monday.

Croft divided volunteers into three groups. He gave one group a report that said Monday blues are for real. He gave the second group a report that denied their existence. The third group received nothing to read. What Croft found was that the first group, which had received the report substantiating Monday blues, was more likely to rate Monday as the worst day in the week. From his research Croft concluded that how people expect to feel affects how they do feel.

What you believe is crucial! Beliefs affect not only what you expect and feel, but what you think and do and become. Beliefs are the grid we use to interpret life.

Depression, Emotions, Expectations,
Feelings, Reality, Truth
Prov. 4:23; John 8:31–32; Rom. 12:1–2;
Eph. 4:23; Phil. 4:4; 2 Thess. 2:10

Date used __________ Place ____________________

According to V. Dion Haynes and Jim Mateja in the *Chicago Tribune,* some astonishing news came forth in the aftermath of the tragic auto accident that killed Princess Diana in 1997. The chauffeur of the car had three times the legal limit of alcohol in his bloodstream. Furthermore, police estimated the car had been going as fast as 120 miles per hour when the crash occurred in the Paris tunnel. Clearly the wrong man was at the wheel of the princess's car.

But that is not unusual for celebrities, reported one security expert. Jerry Hoffman, president of a Cincinnati-based company that builds armored cars and trains drivers, said, "My experience is that a person will spend $150,000 to $200,000 on a limo and then spend no money on training the person to drive it. The driver is hired based on how friendly he is."

No doubt after Diana's death many celebrities began to pay more attention to whether their chauffeur could get them safely to their destination than whether he could carry on a charming conversation.

The same wisdom must be used when we choose the religious beliefs that steer our lives. The issue is not whether our religion makes us feel good. The only question is whether it is trustworthy and thus able to bring us to our hoped-for destination of eternal life with God.

Cults, Deception, Error, False Religions, False Teachers, Gospel, Idols, Purpose, Salvation, Truth, Uniqueness of Christ

John 14:6; 20:31; Acts 4:12; 1 John 5:12

Date used __________ Place ____________________

In January 1997, according to Moira Hodgson in the *New York Times,* Sam Sebastiani Jr., a member of one of California's most prominent winemaking families, died from eating poisonous mushrooms that he had gathered near his home in Santa Rosa, California.

"The mushroom Mr. Sebastiani is thought to have eaten," writes Hodgson, "was an *Amanita phalloides,* also known as the death-cap mushroom. It is the cause of 95 percent of lethal mushroom poisoning worldwide and is fatal more than 35 percent of the time; toxins in its cap destroy the victim's liver by rupturing the cells.

"Experts . . . are warning inexperienced mushroom enthusiasts to leave the picking to trained mycologists, who will not be fooled by poisonous varieties that closely resemble their nonpoisonous cousins."

Roseanne Soloway, a poison control center administrator, says, "A level of presumed expertise is not enough to save your life."

"One of the most sinister aspects of deadly mushroom poisoning," writes Hodgson, "is the delay between ingestion and onset of symptoms. The stronger the poison, the longer it takes to show itself, and by the time a patient is aware of the problem, it may be too late."

Some things you shouldn't attempt to learn by trial and error, for the price of a mistake is far too high. That's the way it is with our beliefs about the meaning of life and our choices about right and wrong. Much is at stake, and the full consequences of our actions may not be seen until it is too late. The only expert you can fully trust is the Bible.

Authority, Beliefs, Choices, Ethics, Guidance,
Knowledge, Lifestyle, Morality, Scripture, Sex
Prov. 14:12; Hos. 4:6; Matt. 7:24–27;
2 Tim. 3:16–17; Heb. 5:11–14

Date used __________ Place ____________________

Bitterness 41

In the early years of the Promise Keepers organization, it exploded in size and impact, and the demands of the ministry put tremendous strain on the marriage of its leader, Bill McCartney. In *From Ashes to Glory* Lyndi McCartney candidly describes how she struggled with bitterness and what terrible destruction it brought into her life:

> I never enjoyed sharing my husband. I always felt cheated. So many times Christians would send me cards or flowers, writing lovely letters saying how much they appreciated me sharing my husband with them. Sometimes my unChristian spirit would take over and I'd want to tell them to "quit borrowing my husband." I really did not like sharing him so much, and I began to resent it. People were always poking into our lives, stealing Bill's time, and I was so angry with him because he would let them do it. . . .
>
> I spent about a year in isolation. The kids were out and on their own, and it was just the two of us in the house. I didn't answer the telephone, and I shut the door on all outsiders. I even shut out friends who loved me. I thought I needed time to myself. . . . I realized we had run amok, and even though thirty years together had generated many great, loving memories, I had to confront my own bitterness. I was hopelessly caught, eyebrow deep, in pain, and I was blind to all the good. I was a wounded, ugly woman. I had made my husband my god and my Savior my sidekick. My life was bleeding profusely. . . . I lost seventy pounds that year—thirty of them in January alone. It was a very scary time. . . . I was totally and completely withdrawn.

Coach McCartney eventually reordered his priorities, and God restored Lyndi McCartney's heart and marriage. The lingering lesson that she has courageously shared with others is that bitterness and isolation are spiritually deadly.

Community, Isolation, Marriage, Resentment
Heb. 10:25; 12:15

Date used __________ Place ____________________

Blame 42

John Killinger tells about the manager of a minor league baseball team who was so disgusted with his center fielder's performance that he ordered him to the dugout and assumed the position himself. The first ball that came into center field took a bad hop and hit the manager in the mouth. The next one was a high fly ball, which he lost in the glare of the sun—until it bounced off his forehead. The third was a hard line drive that he charged with outstretched arms; unfortunately, it flew between his hands and smacked his eye.

Furious, he ran back to the dugout, grabbed the center fielder by the uniform, and shouted, "You idiot! You've got center field so messed up that even I can't do a thing with it!"

Failure, Judging Others

Date used __________ Place ____________________

Blaming God 43

In *Christianity Today* Philip Yancey writes:

When Princess Diana died, I got a phone call from a television producer. "Can you appear on our show?" he asked. "We want you to explain how God could possibly allow such a terrible accident. . . ."

At the 1994 Winter Olympics, when speed skater Dan Jansen's hand scraped the ice, causing him to lose the 500-meter race, his wife, Robin, cried out, "Why, God, again? God can't be that cruel!"

A young woman wrote James Dobson this letter: "Four years ago, I was dating a man and became pregnant. I was devastated! I asked God, 'Why have You allowed this to happen to me?'"

In a professional bout, boxer Ray "Boom-Boom" Mancini slammed his Korean opponent with a hard right, causing a massive cerebral hemorrhage. At a press conference after the Korean's death, Mancini said, "Sometimes I wonder why God does the things he does."

Susan Smith, who pushed her two sons into a lake to drown and then blamed a black carjacker for the deed, wrote in her official confession: "I dropped to the lowest point when I allowed my children to go down that ramp into the water without me. I took off running and screaming, 'Oh God! Oh God, no! What have I done? Why did you let this happen?'"

I once watched a television interview with a famous Hollywood actress whose lover had rolled off a yacht in a drunken stupor and drowned. The actress, who probably had not thought about God in months, looked at the camera, her lovely face contorted by grief, and asked, bizarrely, "How could a loving God let this happen?" Perhaps something similar lay behind the television producer's question. . . . Exposed as frail and mortal, we lash out against someone who is not: God.

Free Will, Goodness of God, Love of God, Problem of Evil,
Questions, Responsibility, Sowing and Reaping
Gal. 6:7–8

Date used __________ Place ____________________

Blindness 44

In 1995 *Jane's International Defense Review* reported that Norinco of China was offering to export a weapon that used laser beams to damage the eyes of enemies. The weapon is called the ZM–87 portable laser "disturber."

According to the *Chicago Tribune*, "Jane's said the company states 'one of its major applications' is 'to injure or dizzy' the eyes of an enemy combatant with high-power laser pulses, and 'especially anybody who is sighting and firing . . . [by means of] an optical instrument, so as to cause him to lose combat ability or result in suppression of his observation and sighting operation.'"

The ZM–87 is effective to a range of two miles.

Blinding a soldier renders him worthless for battle. Satan knows that, and so he too has weapons to blind the eyes.

Lies, Satan, Spiritual Warfare
2 Cor. 4:4

Date used __________ Place ____________________

Blood of Christ 45

Dennis Fulton, former pilot with the Wings of Caring ministry in Zaire, tells of landing a newly purchased Cessna 402 at one of his regular stops in the back country.

As always, the villagers excitedly gathered around the plane, but this time Dennis was approached by two men carrying a live chicken. One had the bird by the feet, and the other had it by the head, and before either the chicken or Dennis knew what was happening, the fowl's head and body parted company. The man with the flopping chicken corpse began swinging it over his head, round and round, with predictable results. Dressed in a freshly pressed white shirt, Dennis was splattered with chicken blood, as were the plane and the villagers.

When Dennis asked what that meant, a native explained that for generations, the splattered blood had signified an end to suffering. To the people of Zaire, the Cessna promised hope and help of all kinds.

In a graphic way, the splattered blood of that chicken, signifying the end of suffering, was a fitting reminder of the blood Christ shed to end the suffering of a world caught in the grip of sin.

Christ, Suffering

Date used __________ Place ____________________

Body of Christ 46

In March of 1981, President Ronald Reagan was shot by John Hinckley, Jr., and was hospitalized for several weeks. Although Reagan was the nation's chief executive, his hospitalization had little impact on the nation's activity. Government continued on.

On the other hand, suppose the garbage collectors in this country went on strike, as they did in Philadelphia. That city was not only in a literal mess, the pile of decaying trash quickly became a health hazard. A three-week nationwide strike would paralyze the country.

Who is more important—the President or a garbage collector?

In the body of Christ, seemingly insignificant ones are urgently needed. As Paul reminds us, "The head cannot say to the feet, 'I don't need you!' On the contrary, those parts of the body that seem to be weaker are indispensable" (1 Cor. 12:21-22).

Spiritual Gifts, Servanthood

Date used __________ Place ____________________

Book of Life 47

Most dictionaries list names of famous people. The editors must make difficult decisions about whom to include and whom to exclude. *Webster's New World Dictionary,* for example, includes Audrey Hepburn but leaves out Spencer Tracy. It lists Bing Crosby, not Bob Hope; Willie Mays, not Mickey Mantle.

Executive editor Michael Agnes explains that names make the cut based on their frequency of use and their usefulness to the reader, but contemporary entertainers are not included.

For that reason, Elton John and Michael Jackson aren't in the dictionary, but Marilyn Monroe and Elvis Presley are.

There is another book far more important than the dictionary. In this book also, some names are included and others excluded. It is called the Book of Life. Only those listed in its pages will enter the glory of heaven and eternal life. The sole criterion for those included: sincere faith in Jesus Christ.

Name, Salvation
Rev. 20:11–15

Date used ________ Place ________________

Brokenness 48

In his book *Broken in the Right Place,* Alan Nelson writes:

My boys are at the age when they like gliders, the cheap, balsa wood airplanes. The thin, light wood is prestamped so that you punch out the airplane and attach the wings to the fuselage. The balsa wood is supposed to break off at the grooves. Sometimes it does not. Occasionally you splinter or break off part of the airplane by accident. When this happens, the planes don't fly as well as they are designed to. Life is delicate, like the balsa plane. When we break in the right areas we will fly higher and smoother than when we break in the wrong places. . . .

When we are broken in the wrong places, we become self-centered. Our broken emotions keep us from loving effectively. We shun future settings where further hurt could take place, like significant relationships, churches, and goal-setting. Or we react defensively to the hurt by overachieving and living a life of abandon. . . . When we are broken in the wrong places, we do not see the fruit of the Spirit.

Look around you. The older you get, the more you see people who have lost the twinkle in their eyes. They have endured tough circumstances, but not successfully. . . . Being broken in the heart, in the soul, where God can do something with your will and character, is a matter of converting, sanctifying the actual pain, and making it a part of the healing salve. You cannot do it on your own. God must. But you must be willing.

Aging, Fear, Self-Centeredness, Testing, Trials
Ps. 51:17; Rom. 5:2–5; James 1:2–4

Date used __________ Place ____________________

Burdens 49

In the Philippines the driver of a carabao wagon was on his way to market when he overtook an old man carrying a heavy load. Taking compassion on him, the driver invited the old man to ride in the wagon. Gratefully the old man accepted.

After a few minutes, the driver turned to see how the man was doing. To his surprise, he found him still straining under the heavy weight, for he had not taken the burden off his shoulders.

Christ offers rest to all who will trust him completely.

Rest, Trust

Date used __________ Place ____________________

Calling 50

In *Discipleship Journal* author and editor Kevin Miller writes:

Jesus had a specific, narrowly defined ministry. He didn't try to do everything. . . . Jesus poured Himself out for people, but within the limits of the calling God the Father had given Him. He focused. . . .

Let me share how this works in my life. . . . One thing I know: God has called me to be a husband. That means He's not going to call me to something that destroys my ability to lovingly care for my wife and my children.

For example, a few years ago, I was invited to join the board of a Christian organization. I really believed in the work, and I wanted to help. To me, even being asked felt like a dream come true. I was ready to start the day before yesterday.

But as I talked with my wife, Karen, she pointed out all the Saturday meetings and the evening phone calls that would come with the position. With her in graduate school, the family already felt stretched, and time for just the two of us was at a premium. She didn't think I should join the board.

I did not want to hear that. I grumped at her and felt irritable inside. How could I say no to something that would please God and perfectly match my interests? For three days, I went back and forth between yes and no, not sure what to do.

What helped me finally make this grueling decision was to pray, "God, what specific things have You called me to do?" One answer was, "Love your wife and children. Support them and help develop their gifts." If I joined the board, I realized, I couldn't fulfill that very well. As much as it hurt to say no, I had to turn the opportunity down. My specific calling as a husband became a protective boundary.

Balance, Boundaries, Burnout, Decisions, Fathers, Focus, God's Will, Guidance, Love, Men, Ministry, Mission, Priorities, Sacrifice, Servanthood

Matt. 14:22–23; 15:24; John 13:34–35; Rom. 12:1–2; Eph. 5:21–33; 6:4

Date used __________ Place ____________________

Caring 51

From 1986 to 1990, Frank Reed was held hostage in a Lebanon cell. For months at a time Reed was blindfolded, living in complete darkness, or chained to a wall and kept in absolute silence. On one occasion, he was moved to another room, and, although blindfolded, he could sense others in the room. Yet it was three weeks before he dared peek out to discover he was chained next to Terry Anderson and Tom Sutherland.

Although he was beaten, made ill, and tormented, Reed felt most the lack of anyone caring. He said in an interview with *Time,* "Nothing I did mattered to anyone. I began to realize how withering it is to exist with not a single expression of caring around [me]. . . . I learned one overriding fact: caring is a powerful force. If no one cares, you are truly alone."

Christians, who are never truly alone, are also fortunate to receive God's gracious care through the church. This care can provide the strength to endure.

Church, Loneliness

Date used __________ Place ____________________

Change 52

Jan Riggenbach writes a newspaper column on gardening. In an article she wrote about how to plant bedding plants, we learn something about Christian growth.

"Giving new bedding plants some rough treatment at planting time," she says, "may be the best thing you can do to help them survive in the garden. When I was new to gardening, I tried to set tomatoes, petunias, and other bedding plants in the garden without disturbing their roots at all. Nowadays, I'm much more ruthless. . . ."

Riggenbach says she squeezes the bottoms of the flexible plastic pots to get the plants out of their container and then she inspects the soil ball.

"If the plant has been growing in its pot so long that the roots are circling the bottom," says Riggenbach, "I jab my finger into the bottom of the soil and pull down to untangle the roots. . . . If the whole pot is filled with circling roots, I have to be merciless. I don't worry if I break some of the roots; that's better than allowing the roots to continue to circle when the plants are growing in the garden. Most bedding plants shrug off this rough treatment."

Christians often resemble rootbound plants. We grow complacent and comfortable where we are. Our roots circle around and around in the same small area, no longer reaching out for life and nourishment and growth. The healthiest thing God can do for us is shake up our roots and put us in new soil.

Comfort, Complacency, Discipline, Fruitfulness, Growth
John 15:1–8

Date used __________ Place ____________________

Change 53

For years, the opening of "The Wide World of Sports" television program illustrated "the agony of defeat" with a painful ending to an attempted ski jump. The skier appeared in good form as he headed down the jump, but then, for no apparent reason, he tumbled head over heels off the side of the jump, bouncing off the supporting structure.

What viewers didn't know was that he chose to fall rather than finish the jump. Why? As he explained later, the jump surface had become too fast, and midway down the ramp, he realized if he completed the jump, he would land on the level ground, beyond the safe sloping landing area, which could have been fatal.

As it was, the skier suffered no more than a headache from the tumble.

To change one's course in life can be a dramatic and sometimes painful undertaking, but change is better than a fatal landing at the end.

Failure, Decisions

Date used __________ Place ____________________

Character 54

In the *South Shore News,* Kathleen Kroll Driscoll was writing about dating and how a woman can figure out what kind of person she's going out with.

She says:

> A theater is an interesting place to analyze someone new in your life. Does he have a phobia about sitting on the aisle? When everyone else is sniffling and crying, is he busy unwrapping licorice and covering up emotions? Does he hog the communal armrest? Does he put his feet on the seat in front? Is he reluctant to ask people to move over one seat so the two of you can sit together? Everything you want to know about your potential mate can be discerned during a movie.

Who we really are cannot be hidden. And the little things often reveal the most.

Discernment, Fruits, Testing
Matt. 12:33–37; 1 Tim. 3:10

Date used __________ Place ____________________

Character 55

The Scriptures often exhort us to be filled with various godly virtues—which means what? How do we know if we are "full of goodness" (Rom. 15:14), for example?

Think a moment about a water-saturated sponge. If we push down with our finger even slightly, water runs out onto the table. We immediately know what fills the interior pockets of the sponge.

The same is true of ourselves. We can tell what fills us on the inside by what comes out under pressure.

Pressure, Tests

Date used __________ Place ____________________

Character 56

Carl Lundquist in *Silent Issues of the Church,* writes:

Henry Wingblade used to say that Christian personality is hidden deep inside us. It is unseen, like the soup carried in a tureen high over a waiter's head. No one knows what's inside —unless the waiter is bumped and he trips!

Just so, people don't know what's inside us until we've been bumped. But if Christ is living inside, what spills out is the fruit of the Spirit.

Fruits of the Spirit, Trials

Date used __________ Place ____________________

Character 57

When you think of someone buying a luxury home with a price tag of more than $300,000, you expect the new home to be of high quality. Such is not always the case, writes Julie Iovine in the *Chicago Tribune*. The preliminary designs for the new home of Michael Eisner, the head of Disney, included one wall that was so thin it would have buckled under its own weight. The $40 million new home of one billionaire software developer had pine siding so vulnerable to decay it started to rot before the home was even completed. It is easy for buyers to mistake luxury for quality. Experts in the home building industry say that "most buyers agonize over the wrong things."

Tom Kligerman, a Manhattan architect, says many buyers "find it boring to spend money on foundations and stud walls. They'd rather spend it on what they can see."

A builder of luxury homes said, "It appears that what sells houses depends on having a tub large enough for at least two people, and probably more; flashy stairs . . . and other glitzy, totally unnecessary elements, as opposed to spatial or constructional quality."

As it is with homes, so it is with people. Too many people put all their effort into image and appearance and pay no attention to the quality of their character.

Appearances, Excellence, Image, Integrity,
Ministry, Quality, Soul, Style
1 Sam. 16:7; Ps. 19:14

Date used __________ Place ____________________

In a story that shows the power of character, Oseola McCarty became something of an American legend in 1995.

Until that year, she had lived in obscurity in the Deep South. She dropped out of school in the sixth grade to help care for an ailing family member and to help her mother with the laundry. After a time she began to do laundry for the business people in the town of Hattiesburg, Mississippi, for fifty cents a load, which amounted to one week of laundry for a family. That's not a lot of money, but Oseola was thrifty and content, and after paying bills each week she deposited what was left in a savings account at the bank.

Year after year Oseola lived a quiet life of integrity. She cared for her grandmother, her aunt, and her mother. She traveled outside of Mississippi only once. She never had an education beyond the sixth grade. She read her Bible each day and kneeled each night to pray to her God. She regularly attended Friendship Baptist Church. She worked and saved.

And then when she was eighty-six years old, the banker sat down with her to talk about what she wanted done with the money in her savings account if she should die. To her astonishment she learned she had a quarter of a million dollars in the bank.

Oseola had lived simply in the past, and she wasn't about to change. She decided to donate some of her money to help other African Americans get what she had had to do without: an education. And so in the summer of 1995 Oseola quietly gave $150,000 to a scholarship fund at the University of Southern Mississippi, not asking that a single brick be named in her honor.

But word of her gift became known, and Oseola's name soon had greater prominence than if the university had named every building on campus after her. She was invited to appear on a spate of TV programs, including interviews with Barbara Walters, *Good Morning America,* and each of the major network news programs. She received numerous honors, including a trip to the White House for the Presidential Citizenship Award and a stop at Harvard for an honorary doctorate of humane letters. Her story was featured on the front page of the *New York Times,* in *Ebony, Jet, People, Guideposts, Christian Reader,* and *Glamour.* She traveled from one end of the country to another to be honored by people who longed to meet the modern-day saint.

Oseola McCarty proves that greatness is measured not by birth or wealth or fame, but by character. We all have the resources to be great in the kingdom, for we all can give ourselves away.

Generosity, Giving, Greatness, Humility,
Money, Persistence, Sacrifice, Saving, Servanthood
Matt. 20:24–28; 2 Cor. 8:9; 9:6–15

Date used __________ Place ____________________

Child Rearing 59

In *New Man,* a pastor tells how on one occasion his firm discipline helped his wayward daughter. His daughter Cori, who had given birth out of wedlock, was chafing at the house rules now put on her by her parents. She was warned that their evening curfew had strict consequences. The pastor writes:

> Once, in the middle of the night, I awoke to the sound of the doorbell ringing. I rushed downstairs and peered through the window. It was Cori, standing on the porch, begging me, "Daddy, Daddy, let me in."
>
> I saw Michael, my grandson, bundled up in a baby carrier next to Cori. I pointed to my watch and closed the curtain. She continued to bang and ring, waking up the neighbors, my wife, and my youngest daughter, Sharryl.
>
> "Daddy, let her in," Sharryl pleaded.
>
> "Haman, the baby is out there," my wife pleaded.
>
> "No," I said. "If we hold the line now, we won't have to do this again."
>
> I wondered about the risk I was taking. I might wound my daughter permanently. My tiny grandson was out there. I might be blamed forever.
>
> For twenty minutes my wife, Sharryl, and Cori begged me to reconsider. "No," I said. "I'm going to bed. You should all do the same."
>
> Cori gave up and spent the night at a friend's house. The next morning she repented, deciding to submit to the house rules and the values of the church. We warmly welcomed her back.

Parents know that at times real love feels unloving.

Consequences, Decisions, Discipline, Fathers, Love, Rules, Tough Love

Pss. 94:12; 119:67–71; Prov. 13:24; 23:13–14; 1 Cor. 11:32; Heb. 12:5–11

Date used __________ Place ____________________

After an interview with singer CeCe Winans, *People Weekly* reported:

Gospel singer CeCe Winans, who was raised in a Christian home and who didn't wear makeup until she was 18, says she isn't about to embrace pop rock—professionally or personally.

"I don't listen to secular music at home," says Winans, 31, who lives in Nashville with her husband and manager, Alvin Love, and their kids Alvin III, 10, and Ashley, 8. "Very seldom do you find a mainstream artist who does only clean music. It's hard for me to wonder whether my children are going to listen to just the clean songs, so it's better to eliminate that music altogether."

CeCe Winans understands that parents are responsible for the environment their children have in the home. And often that means parents must give up something themselves.

Entertainment, Family, Holiness, Home, Music, Purity

Prov. 22:6; Matt. 18:6–9; Eph. 6:4

Date used __________ Place ____________________

Children of God 61

In our entertainment-oriented culture, it's easy to imagine that performing on stage in front of thousands of people would make life complete. Someone who ought to know is Dallas Holm, who has sung on the contemporary Christian music scene for decades. In *Contemporary Christian Magazine,* he tells Devlin Donaldson:

"I have young artists who come up to me and say, 'If I don't get to do what you are doing, then I will never be happy.'

"I have to say to them, 'Then you will never be happy. Happiness isn't based on what you do for him; it's based on who you are in him.'"

Happiness truly is being a child of our Father in heaven.

Happiness, Identity, Performance, Relationship, Works

Rom. 8:28–39; Gal. 2:20–21; Eph. 1:3–14; 1 John 3:1

Date used __________ Place ____________________

Choices 62

In the *New York Times* Barnaby J. Feder reports that in 1994 the Quaker Oats Company, which had posted strong financial earnings for several years, purchased the Snapple drinks business. Although in late 1994 Snapple had been the leader in beverages like fruit drinks and iced teas, the purchase turned out to be a debacle for Quaker Oats and for numerous executives in the company.

In late 1994 Quaker paid $1.7 billion to buy Snapple. A few years later they could sell the company for only $300 million—a loss of $1.4 billion! In the first quarter of 1997 Quaker announced an overall net loss of $1.1 billion owing to its sale of Snapple.

In April 1997 the chairman and chief executive of Quaker, who had promoted the purchase of Snapple, resigned.

Like large corporations choosing what businesses to buy, Christians need to choose their commitments and involvements wisely. Some activities are nothing but a drain.

Busyness, Commitments, Distractions, Habits,
Involvements, Money, Priorities, Sin, Thoughts
1 Cor. 10:23; 2 Cor. 7:1; Eph. 5:8–17; Heb. 12:1–2

Date used __________ Place ____________________

Christ 63

Em Griffin writes, in *Making Friends,* about three kinds of London maps: the street map, the map depicting throughways, and the underground map of the subway. "Each map is accurate and correct," he writes, "but each map does not give the complete picture. To see the whole, the three maps must be printed one on top of each other. However, that is often confusing, so I use only one 'layer' at a time.

"It is the same with the words used to describe the death of Jesus Christ. Each word, like *redemption, reconciliation,* or *justification,* is accurate and correct, but each word does not give the complete picture. To see the whole we need to place one 'layer' on top of the other, but that is sometimes confusing—we cannot see the trees for the whole! So we separate out each splendid concept and discover that the whole is more than the sum of its parts."

Theology, Christ's Death

Date used __________ Place ____________________

Christ's Death 64

In his book *Written in Blood,* Robert Coleman tells the story of a little boy whose sister needed a blood transfusion. The doctor had explained that she had the same disease the boy had recovered from two years earlier. Her only chance for recovery was a transfusion from someone who had previously conquered the disease. Since the two children had the same rare blood type, the boy was the ideal donor.

"Would you give your blood to Mary?" the doctor asked.

Johnny hesitated. His lower lip started to tremble. Then he smiled and said, "Sure, for my sister."

Soon the two children were wheeled into the hospital room—Mary, pale and thin; Johnny, robust and healthy. Neither spoke, but when their eyes met, Johnny grinned.

As the nurse inserted the needle into his arm, Johnny's smile faded. He watched the blood flow through the tube. With the ordeal almost over, his voice, slightly shaky, broke the silence. "Doctor, when do I die?"

Only then did the doctor realize why Johnny had hesitated, why his lip had trembled when he'd agreed to donate his blood. He'd thought giving his blood to his sister meant giving up his life. In that brief moment, he'd made his great decision.

Johnny, fortunately, didn't have to die to save his sister. Each of us however, has a condition more serious than Mary's, and it required Jesus to give not just his blood, but his life.

Love, Sacrifice

Date used __________ Place ____________________

65

A small boy was consistently late coming home from school. His parents warned him that he must be home on time that afternoon, but nevertheless he arrived later than ever. His mother met him at the door and said nothing. His father met him in the living room and said nothing.

At dinner that night, the boy looked at his plate. There was a slice of bread and a glass of water. He looked at his father's full plate and then at his father, but his father remained silent. The boy was crushed.

The father waited for the full impact to sink in, then quietly took the boy's plate and placed it in front of himself. He took his own plate of meat and potatoes, put it in front of the boy, and smiled at his son.

When that boy grew to be a man, he said, "All my life I've known what God is like by what my father did that night."

Fathers, Example

Date used __________ Place ____________________

Christ, Unchanging 66

When Lloyd C. Douglas, author of *The Robe* and other novels, was a university student, he lived in a boarding house, says Maxie Dunnam in *Jesus' Claims—Our Promises.* Downstairs on the first floor was an elderly, retired music teacher, now infirm and unable to leave the apartment.

Douglas said that every morning they had a ritual they would go through together. He would come down the steps, open the old man's door, and ask, "Well, what's the good news?"

The old man would pick up his tuning fork, tap it on the side of his wheelchair, and say, "That's Middle C! It was middle C yesterday; it will be middle C tomorrow; it will be middle C a thousand years from now. The tenor upstairs sings flat, the piano across the hall is out of tune, but my friend, that is middle C!"

The old man had discovered one thing upon which he could depend, one constant reality in his life, one "still point in a turning world." For Christians, the one "still point in a turning world," the one absolute of which there is no shadow of turning, is Jesus Christ.

Gospel, Change

Date used __________ Place ____________________

Christian 67

What is a Christian? In the *Letter to Diognetus,* which dates back to the second century B.C., an anonymous writer describes a strange people who are in the world but not of the world:

Christians are not differentiated from other people by country, language, or customs; you see, they do not live in cities of their own, or speak some strange dialect. . . . They live in both Greek and foreign cities, wherever chance has put them. They follow local customs in clothing, food, and the other aspects of life. But at the same time, they demonstrate to us the unusual form of their own citizenship.

They live in their own native lands, but as aliens. . . . Every foreign country is to them as their native country, and every native land as a foreign country.

They marry and have children just like everyone else, but they do not kill unwanted babies. They offer a shared table, but not a shared bed. They are passing their days on earth, but are citizens of heaven. They obey the appointed laws and go beyond the laws in their own lives.

They love everyone, but are persecuted by all. They are put to death and gain life. They are poor and yet make many rich. They are dishonored and yet gain glory through dishonor. Their names are blackened, and yet they are cleared. They are mocked and bless in return. They are treated outrageously and behave respectfully to others.

When they do good, they are punished as evildoers; when punished, they rejoice as if being given new life. They are attacked by Jews as aliens and are persecuted by Greeks; yet those who hate them cannot give any reason for their hostility.

Persecution, Separation

Date used ____________ Place ________________________

Power can be used in at least two ways: it can be unleashed, or it can be harnessed.

The energy in ten gallons of gasoline, for instance, can be released explosively by dropping a lighted match into the can. Or it can be channeled through a car engine in a controlled burn and used to transport a person 350 miles.

Explosions are spectacular, but controlled burns have lasting effect, staying power.

The Holy Spirit works both ways. At Pentecost, he exploded on the scene; his presence was like "tongues of fire" (Acts 2:3). Thousands were affected by one burst of God's power. But he also works through the church—the institution God began to tap the Holy Spirit's power for the long haul. Through worship, fellowship, and service, Christians are provided with staying power.

Power, Holy Spirit

Date used __________ Place ____________________

Church 69

Gregory Elder writes:

Growing up on the Atlantic Coast, I spent long hours working on intricate sand castles; whole cities would appear beneath my hands.

One year, for several days in a row, I was accosted by bullies who smashed my creations. Finally I tried an experiment: I placed cinder blocks, rocks, and chunks of concrete in the base of my castles. Then I built the sand kingdoms on top of the rocks.

When the local toughs appeared (and I disappeared), their bare feet suddenly met their match.

Many people see the church in grave peril from a variety of dangers: secularism, politics, heresies, or plain old sin. They forget that the church is built upon a Rock (Matt. 16:16), over which the gates of hell itself shall not prevail.

World, Faith

Date used __________ Place ____________________

When it was built for an international exposition in the last century, the structure was called monstrous by the citizens of the city, who demanded it be torn down as soon as the exposition was over.

Yet from the moment its architect first conceived it, he took pride in it and loyally defended it from those who wished to destroy it. He knew it was destined for greatness. Today it is one of the architectural wonders of the modern world and stands as the primary landmark of Paris, France. The architect, of course, was Alexandre Gustave Eiffel. His famous tower was built in 1889.

In the same way we are struck by Jesus' loyalty to another structure—the church—which he entrusted to an unlikely band of disciples, whom he defended, prayed for, and prepared to spread the gospel. To outsiders they (and we) must seem like incapable blunderers. But Jesus, the architect of the church, knows this structure is destined for greatness when he returns.

Creator, Critics

Date used __________ Place ____________________

Church 71

The article "What Good Is a Tree?" in *Reader's Digest* explained that when the roots of trees touch, there is a substance present that reduces competition. In fact, this unknown fungus helps link roots of different trees—even of dissimilar species. A whole forest may be linked together. If one tree has access to water, another to nutrients, and a third to sunlight, the trees have the means to share with one another.

Like trees in a forest, Christians in the church need and support one another.

Unity, Support

Date used __________ Place ______________________

Church 72

In *Witnesses of a Third Way: A Fresh Look at Evangelism,* Robert Neff's chapter includes this story about visiting a church service:

It was one of those mornings when the tenor didn't get out of bed on the right side. . . . As I listened to his faltering voice, I looked around. People were pulling out hymnals to locate the hymn being sung by the soloist. By the second verse, the congregation had joined the soloist in the hymn. By the third verse, the tenor was beginning to find the range. By the fourth verse, it was beautiful. And on the fifth verse the congregation was absolutely silent, and the tenor sang the most beautiful solo of his life.

That is life in the body of Christ, enabling one another to sing the tune Christ has given us.

Support, Spiritual Gifts

Date used __________ Place ____________________

Church 73

David Huxley owns a world record in an unusual category: he pulls jetliners.

On October 15, 1997, for example, he broke his own record at Mascot Airport in Sydney, Australia. He strapped around his upper torso a harness that was attached to a steel cable some fifteen yards long. The other end of the steel cable was attached to the front-wheel strut of a 747 jetliner that weighed 187 tons. With his tennis shoes firmly planted on the runway, Huxley leaned forward, pulled with all his might, and remarkably was able to get the jetliner rolling down the runway. In fact, he pulled the 747 one hundred yards in one minute and twenty-one seconds. A superhuman feat indeed.

The church resembles that 747 jetliner. The strength of a few extraordinary humans can pull the institution of the church for very short distances. Or we can pray until God starts up powerful engines that enable his church to fly thousands of miles on the wings of the Holy Spirit.

Dependence, Evangelism, Fruitfulness, Holy Spirit,
Leadership, Power, Prayer, Revival, Self-Reliance, Strength
Zech. 4:6; Luke 5:4–7; John 21:1–6; Acts 1:4–8; 2:1–47;
Rom. 8:1–14; 2 Cor. 12:7–10

Date used __________ Place ____________________

In her teens, Pulitzer Prize–winning author Annie Dillard went through a season of disillusionment with the church. In *Books & Culture* Philip Yancey writes:

> She got fed up with the hypocrisy of people coming to church mainly to show off their clothes. Wanting to make a major statement, she decided to confront the authority of the church head-on. The senior minister . . . terrified her, so she marched into the assistant minister's office and delivered her spiel about hypocrisy.
>
> "He was an experienced, calm man in a three-piece suit," says Dillard. "He had a mustache and wore glasses. He heard me out and then said, 'You're right, honey, there is a lot of hypocrisy.'"
>
> Annie felt her arguments dissolve. Then the minister proceeded to load her down with books by C. S. Lewis, which, he suggested, she might find useful for a senior class paper. "This is rather early of you, to be quitting the church," he remarked as they shook hands in parting. "I suppose you'll be back soon."
>
> To Annie's consternation, he was right. After plowing through four of the Lewis volumes she fell right back in the arms of the church. Her rebellion had lasted one month.

People should no more assess the church or the gospel by looking at hypocrites than they should test the value of diamonds by looking at a counterfeit. The question is, What is true? not, How have people failed to live up to the truth?

Belief, Church, Disillusionment, Doubt, Gospel, Hypocrites, Rebellion
Matt. 16:18; Eph. 2:19–22; 1 Peter 2:9–10

Date used __________ Place ____________________

Church Attendance 75

Not long ago, the world watched as three gray whales, icebound off Point Barrow, Alaska, floated battered and bloody, gasping for breath at a hole in the ice. Their only hope: somehow to be transported five miles past the ice pack to open sea.

Rescuers began cutting a string of breathing holes about twenty yards apart in the six-inch-thick ice. For eight days they coaxed the whales from one hole to the next, mile after mile. Along the way, one of the trio vanished and was presumed dead. But finally, with the help of Russian icebreakers, the whales Putu and Siku swam to freedom.

In a way, worship is a string of breathing holes the Lord provides his people. Battered and bruised in a world frozen over with greed, selfishness, and hatred, we rise for air in church, a place to breathe again, to be loved and encouraged, until that day when the Lord forever shatters the ice cap.

Worship, Encouragement

Date used __________ Place ____________________

Church Discipline 76

A computer virus on the loose is a computer user's worst nightmare. A virus can destroy everything in a computer's memory. According to S&S Software International and writer James Coates, here is how a computer virus works.

> A computer virus is software, or a piece of programming code, whose purpose is to replicate. . . . Many viruses enter the computer via a floppy disk or are downloaded from another source. . . . Once the computer is infected, the virus checks each time a program is opened to see if the program is clean. If it is, the virus copies itself onto the program. Because viruses need time to spread undetected, most will not affect the proper functioning of the computer right away.

But eventually their destructive power is felt as files are erased or corrupted.

Just as a computer virus spreads through the files of a computer, so sin can spread in the church.

Holiness, Intervention, Spiritual Sickness
1 Cor. 5; Gal. 6:1

Date used __________ Place ____________________

Citizenship 77

On September 15, 1995, Canadian-born pastor Jim Bradford became an American citizen. In the *Pentecostal Evangel* he writes:

In the process of becoming an American citizen I learned that, since the mid–1970s, Canada has recognized the citizenship of any Canadian who has taken out citizenship in another country. I am technically the citizen of two countries—the United States and Canada. It's called dual citizenship.

Jesus described His followers as being part of two kingdoms or two worlds (John 17). Physically, they were a part of this present world and therefore under the rule of human kingdoms. Spiritually, they were also part of a heavenly kingdom, representing a greater allegiance. . . .

By virtue of natural birth, I am a Canadian citizen. To become a citizen of the United States, I had to choose to embrace that privilege and responsibility. And because I am not "naturally" an American by birth, I needed to be naturalized.

By physical birth, I am a citizen of this world; but, as a boy, I met Christ personally and was born again. This rebirth was the result of a choice—to put my faith in Jesus and to turn my primary allegiance over to Him.

Governments, Heaven, Kingdom of God

Matt. 22:21; John 17; Rom. 13:1–7; Eph. 2:19; Phil. 3:20

Date used __________ Place ____________________

Cleansing 78

The American Society for Microbiology studied the hand-washing habits of Americans and found some disturbing results.

According to the Associated Press, the researchers hid in stalls or pretended to comb their hair as they observed 6,333 men and women in restrooms in five cities.

The results: In New York's Penn Station only 60 percent of those using restrooms washed up. At a Braves game in Atlanta 64 percent washed. The study found that women wash their hands more than do men, with 74 percent of women washing their hands after using the toilet versus only 61 percent of men.

"Hand washing in this country has become all but a lost art," said Dr. Michael Osterholm, a Minnesota state epidemiologist.

And that's not good. The Center for Disease Control and Prevention says that hand washing is one of the "most important means of preventing the spread of infection."

To prevent disease, the American Society for Microbiology recommends you wash your hands in the following manner:

—Use warm or hot running water.

—Use soap, preferably antibacterial soap.

—Wash all surfaces thoroughly, including under the fingernails.

—Rub hands together for at least ten to fifteen seconds.

God also has advice on how to be clean—that is, how to be clean within—for our spiritual health likewise depends on it. We can only come clean through Christ.

Blood of Christ, Confession, Conscience, Forgiveness, Guilt, Holiness, Justification by Faith, Purity, Salvation, Shame, Washing, Works

John 13:8; 2 Cor. 7:1; Heb. 10:22; James 4:8; 2 Peter 1:9; 1 John 3:2–3

Date used __________ Place ____________________

Closure 79

Former president George Bush was a Navy pilot during World War II. On one mission, after being hit by Japanese gunfire, he had to bail out of his burning torpedo bomber. That did not go smoothly. As he bailed, he slammed his head against part of the plane, cutting and bruising himself badly, and partially tearing his parachute. He plummeted swiftly to the earth and might have been killed if he had not landed in the ocean.

Mr. Bush received a Distinguished Flying Cross for his troubles, but before he left the Navy he promised himself he would jump out of an airplane again someday and this time get it right.

It took five decades and a stint as president of the United States before he got around to it, but on March 25, 1997, George Bush, age seventy-two, jumped from a plane at 12,500 feet above an army testing base in the desert of Arizona. With him were several professional jumpers from the Parachute Industry Association and the Army's Golden Knights demonstration team. The former president and his "shepherds" sailed without a hitch to the ground, and Mr. Bush made a feather-soft landing just forty yards from the target X.

"It was wonderful," he told onlookers enthusiastically. "I'm a new man. I go home exhilarated."

It took fifty years, but in what had been termed Operation Second Look George Bush had closed the book on a bad memory.

Bringing closure takes many forms. Sometimes it means a long-overdue apology, or the fulfillment of a promise, or finally taking on a frightening spiritual challenge. Sometimes it means handling unfinished business with God himself. Closure is usually difficult, but to be right with ourselves and right with God it needs to be done. God can help us in our own Operation Second Look.

Amends, Challenge, Danger, Fear, Perseverance, Promises, Reconciliation, Regrets, Risk
John 20:24–29; Acts 15:37–38; 2 Cor. 6:1–2

Date used __________ Place ____________________

Commandments 80

In *To My People With Love,* John Killinger writes:

In her beautiful novel about Maine, *The Country of the Pointed Firs,* Sara Orne Jewett describes the ascent of a woman writer on the pathway leading to the home of a retired sea captain named Elijah Tilley. On the way, the woman notes a number of wooden stakes randomly scattered about the property, with no discernible order. Each is painted white and trimmed in yellow, like the captain's house.

Curious, she asks Captain Tilley what they mean. When he first plowed the ground, he says, his plow snagged on many large rocks just beneath the surface. So he set out stakes where the rocks lay in order to avoid them in the future.

In a sense, this is what God has done with the Ten Commandments. . . . He has said, "These are the trouble spots in life. Avoid these, and you won't snag your plow."

Warnings, Ten Commandments

Date used __________ Place ____________________

Commitment 81

In his newspaper column called "Market Report," Bill Barnhart once explained the difference between investors and traders in the stock market.

"A trader in a stock," writes Barnhart, "is making decisions minute-by-minute in the hope of shaving off profits measured in fractions of a dollar. . . . An investor, on the other hand, typically buys or sells a stock based on views about the company and the economy at large."

In other words, traders are wheelers and dealers. They pursue short-term profits. Traders may have no confidence whatsoever in the companies in which they buy stock but they buy, smelling an immediate payoff.

By contrast, investors are in it for the long haul. They "chain themselves to the mast." Investors commit their money to a stock, believing that over a period of years and even decades the stock will pay strong dividends and steadily grow in value. Investors aren't flustered by the typical ups and downs of the market because they believe in the quality of the company, its leaders, and its product.

In the kingdom of God there are also investors and traders. They come to Christ with very different goals. Traders in the kingdom want God to improve their lot in this world. If following Christ means pain or hardship, they sell out.

But investors in the kingdom stay true to Christ no matter what happens in this world, knowing that eternal dividends await them.

Eternal, Feelings, Rewards, Suffering, Temporal
Mark 4:1–20

Date used __________ Place ____________________

Commitment 82

Tim Bowden, in his book *One Crowded Hour* about cameraman Neil Davis, tells about an incident that happened in Borneo during the confrontation between Malaysia and Indonesia in 1964.

A group of Gurkhas from Nepal were asked if they would be willing to jump from transport planes into combat against the Indonesians if the need arose. The Gurkhas had the right to turn down the request because they had never been trained as paratroopers. Bowden quotes Davis's account of the story:

"Now the Gurkhas usually agreed to anything, but on this occasion they provisionally rejected the plan. But the next day one of their NCOs sought out the British officer who made the request and said they had discussed the matter further and would be prepared to jump under certain conditions.

"'What are they?' asked the British officer.

"The Gurkhas told him they would jump if the land was marshy or reasonably soft with no rocky outcrops, because they were inexperienced in falling. The British officer considered this, and said that the dropping area would almost certainly be over jungle, and there would not be rocky outcrops, so that seemed all right. Was there anything else?

"Yes, said the Gurkhas. They wanted the plane to fly as slowly as possible and no more than one hundred feet high. The British officer pointed out the planes always did fly as slowly as possible when dropping troops, but to jump from 100 feet was impossible, because the parachutes would not open in time from that height.

"'Oh,' said the Gurkhas, 'that's all right, then. We'll jump with parachutes anywhere. You didn't mention parachutes before!'"

Any church could use such Gurkha-like commitment and courage.

Courage, Service

Date used __________ Place ____________________

Commitment 83

One Haitian pastor illustrates the need for total commitment to Christ with this parable:

A certain man wanted to sell his house for $2,000. Another man wanted very badly to buy it, but because he was poor, he couldn't afford the full price. After much bargaining, the owner agreed to sell the house for half the original price with just one stipulation: he would retain ownership of one small nail protruding from just over the door.

After several years, the original owner wanted the house back, but the new owner was unwilling to sell. So first the owner went out, found the carcass of a dead dog, and hung it from the nail he still owned. Soon the house became unlivable, and the family was forced to sell the house to the owner of the nail.

The Haitian pastor's conclusion: "If we leave the Devil with even one small peg in our life, he will return to hang his rotting garbage on it, making it unfit for Christ's habitation."

Consecration, Satan

Date used __________ Place ____________________

At the Vietnam Veterans Memorial, that long wall of black marble engraved with the names of those killed in the war, people come to remember their friends and loved ones. Writer Don Moser says that often they leave tokens of their remembrance: flags, sealed letters, pieces of clothing, photos. Volunteers collect these tokens daily and store them at the Vietnam Veterans Memorial Collection.

A book called *Offerings at the Wall* pictures many of these mementos. One man left dog tags, a headband, and a letter that reads, "To all of you here from Echo Company, 1st Marine Regiment, 1st Marine Division . . . I leave you my headband which contains my sweat from the war, my dog tag, and a picture of me and Mike. Another time, another place. I'll never forget you."

A woman left a braid of hair and a picture of a house with an American flag hanging at the porch. Her note read, "Wayne, I think of you every day and miss you so much. I love you."

Written on one flag was this message: "May all of you who died, all of you still missing, and all of you who returned home never be forgotten—Connie."

It's important that we remember. Jesus told us what tokens he wants us to use to remember his death: the bread and the cup. Each has deep meaning for those who love our risen Lord.

Lord's Supper, Memorial, Remembrance
1 Cor. 11:23–26

Date used __________ Place ____________________

Community 85

In October of 1993, in the town of Worcester, Massachusetts, police found an old woman dead on her kitchen floor. This was no ordinary discovery—she had been dead four years. Police speculated she died at age seventy-three of natural causes. That's when her bank transactions ended.

How can someone be so cut off from relationships that no one even notices when he or she dies?

To some extent, it was a mistake. According to the Associated Press, four years earlier, neighbors had called authorities when they sensed something might be wrong. When the police contacted the woman's brother, he said she had gone into a nursing home. Police told the postal service to stop delivering mail. One neighbor paid her grandson to cut the grass because the place was looking run-down. Another neighbor had the utility company come and shut off the water when a pipe froze, broke, and sent water spilling out the door.

To a great extent, though, it was not a mistake.

One friend from the past said, "She didn't want anyone bothering her at all. I guess she got her wish, but it's awfully sad."

Her brother said the family hadn't been close since their mother died in 1979. He added, "Someone should have noticed something before now."

The woman had lived in her house in this middle-class neighborhood for forty years, but none of her neighbors knew her well. "My heart bleeds for her," said the woman who lives across the street. "But you can't blame a soul. If she saw you out there, she never said hello to you."

As this neighborhood shows, a spirit of community only results when all of us reach out to one another. Relationships take effort.

Communication, Family, Friendship
Heb. 10:25; 1 John 1:7

Date used __________ Place ____________________

Community 86

In *Leadership* pastor and author John Ortberg writes:

Psychologist Milton Rokeach once wrote a book called *The Three Christs of Ypsilanti.* He described his attempts to treat three patients at a psychiatric hospital in Ypsilanti, Michigan, who suffered from delusions of grandeur. Each believed he was unique among humankind; he had been called to save the world; he was the messiah. They were full-blown cases of grandiosity, in its pure form.

Rokeach found it difficult to break through, to help the patients accept the truth about their identity. So he decided to put the three into a little community, to see if rubbing against people who also claimed to be the messiah might dent their delusion. A kind of messianic, 12-step recovery group.

This led to some interesting conversations. One would claim, "I'm the messiah, the Son of God. I was sent here to save the earth."

"How do you know?" Rokeach would ask.

"God told me."

One of the other patients would counter, "I never told you any such thing."

Every once in a while, one got a glimmer of reality—never deep or for long. Deeply ingrained was the messiah complex. But what progress Rokeach made was pretty much made by putting them together.

Church, Sanctification, Truth

Prov. 27:17; Eph. 4:15; Heb. 10:24–25

Date used __________ Place ____________________

Community 87

To live in community with others benefits one's health significantly. That is a finding reported in *The Journal of the American Medical Association.*

"Building on a dozen studies correlating friendship and fellowship with health, a new study has found that people with a broad array of social ties are significantly less likely to catch colds than those with sparse social networks," reported the *New York Times* News Service.

"The incidence of infection among people who knew many different kinds of people was nearly half that among those who were relatively isolated, the researchers reported. The lack of diverse social contacts was the strongest of the risk factors for colds that were examined, including smoking, low vitamin C intake and stress."

Researchers have found similar health benefits from community for heart disease patients. In one study Dr. Redford Williams, director of the behavioral medicine research center at Duke University Medical Center, "found that heart disease patients with few social ties are six times as likely to die within six months as those with many relatives, friends and acquaintances."

Reportedly, one of the main beneficiaries of a broadened network of relationships is our immune system. In another study, Dr. Janice Kiecolt-Glaser, director of health psychology at the Ohio State University College of Medicine, and her husband, Dr. Ronald Glaser, a virologist at Ohio State, "have reported that a person's immune response to vaccines increases with the strength of his or her social support."

As always, when God tells us how to live, those guidelines are for our own good. Church involvement contributes to our health!

Church, Health, Isolation, Relationships
Acts 2:42–47; Rom. 12:10; Heb. 10:24–25

Date used __________ Place ____________________

Community 88

According to Bill Jauss and Steve Rosenbloom in the *Chicago Tribune,* on July 19, 1996, Chad Kreuter, a reserve catcher for the Chicago White Sox, severely dislocated and fractured his left shoulder on a play at home. He underwent surgery, and the Sox placed him on the sixty-day disabled list. That's the kind of thing that makes a backup player feel even less like a part of the team.

But quite the opposite happened. Apparently Chad's teammates had a strong liking for him; each player put Chad's number 12 on his ball cap to show support. Chad was a member of the team whether he played or not.

As you can imagine, that meant a lot to Chad. Later in the season when he was able to suit up again, he showed his appreciation by, you guessed it, putting the numbers of each of his teammates on his ball cap.

All devoted to one. One devoted to all. That is what makes a team, and that is what makes the community of Christ.

Body of Christ, Church, Devotion, Loyalty, Team
Acts 2:42–47; Rom. 12:10; 2 Tim. 1:16–18

Date used __________ Place ____________________

Complacency 89

In March of 1994 a German tourist checked into a hotel near Miami International Airport. That night in his room he noticed a foul odor. But travelers must put up with discomforts, so he slept in the bed that night without a complaint to the front desk.

The next morning when he awoke, the odor was only worse. So as he checked out of the hotel, he reported the problem. On Friday, March 11, a maid cleaning the room discovered the source of the odor. Under the bed she found a corpse.

Life is filled with problems, and often it seems the best thing to do is just ignore them. But if we realized how serious and close some problems really are, we would take action.

Apathy, Change, Problems, Repentance
Prov. 1:32; Jer. 6:13–14; 2 Cor. 6:1–2

Date used __________ Place ____________________

Complacency 90

In his book *Identity: Youth and Crisis*, Erik Erikson tells a story he heard from a physician about an old man with a peculiar problem. The old man vomited every morning but had never felt any inclination to consult a doctor. Finally the man's family convinced him to get a checkup.

The doctor asked, "How are you?"

"I'm fine," the man responded. "Couldn't be better."

The doctor examined him and found he was in good shape for his age.

Finally the physician grew impatient and asked, "I hear that you vomit every morning."

The old man looked surprised and said, "Sure. Doesn't everybody?"

Like that old man, we may not realize that the problems we bear daily are abnormal. We've lived with the problems for so long we can't imagine how life could be better.

Abundant Life, Problems, Sin
John 10:10

Date used __________ Place ____________________

Complacency 91

Ronald Meredith, in his book *Hurryin' Big for Little Reasons,* describes one quiet night in early spring:

Suddenly out of the night came the sound of wild geese flying. I ran to the house and breathlessly announced the excitement I felt. What is to compare with wild geese across the moon?

It might have ended there except for the sight of our tame mallards on the pond. They heard the wild call they had once known. The honking out of the night sent little arrows of prompting deep into their wild yesterdays. Their wings fluttered a feeble response. The urge to fly—to take their place in the sky for which God made them—was sounding in their feathered breasts, but they never raised from the water.

The matter had been settled long ago. The corn of the barnyard was too tempting! Now their desire to fly only made them uncomfortable. Temptation is always enjoyed at the price of losing the capacity for flight.

Temptation, Call of God

Date used __________ Place ____________________

Complaints 92

While working in the 1980s on the computing staff of the University of Illinois, computer programmer Steve Dorner created the Eudora e-mail system that in 1997 was used by some 18 million people. To know that so many people are benefiting from his work has to make a programmer feel good. No doubt, millions of these users can't thank Dorner enough for using his skill and sweat to make their communication easier. But not everyone feels that way, and Dorner hears about it, because he now works for the company that owns the program.

Jo Thomas writes in the *New York Times:*

> He gets about 100 e-mail messages a day and says that having 18 million users "is very gratifying, but it can also make me feel a little hunted sometimes.
>
> "I'm the one who has to, in the final analysis, deal with every single problem, and I tend to concentrate on what's wrong," Mr. Dorner said. "There are days when I think that every one of those 18 million people thinks I'm wrong, stupid, and out to get them."

God must feel something like this computer programmer. As the Creator, he takes all kinds of blame from people who don't like his program for their lives. Often these people blame him for their own mistakes. Often they blame him for situations that are for the best, though they cannot begin to understand.

Worst of all, people think God is out to get them, when in fact the opposite is true. God has employed his infinite genius to program goodness into every person's life.

Creator, Goodness of God, Love of God, Pain,
Prayer, Providence, Suffering, Trust, Will of God
Prov. 3:5–6; Hab. 1:2–4; Rom. 8:28, 31; 11:33–36; James 1:5

Date used __________ Place ____________________

Confessing Christ 93

In his autobiography, *Standing Firm,* Dan Quayle, former vice president under George Bush, writes:

> Although I had been raised a Presbyterian, my personal acceptance of Christ occurred in a Methodist church on a Sunday afternoon in 1964, when I was seventeen years old. With about fifteen or twenty other young people, I'd gone through an ecumenical Bible study course, one that alternated between the local Methodist and Presbyterian churches. We talked about Christ having died for our sins and the importance of accepting him as our personal Savior. On this particular Sunday afternoon, our group leader urged each of us to make a personal, open statement about accepting Christ. And in a quiet, peaceful way most of us did. Almost as much as the moment itself, I can still remember how the next day at school we nodded to one another as brother and sister Christians who had publicly professed our faith.

When Jesus ministered on the earth, he called people in public to follow him. Our decision to follow Christ must not remain a secret. Jesus calls us to make a public stand for him.

Born Again, Community, Conversion, Decision,
Family of God, Receiving Christ, Testimony
Matt. 5:14–16; 10:32–33; John 1:12; Rom. 10:8–10

Date used __________ Place ____________________

Confession 94

Workers for the Chicago Transit Authority have minted some interesting terms to describe life on the trains and tracks of the city, says writer Anne Keegan.

The elevated train often runs on a platform built above the city streets. In many places, these platforms are narrow, with just enough width for two trains to pass. If a workman was fixing the tracks when two trains came from different directions, he would have no room to avoid the oncoming trains.

And so, now and then alongside the tracks there is a small platform with a railing, three feet square, projecting out over the street. These small platforms provide a place for those working on the tracks to escape an oncoming train.

Workers for the Chicago Transit Authority call these platforms "fool catchers."

On occasion we all play the fool. We lose our temper or bend the truth or neglect our responsibilities or perhaps even do something criminal. We make decisions that in hindsight we realize were just plain stupid. As the trains of trouble come bearing down on us, we need to remember that God has provided a way of escape. The fool catcher is confession.

Foolishness, Mistakes, Sin

Ps. 51; Prov. 28:13; Luke 18:9–14; 1 John 1:8–10

Date used __________ Place ____________________

Confession 95

An article by Carolyn Hagan in *Child* includes a first-person account by Pulitzer Prize–winning author Alice Walker:

> When I was a little girl, I accidentally broke a fruit jar. Several brothers and a sister were nearby who could have done it. But my father turned to me and asked, "Did you break the jar, Alice?"
>
> Looking into his large, brown eyes, I knew he wanted me to tell the truth. I also knew he might punish me if I did. But the truth inside of me wanted badly to be expressed. "I broke the jar," I said.
>
> The love in his eyes rewarded and embraced me. Suddenly I felt an inner peace that I still recall with gratitude to this day.

In the same way, we find that confessing our sins to our heavenly Father brings us closer to him.

Forgiveness, Guilt, Honesty, Repentance, Truth
Ps. 51; 1 John 1:8–10

Date used __________ Place ____________________

Conflict 96

In the *Chicago Tribune Magazine* writer William Palmer tells a story of conflict that will inspire a knowing nod from anyone who has had a difficult neighbor.

When Mr. Palmer moved into his new house, he and his new neighbor got along just fine. They would smile broadly and wave when they saw each other in the driveway. There was no fence between their yards, and it appeared they would never need one.

The problems began when Palmer's children began stepping in dog droppings in their yard, though they themselves didn't own a dog. The neighbor had two poodles, and Palmer was sure they were the culprits, so one day Palmer brought up the delicate subject. The neighbor denied the poodles were the problem, and before long the two neighbors descended into a messy spiral of antagonism. Droppings were thrown from lot to lot. Angry words were exchanged. Signs were posted.

Eventually the dogs disappeared, but the damage had been done.

In Palmer's mind, the conflict reached its low point when another issue surfaced. One day he received a note from his hostile neighbor suggesting that the dead elm tree that stood squarely on the lot line between them should be cut down. Palmer didn't like the idea of splitting the costs involved and ignored the letter. A few months later he and his wife suddenly heard the sound of a chain saw outside. They looked out their window and watched the dead elm on the lot line as it was sawn vertically down the middle, leaving half of a grotesque dead elm standing on his property. He left it standing for a few years as a conversation piece, then finally cut it down.

What a price we pay for hostility! This tree sawn in half vertically, standing on the lot line between two antagonistic neighbors, is a symbol of the pettiness, craziness, and desolation that so often accompany unresolved conflict.

Anger, Bitterness, Divorce, Hatred, Litigation,
Malice, Neighbors, Property, Revenge
Gal. 5:15; Heb. 12:15

Date used __________ Place ____________________

Conscience 97

In *Focus on the Family,* Rolf Zettersten writes:

> A good friend in North Carolina bought a new car with a voice-warning system. . . . At first Edwin was amused to hear the soft female voice gently remind him that his seat belt wasn't fastened. . . . Edwin affectionately called this voice the "little woman."
>
> He soon discovered his little woman was programmed to warn him about his gasoline. "Your fuel level is low," she said one time in her sweet voice. Edwin nodded his head and thanked her. He figured he still had enough to go another fifty miles, so he kept on driving. But a few minutes later, her voice interrupted again with the same warning. And so it went over and over. Although he knew it was the same recording, Edwin thought her voice sounded harsher each time.
>
> Finally, he stopped his car and crawled under the dashboard. After a quick search, he found the appropriate wires and gave them a good yank. So much for the little woman.
>
> He was still smiling to himself a few miles later when his car began sputtering and coughing. He ran out of gas! Somewhere inside the dashboard, Edwin was sure he could hear the little woman laughing.

People like Edwin learn before long that the little voice inside, although ignored or even disconnected, often tells them exactly what they need to know.

Disobedience, Word of God

Date used __________ Place ____________________

Conscience 98

In *Inside Sports* John Feinstein writes:

In 1994 golfer Davis Love III called a one-stroke penalty on himself during the second round of the Western Open. He had moved his marker on a green to get it out of another player's putting line. One or two holes later, he couldn't remember if he had moved his ball back to its original spot. Unsure, Love gave himself an extra stroke.

As it turned out, that one stroke caused him to miss the cut and get knocked out of the tournament. If he had made the cut and then finished dead last, he would have earned $2,000 for the week. When the year was over, Love was $590 short of automatically qualifying for the following year's Masters. Love began 1995 needing to win a tournament to get into the event.

When someone asked how much it would bother him if he missed the Masters for calling a penalty on himself, Love's answer was simple: "How would I feel if I won the Masters and wondered for the rest of my life if I cheated to get in?"

The story has a happy ending. The week before the 1995 Masters, Love qualified by winning a tournament in New Orleans. Then in the Masters he finished second, earning $237,600.

The only truly satisfying reward is one gained honestly, for a guilty conscience can spoil any gain.

Character, Cheating, Guilt, Honesty, Integrity, Truth

Ps. 15:4; 1 Tim. 1:19; Heb. 13:18

Date used __________ Place ____________________

Conversion 99

Not many conversion stories make it to the pages of the *Wall Street Journal,* but Dr. Marvin Overton's did. A June 6, 1994, article by Robert Johnson shows how true it is that when a person accepts Christ, all things become new.

Dr. Marvin Overton is one of the finest brain surgeons in the nation, a past-president of the Texas Association of Neurosurgeons. In 1992 he began attending a small church in Burnet, Texas, and had a spiritual awakening. About the same time, he began suffering severe, lingering pain in his abdomen. X rays eventually revealed cancer. Several days after the diagnosis, however, tests showed nothing, and Overton has felt fine ever since. Overton was completely healed. The healing crystallized his born-again experience.

Before his conversion he was a skeptic and a rationalist who believed in the power of science. Now, says the *Journal,* Overton has "more answers than questions, a granite certitude about the mind, the brain, and the soul."

Before his conversion he was, by his own description, coldhearted. "I was a good surgeon," said Overton, "but I was coarse. I couldn't shed a tear. My attitude [toward patients] was 'tough.'"

Now he writes notes to friends, notes containing encouraging quotes from Scripture, and he cares enough about patients to ask those scheduled for surgery, "If something goes wrong, are you comfortable that you know God and that you'll go to heaven?"

Before Overton's conversion his god was wine. Not that he was an alcoholic; rather, he owned one of the finest wine collections in the country, over ten thousand bottles of every important vintage made between the late 1700s and 1930. His collection was valued at more than a million dollars. Dr. Overton threw wine-tasting banquets for which French chefs, and hand-carried bottles, were flown in by a Concorde jet. "Wine had become my idol," said Overton. "I worshipped the god Bacchus. . . . I was an excellent heathen."

After Overton's conversion he sold his wine collection, giving much of the proceeds to charity.

Before his conversion Overton was a Fort Worth socialite. Now he is one of the leaders in his small-town, blue-collar church in Burnet, Texas. He even goes door-to-door to tell others about Christ.

What has impressed others most is not his healing but his life. "The question of whether he got an incorrect diagnosis, or whatever, really doesn't matter," said Michael McWhorter, chairman of the American Association of Neurological Surgeons science board. "Who are we to say a miracle didn't happen? Something changed his life."

When a person becomes a fully devoted follower of Jesus Christ, all things become new.

Healing, Witness
John 3:3; 2 Cor. 5:17

Date used __________ Place ____________________

Conversion 100

Campus Life magazine told the conversion story of singer Kathy Troccoli. She grew up with an overprotective mother, and as Kathy got older, she rebelled, abusing alcohol and suffering eating disorders.

Says Kathy, "Maybe you've heard the phrase, 'We are as sick as our secrets.' I was real sick."

While Kathy started out rebelling against an overprotective mom, she wound up rebelling against herself—and at the expense of her own health and self-esteem. Into this swirl of rebellion and alcohol and unhappiness, Jesus came—in the form of a nerd.

At the time, Kathy was partying with her friends and singing in clubs by night.

By day, she was working her summer job at a community pool, and Cindy was her prissy co-worker who read the Bible every day during lunch.

"She was the epitome of a girl that I would not hang out with," says Kathy. "I hung out with harder girls. Tougher. Cindy was kind of frilly. Pink—she was like a pink girl. And when she started telling me about Jesus, I made fun of her. And yet, somewhere deep down inside, I admired her. I was intrigued by her boldness. I liked it that she didn't seem to care what people thought about her. I even suspected she was right, and that I was on the wrong path."

Kathy knew the truth of Christianity hung by a thin thread called faith. She knew there were unanswerable questions, and day after day she fired those questions at frilly Cindy, the Jesus nerd. Finally, one answer, one statement from the pink girl got through. "She said, 'You know, Kath, Jesus is Lord whether you accept him or not.' I went home thinking about that," says Kathy. "I did have this growing sense that if Jesus was real, I had to check him out."

Cindy obliged, giving Kathy a small New Testament. "My other friends thought I was weird," says Kathy, "because I was taking this Bible home, but I did, unapologetically. I read the Gospel of John, plowing right on through, despite a few unanswered questions. When I got to the end, I knew I had to make a decision. If Jesus was who he said he was, I would have to respond. Everything would have to change."

On August 5th [1988], it did.

Everything changed.

Or rather, the changes began.

Addictions, Boldness, Evangelism
2 Cor. 5:17; 1 Thess. 2:3–8

Date used __________ Place ____________________

Conversion 101

In his book *Enjoying God,* Lloyd Ogilvie writes about the conversion of a fellow student named Allistair.

> One summer while finishing his doctoral program, [Allistair] had a carrel next to mine in the library. Often we lunched together and shared thoughtful discussions about faith. Allistair had little experience with the church and had not made a profession of faith in Christ. . . .
>
> Several times our discussions brought Allistair to the edge of the decision to become a Christian. Then he would back off. One day our lunch discussion focused on grace. Near the end of our conversation, I took out my pen and placed it on the table.
>
> "Allistair," I said, "you need to make a decision. When you decide to accept the gift of grace and commit your life to Christ, pick up the pen. . . ."
>
> Allistair sat for more than an hour staring at the pen.
>
> During this time a mutual Scots friend who enjoys God came over to our table. He noticed that we had been silently sitting for a long time.
>
> "What are you lads doing?" he asked with a chuckle.
>
> Allistair looked up and replied intently, "I'm trying to decide whether to become a Christian."
>
> Sensing the intensity of the moment, our friend said, "Why not do it now and get on with your life?" and walked away.
>
> Allistair returned to his silent meditation. I waited and prayed.
>
> Suddenly, as if propelled by an inner compunction, Allistair thrust out his hand and grasped the pen.
>
> "Now is none too soon!" he exclaimed with joy.
>
> God has provided a way for us to have eternal life through Jesus Christ, but we must accept it.

Evangelism, Procrastination, Receiving Christ
John 1:12; 2 Cor. 6:1–2

Date used __________ Place ____________________

Conversion 102

Living without Christ is like driving a car with its front end out of line. You can stay on the road if you grip the steering wheel with both hands and hang on tightly. Any lapse of attention, however, and you head straight for the ditch.

Society in general—educators, political leaders, parents—exhorts us to drive straight and curb our destructive tendencies. But it is a ceaseless struggle.

Coming to Christ is a little like getting a front-end alignment. The pull toward the ditch is corrected from the inside.

Not to say there won't be bumps and potholes ahead that will still try to jar us off the road. Temptations and challenges will always test our alertness to steer a straight course. We can hardly afford to fall asleep at the wheel. But the basic skew in the moral mechanism has been repaired.

Regeneration, Obedience

Date used __________ Place ____________________

Conversion 103

In *Discipleship Journal* author Jean Fleming writes:

> Recently something rapturous happened a few spaces down the church pew from me. The pastor announced that a young boy in our congregation named Crockett had given his heart to Christ that week. Another boy, about four years of age, jumped up on the seat of our pew, thrust his fist into the air, and yelled, "Yeah, Crockett!"
>
> His response was totally unself-conscious; his joy and exuberance exhilarated and rebuked me. His mother had him sitting again in a second. Too bad. The entire congregation should have been standing on the pews.

In the life of any church, history is made when a person receives Christ. These are moments so great they must be celebrated in heaven—and on earth.

Celebration, Community, Enthusiasm,
Expressiveness, Rejoicing, Reserve
Luke 15:1–32; Rom. 12:15

Date used __________ Place ____________________

In his book *The Moral Intelligence of Children,* Harvard professor and Pulitzer Prize-winning author Robert Coles writes:

> Ralph Waldo Emerson once said, "Character is higher than intellect." Marian, a student of mine several years ago, much admired Emerson. She had arrived at Harvard from the Midwest and was trying hard to work her way through college by cleaning the rooms of her fellow students. Again and again she met classmates who had forgotten the meaning of please, of thank you, no matter their high SAT scores. They did not hesitate to be rude, even crude toward her. One day she was not so subtly propositioned by a young man she knew to be very bright. She quit her job, and was preparing to quit going to school. Full of anxiety and anger, she came to see me. "I've been taking all these philosophy courses," she said to me at one point, "and we talk about what's true, what's important, what's good. Well, how do you teach people to be good?"

The answer to that question, according to the Bible, is not education but conversion. No one can learn to be truly good, for only God is perfectly good. The light of true goodness dawns in the heart only when God shines there.

Born Again, Character, Depravity, Education, Ethics, Evil, Flesh, Goodness, Intelligence, Morality, Philosophy, Regeneration, Righteousness, Sin, Sinful Nature

Jer. 31:33; John 3:1–8; Rom. 3:23; 10:3–4; 2 Cor. 5:17; Eph. 2:1–10; Titus 3:3–7

Date used __________ Place ____________________

Conviction 105

When babies are born prematurely, one of the most common critical problems is with their underdeveloped lungs. In September 1996, the *New England Journal of Medicine* reported the results of a pilot study that offered hopeful treatment. The treatment is surprising. In the study, doctors filled the lungs of critically ill premature babies with liquid—an oxygen-rich liquid. Through this liquid the babies actually "breathe."

Normally, when fluid fills the lungs, people drown. But this special oxygen-filled fluid actually saves lives.

In a similar way, there is a sorrow that kills and another sort of sorrow that brings life. Normally, sorrow and depression drown a person's spirit. But like oxygen-filled fluid, sorrow that comes from God brings repentance and life.

Grief, Mourning, Repentance, Sorrow
Matt. 5:4; John 16:8–11; 2 Cor. 7:8–11; James 4:7–10

Date used __________ Place ____________________

Convictions 106

Ken Walker writes in *Christian Reader* that in the 1995 college football season 6-foot–2-inch, 280-pound Clay Shiver, who played center for the Florida State Seminoles, was regarded as one of the best in the nation. In fact, one magazine wanted to name him to their preseason All-America football team. But that was a problem, because the magazine was *Playboy,* and Clay Shiver is a dedicated Christian.

Shiver and the team chaplain suspected that *Playboy* would select him, and so he had time to prepare his response. Shiver knew well what a boon this could be for his career. Being chosen for this All-America team meant that sportswriters regarded him as the best in the nation at his position. Such publicity never hurts athletes who aspire to the pros and to multimillion-dollar contracts.

But Shiver had higher values and priorities. When informed that *Playboy* had made him their selection, Clay Shiver simply said, "No thanks." That's right, he flatly turned down the honor. "Clay didn't want to embarrass his mother and grandmother by appearing in the magazine or give old high school friends an excuse to buy that issue," writes Walker. Shiver further explained by quoting Luke 12:48: "To whom much is given, of him much is required."

"I don't want to let anyone down," said Shiver, "and number one on that list is God."

Compromise, Example, Honor, Leadership,
Purity, Stumbling Blocks, Testimony, World
Matt. 5:13–16; 7:13–14; Rom. 14:13–23; James 4:4; 1 John 2:15–17

Date used __________ Place ____________________

Cooperation 107

CBS radio newsman Charles Osgood told the story of two ladies who lived in a convalescent center. Each had suffered an incapacitating stroke. Margaret's stroke left her left side restricted, while Ruth's stroke damaged her right side. Both of these ladies were accomplished pianists but had given up hope of ever playing again.

The director of the center sat them down at a piano and encouraged them to play solo pieces together. They did, and a beautiful friendship developed.

What a picture of the church's needing to work together! What one member cannot do alone, perhaps two or more could do together—in harmony.

Spiritual Gifts, Church

Date used __________ Place ____________________

Economist Robert Eggert began a monthly newsletter called *Blue Chip Economic Indicators* in 1976, and it is now read by the American president, the chairman of the Federal Reserve, and CEOs of the biggest companies in America. The newsletter attempts to predict the future.

Blue Chip Economic Indicators gives forecasts on economic matters like gross domestic product growth and unemployment rates. How do Robert Eggert and the *Blue Chip* predict the future with an accuracy that motivates subscribers to pay a subscription rate of $498 a year?

Eggert's secret is a simple idea he got in 1969: He gives a consensus forecast. Writer Mark Memmott describes the process:

> On the 15th of each month, he sends a memo to the 75 economists on his list. They include forecasters at such household names as Ford, Chrysler, General Motors, Sears and J. P. Morgan, academics from UCLA and Georgia State, and consultants. He alerts them to special questions he'll be asking. Then, on the first working day of each month, his questionnaires are faxed to all 75.
>
> By the fifth working day of the month, Eggert has crunched the responses, written his analysis and sent the copy to the publisher.

Eggert first experimented with his idea of making a consensus forecast in the early seventies when he was chief economist for RCA. "When I started to average out [other economists'] forecasts, it became apparent the consensus usually had an almost uncanny ability to predict what was coming."

Solomon put it this way: "A wise man listens to advice" (Prov. 12:15).

Advice, Consensus, Decisions, Leadership, Plans, Wisdom
Prov. 12:15; 15:22

Date used __________ Place ____________________

Counterfeits 109

Anything that is extremely valuable will be counterfeited.

Fake gems have been around for thousands of years, but as the technology for making them has advanced, fakes are now harder to detect with the naked eye.

Gem buyers today must be aware of three types of gems that are made to look more valuable than they are.

1. *Synthetic gems,* says writer Vivian Marino, are "lab-grown stones that closely duplicate a natural gem's physical and chemical properties."
2. *Simulated gems* are also manmade. The color of a simulated stone may be similar to that of a natural gem, but it is very different physically and chemically. "Cubic zirconia is a well-known diamond simulation."
3. *Enhanced gems* are natural gems altered in some way to improve their look. "Color can be enhanced through heat, radiation, oils, and chemicals." Other methods used to imitate or enhance the value of stones are "dyeing, waxing, or smoking poor quality stones to make them look richer."

Experts advise buyers to verify a stone's value with gem-testing labs, such as the Gemological Institute of America, before any sales are final. When paying big money for jewels, you want to be very careful about getting the genuine article.

It is the same with truth. We must ensure we are not falling for heresy.

Appearance, Authenticity, Character, Deception, False Prophets, Gospel, Heresy, Integrity, Orthodoxy, Truth

Matt. 7:15–23; 2 Cor. 11:13–15; Gal. 1:6–9; 1 Tim. 3:10

Date used __________ Place ____________________

Courage 110

Rosa Parks, mother of the civil rights movement, was arrested in 1955 for refusing to give her bus seat to a white man. Boycotts and protests followed, and eventually the Supreme Court ruled racial segregation unconstitutional. In *Quiet Strength* she writes:

> I have learned over the years that knowing what must be done does away with fear. When I sat down on the bus that day, I had no idea history was being made—I was only thinking of getting home. But I had made up my mind. After so many years of being a victim of the mistreatment my people suffered, not giving up my seat—and whatever I had to face afterwards—was not important. I did not feel any fear sitting there. I felt the Lord would give me the strength to endure whatever I had to face. It was time for someone to stand up—or in my case, sit down. So I refused to move.

Settle in your mind what is right, and you will find courage in your heart.

Determination, Fear, Leadership, Righteousness
Prov. 28:1; Matt. 5:6

Date used __________ Place ____________________

Courage 111

Peter Cartwright, a nineteenth-century, circuit-riding, Methodist preacher, was an uncompromising man. One Sunday morning when he was to preach, he was told that President Andrew Jackson was in the congregation. Cartwright was warned not to say anything out of line.

When Cartwright stood to preach, he said, "I understand that Andrew Jackson is here. I have been requested to be guarded in my remarks. Andrew Jackson will go to hell if he doesn't repent."

The congregation was shocked and wondered how the president would respond. After the service, President Jackson shook hands with Peter Cartwright and said, "Sir, if I had a regiment of men like you, I could whip the world."

Preaching, Hell

Date used ________ Place ______________

Charles Colson, in *Loving God,* tells the story of Telemachus, a fourth-century Christian.

He lived in a remote village, tending his garden and spending much of his time in prayer. One day he thought he heard the voice of God telling him to go to Rome, so he obeyed, setting out on foot. Weary weeks later, he arrived in the city at the time of a great festival. The little monk followed the crowd surging down the streets into the Colosseum. He saw the gladiators stand before the emperor and say, "We who are about to die salute you." Then he realized these men were going to fight to the death for the entertainment of the crowd. He cried out, "In the name of Christ, stop!"

As the games began, he pushed his way through the crowd, climbed over the wall, and dropped to the floor of the arena. When the crowd saw this tiny figure rushing to the gladiators and saying, "In the name of Christ, stop!" they thought it was part of the show and began laughing.

When they realized it wasn't, the laughter turned to anger. As he was pleading with the gladiators to stop, one of them plunged a sword into his body. He fell to the sand. As he was dying, his last words were, "In the name of Christ, stop!"

Then a strange thing happened. The gladiators stood looking at the tiny figure lying there. A hush fell over the Colosseum. Way up in the upper rows, a man stood and made his way to the exit. Others began to follow. In dead silence, everyone left the Colosseum.

The year was B.C. 391, and that was the last battle to the death between gladiators in the Roman Colosseum. Never again in the great stadium did men kill each other for the entertainment of the crowd, all because of one tiny voice that could hardly be heard above the tumult. One voice—one life—that spoke the truth in God's name.

Sacrifice, Testimony

Date used __________ Place ____________________

Covenant 113

Bruce Shelley in *Christian Theology in Plain Language,* writes:

In modern times we define a host of relations by contracts. These are usually for goods or services and for hard cash. The contract, formal or informal, helps to specify failure in these relationships.

The Lord did not establish a contract with Israel or with the church. He created a covenant. There is a difference.

Contracts are broken when one of the parties fails to keep his promise. If, let us say, a patient fails to keep an appointment with a doctor, the doctor is not obligated to call the house and inquire, "Where were you? Why didn't you show up for your appointment?" He simply goes on to his next patient and has his appointment-secretary take note of the patient who failed to keep the appointment. The patient may find it harder the next time to see the doctor. He broke an informal contract.

According to the Bible, however, the Lord asks: "Can a mother forget the baby at her breast and have no compassion on the child she has borne? Though she may forget, I will not forget you!" (Isa. 49:15).

The Bible indicates the covenant is more like the ties of a parent to her child than it is a doctor's appointment. If a child fails to show up for dinner, the parent's obligation, unlike the doctor's, isn't canceled. The parent finds out where the child is and makes sure he's cared for. One member's failure does not destroy the relationship. A covenant puts no conditions on faithfulness. It is the unconditional commitment to love and serve.

Faithfulness, God's Love

Date used __________ Place ____________________

In the town hall in Copenhagen stands the world's most complicated clock. It took forty years to build at a cost of more than a million dollars. That clock has ten faces, fifteen thousand parts, and is accurate to two-fifths of a second every three hundred years. The clock computes the time of day, the days of the week, the months and years, and the movements of the planets for twenty-five hundred years. Some parts of that clock will not move until twenty-five centuries have passed.

What is intriguing about that clock is that it is not accurate. It loses two-fifths of a second every three hundred years. Like all clocks, that timepiece in Copenhagen must be regulated by a more precise clock, the universe itself. That mighty astronomical clock with its billions of moving parts, from atoms to stars, rolls on century after century with movements so reliable that all time on earth can be measured against it.

Time, God's Sovereignty

Date used __________ Place ____________________

Creation 115

Consider the power and greatness of the One who created the universe and inhabits every square inch.

Begin with our solar system. At the speed of light, 186,000 miles a second, sunlight takes eight minutes to reach the earth. That same light takes five more hours to reach the farthest planet in our solar system, Pluto. After leaving our solar system that same sunlight must travel for four years and four months to reach the next star in the universe. That is a distance of 40 trillion kilometers—mere shoutin' distance in the universe!

The sun resides in the Milky Way Galaxy, which is shaped like a flying saucer, flat and with a bulge in the center. Our sun is roughly 3/4 of the way to the edge of the galaxy. To get a feel for that distance, if our solar system were one inch across, the distance to the center of the Milky Way Galaxy would be 379 miles. Our galaxy contains hundreds of billions of stars.

Yet the Milky Way is but one of roughly one trillion galaxies in the universe. Says astronomer Allan Sandage, "Galaxies are to astronomy what atoms are to physics."

There are twenty galaxies in what is called our local group. The next sort of grouping in the universe is called a supercluster of galaxies. Within our supercluster, the nearest cluster of galaxies, called Virgo, is 50 million light years away. (A light year is the distance light travels in one year. To get a feel for the distance of one light year, if you drove your car at 55 miles per hour, it would take you 12.2 million years to travel one light year.)

Astronomers estimate that the distance across the universe is roughly 40 billion light years and that there are roughly 100 billion trillion stars.

And the Lord Almighty is the Creator of it all. Not a bad day's work.

God's Greatness, God's Power, Omnipresence
Gen. 1; Ps. 33:6–9; John 1:3; Acts 4:24;
Col. 1:16–17; Rev. 4:11

Date used __________ Place ____________________

The more scientists learn about the solar system, the more we see God's hand.

Writing in the journal *Nature,* Benjamin Zuckerman, a professor of astronomy at the University of California at Los Angeles, says that one factor contributing to Earth's ability to sustain life is the size of the largest planet in our solar system: Jupiter. Jupiter, the next neighbor to Earth after Mars, is a giant gaseous planet, with a mass that is 318 times greater than that of Earth and thus a much greater gravitational force.

It is that gravitational force that benefits Planet Earth. When massive objects that could do great harm to our planet hurl through our solar system, Jupiter acts as a sort of vacuum cleaner, sucking comets and asteroids into itself or causing them to veer away from Earth. Without Jupiter, says Zuckerman, Earth would be a sitting duck.

Zuckerman says massive gaseous planets like Jupiter are rare in the universe.

Once again we see God's design in creation. Having a planet like Jupiter nearby may be rare, but it is no coincidence.

God's Wisdom
Gen. 1; Ps. 136:5

Date used __________ Place ____________________

Criticism 117

A young musician's concert was poorly received by the critics. The famous Finish composer Jean Sibelius consoled him by patting him on the shoulder and saying, "Remember, son, there is no city in the world where they have erected a statue to a critic."

Persistence, Reputation

Date used __________ Place ____________________

The Vietnam Veterans Memorial is striking for its simplicity. Etched in a black granite wall are the names of 58,156 Americans who died in that war.

Since its opening in 1982, the stark monument has stirred deep emotions. Some visitors walk its length slowly, reverently, and without pause. Others stop before certain names, remembering their son or sweetheart or fellow soldier, wiping away tears, tracing the names with their fingers.

For three Vietnam veterans—Robert Bedker, Willard Craig, and Darrall Lausch—a visit to the memorial must be especially poignant, for they can walk up to the long ebony wall and find their own names carved in the stone. Because of data-coding errors, each of them was incorrectly listed as killed in action.

Dead, but alive—a perfect description of the Christian.

Death, Christian

Date used __________ Place ____________________

In *Planet in Rebellion,* George Vandeman writes:

It was May 21, 1946. The place: Los Alamos. A young and daring scientist was carrying out a necessary experiment in preparation for the atomic test to be conducted in the waters of the South Pacific atoll at Bikini.

He had successfully performed such an experiment many times before. In his effort to determine the amount of U-235 necessary for a chain reaction—scientists call it the critical mass—he would push two hemispheres of uranium together. Then, just as the mass became critical, he would push them apart with his screwdriver, thus instantly stopping the chain reaction.

But that day, just as the material became critical, the screwdriver slipped. The hemispheres of uranium came too close together. Instantly the room was filled with a dazzling bluish haze. Young Louis Slotin, instead of ducking and thereby possibly saving himself, tore the two hemispheres apart with his hands and thus interrupted the chain reaction.

By this instant, self-forgetful daring, he saved the lives of the seven other persons in the room. . . . As he waited for the car that was to take them to the hospital, he said quietly to his companion, "You'll come through all right. But I haven't the faintest chance myself." It was only too true. Nine days later he died in agony.

Nineteen centuries ago the Son of the living God walked directly into sin's most concentrated radiation, allowed himself to be touched by its curse, and let it take his life. . . . But by that act he broke the chain reaction. He broke the power of sin.

Sacrifice, Sin

Date used __________ Place ____________________

Clarence Jordan, author of the *Cotton Patch* New Testament translation and founder of the interracial Koinonia farm in Americus, Georgia, was getting a red-carpet tour of another minister's church. With pride the minister pointed to the rich, imported pews and luxurious decorations.

As they stepped outside, darkness was falling, and a spotlight shone on a huge cross atop the steeple.

"That cross alone cost us ten thousand dollars," the minister said with a satisfied smile.

"You got cheated," said Jordan. "Times were when Christians could get them for free."

Impressions, Money

Date used __________ Place ____________________

Cross 121

In *Leadership*, pastor and author Tim Keller writes:

Unless we come to grips with the terrible doctrine of hell, we will never even begin to understand the depths of what Jesus did for us on the cross. His body was being destroyed in the worst possible way, but that was a flea bite compared to what was happening to his soul. When he cried out that his God had forsaken him, he was experiencing hell itself.

If an acquaintance denounces you and rejects you—that hurts. If a good friend does the same—the hurt's far worse. However, if your spouse walks out on you, saying, "I never want to see you again," that is far more devastating still. The longer, deeper, and more intimate the relationship, the more torturous is any separation.

But the Son's relationship with the Father was beginning-less and infinitely greater than the most intimate and passionate human relationship. When Jesus was cut off from God, he went into the deepest pit and most powerful furnace, beyond all imagining. And he did it voluntarily, for us.

Atonement, Christ, Hell, Love of God
Isa. 53:1–12; Matt. 27:46; Mark 15:34; Rom. 3:25;
2 Cor. 5:21; 1 Peter 2:24

Date used __________ Place ____________________

According to the *Chicago Tribune,* on June 22, 1997, parachute instructor Michael Costello, forty-two, of Mt. Dora, Florida, jumped out of an airplane at 12,000 feet altitude with a novice skydiver named Gareth Griffith, age twenty-one.

The novice would soon discover just how good his instructor was, for when the novice pulled his rip cord, his parachute failed. Plummeting toward the ground, he faced certain death.

But then the instructor did an amazing thing. Just before hitting the ground, the instructor rolled over so that he would hit the ground first and the novice would land on top of him. The instructor was killed instantly. The novice fractured his spine in the fall, but he was not paralyzed.

One man takes the place of another, takes the brunt for another. One substitutes himself to die so another may live. So it was at the cross, when Jesus died for our sins so that we might live forever.

Atonement, Gratitude, Love, Sacrifice,
Substitutionary Atonement, Teaching

Isa. 53:4–6; Matt. 20:28; Rom. 4:25; 2 Cor. 5:21;
1 Peter 2:24; 1 John 3:16–18

Date used __________ Place ____________________

123

In *Christianity Today* Andrea Midgett writes:

When I think of the cross, I see the arms of Jesus. And I hear him saying, in Matthew, "O Jerusalem, Jerusalem, you who kill the prophets and stone those sent to you, how often I have longed to gather your children together, as a hen gathers her chicks under her wings."

One cold night years ago in North Carolina I went outside to check on some animals then housed in my father's small barn. There was a full moon shining down in bright, brittle light above the pines. It was so cold that the water in the horses' trough had frozen over, unusual for the coastal counties. As I went to get an axe to chop through the ice, I noticed a yard chicken, a hen, perched near the trough, with several biddies tucked under her wings. I was impressed with how she had turned her face and frail body of fluff into the icy wind, her wings outstretched and, it seemed to me, surely tired, for the sake of her children. And I was uplifted by what I took to be a gift and encouragement to my faith, this visual depiction of Jesus' care for me.

But it struck me that those chicks had come to the hen. I don't know if she chased them around the yard first, if some came more willingly than others, or if some were still out there half-frozen. (There were a few late arrivals perched on top of her wings.) I only know the chicks I could see had allowed themselves to be gathered up and protected. They had quit fighting what they had no control over in the first place and said, "You do it, Mom."

And there is Jesus, dying a slow and terrible death, with his arms pulled wide.

The cross is God's passionate invitation to us to come in from the cold.

Good Friday, Invitation, Protection, Receiving Christ
Matt. 23:37; 27:32–50; John 1:12; Eph. 2:16–18

Date used __________ Place ____________________

C. Truman Davis, M.D., in *The Expositer's Bible Commentary* writes: What is crucifixion? A medical doctor provides a physical description: The cross is placed on the ground and the exhausted man is quickly thrown backwards with his shoulders against the wood. The legionnaire feels for the depression at the front of the wrist. He drives a heavy, square wrought-iron nail through the wrist and deep into the wood. Quickly he moves to the other side and repeats the action, being careful not to pull the arms too tightly, but to allow some flex and movement. The cross is then lifted into place.

The left foot is pressed backward against the right foot, and with both feet extended, toes down, a nail is driven through the arch of each, leaving the knees flexed. The victim is now crucified. As he slowly sags down with more weight on the nails in the wrists, excruciating, fiery pain shoots along the fingers and up the arms to explode in the brain—the nails in the wrists are putting pressure on the median nerves. As he pushes himself upward to avoid stretching torment, he places the full weight on the nail through his feet. Again he feels the searing agony of the nail tearing through the nerves between the bones of the feet.

As the arms fatigue, cramps sweep through the muscles, knotting them in deep, relentless, throbbing pain. With these cramps comes the inability to push himself upward to breathe. Air can be drawn into the lungs but not exhaled. He fights to raise himself in order to get even one small breath. Finally carbon dioxide builds up in the lungs and in the blood stream, and the cramps partially subside. Spasmodically he is able to push himself upward to exhale and bring in life-giving oxygen.

Hours of this limitless pain, cycles of twisting, joint-rending cramps, intermittent partial asphyxiation, searing pain as tissue is torn from his lacerated back as he moves up and down against the rough timber. Then another agony begins: a deep, crushing pain deep in the chest as the pericardium slowly fills with serum and begins to compress the heart.

It is now almost over—the loss of tissue fluids reached a critical level—the compressed heart is struggling to pump heavy, thick, sluggish blood into the tissues—the tortured lungs are making a frantic effort to gasp in small gulps of air.

He can feel the chill of death creeping through his tissues. . . . Finally he can allow his body to die.

All this the Bible records with the simple words, "And they crucified him" (Mark 15:24).

What wondrous love is this?

Cross, Christ's Love

Date used __________ Place ____________________

Cults 125

In March 1997 police came to a Rancho Santa Fe, California, mansion and found the corpses of thirty-nine people who had said yes to the wrong thing. They were members of the Heaven's Gate cult, impressionable people who had left homes, friends, and families all across America to follow cult leader Marshall Applewhite. The police found their bodies clothed in black and shrouded in purple. They had committed mass suicide, believing that their souls would leave their bodies and join up with a spaceship that they hoped was trailing behind a comet passing near earth.

In the aftermath of the suicides, journalists talked with individuals who had at one time been proselytized by the cult and had seriously considered joining. Writers Jeff Zeleny and Susan Kuczka reported in the *Chicago Tribune* that a young man named Donald had heard about the cult while he was at the University of Wisconsin. His roommate became a believer. Donald put the cult out of his mind until a few months later when he received a phone call from a representative of Heaven's Gate who offered to send him a videotape entitled "Beyond Human—The Last Call."

"At that time in my life I decided I needed something to grasp on to," he said. Donald responded to the offer and watched the videotape. A few weeks later the cult representative phoned again and offered to send Donald a bus ticket to join the group. Donald thought about it, but eventually he declined, he said, because his girlfriend got upset about it. When the suicides later became public, Donald and his family shuddered with relief.

Just as it is vital to say yes to what is right, it is equally important to say a firm no to what is wrong. The word no can save you.

Deception, False Prophets, False Teaching, Spirit of Error
Mark 13:21–23; Eph. 4:14–15; 2 Peter 2:1; 1 John 4:1–3

Date used __________ Place ____________________

Death 126

Twenty-seven people are banking on the idea that modern science will someday find or engineer a fountain of youth. Those twenty-seven people, all deceased, are "patients" of the Alcor Life Extension Institute in Scottsdale, Arizona, where their bodies—or merely their heads!—have been frozen in liquid nitrogen at minus 320 degrees Fahrenheit awaiting the day when medical science discovers a way to make death and aging a thing of the past.

Ten of the patients paid $120,000 to have their entire body frozen. Seventeen of the patients paid $50,000 to have only their head frozen, hoping that molecular technology will one day be able to grow a whole new body from their head or its cells.

It sounds like science fiction, but it's called cryonics.

As you can imagine, cryonics has its share of critics and skeptics. And of course, Stephen Bridge, president of Alcor, cautions, "We have to tell [people] that we don't even really know if it will work yet."

Nevertheless Thomas Donaldson, a fifty-year-old member of Alcor who hasn't yet taken advantage of its services, brushed aside the naysayers and explained to a reporter why he's willing to give cryonics a try: "For some strange reason, I like being alive. . . . I don't want to die. Okay, guys?"

For those, like Donaldson, who like being alive, God has good news. Jesus Christ has risen from the dead with an eternal, resurrection body. He has conquered death. All those who believe in Jesus will someday also be raised from the dead with an eternal resurrection body. Jesus is the only sure hope of eternal life.

Easter, Hope, Resurrection, Science
John 11:25; 1 Cor. 15

Date used __________ Place ____________________

127

Winston Churchill had planned his funeral, which took place in Saint Paul's Cathedral. He included many of the great hymns of the church and used the eloquent Anglican liturgy. At his direction, a bugler, positioned high in the dome of Saint Paul's, intoned, after the benediction, the sound of "Taps," the universal signal that says the day is over.

But then came a dramatic turn: as Churchill instructed, after "Taps" was finished, another bugler, placed on the other side of the great dome, played the notes of "Reveille"—"It's time to get up. It's time to get up. It's time to get up in the morning."

That was Churchill's testimony that at the end of history, the last note will not be "Taps"; it will be "Reveille."

The worst things are never the last things.

Resurrection, Hope

Date used __________ Place ______________________

Death 128

When John Todd, a nineteenth-century clergyman, was six years old, both his parents died. A kind-hearted aunt raised him until he left home to study for the ministry. Later, this aunt became seriously ill, and in distress she wrote Todd a letter. Would death mean the end of everything, or could she hope for something beyond? Here, condensed from *The Autobiography of John Todd,* is the letter he sent in reply:

It is now thirty-five years since I, as a boy of six, was left quite alone in the world. You sent me word you would give me a home and be a kind mother to me. I have never forgotten the day I made the long journey to your house. I can still recall my disappointment when, instead of coming for me yourself, you sent your servant, Caesar, to fetch me.

I remember my tears and anxiety as, perched high on your horse and clinging tight to Caesar, I rode off to my new home. Night fell before we finished the journey, and I became lonely and afraid. "Do you think she'll go to bed before we get there?" I asked Caesar.

"Oh no!" he said reassuringly, "She'll stay up for you. When we get out o' these here woods, you'll see her candle shinin' in the window."

Presently we did ride out into the clearing, and there, sure enough, was your candle. I remember you were waiting at the door, that you put your arms close about me—a tired and bewildered little boy. You had a fire burning on the hearth, a hot supper waiting on the stove. After supper you took me to my new room, heard me say my prayers, and then sat beside me till I fell asleep.

Some day soon God will send for you, to take you to a new home. Don't fear the summons, the strange journey, or the messenger of death. God can be trusted to do as much for you as you were kind enough to do for me so many years ago. At the end of the road you will find love and a welcome awaiting, and you will be safe in God's care.

Hope, Heaven

Date used __________ Place ____________________

Donald Grey Barnhouse was driving his children to the funeral of their mother. A semitractor trailer truck crossed in front of them at an intersection, momentarily casting a shadow on the car, and Barnhouse asked his children, "Would you rather be struck by the semi or the shadow?"

"The shadow, of course," they replied.

"That's what has happened to us," said Barnhouse. "Mother's dying is only the shadow of death. The lost sinner is struck by the semi of death."

Resurrection, Lostness

Date used __________ Place ____________________

Colin Chapman, in *The Case for Christianity,* quotes Ugandan bishop Festo Kivengere's account of the 1973 execution by firing squad of three men from his diocese:

> February 10 began as a sad day for us in Kabale. People were commanded to come to the stadium and witness the execution. Death permeated the atmosphere. A silent crowd of about three thousand was there to watch.
>
> I had permission from the authorities to speak to the men before they died, and two of my fellow ministers were with me.
>
> They brought the men in a truck and unloaded them. They were handcuffed, and their feet were chained. The firing squad stood at attention. As we walked into the center of the stadium, I was wondering what to say. How do you give the gospel to doomed men who are probably seething with rage?
>
> We approached them from behind, and as they turned to look at us, what a sight! Their faces were all alight with an unmistakable glow and radiance. Before we could say anything, one of them burst out:
>
> "Bishop, thank you for coming! I wanted to tell you. The day I was arrested, in my prison cell, I asked the Lord Jesus to come into my heart. He came in and forgave me all my sins! Heaven is now open, and there is nothing between me and my God! Please tell my wife and children that I am going to be with Jesus. Ask them to accept him into their lives as I did."
>
> The other two men told similar stories, excitedly raising their hands which rattled their handcuffs.
>
> I felt that what I needed to do was to talk to the soldiers, not to the condemned. So I translated what the men had said into a language the soldiers understood. The military men were standing there with guns cocked and bewilderment on their faces. They were so dumbfounded that they forgot to put the hoods over the men's faces!
>
> The three faced the firing squad standing close together. They looked toward the people and began to wave, handcuffs and all. The people waved back. Then shots were fired, and the three were with Jesus.
>
> We stood in front of them, our own hearts throbbing with joy, mingled with tears. It was a day never to be forgotten. Though dead, the men spoke loudly to all of Kigezi District and beyond, so that there was an upsurge of life in Christ, which challenges death and defeats it.

The next Sunday, I was preaching to a huge crowd in the home town of one of the executed men. Again, the feel of death was over the congregation. But when I gave them the testimony of their man, and how he died, there erupted a great song of praise to Jesus! Many turned to the Lord there.

Joy, Witness

Date used __________ Place ____________________

According to the Associated Press and the *Chicago Tribune,* in the span of one year tragedy struck twice in one family. In 1994 Ali Pierce, the fourteen-year-old daughter of John and Anna Pierce of Massachusetts, was diagnosed with liver cancer. She fought the disease bravely for two years, but in November 1996 she succumbed.

Her parents of course were grief-stricken. To deal with his loss, the father sought a constructive way to help others. He started running and set the goal of entering the 1998 Boston Marathon. He intended to take pledges for his run in support of the cancer center where his daughter had died.

On October 11, 1997, Pierce entered a half marathon of thirteen miles in Hollis, New Hampshire. It was the longest race he had ever run. He was fifty-one years old, and so before the race he had a medical exam and was given a clean bill of health.

He almost finished the race. Just ten feet short of the finish line, wearing a baseball cap that said, "In Memory of Ali Pierce," John Pierce crumpled to the pavement, dead of a heart attack.

Death—what a terrible enemy!

Cross, Easter, Grave, Resurrection
Mark 5:35–43; John 11:25; Rom. 6:23;
1 Cor. 15; Heb. 2:14–15; Rev. 21:4

Date used __________ Place ____________________

Death 132

In *Living with Uncertainty* author and church leader John Wimber writes:

> Margie Morton was a woman of wonderful faith. Over the years I had watched her exercise that faith in many different situations. She and her husband were committed members of the church from the very first day.
>
> Margie suffered from brain tumors for a number of years. She had surgery that was somewhat successful, but continued on the long, long journey of this condition.
>
> I was praying for her one day when I sensed the Lord speaking to me. It wasn't an audible voice. Rather, I felt that he gave me some guidelines for ministering to Margie while I sat before him quietly. He said, "You taught Margie how to live. Now you must teach her how to die."
>
> I started sweating immediately. I was not happy to hear those words. I loved Margie greatly and did not want to see her life come to an end.
>
> At the time, her doctors wanted to send her to a hospital in Los Angeles with no real prospect of being healed. They recommended a treatment that might prolong Margie's life but without much quality. She would suffer tremendously, even with the treatment. I shared with her that I thought her remaining weeks could be better spent at home with her children, husband, and loved ones. I told her to share her heart and life with them, and that I thought she would know when it was time to go be with the Lord. I didn't think that Margie would agree, because she was not one to give up without a fight.
>
> However, the next eight weeks she chose to stay home, sharing her life with her family and friends while conscious of her impending death. She did not spend her energies simply fighting cancer.
>
> When it was time, she told her husband that she needed to go to the hospital. When she was in the hospital, her children and husband gathered around the bed and prayed for her. As they left they said, "Well, we'll see you tomorrow, Mom." She responded by saying, "You won't find much."

As soon as they left, she took a shower, and put on her brand-new nightgown. The nurse happened to come in just as she was getting back in bed, and said, "My, how pretty you look! You're all dressed up to go someplace. Where are you going?"

"I'm going to meet my King," Margie replied. Then she died, and did meet her King. That's victory! That's death that has no sting!

Hearing God's Voice, Prayer, Revelation,
Spiritual Gifts, Word of Wisdom
1 Cor. 15

Date used __________ Place ______________________

Death to Self 133

In his book *Broken in the Right Place,* Alan Nelson quotes Paul Cedar:

> In the early 1970s, God called us clearly to leave a very blessed pastoral ministry we were carrying on in Southern California to begin a non-profit ministry which had a particular focus on reaching out and ministering to pastors and local churches. The new ministry was going exceedingly well. However, the "cash flow" was not. . . .
>
> In addition, the enemy brought other attacks upon us which brought embarrassment, discouragement, disillusionment—and even humiliation. . . .
>
> On a given evening, while I was driving alone in my car en route to a ministry engagement, I cried out to God in pain and frustration. . . . I rehearsed for Him all of the sacrifices that we had made for Him in obedience to Him. I reminded Him of the embarrassment and humiliation which we had experienced. Finally, in utter despair I cried out, "Lord, why don't you just take my life!" Immediately, I sensed He was speaking to me in a loving, tender way like a faithful father wanting what was best for His son. I sensed Him saying to me, "Son, I already have taken your life."
>
> Immediately, I was broken before God. I pulled over to the side of the road and sobbed uncontrollably in praise and adoration before God.
>
> Indeed I had given my total life to Him a number of years before. I was His to do whatever He chose to do with. It was at that time on that particular evening that I committed myself anew to die to self and to be alive to God. I so committed my life to Christ that if He chose for me to be a failure, I would attempt to even do that to His glory!

Brokenness, Commitment, Failure, Sacrifice
Rom. 6:12–23; Gal. 2:20

Date used __________ Place ____________________

Death to Self 134

Nichelle Nichols played Uhura in the original *Star Trek* TV program and six *Star Trek* movies. She was one of the first Black women regularly featured on a weekly TV show. As such, she had obstacles to overcome. According to Steve Jones in *USA Today,* a few studio executives were hostile toward her character, which was often diminished by script rewrites, and the studio even withheld tons of her fan mail. After one year on the program, she was fed up. Nichols, who was also an extremely talented professional singer and dancer, told Gene Roddenberry she was going to quit and pursue her performing career.

Before she did, however, she went to a fundraiser for the NAACP. There she happened to meet Dr. Martin Luther King, who urged her not to leave the show. She was a role model for many.

Says Nichols, "When you have a man like Dr. Martin Luther King say you can't leave a show, it's daunting. It humbled my heart, and I couldn't leave. God had charged me with something more important than my own career."

The rest, as they say, is history. Not only did she become a fixture on *Star Trek*, she actually influenced NASA, challenging them to hire Blacks and women for their astronaut corps. She led a 1977 NASA recruitment drive that saw 1,600 women and 1,000 minorities apply within four months.

By giving up her plans to sing and dance, Nichols found the defining role of her career—Uhura—in one of the most popular TV shows ever and influenced a nation.

Like Nichelle Nichols, as we die to ourselves and our own plans so that we can pursue something far more important—the cause of Christ—we find our God-given destiny.

Ministry, Perseverance, Sacrifice, Selfishness, Service
John 12:24–26; 1 Cor. 15:58; Gal. 2:20; 6:9–10

Date used __________ Place ____________________

Deception 135

The Portia spider is a master predator whose chief weapon is deception. To begin with, says Robert R. Jackson in *National Geographic,* the spider looks like a piece of dried leaf or foliage blown into the web. When it attacks other species of spiders, it uses a variety of methods to lure the host spider into striking range.

Sometimes it crawls onto the web and taps the silken threads in a manner that mimics the vibrations of a mosquito caught in the web. The host spider marches up for dinner and instead becomes a meal itself.

The Portia spider can actually tailor its deception for its prey. With a type of spider that maintains its home inside a rolled-up leaf, the Portia dances on the outside of the leaf, imitating a mating ritual.

Jackson writes, "Portia can find a signal for just about any spider by trial and error. It makes different signals until the victim spider finally responds appropriately—then keeps making the signal that works."

Like the Portia spider, Satan's weapon of choice is deception.

Lies, Satan, Stumbling, Temptation

Matt. 4:1–11; John 8:42–45; 2 Cor. 11:14–15

Date used __________ Place ____________________

Dedication 136

In the December 1987 *Life* magazine, Brad Darrach writes:

Meryl Streep is gray with cold. In *Ironweed,* her new movie, she plays a ragged derelict who dies in a cheap hotel room, and for more than half an hour before the scene she has been hugging a huge bag of ice cubes in an agonizing effort to experience how it feels to be a corpse.

Now the camera begins to turn. Jack Nicholson, her derelict lover, sobs and screams and shakes her body. But through take after take—and between takes too—Meryl just lies there like an iced mackerel. Frightened, a member of the crew whispers to the director, Hector Babenco, "What's going on? She's not breathing!"

Babenco gives a start. In Meryl's body there is absolutely no sign of life! He hesitates, then lets the scene proceed. Yet even after the shot is made and the set struck, Meryl continues to lie there, gray and still. Only after 10 minutes have passed does she slowly, slowly emerge from the coma-like state into which she has deliberately sunk.

Babenco is amazed. "Now *that,*" he mutters in amazement, "is acting! *That* is an actress!"

Total dedication amazes people. How wonderful to be so dedicated to Christ that people will say, "Now *that* is a Christian!"

Salt, Testimony

Date used __________ Place ____________________

Deliverance 137

Jeffrey Bils and Stacey Singer reported in the *Chicago Tribune* that on Friday, August 16, 1996, a group of nine children and three adults were enjoying the animals of the Tropic World exhibit at Brookfield Zoo in Chicago. They walked to the large gorilla pit where seven western lowland gorillas live in an environment that resembles their native home, with flowing water, trees, and grass. Then what every mother fears actually happened. Somehow as the group viewed the gorillas from the highest point overlooking the pen, a three-year-old boy climbed up the railing without his mother seeing him. He then tumbled over the railing and fell some twenty-four feet to the concrete floor of the gorilla pit. As he fell his face struck the wall, and when he landed he lay completely still.

At the sight of a toddler at the mercy of gorillas, the crowd immediately began screaming and calling for help. One gorilla, named Binti-Jua, quickly moved toward the boy. Binti-Jua reached down with one arm and picked up the little boy. With him in one arm and her own baby gorilla on her back, she carried the boy some forty feet to the door where the zookeepers enter. When another gorilla moved toward her, Binti-Jua turned away, shielding the boy. Then she gently laid him down at the door of the gorilla pit and waited with him until zookeepers arrived to take him away.

Meanwhile other staff were spraying water at the other gorillas to keep them away. The boy was rushed to the hospital in critical condition, but he soon recovered and returned home.

That the gorilla Binti-Jua saved rather than mauled the little boy was a surprising outcome to a menacing situation. Like Binti-Jua, many things we fear are actually used by God to rescue us. Our God is the God of surprising outcomes, the God who sends astonishing deliverance, the God of Binti-Jua.

Miracles, Prayer, Redemption, Rescue, Salvation, Surprising Outcomes
Exod. 14; Matt. 27–28; Acts 12:1–19; 2 Cor. 1:3–11

Date used __________ Place ____________________

Denial 138

An old story tells of a desert nomad who awakened hungry in the middle of the night. He lit a candle and began eating dates from a bowl beside his bed. He took a bite from one end and saw a worm in it, so he threw it out of the tent. He bit into the second date, found another worm, and threw it away also. Reasoning that he wouldn't have any dates left to eat if he continued, he blew out the candle and quickly ate all the dates.

Many there are who prefer darkness and denial to the light of reality.

Truth, Light

Date used __________ Place ____________________

Depression 139

In his sermon "Overcoming Discouragement," John Yates says:

> Dr. Karl Menninger, the famous psychiatrist, once gave a lecture on mental health and was answering questions from the audience. Someone said, "What would you advise a person to do if that person felt a nervous breakdown coming on?"
>
> Most people thought he would say, "Go see a psychiatrist immediately," but he didn't. To their astonishment, Dr. Menninger replied, "Lock up your house, go across the railroad tracks, find somebody in need, and help that person."

To overcome discouragement, "Don't focus on yourself," concluded Yates. "Get involved in the lives of other people."

Emotions, Giving, Love, Mental Health, Ministry
Acts 20:35

Date used __________ Place ____________________

Devotion 140

Alvin Straight, age seventy-three, lived in Laurens, Iowa. His brother, age eighty, lived several hundred miles away in Blue River, Wisconsin. According to the Associated Press, Alvin's brother had suffered a stroke, and Alvin wanted to see him, but he had a transportation problem. He didn't have a driver's license because his eyesight was bad and he apparently had an aversion to taking a plane, train, or bus.

But Alvin didn't let that stop him. In 1994 he climbed aboard his 1966 John Deere tractor lawn mower and drove it all the way to Blue River, Wisconsin.

Devotion finds a way.

Brotherly Love, Commitment, Persistence, Sacrifice
Rom. 12:10; 2 Tim. 1:16–18

Date used __________ Place ____________________

Devotion 141

According to Reuters news agency, Daniel Lehner and his wife, Remy, were married December 12, 1993. Evidently they believe in doing up anniversaries in a big, big way. Before they even celebrated their first anniversary, they made plans for how they would celebrate their second. They made plans to go to one of their favorite plays—*The Phantom of the Opera,* by Andrew Lloyd Webber—which they had already seen many times.

But just going to the play was not enough to express their love. They wanted to make a grand gesture. So, more than a year in advance, they bought tickets for every seat in the house of New York's Majestic Theater for December 12, 1995. That's 1,609 seats.

With that date still more than a year away, how do you think they celebrated their first anniversary? That's right. They went to see *The Phantom of the Opera.*

Daniel and Remy evidently love each other—and this play—deeply. As they have demonstrated, one of the marks of passionate love is extravagance.

When Jesus walked the earth, there were people who expressed their love to him with extravagance, and Jesus calls us today to love him with extravagant love.

Extravagance, Love for God, Marriage, Worship

2 Sam. 6:14–16; Matt. 16:24–26; Mark 12:30; John 12:1–3; Rom. 12:1

Date used __________ Place ____________________

142

In the 1994 Winter Olympics, held in Norway, twenty-three-year-old Tommy Moe of the United States won the gold on the men's downhill. It was "a beautifully controlled run," said William Oscar Johnson in *Sports Illustrated,* "on which he held tucks and thrust his hands forward in perfect form at places where others had stood up and flailed their arms."

After his victory, Tommy Moe explained his thought processes. "I kept it simple," he said, "focused on skiing, not on winning, not on where I'd place. I remembered to breathe—sometimes I don't."

The winner of the gold medal in the Olympics had to remember the most basic of basics: breathing! He kept it simple.

Likewise as we seek to have a strong walk with God, it doesn't take a rocket scientist to know where we win or lose. Spiritual strength depends on the basics. We need to make sure we're breathing the things of the Spirit.

Basics, Church, Holy Spirit, Prayer, Spiritual Disciplines
Gal. 5:16–26; 1 Thess. 5:16–22; 1 Peter 2:2; Jude 20

Date used __________ Place ____________________

Difficulties 143

On December 29, 1987, a Soviet cosmonaut returned to the earth after 326 days in orbit. He was in good health, which hasn't always been the case in those record-breaking voyages. Five years earlier, touching down after 211 days in space, two cosmonauts suffered from dizziness, high pulse rates, and heart palpitations. They couldn't walk for a week, and after 30 days, they were still undergoing therapy for atrophied muscles and weakened hearts.

At zero gravity, the muscles of the body begin to waste away because there is no resistance. To counteract this, the Soviets prescribed a vigorous exercise program for the cosmonauts. They invented the "penguin suit," a running suit laced with elastic bands. It resists every move the cosmonauts make, forcing them to exert their strength. Apparently the regimen is working.

We often long dreamily for days without difficulty, but God knows better. The easier our life, the weaker our spiritual fiber, for strength of any kind grows only by exertion.

Strength, Work

Date used __________ Place ____________________

According to the Associated Press, on December 14, 1996, a 763-foot grain freighter, the *Bright Field,* was heading down the Mississippi at New Orleans, Louisiana, when it lost control, veered toward the shore, and crashed into a riverside shopping mall. At the time the Riverwalk Mall was crowded with some 1,000 shoppers, and 116 people were injured. The impact of the freighter demolished parts of the wharf, which is the site of two hundred shops and restaurants as well as the adjoining Hilton Hotel.

The ship had lost control at the stretch in the Mississippi that is considered the most dangerous to navigate. After investigating the accident for a year, the Coast Guard reported that the freighter had lost control because the engine had shut down. The engine had shut down because of low oil pressure. The oil pressure was low because of a clogged oil filter. And the oil filter was clogged because the ship's crew had failed to maintain the engine properly.

Furthermore, this failure was not out of character. According to the lead Coast Guard investigator, the ship's owner and crew had failed to test the ship's equipment and to repair long-standing engine problems.

Sudden disasters frequently have a long history behind them.

Caretaking, Consequences, Laziness, Maintenance, Management, Responsibility, Shipwreck, Sluggards, Sowing and Reaping, Stewardship

Gal. 6:7–8; 1 Tim. 4:15–16

Date used __________ Place ____________________

Direction 145

George O. Wood writes that on October 31, 1983, Korean Airlines flight 007 departed from Anchorage, Alaska, for a direct flight to Seoul, Korea. Unknown to the crew, however, the computer engaging the flight navigation system contained a one-and-a-half-degree routing error. At the point of departure, the mistake was unnoticeable. One hundred miles out, the deviation was still so small as to be undetectable. But as the giant 747 continued through the Aleutians and out over the Pacific, the plane strayed increasingly from its proper course. Eventually it was flying over Soviet air space.

Soviet radar picked up the error, and fighter jets scrambled into the air to intercept. Over mainland Russia the jets shot flight 007 out of the sky, and all aboard lost their lives.

Choose your direction well. Although poor choices may hurt you in only minor ways for a while, the longer you go, the more harm they bring.

Beginnings, Commitment, Compromise, Doctrine, Goals, God's Will, Priorities
Prov. 4:25–26; Luke 9:57–62; Rom. 12:2; Phil. 3:7–11; 1 Peter 1:13

Date used __________ Place ____________________

Direction 146

When Andy Griffith, star of the classic television program that bore his name, entered his fifties, he found it increasingly difficult to find work in Hollywood, and his personal finances became tighter and tighter. He wrote in *Guideposts* that finally he and his wife Cindi decided things would be easier if they moved from Los Angeles back to Andy's home state of North Carolina; so they put their home up for sale and waited for a buyer. Unfortunately the real estate market was down, and no one gave them a decent offer for their home. Months passed, and Andy grew depressed.

Then one day the Lord gave Cindi an insight. "Maybe it's a good thing we couldn't sell the house," she said. "Maybe it was God showing us grace. If we moved to North Carolina now, you might indeed never work again. What we need to do is stay here and stoke the fire."

And stoke the fire they did. Day after day they went together to the office of the talent agency that represented Andy. They sat in the lobby, chatted with agents, and went with them to lunch. Eventually the work started to come in: four TV movies that year, including the pilot for *Matlock*, a show that ended up running for nine years.

Sometimes a closed door is a signpost from God. He has a better way for us to go.

Obstacles, Will of God
Acts 16:6–10; Rev. 3:7

Date used __________ Place ____________________

According to the Associated Press, a Dallas, Texas, man had a disagreement with a bank. His home sat adjacent to a tract of land on which the bank planned to build a new facility. The bank wanted to buy his home and knock it down.

The man said no deal. His property was appraised at $86,350, and he claimed the bank had offered only $68,000. The bank claimed it had offered more than that.

Ninety years old, the man had lived in his house for some fifty years. He didn't have to sell his home, and so he decided he wouldn't. The bank wanted to build, and so it decided it would. The result is a new bank building shaped like a horseshoe around the man's home. An automatic teller machine dispenses cash fifteen feet from where he sleeps. The cars of drive-through customers idle in front of his kitchen window.

These two parties may be adjacent to one another, but can scarcely be called neighbors. Those who walk in love do more than coexist; they cooperate.

Church, Community, Cooperation, Fellowship, Flexibility, Harmony, Love, Marriage, Negotiation, Neighbors, Relationships, Stubbornness, Submission
Matt. 22:39; Eph. 5:21; Phil. 2:4; 1 Peter 3:8

Date used __________ Place ____________________

Disasters 148

On March 1, 1997, a series of tornadoes swept through Arkansas, killing twenty-six people and resulting in hundreds of millions of dollars in damage. To protect disaster victims, the Arkansas legislature passed a bill that would bar insurance companies from canceling the coverage of storm victims, and sent the bill to Governor Mike Huckabee for his signature. To the surprise of the legislators, however, the governor refused to sign it, objecting to one phrase in the bill.

The *New York Times* reported, "Mr. Huckabee said that signing the legislation 'would be violating my own conscience' inasmuch as it described a destructive and deadly force as being 'an act of God.' . . . He suggested that the phrase 'acts of God' be changed to 'natural disasters.'"

In a letter to the legislators who drafted the bill, Governor Huckabee, a former Baptist minister, explained, "I feel that I have indeed witnessed many 'acts of God,' but I see His actions in the miraculous sparing of life, the sacrifice and selfless spirit in which so many responded to the pain of others."

Insurance companies have traditionally referred to any natural disaster as an act of God. Who is right?

Such disasters highlight one of the central dilemmas of this life. The Bible portrays God as perfect both in love and in power, yet bad things happen. From our finite and limited perspective, this is a mystery we may never understand in this life.

Acts of God, Death, Love of God, Problem of Evil, Providence, Questions, Sovereignty of God

Exod. 4:11; Deut. 29:29; Job 1; Isa. 45:7; Matt. 6:13; John 9:1–7; Rom. 11:33–36

Date used __________ Place ____________________

Discernment 149

In 1995 Jane Brody reported in the *New York Times* that Boston researchers had demonstrated for the first time that the eye has two functions.

"Just as the human ear controls both hearing and balance," she writes, "the eye . . . not only permits conscious vision but also independently registers light impulses that regulate the body's internal daily clock. Even people who are totally blind and have no perception of light can have normal hormonal responses to bright light." This second function of the eye, which regulates the body's twenty-four-hour clock, keeps in order our biological rhythms, such as sleep.

"Light passes through the retina and travels through a special tract in the optic nerves to a region of the brain called the suprachiasmatic nucleus, the brain's pacemaker. The light impulses then go on to the pineal gland, stopping to release a hormone called melatonin. Melatonin, the so-called hormone of darkness, normally reaches a peak in the blood at night when the lights are out. But when bright light is shown in the eyes, melatonin production shuts down."

According to Jesus, the eye—that is, the eye of the soul—has a third function: "Your eye is the lamp of your body. When your eyes are good, your whole body also is full of light. But when they are bad, your body also is full of darkness. See to it, then, that the light within you is not darkness" (Luke 11:34–35).

The eye of the soul has both moral and spiritual sensibilities, allowing in spiritual darkness or light. As the human body responds to light and darkness, so the human spirit responds to the spiritual light and darkness in our world.

Discernment, Entertainment, Interests, Lust, Morality, Worldliness
Prov. 17:24; Luke 11:34–35; 1 Cor. 2:15–16

Date used __________ Place ____________________

Discipleship 150

David Thomas in *Marriage and Family Living* writes:

Recently our daughter received a document of almost infinite worth to a typical fifteen-year-old: a learner's permit for driving. Shortly thereafter, I accompanied her as she drove for the first time.

In the passenger seat, having no steering wheel and no brakes, I was, in a most explicit way, in her hands—a strange feeling for a parent, both disturbing and surprisingly satisfying.

As she looked to see if the road was clear, we slowly pulled away from the curb. Meanwhile, I checked to determine not only that, but to see if the sky was falling or the earth quaking. If getting from here to there was the only thing that mattered, I would gladly have taken the wheel. But there were other matters of importance here, most of them having to do with my own paternal "letting go."

I experienced a strange combination of weakness and power. My understanding of weakness was simple: she was in control, I was not. But she was able to move to this level of adulthood because of what my wife and I had done. Our power had empowered her. Her new-found strength was attained from us. So as we pulled away from the curb, we all gained in stature.

Parenting, Children

Date used __________ Place ____________________

Discipline 151

In the 1994 Winter Olympics held in Norway, twenty-three-year-old skier Tommy Moe of the United States captured the gold on the men's downhill. It marked a big comeback for Tommy.

He had shown great potential for years but according to *Sports Illustrated,* had a penchant for smoking pot and drinking. In 1986 as a fifteen year old, he was invited to be a part of the U.S. ski team, but when the coaches learned that he had sneaked out of camp to smoke pot, they kicked him off the team.

Tommy's father, an Alaskan construction worker, decided his son needed some discipline and he ordered him to come to Alaska. There he put Tommy to work.

Tommy was on the job at 4 A.M. and he labored under the Alaskan sun for twelve to sixteen hours a day during the long days of Arctic summer. "I worked his rear end off," says Tom Sr. "And then I asked him if he'd rather be doing this or if he'd rather be skiing with the team in Argentina. That straightened him out."

Tommy recalls, "It was mental torture, bad news. It humbled me up pretty fast."

He got serious about ski racing pretty quickly.

Fathers know that children sometimes need discipline and that discipline is hard. But it yields big results.

God the Father, Humility, Sloth
Prov. 6:6–11; Heb. 12:5–13

Date used __________ Place ____________________

Discipline 152

Shaping a child's character is a bit like stone carving.

Smithsonian magazine once did a feature on a master stone carver from England named Simon Verity. Verity learned stone carving by restoring thirteenth-century cathedrals in Great Britain. The four basic tools of his trade are a hammer, a punch, a chisel, and a rasp.

The authors who interviewed Verity and watched him work noticed something interesting.

"Verity listens closely to hear the song of the stone under his careful blows," they write. "A solid strike and all is well. A higher pitched ping and it could mean trouble; a chunk of rock could break off. He constantly adjusts the angle of the chisel and the force of the mallet to the pitch, pausing frequently to run his hand over the freshly carved surface."

In the same way, when parents discipline a child, they must listen with great sensitivity to how the child responds.

Child Rearing, Fathers
Eph. 6:4; Col. 3:21

Date used __________ Place ____________________

153

Dennis Miller writes:

Out of parental concern and a desire to teach our young son responsibility, we require him to phone home when he arrives at his friend's house a few blocks away. He began to forget, however, as he grew more confident in his ability to get there without disaster befalling him.

The first time he forgot, I called to be sure he had arrived. We told him the next time it happened, he would have to come home. A few days later, however, the telephone again lay silent, and I knew if he was going to learn, he would have to be punished. But I did not want to punish him! I went to the telephone, regretting that his great time would have to be spoiled by his lack of contact with his father.

As I dialed, I prayed for wisdom. "Treat him like I treat you," the Lord seemed to say. With that, as the telephone rang one time, I hung up. A few seconds later the phone rang, and it was my son. "I'm here, Dad!"

"What took you so long to call?" I asked.

"We started playing and I forgot. But Dad, I heard the phone ring once, and I remembered."

"I'm glad you remembered," I said. "Have fun."

How often do we think of God as One who waits to punish us when we step out of line? I wonder how often he rings just once, hoping we will phone home.

Parenting, God's Patience

Date used ________ Place ________________

Discipline 154

In *Returning to Your First Love,* author and pastor Tony Evans writes:

> I'll never forget the time my younger brother rebelled against my father. He didn't like my father's rules. . . . Now, little brother was the Maryland state wrestling champion in the unlimited weight class. At 250 pounds, he was big and strong. . . .
>
> My father told my brother to do something. I don't remember what it was, but my brother didn't think he should have to do it. So he frowned, shook his head, and said, "No!"
>
> Dad said, "Oh yes!"
>
> Little brother said, "No!"
>
> My father . . . took him upstairs, and helped him pack his suitcase. My brother jumped bad and said, "Yeah, I'm leaving! I don't have to take this!"
>
> And he walked out of the house. But he forgot a few things. He forgot he didn't have a job. He forgot it was snowing outside. He forgot he didn't have a car. He jumped bad, but he forgot that when you don't have anything, you don't jump bad.
>
> So twenty minutes later . . . knock, knock! Brother was at the door wanting to come home. My father delivered him to the elements that he might be taught respect. . . .
>
> When he was put out, my brother was no longer under the protective custody of our home. He had to fend for himself.

So it is with those who come under church discipline.

Chastisement, Church Discipline, Punishment
Matt. 18:15–18; 1 Cor. 5:1–13; Heb. 12:5–13

Date used __________ Place ____________________

Distraction 155

A former police officer tells of the tactics of roving bands of thieves:

They enter the store as a group. One or two separate themselves from the group, and the others start a loud commotion in another section of the store. This grabs the attention of the clerks and customers. As all eyes are turned to the disturbance, the accomplices fill their pockets with merchandise and cash, leaving before anyone suspects.

Hours—sometimes even days—later, the victimized merchant realizes things are missing and calls the police. Too late.

How often this effective strategy is used by the Evil One! We are seduced into paying attention to the distractions, while evil agents ransack our lives.

Satan, Priorities

Date used __________ Place ______________________

Distractions 156

The cowbird is unique in North America. While some other birds will occasionally lay their eggs in other birds' nests, the cowbird does so exclusively. In Illinois, for example, the little brown cowbird with its mink-colored head is a common sight, but bird experts say you will not find one cowbird nest in the entire state.

And that's becoming a problem, says writer Peter Kendall. The cowbirds are

> prodigious egg-layers: Each female commonly deposits 20 to 40 eggs in dozens of other nests each spring. Cowbird eggs usually hatch more quickly than the other bird's eggs, and the chicks grow more quickly. Because birds tend to feed the largest and loudest of their young first—because they usually would be the healthiest and have the best chance of survival—the host bird spends inordinate time and energy tending to the cowbird.

As a result the cowbird is pushing some other songbirds to extinction.

Like the cowbird, distractions in our lives have a way of intruding themselves and taking over. Distractions can cause the extinction of godly activities.

Church, Devotional Life, Entertainment, Habits, Priorities
Luke 14:15–24; Heb. 10:24–25; 12:1–2

Date used __________ Place ____________________

Distractions 157

According to Jeff Gammage in the *Chicago Tribune,* in the summer of 1996 several thoroughbred racehorses in Kentucky developed foul nasal odors and bloody noses followed by infections in their nostrils. When veterinarians examined the horses, to their astonishment they found small egg-shaped sponges deep in the horses' nasal passages.

Where did the sponges come from?

Authorities determined that someone wanting to fix races had tampered with the horses, inserting the sponges to interfere with the horses' breathing, cut down their oxygen intake, and slow them down. Ten instances of such "sponging" were reported within a nine-month period, and the FBI was called in to investigate.

Like sponges in a thoroughbred's nostrils, sins and distractions weaken a Christian. They take away from what God wants us to be and do. They diminish our ability to breathe of the Holy Spirit.

Commitment, Compromise, Devotion, Entertainment, Habits, Performance, Preoccupations, Priorities, Sins, Strength

Luke 14:15–24; Eph. 5:18; 6:10; Heb. 10:24–25; 12:1–2; 1 Peter 2:2

Date used ________ Place ________________

Diversity 158

The late jazz trumpeter Dizzy Gillespie is remembered not only for his talent but also for how his cheeks puffed out like a frog's as he blew his horn.

Writer Jim Doherty says that one day Gillespie was talking with Chicago Symphony trumpeter Adolph (Bud) Herseth. Herseth, a White man, is known for turning beet red when he plays. Gillespie, who was Black, kidded with Herseth, "Bud, how come your cheeks don't puff out when you play?"

Herseth replied, "Diz, how come your face doesn't get red when you play?"

Two great trumpeters. Two different styles. God has made us all unique, and creation shouts the message that God enjoys that diversity.

Acceptance, Creation, Harmony, Prejudice, Uniqueness
Gen. 1–2; Rom. 12:16; 1 Cor. 12

Date used __________ Place ____________________

159

Richard Conniff writes in *National Geographic* that on January 12, 1997, two Swiss men, Bertrand Piccard and Wim Verstraeten, set out to be the first to circle the earth in a balloon. Their aircraft was called the *Breitling Orbiter,* and it was a high-tech masterpiece, complete with solar power panels and an airtight capsule for pressurized flight at high altitudes that would enable them to fly the jet stream at two hundred miles an hour. Price tag: $1.5 million.

Shortly after liftoff, however, calamity struck. With the cabin sealed tight and pressurized, the pilots suddenly noticed strong kerosene fumes.

Soon they e-mailed their control center: "Kerosene's coming through each pipe on both inside tanks and we cannot tighten them anymore. It is a nightmare. . . . Answer quick."

They were advised to lower their altitude, open the capsule, and hold on until they could reach the coast of Algeria. The fumes proved overwhelming, however, and they were forced to ditch in the Mediterranean.

The cause of the kerosene leak? A clamp, like those used on an automobile radiator hose, had failed. Price tag: $1.16.

It doesn't take much to undermine a great enterprise.

God intends that the Christian life be a triumphant journey, but often we allow small things like doubt or fear to scuttle God's grand plan for us.

Details, Fear, Sin, Small Things, Thoughts, Tongue, Trivialities, Words
Matt. 12:33–37; Mark 11:23; James 1:6; 3:1–12

Date used __________ Place ____________________

Drugs 160

Jonathan Melvoin was a backup keyboard player for the rock group Smashing Pumpkins. On the night of July 11, 1996, he died of a drug overdose. The drug that killed him is a brand of heroin known on the streets as Red Rum—that's murder spelled backwards.

When news of his death hit the media, it caused an astounding reaction among other drug users on Manhattan's Lower East Side. The demand for Red Rum skyrocketed. "When people die from something or nearly die," explained one police official, "all of a sudden, there's this rush to get it because it must be more powerful and deliver a better high."

This is but one more example of how drugs produce their own peculiar brand of insanity.

Addiction, Death, Fear, Pleasure, Self-Deception, Sin
Rom. 6:23; 2 Tim. 3:4; Titus 3:3

Date used __________ Place ____________________

Drunkenness 161

Baseball slugger Mickey Mantle is a tragic picture of how alcohol abuse can destroy what we value most. After treatment at the Betty Ford center, Mantle went public with his story of forty-two years of alcohol abuse. For a man blessed with incredible strength, ability, and good things in life, it is a story of loss.

Alcohol destroyed Mantle's mind. "I could be talking to you and just completely forget my train of thought . . . ," says Mantle. "I'd forget what day it was, what month it was, what city I was in."

Alcohol destroyed Mantle's peace of mind. "I had these weird hangovers—bad anxiety attacks . . . ," he writes. "There were times when I locked myself in my bedroom to feel safe."

Alcohol destroyed Mantle's body. "The doctor . . . said, 'Before long you're just going to have one big scab for a liver,'" recalls Mantle. "'Eventually you'll need a new liver. . . . The next drink you take might be your last.'"

Alcohol diminished Mantle as a baseball player. "The drinking shortened my career . . . ," says Mantle. "Casey [Stengel] had said when I came up, 'This guy's going to be better than Joe DiMaggio and Babe Ruth.' It didn't happen. God gave me a great body to play with, and I didn't take care of it."

Alcohol robbed Mantle of a deep relationship with his four sons. "One of the things I really screwed up, besides baseball," he writes, "was being a father. I wasn't a good family man. I was always out, running around with the guys."

When God warns us against drunkenness, he isn't a spoilsport; he's a lifesaver.

Addictions, Chemical Dependency, Commands, Regret
Eph. 5:18

Date used __________ Place ____________________

Duty 162

Jimmy Carter, the thirty-ninth president of the United States, did not retire to a life of ease when he left the White House in 1981. A committed Christian and longtime Sunday school teacher, Carter began working with Habitat for Humanity and busied himself in many diplomatic peacekeeping missions.

In the *New Yorker,* Carter said:

> When Rosalynn and I left the White House, we decided since I was one of the youngest survivors of the office and we had a lot of years ahead of us, and I was deeply interested in human rights, and I didn't want to just build a library and go back to farming—we would do things that others wouldn't or couldn't do.
>
> To me, this is part of my duty as a human being. It is part of my duty to capitalize on my reputation and fame and influence as a former President of a great nation. And it's exciting. It's unpredictable. It's gratifying. It's adventurous. I just enjoy it.

Whether a former president or a teenager working at McDonald's, we all have a sacred duty to use to the fullest what God has given us. But thankfully it is not a grim duty! God intends that our duties bring us joy.

Human Rights, Responsibility,
Service, Spiritual Gifts
Luke 12:48

Date used __________ Place ____________________

163

Margaret Sangster Phippen wrote that in the mid-1950s her father, British minister W. E. Sangster, began to notice some uneasiness in his throat and a dragging in his leg. When he went to the doctor, he found that he had an incurable disease that caused progressive muscular atrophy. His muscles would gradually waste away, his voice would fail, his throat would soon become unable to swallow.

Sangster threw himself into his work in British home missions, figuring he could still write and he would have even more time for prayer. "Let me stay in the struggle, Lord," he pleaded. "I don't mind if I can no longer be a general, but give me just a regiment to lead." He wrote articles and books, and helped organize prayer cells throughout England. "I'm only in the kindergarten of suffering," he told people who pitied him.

Gradually Sangster's legs became useless. His voice went completely. But he could still hold a pen, shakily. On Easter morning, just a few weeks before he died, he wrote a letter to his daughter. In it, he said, "It is terrible to wake up on Easter morning and have no voice to shout, 'He is risen!'—but it would be still more terrible to have a voice and not want to shout."

Praise, Suffering

Date used __________ Place ____________________

164

Harvey Penick was the golf coach at the University of Texas from 1931 to 1963 and the golf mentor for some of the greats: Ben Crenshaw, Tom Kite, Kathy Whitworth, Betsy Rawls, and Mickey Wright. They returned to Penick even after years on the pro golfers' circuit to seek his help with their putting, chipping, and driving.

Like any good coach, Penick was a careful observer who learned how to golf from watching others. In fact, for decades Penick scribbled his random observations about golf into a notebook. One day he mentioned these golf diaries to a writer named Bud Shrake. Shrake saw the publishing potential in Penick's notebooks and collaborated with him on a book published in 1992 under the title *Harvey Penick's Little Red Book: Lessons and Teachings from a Lifetime in Golf.* The *Little Red Book* sold more than a million copies, becoming the best-selling sports book in history. Penick was eighty-seven years old.

Most older people haven't written a *Little Red Book,* but like Penick observing golfers, they've observed life and learned important things the hard way. A wise person takes seriously the wisdom of older people.

Counsel, Leaders, Learning, Teachability, Wisdom

1 Peter 5:5

Date used __________ Place ____________________

Emptiness 165

According to Lisbeth Levine in the *Chicago Tribune,* for several years TV talk-show host Oprah Winfrey carried on a running public battle against excess pounds that many people can identify with. Having tipped the scales as high as 237 pounds, she tried one diet after another. The weight would come off but then later come right back on.

Then in 1993 Oprah found a new personal trainer named Bob Greene. Greene gave Oprah a ten-step program that included guidelines such as (1) exercise aerobically five to seven days a week, preferably in the morning; (2) exercise at an intensity level of 7 or 8 on a scale of 1 to 10; and (3) work out for twenty to sixty minutes each session.

But Greene's ten steps were not the most important bit of coaching he gave Oprah. He turned the tide for Oprah by helping her understand why she wanted to eat so much. In *People* magazine Oprah said, "For me, food was comfort, pleasure, love, a friend, everything. I consciously work every day at not letting food be a substitute for my emotions."

When we're sad, lonely, feeling empty, eating is one way we can try to fill the void.

Similar to the substitution of excess food for love, we often use things in this world to try to satisfy our true need for God. God designed us to live in relationship with him. Therefore we will feel empty until we love him and walk with him. To substitute things like sex, money, success, and family is to fight a losing battle.

Conversion, Fulfillment, Gospel, Happiness,
Idolatry, Relationship with Christ, Salvation
Exod. 20:3; Isa. 55:1–3; John 4:10–14;
6:35; 7:37–39; Rom. 1:22–25

Date used __________ Place ____________________

Encouragement 166

In June of 1993 the police in South Windsor, Connecticut, pulled over motorists in larger numbers than usual, but not because scofflaws had overrun the city.

One person stopped by a patrolman was Lori Carlson, according to the Reuters news service. As the policeman approached her car, she wondered what she had done wrong. To her amazement the officer handed her a ticket that said, "Your driving was GREAT!—and we appreciate it."

On Wednesday, June 9, the authorities in this Hartford suburb had begun a new program to give safe drivers a two-dollar reward for obeying the speed limit, wearing safety belts, having children in protective seats, and using turn signals.

"You are always nervous when you see the police lights come on," said Carl Lomax, another resident of South Windsor pulled over for good driving. "It takes a second or two to adjust to the officer saying, 'Hey, thanks a lot for obeying the law.' It's about the last thing you would expect."

The police of South Windsor had a good idea. The first thing others should expect from us is encouragement. Our friends, family, and fellow workers will respond best if we not only correct them when they do wrong but thank them for doing right.

Parenting, Relationships, Thanks
1 Thess. 5:11

Date used __________ Place ____________________

Endurance 167

Neil Orchard writes:

I was talking with a farmer about his soybean and corn crops. Rain had been abundant, and the results were evident. So his comment surprised me: "My crops are especially vulnerable. Even a short drought could have a devastating effect."

"Why?" I asked.

He explained that while we see the frequent rains as a benefit, during that time the plants are not required to push roots deeper in search of water. The roots remain near the surface. A drought would find the plants unprepared and quickly kill them.

Some Christians receive abundant "rains" of worship, fellowship, and teaching. Yet when stress enters their lives, many suddenly abandon God or think him unfaithful. Their roots have never pushed much below the surface. Only roots grown deep into God (Col. 2:6–7) help us endure times of drought in our lives.

Prosperity, Trust

Date used __________ Place ____________________

According to the Reuters news agency, in the late 1980s a Hong Kong man was walking near a military firing range when he found a 66-mm anti-tank rocket. He was a gun enthusiast, so he brought it home. He polished the live rocket, which contained twelve ounces of high explosive, and placed it on top of his television.

One day during a probe of attempted robbery charges, the police searched the twenty-two-year-old man's apartment and found and confiscated the rocket. Had the rocket ever fired, it would have demolished the apartment.

Why would someone willfully bring such a deadly force into his living room? Few people have explosives *on top* of their televisions, but many have deadly spiritual weapons *in* their televisions. They bring spiritual danger to themselves and their family when they turn on the tube, because they watch programs that can destroy their values.

Television, Thoughts, Values, Violence

Prov. 4:23; Rom. 12:1–2; Phil. 4:8; 1 John 2:15–17

Date used __________ Place ____________________

Evangelism 169

In the spring of 1992 fourth-grade students in Portland, Maine, carried out a novel experiment. Their teacher, Pamela Trieu, was teaching the kids about the ocean, specifically about the Gulf Stream that flows along the East Coast and then turns toward Europe. According to Reuters, she had the kids put messages with their addresses in empty wine bottles, and then a fisherman took the twenty-one bottles away from shore and threw them into the ocean. They hoped that some of the bottles might drift to England.

Three months later, two bottles washed up in Canada. The class heard nothing else and assumed that the rest of the bottles were lost at sea. Two years passed. Then one of the students, Geoff Hight, received a surprise letter from a girl in Pornichet, France. She found one of their bottles while walking with her father on the beach.

Our efforts at evangelism are often like tossing a bottle with a message into the ocean. We share the gospel with others however we can—giving them a piece of literature, a personal testimony, a prayer with someone in need. We see no response and think our message is forgotten, "lost at sea." But years later we learn that the Spirit of God—like the mighty Gulf Stream—has carried our message to its destination.

Gospel, Patience
Isa. 55:10–11; Rom. 1:16

Date used __________ Place ____________________

Evangelism 170

In *Leadership,* Graham R. Hodges writes:

> When I was a boy milking several cows each morning and night, I dreaded the cocklebur season. In late summer, this prolific weed turned brown, and its seed pods, each armed with dozens of sharp spines, caught in the cows' tails until the animals' fly switchers were transformed into mean whips. One hard switch of such a tail in the milker's face made him lose considerable religion.
>
> So I learned to hate the cocklebur.
>
> Later, comfortably removed from the dairy industry, I learned a remarkable fact about the cocklebur: its sticky seed pod contains several seeds, not just one. And these seeds germinate in different years. Thus, if seed *A* fails to sprout next year because of a drought, seed *B* will be there waiting for the year after next, and seed *C* the year after that, waiting until the right conditions for germination arrive.

Hodges says the genius of the cocklebur pod is much like that of the spiritual seeds we plant in the lives of others. People don't always respond to God's Word immediately. But the seed is planted, and when the time is ripe, it will bring a harvest.

Patience, Reaping, Seeds, Sowing
Isa. 55:10–11; John 4:35–38; Gal. 6:9–10

Date used __________ Place ____________________

Evangelism 171

An old man, walking the beach at dawn, noticed a young man ahead of him picking up starfish and flinging them into the sea. Catching up with the youth, he asked what he was doing. The answer was that the stranded starfish would die if left until the morning sun.

"But the beach goes on for miles, and there are millions of starfish," countered the old man. "How can your effort make a difference?"

The young man looked at the starfish in his hand and then threw it to safety in the waves. "It makes a difference to this one," he said.

Great Commission, Service

Date used __________ Place ____________________

172

Survivor Eva Hart remembers the night, April 15, 1912, on which the Titanic plunged 12,000 feet to the Atlantic floor, some two hours and forty minutes after an iceberg tore a 300-foot gash in the starboard side: "I saw all the horror of its sinking, and I heard, even more dreadful, the cries of drowning people."

Although twenty lifeboats and rafts were launched—too few and only partly filled—most of the passengers ended up struggling in the icy seas while those in the boats waited a safe distance away.

Lifeboat No. 14 did row back to the scene after the unsinkable ship slipped from sight at 2:20 A.M. Alone, it chased cries in the darkness, seeking and saving a precious few. Incredibly, no other boat joined it. Some were already overloaded, but in virtually every other boat, those already saved rowed their half-filled boats aimlessly in the night, listening to the cries of the lost. Each feared a crush of unknown swimmers would cling to their craft, eventually swamping it.

"I came to seek and to save the lost," our Savior said. And he commissioned us to do the same. But we face a large obstacle: fear. While people drown in the treacherous waters around us, we are tempted to stay dry and make certain no one rocks the boat.

Selfishness, Compassion

Date used __________ Place ____________________

Even if people reject the gospel, we still must love them. A good example of this was reported by Ralph Neighbour, pastor of Houston's West Memorial Baptist Church (in *Death and the Caring Community,* by Larry Richards and Paul Johnson):

Jack had been president of a large corporation, and when he got cancer, they ruthlessly dumped him. He went through his insurance, used his life savings, and had practically nothing left.

I visited him with one of my deacons, who said, "Jack, you speak so openly about the brief life you have left. I wonder if you've prepared for your life after death?"

Jack stood up, livid with rage. "You———Christians. All you ever think about is what's going to happen to me after I die. If your God is so great, why doesn't he do something about the real problems of life?" He went on to tell us he was leaving his wife penniless and his daughter without money for college. Then he ordered us out.

Later my deacon insisted we go back. We did.

"Jack, I know I offended you," he said. "I humbly apologize. But I want you to know I've been working since then. Your first problem is where your family will live after you die. A realtor in our church has agreed to sell your house and give your wife his commission.

"I guarantee you that, if you'll permit us, some other men and I will make the house payments until it's sold.

"Then, I've contacted the owner of an apartment house down the street. He's offered your wife a three-bedroom apartment plus free utilities and an $850-a-month salary in return for her collecting rents and supervising plumbing and electrical repairs. The income from your house should pay for your daughter's college. I just wanted you to know your family will be cared for."

Jack cried like a baby.

He died shortly thereafter, so wrapped in pain he never accepted Christ. But he experienced God's love even while rejecting him. And his widow, touched by the caring Christians, responded to the gospel message.

Love, Witness

Date used __________ Place ____________________

Evangelism 174

Roger Storms, pastor of First Christian Church in Chandler, Arizona, tells this story:

One Sunday, a car had broken down in the alley behind our facilities, and the driver had jacked up the car and crawled underneath to work on the problem. Suddenly, we heard him scream for help. The jack had slipped, and the car had come down on top of him.

Someone shouted, "Call 9-1-1!" and a couple of people ran for the phone. Several of our men gathered around the large car and strained to lift it off the trapped man. Nurses from our congregation were rounded up and brought to the scene. Somehow the men were able to ease the car's weight off the man, and he was pulled free. Our nurses checked him over. He was scratched up and shaken, but otherwise okay.

When this man was in peril, people did all they could to help—risking themselves, inconveniencing themselves. Whatever was necessary to save this man, they were ready to try. How we need this same attitude when it comes to rescuing those in greatest peril—the danger of losing life eternally!

Convenience, Sacrifice

Date used __________ Place ____________________

175

One Mercedes Benz TV commercial shows their car colliding with a cement wall during a safety test. Someone then asks the company spokesman why they do not enforce their patent on the Mercedes Benz energy-absorbing car body, a design evidently copied by other companies because of its success.

He replies matter-of-factly, "Because some things in life are too important not to share."

How true. In that category also falls the gospel of salvation, which saves people from far more than auto collisions.

Gospel, Selfishness

Date used __________ Place ____________________

Evangelism 176

On July 15, 1986, Roger Clemens, the sizzling righthander for the Boston Red Sox, started his first All-Star Game. In the second inning he came to bat, something he hadn't done in years because of the American League's designated-hitter rule. He took a few uncertain practice swings and then looked out at his forbidding opponent, Dwight Gooden, who the previous year had won the Cy Young award.

Gooden wound up and threw a white-hot fastball past Clemens. With an embarrassed smile on his face, Clemens stepped out of the box and asked catcher Gary Carter, "Is that what my pitches look like?"

"You bet it is!" replied Carter. Although Clemens quickly struck out, he went on to pitch three perfect innings and be named the game's most valuable player. From that day on, he later said, with a fresh reminder of how overpowering a good fastball is, he pitched with far greater boldness.

Sometimes we forget the Holy Spirit within us and how powerful our witness can be. The gospel has supernatural power—when we speak it in confidence.

Gospel, Boldness

Date used __________ Place ____________________

Evangelism 177

Chris Edwardson, a medical doctor who practices in Dallas, Oregon, writes in the *Pentecostal Evangel:*

> One day a judge came to my office. I asked him what he was really in for because his leg cast didn't need to be checked.
>
> He said, "I just thought maybe you could give me a reason to live." He broke down and cried. I led him to the Lord.
>
> I asked him what prompted him to tell me that. He said, "When you walked into the room, I saw something in your eyes that told me you had what I wanted. Something told me you knew the answer to life. I look in men's faces all day long, judging the truth. I could see that you believed with all your heart that what you were telling me was true. It was enough to convince me I needed it."

Sincere faith is in itself a powerful witness.

Divine Appointments, Light, Salt, Sincerity, Truth, Witnessing
Matt. 5:13–16; 2 Cor. 2:14–17; 1 Peter 3:15

Date used __________ Place ____________________

Evangelism 178

When Jeff Van Gundy, coach of the New York Knicks basketball team, was attending Yale University, he learned an important lesson the hard way. In the *New York Times* Ira Berkow writes:

> Living in a dorm across the quad from Van Gundy in New Haven was the actress Jodie Foster, also a Yale freshman. The twelve students on Van Gundy's floor had put up $100 each and the total would go to the one who got a legitimate date with her.
>
> "I had seen her around," Van Gundy said, "but was too shy to go engage her in conversation and then ask her out."
>
> One evening on his way back to the dorm he was walking by a store that made popcorn, and a voice behind him said, "Geez, that popcorn smells really good." Young Van Gundy turned around, and it was Jodie Foster. "Yeah, it does," he said. And that was it!
>
> "Finally one guy had the guts to ask her out, and she went with him," said Van Gundy, shaking his head in sorrow after all these years. "He got the $1,200.
>
> "But I vowed that I would never be that flustered, or that unprepared, again."

Many opportunities come suddenly, including the chance to tell others the good news of Jesus Christ. We need to be prepared.

Ministry, Opportunity, Preparation, Readiness
1 Peter 3:15

Date used __________ Place ____________________

Evangelism 179

In *Today's Christian Woman,* contemporary Christian singer Susan Ashton tells how God arranged for her to sing about Christ in a setting she never would have dreamed of:

> Garth Brooks's brother Kelly dates a woman who likes my music. One day, after she played my recordings for Kelly, he called Garth and told him he should take me on the road. So he did!
>
> When I got to know Garth better, he admitted he hadn't heard me sing until I stepped on stage in Spain. That night, he was floored—he said he loved my voice and found my song lyrics moving.
>
> But I was scared! I was afraid I might be booed off the stage while the audience screamed, "Garth! Garth!" But incredibly, I received a standing ovation. I was overwhelmed with how open the audience was to me talking about what it means to be a Christian.

While very few of us will bear witness for Christ on a country music stage, God will put each of us in situations we never would have imagined to shine forth his glory and gospel. Your stage may be the cafeteria at work, or a PTA meeting at school, or a conversation with a solitary stranger on a bus. The God who arranged the situation will also empower you to speak. When it happens, be bold!

Boldness, Fear, Witness
Matt. 10; Acts 1:8; 8:26–40; 23:11;
1 Cor. 16:9; Phil. 1:20; 1 Peter 3:15–16

Date used __________ Place ____________________

Evil 180

According to the Associated Press, on June 4, 1961, the K–19, a Soviet nuclear submarine, was conducting a training exercise in the North Atlantic when a pipe carrying coolant to the nuclear reactor burst. In the reactor room the temperature quickly soared to 140 degrees, and the radiation level mounted. The reactor had to be cooled or it would burst, poisoning the sea with radiation.

The captain of the sub, Nikolai Zateyev, called for volunteers to go into the reactor room and weld a new cooling system. The men would work in three-man shifts for five to ten minutes, wearing only raincoats and gas masks for protection.

The first volunteer stumbled out of the reactor room after only five minutes. He tore off his gas mask and vomited. Volunteers continued to go into the reactor, however, and eventually they succeeded in fixing the cooling pipe. The Soviet sub did not explode.

But the radiation had done its harm. The appearance of the men who had gone into the reactor changed. Skin reddened and swelled. Dots of blood appeared on foreheads and scalps. Within two hours, the sailors could not be recognized. Within days eight had died. Within two years, fourteen more eventually died of radiation poisoning.

Like radiation, evil is deadly to the body, soul, and spirit. Just as a raincoat and gas mask could not protect those Russian sailors from radiation, neither can intelligence or education, money or power protect us from the harmful effects of indulgences in evil. Safety can only be found in Jesus Christ and holy living.

Holiness, Occult, Reaping, Sowing
Rom. 6:23; Gal. 6:7–8

Date used __________ Place ____________________

On Monday, December 8, 1997, tragedy struck Heath High School in Paducah, Kentucky. According to Roy Maynard in *World* magazine, a small group of students, who conducted a daily prayer meeting in a hallway near the administrative offices, finished their morning prayers and were about to head off to classes. Shortly after the final amen, it is alleged that a freshman named Michael, whom the prayer group leader had befriended earlier in the year, opened fire on the students with a .22-caliber automatic.

The group's leader, Ben Strong, called out, "Mike, what are you doing?" and walked toward him. After firing ten rounds, Michael finally dropped his gun. Ben Strong walked up and put his arms around the gunman, urging him to calm down.

Three students were killed in the shooting spree, and five were wounded, including one paralyzed.

In the aftermath of the tragedy, pastors and youth ministers were called in to counsel the students. According to one counselor, "The thing the kids are asking most is 'Why?' And all I can tell them is that what Satan means for evil, God can bring good out of. And it's already happening."

"The morning prayer meetings," writes Maynard, "usually attract 25 to 30 kids; on Tuesday morning, nearly half the school—more than 250 students—attended. A number of the youth ministers who have compared notes all say that they've led kids to Christ in the aftermath of the shooting."

Said Ben Strong, "God's the only one we can turn to in something like this, and a lot of people are turning to him. I believe God can bring revival out of this."

Whatever happens, one thing is sure: good can overcome evil. Fifteen-year-old Melissa Jenkins, paralyzed in the shootings, was one of the first victims to send a message to the assailant: "Tell Michael I forgive him."

Forgiveness, Goodness, Murder, Tragedy
Gen. 50:20; Rom. 8:28; 12:21

Date used __________ Place ____________________

Example 182

The power of a person's example is often unseen until years later. Writer Mike Lupica tells of the impact that great athletes of the past had on basketball star Grant Hill.

> In a world of flashy young stars, National Basketball Association rookie Grant Hill is an oddity. He does not draw attention to himself with a big mouth or an act or jewelry or hair or dances or trash talk. He conducts himself with an elegance that seems more uncommon in sports than a solid collective-bargaining agreement.
>
> "When I was young, I remember watching Julius Erving," he says. "The thing I liked best about Doctor J was that he carried himself with class. He never went out of his way to embarrass anybody. I feel like I come from a generation that has the wrong type of heroes. I never got to see Arthur Ashe play tennis, but I saw the way he lived his life after tennis. I always felt that was the type of person I should be looking up to because of his spirit. It's a matter of respect."

Heroes, Respect, Youth
2 Thess. 3:9; 1 Tim. 4:12

Date used __________ Place ____________________

Example 183

On September 19, 1997, a drivers-ed teacher from Durham, North Carolina, gave a lesson he would like to forget. According to the Associated Press, police said the teacher, age thirty-six, had one student driver at the wheel and another in the car when another car cut them off. At that the teacher apparently went into road rage. It is alleged that he ordered the student driver to pursue the other car. When the other car pulled over, the drivers-ed teacher got out of his car and punched the other driver in the face, giving him a bloody nose. The bloodied driver then pulled away.

Amazingly, that wasn't enough for the angry teacher. He again ordered the student to pursue the other car. Eventually the police pulled over the drivers-ed car for speeding, and the motorist with the bloody nose circled back to report to the police what had happened.

The drivers-ed teacher was arrested and charged with simple assault, punishable by up to sixty days in jail. He was released on $400 bail. Later he was suspended from his job and then resigned.

When teachers are the problem, we really have a problem.

Anger, Self-Control, Teachers, Temper
1 Cor. 11:1; James 3:1

Date used __________ Place ____________________

Example 184

In *Everyone's a Coach,* Don Shula, the winningest coach in National Football League history, writes:

> A lot of leaders want to tell people what to do, but they don't provide the example. "Do as I say, not as I do," doesn't cut it. Of course, I'm not about to show players how to run or pass or block or tackle by doing these things myself. My example is in things like my high standards of performance, my attention to detail, and—above all—how hard I work. . . .
>
> During the 1994–95 season, I had what I thought was a calcium spur on my heel. It became so painful to move around on the practice field every day that I began to wear something like a ski boot at practice to reduce some of the pain. I didn't want to take the time to correct the problem until after the season. I can't ask my players to play hurt if I wimp out when I'm hurting a little bit. Finally I had no choice. One day in early December, when I was heading off the field after a practice, I felt something pop. It turned out I'd ruptured my Achilles tendon. . . . The day I had the operation was the first regular-season practice I had missed in my twenty-five years with the Dolphins.

The next day Shula was back at practice getting around in a golf cart. The pin in the hinge of leadership is our example.

Consistency, Dedication, Devotion, Leadership, Sacrifice
1 Cor. 11:1; 1 Tim. 4:12; Titus 2:7; 1 Peter 5:3

Date used __________ Place ____________________

Excellence 185

Gene Stallings tells of an incident when he was defensive backfield coach of the Dallas Cowboys. Two All-Pro players, Charlie Waters and Cliff Harris, were sitting in front of their lockers after playing a tough game against the Washington Redskins. They were still in their uniforms, and their heads were bowed in exhaustion. Waters said to Harris, "By the way, Cliff, what was the final score?"

As these men show, excellence isn't determined by comparing our score to someone else's. Excellence comes from giving one's best, no matter the score.

Winning, Competition

Date used __________ Place ______________________

Integrity is more than not being deceitful or slipshod. It means doing everything "heartily as unto the Lord" (Col. 3:23). In his book *Lyrics,* Oscar Hammerstein II points out one reason why, a reason Christians have always known:

A year or so ago, on the cover of the New York *Herald Tribune* Sunday magazine, I saw a picture of the Statue of Liberty . . . taken from a helicopter, and it showed the top of the statue's head. I was amazed to see the detail there. The sculptor had done a painstaking job with the lady's coiffure, and yet he must have been pretty sure that the only eyes that would see this detail would be the uncritical eyes of sea gulls. He could not have dreamt that any man would ever fly over this head. He was artist enough, however, to finish off this part of the statue with as much care as he had devoted to her face and her arms and the torch and everything that people can see as they sail up the bay. . . .

When you are creating a work of art, or any other kind of work, finish the job off perfectly. You never know when a helicopter, or some other instrument not at the moment invented, may come along and find you out.

Service, Finishing

Date used __________ Place ____________________

Excuses 187

Business consultant James M. Bleech of Jacksonville, Florida, surveyed 110 executives to find out what excuses they hear most from their employees.

Heading the list was "It's not my fault."

The second-place excuse was "It was someone else's fault."

Third, "Something else came up."

The fourth most often used excuse was "I didn't have time" followed by "We've never done it that way before."

Other excuses were "No one told me to do it," "I had too many interruptions," "If only my supervisor really understood," "I will get to it later," and "No one showed me how to do it."

Excuses don't impress anyone, least of all God.

Judgment, Ministry, Work
Matt. 25:14–30; Luke 14:16–24; Rom. 1:20

Date used __________ Place ____________________

Excuses 188

When drivers explain their auto accidents, they can come up with some amazing explanations. Ann Landers gave these humorous examples from insurance reports provided to one insurance company.

"A pedestrian hit me and went under my car."

"The guy was all over the place. I had to swerve a number of times before I hit him."

"The accident occurred when I was attempting to bring my car out of a skid by steering into the other vehicle."

"As I approached the intersection, a stop sign suddenly appeared in a place where no stop sign had ever appeared before. I was unable to stop in time to avoid the accident."

"The telephone pole was approaching fast. I was attempting to swerve out of its path when it struck my front end."

"To avoid hitting the bumper of the car in front, I struck the pedestrian."

"An invisible car came out of nowhere, struck my vehicle and vanished."

"The pedestrian had no idea which direction to go, so I ran him over."

The excuses we try to give God sound just as lame.

Failure, Rationalization, Sin
Prov. 19:3; Luke 10:29; 14:15–24

Date used __________ Place ____________________

Extra Mile 189

Christian financial consultant and author Larry Burkett tells in *Business by the Book* about going the extra mile.

In 1984 he leased an office in a building that proved to be a nightmare. The foundation had not been properly constructed, and the office building was literally sinking several inches a year into the ground. After more than three years of putting up with assorted problems, including power failures and several weeks without water, Burkett moved his business to another location.

Two months later Burkett received a call from his former landlord who demanded that Burkett remodel and repaint his former office space. Burkett said no, feeling he had already been more than fair with the landlord, but the former landlord continued to call with his demands. Burkett consulted an attorney who agreed that Burkett had fulfilled his responsibility and should not do anything further. Burkett writes,

> The Lord used my oldest son to offer me some counsel. He reminded me that the man and his wife had lost their only child a few years earlier and still suffered from that tragedy. We had often commented that we would like to help them. . . . My son suggested that this might be an opportunity to go that extra mile the Lord suggested.
>
> As I considered that, I had to agree with his conclusion. We decided to commit several thousand dollars to restore a virtually nonusable building.

Going the extra mile doesn't usually make good business sense, but it makes great spiritual sense.

Business, Grace
Matt. 5:38–42

Date used __________ Place ____________________

Failure 190

Fred Astaire was without dispute one of the top singers, dancers, and actors of all time. In *Top Hat, Swing Time, Holiday Inn,* and other famous movies, he danced and crooned his way into people's hearts worldwide.

But in 1932, when Astaire was starting out, a Hollywood talent judge wrote on his screen test: "Can't act. Can't sing. Can dance a little."

As Christians, we may fail badly. *What kind of a Christian would do that?* we think. *How can I ever serve Christ again?*

But we develop in the Christian life when we leave those failures behind and daily use our God-given gifts for him. In time, those failures will be forgotten footnotes.

Spiritual Gifts, Perseverance

Date used __________ Place ____________________

In the October 1993 issue of *Life* magazine, a photo by Scott Threlkeld shows three teenage boys who have jumped from a thirty-foot-high cypress branch toward a dark Louisiana pond. Threlkeld evidently climbed the tree and shot from above the shirtless, soaring Huck Finns, for we look down on the boys and the pond.

There's something inspiring, even spiritual, about this picture.

The lanky boy on the right shows the least confidence, jumping feet first, knees bent and legs spread, ungainly arms flapping like a drunken stork about to make a crash landing.

The middle boy dives head first, arms spread stiffly straight and perpendicular, like the wings of a Piper Cub airplane. His head is slightly ducked and to the right, as if he were approaching the runway against a side wind. He is in a hurry to reach the water.

The third boy also dives head first but he isn't hurrying toward the tunnel-dark pond. He is floating. His head is up. His body is in a relaxed arch, both knees slightly bent, legs slightly apart. His arms are nonchalantly straight, hanging from his shoulders in an upside-down V. Poised and self-assured, as playful as an acrobat on the flying trapeze, he knows exactly where he is and, it appears, waits until the last moment to lift his arms, duck his head, and slip into the water.

No matter their kinesthetic sense or style, each of these three boys did a challenging thing: He took a scary leap.

Granted, high dives into country backwaters aren't always wise, but sometimes to follow God we must take a similar leap of faith. When we do, we will find that the kingdom of God is in the pond.

Fear, Ministry, Obedience, Risk, Service
Matt. 14:22–33; Heb. 11:8–10

Date used __________ Place ____________________

Faith 192

An illustration of the balance between faith and works lies hidden within any tree. Leaves use up nutrients in the process of photosynthesis. As the leaves consume nutrients in the sap, a suction is formed, which draws more sap from the roots. Without the sap, the leaves and branches would die. But the continual flow of this sap comes only as it is used up by the work of the leaf.

Likewise, through faith we draw life from Christ. But a continual supply of fresh spiritual nutrients depends on our willingness to "consume" the old supply through our acts of obedience, through our works.

Good Works, Power

Date used __________ Place ____________________

Faith 193

In April 1988 the evening news reported on a photographer who was a skydiver. He had jumped from a plane along with numerous other skydivers and filmed the group as they fell and opened their parachutes. On the film shown on the telecast, as the final skydiver opened his chute, the picture went berserk. The announcer reported that the cameraman had fallen to his death, having jumped out of the plane without his parachute. It wasn't until he reached for the absent ripcord that he realized he was freefalling without a parachute.

Until that point, the jump probably seemed exciting and fun. But tragically, he had acted with thoughtless haste and deadly foolishness. Nothing could save him, for his faith was in a parachute never buckled on. Faith in anything but an all-sufficient God can be just as tragic spiritually. Only with faith in Jesus Christ dare we step into the dangerous excitement of life.

Self-Reliance, Preparation

Date used __________ Place ____________________

Faith 194

The African impala can jump to a height of over 10 feet and cover a distance of greater than 30 feet. Yet these magnificent creatures can be kept in an enclosure in any zoo with a 3-foot wall. The animals will not jump if they cannot see where their feet will fall.

Faith is the ability to trust what we cannot see, and with faith we are freed from the flimsy enclosures of life that only fear allows to entrap us.

Spiritual Perception, Vision

Date used __________ Place ____________________

This piece was heard on National Public Radio's *Morning Edition* on November 2, 1988:

> In 1958, America's first commercial jet air service began with the flight of the Boeing 707. A month after that first flight, a traveler on a piston-engine, propeller-driven DC-6 airliner struck up a conversation with a fellow passenger. The passenger happened to be a Boeing engineer. The traveler asked the engineer about the new jet aircraft, whereupon the engineer began speaking at length about the extensive testing Boeing had done on the jet engine before bringing it into commercial service. He recounted Boeing's experience with engines, from the B-17 to the B-52.
>
> When his traveling companion asked him if he himself had yet flown on the new 707 jet airliner, the engineer replied, "I think I'll wait until it's been in service awhile."

Even enthusiastic talking about our faith doesn't mean much if we aren't also willing to put our lives where our mouth is.

Trust, Testimony

Date used __________ Place ____________________

Faith 196

Donner Atwood, in *Reformed Review,* writes:

During the terrible days of the Blitz, a father, holding his small son by the hand, ran from a building that had been struck by a bomb. In the front yard was a shell hole. Seeking shelter as soon as possible, the father jumped into the hole and held up his arms for his son to follow.

Terrified, yet hearing his father's voice telling him to jump, the boy replied, "I can't see you!"

The father, looking up against the sky tinted red by the burning buildings, called to the silhouette of his son, "But I can see you. Jump!"

The boy jumped, because he trusted his father.

The Christian faith enables us to face life or meet death, not because we can see, but with the certainty that we are seen; not that we know all the answers, but that we are known.

Father God, God's Knowledge

Date used __________ Place ____________________

Faith 197

Imagine a family of mice who lived all their lives in a large piano. To them in their piano-world came the music of the instrument, filling all the dark spaces with sound and harmony. At first the mice were impressed by it. They drew comfort and wonder from the thought that there was Someone who made the music—though invisible to them—above, yet close to them. They loved to think of the Great Player whom they could not see.

Then one day a daring mouse climbed up part of the piano and returned very thoughtful. He had found out how music was made. Wires were the secret; tightly stretched wires of graduated lengths that trembled and vibrated. They must revise all their old beliefs: none but the most conservative could any longer believe in the Unseen Player.

Later, another explorer carried the explanation further. Hammers were now the secret, numbers of hammers dancing and leaping on the wires. This was a more complicated theory, but it all went to show that they lived in a purely mechanical and mathematical world. The Unseen Player came to be thought of as a myth.

But the pianist continued to play.

Doubt, God's Sovereignty

Date used __________ Place ____________________

Reprinted from the *London Observer*

Faith 198

Author Marshall Shelley, who suffered the deaths of two of his children, writes in *Leadership:*

Even as a child, I loved to read, and I quickly learned that I would most likely be confused during the opening chapters of a novel. New characters were introduced. Disparate, seemingly random events took place. Subplots were complicated and didn't seem to make any sense in relation to the main plot.

But I learned to keep reading. Why? Because you know that the author, if he or she is good, will weave them all together by the end of the book. Eventually, each element will be meaningful.

At times, such faith has to be a conscious choice.

Even when I can't explain why a chromosomal abnormality develops in my son, which prevents him from living on earth more than two minutes. . . .

Even when I can't fathom why our daughter has to endure two years of severe and profound retardation and continual seizures. . . .

I choose to trust that before the book closes, the Author will make things clear.

Confusion, Death, Mourning, Trials, Trust
Prov. 3:5–6; Mark 4:35–41; 2 Cor. 5:7; Heb. 11

Date used __________ Place ____________________

In 1972 NASA launched the exploratory space probe Pioneer 10. According to Leon Jaroff in *Time,* its primary mission was to reach Jupiter, photograph the planet and its moons, and beam data to Earth about Jupiter's magnetic field, radiation belts, and atmosphere. Scientists regarded this as a bold plan, for at this time no probe had ever gone beyond Mars, and they feared the asteroid belt would destroy Pioneer 10 before it could reach its target.

But Pioneer 10 accomplished its mission and much more. Swinging past the giant planet in November 1973, Pioneer 10 was then hurled by Jupiter's immense gravity at a higher rate of speed toward the edge of the solar system. At 1 billion miles from the sun Pioneer 10 passed Saturn, then swept past Uranus at some 2 billion miles, Neptune at nearly 3 billion miles, Pluto at almost 4 billion miles. By 1997, twenty-five years after its launch, Pioneer 10 was more than 6 billion miles from the sun. (Not bad for a device that was designed to have a useful life of only three years.)

And despite that immense distance, Pioneer 10 was still beaming back radio signals that scientists on Earth could decipher. "Perhaps most remarkable," writes Jaroff, "those signals emanate from an 8-watt transmitter, which radiates about as much power as a bedroom night light, and take more than nine hours to reach Earth."

Even a faint message can travel a long way. Similarly, even prayers with small faith can reach the heart of God, whose great strength can work the impossible.

Expectations, Mustard Seed, Perseverance,
Persistence, Prayer, Weakness
Matt. 17:20–21; Luke 17:5–6

Date used __________ Place ____________________

Faithfulness of God 200

In *Christianity Today,* Philip Yancey writes:

I remember my first visit to Old Faithful in Yellowstone National Park. Rings of Japanese and German tourists surrounded the geyser, their video cameras trained like weapons on the famous hole in the ground. A large, digital clock stood beside the spot, predicting 24 minutes until the next eruption.

My wife and I passed the countdown in the dining room of Old Faithful Inn overlooking the geyser. When the digital clock reached one minute, we, along with every other diner, left our seats and rushed to the windows to see the big, wet event.

I noticed that immediately, as if on signal, a crew of busboys and waiters descended on the tables to refill water glasses and clear away dirty dishes. When the geyser went off, we tourists oohed and aahed and clicked our cameras; a few spontaneously applauded. But, glancing back over my shoulder, I saw that not a single waiter or busboy—not even those who had finished their chores—looked out the huge windows. Old Faithful, grown entirely too familiar, had lost its power to impress them.

Few things are more quickly taken for granted than God's faithfulness. But few things are more important. God's faithfulness deserves our untiring praise and wonder.

Familiarity, Thanksgiving, Wonder, Worship
Ps. 145; Luke 17:11–19; Heb. 10:23

Date used __________ Place ____________________

201

Brent Philip Waters in *The Christian Ministry* writes:

A favorite nursery rhyme is the familiar tale of an egg that takes an unfortunate tumble:

Humpty Dumpty sat on a wall, Humpty Dumpty had a great fall. All the king's horses and all the king's men couldn't put Humpty together again.

According to those who know about such things, this piece of wisdom is a relic thousands of years old. Versions have appeared in eight European languages.

In its primitive stages, however, Humpty Dumpty was a riddle. It asked the question: what, when broken, can never be repaired, not even by strong or wise individuals? As any child knows, an egg. Regardless of how hard we try, a broken egg can never be put back together again. We simply have to learn to live with the mess.

There is a Humpty Dumpty story in the Bible. We call it the Fall.

Adam and Eve eat the forbidden fruit. They claim they possess the necessary wisdom to be like God. When the dust settles, Adam and Eve are not perched on a lofty plane. They have fallen. Regardless of how hard we try, things can never be put back together again.

Our contemporary fall is seen in the feeling that things just don't work anymore. Our lives appear out of control. Changes come faster than our ability to cope. Broken eggs are an appropriate symbol. Wherever we step we hear the crunch of fragile shells beneath our feet.

Brokenness, Sin

Date used __________ Place ____________________

202

Where do all these computer viruses come from anyway? What sort of a sick mind would intentionally mess up the computer data of others?

John Norstad, a Northwestern University systems engineer and computer guru who invented "Disinfect," a software program that protects computers from viruses, once discovered the source of many of the computer viruses. In an interview with writer Peter Gorner, Norstad said:

I went to a conference in Europe in 1992 and met most of my counterparts in the PC anti-viral community. One fellow was a Bulgarian who told us about the Bulgarian virus-writing factory.

Evidently, during the Communist heyday, the KGB trained and paid PC programmers to break Western copy-protection schemes. It was an official piracy program. Then, when the government fell in Bulgaria, all these people were out of work and bitter. So they formed virus-writing clubs and set about infecting the PC community worldwide. A significant percentage of the PC viruses came out of a group of disaffected hackers who had formerly worked for the Communists.

Computer viruses are a lot like false teachings about God and morality: they destroy what is valuable. Where do all the false teachings come from? According to the apostle Paul, many come from a group of malicious spirits called demons. They intentionally pump error into the world to deceive and destroy people.

Deceiving Spirits, Deception, Demons, Satan
John 8:44; 1 Tim. 4:1

Date used __________ Place ____________________

Falsehood 203

Falsehoods have a way of taking on an air of truth the more they're quoted. Consider one commonly quoted statistical falsehood. In *Better Families,* J. Allan Petersen writes:

> Pollster Louis Harris has written, "The idea that half of American marriages are doomed is one of the most specious pieces of statistical nonsense ever perpetuated in modern times.
>
> "It all began when the Census Bureau noted that during one year, there were 2.4 million marriages and 1.2 million divorces. Someone did the math without calculating the 54 million marriages already in existence, and presto, a ridiculous but quotable statistic was born."
>
> Harris concludes, "Only one out of eight marriages will end in divorce. In any single year, only about 2 percent of existing marriages will break up."

As this statistical example shows, falsehoods are tenacious. Just because it's said doesn't mean it's so.

Divorce, Marriage, Statistics, Truth
Prov. 30:8; 1 John 4:6

Date used __________ Place ____________________

Family 204

According to Reuters, one judge in London, England, awarded a divorce to a fifty-six-year-old woman apparently because her husband was a cheapskate. The woman's husband charged her $7.50 to repaint the living room of their London home. When his married daughter came to visit, he demanded that she pay eight cents to use the shower. He collected seventy-five cents a week from his family to pay for the electricity used when they watched television. When the couple was first married in 1947, he refused to take her on a honeymoon. He never gave her a birthday present.

In good English style the judge said that the man "had very peculiar ideas about family finances."

The divorce was the final nail in the coffin of a relationship that had died long, long before. Stinginess kills a relationship. Marriage and family life are based on unselfish giving. If you stop giving, you destroy love.

Giving, Husbands, Marriage, Money, Stinginess
Matt. 20:26–28; 2 Cor. 8:9; Eph. 5:25

Date used __________ Place ____________________

Family 205

In an interview for *Today's Christian Woman*, writer and speaker Carol Kent says:

> One day when [my son] Jason was young, we were eating breakfast together. I had on an old pair of slacks and a fuzzy old sweater. He flashed his baby blues at me over his cereal bowl and said, "Mommy, you look so pretty today."
>
> I didn't even have makeup on! So I said, "Honey, why would you say I look pretty today? Normally I'm dressed up in a suit and high heels."
>
> And he said, "When you look like that, I know you're going some place; but when you look like this, I know you're all mine."

Nothing can replace the beauty of being together with those we love.

Beauty, Busyness, Love, Mothers, Priorities

Prov. 31:10–31; John 17:24

Date used __________ Place ____________________

Families don't grow strong unless parents invest precious time in them. In *New Man* Gary Oliver writes about a difficult decision made by professional baseball player Tim Burke concerning his family:

From the time Burke can first remember, his dream was to be a professional baseball player. Through years of sacrifice and hard work he achieved that goal.

While a successful pitcher for the Montreal Expos, he and his wife wanted to start a family but discovered they were unable to have children. After much prayer, they decided to adopt four special-needs international children. This led to one of the most difficult decisions of Tim's life.

He discovered that his life on the road conflicted with his ability to be a quality husband and dad. Over time it became clear that he couldn't do a good job at both. After more prayer and soul-searching, he made what many considered an unbelievable decision: he decided to give up professional baseball.

When he left the stadium for the last time, reporters wanted to know why he was retiring. "Baseball is going to do just fine without me," he said. "It's not going to miss a beat. But I'm the only father my children have. I'm the only husband my wife has. And they need me a lot more than baseball does."

Choices, Decisions, Devotion, Marriage, Parenting, Priorities, Sacrifice
Eph. 5:25; 6:4

Date used __________ Place ____________________

In *The Effective Father,* Gordon MacDonald writes:

It is said of Boswell, the famous biographer of Samuel Johnson, that he often referred to a special day in his childhood when his father took him fishing. The day was fixed in his mind, and he often reflected upon many things his father had taught him in the course of their fishing experience together.

After having heard of that particular excursion so often, it occurred to someone much later to check the journal that Boswell's father kept and determine what had been said about the fishing trip from the parental perspective. Turning to that date, the reader found only one sentence entered: "Gone fishing today with my son; a day wasted."

Children, Teaching

Date used __________ Place ____________________

Father's Day 208

A grown man awaiting surgery in the hospital was talking with his father. "Dad," he said, "I sure hope I can be home for Father's Day. I felt awful years ago when I was 10, because I never gave you a gift that year."

The father replied, "Mark, I remember that Saturday before Father's Day. I saw you in the store. I watched as you picked up the cigars and stuffed them in your pocket. I knew you had no money, and I was sad because I thought you were going to run out of the store without paying. But as soon as you hid the cigars, you pulled them out and put them back.

"When you stayed out playing all the next day because you had no present, you probably thought I was hurt. You're wrong. When you put the cigars back and decided not to break the law, Mark, you gave me the best present I ever received."

Honesty, Gifts

Date used __________ Place ____________________

A Chicago bank once asked for a letter of recommendation on a young Bostonian being considered for employment.

The Boston investment house could not say enough about the young man. His father, they wrote, was a Cabot; his mother was a Lowell. Further back was a happy blend of Saltonstalls, Peabodys, and others of Boston's finest families. His recommendation was given without hesitation.

Several days later, the Chicago bank sent a note saying the information supplied was altogether inadequate. It read: "We are not contemplating using the young man for breeding purposes. Just for work."

Neither is God a respecter of persons but uses those from every family, nation, and race who want to work for his kingdom.

Partiality, Service

Date used __________ Place ____________________

Fear 210

Have you ever feared driving over a high bridge? If so, you're not alone. In fact, some people are so afraid of bridges that they will drive hours out of their way to avoid them. Others try to cross but have a panic attack in the middle of a bridge and can't go on. They block traffic.

Because of this the operators of some of the longest and highest spans in America now offer a driving service. On request, one of the bridge attendants will get behind the wheel and drive the car over the bridge.

In 1991 Michigan's Timid Motorist Program assisted 830 drivers across the Mackinac Bridge, which is five miles long and rises two hundred feet above the water.

At Maryland's Chesapeake Bay Bridge, which is over four miles long and rises two hundred feet above the water, authorities took the wheel and helped one thousand fearful motorists.

Bridges aren't the only things causing fear in people's hearts. In any terrifying situation the way to get over the paralysis of fear is to do like these motorists—turn the wheel over to someone else. Turn the situation over to God and then trust him. You have to cross that bridge, but you're not doing it alone, and God is the One in control.

Panic, Prayer, Trust
Ps. 56:3; 1 Peter 5:7

Date used __________ Place ____________________

Fear 211

On August 14, 1989, *Time* reported the sad story of a man from East Detroit who died of fear. He had taken a number of fur-trapping expeditions over the years and had been bitten by his share of ticks. Then he heard about Lyme disease, which is carried by deer ticks. He became obsessed with the fear that he had been bitten in the past by a tick with the disease and that he had passed the disease to his wife.

Doctors tested him and assured him he didn't have Lyme disease and that, even if he did, the disease was virtually impossible to transmit to his wife. But the man didn't believe the doctors. Paranoid, because of the disease, the man killed his wife and then himself.

The police found the man's mailbox jammed with material describing Lyme disease and a slip confirming a doctor's appointment for yet another Lyme-disease test.

Fear distorts a person's sense of reality. Fear consumes a person's energy and thoughts. Fear controls.

Faith, Trust, Worry
Mark 4:40; John 14:27

Date used __________ Place ______________________

Fear 212

Picture this: Eric Valli, a professional photographer, is dangling by a nylon rope from a 395-foot cliff in Nepal. Nearby on a rope ladder is another man, Mani Lal, doing what he has done for decades: hunting honey. Here in the Himalayan foothills, the cliffs shelter honeycombs of the world's largest honeybee.

At the moment, thousands of them are buzzing around both men. Lal, a veteran of hundreds of such attacks, is calm. Not so Mr. Valli. Describing that moment in *National Geographic,* he says, "There were so many bees I was afraid I might freak out. But I knew if I did, I would be dead. So I took a deep breath and relaxed. Getting stung would be better than finding myself at the bottom of the cliff." He overcame his fears and won a photo competition for his efforts.

Fear can send a person plummeting to destruction. Some believers, fearing the stings of persecution, testing, and temptation, have compromised their faith and slipped from the lifeline of Christ—which is why the Bible teaches us to fear God alone.

Reverence, Persecution

Date used __________ Place ____________________

213

According to the Associated Press, in June 1997 an employee at a Massachusetts store found a $20 bill on the washroom floor with a note folded inside.

"HELP KIDNAPPED CALL HIGHWAY PATROL," the note said on one side, and listed two Oklahoma phone numbers. "MY FORD VAN CREAM & BLUE OKLA," it said on the other side.

The police were notified, and after they determined the names of the elderly couple registered at those phone numbers, Floyd and Rita Rupp, they put out an all-points bulletin. The media published photos and descriptions of the missing couple. The two daughters of the couple sat anxiously by their phones waiting for news as the interstate police search lasted twenty-four hours.

Then a phone call was received at the office of Mr. Rupp. The office manager heard a familiar voice report, "I'm sitting here enjoying the view of the ocean."

It was none other than the missing man.

"You have no idea what's going on, do you?" said the office manager.

No, he didn't, but when he found out, he and his wife were quite embarrassed. It turned out his wife had been feeling insecure about the drive back to Oklahoma, which she would be making alone. She had written the kidnap note and kept it in her purse just in case she needed it. It had accidentally fallen out of her purse in the store washroom.

When our fears—and our elaborate efforts to find security—are brought into the open, what once terrified us can seem silly. The basis for a strong sense of security is a deep trust in God.

Danger, Fear, Peace, Security, Trust
Ps. 46:1–3

Date used __________ Place ____________________

Fear 214

An aerosol propellant called 1,1,1 trichloroethane, which has been used in spray cans of household cleaners, is toxic when the product is used improperly. John Broder writes in the *New York Times:*

> In the early 1980's, teenagers discovered they could get high by spraying the cleaner into a plastic bag and breathing the propellant fumes.
>
> The label on the can clearly warned of death or serious injury if the product was inhaled, said Victor E. Schwartz, a Washington lawyer, but some young people ignored it, leading to at least one death. The company wanted to make the warning larger, but Mr. Schwartz argued against it, saying that teenagers would then assume that there was more of the propellant in the product.
>
> "What do kids worry about more than death or injury?" Mr. Schwartz asked his clients. "How they look, of course. So we wrote the warning to say that sniffing the stuff could cause hair loss or facial disfigurement. It doesn't, but it scared the target audience and we haven't had a liability claim since then."

What we fear controls us. What we fear results from our values. What is most important to you?

Warnings, Worry
Matt. 6:25–34; 1 Peter 3:14

Date used __________ Place ____________________

At 7:00 on Thursday night, December 5, 1996, at a dinner in Washington sponsored by the American Enterprise Institute, Alan Greenspan, the chairman of the Federal Reserve Board, gave a speech that to the average person would be nothing more than boring, economic mumbo jumbo. But not to investors with thousands, millions, or billions of dollars in the stock and bond markets.

In that speech Greenspan uttered ten sentences that in less than an hour began to shake markets around the financial world. The stock market in Australia, which was trading at the time, suddenly took a nose dive when news of Greenspan's comments came over the newswires; a whopping 2.91 percent of its total value was lost by the end of the trading day. Japan's markets tumbled 3.19 percent in value, Germany 4.05 percent. "A little over 14 hours after Mr. Greenspan rose to give his speech," wrote Richard Stevenson in the *New York Times,* "the New York Stock Exchange opened, and the Dow-Jones industrial average was soon down more than 144 points."

What did Greenspan say in those ten sentences that shook the financial world? For one thing, he used the word *bubble*, suggesting that the stock market at the time may have been overheated and overvalued by speculation. "In financial markets, one of the nastiest things that can be said about a rising market," wrote Floyd Norris, "is that it is a 'bubble,' conjuring images of a burst that would wipe out most of the gains in an instant."

As this episode shows, when the chairman of the Federal Reserve Board talks, investors listen. Their money is at stake. The chairman has the power to adjust interest rates, which dramatically affect the economy and investments.

In a similar way, when God talks, the wise person listens, for far more than money is at stake.

Obedience, Reverence, Word of God
Exod. 19–20; Isa. 66:2; Phil. 2:12–13; 1 Peter 1:17

Date used __________ Place ____________________

Fear of God 216

In 1996 U.S. astronaut Shannon Lucid spent 188 days in space along with two cosmonauts from the former Soviet Union. One night after supper she and the two cosmonauts began talking about their childhoods and what life was like for them during the Cold War between the United States and the Soviet Union.

Lucid and the cosmonauts surprised each other. She told them she had grown up fearful of the Soviet Union, and most American adults would have felt the same way. But the cosmonauts said they had been equally afraid of the United States.

What? Afraid of the United States? The idea that Russians would think we wanted to destroy them is incredible to Americans.

These Russian cosmonauts resemble those who do not know God. They think that God wants to harm them, but nothing could be farther from the truth. Although there is a spiritual cold war going on, in which those who do not know Christ are indeed God's enemies because of their sins, they are not enemies that God wants to destroy. They are enemies that God dearly wants to make his friends.

Fear, Love of God, Peace, Reconciliation
John 3:16; Eph. 2:1–9

Date used __________ Place ____________________

Fellowship 217

In the fall of the year, Linda, a young woman, was traveling alone up the rutted and rugged highway from Alberta to the Yukon. Linda didn't know you don't travel to Whitehorse alone in a rundown Honda Civic, so she set off where only four-wheel-drives normally venture. The first evening she found a room in the mountains near a summit and asked for a 5 A.M. wakeup call so she could get an early start. She couldn't understand why the clerk looked surprised at that request, but as she awoke to early-morning fog shrouding the mountain tops, she understood.

Not wanting to look foolish, she got up and went to breakfast. Two truckers invited Linda to join them, and since the place was so small, she felt obliged. "Where are you headed?" one of the truckers asked.

"Whitehorse."

"In that little Civic? No way! This pass is *dangerous* in weather like this."

"Well, I'm determined to try," was Linda's gutsy, if not very informed, response.

"Then I guess we're just going to have to hug you," the trucker suggested.

Linda drew back. "There's no way I'm going to let you touch me!"

"Not like that!" The truckers chuckled. "We'll put one truck in front of you and one in the rear. In that way, we'll get you through the mountains." All that foggy morning Linda followed the two red dots in front of her and had the reassurance of a big escort behind as they made their way safely through the mountains.

Caught in the fog in our dangerous passage through life, we need to be "hugged." With fellow Christians who know the way and can lead safely ahead of us, and with others behind, gently encouraging us along, we, too, can pass safely.

Church, Accountability

Date used __________ Place ____________________

Fighting 218

National Geographic included a photograph of the fossil remains of two saber-toothed cats locked in combat. To quote the article: "One had bitten deep into the leg bone of the other, a thrust that trapped both in a common fate. The cause of the death of the two cats is as clear as the causes of extinction of their species are obvious."

When Christians fight each other, everybody loses. As Paul put it, "If you keep on biting and devouring each other, watch out or you will be destroyed by each other" (Gal. 5:15).

Conflict, Forgiveness

Date used __________ Place ____________________

Finish 219

According to Tim Franklin in the *Chicago Tribune,* in the 1996 summer Olympics in Atlanta, the U.S. women's softball team lost only one game, and it was a game they should have won. Here's why.

In the fifth inning, with the score tied 0–0, U.S. player Dani Tyler clubbed a home run over the fence. She took her home run trot around the bases, and when she reached home, amid the excitement and congratulations and high-fives from her teammates, she failed to tag home plate. When she reached the dugout, the opposing team of Australians tagged home, and the umpire at first base agreed that she had stepped right over the plate.

Tyler had to return to third base, where she was stranded. The score remained 0–0 until the end of regulation play.

The U.S. scored a run in the top half of the tenth inning. Then in the bottom of the inning, one strike away from defeat, an Australian player hit a two-run homer to win the game for Australia. The loss was an emotional blow to the American team, and especially to Dani Tyler. "I just can't believe I missed it," she said after the game. "I didn't know anything about it until I was in the dugout."

How easy it is to feel that if we have started well, the job is done. We knock the ball over the fence and assume the rest will take care of itself. Not so! How we finish is crucial.

Carelessness, Completeness, Details, Law,
Obedience, Perseverance, Persistence, Righteousness
Matt. 10:22; 2 Tim. 4:7; James 2:10

Date used __________ Place ____________________

Fire 220

On the prairies of the Midwest, a grass fire can be a good thing.

"To ask whether a prairie needs fire is to wonder whether it needs water," says writer Cindy Schreuder. "Burns stimulate the growth of grasses and forbs, return nutrients to the soil, expose seed beds to the sun and suppress invading trees and shrubs."

During the 1960s, as people in the prairie restoration movement saw the benefits of a regular prairie fire, the practice of intentionally setting such fires became widespread. Schreuder describes one such fire:

> Pushed forward by the wind, the flames raced across the prairie. Thick, dead grass stalks wavered for just a moment before buckling and falling into flames. . . .
>
> Nineteenth-century settlers spoke of the violence of the burns, their noise, heat, power and attraction. They are reactions modern-day scientists share. "A prairie burning is something like a great thunderstorm—you experience the raw power of nature," said [Stephen Packard, science director for the Nature Conservancy, Illinois]. "After you've burned it off, nothing is left. It's so pure. Every leaf that emerges is new and shiny and wet. Every flower petal is perfect. It reminds you of being young."

In the same way, God's consuming fire brings new life when we willingly let him burn the fields of our hearts.

Altar, Cleansing, Holiness, Purging, Repentance, Revival, Sacrifice
Mal. 3:3; Heb. 12:29; James 4:6–10; 1 Peter 4:17

Date used __________ Place ____________________

221

Mountain goats live in a precarious environment. One wrong move and they can fall to their deaths. Young mountain goats can be in special danger because of their playfulness.

Douglas Chadwick in *National Geographic* writes that the kids of mountain goats are "born to romp—and leap, twist, skip, prance. . . . High spirits and wandering attention can be fatal for young goats. Fortunately, nannies dote on their offspring, tending them from the downhill side to block falls. . . ."

What a beautiful image for how mature Christians should care for new believers. New Christians will stumble and fall on occasion—that is certain—so we must tend them from the downhill side, ready to block them when they fall. Tending from the downhill side means staying in regular communication.

Discipleship, Growth
Gal. 6:1

Date used __________ Place ____________________

In *Restoring Your Spiritual Passion,* Gordon MacDonald writes:

> One memory that burns deep within is that of a plane flight on which I was headed toward a meeting that would determine a major decision in my ministry. I knew I was in desperate need of a spiritual passion that would provide wisdom and submission to God's purposes. But the passion was missing because I was steeped in resentment toward a colleague.
>
> For days I had tried everything to rid myself of vindictive thoughts toward that person. But, try as I might, I would even wake in the night, thinking of ways to subtly get back at him. I wanted to embarrass him for what he had done, to damage his credibility before his peers. My resentment was beginning to dominate me, and on that plane trip I came to a realization of how bad things really were. . . .
>
> As the plane entered the landing pattern, I found myself crying silently to God for power both to forgive and to experience liberation from my poisoned spirit. Suddenly it was as if an invisible knife cut a hole in my chest, and I literally felt a thick substance oozing from within. Moments later I felt as if I'd been flushed out. I'd lost negative spiritual weight, the kind I needed to lose: I was free. I fairly bounced off that plane and soon entered a meeting that did in fact change the entire direction of my life.

Spiritual passion cannot coexist with resentments. The Scriptures are clear. The unforgiving spirit saps the energy that causes Christian growth and effectiveness.

Anger, Prayer, Resentment, Thoughts
Matt. 6:12; Eph. 4:30–32

Date used __________ Place ____________________

Forgiveness 223

Richard Hoefler's book *Will Daylight Come?* includes a homey illustration of how sin enslaves and forgiveness frees.

A little boy visiting his grandparents was given his first slingshot. He practiced in the woods, but he could never hit his target.

As he came back to Grandma's backyard, he spied her pet duck. On an impulse he took aim and let fly. The stone hit, and the duck fell dead.

The boy panicked. Desperately he hid the dead duck in the woodpile, only to look up and see his sister watching. Sally had seen it all, but she said nothing.

After lunch that day, Grandma said, "Sally, let's wash the dishes."

But Sally said, "Johnny told me he wanted to help in the kitchen today. Didn't you, Johnny?" And she whispered to him, "Remember the duck!" So Johnny did the dishes.

Later Grandpa asked if the children wanted to go fishing. Grandma said, "I'm sorry, but I need Sally to help make supper." Sally smiled and said, "That's all taken care of. Johnny wants to do it." Again she whispered, "Remember the duck." Johnny stayed while Sally went fishing.

After several days of Johnny doing both his chores and Sally's, finally he couldn't stand it. He confessed to Grandma that he'd killed the duck.

"I know, Johnny," she said, giving him a hug. "I was standing at the window and saw the whole thing. Because I love you, I forgave you. I wondered how long you would let Sally make a slave of you."

Confession, Bondage

Date used __________ Place ____________________

Forgiveness 224

In an article in *Guideposts,* Corrie ten Boom told of not being able to forget a wrong that had been done to her. She had forgiven the person, but she kept rehashing the incident and so, couldn't sleep. Finally Corrie cried out to God for help in putting the problem to rest. She writes:

His help came in the form of a kindly Lutheran pastor to whom I confessed my failure after two sleepless weeks. "Up in that church tower," he said, nodding out the window, "is a bell which is rung by pulling on a rope. But you know what? After the sexton lets go of the rope the bell keeps on swinging. First 'ding,' then 'dong.' Slower and slower until there's a final dong and it stops. I believe the same thing is true of forgiveness. When we forgive, we take our hand off the rope. But if we've been tugging at our grievances for a long time, we mustn't be surprised if the old angry thoughts keep coming for a while. They're just the ding-dongs of the old bell slowing down."

And so it proved to be. There were a few more midnight reverberations, a couple of dings when the subject came up in my conversations. But the force—which was my willingness in the matter—had gone out of them. They came less and less often and at last stopped altogether. And so I discovered another secret of forgiveness: we can trust God not only above our emotions, but also above our thoughts.

Emotions, Memories

Date used __________ Place ____________________

Forgiveness 225

In his book, *Lee: The Last Years,* Charles Bracelen Flood reports that after the Civil War, Robert E. Lee visited a Kentucky lady who took him to the remains of a grand old tree in front of her house. There she bitterly cried that its limbs and trunk had been destroyed by Federal Artillery fire. She looked to Lee for a word condemning the North or at least sympathizing with her loss.

After a brief silence, Lee said, "Cut it down, my dear Madam, and forget it."

It is better to forgive the injustices of the past than to allow them to remain, let bitterness take root, and poison the rest of our life.

Bitterness, Injustice

Date used __________ Place ____________________

Forgiveness 226

Senator Mark Hatfield recounts the following history:

James Garfield was a lay preacher and principal of his denominational college. They say he was ambidextrous and could simultaneously write Greek with one hand and Latin with the other. In 1880, he was elected president of the United States, but after only six months in office, he was shot in the back with a revolver. He never lost consciousness. At the hospital, the doctor probed the wound with his little finger to seek the bullet. He couldn't find it, so he tried a silver-tipped probe. Still he couldn't locate the bullet.

They took Garfield back to Washington, D.C. Despite the summer heat, they tried to keep him comfortable. He was growing very weak. Teams of doctors tried to locate the bullet, probing the wound over and over. In desperation they asked Alexander Graham Bell, who was working on a little device called the telephone, to see if he could locate the metal inside the president's body. He came, he sought, and he too failed.

The president hung on through July, through August, but in September he finally died—not from the wound but from infection. The repeated probing, which the physicians thought would help the man, eventually killed him.

So it is with people who dwell too long on their sin and refuse to release it to God.

Sin, Christ's Work

Date used __________ Place ____________________

Forgiveness 227

In 1982 would-be assassin John Hinckley shot President Ronald Reagan. Reagan underwent surgery and recovered, and through the entire ordeal Reagan's daughter Patti Davis saw God at work. In *Angels Don't Die* she writes:

> I give endless prayers of thanks to whatever angels circled my father, because a Devastator bullet, which miraculously had not exploded, was found a quarter inch from his heart. The following day my father said he knew his physical healing was directly dependent on his ability to forgive John Hinckley. By showing me that forgiveness is the key to everything, including physical health and healing, he gave me an example of Christ-like thinking.

The same grace of God that protects and heals us also calls us to forgive those who hurt us the most.

Christlikeness, Grace, Mercy, Protection, Providence
Matt. 6:12; 18:21–35

Date used __________ Place ____________________

228

Jimmy Carter ran for president of the United States against Ronald Reagan in 1980. According to David Wallis in the *New York Times Magazine,* prior to a televised debate between the two candidates, columnist George Will came upon Carter's debate notes and sneaked them to the Reagan camp. Many pundits felt that Reagan won that debate, and he went on to win the election. Carter did not forget what George Will had done to him.

In a 1997 interview with Wallis, Carter said:

> I was teaching forgiveness one day in Sunday school, and I tried to go through my memory about people for whom I had a resentment. George Will was one of those people, so I wrote him a note. I asked myself, What do we have in common, and I had known that he had written a book about baseball, which I had refused to read. I went to a bookstore and found a remaindered copy. Paid a dollar for it. So I wrote him a note and told him the facts: that I had a feeling of resentment toward him, that I had found his book delightful and I hoped that we would be permanently reconciled.
>
> He wrote me back a nice, humorous note. He said his only regret was that I didn't pay full price for his book.

Anyone can hold a grudge. It takes character to initiate reconciliation.

Grudges, Reconciliation, Resentment
Matt. 5:23–26; 18:15–35; Col. 3:13

Date used __________ Place ____________________

Forgiveness 229

In *Running on Empty,* Jill Briscoe writes:

A woman I met at a conference told me how she was sexually abused as a small child by her father. She grew up, overcame the emotional damage that had been done, and eventually married a missionary. Years later, after her children were fully grown, she received a letter from her father telling her he had become a Christian and had asked God for forgiveness and received it. He had, moreover, realized he had sinned dreadfully against her, and was writing to ask for her pardon.

Feelings she didn't know were there suddenly surfaced. It wasn't fair! He should pay for what he had done, she thought bitterly. It was all too easy. And now he was going to be part of the family! She was sure her home church was busy killing the fattened calf for him and that she would be invited to the party! She was angry, resentful. . . .

Then she had a dream. She saw her father standing on an empty stage. Above him appeared the hands of God holding a white robe of righteousness. She recognized it at once, for she was wearing one just like it! As the robe began to descend toward her father, she woke up crying out, "No! It isn't fair! What about me?"

The only way she could finally rejoice, as her heavenly Father pleaded with her to do, was to realize that her earthly father was now wearing the same robe that she was. They were the same in God's sight. It had cost his Son's life to provide both those robes. As she began to see her father clothed with the garments of grace, she was able to begin to rejoice.

Bitterness, Family, Grace, Mercy,
Righteousness, Sexual Abuse
Matt. 18:21–35; Luke 15:11–32

Date used __________ Place ____________________

Forgiveness 230

In August 1995 a scene occurred in Burma, now called Myanmar, that fifty years earlier no one could ever have imagined. It happened at the bridge over the Kwai River. During World War II the Japanese army had forced Allied prisoners of war from Britain, Australia, and the Netherlands to build a railroad. The Japanese soldiers committed many atrocities, and some sixteen thousand Allied POWs died building what has been called Death Railway.

But after the war, a former Japanese army officer named Nagase Takashi went on a personal campaign to urge his government to admit the atrocities committed.

After many years of effort, the result of his crusade was a brief ceremony in 1995 at the infamous bridge. On one side of the bridge were fifty Japanese, including five war veterans, and Mr. Takashi. Eighteen schoolteachers from Japan carried two hundred letters written by children expressing sadness for what had happened during the war.

At the other side of the bridge were representatives of Allied soldiers: Two old soldiers from Britain who declared the business of fifty years ago finished at last. A young woman from Australia who came to deliver, posthumously, her father's forgiveness. A son of a POW who came to do the same. And there was 73-year-old Australian David Barrett, who said he made the pilgrimage because he felt that to continue hating would destroy him.

The two groups began to walk the narrow planks of the black iron bridge toward one another. When they met in the center, they shook hands, embraced, shed tears. Yuko Ikebuchi, a schoolteacher, handed the letters from the Japanese children to the veterans, and in tears turned and ran without a word.

Forgiveness can transform the very place where atrocities have occurred into something beautiful—a display of God's mercy.

Confession, Peacemakers, Reconciliation
Matt. 5:9, 23–26; 18:21–35

Date used __________ Place ____________________

Freedom 231

In *The Grace Awakening,* Charles Swindoll recalls the sense of freedom he had when as a teenager he first received his driver's license. His dad rewarded him.

> "Tell you what, son . . . you can have the car for two hours, all on your own." Only four words, but how wonderful: "All on your own."
>
> I thanked him. . . . My pulse rate must have shot up to 180 as I backed out of the driveway and roared off. While cruising along "all on my own," I began to think wild stuff—like, *This car can probably do 100 miles an hour. I could go to Galveston and back twice in two hours if I averaged 100 miles an hour. I can fly down the Gulf Freeway and even run a few lights. After all, nobody's here to say "Don't!"* We're talking dangerous, crazy thoughts! But you know what? I didn't do any of them. I don't believe I drove above the speed limit. In fact, I distinctly remember turning into the driveway early. . . . I had my dad's car all to myself with a full gas tank in a context of total privacy and freedom, but I didn't go crazy. Why? My relationship with my dad and my grandad was so strong that I couldn't, even though I had a license and nobody was in the car to restrain me. Over a period of time, there had developed a sense of trust, a deep love relationship that held me in restraint.

In the same way, our love for Christ keeps us from abusing the freedom he gives us.

Fathers, Love, Sin, Trust
Gal. 5; 1 Peter 2:16

Date used __________ Place ____________________

The Grace Awakening, Charles Swindoll, 1990, Word, Dallas, Texas.

Freedom 232

Charles Simpson, in *Pastoral Renewal,* writes:

I met a young man not long ago who dives for exotic fish for aquariums. He said one of the most popular aquarium fish is the shark. He explained that if you catch a small shark and confine it, it will stay a size proportionate to the aquarium. Sharks can be six inches long yet fully matured. But if you turn them loose in the ocean, they grow to their normal length of eight feet.

That also happens to some Christians. I've seen the cutest little six-inch Christians who swim around in a little puddle. But if you put them into a larger arena—into the whole creation—only then can they become great.

Missions, Growth

Date used __________ Place ____________________

Fruitfulness 233

According to Julie Iovine in the *New York Times,* in the 1990s many owners of small farms in America began to reduce their wholesale farming to a mere sideline and instead started using their property for another purpose: entertainment farming. Other terms for this new way to make a living on the farm are agritainment and agritourism.

Entertainment farmers attract paying customers to their property with country bands, hay-bale mazes, petting corrals, and tricycle courses. City-dwelling families eager for a feel of life on the farm can pay $12 for admission, food, and amusements. It can cost a child $1 to frolic in a pile of straw or pick a flower. Some farms have mazes cut into their cornfields that can take a person forty-five minutes to navigate. Iovine reports that one farmer in Arizona makes up to $15,000 on a good weekend.

In 1994 Alaska and Oklahoma introduced agritourism as official parts of their state tourism policies.

The catalyst for many of these farmers to take up agritainment was economic pressure.

Sometimes a Christian, or a church, can resemble an entertainment farmer. For whatever reason, we are diverted from the central purpose of producing a crop. Fruitfulness is God's will for every Christian and every church.

Complacency, Discipleship, Evangelism, Growth, Maturation, Missions, Outreach, Repentance
Matt. 3:8; 28:18–20; John 4:34–38; 15:1–17; Rom. 12:1–2; Gal. 5:22–26; 6:9–10; Heb. 5:11–6:3

Date used __________ Place ____________________

Fruitfulness 234

According to *National Wildlife,* each week people in the United States generate four million tons of trash. During the holiday season between Thanksgiving and Christmas, though, we throw out even more—five million tons per week—and a high percentage of that trash is simply wasteful.

For example, if each person in America throws away just one bite of Thanksgiving turkey, that comes out to 8.1 million pounds of edible turkey in the trash can. If each person throws away one tablespoon of stuffing, 16.1 million pounds of edible stuffing is wasted.

And then, of course, there's all that wrapping paper. The average U.S. consumer gift-wraps twenty packages during the holidays. If each person wrapped just three of those packages with recycled wrap, the amount of paper saved would cover 45,000 football fields.

New Year celebrations add to the trash heap. After the Times Square New Year's Eve celebration, for example, the New York sanitation department cleans up forty-two tons of extra garbage.

Environmentalists aren't the only ones bothered by the waste of valuable resources. God, too, hates waste. He doesn't want to see valuable resources he bestows on individuals—such as spiritual gifts, time, money, ability, and vitality—lost and unused. The Lord commands that we bear fruit in this life.

Excess, Giving, Money, Spiritual Gifts, Stewardship, Waste
Matt. 25:14–30; Luke 12:48; 13:6–9; John 6:12; 15:1–8

Date used __________ Place ____________________

André-François Raffray, a retired lawyer in Arles, France, made what any reasonable businessman would say was a sound financial decision. According to the *Chicago Tribune,* for a five-hundred-dollar-a-month annuity, he bought the rights to take over an apartment in Arles, France, on the death of its current resident. The woman living in the apartment was Jeanne Calment, age ninety. Actuarial tables predicting the mathematical probabilities of Jeanne Calment's life span were clearly on the lawyer's side.

Thirty years later and $180,000 poorer, Raffray had still not moved into the apartment. On Tuesday, February 21, 1995, Jeanne Calment celebrated her 120th birthday. She was verifiably the oldest person in the world. Each year on her birthday she sends Raffray a card that jokingly says, "Sorry I am still alive."

How little control we humans have of the future!

Aging, Control, Death, Foreknowledge, Sovereignty of God
Ps. 31:15; Isa. 41:21–27; Acts 2:23; 1 Peter 1:2

Date used __________ Place ____________________

Gentleness 236

In *Honest to God,* Bill Hybels writes:

Recently my brother and I spent a lunch hour discussing the mark our dad left on our lives. . . .

Dan and I reminisced about the times we had sailed with him on Lake Michigan. We remembered violent storms with fifty-mile-an-hour winds. All the other sailors would dash for the harbor, but Dad would smile from ear to ear and say, "Let's head out farther!"

We talked about the tough business decisions we had seen him make. We winced when we remembered his firm hand of discipline that blocked our rebellious streaks. We never doubted it. Dad was strong, tough, and thoroughly masculine.

Yet for twenty-five years he spent nearly every Sunday afternoon standing in front of a hundred mentally retarded women at the state mental hospital. Gently and patiently he led them in a song service. Few of them could even sing, but he didn't care. He knew it made them feel loved. Afterward he stood by the door while each of those disheveled, broken women planted kisses on his cheek. As little guys, Dan and I had the unspeakable privilege of watching our six-foot-three, two-hundred-twenty-pound, thoroughly masculine dad treat these forgotten women with a gentleness that marked us.

Fathers, Love, Masculinity, Strength
Matt. 11:29; Eph. 4:2

Date used __________ Place ____________________

Giving 237

According to the Associated Press, in October 1994, Harvard University Law School announced it had just received the largest cash gift ever given to a law school: a cool thirteen million dollars.

The donors were Gustave and Rita Hauser. What was it that inspired such generosity? Romance and gratitude. Back in 1955 Gustave and Rita met at the law school. The day after final exams in 1956, they married. They went on to become highly successful in business. Hauser, who is chairman and CEO of Hauser Communications and formerly head of the Warner Bros. cable unit, was one of the pioneers of cable television and a developer of the Nickelodeon channel. Gustave Hauser never did practice law. It seems his deep gratitude to Harvard was because of its role as matchmaker. Said Hauser at a ceremony announcing the donation, "The school had a unique role in bringing us together."

When we are given much—and are mature enough to be grateful—we naturally want to give much. God gave us his only Son, Jesus Christ. It is no wonder, then, that we find great joy in giving back to God our time, energy, abilities, and money. We owe God everything.

Devotion, Generosity, Gratitude, Love, Offering, Sacrifice
Matt. 10:8; 2 Cor. 5:14–15; Gal. 2:20

Date used __________ Place ____________________

238

In *Leadership,* pastor and author Stu Weber writes:

My youngest son is the third of three boys. The first two are high-powered; the third is not any less high-powered, but he's the third out of three. By the time you've had a brother who's All-Conference this and another brother who's All-Conference that, there's not much left for you to do.

As a father, I worried about our caboose. He is the most sensitive of the three. To encourage him, I spent a lot of time with him in the outdoors—camping, hunting, fishing. Anybody who has spent time in the outdoors knows that a pocketknife is essential gear—the man with the best blade gets the job done. So, whenever you're setting up camp, you're always looking for the knife.

My son Ryan had a pocketknife that became his identity. His older brothers always had to ask him to use the knife as we were setting up camp. That became his status in the tribe. He was the man with the blade.

My birthday came around one year, and my family was planning a party for me. Earlier in the afternoon my youngest walked into my office at home where I was studying. At first I didn't hear him; I felt him—I could sense his presence—and I turned around.

He had chosen this moment because he wanted to give me a birthday present but not at the birthday party. He wanted it to be just me and him. He handed me a present, and I opened it—it was his knife.

When we want to express our love for God, we also delight in giving him what is most important to us.

Children, Fathers, Intimacy, Love for God
Num. 18:29; John 3:16; 12:1–8

Date used __________ Place ____________________

According to *USA Today,* on Wednesday, November 23, 1994, a couple named Sandy and Theresa boarded TWA flight 265 in New York to fly to Orlando and see Disney World. Theresa was almost seven months pregnant. Thirty minutes into the flight, Theresa doubled over in pain and began bleeding. Flight attendants announced that they needed a doctor, and a Long Island internist volunteered.

Theresa soon gave birth to a boy. But the baby was in trouble. The umbilical cord was wrapped tightly around his neck, and he wasn't breathing. His face was blue.

Two paramedics rushed forward to help, one of whom specialized in infant respiratory procedures. He asked if anyone had a straw, which he wanted to use to suction fluid from the baby's lungs. The plane did not stock straws, but a flight attendant remembered having a straw left over from a juice box she had brought on board the plane. The paramedic inserted the straw in the baby's lungs as the internist administered CPR. The internist asked for something he could use to tie off the umbilical cord. A passenger offered a shoelace.

Four minutes of terror passed. Then the little baby whimpered. Soon the crew was able to joyfully announce that it was a boy, and everyone on board cheered and clapped.

The parents gave the little boy the name Matthew. Matthew means "Godsent." The people on board the plane "were all godsends," the father said.

Indeed, God had met the need through people who gave what they had and did what they could. God usually meets needs through people.

Body of Christ, Church, Needs, Spiritual Gifts, Teamwork

Rom. 12:3–8; 1 Cor. 12; 2 Cor. 8–9

Date used __________ Place ____________________

Giving 240

A Tampa chiropractor had paid alimony to his former wife for a long time. In 1994 he came to his final alimony payment of $182. He didn't just want to send his money; he wanted to send a message. So in large scale he drew a check on the back of a pinstripe shirt. On the memo line of his shirt-check, he wrote, "Here it is—the shirt off my back!" The bank cashed it.

When there is no love, giving leads to bitterness.

Bitterness, Love for God, Money, Resentment
2 Cor. 9:7

Date used __________ Place ____________________

241

Charles Spurgeon and his wife, according to a story in *The Chaplain* magazine, would sell, but refused to give away, the eggs their chickens laid. Even close relatives were told, "You may have them if you pay for them." As a result, some people labeled the Spurgeons greedy and grasping.

They accepted the criticisms without defending themselves, and only after Mrs. Spurgeon died was the full story revealed: All the profits from the sale of eggs went to support two elderly widows. Because the Spurgeons were unwilling to let their left hand know what the right hand was doing (Matt. 6:3), they endured the attacks in silence.

Money, Good Works

Date used __________ Place ____________________

In Other Words, a publication of the Wycliffe Bible Translators, recently told a story about Sadie Sieker, who served for many years as a house-parent for missionaries' children in the Philippines.

Sadie loved books. Though she gladly loaned out some, others she treasured in a footlocker under her bed. Once, in the quiet of the night, Sadie heard a faint gnawing sound. After searching all around her room, she discovered that the noise was coming from her footlocker. When she opened it, she found nothing but an enormous pile of dust. All the books she had kept to herself had been lost to termites.

What we give away, we keep. What we hoard, we lose.

Selfishness, Treasures

Date used __________ Place ____________________

Giving 243

For decades various universities, hospitals, and other charitable organizations had received huge financial gifts—as high as $30 million to one recipient—from an anonymous donor. The gifts came in cashier's checks so that the recipient could not trace the source. But in 1997 this secret giver was forced to reveal himself when he sold his company, and a lawsuit over the sale disclosed his anonymous donations.

His name is Charles F. Feeney, one of the cofounders of a company called Duty Free Shoppes, which sells luxury items in airports and in the mid-nineties had sales of more than $3 billion annually. According to writer Judith Miller in the *New York Times,* over a fifteen-year period Feeney's two charitable foundations gave away some $600 million, leaving himself some $5 million. In 1997 the proceeds from the sale of Duty Free Shoppes and other business assets—some $3.5 billion—also went into Feeney's charitable foundations.

Mr. Feeney reluctantly explained his generosity. "I simply decided I had enough money," he said. "It doesn't drive my life. I'm a what-you-see-is-what-you-get kind of guy."

Indeed, the lawyer who advised him in the setting up of his charitable foundations said, "He doesn't own a house. He doesn't own a car. He flies economy. And I think his watch cost about $15."

But the most extraordinary part of Feeney's giving was his absolute commitment to secrecy. Said one doctor associated with a school of medicine, "Anonymous giving, giving that is not dependent on ego, is just really rare."

It is important both to give and to give in the right way. According to Jesus, the right way to give is in secrecy.

Generosity, Money, Secrecy, Simplicity
Matt. 6:3–4

Date used __________ Place ____________________

According to David Dunlap in the *New York Times*, in 1997 during the construction of a new $6 million children's zoo in New York's Central Park, the administrators received some very bad news. The couple that had agreed to donate half of the money for the project decided to rescind their gift of $3 million.

The problem was the plaque that would acknowledge their gift. The commission that decided on such things said it would be just two inches tall and be placed on a center pier in the gateway of the zoo. Flanking the gateway would be two piers that acknowledged another couple who had donated $500,000 for the original zoo and the gateway itself thirty-six years earlier.

It was proposed that the names of these original donors be eradicated from the gateway and replaced by the names of the new donors. When the commission refused, the couple rescinded their gift.

"We were not talking about neon lights," the couple told the *New York Times*. "We were talking about a very modest plaque that would give acknowledgment to a very sizable gift by anybody's standard."

Although this donation certainly turned sour, in the secular arena it is not frowned upon to donate to a cause with the expectation of some sort of recognition. Not so when we give to God. Those who want rewards in heaven should seek no plaques on earth.

Credit, Motives, Recognition
Matt. 6:1–4; 1 Cor. 4:5

Date used __________ Place ____________________

In 1976 six men took over a Nebraska-based company called Bethesda Care Centers, which administered fifteen nursing homes and two acute-care centers. The company had recently lost $3 million and was facing bankruptcy. These six unlikely men were about to turn this ailing company into a showcase of God's grace.

Previously the six had been, respectively, a biology teacher, a math teacher, a rancher, a used-car salesman, a construction worker, and an accountant—not exactly Harvard Business School graduates! But these men were Christians, and they had the gifts of faith and giving. Despite the company's dire financial picture, one of the first things the six did was donate $5,000 to a missionary in Calcutta, India.

Four years later the company was in the black. "And by 1988," writes Ron Barefield in the *Pentecostal Evangel,* "the company had grown to 34 successful nursing homes in seven states. They were so successful that a lucrative offer to sell the homes was received.

"The offer was accepted, but the sixsome had a decision to make. They could take the funds and build personal estates. It is done every business day. If they did that, however, Uncle Sam would have taken a $25 million bite out of the proceeds.

"So, they opted for a corporate not-for-profit restructuring which put the $25 million to work for Father God instead of Uncle Sam—a separation of church funds from state that has greatly benefited the cause of world evangelism. The proceeds of the 1988 sale are invested in stocks, buildings, shopping centers, assisted-living facilities, radio stations, and land development, generating funds that are invested in the Kingdom."

These six men turned themselves and their company into financiers of God's work. Their personal and business goals are to give as much to missions as they can—to bankroll the work of the gospel. From 1976 to 1996 they gave away $35 million. In 1995 alone they gave $5 million to ministries in their denomination.

Says Dave Burdine, who is one of the six, "We're just common people who like to work and play but have a passion for the lost and want to reach as many people as we can with the gospel."

They have definitely put their money where their hearts are. They have allowed their story to be told for one reason: to encourage others to follow their example. At whatever level, large or small, each of us has the opportunity to be a part of financing the work of God.

Business, Generosity, Gospel, Missions, Money, Vocation, Work

Hag. 1:2–15; Luke 8:1–3; 12:16–21; Rom. 12:8; 2 Cor. 9:6–11; Eph. 4:28

Date used __________ Place ____________________

Glorification 246

During his championship years with the Chicago Bulls, Michael Jordan was motivated by many things. One motivation most people did not hear about was his desire to win for the sake of the new players and coaches who had never been on a championship team.

So it was in 1997 when the Bulls pursued their fifth championship. Assistant coach Frank Hamblen was new to the team that season. Before coming to the Bulls he had been an assistant coach on various teams for twenty-five years, but did not own a championship ring. He was now fifty years old.

Jordan told writer Melissa Isaacson of the *Chicago Tribune,* "He's been around the league for so long, on a lot of teams and made some great contributions . . . and then not to be on a championship team. . . . That will be my gift to Hamblen. That's part of my motivation."

Hamblen said, "Michael came to me early in the season and told me it was a big motivation for him to win so that I can get a ring. When the best basketball player in the world tells you that, well, it certainly made me feel special."

The Bulls did win it all in 1997, and Frank Hamblen got his ring.

Jesus Christ has a similar desire for us. He is determined to carry us to victory. He wants to see us glorified with him. He wants us to share the glory of his triumphant kingdom. When the Lord of heaven and earth tells us that, well, it certainly makes us feel special.

Goodness, Grace, Heaven, Kingdom,
Overcomers, Victory, Winning
Rom. 8:30, 37; 1 Cor. 3:21–23; 2 Cor. 2:14;
Eph. 1:3–14; 2:6–7; 1 Peter 1:13

Date used __________ Place ____________________

247

It was a fog-shrouded morning, July 4, 1952, when a young woman named Florence Chadwick waded into the water off Catalina Island. She intended to swim the channel from the island to the California coast. Long-distance swimming was not new to her; she had been the first woman to swim the English Channel in both directions.

The water was numbing cold that day. The fog was so thick she could hardly see the boats in her party. Several times sharks had to be driven away with rifle fire. She swam more than fifteen hours before she asked to be taken out of the water. Her trainer tried to encourage her to swim on since they were so close to land, but when Florence looked, all she saw was fog. So she quit . . . only one-half mile from her goal.

Later she said, "I'm not excusing myself, but if I could have seen the land, I might have made it." It wasn't the cold or fear or exhaustion that caused Florence Chadwick to fail. It was the fog.

Many times we too fail, not because we're afraid or because of the peer pressure or because of anything other than the fact that we lose sight of the goal. Maybe that's why Paul said, "I press toward the mark for the prize of the high calling of God in Christ Jesus" (Phil. 3:14).

Two months after her failure, Florence Chadwick walked off the same beach into the same channel and swam the distance, setting a new speed record, because she could see the land.

Failure, Perseverance

Date used __________ Place ____________________

God the Father 248

On Saturday, September 18, 1982, the U.S. government released the results of a sad investigation. The government determined that an army soldier stationed in Korea had been a defector to the Communists. According to the investigation, on August 28, 1982, this twenty-year-old private willingly crossed the Korean Demilitarized Zone into North Korea "for motives that are not known." His fellow American soldiers pleaded with him to turn back, but he did not respond.

The day after the findings were released, the parents of the young man held a press conference on the lawn of their St. Louis home. Wiping tears from his eyes, the father said that they had accepted the fact that their son was indeed a defector. "He has lost his credibility in this country, even with me," said the man. But then he showed the heart of a father. "I still love my son," he said, "and want him back."

God is like this father. You may have turned away from him, but if you will come back, the door is open, and the light is on. Come home, says the Father. Please come home.

Forgiveness, Love of God, Mercy
Luke 15:11–24; John 3:16; Rom. 5:8; Rev. 22:17

Date used __________ Place ____________________

God's Goodness 249

Everyone is familiar with Sherlock Holmes, his faithful companion Dr. Watson, and Holmes's keen power of observation that solved countless crimes. Yet few of us know that Holmes thought deduction and observation were even more necessary to religion.

Tucked away in *The Adventure of the Naval Treaty,* Holmes is found studying a rose. Watson narrates: "He walked past the couch to an open window and held up the drooping stalk of a moss rose, looking down at the dainty blend of crimson and green. It was a new phase of his character to me, for I had never before seen him show an interest in natural objects.

"'There is nothing in which deduction is so necessary as in religion,' said he, leaning with his back against the shutters. . . . 'Our highest assurance of the goodness of Providence seems to me to rest in the flowers. All other things, our powers, our desires, our food, are really necessary for our existence in the first instance. But this rose is an extra. Its smell and its color are an embellishment of life, not a condition of it. It is only goodness which gives extras, and so I say again that we have much to hope from the flowers.'"

What other "extras" should we be observing and thanking God for this year?

Thankfulness, Faith

Date used __________ Place ____________________

God's Greatness 250

Leave it to a children's book to help us see how big our universe is. In a book entitled *Is a Blue Whale the Biggest Thing There Is?* Robert Wells takes us from a size we can grasp to one we can't.

The largest animal on earth is the blue whale. Just the flippers on its tail are bigger than most animals on earth.

But a blue whale isn't anywhere near as big as a mountain. If you put one hundred blue whales in a huge jar, you could put millions of whale jars inside a hollowed-out Mount Everest.

But Mount Everest isn't anywhere near as big as the earth. If you stacked one hundred Mount Everests on top of one another, it would be just a whisker on the face of the earth.

And the earth isn't anywhere near as big as the sun. You could fit one million earths inside of the sun.

But the sun, which is a medium-size star, isn't anywhere near as big as a red supergiant star called Antares. Fifty million of our suns could fit inside of Antares.

But Antares isn't anywhere near as big as the Milky Way galaxy. Billions of stars, including supergiants like Antares, as well as countless comets and asteroids, make up the Milky Way galaxy.

But the Milky Way galaxy isn't anywhere near as big as the universe. There are *billions* of other *galaxies* in the universe.

And yet, filled with billions of galaxies, the universe is almost totally empty. The distances from one galaxy to another are beyond our imagination.

And the Creator of this universe is God, who with a Word spoke it all into being, who is present everywhere in this universe and beyond, who upholds it all with his mighty power. Great is our God and greatly to be praised!

Creation, Omnipresence, Power of God
Gen. 1; Ps. 19:1–6; Isa. 40:18–26; John 1:1–3

Date used __________ Place ____________________

God's Love 251

Pete Rose, one-time star of baseball's Cincinnati Reds, holds the record for the most hits by a player: 4,256. He is better remembered, though, for his style of play. On every single pitch Rose gave it 110 percent, no matter whether his team was winning or losing by ten runs, or whether it was the World Series or the preseason. Pete Rose's nickname was Charlie Hustle.

Rose's son, Pete Rose, Jr., played minor league baseball for the South Bend Silver Hawks. One of the owners of the team, Stuart N. Robinson, told *Sports Illustrated*, "Last year I saw Big Pete. . . . I fell in step with him, identified myself and my South Bend connection, and gave Big Pete my observations of Pete Jr. He never looked at me, or smiled, or broke stride. All he said was, 'Did he hustle?'"

We learn a lot about a father by what he looks for in his son. Our heavenly Father asks one question about his children: Are they walking in love? By that question we see the values of God himself.

Fathers, Imitating God, Love
John 13:34–35; 15:9–17; 1 John 4:7–12

Date used __________ Place ____________________

Several years ago an eastern paper reported this story:

One evening a woman was driving home when she noticed a huge truck behind her that was driving uncomfortably close. She stepped on the gas to gain some distance from the truck, but when she sped up, the truck did too. The faster she drove, the faster the truck did.

Now scared, she exited the freeway. But the truck stayed with her. The woman then turned up a main street, hoping to lose her pursuer in traffic. But the truck ran a red light and continued the chase.

Reaching the point of panic, the woman whipped her car into a service station and bolted out of her auto screaming for help. The truck driver sprang from his truck and ran toward her car. Yanking the back door open, the driver pulled out a man hidden in the backseat.

The woman was running from the wrong person. From his high vantage point, the truck driver had spotted a would-be rapist in the woman's car. The chase was not his effort to harm her but to save her even at the cost of his own safety.

Likewise, many people run from God, fearing what he might do to them. But his plans are for good not evil—to rescue us from the hidden sins that endanger our lives.

God's Goodness, Sin

Date used __________ Place ____________________

God's Work 253

Gregory Wiens writes:

One afternoon while playing on a wooden picnic table, 4 1/2-year-old Jordon ran a splinter into his finger. Sobbing, he called his father (me) at the office. "I want God to take the splinter out," he said.

I told him his mother could remove it very easily. But he wanted God to do it because when Mom takes a splinter out, it hurts. He wanted God to remove it "by himself."

When I got home an hour later, the splinter was still there so I proceeded to remove it, and I tried to teach Jordon that sometimes God uses others to do his work. And sometimes it is painful.

Church, Healing

Date used __________ Place ____________________

Bodie Thoene, coauthor of bestselling Christian fiction such as the *Zion Chronicles,* once worked for John Wayne as a script writer. In *Today's Christian Woman,* Thoene tells how that opportunity came about.

> By the time I was nineteen, I was commuting to Los Angeles and doing feature articles on different stunt men and other film personalities for magazines. Four years later, an article I co-wrote with John Wayne's stuntman won the attention of the Duke himself. One day he called and invited [my husband,] Brock, and me to come to his house. He talked to us as if we were friends, showing keen interest in us as individuals. From that day on, I began writing for his film company, Batjac Productions. Brock helped me with the historical research.
>
> We were awestruck. Here was this man who had been in film for fifty years and he takes a young couple with small children under his wing! Once I asked him, "Why are you doing this? You're so good to us."
>
> He replied, "Because somebody did it for me."

Goodness doesn't originate with us. We receive, and then we give. God is good to all, enabling all to be good to others.

Generosity, Giving
Matt. 5:43–48; 10:8; 1 John 4:19

Date used __________ Place ____________________

Goodness 255

One of the great heartbreaks of the 1988 Winter Olympics was the story of speed skater Dan Jansen. Just hours before his race he received the news that his sister, who had been fighting leukemia for more than a year, had just died. Bearing the weight of his sorrow, Dan laced on his skates to race for his sister. When the gun sounded, he sprinted from the starting line, only to slip and fall in the first turn. Four days later, in the 1,000-meter race, he fell again. The whole country mourned with him.

Many Americans sent Dan letters of consolation. According to *Sports Illustrated,* not long after returning home, Jansen received a letter from Mark Arrowood, a disabled thirty-year-old from Doylestown, Pennsylvania. Mark wrote:

> Dear Dan, I watched you on TV. I'm sorry that you fell 2 times. I am in Special Olympics. I won a gold medal at Pa. State Summer Olympics right after my Dad died seven years ago. . . . Before we start the games we have a saying that goes like this. "Let me win but if I can't win let me be brave in the attempt." . . . I want to share one of my gold medals with you because I don't like to see you not get one. Try again in four more years.

Inside the envelope, Dan Jansen found a gold medal that Mark Arrowood had won in a track-and-field event.

Those who share their blessings are the greatest champions of all. Goodness is greatness.

Giving, Kindness, Love, Sharing
Acts 2:44–45; Gal. 5:22–23; 2 Peter 1:5–8

Date used __________ Place ____________________

In *Robins Reader,* Frank W. Mann Jr. writes:

> An enlightening pastime is to make a list of favorite things that impact the senses. . . . It sharpens our appreciation of these golden moments in time.
>
> For example, one person's list of ten favorite sounds: a distant train whistle; a mother talking to her new baby; the scrunch of leaves on a bright autumn day; seagulls crying; a hound baying in the woods at night; the absolute silence of a mountain lake at sunset; a crackling fire on a bitter day; a stadium crowd singing the national anthem; the screech of an airplane's tires as they touch down; his wife's voice at morning.

God gave us our five senses and then he filled his creation with pleasures for each sense. God is exceedingly good.

Pleasure, Thanksgiving
Ps. 34:8; Prov. 20:12; 1 Tim. 4:4

Date used __________ Place ____________________

Phil Knight founded the Nike shoe company in 1972, and in less than two decades it became one of the strongest and most well-recognized companies in the world. Unique and unforgettable advertising is what powered its phenomenal corporate growth.

When you think of classic Nike advertising, you think of superstar athletes—Michael Jordan, Charles Barkley, and Bo Jackson—and you think of the phrase "Just Do It." You think of Spike Lee muttering about Michael Jordan, "It's gotta be the shoes" or Charles Barkley announcing, "Just because I can dunk a basketball doesn't mean I should raise your kids."

In 1994 the Cannes International Advertising Festival recognized the consistent creativity and impact of Nike advertising by naming Nike advertiser of the year.

That is unimaginable to anyone who knew how Nike CEO Phil Knight felt about advertising back in 1981. That's when Phil Knight first hired a new ad agency. When Knight met with the ad agency's president, Knight told him to his face, "I hate advertising."

The greatest advertiser in the world once hated advertising! The company made by advertising started its relationship with its ad agency skeptical and dubious.

In the same way, many people who once hated the gospel of Jesus Christ now love that gospel. It has brought them all the good they now enjoy.

Change, Evangelism, Repentance
Mark 1:15; John 9:25; Rom. 1:16

Date used __________ Place ____________________

In *World Vision,* writer Tony Campolo tells of taking an airplane from California to Philadelphia one stormy night. It was late, but when the man in the next seat learned that Campolo was a Christian, he wanted to talk. "I believe that going to heaven is like going to Philadelphia," the man said. You can get there by airplane, by train, by bus, by automobile. There are many ways to get to Philadelphia. Campolo writes:

> As we started descending into Philadelphia, the place was fogged in. The wind was blowing, the rain was beating on the plane, and everyone looked nervous and tight. As we were circling in the fog, I turned to the theological expert on my right. "I'm certainly glad the pilot doesn't agree with your theology," I said.
>
> "What do you mean?" he asked.
>
> "The people in the control booth are giving instructions to the pilot: 'Coming north by northwest, three degrees, you're on beam you're on beam, don't deviate from beam.' I'm glad the pilot's not saying, 'There are many ways into the airport. There are many approaches we can take.' I'm glad he is saying, 'There's only one way we can land this plane, and I'm going to stay with it.'"

There is only one way to God, and that is through Jesus Christ.

Evangelism, Salvation

John 14:6; Acts 4:12; 1 John 5:12

Date used __________ Place ____________________

Gospel 259

In *The Whisper Test,* Mary Ann Bird writes:

> I grew up knowing I was different, and I hated it. I was born with a cleft palate, and when I started school, my classmates made it clear to me how I looked to others: a little girl with a misshapen lip, crooked nose, lopsided teeth, and garbled speech.
>
> When schoolmates asked, "What happened to your lip?" I'd tell them I'd fallen and cut it on a piece of glass. Somehow it seemed more acceptable to have suffered an accident than to have been born different. I was convinced that no one outside my family could love me.
>
> There was, however, a teacher in the second grade that we all adored—Mrs. Leonard by name. She was short, round, happy—a sparkling lady.
>
> Annually we had a hearing test. . . .
>
> Mrs. Leonard gave the test to everyone in the class, and finally it was my turn. I knew from past years that as we stood against the door and covered one ear, the teacher sitting at her desk would whisper something, and we would have to repeat it back—things like "The sky is blue" or "Do you have new shoes?" I waited there for those words that God must have put into her mouth, those seven words that changed my life. Mrs. Leonard said, in her whisper, "I wish you were my little girl."

God says to every person deformed by sin, "I wish you were my son" or "I wish you were my daughter."

Acceptance, Grace, Love of God, Mercy, Sin
Rom. 5:8; Eph. 2:1–5

Date used __________ Place ____________________

In *Christianity Today,* Wendy Murray Zoba says that one of the more effective evangelistic tools that Campus Crusade for Christ has developed is the *Jesus* film. She writes:

> Several years ago in Peru, during the insurgence of the Sendero Luminoso (Shining Path), a Wycliffe couple was traveling to show the film in a village. Their vehicle was intercepted by the Senderos, and they feared for their lives (with just cause). Instead of killing them, however, the terrorists decided to seize their equipment, including the film projector. The husband boldly suggested that they might as well take the film reels too.
>
> Some time later, a man contacted them to say that he had been among the Senderos who had robbed them. He told them they watched the film seven times (out of sheer boredom), and some had been converted through it. He came to apologize and to tell of his ministry in preaching and evangelism.

Not even a cold-blooded terrorist can withstand the white-hot power of the gospel.

Evangelism
Rom. 1:16

Date used __________ Place ____________________

Gossip 261

Who can forget the 1994 tabloid headline "Killer Bug Ate My Face"? Although the reporting was sensational, the stories were based on seven real cases of invasive strep A bacteria in Gloucestershire, England.

When invasive strep A (which is not the same as strep throat) takes hold in a victim's body, necrotizing fasciitis can begin, which means that the flesh starts to die at an incredible rate of several inches per hour. Meanwhile toxic shock can set in, shutting down organs and causing death.

Geoffrey Cowley describes scientifically what happens after the deadly microbes take hold in a victim's body.

> The bacteria then multiply rapidly, producing toxins in the process. For three days, the patient may suffer swollen lymph nodes, a rising fever and excruciating pain at the site of infection. Penicillin can stop the attack at this stage, but by day four, infected tissues start dying. Bacteria soon saturate the bloodstream, destroying muscles and organs and sending the body into shock. Death can follow within hours. . . . Invasive strep is rare, but it's also unforgiving.

Is there any counterpart to the strep A bacteria in the body of Christ? Yes. Nothing can so quickly eat the flesh of the church as sins of the tongue: gossip, slander, criticism of leaders, and bad reports.

Body of Christ, Grumbling, Tongue
Prov. 16:28; Eph. 4:29–31; James 3:5–7; 5:9

Date used __________ Place ____________________

According to the Associated Press, on a windy day in March 1997 a father and his son came to Valley Forge National Historical Park, where George Washington stationed the Revolutionary Army during the difficult winter of 1777–1778. The father and son had something much less historic in mind: they wanted to launch a model rocket. At first they tried using electric ignition wires to light the fuse, but to no avail. So they tried lighting the fuse with a common sparkler, the kind seen on the Fourth of July.

That's when the trouble began. Sparks ignited a grass fire, and the winds quickly spread the blaze, burning one field where Revolutionary War soldiers had trained, and coming within a half mile of George Washington's headquarters. Thirty units from twelve fire departments fought the blaze for an hour before bringing it under control, and in the end over thirty acres were charred. The man with the sparkler was charged with destruction of government property and use of fireworks.

Like that sparkler, gossip never seems as dangerous as it really is.

Criticism, Slander, Tongue
Prov. 26:20; Eph. 4:29; James 3:3–12

Date used __________ Place ____________________

Government 263

In the early nineties, the leaning Tower of Pisa began to lean too far. Seeing that the 180-foot-high tower would soon become dangerous, engineers designed a system to salvage the twelfth-century landmark by holding the lean constant.

First the engineers injected supercold liquid nitrogen into the ground to freeze it and thereby minimize dangerous ground vibrations during the work that followed. Then they plan to install cables to pull the structure more upright. Engineers hope that the underground cable network will pull the tower toward center by at least an inch.

Left to itself, our world resembles the leaning Tower of Pisa: tilting and heading to catastrophe. To prevent total anarchy, God establishes governments to maintain order. Governments and their laws function like the steel cables that will hold the leaning tower. The tower still leans. It's not perfect. But the cables prevent total destruction.

Authority, Law, Rulers, Submission, Taxes
Rom. 13:1–7; 1 Peter 2:13–17

Date used __________ Place ____________________

In *The Christian Reader,* Paul Francisco writes:

When I was a child, our church celebrated the Lord's Supper every first Sunday of the month. At that service, the offering plates were passed twice: before the sermon for regular offerings, and just prior to Communion for benevolences. My family always gave to both, but they passed a dime to me to put in only the regular offering.

One Communion Sunday when I was nine, my mother, for the first time, gave me a dime for the benevolent offering also. A little later when the folks in our pew rose to go to the Communion rail, I got up also. "You can't take Communion yet," Mother told me.

"Why not?" I said. "I paid for it!"

This child's humorous story shows a very adult attitude. We may think we can earn God's salvation.

Communion, Faith, Jesus Christ, Salvation, Works
Rom. 3:21–25; Eph. 2:8–9

Date used __________ Place ____________________

According to the *Chicago Tribune,* in the summer of 1994, Marcio da Silva, a love-struck Brazilian artist, was distraught over the breakup of a four-year relationship with his girlfriend, Katia de Nascimento. He tried to win back her love by a gesture of great devotion. He walked on his knees for nine miles. With pieces of car tires tied to his kneecaps, the twenty-one-year-old man shuffled along for fourteen hours before he reached her home in Santos, Brazil. He was cheered on by motorists and passersby, but when he reached the end of his marathon of love thoroughly exhausted, the nineteen-year-old woman of his dreams was not impressed. She had intentionally left her home to avoid seeing him.

Some people try similar acts of devotion to impress God and earn salvation. Like Katia de Nascimento, God is not impressed. The only thing that brings the forgiveness of sin is faith in Jesus Christ, not sacrificial deeds.

Faith, Gospel, Sacrifice, Salvation, Works
Rom. 10:1–4; Eph. 2:8–9

Date used __________ Place ____________________

Pilot William Langewiesche writes in *Atlantic Monthly:*

> In clouds or on black nights, when they cannot see outside, pilots keep their wings level by watching an artificial horizon on the instrument panel. The artificial horizon is a gyroscopically steadied line, which stays level with the earth's surface.

Langewiesche says that pilots sometimes become confused about what the instruments are telling them. He says:

> As turbulence tilts the airplane to the left, the pilots, tilting with it, notice the artificial horizon line dropping to the right. Reacting instinctively to the indication of motion, they sometimes try to raise the line as if it were a wing. The result of such a reversal is murderous. Pilots steer to the left just when they should steer to the right, and then in confusion they steer harder. While cruising calmly inside clouds, I have had student pilots suddenly try to flip the airplane upside down.

The same kind of disorientation can happen when we seek God's acceptance. When we see how far short we fall of God's will, we can try harder and harder to be good, hoping that if we become almost perfect, God will accept us. But that's precisely the opposite of what we need to do. Instead we should trust in God's grace.

Legalism, Righteousness, Salvation, Trust, Works
Rom. 10:2–4; Gal. 5:1–6; Eph. 2:8–9

Date used __________ Place ____________________

In *The Grace Awakening,* Charles Swindoll writes:

I vividly remember my last spanking. It was on my thirteenth birthday, as a matter of fact. Having just broken into the sophisticated ranks of the teen world, I thought I was something on a stick. My father wasn't nearly as impressed as I was with my great importance and new-found independence. I was lying on my bed. He was outside the window on a muggy October afternoon in Houston, weeding the garden. He said, "Charles, come out and help me weed the garden." I said something like: "No . . . it's my birthday, remember?" My tone was sassy and my deliberate lack of respect was eloquent. I knew better than to disobey my dad, but after all, I was the ripe old age of thirteen. He set a new 100-meter record that autumn afternoon. He was in the house and all over me like white on rice, spanking me all the way out to the garden. As I recall, I weeded until the moonlight was shining on the pansies.

That same night he took me out to a surprise dinner. He gave me what I deserved earlier. Later he gave me what I did not deserve. The birthday dinner was grace.

Child Rearing, Discipline, Fathers, Obedience
Eph. 2:8–9; Heb. 12:5–11

Date used __________ Place ____________________

The Grace Awakening, Charles Swindoll, 1990, Word, Dallas, Texas.

In Warren Wiersbe's *Meet Yourself in the Psalms,* he tells about a frontier town where a horse bolted and ran away with a wagon carrying a little boy. Seeing the child in danger, a young man risked his life to catch the horse and stop the wagon.

The child who was saved grew up to become a lawless man, and one day he stood before a judge to be sentenced for a serious crime. The prisoner recognized the judge as the man who, years before, had saved his life; so he pled for mercy on the basis of that experience.

But the words from the bench silenced his plea, "Young man, then I was your savior; today I am your judge, and I must sentence you to be hanged."

One day Jesus will say to rebellious sinners, "During that long day of grace, I was the Savior, and I would have forgiven you. But today I am your Judge. Depart from me, ye cursed, into everlasting fire!"

Judgment, Salvation

Date used __________ Place ____________________

Grace 269

Lillie Baltrip is a good bus driver. In fact, according to the Fort Worth *Star-Telegram* of June 17, 1988, the Houston school district nominated her for a safe-driving award. Her colleagues even trusted her to drive a busload of them to an awards ceremony for safe drivers. Unfortunately, on the way to the ceremony, Lillie turned a corner too sharply and flipped the bus over, sending herself and sixteen others to the hospital for minor emergency treatment.

Did Lillie, accident free for the whole year, get her award anyway? No. Award committees rarely operate on the principle of grace. How fortunate we are that even when we don't maintain a spotless liferecord, our final reward depends on God's grace, not on our performance!

Good Works, Failure

Date used ________ Place ____________________

Belden C. Lane writes in the *Christian Century* about English raconteur T. H. White, who recalls in *The Book of Merlyn* a boyhood experience:

"My father made me a wooden castle big enough to get into, and he fixed real pistol barrels beneath its battlements to fire a salute on my birthday, but made me sit in front the first night . . . to receive the salute, and I, believing I was to be shot, cried." How many times have we, too, misinterpreted the ambiguity of life and thought ourselves to be "shot" when delight was intended?

One translation of Psalm 94:19 reads, "In the middle of all my troubles, you roll me over with rollicking delight." The psalmist is right; God's festive gaiety is somehow to be discerned in the midst of our own troubled fears. God often plays rough before breaking into laughter, and only a bold and rowdy playfulness can draw the whole of what we are to such a God. Yet, we're not always able to grasp the truth. Ever expecting to be shot, we are so often dumbfounded by a grace we can't conceive.

Fear, Trials

Date used __________ Place ____________________

In his book *In the Grip of Grace,* Max Lucado writes:

In my first church, we had more than our share of southern ladies who loved to cook. I fit in well because I was a single guy who loved to eat. Our potlucks were major events.

I counted on those potluck dinners for my survival. While others were planning what to cook, I was studying my kitchen shelves to see what I could offer. The result was pitiful: one of my better offerings was an unopened sack of chips, another time I took a half-empty jar of peanuts.

Wasn't much, but no one ever complained. Those ladies would take my jar of peanuts and set it on the long table with the rest of the food and hand me a plate. "Go ahead. Don't be bashful. Fill up your plate." And I would! Mashed potatoes and gravy. Roast beef. Fried chicken. I came like a pauper and ate like a king!

The apostle Paul would have loved the symbolism of those potlucks. He would say that Christ does for us precisely what those women did for me.

Community, Salvation, Works
Isa. 64:6; Rom. 3–5; Eph. 2:8–10

Date used __________ Place ____________________

In his sermon "Why Christ Had to Die," author and pastor Stuart Briscoe says:

Many years ago when the children were small, we went for a little drive in the lovely English countryside, and there was some fresh snow. I saw a lovely field with not a single blemish on the virgin snow. I stopped the car, and I vaulted over the gate, and I ran around in a great big circle striding as wide as I could. Then I came back to the kids, and I said, "Now, children, I want you to follow in my footsteps. So I want you to run around that circle in the snow, and I want you to put your feet where your father put his feet."

Well, David tried and couldn't quite make it. Judy, our overachiever, was certain she would make it; she couldn't make it. Pete, the little kid, took a great run at it, put his foot in my first footprint and then strode out as far as he could and fell on his face. His mother picked him up as he cried.

She said to me, "What are you trying to do?"

I said, "I'm trying to get a sermon illustration."

I said, "Pete, come here." I picked up little Peter and put his left foot on my foot, and I put his right foot on my foot. I said, "Okay, Pete, let's go." I began to stride one big stride at a time with my hands under his armpits and his feet lightly on mine.

Well, who was doing it? In a sense, he was doing it because I was doing it. In a sense there was a commitment of the little boy to the big dad, and some of the properties of the big dad were working through the little boy.

In exactly the same way, in our powerlessness we can't stride as wide as we should. We don't walk the way we should. We don't hit the target the way we ought. It isn't that at every point we are as bad as we could be. It's just that at no point are we as good as we should be. Something's got to be done.

The message of Easter is it has been done. You can be justified. You can be saved from wrath. You can be saved by his life. All that is the message of grace—God offering you what you don't deserve.

Depravity, Easter, Faith, Justification,
Original Sin, Powerlessness, Righteousness, Sin
Jer. 33:16; Rom. 3:10–26; 4:1–25; Eph. 2:8–10

Date used __________ Place ____________________

In *Pursuit* author and evangelist Luis Palau writes:

Thank God His grace isn't "fair." A couple of years ago, one of my nephews (I'll call him Kenneth) was near death. He had AIDS. During a family reunion in the hills of northern California, Kenneth and I broke away for a short walk. He was a hollow shell, laboring for breath.

"Kenneth, you know you're going to die any day," I said. "Do you have eternal life? Your parents agonize. I must know."

"Luis, I know God has forgiven me and I'm going to heaven."

For several years, since his early teens, Kenneth had practiced homosexuality. More than that, in rebellion against God and his parents, he flaunted his lifestyle.

"Kenneth, how can you say that?" I replied. "You rebelled against God, you made fun of the Bible, you hurt your family terribly. And now you say you've got eternal life, just like that?"

"Luis, when the doctor said I had AIDS, I realized what a fool I'd been."

"We know that," I said bluntly, but deliberately, because Kenneth knew full well that the Bible teaches that homosexual behavior is sin. "But did you really repent?"

"I did repent, and I know God has had mercy on me. But my dad won't believe me."

"You've rebelled in his face all your life," I said. "You've broken his heart."

Kenneth looked me straight in the eye. "I know the Lord has forgiven me."

"Did you open your heart to Jesus?"

"Yes. Luis! Yes!"

As we put our arms around each other and prayed and talked some more, I became convinced that Jesus had forgiven all of Kenneth's rebellion and washed away all his sin. Several short months later, he went to be with the Lord at age twenty-five.

My nephew, like the repentant thief on the cross, did not deserve God's grace. I don't either. None of us do. That's why grace is grace—unmerited favor.

AIDS, Conversion, Forgiveness,
Homosexuality, Rebellion
Luke 23:43

Date used __________ Place ____________________

274

In 1997 *Fortune* magazine said Bill Gates, CEO of Microsoft, was the richest American in history, with personal wealth of some $35 billion. According to Carey Goldberg in the *New York Times,* in February of 1997 Mr. Gates spoke to 1,500 people in Seattle at the annual convention of the American Association for the Advancement of Science. After Mr. Gates's speech, Dr. John Cantwell Kiley, a medical doctor with a Ph.D. in philosophy, stood up and asked a question. If Bill Gates were blind, Kiley asked, would he trade all of his billions to have his sight restored?

The reply of Bill Gates shows where true value lies. He said that he would trade all his money for his sight, and then he offered his e-mail address for further discussion.

If we have nothing else, if we have our sight, our hearing, our mobility, our hands and fingers—our health, we have much to be grateful for, because they are a priceless gift from God.

Contentment, Goodness of God, Money, Thanksgiving, Values
Prov. 20:12; Luke 17:11–19; Rom. 11:36; 1 Thess. 5:18

Date used __________ Place ____________________

Greed 275

A chapter heading in Calvin Miller's book *A Requiem for Love* reads:

A beggar asked a millionaire,
"How many more dollars
Would it take to
Make you truly happy?"

The millionaire,
Reaching his gnarled hands
Into the beggar's cup, replied,
"Only one more!"

Money, Happiness

Date used __________ Place ____________________

Clovis Chappell writes in his book of sermons *Feminine Faces:*

When Pompeii was being excavated, there was found a body that had been embalmed by the ashes of Vesuvius. It was that of a woman. Her feet were turned toward the city gate, but her face was turned backward toward something that lay just beyond her outstretched hands.

The prize for which those frozen fingers were reaching was a bag of pearls. Maybe she herself had dropped them as she was fleeing for her life. Maybe she had found them where they had been dropped by another. But, be that as it may, though death was hard at her heels, and life was beckoning to her beyond the city gates, she could not shake off their spell. She had turned to pick them up, with death as her reward. But it was not the eruption of Vesuvius that made her love pearls more than life. It only froze her in this attitude of greed.

Treasures, Possessions

Date used __________ Place ____________________

Grief 277

Author Edgar Jackson poignantly describes grief:

Grief is a young widow trying to raise her three children, alone.

Grief is the man so filled with shocked uncertainty and confusion that he strikes out at the nearest person.

Grief is a mother walking daily to a nearby cemetery to stand quietly and alone a few minutes before going about the tasks of the day. She knows that a part of her is in the cemetery, just as part of her is in her daily work.

Grief is the silent, knife-like terror and sadness that comes a hundred times a day, when you start to speak to someone who is no longer there.

Grief is the emptiness that comes when you eat alone after eating with another for many years.

Grief is teaching yourself to go to bed without saying good night to the one who has died.

Grief is the helpless wishing that things were different when you know they are not and never will be again.

Grief is a whole cluster of adjustments, apprehensions, and uncertainties that strike life in its forward progress and make it difficult to redirect the energies of life.

Death, Mourning

Date used __________ Place ____________________

278

In *A Slow and Certain Light,* Elisabeth Elliot tells of two adventurers who stopped by to see her, all loaded with equipment for the rain forest east of the Andes. They sought no advice, just a few phrases to converse with the Indians.

She writes: "Sometimes we come to God as the two adventurers came to me—confident and, we think, well-informed and well-equipped. But has it occurred to us that with all our accumulation of stuff, something is missing?"

She suggests that we often ask God for too little. "We know what we need—a yes or no answer, please, to a simple question. Or perhaps a road sign. Something quick and easy to point the way.

"What we really ought to have is the Guide himself. Maps, road signs, a few useful phrases are good things, but infinitely better is Someone who has been there before and knows the way."

Prayer, Direction

Date used __________ Place ____________________

Guidance 279

Perhaps you have spent some time in a sailboat. Relying on the boat to stay afloat, you slide across the water propelled by a gentle breeze. Yet within the confines of the shores, you have the opportunity and responsibility of guiding the rudder to determine the direction of travel.

Is that not similar to living within the will of God? As Christians we must rest upon God to sustain us, and upon the breath of his Spirit to empower us. Yet within his moral boundaries, we each have the opportunity and responsibility to determine our course.

God's Will, Decisions

Date used __________ Place ____________________

Bob Mumford, in *Take Another Look at Guidance,* compares discovering God's will with a sea captain's docking procedure:

A certain harbor in Italy can be reached only by sailing up a narrow channel between dangerous rocks and shoals. Over the years, many ships have been wrecked, and navigation is hazardous.

To guide the ships safely into port, three lights have been mounted on three huge poles in the harbor. When the three lights are perfectly lined up and seen as one, the ship can safely proceed up the narrow channel. If the pilot sees two or three lights, he knows he's off course and in danger.

God has also provided three beacons to guide us. The same rules of navigation apply—the three lights must be lined up before it is safe for us to proceed. The three harbor lights of guidance are:

1. The Word of God (objective standard)
2. The Holy Spirit (subjective witness)
3. Circumstances (divine providence)

Together they assure us that the directions we've received are from God and will lead us safely along his way.

God's Will, Holy Spirit

Date used __________ Place ____________________

Guidance 281

Author Gary Thomas, founder of the Center for Evangelical Spirituality, writes in *Discipleship Journal:*

When my wife and I prayed extensively about buying a house, we gave God many opportunities to close the door. God appeared to bless the move. Five years later, our house is worth considerably less than what we paid for it.

"Why didn't God stop us?" my wife and I kept wondering. After all, we had given Him plenty of opportunities. But one day as my wife was praying, she sensed God asking her, "Have you ever considered the possibility that I wanted you in that neighborhood to minister there rather than to bolster your financial equity?"

We thought of the people we have been able to reach, and then asked ourselves, are we willing to surrender to a God who would lead us to make a decision that turned out to be undesirable financially but profitable spiritually? Does obedience obligate God to bless us, or can obedience call us to sacrifice? Think about the cross before you answer that one.

Availability, Blessing, Cross, Evangelism, God's Leading, God's Will, Loss, Money, Outreach, Prosperity, Sacrifice, Surrender

Gen. 12:1–10; Exod. 5:1–23; Rom. 12:2; 2 Cor. 6:3–10

Date used __________ Place ____________________

Guilt 282

For some time the *Chicago Tribune Magazine* ran a column about people's jobs. A writer would interview an average cop or baker or legal secretary about what it was like to do his or her work. One column told the story of a man named Neil Boyle who read depositions in jury trials. Boyle told of one crazy lawsuit he had seen.

> A hospital-supply corporation falsified its annual reports so that the shareholders thought it was doing better financially than it was. An auditing firm came in, but the company manipulated its inventory, moving the same goods to whatever warehouse the firm was inspecting. When the fraud was finally discovered, the corporation sued the auditing firm for not catching them! The auditing firm eventually won, but it took 11 years.

Some people will never acknowledge their guilt.

Blame, Confession, Deception, Justice
1 John 1:8–10

Date used __________ Place ____________________

According to *Time* magazine, in 1970 Katherine Power, a student at Brandeis University in Boston, was a leader of the radical National Student Strike Force. She and several others planned to raise money to buy arms for the Black Panthers by robbing a bank.

Kathy drove the getaway car. But the robbery went awry. A silent alarm was quickly answered by patrolman Walter Schroeder. Shots were fired by one of Kathy's accomplices, and patrolman Schroeder was killed.

That night Kathy began what would be twenty-three years of life on the lam. Listed as armed and "very dangerous," she was on the FBI's most-wanted list.

In the late 1970s, Power moved to Oregon. There she assumed the name Alice Metzinger, settled down, started a new life in the restaurant business, bought a house, gave birth to her son, and married. She was an active part of the community and seemingly had every reason to be at peace.

But at age forty-four Kathy Power was desperately tired, tormented by guilt, and chronically depressed. Finally Kathy did the only thing she felt could end her agony. In September 1993 she turned herself in to Boston police. She explained why this was so important: "I am now learning to live with openness and truth," she said, "rather than shame and hiddenness."

Shame and guilt are feelings from which you cannot run and cannot hide. Freedom comes only by facing up to the truth—with people and with God.

Confession, Depression, Shame, Truth
Heb. 10:22; James 5:16; 1 John 1:9

Date used __________ Place ____________________

In *Fearfully and Wonderfully Made,* Dr. Paul Brand and Philip Yancey write:

Amputees often experience some sensation of a phantom limb. Somewhere, locked in their brains, a memory lingers of the nonexistent hand or leg. Invisible toes curl, imaginary hands grasp things, a "leg" feels so sturdy a patient may try to stand on it.

For a few, the experience includes pain. Doctors watch helplessly, for the part of the body screaming for attention does not exist.

One such patient was my medical school administrator, Mr. Barwick, who had a serious and painful circulation problem in his leg but refused to allow the recommended amputation.

As the pain grew worse, Barwick grew bitter.

"I hate it! I hate it!" he would mutter about the leg. At last he relented and told the doctor, "I can't stand it anymore. I'm through with that leg. Take it off." Surgery was scheduled immediately.

Before the operation, however, Barwick asked the doctor, "What do you do with legs after they're removed?"

"We may take a biopsy or explore them a bit, but afterwards we incinerate them," the doctor replied.

Barwick proceeded with a bizarre request: "I would like you to preserve my leg in a pickling jar. I will install it on my mantle shelf. Then, as I sit in my armchair, I will taunt that leg, 'Hah! You can't hurt me anymore!'"

Ultimately, he got his wish. But the despised leg had the last laugh.

Barwick suffered phantom limb pain of the worst degree. The wound healed, but he could feel the torturous pressure of the swelling as the muscles cramped, and he had no prospect of relief. He had hated the leg with such intensity that the pain had unaccountably lodged permanently in his brain.

To me, phantom limb pain provides wonderful insight into the phenomenon of false guilt. Christians can be obsessed by the memory of some sin committed years ago. It never leaves them, crippling their ministry, their devotional life, their relationships with others. They live in fear that someone will discover their past. They work overtime trying to prove to God they're truly repentant. They erect barriers against the enveloping, loving grace of God.

Unless they experience the truth in 1 John 3:19–20 that "God is greater than our conscience," they become as pitiful as poor Mr. Barwick, shaking a fist in fury at the pickled leg on the mantle.

Conscience, Forgiveness

Date used __________ Place ____________________

According to the Casper, Wyoming, *Star-Tribune,* Charles Taylor was brought into the courtroom of Judge James Fleetwood. Taylor was accused of robbing a shoe store at knifepoint, taking a pair of tan hiking boots and $69. During the trial Taylor propped his feet up on the defense table. The judge looked over and did a double take. Taylor was wearing a pair of tan hiking boots. Surely, nobody would be so stupid as to wear the boots he stole to his trial, the judge thought.

Nevertheless, as the jury deliberated, the judge had an FBI agent call the shoe store. He learned that the stolen boots were size 10 1/2 from Lot 1046. They checked the boots that Taylor wore to trial and found that they were size 10 1/2 from Lot 1046.

The jury found Taylor guilty, and the judge sent him back to jail in his stocking feet.

Some transgressors are either very stupid or very brazen about their crimes. Before God their judge, defiant sinners oftentimes are both.

Brazenness, Conscience, Defiance,
Judgment, Lawlessness, Rebelliousness
Rom. 1:18–3:8; Rev. 9:20–21; 16:8–21

Date used __________ Place ____________________

Guilt 286

You just can't deny the obvious. That's what a man named Daron discovered, according to Mitchell May in the *Chicago Tribune.*

Police had a warrant out on Daron for possession of a controlled substance with intent to deliver. On August 4, 1997, in Champaign, Illinois, police stopped Daron as he left an apartment in an area of town known for drug trafficking. The police asked his name. Daron claimed his name was John Henry Jones.

The police didn't believe him. Like Sherlock Holmes, they were observant. They pointed to a tattoo on his arm. The tattoo said, "Daron."

Oops!

Thinking fast, Daron claimed it was the name of his girlfriend.

Needless to say, the police could not be snookered, and they took him into custody.

Often we do not want to own up to who we are or what we have done. But the truth cannot be denied forever. Like Daron's tattoo, the guilt of our sins cannot be hidden. Sooner or later our identity will come into the open.

Accountability, Blame, Deception, Denial,
Identity, Name, Responsibility, Shame, Sin
Ps. 51; Isa. 59:12; John 4:16–19;
Rom. 5:12–14; 1 Tim. 5:24–25; Heb. 4:13

Date used __________ Place ____________________

Habits 287

In *Pulpit Digest* William H. Willimon used this illustration:

Philip Haille wrote of the little village of Le Chambon in France, a town whose people, unlike others in France, hid their Jews from the Nazis. Haille went there, wondering what sort of courageous, ethical heroes could risk all to do such extraordinary good. He interviewed people in the village and was overwhelmed by their *ordinariness*. They weren't heroes or smart, discerning people.

Haille decided that the one factor that united them was their attendance, Sunday after Sunday, at their little church, where they heard the sermons of Pastor Trochme. Over time, they became by habit people who just knew what to do and did it. When it came time for them to be courageous, the day the Nazis came to town, they quietly did what was right.

One old woman, who faked a heart attack when the Nazis came to search her house, later said, "Pastor always taught us that there comes a time in every life when a person is asked to do something for Jesus. When our time came, we knew what to do."

The habits of the heart are there when they are most needed.

Courage, Church Attendance

Date used __________ Place ____________________

Is money the key to happiness? Consider what it did for Buddy Post, of Oil City, Pennsylvania. According to the Associated Press and *Chicago Tribune*, in 1988 he won a jackpot of $16.2 million in the Pennsylvania Lottery. That was the beginning of his misery.

His landlady claimed that she shared the winning ticket with Post and successfully sued him for one-third of the money.

Post started an assortment of business ventures with his siblings, all of which failed.

In 1991 he was sentenced to six months to two years in prison for assault. Post claimed that he had simply fired a gun into his garage ceiling to scare off his stepdaughter's boyfriend, who was arguing with him over business and ownership of Post's pickup.

In 1993 Post's brother was convicted of plotting to kill Buddy and his wife to gain access to the lottery money.

In 1994 Post filed for bankruptcy.

Post's wife left him, and the court ordered that Post pay $40,000 a year in support payments.

Post finally had enough. To pay off a mountain of legal fees, he tried in September 1996 to sell off the rights to the seventeen future payments from his jackpot, valued at some $5 million. But the Pennsylvania Lottery tried to block the sale.

"Money didn't change me," says Post. "It changed people around me that I knew, that I thought cared a little bit about me. But they only cared about the money."

Greed, Money
1 Tim. 6:6–10

Date used __________ Place ____________________

Hardness 289

Cardiologists are hunting for a way to clear arteries clogged by plaque. They've tried using lasers to burn through the plaque. They've experimented with rotating burrs to grind away the plaque. They've even tried using rotating knives to cut away plaque. None of these methods have succeeded.

At the annual meeting of the American Heart Association in 1993, researchers reported on another experimental device that would work like a tiny jackhammer inside the arteries. Writer Jon Van says the device is inserted into the coronary arteries via a tiny wire called a catheter. There it emits low-frequency, ultrasound energy, vibrating the jackhammer-like tip of the probe at 19,500 times a second, about one-thousandth of an inch back and forth each time. After the jackhammer has done its work, a balloon is inserted into the narrowed artery and expanded to open the artery.

In twenty-nine test cases, the jackhammer seemed to accomplish something the other methods could not. It broke down the calcium and gristle in the hard plaque without harming the soft walls of the artery.

Hardening of the arteries is the enemy of the heart. A dangerous hardness can also develop in our spiritual lives, a hardness that constricts the life-giving love of God in our lives. If your heart has been hardened, there is no better "jackhammer" than to humble yourself before the Lord.

Anger, Heart, Humility, Prayer, Repentance
Eph. 4:17–19; Heb. 3:13; 1 Peter 5:6

Date used __________ Place ____________________

Hatred 290

In November 1996 *Sports Illustrated* reported a bizarre story of competitiveness gone too far. According to the magazine, in a New Mexico high school football game between Albuquerque Academy and St. Pius X on October 12, 1996, several of the Academy players found themselves with strange cuts, slashes, and scratches on their arms and hands. One boy was bleeding freely from three cuts that later required ten stitches to close. Another boy told his coaches, "It feels like they've got razor blades out there."

Well, almost. Referee Steve Fuller inspected the equipment of the opposing team. What he found on the helmet of the offensive center were two chin-strap buckles sharpened to a razor's edge. In the investigation that followed, the offending player's father, a pediatric dentist, admitted to milling the buckles. He had been angered in the previous game by what he thought was excessive head-slapping against his son by opposing linemen. This was his solution.

Sports Illustrated reported, "Several observers describe the father, who was working on the sideline chain gang during the Albuquerque Academy–St. Pius game, as a hothead. He was so vocal in his criticism of the officiating during St. Pius's game against Capital High on Sept. 28 that he was asked to leave the sideline crew."

Hatred and anger—they're as ugly and violent as those razor-sharp buckles.

Aggression, Anger, Competition, Revenge
Gal. 5:20; James 1:20; 1 John 2:11; 3:12–15

Date used __________ Place ____________________

Hatred of Evil 291

In May 1994 the Associated Press carried a story about one person's unusual war on sin. At the public library in Coquille, Oregon, library workers discovered at least a dozen books in which entire pages had been blanked out by a patron wielding white correction fluid. The unknown, self-appointed censor painted over naughty phrases and sexually explicit passages. "They've marked everything from love-swept romances to best sellers," said librarian Molly DePlois.

While conducting a war with white-out is probably not what God had in mind, Scripture *does* call us to hate what is evil.

Evil, Holiness, Purity, World
Rom. 12:9; James 1:27

Date used __________ Place ____________________

Healing 292

In the *Pentecostal Evangel* church leader George O. Wood writes:

Have you ever heard a healing take place? I have. I listened to an audiotape of Duane Miller teaching his Sunday school class from the text of Psalm 103 at the First Baptist Church in Brenham, Texas, on January 17, 1993. Duane prematurely retired from pastoring three years earlier because of a virus which penetrated the myelin sheath around the nerves in his vocal cords, reducing his speech to a raspy whisper. . . .

Teaching his class that day with a special microphone resting on his lips, he reaffirmed his belief in divine healing and that miracles had not ended with the Book of Acts. Listening to the tape, at times you can barely understand his weakly spoken wheezy words of faith. The miracle happened at verse 4 when he said, "I have had and you have had in times past pit experiences."

On the word *pit* his life changed—the word was as clear as a bell, in contrast to the imperfect enunciation of the preceding word *past.* He paused, startled; began again and stopped. He said a few more words—all in a normal clear tone—and stopped again. The class erupted with shouts of joy, astonishment, and sounds of weeping. God completely healed him as he was declaring the truth in this psalm. (You can read the full account in Miller's book *Out of the Silence,* Nelson Publishers.)

Faith, Miracles

Exod. 15:26; Ps. 103:1–5; Matt. 8:17; James 5:14–16

Date used __________ Place ____________________

Healing 293

In 1993 the late author and church leader John Wimber found he had inoperable cancer and underwent radiation treatments. The cancer went into remission. In *Living with Uncertainty* he writes about going without a miraculous healing for himself even though he had seen others dramatically healed by God. He relates this account:

I was speaking in South Africa at a large conference. A friend, John McClure, was with me, and we were asked to go to the home of a lady of the church. She was dressed beautifully but was very emaciated, weighing only 85 pounds. She had been sent home from the hospital to die. Her body was full of cancer. Her only hope of survival was divine intervention.

We prayed for her, but not with great fervency. John had confidence that she would be healed. I felt nothing.

That night she woke up with a vibrant, tingling feeling throughout her body. For the next four hours her body was full of intense heat. She tried to call out to her husband in the next room but couldn't raise her voice loud enough for him to hear.

Alone and frightened, she crawled into the bathroom, her body racked with pain. At the time she thought, "O my God. My body is coming apart and I'm dying." Without knowing it, she eliminated from her body a number of large tumors. Finally, exhausted from the night's events, she fell back asleep. She didn't know if she'd wake up.

But half an hour later she woke up incredibly refreshed. Later her husband woke up to the smell of freshly brewed coffee. "What are you doing?" he asked, astonished to see his wife on her feet and preparing breakfast.

She replied with sudden understanding: "God has healed me."

Two days later she reported to her doctors, who gave her a clean bill of health. They couldn't find a cancer in her body. God had completely delivered her of all of it.

Without much energy to pray on our part and without any desperation or faith on her part, the Lord chose to heal this woman's cancer-infested body through divine means. That's God, and that is sometimes how he does it.

Faith, Miracles, Prayer, The Supernatural
Exod. 15:26; Ps. 103:3; Matt. 8:17; James 5:13–16

Date used __________ Place ____________________

In his book *When You're All Out of Noodles,* Ken Jones writes about a lesson he learned one day at the office.

> [When I walked into my office,] I noticed something I had never seen before. It was round, about the size of a dessert plate, and plugged into the wall, giving out a constant noise. It wasn't a loud noise, just constant. *What in the world is that thing?* I thought as I stopped to stare.
>
> I finally asked the receptionist about it. She said, "It's an ambient noise generator. If it's too quiet in here, we can distinguish the voices in the counseling offices, and we want to protect their privacy. So we bought the noise generator to cover the voices."
>
> Her explanation made perfect sense to me, but didn't it have to be louder to mask the conversations, I asked. "No," she said. "The constancy of the sound tricks the ear so that what is being said can't be distinguished."
>
> *Interesting,* I thought. *Very interesting.* One kind of noise to cover the sound of another. It made me think and pray.
>
> *No wonder, Lord. No wonder I strain to hear what you have to say to me. . . . The constancy of sound—little noises, soft, inward, ambient thoughts and fears and attitudes—tricks the ears of my inner man and masks your still, small voice.*

God isn't silent. We just have trouble hearing him.

Listening, Silence, Solitude, Spiritual Discernment, Spiritual Disciplines
1 Kings 19:9–13; Ps. 46:10

Date used __________ Place ____________________

Heart 295

In December 1995 NASA's Galileo space probe parachuted into the atmosphere of Jupiter. Paul Hoversten writes in *USA Today* that Galileo's mission was to radio data back to Earth on the nature of this gaseous planet. Through telescopes astronomers have long seen tremendous storms on the surface of Jupiter. The winds of these storms have been blowing at some four hundred miles per hour for literally hundreds of years. Scientists wondered, was sunlight driving these storms, as happens on Earth, or was there some sort of reaction going on within the planet, as happens in the stars?

Galileo found the answer to that question. It discovered temperatures ranging from a chilling minus 171 degrees at the cloud tops to a sizzling 305 degrees closer to the core. More important, it found that the superhot core of the planet is the source of the centuries-long storms. The storm winds actually swirl ten thousand miles deep into the planet.

Andrew Ingersoll of the California Institute of Technology explained, "The winds we see at the cloud tops are just the tip of the iceberg. Jupiter's whole fluid interior is in motion just as rapidly as winds at the surface. . . . This helps us explain why you can have 300-year-old storms and jet streams that last for hundreds of years. You've got so much inertia behind it, it's like a giant flywheel spinning forever."

The core of Jupiter is the engine of the planet. So it is with a person. The only way to really change a person is to change the heart.

Emotions, Habits, Motivation, New Creation,
Repentance, Sinful Nature, Tongue, Zeal
Matt. 15:18–20; Luke 6:45; John 3:3; 2 Cor. 5:17

Date used __________ Place ____________________

Heaven 296

Dave Dravecky pitched for the San Francisco Giants in the 1980s. In 1988 doctors discovered a tumor in his pitching arm. In 1991 Dravecky's arm finally had to be amputated.

In *When You Can't Come Back,* Dave Dravecky writes about his sense of loss.

> I miss doing things with my own two hands, and—of course—I really miss baseball. There is a scene in the movie *Field of Dreams* where Shoeless Joe Jackson—one of the eight White Sox players banned from baseball for conspiring to lose the 1919 World Series—said, "Getting thrown out of baseball was like having part of me amputated. I'd wake up at night with the smell of the ballpark in my nose, the cool of the grass on my feet. Man, I did love this game. I'd have played for food money. It was a game. The sounds, the smells. I'd have played for nuthin'."

Dravecky comments, "That scene had a powerful effect on me. I missed those feelings too. The feel of stitched seams as you cradle a new ball in your hand. The smell of seasoned leather as you bring the glove to your face. The sound of a bat cracking out a base hit. I'd have played for food money. I'd have played for nuthin'."

How painful it is to lose what we love. Unfortunately in this fallen world, our lives are touched by loss over and over again. God wants us to enjoy what we love for all eternity, to never experience loss. That is the promise of heaven.

Eternal, Loss, Temporal, World

Matt. 6:19–21; 10:37–39; 16:23–27; 2 Cor. 4:16–18; Rev. 21:1–5

Date used __________ Place ____________________

Heaven 297

In *Six Hours One Friday,* Max Lucado wrote of a friend named Joy who taught a Sunday school class in an underprivileged area. Joy had in her class a timid, nine-year-old girl named Barbara. Max writes:

> [Barbara's] difficult home life had left her afraid and insecure. For the weeks that my friend was teaching the class, Barbara never spoke. Never. While the other children talked, she sat. While the others sang, she was silent. While the others giggled, she was quiet.
>
> Always present. Always listening. Always speechless.
>
> Until the day Joy gave a class on heaven. Joy talked about seeing God. She talked about tearless eyes and deathless lives.
>
> Barbara was fascinated. She wouldn't release Joy from her stare.
>
> She listened with hunger. Then she raised her hand. "Mrs. Joy?"
>
> Joy was stunned. Barbara had never asked a question. "Yes, Barbara?"
>
> "Is heaven for girls like me?"

Barbara couldn't be more qualified.

Children, Hope
Matt. 19:14; Eph. 1:11–14

Date used __________ Place ____________________

John M. Drescher, in *Pulpit Digest,* writes:

When John Owen, the great Puritan, lay on his deathbed his secretary wrote (in his name) to a friend, “I am still in the land of the living.”

“Stop,” said Owen. “Change that and say, ‘I am yet in the land of the dying, but I hope soon to be in the land of the living.’”

Death, Eternal Life

Date used __________ Place ____________________

Heaven 299

In *Preaching Today* Leith Anderson says:

My family and I have lived in the same house for seventeen years. We've lived there more than twice as long as I have lived at any other address in my entire life. I'll sometimes refer to it as "our house," but more often I refer to it as "home." What makes it home isn't the address or the lot or the garage or the architecture. What makes it home is the people.

You may live in a bigger or newer or better house than we live in, but as nice as your house may be, I would never refer to your house as home because the people who are most important to me don't live there. So what makes home home is the people in the relationships.

And what makes heaven heaven is not streets made out of gold, great fountains, lots of fun, and no smog. That all may well be. Actually, I think that heaven is far greater than our wildest imagination. The same God who designed the best of everything in this world, also designed heaven, only he took it to a far greater extent than anything we've ever seen. Yet, that's still not what makes heaven heaven.

What makes heaven heaven is God. It is being there with him.

Death, Home, Hope, Inheritance, Love for God
John 17:24; 1 Thess. 4:17; Rev. 21:1–4

Date used __________ Place ____________________

Heaven 300

In *Preaching Today* writer Joni Eareckson Tada recalls the comment of one boy at the end of a retreat for the handicapped when participants were asked to tell what the week had meant to them:

Little freckle-faced, red-haired Jeff raised his hand. We were so excited to see what Jeff would say, because Jeff had won the hearts of us all at family retreat. Jeff has Down's syndrome. He took the microphone, put it right up to his mouth, and said, "Let's go home."

Later, his mother told me, "Jeff really missed his dad back home. His dad couldn't come to family retreat because he had to work." Even though Jeff had had a great time, a fun-filled week, he was ready to go home because he missed his daddy.

This world is pleasant enough. But would we really want it to go on forever as a family retreat? I don't think so. I'm with Jeff. I miss my Daddy, my Abba Father. My heart is longing to go home.

The hope of being with God in heaven is one of the strong pillars of the Christian life.

Death, Father God, Hope
Rom. 8:15–16; 1 Cor. 13:13; 1 John 2:15

Date used __________ Place ____________________

Heaven 301

U.S. astronaut Shannon Lucid desperately wanted to go home. She had spent six months on the Russian Mir space station, from March to September 1996. Her ride home was delayed six weeks by two hurricanes and assorted mechanical problems with the shuttle booster rockets, making her stay in space the longest of any American astronaut, man or woman. Nevertheless she faced each setback with patient good cheer and a stiff upper lip.

But as the days wore on, she knew where she would rather be. Eventually she admitted she wanted to return home to see her family, to feel the sun and wind on her face, and to check out the new books published in the last six months. Prior to being picked up for her return to Earth by the space shuttle Atlantis, Shannon Lucid quipped, "You can rest assured I am not going to be on the wrong side of the hatch when they close it."

There is another important door in Shannon Lucid's future—and in each of ours as well. It is the door of heaven. If our heart is set on going home to heaven, we will do whatever is necessary to ensure we are on the right side of heaven's door when it shuts for the last time.

Door, Repentance, Treasures
Matt. 6:19–21; Luke 13:22–30

Date used __________ Place ____________________

Hindrances 302

It was to be a majestic evening. On Friday, October 18, 1991, the world-class Chicago Symphony presented the final concert in its year-long celebration of the symphony's one hundredth year. For the first time in United States symphony history, the present conductor and two former conductors of an orchestra stood on the same stage: Rafael Kubelik, Georg Solti, and Daniel Barenboim. At a centenary celebration dinner before the concert, patrons had received souvenir clocks as gifts. As Daniel Barenboim sat down at the piano and Georg Solti lifted his baton to begin Tchaikovsky's First Piano Concerto, a great sense of drama filled Chicago's historic Orchestra Hall. And the beauty of the music took over.

A few minutes later, however, at 9:15 P.M., the music began to unravel. Out in the auditorium a little beep sounded. Then another, and another. Little beeps were sounding everywhere. Barenboim and the symphony plowed ahead, but everyone was distracted and the music suffered.

Finally, after the first movement ended, Henry Fogel, the executive director of the symphony, walked on stage to explain what had happened. The manufacturer of the souvenir clocks presented at the pre-concert dinner had set the alarms to go off at 9:15.

Now there was only one way to get on with the concert. Fogel asked everyone who had one of the clocks to check them in with an usher.

Trivial things have terrible power to disrupt—or even make a farce—of what is important.

Distractions, Eternal, Materialism, Priorities, Temporal, Values
Luke 8:14; Phil. 3:7–8; Heb. 12:1

Date used __________ Place ____________________

Hindrances 303

In Jules Verne's novel *The Mysterious Island,* he tells of five men who escape a Civil War prison camp by hijacking a hot-air balloon. As they rise into the air, they realize the wind is carrying them over the ocean. Watching their homeland disappear on the horizon, they wonder how much longer the balloon can stay aloft.

As the hours pass and the surface of the ocean draws closer, the men decide they must cast overboard some of the weight, for they had no way to heat the air in the balloon. Shoes, overcoats, and weapons are reluctantly discarded, and the uncomfortable aviators feel their balloon rise. But only temporarily. Soon they find themselves dangerously close to the waves again, so they toss their food. Better to be high and hungry than drown on a full belly!

Unfortunately, this, too, is only a temporary solution, and the craft again threatens to lower the men into the sea. One man has an idea: they can tie the ropes that hold the passenger car and sit on those ropes. Then they can cut away the basket beneath them. As they sever the very thing they had been standing on, it drops into the ocean, and the balloon rises.

Not a minute too soon, they spot land. Eager to stand on terra firma again, the five jump into the water and swim to the island. They live, spared because they were able to discern the difference between what really was needed and what was not. The "necessities" they once thought they couldn't live without were the very weights that almost cost them their lives.

The writer to the Hebrews says, "Let us throw off everything that hinders and the sin that so easily entangles" (Heb. 12:1).

Priorities, Sin

Date used __________ Place ____________________

Holding On 304

On a commuter flight from Portland, Maine, to Boston, Henry Dempsey, the pilot, heard an unusual noise near the rear of the small aircraft. He turned the controls over to his co-pilot and went back to check it out.

As he reached the tail section, the plane hit an air pocket, and Dempsey was tossed against the rear door. He quickly discovered the source of the mysterious noise. The rear door had not been properly latched prior to takeoff, and it flew open. He was instantly sucked out of the jet.

The co-pilot, seeing the red light that indicated an open door, radioed the nearest airport, requesting permission to make an emergency landing. He reported that the pilot had fallen out of the plane, and he requested a helicopter search of that area of the ocean.

After the plane landed, they found Henry Dempsey—holding onto the outdoor ladder of the aircraft. Somehow he had caught the ladder, held on for ten minutes as the plane flew 200 mph at an altitude of 4,000 feet, and then, at landing, kept his head from hitting the runway, which was a mere twelve inches away. It took airport personnel several minutes to pry Dempsey's fingers from the ladder.

Things in life may be turbulent, and you may not feel like holding on. But have you considered the alternative?

Perseverance, Trials

Date used __________ Place ____________________

305

According to writer Lisa Belcher-Hamilton, Fred Rogers, of the television program *Mister Rogers' Neighborhood,* took courses on how to preach during his time in seminary. Said Rogers:

> Years ago my wife and I were worshiping in a little church with friends of ours. We were on vacation, and I was in the middle of my homiletics course at the time.
>
> During the sermon I kept ticking off every mistake I thought the preacher—he must have been eighty years old—was making. When this interminable sermon finally ended, I turned to one of my friends, intending to say something critical about the sermon. I stopped myself when I saw the tears running down her face.
>
> She whispered to me, "He said exactly what I needed to hear." That was really a seminal experience for me. I was judging and she was needing, and the Holy Spirit responded to need, not judgment.

Although we must always give ministry our best effort, we must never forget that the Holy Spirit can work through even the most faulty instrument.

Criticism, Judging, Ministry, Preaching
Matt. 7:1–2; Eph. 4:29–32

Date used __________ Place ____________________

In *Flying Closer to the Flame*, Charles Swindoll writes:

Some years ago my phone rang in the middle of the day on a Friday. It was someone from our older daughter's school telling me that Charissa had been in an accident. She had been practicing a pyramid formation with her cheerleading squad when someone at the bottom slipped, causing the whole human pyramid to collapse. Charissa had been at the top and, consequently, fell the farthest, hitting the back of her head with a sharp jolt. Her legs and arms had gone numb, and she was unable to move even her fingers. After notifying the paramedics, the school official had called me.

My wife, Cynthia, was away at the time, so I raced to the school alone, not knowing what I'd find or how serious our daughter had been injured. En route, I prayed aloud. I called out to the Lord like a child trapped in an empty well. I told Him I would need Him for several things: to touch my daughter, to give me strength, to provide skill and wisdom to the paramedics. Tears were near the surface, so I asked Him to calm me, to restrain the growing sense of panic within me.

As I drove and prayed, I sensed the most incredible realization of God's presence. It was almost eerie. The pulse that had been thumping in my throat returned to normal. When I reached the school parking lot, even the swirling red and blue lights atop the emergency vehicle didn't faze my sense of calm.

I ran to where the crowd had gathered. By that time the paramedics had Charissa wrapped tightly on a stretcher, her neck in a brace. I knelt beside her, kissed her on the forehead, and heard her say, "I can't feel anything below my shoulders. Something snapped in my back, just below my neck." She was blinking through tears.

Normally, I would have been borderline out of control. I wasn't. Normally, I would have been shouting for the crowd to back away or for the ambulance driver to get her to the hospital immediately! I didn't. With remarkable ease, I stroked the hair away from her eyes and whispered, "I'm here with you, sweetheart. So is our Lord. No matter what happens, we'll make it through this together. I love you, Charissa." Tears ran down the side of her face as she closed her eyes.

Calmly, I stood and spoke with the emergency medical personnel. We agreed on which hospital she should go to and what route we would take. I followed in my car, again sensing the Spirit's profound and sovereign presence. Cynthia joined me at the hospital, where we waited for the x-rays and the radiologist's report. We prayed, and I told her of my encounter with the Spirit's wonderful presence.

In a few hours we learned that a vertebrae in Charissa's back had been fractured. The doctors did not know how much damage had been done to the nerves as a result of the fall and fracture. Neither did they know how long it would take for the numbness to subside or if, in fact, it would. The physicians were careful with their words, and I can still remember how grim both of them seemed. We had nothing tangible to rely on, nothing medical to count on, and nothing emotional to lean on . . . except the Spirit of God, who had stayed with us through the entire ordeal.

Sunday was just around the corner (it always is). I was exhausted by Saturday night, but again God's Spirit remained my stability. In human weakness and with enormous dependence, I preached on Sunday morning. The Lord gave me the words, and He proved His strength in my weakness. (I am told by our audio tape department that that particular message remains one of the most requested sermons on tape of all the messages I've delivered since I first became pastor of the church back in 1971.)

Amazing! God the Holy Spirit filled me, took full control, gave great grace, calmed fears, and ultimately brought wonderful healing to Charissa's back. Today she is a healthy, happy wife and mother of two, and the only time her upper back hurts is when she sneezes! When that happens and I'm with her, I usually look at her and ask, "Did that hurt?" Invariably, she nods and says, "Yeah, it did." I smile, she smiles back, and for a moment we mentally return to that original scene where she and I felt a very real awareness of the Spirit's presence.

Crisis, Peace, Prayer, Presence of God
John 14:26–27; Gal. 5:22–23; Phil. 4:6–7

Date used __________ Place ____________________

Flying Closer to the Flame, Charles Swindoll, 1993, Word, Dallas, Texas.

In his book *Enjoying God,* Lloyd Ogilvie writes:

An elder at my church realized his need for the sealing of the Spirit long after he committed his life to Christ years ago. His exemplary character and generosity made him a shoo-in for nomination and election to eldership. However, no one knew how uncertain he was about his relationship to Christ because he had kept that hidden beneath a polished exterior. He didn't anticipate that being part of the elders' prayer ministry at the end of our worship services would confront him with his own insecure relationship with Christ. When people came to pray with him, he keenly saw that something was missing in his own life. He had never allowed Christ to break through his inner hard shell of self-sufficiency. Being called to minister to others forced him to see that he was in over his head spiritually. What he was asked to pray for in others he needed himself.

Fortunately, my friend began to talk about his spiritual emptiness, although it was not easy for him to admit his neediness. He had spent his entire life convincing others that he was adequate.

As we talked, I shared with him the power of the Spirit-filled life. He'd heard hundreds of sermons about the Spirit, but the words never penetrated his shell. Now Christ was breaking the shell, allowing my elder friend to receive what Christ had longed to give him for years—the Spirit. We knelt and prayed together while he asked to receive the security and strength of being sealed. And Christ was faithful. Into the soft wax of this man's ready heart, He pressed the seal of His indwelling presence.

Emptiness, Security, Self-Sufficiency
Rom. 8:13–16; Eph. 5:18

Date used __________ Place ____________________

308

Gordon Brownville's *Symbols of the Holy Spirit* tells about the great Norwegian explorer Roald Amundsen, the first to discover the magnetic meridian of the North Pole and to discover the South Pole. On one of his trips, Amundsen took a homing pigeon with him. When he had finally reached the top of the world, he opened the bird's cage and set it free.

Imagine the delight of Amundsen's wife, back in Norway, when she looked up from the doorway of her home and saw the pigeon circling in the sky above. No doubt she exclaimed, "He's alive! My husband is still alive!"

So it was when Jesus ascended. He was gone, but the disciples clung to his promise to send them the Holy Spirit. What joy, then, when the dovelike Holy Spirit descended at Pentecost. The disciples had with them the continual reminder that Jesus was alive and victorious at the right hand of the Father. This continues to be the Spirit's message.

Christ's Ascension, Signs

Date used __________ Place ____________________

Holy Spirit 309

In the *Pentecostal Evangel* Paul Grabill, a pastor in State College, Pennsylvania, interviewed Eric Harrah, a recent convert to Christ. Harrah had previously been the owner and partner in twenty-six abortion clinics, making him the second largest abortion provider in the United States. He received Christ late in 1997, and the supernatural working of the Holy Spirit through a believer named Steve Stupar played a part in his decision. Harrah recalls:

A week before I gave my life back to Christ, we were sitting at a restaurant and Steve said the Holy Spirit had revealed three things to him and he wanted to confirm them. He said, "The name John keeps coming up. What does that name mean to you?"

I said, "That's my grandfather's name. He is dying with lung cancer."

He said, "I saw a girl in a plaid outfit and a white shirt. Do you know who that would have been?"

As soon as he said that I knew it was my sister. I remember the picture explicitly because my grandfather has her school picture in which she is wearing a plaid outfit and a white shirt. I wasn't too impressed because people knew I had a sister and everybody knew who my grandfather was.

Then he said, "The Holy Spirit revealed to me a plate that had blue pills on it with white bands. Does that mean anything to you?"

I denied it at first, but later called him and told him what the significance was. About a week before, I had come home with some joint pains. I went to my kitchen to get some pain medication. One of the bottles contained the blue pills with the white band. I went to take one, and just said to myself, Enough is enough—tonight is a good night to die. I reached up into my cabinet and got a plate out and dumped all the blue pills onto the plate. I got my other medication and dumped them all out on the plate too. When I went to put the first pill in my mouth, my dog barked and looked up at me as if to say, What about me? Who's going to take care of me? I knew nobody would, so I put the pills back in their containers. . . .

It was amazing to me that the Holy Ghost revealed that to him. That is when I knew it was time to give in.

One reason God gives us the power of the Holy Spirit is to help us win lost people to Christ.

Evangelism, Power, Spiritual Gifts,
The Supernatural, Word of Knowledge
Acts 1:8; 1 Cor. 2:4–5; 12:1–31; 14:24–25

Date used __________ Place ____________________

Holy Spirit 310

The monarch butterfly is a familiar sight in most of the United States. Few butterflies can compare with the beauty of its orange, yellow, and black wings. Each year people in many regions of the United States enjoy the unique pleasure of seeing thousands of monarch butterflies fill the sky in their annual migration south. They spend the winter in forests of fir trees in the volcanic highlands of south-central Mexico. Environmentalists have identified nine areas where the monarchs cluster in colonies, and Mexico has designated five of these sites as sanctuaries of protection.

But that isn't enough, say researchers. The sanctuaries cover only sixty-two square miles. Meanwhile poor farmers and commercial loggers are clearing fir forests, at times even in the restricted zones, putting increasing pressure on existing butterfly colonies. Lincoln Brower of the University of Florida said, "We're not going to have a monarch migration in twenty years if those reserves aren't expanded and protected."

Like these beautiful, fragile monarch butterflies coming to their winter home, God's Spirit usually fills our hearts in gentle ways. We must intentionally keep a sanctuary for him, for many things would encroach upon his home in us. Our sense of his manifest presence, our ability to hear his thoughts, our awareness of his direction—all can be lost if we do not safeguard a place for him.

Direction, God's Presence, God's Voice, Silence,
Solitude, Spiritual Disciplines, Spiritual Perception
1 Kings 19:9–13; Eph. 4:30; 5:18

Date used __________ Place ____________________

311

In his book *Integrity,* Ted Engstrom tells this story:

For Coach Cleveland Stroud and the Bulldogs of Rockdale County High School [Conyers, Georgia], it was their championship season: 21 wins and 5 losses on the way to the Georgia boy's basketball tournament last March, then a dramatic come-from-behind victory in the state finals.

But now the new glass trophy case outside the high school gymnasium is bare. Earlier this month the Georgia High School Association deprived Rockdale County of the championship after school officials said that a player who was scholastically ineligible had played 45 seconds in the first of the school's five postseason games.

"We didn't know he was ineligible at the time; we didn't know it until a few weeks ago," Mr. Stroud said. "Some people have said we should have just kept quiet about it, that it was just 45 seconds and the player wasn't an impact player. But you've got to do what's honest and right and what the rules say. I told my team that people forget the scores of basketball games; they don't ever forget what you're made of."

Integrity, Reputation

Date used __________ Place ____________________

Honor 312

On September 22, 1997, the U.S. Army commissioned West Point's first black cadet—123 years after expelling him. James Webster Smith, a former slave, entered the U.S. Military Academy in 1870. For the next four years he was harassed for the color of his skin. White students refused to talk to him. He was forced to eat by himself, and others poured slop on him. Twice he was court-martialed. He had to repeat a year. Finally the academy expelled him after his junior year for failing an exam. Smith died of tuberculosis at age twenty-six. That seemingly was the sad final note for a life scarred by injustice.

But 123 years later the Army endeavored to some degree to right its wrong. Because he had no known descendants, the commissioning certificate and gold second lieutenant's bars of James Webster Smith were presented to South Carolina State University. In the end a courageous man finally received his due.

In this world people who deserve honor may temporarily receive dishonor. But it is only temporary. Eventually such people will be vindicated. Honor will come. Sometimes the honor that is deserved comes in this world, but that honor always comes in the kingdom of God. That honor, which comes from God, is what really matters.

Discrimination, Name, Persecution, Prejudice, Shame, Vindication
Matt. 5:10–12; John 12:26; Rom. 2:5–11;
1 Cor. 4:8–13; 2 Cor. 4:1–18; 6:3–10

Date used __________ Place ____________________

313

In *Imaginary Homelands* author Salman Rushdie writes of one of the family traditions of his home:

> In our house, whenever anyone dropped a book, it was required to be not only picked up but also kissed, by way of apology for the act of clumsy disrespect. I was as careless and butterfingered as any child, and accordingly I kissed a large number of books.
>
> Devout households in India still contain persons in the habit of kissing holy books. But we kissed everything. We kissed dictionaries and atlases. We kissed novels and Superman comics. If I'd ever dropped the telephone directory, I'd probably have kissed that too.

Is it any surprise that Salman Rushdie grew up to become an author? What we honor defines us.

Child Rearing, Honor, Respect, Reverence, Worship
Eph. 6:2

Date used __________ Place ____________________

Hope 314

We can learn something about Christian hope from fishermen. In *Pavlov's Trout,* Paul Quinnett writes:

> It is better to fish hopefully than to catch fish.
>
> Fishing is hope experienced. To be optimistic in a slow bite is to thrive on hope alone. When asked, "How can you fish all day without a hit?" the true fisherman replies, "Hold it! I think I felt something." If the line goes slack, he says, "He'll be back!"
>
> When it comes to the human spirit, hope is all. Without hope, there is no yearning, no desire for a better tomorrow, and no belief that the next cast will bring the big strike.

According to the Bible, the Christian life is also hope experienced. A hopeless Christian is a contradiction in terms.

Discouragement, Evangelism, Prayer
Rom. 4:18; 15:13; 1 Cor. 13:13; Col. 1:27

Date used __________ Place ______________________

Hope 315

Strong leaders never lose hope.

The story is told of a great, never-say-die general who was taken captive and thrown into a deep, wide pit along with a number of his soldiers. In that pit was a huge pile of horse manure.

"Follow me," the general cried to his men as he dove into the pile, "There has to be a horse in here somewhere!"

Leadership, Optimism, Trials

Rom. 8:24–25; Col. 1:27; James 1:2–4

Date used __________ Place ____________________

Hope 316

In *Christianity Today*, David Neff writes:

About five years ago, Christian social critic Richard John Neuhaus was being driven from the Pittsburgh airport to a speaking engagement. During the drive, one of his hosts persisted in decrying the disintegration of the American social fabric and the disappearance of Christian values from our culture. Cases in point were too numerous to mention, but Pastor Neuhaus's host tried anyway. After the tedious drive, Neuhaus offered these words of advice: "The times may be bad, but they are the only times we are given. Remember, hope is still a Christian virtue, and despair is a mortal sin."

Cynicism, Despair, Negativism
Rom. 8:24–25; 1 Cor. 13:13; Col. 1:27

Date used __________ Place ____________________

Hope 317

In 1997 the journal of the American Heart Association reported on some remarkable research. According to the *Chicago Tribune,* Susan Everson of the Human Population Laboratory of the Public Health Institute in Berkeley, California, found that people who experienced high levels of despair had a 20 percent greater occurrence of atherosclerosis—the narrowing of their arteries—than did optimistic people. "This is the same magnitude of increased risk that one sees in comparing a pack-a-day smoker to a non-smoker," said Everson. In other words, despair can be as bad for you as smoking a pack a day!

That is just one more reason why God calls us to choose hope and faith. The Christian life contributes to good health, for God gives us a legitimate basis for hope.

Despair, Health
Rom. 15:13; 1 Cor. 13:13

Date used __________ Place ____________________

Humility 318

In *Guideposts,* Ronald Pinkerton describes a near accident he had while hang gliding. He had launched his hang glider and been forcefully lifted 4,200 feet into the air. As he was descending, he was suddenly hit by a powerful new blast of air that sent his hang glider plummeting toward the ground.

> I was falling at an alarming rate. Trapped in an airborne riptide, I was going to crash! Then I saw him—a red-tailed hawk. He was six feet off my right wingtip, fighting the same gust I was. . . .
>
> I looked down: 300 feet from the ground and still falling. The trees below seemed like menacing pikes.
>
> I looked at the hawk again. Suddenly he banked and flew straight downwind. Downwind! If the right air is anywhere, it's upwind! The hawk was committing suicide.
>
> Two hundred feet. From nowhere the thought entered my mind: *Follow the hawk*. It went against everything I knew about flying. But now all my knowledge was useless. I was at the mercy of the wind. I followed the hawk.
>
> One hundred feet. Suddenly the hawk gained altitude. For a split second I seemed to be suspended motionless in space. Then a warm surge of air started pushing the glider upward. I was stunned. Nothing I knew as a pilot could explain this phenomenon. But it was true: I was rising.

On occasion we all have similar "downdrafts" in our lives, reversals in our fortunes, humiliating experiences. We want to lift ourselves up, but God's Word, like that red-tailed hawk, tells us to do just the opposite. God's Word tells us to dive—to humble ourselves under the hand of God. If we humble ourselves, God will send a thermal wind that will lift us up.

Ego, Instincts, Scripture, Trials
Luke 18:9–14; James 4:10

Date used __________ Place ____________________

Humility 319

Few people have the privilege of a private audience with Pope John Paul II. One who did was journalist Tim Russert, NBC News Washington bureau chief, *Meet the Press* moderator, and former altar boy. In the *St. Anthony Messenger,* James W. Arnold relates Russert's story.

> I'll never forget it. I was there to convince His Holiness it was in his interest to appear on the *Today* show. But my thoughts soon turned away from NBC's ratings toward the idea of salvation. As I stood there with the Vicar of Christ, I simply blurted, "Bless me, Father!"
>
> He put his arm around my shoulders and whispered, "You are the one called Timothy, the man from NBC?"
>
> I said, "Yes, yes, that's me."
>
> "They tell me you're a very important man."
>
> Taken aback, I said, "Your Holiness, there are only two of us in this room, and I am certainly a distant second."
>
> He looked at me and said, "Right."

It's always wise to know your place.

Blessing, Position, Status
Luke 14:7–11

Date used __________ Place ____________________

Humility 320

The *Handbook of Magazine Article Writing* contains this illustration by Philip Barry Osborne:

Alex Haley, the author of *Roots,* has a picture in his office, showing a turtle sitting atop a fence. The picture is there to remind him of a lesson he learned long ago: "If you see a turtle on a fence post, you know he had some help."

Says Alex, "Any time I start thinking, *Wow, isn't this marvelous what I've done!* I look at that picture and remember how this turtle—me—got up on that post."

Help, Success

Date used __________ Place ____________________

In *People Weekly* Richard Jerome and Elizabeth McNeil write:

> Violin virtuoso Joshua Bell is that rare prodigy who has matured into a world-class musician and an acclaimed interpreter of Mozart, Beethoven and Tchaikovsky. The 29-year-old Bell has always been driven, even while growing up in Bloomington, Ind. Whether it was chess, computers, video games or the violin, Bell had a need to master his environment.
>
> In some quarters, he's already arrived at his pinnacle. Years ago back home in Bloomington, a twelve-year-old boy approached him and announced, "You're Joshua Bell. You're famous."
>
> "Well, ummm, not really," Bell replied.
>
> "Yes, really," the kid insisted. "Your name is on every video game in the arcade as the highest scorer."

Greatness is measured in different ways by different people. The kingdom of heaven, too, has its own standard of greatness: namely, humility and servanthood.

Greatness, Servanthood, Success
Matt. 18:1–4; 20:26–28; Phil. 2:1–11; 3:4–11

Date used __________ Place ____________________

Humility 322

One of the most decisive moments in our lives is when we admit our need. That admission is what it took to turn Tracey Bailey around. Bailey writes in *Guideposts* that in 1993 he stood in the White House Rose Garden in the presence of the president of the United States to receive the National Teacher of the Year Award. He had come a long way. Some fifteen years earlier he had stood as a teenager in the presence of a county judge in an Indiana courtroom to be sentenced to jail. Bailey had gone on a drunken rampage with friends, vandalizing a high school, had been caught and found guilty. Nevertheless Bailey stood before the judge with his head held high, the words of his high school wrestling coach ringing in his ears: "Don't you ever hang your head. Don't admit defeat. The minute you do, it's over."

The judge looked at the proud teenager and stunned the courtroom with Bailey's sentence: five years in the Indiana youth center, a prison one step below the state penitentiary.

Tracey Bailey went to jail with his head still held high, but it took only a few months for reality to set in. One day as he sat in solitary confinement in a cell with nothing more than a metal cot, a sink, and a toilet, he realized what a mistake he had made. He began to weep. More important, he began to pray to God. "God, I need help," he said. "I am defeated without you."

That was the turning point for Tracey Bailey. He joined a prison Bible study and began taking college correspondence courses. After fourteen months in jail he was released on probation, and after further college studies he became a science teacher in Florida. With these words he summarizes the lesson he had learned in life: "I bowed my head and tasted victory."

Brokenness, Confession, Contriteness, Dependence, Need

Ps. 40:1–2; Isa. 66:2; Dan. 4; 1 Peter 5:5–6; 1 John 1:9

Date used __________ Place ____________________

Hypocrisy 323

According to Reuters news agency, on April 28 at the 1992 Galveston County Fair and Rodeo, a steer named Husker, weighing in at 1,190 pounds, was named grand champion. The steer was sold at auction for $13,500 and slaughtered a few days after the competition. When veterinarians examined the carcass, said a contest official, they found something suspicious. They discovered evidence of what is called "airing."

To give steers a better appearance, competitors have been known to inject air into their animals' hides with a syringe or a needle attached to a bicycle pump. Pump long enough, and they've got themselves what looks like a grand champion steer, though of course it's against the rules.

The Galveston County Fair and Rodeo Association withdrew the championship title and sale money from Husker.

A pumped-up steer is like a hypocritical person. Hypocrites appear more virtuous than they are.

Boasting, Knowledge, Pride
1 Cor. 8:1

Date used __________ Place ____________________

Hypocrisy 324

The *Queen Mary* was the largest ship to cross the oceans when it was launched in 1936. Through four decades and a world war she served until she was retired, anchored as a floating hotel and museum in Long Beach, California.

During the conversion, her three massive smokestacks were taken off to be scraped down and repainted. But on the dock they crumbled.

Nothing was left of the 3/4-inch steel plate from which the stacks had been formed. All that remained were more than thirty coats of paint that had been applied over the years. The steel had rusted away.

When Jesus called the Pharisees "whitewashed tombs," he meant they had no substance, only an exterior appearance.

Appearances, Character

Date used __________ Place ____________________

Hypocrisy 325

In *Christian Reader* Jim Corley tells of a conversation he had with a friend named Alex who attended his church. Alex was struggling over his many failures to live the Christian life the way he knew he should. One day they met at the car dealership where Alex worked. Corley writes:

That day in his office Alex got straight to the point. "Jim, I feel like a hypocrite every time I go to church because I fail to live for Christ so often."

"Alex, what do you call this part of the dealership?" I asked, nodding to the area outside his cubicle.

"You mean the showroom?"

I smiled. "Yes. And what's behind the showroom, past the parts counter?"

"The service department," Alex said confidently.

"What if I told you I didn't want to bring my car to the service department because it was running rough?"

"That would be crazy! That's the whole point of service departments—to fix cars that aren't running right."

"You're absolutely right," I replied. "Now, let's get back to our initial conversation. Instead of thinking of church as a showroom where image is everything, start thinking of it as God's service department. Helping people get back in running order with God is what the church is all about."

Church, Discipleship, Failure, Guilt, Obedience, Sin
Matt. 9:9–13; 1 John 1:7–10

Date used __________ Place ____________________

Hypocrisy 326

According to the *Chicago Tribune,* a man named Joe from Rockford, Illinois, ran a live Internet sex site called Video Fantasy. Joe had a ten-year-old son. On his home computer Joe installed filtering software to limit the surfing that his son could do on the Internet.

Joe explained, "It's not that I keep him sheltered, but my wife and I pay close attention to what he reads, what he watches on TV and what he does on the computer because we have a responsibility to him to be the best parents we can."

Joe's sense of responsibility to his son is commendable. Joe's sense of responsibility to the children of other parents (and the parents themselves!) is deplorable.

Can there be a more stark illustration of hypocrisy?

Golden Rule, Pornography, Responsibility, Stumbling Blocks, Voyeurism
Matt. 7:12; 18:5–7; 23:28; 1 Tim. 4:2; 1 Peter 2:1

Date used __________ Place ____________________

Idolatry 327

Fans can go to the extreme in their devotion to musical performers.

In the April 25, 1994, news section of *Christianity Today,* it was reported that some fans of Elvis Presley were actually revering the king of rock and roll as a god. Pockets of semi-organized Elvis worship had taken hold in New York, Colorado, and Indiana. Worshipers raised their hands, spelled and then chanted Presley's name, worked themselves into a fervor, and prayed to the deceased star.

At the First Presleyterian Church of Denver, a Reverend Mort Farndu said that Elvis worship was spreading. Followers believe Elvis watches over them. If someone reports seeing Presley, the high priests at the Church of the Risen Elvis in Denver hold Elvis worship services. They enshrined a look-alike doll of Elvis in an altar surrounded by candles and flowers.

Idolatry is alive and well in America.

Music, Ten Commandments
Exod. 20:3; Rom. 1:18–23

Date used __________ Place ____________________

Idolatry 328

When does sports as entertainment become sports as idolatry? Consider this banner seen at Lambeau Field in 1996, the season the Green Bay Packers won the Super Bowl in New Orleans and their quarterback Brett Favre was named the most valuable player:

Our Favre who art in Lambeau, hallowed be thy arm. The Bowl will come, it will be won, in New Orleans as it is in Lambeau. Give us this Sunday our weekly win. And give us many touchdown passes. But do not let others pass against us. Lead us not into frustration, but deliver us to Bourbon Street. For thine is the MVP, the best of the NFL, and the glory of the cheeseheads, now and forever. Go get 'em!

Apparently some fans recognize their team support for what it really is: worship.

Worship

Exod. 20:3, Matt. 6:24, Mark 12:30, James 4:4, 1 John 5:21

Date used __________ Place ____________________

329

According to Peter Kendall in the *Chicago Tribune,* Ruben Brown, age sixty-one, was known on the south and west sides of Chicago, as the friendly neighborhood cockroach exterminator with "the Mississippi stuff." The Mississippi stuff was a pesticide Brown had bought hundreds of gallons of in the South, and it really did the trick on roaches. Brown went from door to door with his hand sprayer, and his business grew as satisfied customers recommended the remarkably effective exterminator to others.

In the process, however, Brown is alleged to have single-handedly created an environmental catastrophe. The can-do pesticide—methyl parathion—is outlawed by the EPA for use in homes. Southern farmers use it on boll weevils in their cotton fields, and within days the pesticide chemically breaks down into harmless elements. Not so in the home. There the pesticide persists as a toxic chemical that can harm the human neurological system with effects similar to lead poisoning.

The EPA was called into Chicago for the cleanup. Drywall, carpeting, and furniture sprayed with the pesticide had to be torn out and hauled to a hazardous-materials dump. The U.S. Environmental Protection Agency estimated that the total cost of the cleanup would be some $20 million, ranking this as one of the worst environmental nightmares in Illinois history.

Brown was charged with two misdemeanors. He apparently didn't know much about the pesticide he sprayed so liberally. Brown's attorney said, "It's a tragedy. It is one of those situations where he did a lot of harm, but his intention in no way matches the damage he has done. He is a family man and handled it with his own hands. Do you think he knew how toxic it was?"

What you don't know can hurt you. That is true both of pesticides and of false teaching.

Doctrine, Error, False Teaching, Knowledge, Mistakes, Study, Teachers
Ezra 7:10; Matt. 4:4; Eph. 4:14; 1 Tim. 4:1–16; 6:3–5; 2 Tim. 2:15–17; 3:14–17; Heb. 5:14; James 3:1; Rev. 2:20

Date used __________ Place ____________________

Image 330

In a *New York Times* book review of *John Wayne's America,* by Garry Wills, writer Michiko Kakutani illustrates what a powerful effect the movie image of John Wayne has had on American men. General Douglas MacArthur thought John Wayne was the model of the American soldier. Critic Eric Bentley thought he was the most important man in America. Politicians like Ronald Reagan imitated his manner. And phrases like "Saddle up!" and "Lock and load!" have become battle cries for some.

But Garry Wills's book points out that the real man behind the legend was not always what he appeared. "Wills notes that the big-screen warrior," says Kakutani, "who denounced those who refused to serve in Vietnam as 'soft,' got out of serving in World War II so he could focus on his career; that the star of so many horse epics actually hated horses; that the indomitable man of the West was born in Iowa with the very unmacho name of Marion Morrison. Indeed this volume's central narrative traces John Wayne's creation of a mythic persona: an invented self that projected an aura of authority, autonomy and slumberous power."

We expect film stars to create an image; that is part of the business. But a false image is never the business of real life.

Entertainment, Hypocrisy, Myth, Perception, Reality, Truth
John 1:47

Date used __________ Place ____________________

Imitating God 331

On September 6, 1995, Cal Ripken Jr. broke the baseball record that many believed would never be broken: Lou Gehrig's iron-man feat of playing in 2,131 consecutive games. Ripken gives much of the credit for his accomplishments to the example and teaching of his father Cal Ripken Sr. who played minor league baseball, and coached and managed for the Orioles.

During the 1996 season Ripken Sr. was inducted into the Orioles Hall of Fame. After he gave his acceptance speech, the son came to the microphone, an emotional moment recalled in his book *The Only Way I Know:*

> It was difficult. I wasn't certain I could say what I wanted about my father and what he means to me. So I told a little story about my two children, Rachel, six at the time, and Ryan, then three. They'd been bickering for weeks, and I explained how one day I heard Rachel taunt Ryan, "You're just trying to be like Daddy."
>
> After a few moments of indecision, I asked Rachel, "What's wrong with trying to be like Dad?"
>
> When I finished telling the story, I looked at my father and added, "That's what I've always tried to do."

What could be more right than to try to be like your heavenly Father? It brings true and lasting greatness.

Example, Fathers, Greatness, Holiness, Imitation
Matt. 5:48; 20:25–28; Luke 6:36; Eph. 5:1–2; 1 Peter 1:16

Date used __________ Place ____________________

Incarnation 332

In the *New York Times Magazine,* Nancy V. Raine told a story she heard twenty-five years earlier from a friend named George.

> In those days, work crews marked construction sites by putting out smudge pots with open flames. George's four-year-old daughter got too close to one and her pants caught fire like the Straw Man's stuffing. The scars running the length and breadth of Sarah's legs looked like pieces of a jigsaw puzzle. In the third grade she was asked, "If you could have one wish, what would it be?" Sarah wrote: "I want everyone to have legs like mine."

When we suffer pain, we want others to understand. We want others to be like us so they can identify with us. We don't want to be alone.

God does understand. When Jesus became a man, he did something far more difficult than having legs like Sarah's.

Handicap, High Priest, Loneliness, Pain, Sympathy
John 1:14; Heb. 2:10; 4:14–5:3

Date used __________ Place ____________________

Independence 333

The March 2, 1995, issue of the *New England Journal of Medicine* reported an extraordinary case of self-treatment.

A plastic surgeon was repairing an examining-room lamp and was accidently shocked. Soon he felt dizzy, and his heart was pounding. He shakily dragged himself into his operating room and hooked himself up to a heart monitor, which showed his heart was racing at 160 beats a minute. The doctor diagnosed himself as suffering atrial fibrillation, which is potentially life threatening.

His operating room was equipped with a defibrillator, which is an electronic device that applies an electric shock to restore the rhythm of the heart. But the device was hardly designed for self-use.

Nevertheless the forty-year-old doctor quickly grabbed a tube of petroleum jelly and smeared the jelly on his bare chest. Then he grabbed the paddles of the defibrillator and pressed them to his chest. He gave himself two shocks of 100 watt-seconds (100 joules). The jolts of electricity knocked him right off the operating table, but his normal heart rhythm was restored.

Amin Karim of Baylor College of Medicine in Houston, who reported this case to the *Journal,* said this man probably would have been better off dialing 911 for an ambulance. "What if he passed out?" said Karim. "He could have put himself into a more dangerous rhythm."

Like this doctor, when we enter a crisis, we often want to rely on ourselves rather than call for help. But extreme independence is risky at best and dangerous at worst.

Church, Crisis, Faith, Prayer, Self-Reliance, Works
2 Chron. 14:11; Prov. 28:26; Rom. 10:3; 2 Cor. 1:9

Date used __________ Place ____________________

On November 20, 1988, the *Los Angeles Times* reported:

A screaming woman, trapped in a car dangling from a freeway transition road in East Los Angeles was rescued Saturday morning. The 19-year-old woman apparently fell asleep behind the wheel about 12:15 A.M. The car, which plunged through a guard rail, was left dangling by its left rear wheel. A half dozen passing motorists stopped, grabbed some ropes from one of their vehicles, tied the ropes to the back of the woman's car, and hung on until the fire units arrived. A ladder was extended from below to help stabilize the car while firefighters tied the vehicle to tow trucks with cables and chains.

"Every time we would move the car," said one of the rescuers, "she'd yell and scream. She was in pain."

It took almost 2 1/2 hours for the passers-by, CHP officers, tow truck drivers, and firefighters—about 25 people in all —to secure the car and pull the woman to safety.

"It was kinda funny," L.A. County Fire Capt. Ross Marshall recalled later. "She kept saying, 'I'll do it myself.'"

There are times when self-sufficiency goes too far.

Self-Sufficiency, Help

Date used __________ Place ____________________

Influence 335

In the November 1987 *Reader's Digest,* Betty Wein retells an old tale she heard from Elie Wiesel:

A just man comes to Sodom hoping to save the city. He pickets. What else can he do? He goes from street to street, from marketplace to marketplace, shouting, "Men and women, repent. What you are doing is wrong. It will kill you; it will destroy you."

They laugh, but he goes on shouting, until one day a child stops him. "Poor stranger, don't you see it's useless?"

"Yes," the just man replies.

"Then why do you go on?" the child asks.

"I was convinced that I would change them. Now I go on shouting because I don't want them to change me."

Testimony, Evil

Date used ________ Place ________________

Integrity 336

In *The Wall Street Journal* Emory Thomas Jr. writes:

Ernest "Bud" Miller, president and chief executive officer of Arvida, a real-estate company, closed regional offices, reorganized departments, and cut his work force of 2,600 in half. In the process he turned a money-losing company into a profitable one. But despite the trimming, Miller believed one layer of fat remained. So last March he resigned.

"I couldn't justify me to me," says Miller. "I couldn't look at the people I let go and say I applied a different standard to me. Every fiber of my person wanted to stay. But professionally this was the decision that had to be made."

The move eliminated one of the two senior jobs at the company. The chief operating officer of Arvida became the chief executive.

Miller, 53, gave up an "upper six-figure" salary package.

The greatest test of integrity is whether we will do what is right at our own expense.

Authority, Leadership, Sacrifice, Selflessness, Servanthood
Matt. 20:26–28; Phil. 2:2–8, 19–24

Date used __________ Place ____________________

Intimacy with God 337

Marsha Kaitz, a psychology professor at Hebrew University in Jerusalem, did a test to see how well mothers know their babies. According to the Associated Press, the forty-six mothers chosen for the test had all given birth in the previous five to seventy-nine hours. They all had breast-fed their newborn.

Each mother was blindfolded and then asked to identify which of three sleeping babies was her own. Nearly seventy percent of the mothers correctly chose their baby. Most of the mothers said they knew their child by the texture or temperature of the infant's hand. The women apparently learned the identifying features during routine contact, said Kaitz, because they weren't allowed to study their babies to prepare for the experiment.

The Lord knows you even better than a mother knows her baby.

Calling, Knowledge, Mothers
Ps. 131; 139; John 1:47–48

Date used __________ Place ____________________

Isolation 338

In January of 1997 astronomers announced they had made another discovery through the orbiting Hubble space telescope. As scientists peered at a cluster of some 2,500 galaxies called Virgo, they saw for the first time heavenly bodies that had been theorized for some time. What they saw, writes John Noble Wilford, were lone stars without a galaxy to call home. These isolated stars drift more than 300,000 light years from the nearest galaxy—that's three times the diameter of the Milky Way Galaxy.

"Somewhere along the way," writes Wilford in the *New York Times,* "they wandered off or were tossed out of the galaxy of their birth, out into the cold, dark emptiness of intergalactic space. . . . Astronomers theorize that these isolated stars were displaced from their home galaxies as a result of galactic mergers or tidal forces from nearby galaxies. There they drifted free of the gravitational influence of any single galaxy."

Like these isolated, wandering stars, Christians can drift from the community of Christ. But God never created us for the cold of isolation. He created us to be together in deep devotion to one another. He made us for the warmth of fellowship. He designed us to live in community.

Church, Community, Fellowship, Togetherness
Acts 2:42–47; Rom. 12:10; Heb. 10:24–25

Date used __________ Place ____________________

At the 1994 Winter Olympics, held in Hamar, Norway, the name Dan took on very special meaning.

At his first Olympics in 1984 as an eighteen year old, Dan Jansen finished fourth in the 500 meters, beaten for a bronze medal by only sixteen one hundredths of a second, and he finished sixteenth in the 1,000.

At his second Olympics in Calgary in 1988, on the morning he was to skate the 500 meters, he received a phone call from America. His twenty-seven-year-old sister, Jane, had been fighting leukemia for over a year. She was dying. Dan spoke to her over the phone, but she was too sick to say anything in return. Their brother Mike relayed Jane's message: She wanted Dan to race for her. Before Dan skated that afternoon, however, he received the news that Jane had died. When he took to the ice, perhaps he tried too hard for his sister. In the 500 meters, he slipped and fell in the first turn. He had never fallen before in a race. Four days later in the 1,000, he fell again, this time, of all places, in the straightaway.

At his third Olympics in 1992, he was expected to win the 500 meters, where he had already set world records. For four years he had been regarded as the best sprinter in the world. But he had trouble in the final turn and he finished fourth. In the 1,000 he tied for twenty-sixth.

At his fourth Olympics in 1994, Dan again was expected to win in the 500 meters, which was his specialty. Again tragedy struck. He didn't fall, but in the beginning of the final turn he fleetingly lost control of his left skate and put his hand down, slowing him just enough to finish in eighth place. Afterward, he apologized to his home town of Milwaukee.

He had one race left, the 1,000 meter. One more race and then he would retire. At the midway point of the race, the clock showed he was skating at a world-record pace, and the crowd, including his wife and father, cheered. But with 200 meters to go, the hearts of the fans skipped a beat. Dan Jansen slipped. He didn't fall, but he slipped, touched his hand to the ice, regained control, and kept skating. When Dan crossed the finish line, he looked at the scoreboard and saw WR beside his name—world record. In his last race, Dan Jansen had finally won the gold medal.

Later that day as he stood on the award stand, Dan looked heavenward, acknowledging his late sister, Jane.

Jansen was asked to skate a victory lap. The lights were turned out, and a single spotlight illuminated Dan's last lap around the Olympic track, with a gold medal around his neck, roses in one arm, and his baby daughter—named Jane—in his other arm.

In the closing ceremony of the 1994 Olympics, Dan Jansen was chosen to carry the U.S. flag.

"Late in the afternoon of February 18, 1994," said writer Philip Hersh, "after Jansen had won the gold medal that eluded him in seven previous races over four Olympics and a decade, someone put a hand-lettered sign in the snow on the side of the main road from Lillehammer to Hamar. The sign said simply, 'Dan.' It spoke volumes about what the world thought about the man whose Olympic futility had finally ended in triumph."

Sometimes a name, a name alone, says it all. So it is when in praise we simply say, "Jesus."

Name, Perseverance, Praise
Ps. 138:2; Acts 3:16; 4:12

Date used __________ Place ____________________

In the *Christian Reader* Andy Woodland writes:

Working as Bible translators in Asia, we had come to two verses spoken by Jesus to his disciples: "I will pray the Father, and he will give you another Counselor . . ." (John 14:16 RSV) and "In that day you will ask in my name; and I do not say to you that I shall pray the Father for you" (John 16:26 RSV). Our immediate thought was to use the common vernacular for "pray" or "beg," but our cotranslator had a better idea.

"Use the phrase *do paarat,*" he suggested. "It's a recommendation an influential person brings on behalf of someone else." Not until a trip to the hospital in our adopted country did I fully understand its meaning.

My wife, Ellie, and I had been asked to help a friend's daughter experiencing post-natal complications. Ellie found the girl, her mother, and mother-in-law waiting in the ward. I stayed outside with the father.

Immediately, he turned to me and said, "You must tell Ellie to speak to the doctor and *do paarat* on my daughter's behalf. We are just poor people from a minority group. They won't respect us or treat us well. But if you *do paarat,* they will give us proper treatment." Ellie agreed, not knowing if it would make a difference.

Thankfully, the doctors did listen and the girl recovered quickly. For us, it was a humbling illustration of how Jesus comes before the Father on our behalf.

Advocate, High Priest, Intercession, Prayer
John 14:16; 16:26; Heb. 4:14–5:10; 1 John 2:1–2

Date used __________ Place ____________________

On Tuesday, April 18, 1995, superstar Joe Montana announced his retirement from pro football after sixteen seasons. To salute him, twenty thousand residents of San Francisco filled the downtown area for a ceremony in Montana's honor.

Television announcer John Madden came to the podium and gave his opinion of Montana's skills: "This is the greatest quarterback who's ever played the game."

At one point in the ceremonies when Bill Walsh, Montana's long-time coach at the 49ers, was at the microphone, a fan yelled, "We love you, Joe."

Walsh knew that hadn't always been the case. "You weren't saying that in 1979," he replied to the fan. "Then you were saying, 'Where'd you get this guy who looks like a Swedish placekicker?'"

In 1979 Joe Montana was merely a third-round draft pick out of Notre Dame. Scouts said he had a weak arm. He was skinny. He lacked the muscular build of most football players.

But when Joe Montana stepped into the pros, he entered his element. He threw passes with perfect timing. He was the master of the two-minute drill. He went on to win four Super Bowls, helping turn the derelict 49ers into the dominant team of the 1980s.

Joe Montana was at first unimpressive to many people but was destined to be the greatest. In an infinite way, those words also describe Jesus Christ.

Appearance, Humility, Incarnation, Lordship of Christ
Isa. 53:2–3; Matt. 11:29; Phil. 2:6–11

Date used __________ Place ____________________

342

In *Discipleship Journal* Paul Thigpen writes:

I remember coming home one afternoon to discover that the kitchen I had worked so hard to clean only a few hours before was now a terrible wreck. My young daughter had obviously been busy "cooking," and the ingredients were scattered, along with dirty bowls and utensils, across the counters and floor. I was not happy with the situation.

Then, as I looked a little more closely at the mess, I spied a tiny note on the table, clumsily written and smeared with chocolatey fingerprints. The message was short—"I'm makin sumthin 4 you, Dad"—and it was signed, "Your Angel."

In the midst of that disarray, and despite my irritation, joy suddenly sprang up in my heart, sweet and pure. My attention had been redirected from the problem to the little girl I loved. As I encountered her in that brief note, I delighted in her. With her simple goodness in focus, I could take pleasure in seeing her hand at work in a situation that seemed otherwise disastrous.

The same is true of my joy in the Lord. Many times life looks rather messy; I can't find much to be happy about in my circumstances. Nevertheless, if I look hard enough, I can usually see the Lord behind it all, or at least working through it all, "makin sumthin" for me.

Confusion, God's Love, Problems, Purpose, Trials

John 5:17; 16:33; Rom. 5:3–5; 8:28–39; Phil. 2:12–13; 4:4; James 1:2–4

Date used __________ Place ____________________

Judging Others 343

At the turn of the century, the world's most distinguished astronomer was certain there were canals on Mars. Sir Percival Lowell, esteemed for his study of the solar system, had a particular fascination with the Red Planet.

When he heard, in 1877, that an Italian astronomer had seen straight lines crisscrossing the Martian surface, Lowell spent the rest of his years squinting into the eyepiece of his giant telescope in Arizona, mapping the channels and canals he saw. He was convinced the canals were proof of intelligent life on Mars, possibly an older but wiser race than humanity.

Lowell's observations gained wide acceptance. So eminent was he, none dared contradict him.

Now, of course, things are different. Space probes have orbited Mars and landed on its surface. The entire planet has been mapped, and no one has seen a canal. How could Lowell have "seen" so much that wasn't there?

Two possibilities: (1) he so wanted to see canals that he did, over and over again, and (2) we know now that he suffered from a rare eye disease that made him see the blood vessels in his own eyes. The Martian "canals" he saw were nothing more than the bulging veins of his eyeballs. Today the malady is known as "Lowell's syndrome."

When Jesus warns that "in the same way you judge others, you will be judged" and warns of seeing "the speck of sawdust" in another's eye while missing the plank in our own (Matt. 7:1–3), could he not be referring to the spiritual equivalent of Lowell's syndrome? Over and over, we "see" faults in others because we don't want to believe anything better about them. And so often we think we have a first-hand view of their shortcomings, when in fact our vision is distorted by our own disease.

Criticism, Spiritual Perception

Date used __________ Place ____________________

344

The following story appeared in the newsletter *Our America:*

Dodie Gadient, a schoolteacher for thirteen years, decided to travel across America and see the sights she had taught about. Traveling alone in a truck with camper in tow, she launched out. One afternoon rounding a curve on I-5 near Sacramento in rush-hour traffic, a water pump blew on her truck. She was tired, exasperated, scared, and alone. In spite of the traffic jam she caused, no one seemed interested in helping.

Leaning up against the trailer, she prayed, "Please God, send me an angel . . . preferably one with mechanical experience." Within four minutes, a huge Harley drove up, ridden by an enormous man sporting long, black hair, a beard, and tattooed arms. With an incredible air of confidence, he jumped off and, without even glancing at Dodie, went to work on the truck. Within another few minutes, he flagged down a larger truck, attached a tow chain to the frame of the disabled Chevy, and whisked the whole 56-foot rig off the freeway onto a side street, where he calmly continued to work on the water pump.

The intimidated schoolteacher was too dumbfounded to talk. Especially when she read the paralyzing words on the back of his leather jacket: "Hell's Angels—California." As he finished the task, she finally got up the courage to say, "Thanks so much," and carry on a brief conversation.

Noticing her surprise at the whole ordeal, he looked her straight in the eye and mumbled, "Don't judge a book by its cover. You may not know who you're talking to." With that, he smiled, closed the hood of the truck, and straddled his Harley. With a wave, he was gone as fast as he had appeared.

Given half a chance, people often crawl out of the boxes into which we've relegated them.

Angels, Prayer

Date used __________ Place ____________________

Judging Others 345

In *Your Health* Al Hinman writes:

> A spotless kitchen may harbor as many bacteria as a less tidy one, says a surprising new finding from the University of Arizona, in Tucson. That's because the most germ-laden object in a kitchen is often the sponge. Researchers tested sponges and dishrags collected from five hundred kitchens across the U.S. and found that as many as one out of five contained salmonella bacteria. Almost two thirds had at least some other bacteria that, when ingested, could make people ill.

Some attempts to cleanse can cause more harm than good. So it is when a pharisaical attitude prevails. Condemnation, self-righteousness, and judgmentalism are the salmonella of the soul.

Condemnation, Conscience, Faultfinding
Pharisaism, Self-Righteousness
Matt. 7:1–5; Rom. 14; Gal. 6:1

Date used __________ Place ______________________

After a three-month summer recess, on October 3, 1994, the Supreme Court of the United States opened its 1994–95 term. According to the New York Times News Service, the court's legal business for that first day could be summed up with one word: *no*. The court announced it had refused to hear more than 1,600 cases. The names and docket numbers of the rejected appeals covered sixty-eight typewritten pages. For those cases, that was the last court of appeal, the final word.

There's something terribly final about judgment. The Supreme Court says no, and that's it. No appeals. No arguments. The books are sealed, and the decision is final.

On the great day of judgment there will also be a terrible crescendo of no's. "No, you cannot enter my kingdom." And the doors will be shut forever. No appeal. No time to change one's mind. Those who have rejected Jesus Christ will have forever lost their opportunity for eternal life.

Eternal Life, Repentance, Salvation
Matt. 25:1–13; 2 Cor. 6:1–2; Rev. 20:11–15

Date used __________ Place ____________________

Judgment 347

To learn how Americans feel about prayer, *Life* magazine once interviewed dozens of people. One person they talked to was a prostitute, age twenty-four, in White Pine County, Nevada.

"I don't think about my feelings a lot," she said. "Instead I lie in my bed and think onto him. I meditate because sometimes my words don't come out right. But he can find me. He can find what's inside of me just by listening to my thoughts. I ask him to help me and keep me going.

"A lot of people think working girls don't have any morals, any religion. But I do. I don't steal. I don't lie. The way I look at it, I'm not sinning. He's not going to judge me. I don't think God judges anybody."

Few notions are more comforting than the idea that God judges no one. The problem is that soothing idea is false.

Morals, Prayer, Self-Deception
Rom. 14:10–12

Date used __________ Place ____________________

In *Is It Real When It Doesn't Work?* Doug Murren and Barb Shurin recount:

> Toward the end of the nineteenth century, Swedish chemist Alfred Nobel awoke one morning to read his own obituary in the local newspaper: "Alfred Nobel, the inventor of dynamite, who died yesterday, devised a way for more people to be killed in a war than ever before, and he died a very rich man."
>
> Actually, it was Alfred's older brother who had died; a newspaper reporter had bungled the epitaph.
>
> But the account had a profound effect on Nobel. He decided he wanted to be known for something other than developing the means to kill people efficiently and for amassing a fortune in the process. So he initiated the Nobel Prize, the award for scientists and writers who foster peace.
>
> Nobel said, "Every man ought to have the chance to correct his epitaph in midstream and write a new one."

Few things will change us as much as looking at our life as though it is finished.

Repentance, Death

Date used __________ Place ____________________

Judgment 349

How do you get a great parking space at a New York Yankees baseball game? One man thought he had a way. According to the Fresno, California *Bee,* this man pulled his car into the VIP parking lot and casually told the attendant that he was a friend of George Steinbrenner, owner of the Yankees. Unfortunately for the imposter, the person attending the parking lot that day was George Steinbrenner himself, doing some personal investigation of traffic problems at the stadium.

The surprised imposter looked at Steinbrenner and said, "Guess I've got the wrong lot." You can be sure that he did not park in the VIP lot that day or ever.

The owner knows his friends. The owner determines who gets in the VIP lot.

God also knows who his friends are and who the imposters are.

Imposters, Heaven, Love for God, Obedience
Matt. 7:21–23

Date used __________ Place ____________________

Judgment 350

According to the Associated Press, in fall 1997 the journal *Cell* reported on an experiment that may have far-reaching potential for fighting disease. Dr. John Rose and his research team at Yale Medical School had successfully altered the genes of a virus that normally infects livestock and turned it into a virus that specifically and exclusively attacks AIDS-infected cells and destroys them. In other words, they created smart bombs out of a virus. They used infection against infection.

The experiments were successful in the test tube and had yet to be tried on animals or humans.

Just as viruses can be designed to kill viruses, one of the ways God judges evil is to withdraw his protection and allow evil to come against what is evil.

Demons, Evil, Punishment, Satan, Sowing and Reaping
1 Sam. 18:10; Ps. 109:6; Jer. 4; 1 Cor. 5:1–5; Gal. 6:7–8

Date used __________ Place ____________________

Judgment Day 351

In the spring of 1995 columnist Charles Krauthammer wrote an article explaining why the 1994 baseball strike dealt a fatal blow to many fans.

> The cancellation of the [World] Series reduced the entire '94 season to meaninglessness, a string of exhibition games masquerading for a while as a "championship season." No championship, no season.
>
> The real scandal of the '94 season is not the games that were canceled but the games that were played. The whole season was a phony. The fans who invested dollars and enthusiasm in the expectation that the winners and losers and homers and averages would count were cheated.
>
> More than cheated. By canceling the season in a dispute over money, the players and owners mocked the fan who really cared whether Ken Griffey broke Roger Maris's record or Tony Gwynn hit .400.

Hitting records and the World Series give meaning to the regular season. Judgment day gives meaning to life. Because God will call every deed into account, everything we do matters.

Meaning, Obedience, Significance, Ten Commandments
Eccles. 12:13–14; Rom. 14:10–12; Rev. 20:11–15

Date used __________ Place ____________________

The name Al Capone brings to mind crime, gangsters terrorizing a city, and Scarface himself beating three of his wayward subordinates to death with a baseball bat.

But that view of Capone wasn't always the case.

During the 1920s many people viewed Al Capone as a respected citizen, a sort of Robin Hood, says writer Ron Grossman. In 1930 students at Northwestern University's Medill School of Journalism were asked to name "the outstanding personages of the world." Capone made the list, along with George Bernard Shaw, Mahatma Gandhi, and Albert Einstein.

But Capone's days of power were short-lived.

In 1931 he attended a football game at Northwestern University. In years past when he attended sporting events, he often was saluted by fans. But this time he was booed out of the stands and left the stadium in humiliation.

In 1931, after only six years as mob boss in Chicago, Capone was convicted of income tax evasion. He ended up in Alcatraz. Eight years later when he was released from prison, he was suffering from the advanced stages of syphilis. He lived as a recluse, dying in 1947.

During his time at Alcatraz, Capone worked in the prison shoe shop and shared a cell with a convict who worked on the prison newspaper. Capone told his cellmate one evening, "I'm supposed to be a big shot and I've wound up in the shoe shop; you're supposed to be a safe cracker and now you write editorials. What kind of a screwed-up, lousy world is this?"

This world is a place where those who violate God's law may flourish for a season, but their days are numbered. Sooner or later, on this earth or at the great judgment seat, evildoers pay for their evil deeds.

Judgment, Law of God, Reaping, Sowing
Ps. 37; 73

Date used __________ Place ____________________

Justice 353

Life is unjust. Upon accepting an award, the late Jack Benny once remarked, "I really don't deserve this. But I have arthritis, and I don't deserve that either."

Suffering, Rights

Date used __________ Place ____________________

In the 1990s Chee Soon Juan was one of the few opposition politicians in the Parliament of Singapore. The ruling People's Action Party had an iron grip on the country, holding 77 of 81 seats, and had been in power since 1959. Through authoritarian means the People's Action Party had brought great prosperity to the country, but political opponents like Chee Soon Juan felt that the time had come to loosen up.

The People's Action Party did not take kindly to dissidents, though, and for many years the way it had gotten rid of them was financial. For one reason or another, party opponents would be sued, fined, and financially broken.

In 1993 Chee Soon Juan was forced to sell his home to pay a defamation suit brought against him by a member of the ruling party.

In 1996 the harassment continued. Chee Soon Juan made a report to Parliament, and to his regret it contained a statistical error. According to Seth Mydans in the *New York Times,* Chee Soon Juan reported that "government spending on health care had fallen from 40 percent of the nation's total costs in 1970 to 5 percent in 1990. The actual 1990 figure was 25 percent."

When party officials discovered the error, they pounced on it. Chee Soon Juan was accused of perjury, misconduct, and giving false information to Parliament. He blamed it on a typing error. Late in 1996 "the Parliamentary Privileges Committee issued a 196-page report on Mr. Chee's statistical error and found him guilty as charged." He was fined $18,000.

In Singapore that may be legal, but most people would agree it is unjust. And injustice grieves the heart of God.

Control, Error, Fairness, Forgiveness, Injustice, Mistakes, Oppression, Parenting, Punishment, Retribution, Vengeance

Prov. 29:14; Isa. 11:4; Micah 6:8; Matt. 23:23

Date used __________ Place ____________________

Kindness 355

According to the Associated Press, Chuck Wall, a human relations instructor at Bakersfield College in California, was watching the news one day when a cliché from a broadcaster stuck in his mind: "Another random act of senseless violence."

Wall got an idea. He gave an unusual assignment to his students. They were to do something out of the ordinary to help someone and then write an essay about it. Then Wall dreamed up a bumper sticker that said, "Today, I will commit one random act of senseless KINDNESS . . . Will You?" The students sold the bumper stickers, which a bank and union paid to have printed, for one dollar each, and the profits went to a county Braille center.

For his random act of kindness one student paid his mother's utility bills.

Another student bought thirty blankets from the Salvation Army and took them to homeless people gathered under a bridge.

The idea took hold. The bumper sticker was slapped on all 113 county patrol cars. It was trumpeted from pulpits, in schools, and in professional associations.

After seeing the success of the idea, Chuck Wall commented, "I had no idea it would erupt like it has. I had no idea our community was in such need of something positive."

In this negative and dark world, we each can do acts of kindness to bring some light.

Golden Rule, Love, Violence
Matt. 5:14–16; 25:31–46; Gal. 5:22–23

Date used __________ Place ____________________

In his book *Pleasures Forevermore,* Phillip Keller writes:

For two weeks it had snowed off and on almost every day. I was beginning to weary of shoveling snow, cleaning giant cornices of snow off the roof, knocking snow off each block of wood carried in for the heater, cleaning snow from doorways and driveways. It seemed there was no end to snow, snow, snow. I even wondered where room could be found to pile the wind-driven drifts.

Then it happened. Suddenly one day I came home gingerly through the gathering gloom to find that all the driveway, the sidewalks, and even the doorways had been shoveled clean.

Stunned, I paused momentarily in the drive. It simply seemed too good to believe. The bare pavement appeared almost unreal. The huge piles of snow heaped up on every side astonished me.

Did someone, with more strength than I, care enough to come over and do this job out of sheer goodwill and heartwarming concern? Yes, someone did, and he did it with gusto.

I learned later that it was a young man from town, ten miles away. With enormous energy and strong muscles he had moved mountains of snow on my behalf. With this one gracious act of generosity he had not only saved my aching old back, but he had broken the back of winter.

In a warm and wonderful way my spirit welled up with profound gratitude. What a lift our Father gave me through that young man's strong arms!

Then another evening the doorbell rang. I went to see who was there. Cold wind tugged at the eaves and swirled around the door. I opened it carefully to keep out the formidable frost.

Standing there all wrapped up in wool cap, mitts, and thick winter jacket stood a neighbor. His bright blue eyes sparkled above crimson cheeks. "Just brought you a wee treat," he muttered, pushing a covered basket of food toward me. "I won't come in just now—too much winter." And he was gone.

Softly I unwrapped the unexpected gift. It steamed hot and pungent and tantalizing . . . a fresh, home-baked meat pie, drawn from the oven only moments before. Beside it was a piping hot bowl of rich dark gravy. What a feast! What a banquet to nourish one's body battling midwinter ice and sleet! . . .

Every mouthful of the delicious meal was relished. Every particle of pie was consumed with contentment. Every drop of gravy was licked up with glorious delight. It was a meal that will be remembered to the end of my days.

That night I curled up like a cat and slept for nine hours solid. I had peace and rest and deep, deep joy . . . besides quickened faith in the gentle goodness of generous neighbors.

In this weary old world there are still some sterling souls who really do love their neighbors as they love themselves.

Golden Rule, Love, Neighbors
Matt. 7:12; Gal. 5:22

Date used __________ Place ____________________

Taken from the title *Pleasures Forevermore* by Phillip Keller.

Kindness 357

According to writer Jon Van, at the 1995 annual meeting of the American Association for the Advancement of Science, researchers revealed the results of a study that show how important kindness is in day-to-day relations.

In the experiment researchers gave forty-four doctors the symptoms of a hypothetical patient and then asked for each doctor's diagnosis of the illness. But the real point of the study was not how well the doctors could diagnose illness. Before the experiment began, researchers gave half of the doctors a bag of candy, saying it was a token of appreciation for their involvement in the study. The other doctors received nothing.

Alice Isen, a Cornell University psychologist, said the doctors receiving the candy were far more likely to correctly diagnose the patient's problem. "Pleasant-feeling states give rise to altruism, helpfulness, and improved interpersonal processes," she explained.

When God tells us to be kind to others, as always, he has a good idea. Kindness is God's program for making our world work better.

Affirmation, Encouragement, Thanks
Gal. 5:22–23; Col. 3:12

Date used __________ Place ____________________

In *Conspiracy of Kindness* Steve Sjogren writes:

On a typical hot, humid summer day in Cincinnati, Joe Delaney and his eight-year-old son were in the backyard playing catch. As the two lobbed the ball back and forth, Joe could tell something was on Jared's mind. At first they talked about Reds' baseball, friends, and summer vacation. Then the conversation took a more serious turn, and Joe felt like a backyard ballplayer who suddenly found himself in the major leagues.

"Dad, is there a God?"

Joe had the same helpless feeling he experienced on the high school baseball team when he lost sight of a fly ball in the blazing sun. He didn't know whether to move forward, backward, or just stay put. A string of trite answers raced through his mind. In the end Joe opted for honesty. "I don't know, Jared," he replied as the ball landed solidly in his glove.

Joe's agnosticism failed to stifle his son's curiosity. Jared dug a little deeper. "If there is a God, how would you know him?"

"I really have no idea, Jared. I only went to church a couple of times when I was a kid, so I don't know a lot about these kinds of things."

Jared seemed deep in thought for a few minutes as the game of catch continued. Suddenly, he headed for the house. "I'll be right back," he yelled over his shoulder. "I have to get something." Jared soon returned with a Mylar helium balloon fresh from the circus along with a pen and an index card.

"Jared, what in the world are you doing?" Joe asked.

"I'm going to send a message to God—airmail," the boy earnestly replied.

Before Joe could protest, his son had started writing. "Dear God," Jared wrote on the index card, "if you are real and if you are there, send people who know you to Dad and me."

Joe kept his mouth shut, not wanting to dampen his son's enthusiasm. *This is silly*, he thought as he helped Jared fasten the card to the balloon's string. *But God, I hope you're watching*, he added to his silent petition. After Jared let go of the balloon, father and son stood with their faces to the sky and watched it sail away.

Two days later I became part of the answer to this unusual inquiry. Joe and Jared pulled into the free car wash that our church was holding as part of our outreach into the community on this particular Saturday morning. “How much?” Joe asked as he neared the line of buckets, sponges, and hoses.

“It’s free,” I told him. “No strings attached.”

“Really!” Joe exclaimed. He seemed intrigued with the idea of getting something for nothing. “But why are you doing this?”

“We just want to show you God’s love in a practical way.”

It was as if that simple statement opened a hidden door to Joe’s heart. The look on his face was incredulous. “Wait a minute!” he practically shouted. “Are you guys Christians?”

“Yeah, we’re Christians,” I replied.

“Are you the kind of Christians who believe in God?”

I couldn’t help but smile. “Yes, we’re that kind of Christians.”

After directing a big grin at Jared, Joe proceeded to tell me the story of releasing the helium balloon with its message only days earlier. “I guess you’re the answer to one of the strangest prayers God’s ever received,” Joe said.

How often it is that our acts of kindness are an answer to someone’s deepest prayer.

Evangelism, Outreach, Prayer, Providence
Matt. 5:14–16; Gal. 6:10

Date used __________ Place ____________________

Kindness 359

In his book *I Was Wrong* former PTL president and television personality Jim Bakker, who was sent to prison for fraud, writes:

> Not long after my release from prison, I joined Franklin Graham and his family at his parents' old log mountain home for dinner. Ruth Graham (Billy's wife) had prepared a full-course dinner. We talked and laughed and enjoyed a casual meal together like family.
>
> During our conversation, Ruth asked me a question that required an address. I reached into my back pocket and pulled out an envelope. My wallet had been taken when I went to prison. I had not owned a wallet for over four-and-a-half years.
>
> As I fumbled through the envelope, Ruth asked tenderly, "Don't you have a wallet, Jim?"
>
> "This is my wallet," I replied.
>
> Ruth left the room, returning with one of Billy's wallets. "Here is a brand-new wallet Billy has never used. I want you to have it," she said.
>
> I still carry that wallet to this day. Over the years I have met thousands of wonderful Christian men and women, but never anyone more humble, gracious, and in a word, "real" than Ruth Graham and her family.

Kindness does not have to be extravagant to mean a great deal to people.

Acceptance, Community, Love, Giving, Grace, Mercy, Sharing, Sincerity
Gal. 5:22; Col. 3:12; 2 Peter 1:7

Date used __________ Place ____________________

In *Running on Empty*, author and speaker Jill Briscoe writes:

> I had been traveling for two weeks straight, speaking at meetings. Somehow the tight schedule allowed only time for talking and not much for eating! Whenever it was mealtime, I found myself on one more airplane. On this particular day it was hot, it was summer, and I was tired and hungry. My flight had been delayed, and by the time I arrived at the next conference center, I discovered that my hosts had gone to bed. (In the morning I learned that because of the delayed flight, they presumed I would not be coming until the following day—hence, no welcoming committee.) I wandered around the large dining room, hoping to find something to eat, but all the doors into the kitchen had been locked. "Lord," I prayed, "I really don't care what I eat, but I need something—and while I'm talking to you about this, I've got a yearning for peaches! Oh, for a lovely, refreshing, juicy peach!" Then I smiled. That was just the sort of prayer I counseled others against offering! I sighed, picked up my bags, and went to my assigned cabin.
>
> When I arrived at my room . . . a basket of peaches sat on the doorstep smiling up at me! I lifted them up and felt my loving Lord's smile. (It could have been oranges and apples, you know!) Never before or since have I received a whole basket of delicious, fresh peaches. . . . The Lord provided a sweet touch that reminded me of his great love.

If we will notice the little things, we will see there is no limit to God's kindness.

Love of God, Needs, Prayer, Providence, Provision, Wants
Pss. 23:1; 37:4; 107:4–9; Matt. 7:7–8; Titus 3:4

Date used __________ Place ____________________

Kingdom of God 361

The Internet is now a household word. James Coates writes that the Internet began in 1962 when Paul Baran, an engineer at the Rand Corporation think tank, found a way to move messages through a network of Defense Department computers. In 1968 the Department of Defense commissioned the Advanced Research Projects Agency to build the ARPAnet. In 1971 only twenty-three computers were on the ARPAnet.

In 1981 IBM introduced the personal computer, bringing the computer to the home. By 1984 more than one thousand computers were on the Internet.

In 1986 the ARPAnet became part of the NSFnet, which was sponsored by the National Science Foundation. This became the Internet backbone.

In 1989 more than one hundred thousand computers were on the Internet.

In 1992 more than one million computers were on the Internet. That year the Internet society was chartered to loosely govern the Internet.

In 1993 the first graphic face, called Mosaic, was put on the Internet, which made it more accessible.

In 1994 local Internet access providers and on-line services greatly expanded their Internet services.

In 1995 experts estimated that thirty million computers were on the Internet.

The kingdom of God is like the Internet. It began small with only a few disciples following Jesus. But it has spread for two thousand years, person to person, culture to culture, with more and more people getting on-line with God.

Church, Gospel, Growth
Matt. 13:31–33; Col. 1:6

Date used __________ Place ____________________

On December 6, 1865, just months after the Civil War ended, the thirteenth amendment outlawing slavery was ratified and became the law of the land. But that didn't mean every state approved the ratification of the amendment. Mississippi's state legislature, for example, was dominated by whites bitter over the defeat of the Confederacy, and they rejected the measure. One hundred and thirty years passed before Mississippi took action. By 1995 Mississippi was the only state in the Union that had not approved the ratification of the thirteenth amendment.

Finally, on Thursday, February 16, 1995, the Mississippi Senate voted unanimously to outlaw slavery by approving the ratification of the thirteenth amendment to the Constitution.

Senator Hillman Frazier, a member of Mississippi's Legislative Black Caucus, said, "I think it's very important for us to show the world that we have put the past behind us."

Just as there was a delay in some states ratifying an end to slavery in the United States, so there is now a delay in people accepting God's kingdom. But God's kingdom will one day hold sway over all the world, and his kingdom brings freedom.

Freedom, Liberty, Lordship of Christ
Matt. 4:17; John 3:1–7; 8:31–36; Gal. 5

Date used __________ Place ____________________

Kingdom of God 363

"While serving as a missionary in Laos," tells John Hess-Yoder, "I discovered an illustration of the kingdom of God.

"Before the colonialists imposed national boundaries, the kings of Laos and Vietnam reached an agreement on taxation in the border areas. Those who ate short-grain rice built their houses on stilts, and decorated them with Indian-style serpents were considered Laotians. On the other hand, those who ate long-grain rice built their houses on the ground, and decorated them with Chinese-style dragons were considered Vietnamese.

"The exact location of a person's home was not what determined his or her nationality. Instead, each person belonged to the kingdom whose cultural values he or she exhibited."

So it is with us: we live in the world, but as part of God's kingdom, we are to live according to his kingdom's standards and values.

Values, World

Date used __________ Place ____________________

Knowing God 364

Nikola Tesla is the scientist who invented the method of generating electricity in what we call alternating current. Many people regard him as a greater scientific genius than the better known Alexander Graham Bell.

Author Philip Yancey tells an interesting anecdote about Tesla. During storms Tesla would sit on a black mohair couch by a window. When lightning struck, he would applaud—one genius recognizing the work of another. Tesla could appreciate better than anyone the wonder of lightning because he had spent years researching electricity.

In a similar way, the more we know God and his Word, the more deeply we will applaud his mighty deeds.

Creation, Power of God, Praise
Eph. 1:3–14

Date used __________ Place ____________________

Knowing God 365

In *The Cure for a Troubled Heart* author and pastor Ron Mehl writes:

I heard once about a dear, saintly old woman who was gradually losing her memory. Details began to blur. . . . Throughout her life, however, this woman had cherished and depended on the Word of God, committing to memory many verses from her worn King James Bible.

Her favorite verse had always been 2 Timothy 1:12: "For I know whom I have believed, and am persuaded that he is able to keep that which I have committed unto him against that day."

She was finally confined to bed in a nursing home, and her family knew she would never leave alive. As they visited with her, she would still quote verses of Scripture on occasion—especially 2 Timothy 1:12. But with the passing of time, even parts of this well-loved verse began to slip away.

"I know whom I have believed," she would say. "He is able to keep . . . what I have committed . . . to him."

Her voice grew weaker. And the verse became even shorter. "What I have committed . . . to him."

As she was dying, her voice became so faint family members had to bend over to listen to the few whispered words on her lips. And at the end, there was only one word of her life verse left.

"Him."

She whispered it again and again as she stood on the threshold of heaven. "Him . . . Him . . . Him."

It was all that was left. It was all that was needed.

Aging, Death, Security, Trust
John 10:27–29; 2 Tim. 1:12

Date used __________ Place ____________________

Writer T. H. Watkins is in love with the unique region of the Southwest United States called the Four Corners. The Four Corners is the only place in the country where four states join at one point: Utah, Colorado, New Mexico, and Arizona. The region around that point is one of breathtaking beauty: graceful sand dunes, striking deserts, buttes that glow orange in the morning light, deep canyons, snow-covered mountains, fog-shrouded valleys, vertical rock, sandstone wedges jutting into the sky. It is a terrain so unusual in its character that those who explore there never weary of it.

Watkins writes in *National Geographic* that this area of 100,000 square miles is "endlessly various and fascinating in its forms. Much of this I have come to think of as my own country. . . .

"I have spent several years exploring this western landscape, driving its roads, flying over it, hiking into its canyons, camping along its rivers, soaking it up, taking it in, sometimes writing about it, most of the time just thinking about its warps and tangles of rock and sky. This is not an idle passion. It stems from a deeply held conviction that the Four Corners country has something essential to offer us."

Watkins's relationship with this landscape is much like the joy that is ours as we seek to know God. God invites us to spend this life and all eternity getting to know his inexhaustible character and nature.

Devotional Life, Spiritual Disciplines, Transcendence
Exod. 33:18–34:7; Jer. 9:23–24; Hosea 6:6;
John 17:3, 24–26; Phil. 3:10

Date used __________ Place ____________________

367

Timothy Munyon writes:

While living in Florida, I had several friends who worked cleaning rooms at a nationally known inn located directly on the white sands of the Gulf of Mexico. They spent their work breaks running barefoot in the sand. The problem was the inn required all employees to wear shoes at all times while working.

I noticed the employees responded in one of two ways.

The majority thought the rule restricted their freedom. The rooms had shag carpeting, delightful to bare toes, and just a few steps away lay the beach. To them the rule to wear shoes was nothing more than employer harassment.

But a minority of the employees looked at the rule differently. Sometimes late night parties would produce small pieces of broken glass. Occasionally a stickpin would be found hidden in the deep shag piles. Some knew the pain of skinning bare toes on the steel bed frame while making a bed. This minority saw the rule as protection, not restriction.

Were God's laws written to make life miserable? Or were they written by a loving heavenly Father who cares about his children?

Freedom, God's Love

Date used __________ Place ____________________

368

In *Who Will Deliver Us?* Paul F. M. Zahl writes:

A duck hunter was with a friend in the wide-open land of southeastern Georgia. Far away on the horizon he noticed a cloud of smoke. Soon he could hear crackling as the wind shifted. He realized the terrible truth: a brushfire was advancing, so fast they couldn't outrun it.

Rifling through his pockets, he soon found what he was looking for—a book of matches. He lit a small fire around the two of them. Soon they were standing in a circle of blackened earth, waiting for the fire to come.

They didn't have to wait long. They covered their mouths with handkerchiefs and braced themselves. The fire came near—and swept over them. But they were completely unhurt, untouched. Fire would not pass where fire had already passed.

The law is like a brushfire. I cannot escape it. But if I stand in the burned-over place, not a hair of my head will be singed. Christ's death is the burned-over place. There I huddle, hardly believing yet relieved. The law is powerful, yet powerless: Christ's death has disarmed it.

Atonement, Christ's Death

Date used __________ Place ____________________

Lawlessness 369

On the Fox River and Chain o' Lakes waterways of northern Illinois, officials annually face an expensive problem. Of the roughly six hundred buoys on these waterways, not one is expected to last the entire season. Each year the attrition rate for the lighted plastic buoys has been 125 percent.

What happens to them? Officials say the buoys are willfully smashed to pieces by vandals.

In so doing, boaters are only hurting themselves and others, of course. The buoys are there "to provide safety and direction for boaters," says writer Stephen Lee in the *Chicago Tribune*. "Some mark no-wake zones where powerboaters must go at slower speeds. They delineate shallow areas where boating could be dangerous, and show the way to mouths of channels."

Smashing buoys may bring laughs, but it is an expensive hobby. An agency ordinance levies a $1,000 fine on boaters convicted of maliciously vandalizing buoys.

Like vandals smashing buoys, many people take great delight in running over the commands of God. The Bible calls this the spirit of lawlessness. God's commands are given for our safekeeping, yet the sinful nature within us hates them nonetheless.

Commandments, Disobedience, Lawlessness, Rebellion, Ten Commandments

Rom. 1–3; 1 Cor. 7:19; James 2:8–11; 1 John 3:4

Date used __________ Place ____________________

In August 1994 a ship, the *Columbus Iselin,* doing environmental research ran aground off the Florida Keys and—ironically—spilled two hundred gallons of diesel fuel.

Siobhan McCready of the University of Miami said the ship was collecting "chemical, physical, and biological data on the currents of the Florida Straits." The data would be used to manage ocean oil spills.

When the *Columbus Iselin* hit a reef and punctured its two fuel tanks, it was working in the Looe Key National Marine Sanctuary—where the coral formations are famous.

Adding to the problem, efforts to pull the ship free from the reef spread a huge plume of sand, which can kill live coral.

Just as an environmental research boat can pollute the very waters it hopes to preserve, church leaders who fail morally can harm the people who follow them.

Deacons, Elders, Judgment, Moral Failure, Teachers
1 Tim. 3:1–13; Titus 1:5–9; James 3:1–2

Date used __________ Place ____________________

Leadership 371

Scott Turow begins his novel *Presumed Innocent* with the words of a prosecuting attorney named Rusty. Rusty is explaining his approach to the jury when he is in court. Rusty says:

> This is how I always start:
>
> "I am the prosecutor.
>
> "I represent the state. I am here to present to you the evidence of a crime. Together you will weigh the evidence. You will deliberate upon it. You will decide if it proves the defendant's guilt.
>
> "This man—" and here I point. . . .
>
> If you don't have the courage to point . . . you can't expect them to have the courage to convict.
>
> And so I point. I extend my hand across the courtroom. I hold one finger straight. I seek the defendant's eye. I say:
>
> "This man has been accused. . . ."

Scott Turow shows in the courtroom a principle that holds true in all of life. People need leaders to galvanize their courage. People need leaders to point, to take a stand, to say what they believe.

Courage, Preaching
1 Cor. 11:1; 2 Tim. 4:2

Date used __________ Place ____________________

Leadership 372

In *The Last Days Newsletter,* Leonard Ravenhill tells about a group of tourists visiting a picturesque village who walked by an old man sitting beside a fence. In a rather patronizing way, one tourist asked, "Were any great men born in this village?"

The old man replied, "Nope, only babies."

A frothy question brought a profound answer. There are no instant heroes—whether in this world or in the kingdom of God. Growth takes time, and as 1 Timothy 3:6 and 5:22 point out, even spiritual leadership must be earned.

Beginnings, Growth

Date used __________ Place ____________________

373

Bruce Larson, in his book *Wind and Fire,* points out some interesting facts about sandhill cranes:

These large birds, who fly great distances across continents, have three remarkable qualities. First, they rotate leadership. No one bird stays out in front all the time. Second, they choose leaders who can handle turbulence. And then, all during the time one bird is leading, the rest are honking their affirmation. That's not a bad model for the church. Certainly we need leaders who can handle turbulence and who are aware that leadership ought to be shared. But most of all, we need a church where we are all honking encouragement.

Encouragement, Church

Date used __________ Place ____________________

In *Everyday Discipleship for Ordinary People,* Stuart Briscoe writes:

One of my young colleagues was officiating at the funeral of a war veteran. The dead man's military friends wished to have a part in the service at the funeral home, so they requested the pastor to lead them down to the casket, stand with them for a solemn moment of remembrance, and then lead them out through the side door. This he proceeded to do, but unfortunately the effect was somewhat marred when he picked the wrong door. The result was that they marched with military precision into a broom closet, in full view of the mourners, and had to beat a hasty retreat covered with confusion.

This true story illustrates a cardinal rule or two. First, if you're going to lead, make sure you know where you're going. Second, if you're going to follow, make sure that you are following someone who knows what he is doing!

Followers, Competence

Date used __________ Place ____________________

One of the shocking legal developments of the late 1990s was the settlement between the tobacco industry and the attorneys general of numerous states. After the $360 billion settlement, the *Wall Street Journal* published an article by Alix M. Freedman and Suein L. Hwang that gave credit for this change in the tobacco industry's fortunes to the largely independent actions of seven individuals.

According to the writers, Jeffrey Nesbitt was a spokesman for the Food and Drug Administration. As he watched his father, a heavy smoker, dying from cancer and his youngest brother becoming more devoted to cigarettes, he pressed his colleagues at the administration to take initiatives to regulate the tobacco industry. They were reluctant because they did not think they could succeed, but eventually they took up the fight.

Michael Lewis was a small-town lawyer in Mississippi. As he rode a hospital elevator following a visit to a smoker suffering from heart disease, he got an idea for a new way to sue the tobacco companies. In the past the tobacco industry had always won legal suits because they had been brought by individuals, and juries had decided that individuals were responsible for their own decisions. This Mississippi lawyer's idea was for states to sue the companies to recover state money used to pay Medicaid bills for the care of those suffering from smoking-related diseases.

Jeffrey Wigand was a researcher who had once worked for one of the big tobacco companies. The companies had long claimed that nicotine was not addictive. As a former insider, Wigand blew the whistle on the companies, showing that they did know of nicotine's effects and even designed cigarettes to enhance that addictive power.

Walt Bogdanich was an ABC television producer who championed a 1994 exposé that showed that tobacco companies carefully controlled the level of nicotine in their product.

Presidential advisor Dick Morris, who had watched his mother's health fall apart due to a three-pack-a-day habit, convinced President Clinton to put his weight behind the FDA's anti-youth-smoking initiative. Morris provided the polls that showed overwhelming support for such a move, proving that it was politically viable.

Bennett LeBow, a financier who controlled one of the tobacco companies, was the first to bolt from the ranks of Big Tobacco. He led his company to unilaterally settle with the attorneys general of four states. Then he officially admitted that nicotine is addictive and agreed to stamp warnings to that effect on cigarette packages.

Grady Carter was a smoker who had tried for more than twenty-five years to quit. He succeeded only after finding he suffered from lung cancer. Then he filed a personal suit against one of the tobacco companies and was the first to win such a case.

As these seven men show, individuals who take action can make a huge difference—even in causes thought impossible.

Activism, Change, Commitment, Initiative,
Ministry, Prayer, Revival, Zeal
Esther 4:14; Matt. 28:18–20; Acts 17:6

Date used __________ Place ____________________

376

On August 1, 1970, W. Lain Guthrie, a commercial airline pilot, decided he had had enough. He had dumped his last load of kerosene into the environment. Holcomb Noble writes in the *New York Times* that at that time the airline industry practice was to dump waste kerosene during takeoff or at high altitudes. Airline officials claimed that the kerosene evaporated and caused no harm to the environment, but Guthrie did not buy it. He claimed that in peak seasons as much as five hundred gallons of fuel was dumped every day over his home airport of Miami.

And so on his thirtieth anniversary as a pilot, he celebrated by following his conscience. He refused to take off until the waste fuel accumulated from the previous flight was pumped out of his jet. In subsequent flights he continued his demand, and two months later he was fired for insubordination. By now, however, he had become a cause célèbre, as other pilots rallied around him and also refused to dump fuel. Finally the airline backed down and rehired Guthrie at full pay. Soon the airline industry as a whole ceased the practice of aerial fuel dumping.

For wrongs to be righted, the question often is who will lead the way and be the first to pay the price of following his or her conscience. For some people it means deciding that they have told their last lie or cut their last corner. When we follow our conscience, it just may be that many other people will be encouraged to follow theirs. But even if others do not, the day we choose to do what we think is right is a cause for celebration.

Conscience, Conviction, Environment, Taking a Stand
Exod. 32:26

Date used __________ Place ____________________

In *Moody* magazine, pastor and author Leith Anderson writes:

[My wife], Charleen, and I grew up together and dated through high school and college. We've been married for most of our lives, but we've never drafted a list of rules for our lives together. Don't misunderstand, we are both committed to Jesus Christ as Lord and to the Holy Spirit as our guide. We hold God's moral law in highest value—truth, morality, honesty, honoring of parents, and preserving life.

When we first married, we could not have anticipated all that would be included in "better and worse, richer and poorer, sickness and health." There is no way that any set of rules or any book on marriage could have told us what to do. We've based our decisions on a relationship of commitment, love, and growing to know each other better every day.

That's the way the Christian life is to be lived—by relationship, not rules. The Christian's relationship with God is based on love and commitment, holding God's moral law in highest regard but depending on the grace of God to live out His morality in everyday circumstances. Every relationship is a bit different, so there is freedom. Every relationship learns and grows through experience. Life by the Spirit, not by the rules.

Holy Spirit, Rules
Gal. 5:22–25; Col. 2:6–7

Date used __________ Place ____________________

Legalism 378

United Parcel Service takes pride in the productivity of its delivery men and women. On average, a UPS driver delivers four hundred packages every working day. The company gets such high productivity by micromanaging the details of a deliveryman's routine.

Writing in the *Wall Street Journal,* Robert Frank says:

"With a battalion of more than 3,000 industrial engineers, the company dictates every task for employees. Drivers must step from their trucks with their right foot, fold their money face-up, and carry packages under their left arm."

UPS "tells drivers how fast to walk (three feet per second), how many packages to pick up and deliver a day (400, on average), even how to hold their keys (teeth up, third finger)."

"Those considered slow are accompanied by supervisors, who cajole and prod them with stopwatches and clipboards."

This approach may work well in the package delivery business, but it is a complete failure in spiritual business. When spiritual leaders imitate these industrial engineers, controlling every movement of their followers, it leads to legalism and bondage. The Christian life, on the other hand, is engineered by God as a life of freedom in the Spirit.

Freedom, Obedience, Spirituality
Gal. 2:19–21; 5:1

Date used __________ Place ____________________

Moderate exercise is good for you, right? Not necessarily. One study suggests that exercise may do more harm than good if you are being forced to work out against your will.

According to Jon Van and Ron Kotulak in the *Chicago Tribune,* University of Colorado researcher Monika Fleshner focused an experiment on the effects of forced and unforced exercise on the immune system, that part of the body that fights off colds and infectious diseases.

Fleshner studied two groups of lab animals. One group was allowed to run on exercise wheels whenever they liked. The result was an improved response of their immune systems. A similar improvement in the human immune system's response is seen after moderate exercise.

On the other hand, the other group of lab animals was forced to run; their immune systems responded negatively in several ways, including having reduced levels of antibodies. The negative effects likely resulted from the stress of being forced to exercise.

The negative effect of forced exercise is similar to the spiritual harm of legalism. When people are forced to follow a code instead of freely choosing to obey out of love, they stay immature rather than mature.

Freedom, Manipulation, Obedience, Righteousness, Submission, Will
Matt. 5:6; John 14:23–24; 2 Cor. 9:7;
Gal. 3:1–14; 4:1–11; 5:1–15; Phil. 2:12–13

Date used __________ Place ____________________

Lies 380

In *The Christian Reader,* Lynn Austin writes:

Sometimes Satan makes a little white lie seem like an easy way out of a problem. I know.

My five-year-old son had been looking forward to visiting the planetarium while on vacation, but when we arrived, we learned that children under age 6 were not admitted.

"Let's pretend you had a birthday," I told him. "If the ticket man asks how old you are, I want you to say, 'I'm 6.'"

I made him practice it until he sounded convincing, then bought the tickets without any problems. When the show ended, we moved on to the museum. There a large sign read, "Children 5 and under admitted free." To avoid a $5 admission fee, I had to convince my son to forget his pretend birthday.

The consequences of my lie became apparent as we walked up the steps to our last destination, the aquarium. "Wait a minute, Mom," my son said with a worried look. "How old am I now?"

I knew that I had fallen for the "way that seems right to a man, but in the end it leads to death" (Prov. 14:12).

Child Rearing, Mothers
Prov. 22:6; Col. 3:9

Date used __________ Place ____________________

Some scientists, according to a story by Harold Bredesen, decided to develop a fish that could live outside of water. So, selecting some healthy red herring, they bred and crossbred, hormoned and chromosomed until they produced a fish that could exist out of water.

But the project director wasn't satisfied. He suspected that though the fish had learned to live on dry land, it still had a secret desire for water.

"Re-educate it," he said. "Change its very desires."

So again they went to work, this time retraining even the strongest reflexes. The result? A fish that would rather die than get wet. Even humidity filled this new fish with dread.

The director, proud of his triumph, took the fish on tour. Well, quite accidentally, according to official reports, it happened—the fish fell into a lake. It sank to the bottom, eyes and gills clamped shut, afraid to move, lest it become wetter. And of course it dared not breathe; every instinct said no. Yet breathe it must.

So the fish drew a tentative gill-full. Its eyes bulged. It breathed again and flicked a fin. It breathed a third time and wriggled with delight. Then it darted away. The fish had discovered water.

And with that same wonder, men and women conditioned by a world that rejects God, discover him. For in him we live and move and have our being.

Rejecting God, Conversion

Date used __________ Place ____________________

Peter W. Law in *A Portrait of My Father* writes:

Imagine you are on holiday, and you have an apartment overlooking the sand and surf. Sitting on the table in your room is a fishbowl, and inside the bowl is a small goldfish. Each day you swim and sunbake and enjoy soaking up the delights of vacationing. Before long, however, you begin to feel sorry for little Goldie who is all alone in his bowl while you go out having fun in the sun. To make up for this injustice, you promise Goldie a little of the action. "Tomorrow," you tell the goldfish, "you will begin to enjoy life, too."

The next day you take a washcloth, lift the fish from the bowl, place it in the cloth, wrap it up, and put the living bundle into your pocket before leaving for the beach.

As you reach the spot where you are accustomed to spending your day, you can feel the sun's heat beating down upon your back. Excitedly you take your gilled companion from your pocket, lay out the washcloth on the sand, place the fish on the cloth, stand back, and say, "Now this is the life, Goldie; live it up!"

Can anything be more ridiculous or more foolish? Being in the sun on the hot beach is no environment for a goldfish—or any fish! It will die there, not live. It was never intended to be in that environment. For people, a relationship with God as Father is the only correct environment for life.

Enjoyment, Knowing God

Date used __________ Place ____________________

Life Span 383

According to the *Chicago Tribune*, on February 21, 1995, Jeanne Calment of Arles, France, celebrated her 120th birthday. She was verifiably the oldest person in the world and had become somewhat of a celebrity in France. France's minister of health came to her birthday party. Three books had been written about her.

Medical scientists have researched her life to try to discover the secret of her longevity. They found that for years she ate two pounds of chocolate a week. She smoked moderately until age 117. She cooked with olive oil. She took vigorous walks and even rode her bike through the streets of Arles until she was 100.

At age 110 she said with good humor, "I had to wait 110 years to become famous. I intend to enjoy it as long as possible."

But by age 120 she was confined to a wheelchair. "I see badly," she said, "I hear badly, I can't feel anything, but everything's fine."

Someone asked Calment what kind of future she expected. Still displaying her good humor, she replied, "A very short one."

She speaks for us all. Even if we are young and have a hundred years to live, the body has limits, and even a long life is short.

Aging, Body, Death, Mortality

Gen. 5:27; Ps. 90:10; 144:4; 1 Cor. 15; 1 Peter 1:24–25

Date used __________ Place ____________________

Bob Woods, in *Pulpit Digest,* tells the story of a couple who took their son, 11, and daughter, 7, to Carlsbad Caverns. As always, when the tour reached the deepest point in the cavern, the guide turned off all the lights to dramatize how completely dark and silent it is below the earth's surface.

The little girl, suddenly enveloped in utter darkness, was frightened and began to cry.

Immediately was heard the voice of her brother: "Don't cry. Somebody here knows how to turn on the lights."

In a real sense, that is the message of the gospel: light is available, even when darkness seems overwhelming.

Darkness, Fear

Date used __________ Place ____________________

In *Moody,* pastor and author Dan Schaeffer writes:

In a popular Christmas movie called *Home Alone,* a family plans a European vacation for Christmas. The relatives all arrive for the big event, but the youngest son is feeling slighted. Easily ignored in all the last-minute details, he rebels and gets in trouble. He's sent to a room in the attic. While there, in a tantrum, he wishes his family and everyone else would go away, so he could be all alone.

In a bizarre plot twist, the family overlooks the little boy in the attic, leaves for the airport, and gets on the plane, all the while believing he is with them. When the boy wakes in the morning, he discovers no one there, and believes his wish has been granted. He is delighted.

For the next few days, he lives alone, while his mother and family try frantically to return to him. At first the boy is delirious with joy, as he has full run of the house. He eats all the junk food he wants, watches whatever movie he wants, sleeps wherever he wants, and doesn't have to answer to anyone.

Then burglars try to break into the house, and he finds himself involved in simply keeping his home safe. After the burglars have been taken care of, he realizes he is now lonely and alone. It wasn't what he thought it would be, this life without his parents. He becomes sorry he had treated them so badly, and desperately wants them back again.

Schaeffer writes that this story is similar to how people relate to God. Often we resent God's authority and want our freedom. When we exercise our freedom, we may have fun for a while, but we end up with a life of fear and loneliness. Without God we are home alone.

Alienation, Emptiness, Fear, Freedom, Hell,
Human Condition, Independence, Rebellion
Gen. 3

Date used __________ Place ____________________

Lordship of Christ 386

The captain of the ship looked into the dark night and saw faint lights in the distance. Immediately he told his signalman to send a message: "Alter your course 10 degrees south."

Promptly a return message was received: "Alter your course 10 degrees north."

The captain was angered; his command had been ignored. So he sent a second message: "Alter your course 10 degrees south—I am the captain!"

Soon another message was received: "Alter your course 10 degrees north—I am seaman third class Jones."

Immediately the captain sent a third message, knowing the fear it would evoke: "Alter your course 10 degrees south—I am a battleship."

Then the reply came: "Alter your course 10 degrees north—I am a lighthouse."

In the midst of our dark and foggy times, all sorts of voices are shouting orders into the night, telling us what to do, how to adjust our lives. Out of the darkness, one voice signals something quite opposite to the rest—something almost absurd. But the voice happens to be the Light of the World, and we ignore it at our peril.

Pride, Submission

Date used __________ Place ____________________

Lordship of Christ 387

There is a picture hanging crookedly on your living-room wall. It bothers you, so you walk to the picture and push up the side that is hanging low. You step back, squint your eyes, and decide now the picture is straight. You leave the room feeling good about getting things to look the way they should.

The next day you walk through the living room and are surprised to see the picture is once again hanging as crookedly as it did yesterday before you straightened it. You conclude you must have failed to get it really level the day before. Again you push up the side hanging low, step back, eyeball the picture, and decide this time you have it right.

The next day to your great frustration you find the picture hanging crookedly again. You are sure you had it right the day before. You push it straight and walk away wondering whether it will be crooked again tomorrow.

The next day it is crooked again. What's going on! Then it dawns on you. Perhaps the wire on the back of the picture is not centered on the wall hook. You take hold of the picture, slide it to the left a fraction of an inch, and then level it.

The next day when you return to the living room, you find your picture hanging straight and true the way you left it the day before.

A picture will stay level only if it is centered on the hook. Without that, any corrections are temporary. In the same way, until we center ourselves in Jesus Christ, no matter how hard we try to straighten out our lives they will eventually fall out of line.

Balance, Conversion, Morality, Regeneration,
Repentance, Self-Improvement, Will Power
2 Cor. 5:15; Phil. 1:21; 1 Peter 3:15

Date used __________ Place ____________________

388

On Sunday, December 22, 1996, Carnell Taylor was working on a paving crew repairing the Interstate 64 bridge over the Elizabeth River in Virginia. The road was icy, and a pickup truck slid out of control and hit Taylor, knocking him off the bridge. He fell seventy feet and hit the cold waters of the river below. His pelvis and some of the bones in his face were broken.

Joseph J. Brisson, the captain of a barge passing by at that moment, saw Taylor fall and quickly had to make a life-or-death decision. He knew Taylor would drown before he and his crew could launch their small boat and reach him. The numbingly cold water and strong currents of the river could kill him if he dived in to rescue Taylor. He had a family, and Christmas was three days away.

Brisson decided to risk his life for a man he had never met. He dived into the river, swam to Taylor, and grabbed hold of him. "Don't worry, buddy," he said, "I got you." Brisson held Taylor's face above the water and encouraged him to keep talking. Then he took hold of a piece of wood in the water and slid it under Taylor to help keep him afloat. The current was too strong for them to swim to safety, and eventually the cold caused Brisson to lose his grip on Taylor. So Brisson wrapped his legs around the injured man's waist and held on.

After nearly thirty minutes the crew from the barge was finally able to reach the two men and pull them from the water into the small boat. Taylor was hospitalized for broken bones. Brisson, the hero, was treated for mild hypothermia.

Brisson later told the Associated Press he knew what he had to do when he saw the man fall. "I have a family," he said. "I thought about that. But I thought about how life is very important. I'm a Christian man, and I couldn't let anything happen to him."

In this perilous rescue, Joseph Brisson shows us the heart of God. The God of love knows better than anyone the tremendous value of a human being and his or her eternal soul. For even one person Jesus was willing to leave the safety and joy of his family in heaven and give himself to save others.

Christmas, Courage, Evangelism, Incarnation, Love, Love of God, Redemption, Rescue, Risk, Sacrifice, Salvation, Sanctity of Life, Security of Believer, Selflessness

Luke 15; John 3:16; John 10:27–29

Date used __________ Place ____________________

Lost People 389

Hall of Famer Walter Payton holds the NFL record for rushing yards, and in 1985 he climaxed his career by winning Super Bowl XX with the Chicago Bears. One of Payton's cherished possessions was his Super Bowl ring commemorating their triumph. According to writer Fred Mitchell in the *Chicago Tribune,* each ring was distinctive, marked with the player's name, uniform number, and position.

In the winter of 1996, Walter's invaluable ring disappeared. It happened when he delivered a motivational speech to a high school basketball team he had worked closely with for years. To give an object lesson on the importance of trust, he entrusted his ring to one of the players for the weekend. Reportedly, when friends of that player came to the boy's house to see the ring, it disappeared.

At first, because of his close relationship with the school, Payton did not report the theft to the authorities. Exercising remarkable patience, he hoped the boys would get the ring back for him. But after five months he could wait no longer. He had to have his keepsake ring back. So he reported the theft to the police and offered a reward for information leading to its recovery.

One of the most painful experiences in life is to lose what we highly value. That is precisely what happened to God. The people whom God made in his image became lost through sin. Lost people matter to God.

Evangelism, Love of God, Stealing, Stewardship, Trust

Matt. 28:18–20; Luke 15:1–32; 19:1–10; Rom. 2:4; 1 Tim. 2:4; 2 Peter 3:9

Date used __________ Place ____________________

Lostness 390

A novel by Madeleine L'Engle is entitled *A Severed Wasp.* The title, which comes from one of George Orwell's essays, offers a graphic image of human lostness.

Orwell describes a wasp that "was sucking jam on my plate and I cut him in half. He paid no attention, merely went on with his meal, while a tiny stream of jam trickled out of his severed esophagus. Only when he tried to fly away did he grasp the dreadful thing that had happened to him."

The wasp and people without Christ have much in common. Severed from their souls, but greedy and unaware, people continue to consume life's sweetness. Only when it's time to fly away will they grasp their dreadful condition.

Pleasures, World

Date used __________ Place ____________________

In *Rhythms of the Heart,* Phil Hook writes:

> My mother and I did not "mix." I chose a typical teenage solution to the problem—silence.
>
> I would leave for school in the morning, come home to eat, then leave again. When I was finally home late at night, I read books.
>
> Invariably, my mother would come downstairs and ask me if I wanted a sandwich. I grunted my assent. She cooked egg and bacon sandwiches for me night after night until I left home for good.
>
> Years later, when our relationship was mended, she told me why she had made all those sandwiches. "If you would ever talk to me, it was while I made that sandwich," she said.

Hook writes, "I've learned love is found in a consistent display of interest, commitment, sacrifice, and attention."

Child Rearing, Kindness, Mothers, Teenagers
John 13:1–17; Titus 2:4–5

Date used __________ Place ____________________

On the morning of Sunday, November 8, 1987, Irishman Gordon Wilson took his daughter Marie to a parade in the town of Enniskillen, Northern Ireland.

As Wilson and his twenty-year-old daughter stood beside a brick wall waiting for English soldiers and police to come marching by, a bomb planted by IRA terrorists exploded from behind, and the brick wall tumbled on them. The blast instantly killed half a dozen people and pinned Gordon and his daughter beneath several feet of bricks. Gordon's shoulder and arm were injured. Unable to move, Gordon felt someone take hold of his hand. It was his daughter Marie.

"Is that you, Dad?" she asked.

"Yes, Marie," Gordon answered.

He heard several people begin screaming.

"Are you all right?" Gordon asked his daughter.

"Yes," she said. But then she, too, began to scream. As he held her hand, again and again he asked if she was all right, and each time she said yes.

Finally Marie said, "Daddy, I love you very much."

Those were her last words. Four hours later she died in the hospital of severe spinal and brain injuries.

Later that evening a BBC reporter requested permission to interview Gordon Wilson. After Wilson described what had happened, the reporter asked, "How do you feel about the guys who planted the bomb?"

"I bear them no ill will," Wilson replied. "I bear them no grudge. Bitter talk is not going to bring Marie Wilson back to life. I shall pray tonight and every night that God will forgive them."

In the months that followed, many people asked Wilson, who later became a senator in the Republic of Ireland, how he could say such a thing, how he could forgive such a monstrous act.

Wilson explained, "I was hurt. I had just lost my daughter. But I wasn't angry. Marie's last words to me—words of love—had put me on a plane of love. I received God's grace, through the strength of his love for me, to forgive."

For years after this tragedy, Gordon Wilson continued to work for peace in Northern Ireland.

Love can do miracles. Just as Marie Wilson's last words to her father lifted him onto the plane of love, so God's love for us lifts us onto a whole different plane, enabling us to love others no matter how they treat us.

Bitterness, Enemies, Forgiveness, Peace
Matt. 5:38–48; Rom. 12:21

Date used __________ Place ____________________

Bruce Thielemann tells the story of a church elder who showed what it means to follow Jesus.

A terrible ice storm had hit Pittsburgh, making travel almost impossible. At the height of the storm, a church family called their pastor about an emergency. Their little boy had leukemia and he had taken a turn for the worst. The hospital said to bring the boy in, but they could not send an ambulance, and the family did not own a car.

The pastor's car was in the shop, so he called a church elder. The elder immediately got in his car and began the treacherous journey. The brakes in his car were nearly useless. It was so slick that he could not stop for stop signs or stop lights. He had three minor accidents on the way to the family's house.

When he reached their home, the parents brought out the little boy wrapped in a blanket. His mother got in the front seat and held her son, and the father got in the back. Ever so slowly they drove to the hospital. Says Thielemann:

> They came to the bottom of a hill and as they managed to skid to a stop, he tried to decide whether he should try to make the grade on the other side, or whether he should go to the right and down the valley to the hospital. And as he was thinking about this, he chanced to look to the right and he saw the face of the little boy. The youngster's face was flushed, and his eyes wide with fever and with fear. To comfort the child, he reached over and tousled his hair. Then it was that the little boy said to him, "Mister, are you Jesus?" Do you know in that moment he could have said yes. For him to live was Jesus Christ.
>
> People who piddle around with life never know moments like that.

Loving as Jesus loved requires courage.

Courage, Risk, Sacrifice

Matt. 25:31–46; Luke 10:30–37; John 13:34–35; 15:13

Date used __________ Place ____________________

In his book *The Ten Laws of Lasting Love,* Paul Pearsall describes an important episode in a battle he faced against cancer.

> Any time a doctor came with news of my progress, my wife would join with me in a mutual embrace. The reports were seldom good during the early phases of my illness, and one day a doctor brought particularly frightening news. Gazing at his clipboard, he murmured, "It doesn't look like you're going to make it."
>
> Before I could ask a question of this doomsayer, my wife stood up, handed me my robe, adjusted the tubes attached to my body and said, "Let's get out of here. This man is a risk to your health." As she helped me struggle to the door, the doctor approached us. "Stay back," demanded my wife. "Stay away from us."
>
> As we walked together down the hall, the doctor attempted to catch up with us. "Keep going," said my wife, pushing the intravenous stand. "We're going to talk to someone who really knows what is going on." Then she held up her hand to the doctor. "Don't come any closer to us."
>
> The two of us moved as one. We fled to the safety and hope of a doctor who did not confuse diagnosis with verdict. I could never have made that walk toward wellness alone.

According to the "love chapter" in the Bible, love protects.

Cancer, Faith, Hope, Marriage, Protection

Mark 5:35–43; 1 Cor. 13:7; Gal. 6:2

Date used __________ Place ____________________

Mother Teresa of Calcutta, India, was the keynote speaker at the 1994 National Prayer Breakfast in Washington, D.C. The scene was unforgettable: On either side of the podium sat President Clinton, Vice President Gore, and other dignitaries. Aids rolled the frail, eighty-three-year-old Mother Teresa to the podium in a wheelchair and had to help her stand to her feet. She stood on a special platform, and even with that the four-foot-six-inch woman could hardly reach the microphone.

Nevertheless her words sent shock waves through the auditorium. She rebuked America and its leaders for the policy of abortion.

"Mother Teresa said that America has become a selfish nation," writes Philip Yancey, "in danger of losing the proper meaning of love: 'giving until it hurts. . . .'"

Mother Teresa said, "If we accept that a mother can kill even her own child, how can we tell other people not to kill each other? . . . Any country that accepts abortion is not teaching its people to love but to use any violence to get what they want."

Mother Teresa pleaded with pregnant women who don't want their children: "Please don't kill the child," she said. "I want the child. Please give me the child. I want it. I will care for it."

She means what she says. Mother Teresa has already placed three thousand children with families in Calcutta.

She is a model of self-sacrificing love, speaking out on behalf of the weak and giving herself to serve them.

Abortion, Conviction, Courage, Sacrifice
John 15:13

Date used __________ Place ____________________

396

In *The Christian Leader,* Don Ratzlaff retells a story Vernon Grounds came across in Ernest Gordon's *Miracle on the River Kwai.* The Scottish soldiers, forced by their Japanese captors to labor on a jungle railroad, had degenerated to barbarous behavior, but one afternoon something happened:

A shovel was missing. The officer in charge became enraged. He demanded that the missing shovel be produced, or else. When nobody in the squadron budged, the officer got his gun and threatened to kill them all on the spot. . . . It was obvious the officer meant what he had said. Then, finally, one man stepped forward. The officer put away his gun, picked up a shovel, and beat the man to death. When it was over, the survivors picked up the bloody corpse and carried it with them to the second tool check. This time, no shovel was missing. Indeed, there had been a miscount at the first checkpoint.

The word spread like wildfire through the whole camp. An innocent man had been willing to die to save the others! . . . The incident had a profound effect. . . . The men began to treat each other like brothers.

When the victorious Allies swept in, the survivors, human skeletons, lined up in front of their captors . . . (and instead of attacking their captors) insisted: "No more hatred. No more killing. Now what we need is forgiveness."

Sacrificial love has transforming power.

Forgiveness, Sacrifice

Date used __________ Place ____________________

J. Allan Peterson, in *The Myth of the Greener Grass,* writes:

Newspaper columnist and minister George Crane tells of a wife who came into his office full of hatred toward her husband. "I do not only want to get rid of him; I want to get even. Before I divorce him, I want to hurt him as much as he has me."

Dr. Crane suggested an ingenious plan. "Go home and act as if you really loved your husband. Tell him how much he means to you. Praise him for every decent trait. Go out of your way to be as kind, considerate, and generous as possible. Spare no efforts to please him, to enjoy him. Make him believe you love him. After you've convinced him of your undying love and that you cannot live without him, then drop the bomb. Tell him that you're getting a divorce. That will really hurt him."

With revenge in her eyes, she smiled and exclaimed, "Beautiful, beautiful. Will he ever be surprised!"

And she did it with enthusiasm. Acting "as if." For two months she showed love, kindness, listening, giving, reinforcing, sharing.

When she didn't return, Crane called. "Are you ready now to go through with the divorce?"

"Divorce!" she exclaimed. "Never! I discovered I really do love him." Her actions had changed her feelings. Motion resulted in emotion. The ability to love is established not so much by fervent promise as often repeated deeds.

Divorce, Marriage

Date used __________ Place ____________________

Ian Pitt-Watson adapts this portion from *A Primer for Preachers:*

There is a natural, logical kind of loving that loves lovely things and lovely people. That's logical. But there is another kind of loving that doesn't look for value in what it loves, but that "creates" value in what it loves. Like Rosemary's rag doll.

When Rosemary, my youngest child, was three, she was given a little rag doll, which quickly became an inseparable companion. She had other toys that were intrinsically far more valuable, but none that she loved like she loved the rag doll.

Soon the rag doll became more and more rag and less and less doll. It also became more and more dirty. If you tried to clean the rag doll, it became more ragged still. And if you didn't try to clean the rag doll, it became dirtier still.

The sensible thing to do was to trash the rag doll. But that was unthinkable for anyone who loved my child. If you loved Rosemary, you loved the rag doll—it was part of the package.

"If anyone says, 'I love God' yet hates his brother or sister, he is a liar" (1 John 4:20).

"Love me, love my rag dolls," says God, "including the one you see when you look in the mirror. This is the finest and greatest commandment."

Church, Unlovable People

Date used __________ Place ____________________

Booker T. Washington was born a slave. Later freed, he headed the Tuskegee Institute and became a leader in education. In his autobiography, he writes:

The most trying ordeal that I was forced to endure as a slave boy . . . was the wearing of a flax shirt. In that portion of Virginia where I lived, it was common to use flax as part of the clothing for the slaves. That part of the flax from which our clothing was made was largely the refuse, which of course was the cheapest and roughest part.

I can scarcely imagine any torture, except, perhaps, the pulling of a tooth, that is equal to that caused by putting on a new flax shirt for the first time. It is almost equal to the feeling that one would experience if he had a dozen or more chestnut burrs, or a hundred small pin-points, in contact with his flesh. . . . But I had no choice, I had to wear the flax shirt or none. . . .

My brother John, who is several years older than I am, performed one of the most generous acts that I have ever heard of one slave relative doing for another. On several occasions when I was being forced to wear a new flax shirt, he generously agreed to put it on in my stead and wear it for several days, till it was "broken in."

Sacrifice, Help

Date used __________ Place ____________________

Love 400

Rubel Shelly tells this story:

Jason Tuskes was a 17-year-old high school honor student. He was close to his mother, his wheelchair-bound father, and his younger brother. Jason was an expert swimmer who loved to scuba dive.

He left home on a Tuesday morning to explore a spring and underwater cave near his home in west central Florida. His plan was to be home in time to celebrate his mother's birthday by going out to dinner with his family that night.

Jason became lost in the cave. Then, in his panic, he apparently got wedged into a narrow passageway. When he realized he was trapped, he shed his yellow metal air tank and unsheathed his diver's knife. With the tank as a tablet and the knife as a pen, he wrote one last message to his family: I LOVE YOU MOM, DAD, AND CHRISTIAN. Then he ran out of air and drowned.

A dying message—something communicated in the last few seconds of life—is something we can't ignore. God's final words to us are etched on a Roman cross. They are blood red. They scream to be heard. They, too, say, "I love you."

God's Love, Christ's Blood

Date used __________ Place ____________________

In 1996 Disney came out with the movie *101 Dalmatians,* and it was a box-office success. Many viewers fell in love with the cute spotted puppies on the big screen and decided to get one for themselves. When they brought those adorable little puppies home, however, they found that living with a dalmatian is an entirely different experience from watching one on the movie screen. Soon, according to the Associated Press, all over the United States dog shelters saw a dramatic increase in the number of dalmatians being abandoned by their owners. A Florida organization called Dalmatian Rescue took in 130 dalmatians in the first nine months of 1997; usually they get that many dogs in two and a half years.

Dalmatians can be a challenge to own for several reasons. Dalmatians grow to be big dogs, weighing as much as seventy pounds. They are rambunctious and require a lot of exercise. They can be moody, becoming restless and even destructive if they don't get enough activity. They shed year-round, and 10 percent of dalmatians are born deaf.

Tracey Carson, a spokeswoman for the Wisconsin Humane Society, says, "Although Dalmatians are beautiful puppies, and can be wonderful dogs, you have to know what you're getting into."

Whether with pets or with people, infatuation with someone's appearance is a poor foundation for a relationship.

Appearance, Commitment, Expectations, Faithfulness, Illusions, Infatuation, Marriage, Relationships, Romance
Rom. 12:10; 1 Cor. 13:7–8

Date used __________ Place ____________________

Rita Price writes in a 1995 issue of the *Columbus Dispatch:*

Katie Fisher, 17, pulled her unruly lamb into the arena of the Madison County Junior Livestock Sale last July. With luck the lamb would fetch some spending money—and she wouldn't collapse as she had during another livestock show the day before.

Fisher had been battling Burkitt's lymphoma, a fast-growing malignancy, since February. She had endured many hospitalizations and months of chemotherapy. "Sometimes, in the beginning, it hurt so bad all she could do was pace," said her 12-year-old sister, Jessica.

Selling the lamb did raise pin money for Fisher.

"We sort of let folks know that Katie had a situation that wasn't too pleasant," said auctioneer Roger Wilson, who hoped his introduction would push the price-per-pound above the average of $2. It did—and then some.

The lamb sold for $11.50 per pound. Then the buyer gave it back. That started a chain reaction. Families bought it and gave it back; businesses bought it and gave it back.

"The first sale is the only one I remember. After that, I was crying too hard," said Katie's mother, Jayne Fisher. "Everyone kept saying, 'Re-sell! Re-sell!'"

"We sold that lamb 36 times," said Wilson. And the last buyer gave back the lamb for good. The effort raised more than $16,000, which went into a fund to help pay Katie's medical expenses.

It is blessed both to give and to receive.

Giving, Mercy, Sacrifice
Acts 20:35; Gal. 6:2; 1 John 3:16–18

Date used __________ Place ____________________

Researcher Beppino Giovanella knows what it means to give himself on behalf of others. In *Johns Hopkins Magazine* Melissa Hendricks writes:

> Nobody put a gun to Beppino Giovanella's head and said, "Take this or else." It was the desire to find a safe but effective dosage that made the biologist swallow a gelatin capsule containing 100 milligrams of an experimental cancer drug. Like a modern-day Dr. Jekyll, Giovanella, director of laboratories for the Stehlin Foundation in Houston, chose himself as a guinea pig. Partly as a result of his self-experiment, the drug is now in clinical trials.
>
> Science is rich with stories of self-experiments, but today an investigator like Giovanella, who has tested several drugs on himself without seeking formal approval of his institution, is a rare bird. As a result of his latest experiment, he temporarily lost his hair. But he did find that cancer drug doses effective in animals are too much for humans.
>
> "As a biologist, you become acutely aware that drugs at times act very differently from one species to another," Giovanella says. "That is why I always test new drugs on myself first. It wouldn't be very nice to risk another person before I risk myself."

Love is considerate.

Golden Rule, Self-Sacrifice
1 Cor. 13:7; James 3:17–18

Date used __________ Place ____________________

How do we love someone who stumbles?

In a *Leadership* profile of pastor and author Stu Weber, Dave Goetz writes:

> Growing up, Weber developed a temper, which blossomed in high school and college. "And then I went in the military," Weber said, "which doesn't do a lot to curb your temper and develop relational skills."
>
> Early in his ministry, he stopped playing church-league basketball altogether; his temper kept flaring, embarrassing himself and the church. A decade passed. "I hadn't had a flash of temper for years," Weber said. "I thought, the Lord has been good. I'm actually growing."
>
> Then his oldest son made the high school varsity basketball squad. "I began living my life again through my son." Weber terrorized the referees. On one occasion, seated in the second row, Weber wound up on the floor level, with no recollection of how he got there. He received nasty letters from church members, who, he says now, "were absolutely right on."
>
> But then he got another note: "Stu, I know your heart. I know that's not you. I know that you want to live for Christ and his reputation. And I know that's not happened at these ballgames. If it would be helpful to you, I'd come to the games with you and sit beside you."
>
> It was from one of his accountability partners.
>
> "Steve saved my life," Weber said. "It was an invitation, a gracious extension of truth. He assumed the best and believed in me."

When we love others, we believe in and hope the best for them even when they fail.

Accountability, Anger, Belief, Community, Devotion, Discipleship, Failure, Forbearance, Loyalty, Men, Stumbling, Support, Temper

Rom. 12:10; 1 Cor. 13:7; Col. 3:8, 12–14

Date used __________ Place ____________________

Love, for enemies 405

In *Context,* Martin Marty retells a parable from the *Eye of the Needle* newsletter:

A holy man was engaged in his morning meditation under a tree whose roots stretched out over the riverbank. During his meditation he noticed that the river was rising, and a scorpion caught in the roots was about to drown. He crawled out on the roots and reached down to free the scorpion, but every time he did so, the scorpion struck back at him.

An observer came along and said to the holy man, "Don't you know that's a scorpion, and it's in the nature of a scorpion to want to sting?"

To which the holy man replied, "That may well be, but it is my nature to save, and must I change my nature because the scorpion does not change its nature?"

Evangelism, Perseverance

Date used __________ Place ____________________

Love, for enemies 406

In *The Grace of Giving,* Stephen Olford tells of a Baptist pastor during the American Revolution, Peter Miller, who lived in Ephrata, Pennsylvania, and enjoyed the friendship of George Washington.

In Ephrata also lived Michael Wittman, an evil-minded sort who did all he could to oppose and humiliate the pastor.

One day Michael Wittman was arrested for treason and sentenced to die. Peter Miller traveled seventy miles on foot to Philadelphia to plead for the life of the traitor.

"No, Peter," General Washington said, "I cannot grant you the life of your friend."

"My friend!" exclaimed the old preacher. "He's the bitterest enemy I have."

"What?" cried Washington. "You've walked seventy miles to save the life of an enemy? That puts the matter in a different light. I'll grant your pardon." And he did. Peter Miller took Michael Wittman back home to Ephrata—no longer an enemy, but a friend.

Grace, Enemies

Date used __________ Place ____________________

Love, for enemies 407

In *The Northwestern Lutheran,* Joel C. Gerlach writes:

Eight times the Ministry of Education in East Germany said no to Uwe Holmer's children when they tried to enroll at the university in East Berlin. The Ministry of Education doesn't usually give reasons for its rejection of applications for enrollment. But in this case the reason wasn't hard to guess.

Uwe Holmer, the father of the eight applicants, is a Lutheran pastor at Lobetal, a suburb of East Berlin. For 26 years the Ministry of Education was headed by Margot Honecker, wife of East Germany's premier, Erich Honecker. . . . [Then] when the Berlin wall cracked ... Honecker and his wife were unceremoniously dismissed from office. He is now under indictment for criminal activities during his tenure as premier.

At the end of January the Honeckers were evicted from their luxurious palace in Vandlitz, an exclusive suburb of palatial homes reserved for the VIPs in the party. The Honeckers suddenly found themselves friendless, without resources, and with no place to go. None of their former cronies showed them any of the humanitarianism communists boast about. No one wanted to identify with the Honeckers. . . .

Enter Uwe Holmer. Remembering the words of Jesus, "If someone strikes you on the right cheek, turn to him the other also," Holmer extended an invitation to the Honeckers to stay with his family in the parsonage of the parish church in Lobetal. . . .

Pastor Holmer has not reported that the Honeckers have renounced their atheism and professed faith in Jesus as Savior and Lord. But at least they fold their hands and bow their heads when the family prays together. Who knows what the Holmers' faith-in-action plan will lead to before this extraordinary episode ends?

Enemies, Evangelism

Date used __________ Place ____________________

A factory employee named Kenneth worked for the largest manufacturer in Illinois for twenty-four years. The wages and benefits paid at his factory were double what the average factory job paid in America. He had steady work. He was forty-four years old, yet he had never attended a union meeting. He was a contented, middle-class worker—until 1992.

From 1992 until 1994 you could find Kenneth at the end of the day shift parading through the factory, holding an American flag along with two other workers, chanting, "No contract. No peace. No contract. No peace." Kenneth called out the cadences for about one hundred middle-age marchers.

What turned a contented worker into a thorn in this manufacturer's side? The turning point came in 1992, after the union had been on strike for nearly six months, when the company threatened to replace its striking workers.

That did something to Kenneth. It turned him bitterly against his company. Kenneth angrily explains, "I finally realized two years ago, when they threatened to replace us, that as far as they are concerned, I am nothing to them."

I am nothing to them—Kenneth's whole attitude changed when he concluded, whether rightly or wrongly, that he had no worth to the company, that he was replaceable, that they didn't care about him as a person. Even the toughest, manliest laborer in America craves loyalty, craves to have others care.

There is only one place where we are assured of that. God values us and cares for us so much that even when we "went on strike"—rejecting his will for our lives—instead of rejecting us in return, he sent his Son to die for our sins.

Bitterness, Faithfulness, Men, Significance
John 3:16; Rom. 12:10; 1 Peter 5:7

Date used __________ Place ____________________

In his book *Enjoying God,* Lloyd Ogilvie writes:

My formative years ingrained the quid pro quo into my attitude toward myself: *do and you'll receive; perform and you'll be loved*. When I got good grades, achieved, and was a success, I felt acceptance from my parents. My dad taught me to fish and hunt and worked hard to provide for us, but I rarely heard him say, "Lloyd, I love you." He tried to show it in actions, and sometimes I caught a twinkle of affirmation in his eyes. But I still felt empty.

When I became a Christian, I immediately became so involved in discipleship activities that I did not experience the profound healing of the grace I talked about theoretically. . . .

I'll never forget as long as I live the first time I really experienced healing grace. I was a postgraduate student at the University of Edinburgh. Because of financial pressures I had to accordion my studies into a shorter than usual period. Carrying a double load of classes was very demanding, and I was exhausted by the constant feeling of never quite measuring up. No matter how good my grades were, I thought they could be better. Sadly, I was not living the very truths I was studying. Although I could have told you that the Greek words for grace and joy are *charis* and *chara,* I was not experiencing them.

My beloved professor, Dr. James Stewart, that slightly built dynamo of a saint, saw into my soul with x-ray vision. One day in the corridor of New College he stopped me. He looked me in the eye intensely. Then he smiled warmly, took my coat lapels in his hands, drew me down to a few inches from his face, and said, "Dear boy, you are loved now!"

God loves us *now,* not when we get better. God loves us *now,* as we are.

Acceptance, Fathers, Grace, Joy
John 3:16; Rom. 5:8; 1 Peter 1:8; 1 John 4:7–10

Date used __________ Place ____________________

Loyalty 410

Jackie Robinson was the first black person to play major league baseball. While breaking baseball's color barrier, he faced jeering crowds in every stadium.

While playing one day in his home stadium in Brooklyn, he committed an error. His own fans began to ridicule him. He stood at second base, humiliated, while the fans jeered.

Then shortstop "Pee Wee" Reese came over and stood next to him. He put his arm around Jackie Robinson and faced the crowd. The fans grew quiet. Robinson later said that arm around his shoulder saved his career.

Encouragement, Failure

Date used __________ Place ____________________

Loyalty 411

In the December 31, 1989 *Chicago Tribune,* the editors printed their photos of the decade. One of them, by Michael Fryer, captured a grim fireman and paramedic carrying a fire victim away from the scene.

The blaze, which happened in Chicago in December 1984, at first seemed routine. But then firefighters discovered the bodies of a mother and five children huddled in the kitchen of an apartment.

Fryer said the firefighters surmised, "She could have escaped with two or three of the children but couldn't decide whom to pick. She chose to wait with all of them for the firefighters to arrive. All of them died of smoke inhalation."

There are times when you just don't leave those you love.

Love, Mothers

Date used __________ Place ____________________

Lust 412

Radio personality Paul Harvey tells the story of how an Eskimo kills a wolf. The account is grisly, yet it offers fresh insight into the consuming, self-destructive nature of sin:

First, the Eskimo coats his knife blade with animal blood and allows it to freeze. Then he adds another layer of blood, and another, until the blade is completely concealed by frozen blood.

Next, the hunter fixes his knife in the ground with the blade up. When a wolf follows his sensitive nose to the source of the scent and discovers the bait, he licks it, tasting the fresh frozen blood. He begins to lick faster, more and more vigorously, lapping the blade until the keen edge is bare. Feverishly now, harder and harder the wolf licks the blade in the arctic night. So great becomes his craving for blood that the wolf does not notice the razor-sharp sting of the naked blade on his own tongue, nor does he recognize the instant at which his insatiable thirst is being satisfied by his "own" warm blood. His carnivorous appetite just craves more—until the dawn finds him dead in the snow!

It is a fearful thing that people can be "consumed by their own lusts."

Self-Destruction, Sin

Date used __________ Place ____________________

Lust 413

In one movie some shipwrecked men are left drifting aimlessly on the ocean in a lifeboat. As the days pass under the scorching sun, their rations of food and fresh water give out. The men grow deliriously thirsty. One night while the others are asleep, one man ignores all previous warnings and gulps down some salt water. He quickly dies.

Ocean water contains seven times more salt than the human body can safely ingest. Drinking it, a person dehydrates because the kidneys demand extra water to flush the overload of salt. The more salt water someone drinks, the thirstier he gets. He actually dies of thirst.

When we lust, we become like this man. We thirst desperately for something that looks like what we want. We don't realize, however, that it is precisely the opposite of what we really need. In fact, it can kill us.

Thirst, Deception

Date used __________ Place ____________________

Lying 414

Jazz musician Billy Tipton was a gifted pianist and saxophonist who got his start during the big band era of the 1930s.

According to *Time* magazine, Billy had a few peculiarities: He refused to give his social security number to his booking agent. His three adopted sons could not recall a time when he went swimming with them. He would never visit a doctor even when suffering serious illness.

When Tipton died in 1989 at age seventy-four, the family found out why. The funeral director told one of the adopted sons that Billy Tipton was a woman. Tipton began living a lie because during the big band era, women were allowed to sing but rarely played in the band.

That kind of sexism is sad. But Billy Tipton's story is sad in another way. No matter what a person's motives are for lying, when the truth comes out, confusion, hurt, and shame are inescapable.

Ambition, Identity, Secrets, Shame, Truth
Ps. 51:6; Prov. 12:19

Date used __________ Place ______________________

415

Early in 1996 the body of the former ambassador to Switzerland was buried in Arlington Cemetery, America's graveyard of war heroes. His granite tombstone read, "S1C [Seaman First Class] U.S. Merchant Marine."

But according to Don Van Natta Jr. and Elaine Sciolino in the *New York Times,* on December 11, 1997, cemetery workers hauled that tombstone away, and they exhumed the casket. The reason: the man had lied. For years he told others he had served on the Coast Guard ship *Horace Bushnell* during World War II. He said the Germans torpedoed the ship, and he had been thrown overboard, sustaining a head injury. In fact, records showed that at the time he said he was serving in the Merchant Marine he was actually attending Wilbur Wright College in Chicago. The Coast Guard had no record of his serving in the Merchant Marine, and of course he had never earned the rank of seaman first class.

Somehow his lie was not discovered when the State Department investigated his background, and he was approved as an ambassador. Somehow his body was permitted to be buried in Arlington Cemetery with a tombstone engraved with a lie. But to no surprise, the truth eventually came out.

The truth always will.

Character, Deception, Falsehood, Integrity, Truth
Matt. 10:26; Luke 12:1–3; Eph. 5:8–14

Date used __________ Place ____________________

Man’s Nature 416

A school teacher lost her life savings in a business scheme that had been elaborately explained by a swindler. When her investment disappeared and her dream was shattered, she went to the Better Business Bureau.

“Why on earth didn’t you come to us first?” the official asked. “Didn’t you know about the Better Business Bureau?”

“Oh, yes,” said the lady sadly. “I’ve always known about you, but I didn’t come because I was afraid you’d tell me not to do it.”

The folly of human nature is that even though we know where the answers lie—God’s Word—we don’t turn there for fear of what it will say.

Bible, God’s Will

Date used __________ Place ____________________

Californians Randy Curlee and Victoria Ingram became engaged in February 1994. According to the *Chicago Tribune,* a short time later, Randy received bad news from his doctor. Randy had suffered from diabetes since he was twelve; he was now forty-six, and the doctor said the diabetes had ruined his kidneys. He would need a transplant to save his life.

Randy brought his fiancée, Victoria, to hear what the doctor was saying so she would understand how his diabetes would affect their future. The doctor said that each year only four thousand kidneys become available to the thirty-six thousand people who need a transplant. Usually family members provide the best match for a transplant, but none of Randy's family matched his profile well.

Victoria spoke up, "Why don't you test me?" The doctor gave her the tests, and the couple went home and forgot about it.

Then the phone rang. Randy's doctor reported that their immune systems were an identical match.

So the couple made plans to be married on October 11, 1994, and the next day to have the transplant surgery. At the last minute, the surgery had to be delayed because Victoria's kidney was nicked by a catheter during testing. But one month after becoming man and wife, in a five-and-a-half-hour operation at Sharp Memorial Hospital in San Diego, Victoria gave her husband, Randy, her left kidney. It was believed to be the first organ swap between husband and wife in the United States.

Randy and Victoria's marriage literally depended on her sacrifice for its survival. In a sense, so does every marriage. Marriages survive and thrive when spouses focus on what they can give to their partner more than on what they can get.

Love, Sacrifice
John 13:34–35; Eph. 5:22–33

Date used __________ Place ____________________

Marriage 418

In *Focus on the Family Newsletter,* Dr. James Dobson writes:

What should a woman do for a man that will relate directly to his masculine nature? In a word, she can build his confidence. This vital role is best illustrated by one of my favorite stories told by my friend E. V. Hill. Dr. Hill is a dynamic black minister and the senior pastor at Mt. Zion Missionary Baptist Church in Los Angeles. He lost his precious wife, Jane, to cancer a few years ago. In one of the most moving messages I've ever heard, Dr. Hill spoke about Jane at her funeral and described the ways this "classy lady" made him a better man.

As a struggling young preacher, E. V. had trouble earning a living. That led him to invest the family's scarce resources, over Jane's objections, in the purchase of a service station. She felt her husband lacked the time and expertise to oversee his investment, which proved to be accurate. Eventually, the station went broke, and E. V. lost his shirt in the deal.

It was a critical time in the life of this young man. He had failed at something important, and his wife would have been justified in saying, "I told you so." But Jane had an intuitive understanding of her husband's vulnerability. Thus, when E. V. called to tell her that he had lost the station, she said simply, "All right."

E. V. came home that night expecting his wife to be pouting over his foolish investment. Instead, she sat down with him and said, "I've been doing some figuring. I figure that you don't smoke and you don't drink. If you smoked and drank, you would have lost as much as you lost in the service station. So, it's six in one hand and a half-dozen in the other. Let's forget it."

Jane could have shattered her husband's confidence at that delicate juncture. The male ego is surprisingly fragile, especially during times of failure and embarrassment. That's why E. V. needed to hear her say, "I still believe in you," and that is precisely the message she conveyed to him.

Shortly after the fiasco with the service station, E. V. came home one night and found the house dark. When he opened the door, he saw that Jane had prepared a candlelight dinner for two.

"What meaneth thou this?" he said with characteristic humor.

"Well," said Jane, "we're going to eat by candlelight tonight."

E. V. thought that was a great idea and went into the bathroom to wash his hands. He tried unsuccessfully to turn on the light. Then he felt his way into the bedroom and flipped another switch. Darkness prevailed. The young pastor went back to the dining room and asked Jane why the electricity was off. She began to cry.

"You work so hard, and we're trying," said Jane, "but it's pretty rough. I didn't have quite enough money to pay the light bill. I didn't want you to know about it, so I thought we would just eat by candlelight."

Dr. Hill described his wife's words with intense emotion: "She could have said, 'I've never been in this situation before. I was reared in the home of Dr. Caruthers, and we never had our light cut off.' She could have broken my spirit; she could have ruined me; she could have demoralized me. But instead she said, 'Somehow or another we'll get these lights on. But let's eat tonight by candlelight.'"

Courage, Forgiveness, Wives
1 Cor. 13:4–7; Eph. 5:22–33

Date used __________ Place ____________________

Marriage 419

A braid appears to contain only two strands of hair. But it is impossible to create a braid with only two strands. If the two could be put together at all, they would quickly unravel.

Herein lies the mystery: What looks like two strands requires a third. The third strand, though not immediately evident, keeps the strands tightly woven.

In a Christian marriage, God's presence, like the third strand in a braid, holds husband and wife together.

Unity, God's Presence

Date used __________ Place ____________________

In *On This Day* by Carl D. Windsor, the page for Valentine's Day includes this anecdote:

Even the most devoted couple will experience a stormy bout once in a while. A grandmother, celebrating her golden wedding anniversary, once told the secret of her long and happy marriage. "On my wedding day, I decided to make a list of ten of my husband's faults which, for the sake of our marriage, I would overlook," she said.

A guest asked the woman what some of the faults she had chosen to overlook were. The grandmother replied, "To tell you the truth, my dear, I never did get around to listing them. But whenever my husband did something that made me hopping mad, I would say to myself, *Lucky for him that's one of the ten!*"

Faultfinding, Forbearance

Date used __________ Place ____________________

Ruth Ryan, wife of Hall of Fame pitcher Nolan Ryan, had one moment she looked forward to in every one of her husband's games. In *Covering Home,* she writes:

> It probably happened the first time on the high-school baseball diamond in Alvin, Texas, in the mid-1960s. Then it happened repeatedly for three decades after that. Inevitably, sometime during a game, Nolan would pop up out of the dugout and scan the stands behind home plate, looking for me. He would find my face and grin at me, maybe snapping his head up in a quick nod as if to say, There you are; I'm glad. I'd wave and flash him a smile. Then he'd duck under the roof and turn back to the game.
>
> It was a simple moment, never noted in record books or career summaries. But of all the moments in all the games, it was the one most important to me.

Those who love us long for us to acknowledge them, to give them our attention. This is true not only in marriage and family, but in our relationship with God. Throughout our days, in both the big and small moments, God enjoys it when we "step out of the dugout" and smile in his direction.

Acknowledging God, Attention, Love, Prayer, Support, Thanksgiving
Prov. 3:5–6; Eph. 5:25

Date used __________ Place ____________________

In *Discipleship Journal* Navigator staff member Skip Gray writes:

When Joseph Ton was a pastor in Romania he was arrested by the secret police for publishing a sermon calling for the churches to refuse to submit to the communist government's demand for control over their ministries. When an official told him he must renounce his sermon, he replied, "No, sir! I won't do that!"

The official, surprised that anyone would respond so forcefully to the secret police, said, "Aren't you aware that I can use force against you?"

"Sir, let me explain that to you," Ton said. "You see, your supreme weapon is killing. My supreme weapon is dying. . . . You know that my sermons are spread all over the country on tapes. When you kill me, I only sprinkle them with my blood. They will speak 10 times louder after that, because everybody will say, 'That preacher meant it because he sealed it with his blood.' So go on, sir, kill me. When you kill me, I win the supreme victory." The secret police released him, knowing his martyrdom would be far more of a problem than his sermon.

Conviction, Courage, Death, Leadership, Persecution, Sacrifice, Witness
John 15:18–16:4; Acts 7:54–8:4; Phil. 1:20

Date used __________ Place ____________________

Materialism 423

The story is told of a prosperous, young investment banker who was driving a new BMW sedan on a mountain road during a snowstorm. As he veered around one sharp turn, he lost control and began sliding off the road toward a deep precipice. At the last moment he unbuckled his seat belt, flung open his door, and leaped from the car, which then tumbled down the ravine and burst into a ball of flames.

Though he had escaped with his life, the man suffered a ghastly injury. Somehow his arm had been caught near the hinge of the door as he jumped and had been torn off at the shoulder.

A trucker saw the accident in his rearview mirror. He pulled his rig to a halt and ran to see if he could help. He found the banker standing at the roadside, looking down at the BMW burning in the ravine below.

"My BMW! My new BMW!!" the banker moaned, oblivious to his injury.

The trucker pointed at the banker's shoulder and said, "You've got bigger problems than that car. We've got to find your arm. Maybe the surgeons can sew it back on!"

The banker looked where his arm had been, paused a moment, and groaned, "Oh no! My Rolex! My new Rolex!!"

God gives us material possessions so we will enjoy them, not so we will worship them.

Greed, Priorities, Values
Luke 12:13–21

Date used __________ Place ____________________

Materialism 424

Fortune magazine quotes a comment made by billionaire H. Ross Perot:

"Guys, just remember, if you get real lucky, if you make a lot of money, if you go out and buy a lot of stuff—it's gonna break. You got your biggest, fanciest mansion in the world. It has air conditioning. It's got a pool. Just think of all the pumps that are going to go out. Or go to a yacht basin any place in the world. Nobody is smiling, and I'll tell you why. Something broke that morning. The generator's out; the microwave oven doesn't work. . . . Things just don't mean happiness."

Treasures, Happiness

Date used __________ Place ____________________

Materialism 425

In the syndicated cartoon "Mister Boffo" Joe Martin pictures a middle-aged man lying on a psychologist's couch. The psychologist sits on a chair next to him, listens intently, and writes in a notebook. The man on the couch has a problem. "I drive a Mercedes," he says, "I have a beachhouse in Bermuda, a 12-room penthouse, a 90-foot yacht. My clothes are made by the finest tailors in London. I have a world-class wine cellar. And yet I'm still not happy."

The psychologist asks, "Do you have a Rolex?"

Abruptly the troubled man raises his head from the couch, points his finger in the air, and declares, "Why no, I don't!"

Such is the folly of those who pursue happiness in material possessions. They will always be one purchase away from a happy life.

Greed, Happiness, Possessions
Exod. 20:17; Luke 12:15

Date used __________ Place ____________________

Men are strong in different ways.

Sports Illustrated once did a profile on a champion arm wrestler named Dave Patton. According to the article Patton hadn't lost an arm-wrestling match in some twelve years. He weighed a mere 160 pounds but easily defeated men twice his size.

Patton trained obsessively. He did exactly 756 bicep curls per session, pushing his pain threshold to the outer limits. For fun he ventured onto the streets of Manhattan, set up a table, and challenged all comers to a prize of one thousand dollars to whoever could beat him. No one of any size ever had.

In the article Tom Junod describes the feats of strength of other men.

> Moe Baker of Bristol, Connecticut, . . . not only had 18-inch forearms but could also jump straight out of a 55-gallon drum without ever touching the sides. Cleve Dean, a 600-pound hog farmer from Georgia, was a he-man, too, because he could pick up a full-grown sow under each arm and walk around. . . . And the legendary Mac Batchlor, from Los Angeles, was a he-man because he could fold four bottle caps in half simply by placing them on his fingers and closing his fist.

These are strong men. God wants men to be strong—but strong in a way that matters.

Power, Strength
1 Cor. 16:13; Eph. 6:10

Date used __________ Place ____________________

Mercy 427

In *Reader's Digest* Jim Williams of Butte, Montana, writes:

> I was driving too fast late one night when I saw the flashing lights of a police car in my rearview mirror. As I pulled over and rolled down the window of my station wagon, I tried to dream up an excuse for my haste. But when the patrolman reached the car, he said nothing. Instead, he merely shined his flashlight in my face, then on my seven-months-pregnant wife, then on our snoozing 18-month-old in his car seat, then on our three other children, who were also asleep, and lastly on the two dogs in the very back of the car. Returning the beam of light to my face, he then uttered the only words of the encounter.
>
> "Son," he said, "you can't afford a ticket. Slow it down." And with that, he returned to his car and drove away.

Sometimes mercy triumphs over law. So it is for sinners who call out to Jesus.

Grace, Law, Salvation
Luke 18:9–14; Rom. 11:32; James 2:12

Date used __________ Place ____________________

At the Wright Patterson Air Force base in Dayton, Ohio, researchers hope they will develop the means for pilots to fly airplanes with their minds. The project is called brain-actuated control.

Writers Ron Kotulak and Jon Van say this is how it could work. The pilot would wear scalp monitors that pick up electrical signals from various points on his head. The scalp monitors would be wired to a computer. Using biofeedback techniques, the pilot would learn to manipulate the electrical activity created by his or her thought processes. The computer would translate the electrical signals into mechanical commands for the airplane.

Imagine being able to bank an airplane's wings, accelerate, and climb another ten thousand feet, all by controlling what you think.

Although controlling airplanes with the mind is yet to be developed, our mind already has tremendous control of one thing: our behavior. Our thoughts sooner or later lead to our actions.

Heart, Self-Control, Thoughts
Prov. 4:23; Rom. 13:14; James 1:14–15

Date used __________ Place ____________________

According to an October 29, 1994, story from the Reuters news agency, a Chinese woman named Zhang Meihua began to suffer mysterious symptoms when she turned twenty. She was losing the ability to nimbly move her legs and arms. Doctors could not find the cause, and the symptoms continued.

Two decades passed, and Zhang began to also suffer from chronic headaches. Again she sought help from the doctors. This time a CAT scan and an X ray found the source of the woman's mysterious symptoms. A rusty pin was lodged in her head. The head of the pin was outside the skull, and the shaft penetrated into her brain. Doctors performed surgery and successfully extracted the pin.

The Xinhua news agency reported the doctors expressed amazement that the woman "could live for so long a time with a rusty pin stuck in her brain." After noting the position of the pin in her skull, they speculated that the pin had entered her skull sometime soon after birth and before her skull had hardened. Zhang, now fully recovered, said she "had no memory of being pierced by a pin in the head."

Like the rusty pin in that woman's brain, unwholesome thoughts, bad attitudes, and painful memories can lodge in our minds and cause chronic problems. God tells us to renew our minds.

Attitudes, Health, Thoughts
Rom. 12:1–2; Phil. 4:8–9

Date used __________ Place ____________________

In a *Forbes* article about Harry Quadracci and the Quad/Graphics printing company, Phyllis Berman writes about the kind of employees the company hires.

> A good many people whom society would dismiss as losers have been given a chance at Quad/Graphics, and they are grateful.
>
> "We hire people who have no education and little direction," Quadracci explains. "They are the kind of people who look at their shoes when they apply for a job. They join the firm not for its high wages—starting salaries on the floor are only about $7.50 an hour—but because we offer them a chance to make something out of themselves."

Like this businessman, God delights in calling workers who look at their shoes when they apply for the job. God gives great responsibility to people whom the world thinks little of.

Calling, Confidence, Losers, Pride, Salvation, Spiritual Gifts
Exod. 3; 1 Cor. 1:18–31; 2 Cor. 3:5–6

Date used __________ Place ____________________

Ministry 431

We can learn something about effective ministry from a famous trumpet player for the Chicago symphony.

Adolph (Bud) Herseth is regarded as "the premier orchestral trumpeter of his time, and perhaps of all time," wrote Jim Doherty in 1994. Herseth has played first trumpet for the world-class Chicago Symphony for nearly fifty years.

"Fellow musicians hail him as 'a legend,' 'a phenomenon' and the 'prototype,'" says the writer. "Critics knock themselves out singing his praise. He is a hero to brass students at music schools. Wherever the Chicago goes on tour, young players mob him."

Doherty continues:

> Early in his career, a car accident cost him a half-dozen front teeth and split his lower lip so badly thirteen stitches were needed to close it. A mere mortal might have feared the end of his playing days. Bud had his mouth rebuilt and six weeks later resumed his seat. His lip was numb and his mouthpiece felt funny, yet somehow he produced the same gorgeous sound. He can't explain it.
>
> That pretty much sums up Bud's whole approach. He refuses to make a big deal about "technique." Playing has less to do with the mouth than the ear, he says. "You have to start with a very precise sense of how something should sound. Then, instinctively, you modify your lip and your breathing and the pressure of the horn to obtain that sound."

Techniques and rules are not the key to playing the trumpet, nor are they the key to serving Christ. First and foremost, you've got to hear it. You've got to know what the "music" of ministry sounds like. Techniques are secondary.

Discipleship, Holy Spirit, Legalism, Spiritual Discernment,
Technique, Training, Vision
Mark 3:13–15

Date used __________ Place ____________________

The highest honor a French chef can attain is to have his restaurant listed as a three-star restaurant in the Michelin Guide to fine eating. According to the *Chicago Tribune,* the 1995 Guide added a twentieth restaurant to its three-star listing: the Auberge de l'Eridan in Annecy, France.

The owner and self-taught chef, Marc Veyrat, is a culinary maverick. His unorthodox ideas got him kicked out of three hotel culinary schools, and local hotels would not even take him on as an apprentice in the kitchen.

Veyrat is from the French Alps. Alpine herbs, such as caraway, cumin, wild thyme, and chenopodium, are key ingredients in his recipes. Once a week at dawn Veyrat ventures into the mountains to pick the herbs.

"I know I'm not a traditional chef," says Veyrat. "I'm a student of nature, because before you love cuisine, you have to love the ingredients."

The teaching of God's Word is much like preparing fine food. Before you can bring people the gospel, you first must love the Word.

Creativity, Love, Preaching, Study, Teaching
Rom. 1:9; 1 Tim. 4:15–16; 2 Tim. 3:14; 4:2

Date used __________ Place ____________________

Ministry 433

The *Times-Reporter* of New Philadelphia, Ohio, reported in September 1985 a celebration at a New Orleans municipal pool. The party around the pool was held to celebrate the first summer in memory without a drowning at any New Orleans city pool. In honor of the occasion, two hundred people gathered, including one hundred certified lifeguards.

As the party was breaking up and the four lifeguards on duty began to clear the pool, they found a fully dressed body in the deep end. They tried to revive Jerome Moody, thirty-one, but it was too late. He had drowned surrounded by lifeguards celebrating their successful season.

I wonder how many visitors and strangers are among us drowning in loneliness, hurt, and doubt, while we, who could help them, don't realize it. We Christians have reason to celebrate, but our mission, as the old hymn says, is to "rescue the perishing." And often they are right next to us.

Evangelism, Mission

Date used __________ Place ____________________

Rusty Stevens, a Navigators director in Virginia Beach, Virginia, tells this story:

As I feverishly pushed the lawn mower around our yard, I wondered if I'd finish before dinner. Mikey, our 6-year-old, walked up and, without even asking, stepped in front of me and placed his hands on the mower handle. Knowing that he wanted to help me, I quit pushing.

The mower quickly slowed to a stop. Chuckling inwardly at his struggles, I resisted the urge to say, "Get out of here, kid. You're in my way," and said instead, "Here, Son. I'll help you." As I resumed pushing, I bowed my back and leaned forward, and walked spread-legged to avoid colliding with Mikey. The grass cutting continued, but more slowly, and less efficiently than before, because Mikey was "helping" me.

Suddenly, tears came to my eyes as it hit me: *This is the way my heavenly Father allows me to "help" him build his kingdom!* I pictured my heavenly Father at work seeking, saving, and transforming the lost, and there I was, with my weak hands "helping." My Father *could* do the work by himself, but he doesn't. He chooses to stoop gracefully to allow me to co-labor with him. Why? For *my* sake, because he wants me to have the privilege of ministering with him.

Service, Evangelism

Date used __________ Place ____________________

In the early 1990s large numbers of upscale professionals and independent freelancers began moving from the cities to the country. When those accustomed to the conveniences of suburban and city living arrived in rural areas, many were in for a big surprise, writes Patrick O'Driscoll in *USA Today*. "Your neighbor's cattle may stink," he writes. "You may have to haul your own trash to the dump. The mail carrier might not deliver daily, or perhaps not at all. Power or phone lines may not reach your property. The fire department or ambulance may not come quickly enough in an emergency. And, yes, your remote mountain road may not get plowed—or paved, for that matter."

Life in rural America had hardships naive newcomers never expected. Some of these city slickers called to complain. One county commissioner named John Clarke of Larimer County, Colorado, got so many cranky calls that he finally decided to warn people who were planning to move to the country about the realities that awaited them. He wrote a thirteen-page booklet called "The Code of the West: The Realities of Rural Living." Some of the warnings went like this:

"Animals and their manure can cause objectionable odors. What else can we say?"

"If your road is gravel, it is highly unlikely that Larimer County will pave it in the foreseeable future. . . . Gravel roads generate dust. . . . Dust is still a fact of life for most rural residents."

"The topography of the land can tell you where the water will go in case of heavy precipitation. When property owners fill in ravines, they have found that the water that drained through that ravine now drains through their house."

Clarke's motive in writing the booklet wasn't to keep newcomers away. "We just want them to know what to expect," he says.

Just as moving from the city to the country may bring unexpected hardships, so does becoming an active worker in the church. We too need to know what to expect. Don't be surprised by people problems or organizational glitches that arise when you are involved in a volunteer work force. Even with these vexations, though, working for Christ is as beautiful as a gentle stream flowing through a mountain valley.

Change, Complaining, Expectations, Hardship,
Problems, Reality, Spiritual Warfare
Phil. 1:28–30; 2 Tim. 2:3

Date used ___________ Place ______________________

436

In 1996 the U.S. auto industry celebrated its one hundredth anniversary. In observance, *Chicago Tribune* auto writer Jim Mateja selected what he called the "10 That Made a Difference." These were the ten vehicles that had made the most significant contributions in their time and whose reputations live on:

1. 1896 Duryea Motor Wagon. For the first time more than one vehicle was manufactured from the same design (thirteen the first year).
2. 1901 Curved Dash Olds. This was the first mass-produced vehicle (425 the first year).
3. 1908 Ford Model T. Known as the Tin Lizzie, this car put America on the road.
4. 1941 Willys Jeep. The jeep helped win World War II and proved to be the forerunner of the sport-utility vehicle.
5. 1949 Volkswagen Beetle. This was "The People's Car," and in 1973 it overtook the Ford Model T as the world's best-selling car.
6. 1953 Chevrolet Corvette.
7. 1964 Pontiac GTO.
8. 1964 Ford Mustang. The Mustang set a first-year record of 417,000 sales, and drew a cult following.
9. 1984 Chrysler minivan. It replaced the station wagon as a people carrier.
10. 1986 Ford Taurus. By 1992 it was the industry's top-selling car.

Ten cars that made a big difference in the auto world.

Like these cars, each of us is called to make a difference in our world. We are change agents. God calls us to be salt, light, ambassadors for Christ. He wants each of us to leave our workplace, family, neighborhood, church a better place than when we came.

Change Agents, Evangelism, Fruitfulness, Leadership, Light, Outreach, Salt, Vision

Matt. 5:13–16; 28:18–20; John 15:8; Acts 1:8; 17:6; 1 Cor. 15:58

Date used __________ Place ____________________

437

At the 1997 Brickyard 400 auto race, NASCAR driver Lake Speed learned firsthand the amazing effect of prayer. His car had been having mechanical problems. Sitting on the track in preparation for a qualifying run, he waited in frustration because his car wouldn't start. Meanwhile he prayed. Finally his crew chief Jeff Buice took out a wrench and hand-cranked the engine Model-A style. The car started, and Lake Speed roared onto the track to post the second fastest qualifying time of the day.

Victor Lee writes in *Sports Spectrum:*

Later, when Speed returned to the pits to get ready for a final practice session, he found his crew tearing out the engine. Shocked, he asked what was going on.

"Lake, that engine was blown before you qualified," Buice said, noting that it had blown during NASCAR pre-race inspection. Lake looked more closely. Oil was everywhere.

Buice continued, "I wasn't going to tell you anything, because time had run out. But I was already trying to figure out how I was going to spend Saturday. Even if it started, I surely didn't expect it to make a lap, and surely not to run good enough to make the race."

Lake's assessment: "God did a major mechanical miracle. I always pray right before the race. Sitting on that track, when it didn't start, I prayed, 'Lord, I don't know what's going on here, but if there's any way, I'd like this thing to start.'"

Driver Lake Speed went on to finish twelfth in the race, his second best finish in 1997.

You may say this has a perfectly natural explanation; or you may call it a miracle; but without question according to the automobile experts on the scene this was a remarkable event that followed prayer. Funny, but remarkable events and coincidences often follow prayer.

Impossibilities, Prayer, The Supernatural
Gen. 18:14; Matt. 19:26

Date used __________ Place ____________________

438

In the *Pentecostal Evangel* missionary Ian Hall tells the story of a Romanian woman named Cristina Ardeleanu, whom he met during a preaching crusade:

In March 1992 Cristina was in the hospital with an ectopic pregnancy. Before she learned she was pregnant, the fetus died and began to decompose in her body. Cristina was not expected to live.

My wife Sheila and I went to the hospital to pray for Cristina, and God healed her. Still, in their attempts to save her life, doctors removed most of her uterus and one ovary. They told her she would never bear a child.

Cristina's strength returned, and by May she was back in church. I was holding another series of meetings there, and she and her husband Stefan came forward for prayer.

"Will you pray that God will give us a child?" they asked. Knowing Cristina's diagnosis, they were hoping to adopt.

I began to pray, but suddenly I found myself prophesying: "In one year you will stand in this place holding a son born of your own body."

"Why did you say that?" Sheila asked later. "You know she can't bear children. You've really put yourself out on a limb."

I knew my predicament all too well. The words that came from my lips had astonished everyone, including me.

That year I returned to the area from time to time, but Stefan and Cristina said nothing of a baby. Although I was troubled at first, in time I stopped thinking about the prophecy.

In May 1993 I was conducting services again in the Cimpulung church. The pastor announced that a baby would be dedicated and informed me that I was to pray for the child. But as I surveyed the audience, I couldn't see anyone with a baby.

Then from the farthest corner of the church I saw Stefan and Cristina approaching, holding the son born to them 6 weeks earlier. As with Hannah of the Bible, the Ardeleanus had received their promise—and they named him Samuel.

Childbirth, Healing, Holy Spirit, Pregnancy,
Promise, Prophecy, The Supernatural, Word of Knowledge
1 Sam. 1; Acts 2:17–18; 21:10–11; 1 Cor. 12; 14; James 5:14–16

Date used __________ Place ____________________

Baseball fans will talk about the first game of the 1996 American League championship series between the New York Yankees and the Baltimore Orioles for years to come. The game was played in New York. Going into the bottom of the eighth inning Baltimore led 4–3. With one out and Armando Benitez on the mound, Yankee Derek Jeter hit a towering blast to right field. Orioles right fielder Tony Tarasco ran back to the wall and timed his jump perfectly to snatch the ball before it hit high off the right-field fence.

But before the ball landed safely in his glove, the unexpected happened. “To me it was a magic trick,” said Tarasco later, “because the ball just disappeared out of midair.”

Not quite. A twelve-year-old boy from New Jersey named Jeff Maier had skipped school that day to come to the game and was seated in the front row in right field. When that towering fly ball fell straight in front of him, he did what any Yankee fan would do: he reached out over the wall with his baseball glove and scooped the ball into the stands.

The “magic” continued. The umpire erroneously called it a home run, tying the score. The game went into extra innings, and in the bottom of the eleventh Yankee Bernie Williams hit the home run that won the game, giving the Yankees a 1–0 lead in the series. Afterward the Orioles called the fan interference an outrage. Yankee fans called it a miracle. The Yankees went on to win the series 4 games to 1.

Like the Yankees, sometimes we need outside intervention. We need God to reach out and break the rules of nature to help us. Miracles are possible for those who pray and believe.

Angels, Deliverance, Healing, Impossibilities, Prayer
Matt. 19:26; Mark 9:23; 10:27; Acts 12:1–11

Date used __________ Place ____________________

Author and professor Phillip Johnson has waged an all-out war on the theory of Darwinian evolution. In a *Christianity Today* article titled "The Making of a Revolution," Tim Stafford tells how Johnson took up the cause:

> In the fall of 1987, Phillip Johnson, a middle-aged law professor at the University of California, Berkeley, began a sabbatical year in England. His distinguished academic career had specialized in criminal law and lately branched out into more philosophical fields of legal theory. Nevertheless, Johnson could not shake the feeling that his life amounted to a wasted talent, that he had used a first-class mind for only second-class occupations. He was "looking for something to do the rest of his life" and talked about it with his wife, Kathie, as they hiked around the green fields of England. "I pray for an insight," he told her. "I'd like to have an insight that is worthwhile, and not just be an academic who writes papers and spins words."
>
> In London, Johnson's daily path from the bus stop to his office at University College took him by a scientific bookstore. "Like a lot of people," Johnson says, "I couldn't go by a bookstore without going in and fondling a few things." The very first time he walked by he saw and purchased the powerful, uncompromising argument for Darwinian evolution by Richard Dawkins, *The Blind Watchmaker.* Johnson devoured it and then another book, Michael Denton's *Evolution: A Theory in Crisis.* "I read these books, and I guess almost immediately I thought, This is it. This is where it all comes down to, the understanding of creation."
>
> Johnson began a furious reading program, absorbing the literature on Darwinian evolution. Within a few weeks, he told his wife, "I think I understand this stuff. I know what the problem is. But fortunately, I'm too smart to take it up professionally. I'd be ridiculed. Nobody would believe me. They would say, 'You're not a scientist, you're a law professor.' It would be something, once you got started with it, you'd be involved in a lifelong, never-ending battle."

"That," says Phillip Johnson, remembering back with a smile, "was of course irresistible. I started to work the next day."

Every Christian needs a great mission worth giving one's life for.

Cause, Challenge, Defining Moments, Direction, Leadership, Prayer, Purpose, Spiritual Gifts, Vision

Matt. 4:18–22; Rom. 12:1–2; Phil. 2:12–13; 3:7–14; 1 Peter 4:10

Date used __________ Place ____________________

441

Philip Yancey in *World Concern Update* writes:

I don't know what comes to your mind when you hear the word *fat,* but I have a good idea. In America fat is nearly always a dirty word. We spend billions of dollars on pills, diet books, and exercise machines to help us lose excess fat. I hadn't heard a good word about fat in years—that is, until I met Dr. Paul Brand.

"Fat is absolutely gorgeous," says Brand, a medical doctor who has worked with lepers in India. "When I perform surgery, I marvel at the shimmering, lush layers of fat that spread apart as I open up the body. Those cells insulate against cold, provide protection for the valuable organs underneath, and give a firm, healthy appearance to the whole body." I had never thought of fat quite like that!

"But those are just side benefits," he continues. "The real value of fat is as a storehouse. Locked in those fat cells are the treasures of the human body. When I run or work or expend any energy, fat cells make that possible. They act as banker cells. It's absolutely beautiful to observe the cooperation among those cells!"

Dr. Brand applies the analogy of fat to the body of Christ. Each individual Christian in a relatively wealthy country like America is called to be a fat cell. America has a treasure house of wealth and spiritual resources. The challenge to us, as Christians, is to wisely use those resources for the rest of the body.

Ever since talking to Dr. Brand, I have taken sort of a whimsical pleasure once each month in thinking of myself as a fat cell—on the day I write out checks for Christian organizations. It has helped my attitude. No longer do I concentrate on how I could have used that money I am giving away; rather, I contemplate my privilege to funnel those resources back into Christ's body to help accomplish his work all around the world.

Stewardship, Body of Christ

Date used __________ Place ____________________

Money 442

In the spring of 1995 congressional Democrats and Republicans were battling over the national budget. According to Reuters, one portion of a tax-cut bill stirred up a storm of controversy. The debated provision was designed to crack down on wealthy Americans who renounce U.S. citizenship to avoid taxes. That's right. Some American billionaires actually move their citizenship to another country to save money. One politician referred to them as "Benedict Arnold billionaires."

Money can do terrible things to a person's loyalties.

Greed, Idolatry, Loyalty
Matt. 6:19–24; 1 Tim. 6:6–10

Date used __________ Place ____________________

Money 443

Money can't buy happiness. You've probably heard that cliché in the mouths of the old and the wise, but now even social scientists are saying that money doesn't make you happy.

According to writers Ron Kotulak and Jon Van, an international study based on information gathered in thirty-nine countries and published in the journal *Social Indicators Research* concluded that the more money people make, the more they want, so happiness keeps eluding them.

The study said, "Neither increasing income at the individual level nor country level were accompanied by increases in subjective well-being."

In fact the researchers found that rapid increases in wealth resulted in less, not more, happiness.

Ed Diener, a University of Illinois psychologist, said, "A lot of people think, *If only I had a million dollars, I'd be happy.* It could be true for an individual, but for most people, on average, it appears not to be true."

Coveting, Greed, Happiness
Luke 16:13–15; Heb. 13:5–6

Date used __________ Place ____________________

Money 444

In *I Talk Back to the Devil,* A. W. Tozer reminds us:

> Money often comes between men and God. Someone has said that you can take two small ten-cent pieces, just two dimes, and shut out the view of a panoramic landscape. Go to the mountains and just hold two coins closely in front of your eyes—the mountains are still there, but you cannot see them at all because there is a dime shutting off the vision in each eye.

It doesn't take large quantities of money to come between us and God; just a little, placed in the wrong position, will effectively obscure our view.

Spiritual Perception, Idolatry

Date used __________ Place ____________________

Money 445

Many people think money is security, but 1 Timothy 6:9 warns that it can be just the opposite. A few years ago, columnist Jim Bishop reported what happened to people who won the state lottery:

> Rosa Grayson of Washington won $400 a week for life. She hides in her apartment. For the first time in her life, she has "nerves." Everyone tries to put the touch on her. "People are so mean," she said. "I hope you win the lottery and see what happens to you."
>
> When the McGugarts of New York won the Irish Sweepstakes, they were happy. Pop was a steamfitter. Johnny, twenty-six, loaded crates on docks. Tim was going to night school. Pop split the million with his sons. They all said the money wouldn't change their plans.
>
> A year later, the million wasn't gone; it was bent. The boys weren't speaking to Pop, or to each other. Johnny was chasing expensive race horses; Tim was catching up with expensive girls. Mom accused Pop of hiding his poke from her. Within two years, all of them were in court for nonpayment of income taxes. "It's the Devil's own money," Mom said. Both boys were studying hard to become alcoholics.

All these people hoped and prayed for sudden wealth. All had their prayers answered. All were wrecked on a dollar sign.

Coveting, Happiness

Date used __________ Place ____________________

When you go to a doctor for your annual check-up, he or she will often begin to poke, prod, and press various places, all the while asking, "Does this hurt? How about this?"

If you cry out in pain, one of two things has happened. Either the doctor has pushed too hard, without the right sensitivity. Or, more likely, there's something wrong, and the doctor will say, "We'd better do some more tests. It's not supposed to hurt there!"

So it is when pastors preach on financial responsibility, and certain members cry out in discomfort, criticizing the message and the messenger. Either the pastor has pushed too hard, or perhaps there's something wrong. In that case, I say, "My friend, we're in need of the Great Physician because it's not supposed to hurt there."

Preaching, Stewardship

Date used __________ Place ____________________

447

In *Success, Motivation and the Scriptures* William H. Cook describes a meeting in 1923 of a group of business tycoons. Together these men controlled unthinkable sums of wealth, and for years the media had trumpeted their success stories. On this day in Chicago they assembled to enjoy their mutual success. Dr. Cook relays what happened to these men in the years that followed.

Charles Schwab, the president of the largest independent steel company, lived on borrowed money the last five years of his life and died penniless.

Richard Whitney, the president of the New York Stock Exchange, served time in Sing Sing Prison.

Albert Fall, a former member of the President's Cabinet, was pardoned from prison so he could die at home.

Jesse Livermore, the greatest bear on Wall Street, committed suicide.

Leon Fraser, the president of the Bank of International Settlement, committed suicide.

Ivan Krueger, head of the world's greatest monopoly, committed suicide.

The success they celebrated proved illusory.

Success, Power

Date used __________ Place ____________________

According to the Associated Press, in the summer of 1996 a man named Joe from Janesville, Wisconsin, received a check from the Social Security Administration for $40,945. Though entitled to the money, Joe was not supposed to receive that check directly. Rather, the check was supposed to go to him through a responsible payee. That's because Joe has an IQ of about 70 and suffers manic depression. Although he had worked some menial jobs here and there, he was unemployed and mildly retarded. Joe also had a gambling problem.

As you might guess, that was his undoing. Whenever Joe felt down, he told his live-in girlfriend he was going on an errand, and he would end up being gone for days on a gambling binge at the casino in Baraboo. Joe often felt down, and so the money didn't last long. In a few weeks he had blown all of the $40,000.

That isn't the way Joe had planned to spend the money. He had planned to buy a house and provide for his three children. Instead, he blew a great opportunity to get ahead. In the end, he blamed the Social Security Administration.

The government won't be giving any more money directly to Joe. Those who can't manage money cannot expect to be given even more.

The same principle applies to us all. God entrusts what is valuable to those who prove their ability to manage it.

Faithfulness, Gambling, Management, Stewardship, Waste
Matt. 25:14–30; Luke 16:1–13; 1 Cor. 4:1–4; 1 Tim. 1:12

Date used __________ Place ____________________

Money 449

The Bible says we are to be free of the love of money. Campus Crusade for Christ's founder Bill Bright and his wife Vonette are sterling examples of this attitude.

A 1997 *Christianity Today* article by Wendy Murray Zoba says that although Campus Crusade had worldwide revenues in 1996 of $300 million, Bill Bright, at age seventy-five, and his wife Vonette, still raise their own monthly support from individual donors just like any other Campus Crusade staff person. Together they earn $48,000 annually ($29,000 for Bill and $19,000 for Vonette). After Bill won the Templeton Award for Progress in Religion in 1996, he relinquished the prize money—in excess of $1 million—for the purpose of developing a ministry of prayer and fasting.

"He recently liquidated $50,000 of his retirement funds," writes Zoba, "to help start up a training center in Moscow. All royalties from his books go to Campus Crusade; he does not accept speaking fees and has no savings account (though Vonette has a small one). The luxury condo they live in was donated to CCC (they pay $1,000 a month rent). They do not own a car, and they have no property."

Giving

Matt. 6:19–21; 1 Tim. 3:3; Heb. 13:5

Date used __________ Place ____________________

George Will writes in *Men at Work:*

> Baseball umpires are carved from granite and stuffed with microchips. . . . They are professional dispensers of pure justice. Once when Babe Pinelli called Babe Ruth out on strikes, Ruth made a populist argument. Ruth reasoned fallaciously (as populists do) from raw numbers to moral weight: "There's 40,000 people here who know that last one was a ball, tomato head."
>
> Pinelli replied with the measured stateliness of John Marshall: "Maybe so, but mine is the only opinion that counts."

Christians are also pressed by the weight of numbers aligned against the moral law of God. But the Christian knows that in the end, only one opinion counts: that of the beneficent Umpire of all human affairs.

Judgment, Opinions

Date used __________ Place ____________________

Morality 451

In *Words We Live By,* Brian Burrell tells of an armed robber named Dennis Lee Curtis who was arrested in 1992 in Rapid City, South Dakota. Curtis apparently had scruples about his thievery. In his wallet the police found a sheet of paper on which was written the following code, sort of a robber's rules:

1. I will not kill anyone unless I have to.
2. I will take cash and food stamps—no checks.
3. I will rob only at night.
4. I will not wear a mask.
5. I will not rob mini-marts or 7-Eleven stores.
6. If I get chased by cops on foot, I will get away. If chased by a vehicle, I will not put the lives of innocent civilians on the line.
7. I will rob only seven months out of the year.
8. I will enjoy robbing from the rich to give to the poor.

This thief had a sense of morality, but it was flawed. When he stood before the court, he was not judged by the standards he had set for himself but by the higher law of the state.

Likewise when we stand before God, we will not be judged by the code of morality we have written for ourselves but by God's perfect law.

Codes, Ethics, Judgment, Justice, Law, Righteousness, Standards, Stealing, Ten Commandments, Truth

Isa. 64:6; Rom. 3:10–23

Date used __________ Place ____________________

John Killinger's book *Lost in Wonder, Love, and Praise* includes the following affirmation:

I believe in Jesus Christ, the Son of the living God,
who was born of the promise to a virgin named Mary.
I believe in the love Mary gave her Son,
that caused her to follow him in his ministry
and stand by his cross as he died.
I believe in the love of all mothers,
and its importance in the lives of the children they bear.
It is stronger than steel, softer than down,
and more resilient than a green sapling on the hillside.
It closes wounds, melts disappointments,
and enables the weakest child to stand tall
and straight in the fields of adversity.
I believe that this love, even at its best,
is only a shadow of the love of God,
a dark reflection of all that we can expect of him,
both in this life and the next.
And I believe that one of the most beautiful sights
in the world is a mother who lets this greater love
flow through her to her child,
blessing the world with the tenderness of her touch
and the tears of her joy.

Love, Children

Date used __________ Place ____________________

A lady answered the knock on her door to find a man with a sad expression.

"I'm sorry to disturb you," he said, "but I'm collecting money for an unfortunate family in the neighborhood. The husband is out of work, the kids are hungry, the utilities will soon be cut off, and worse, they're going to be kicked out of their apartment if they don't pay the rent by this afternoon."

"I'll be happy to help," said the woman with great concern. "But who are you?"

"I'm the landlord," he replied.

Mercy, Giving

Date used __________ Place ____________________

454

When we feel desperate, we sometimes do dangerous things.

In the fall of 1993 Armenia was a country desperate for power sources. The country was entering its third winter under a near-total oil and gas blockade imposed by neighboring Azerbaijan as a weapon in the war between the two former Soviet republics. To survive, the people of Armenia had been cutting down trees for fuel to heat their homes—over 1.5 million trees were lost during the previous winter. As a result, the government was considering the unthinkable: starting up a rusting Soviet nuclear reactor shut down in 1989 because it was unsafe.

The Medzamor nuclear plant was built in the 1970s. The outdated plant had no containment building to control the effects of an accidental radiation leak. The plant was in a known earthquake zone located a mere twenty-five miles from Armenia's capital city, Yerevan, and so any accident would expose hundreds of thousands of people to deadly radiation.

In desperation, people often choose things they live to regret. Turning to sin in a time of need is like pinning your hopes on a rusty, outdated, nuclear power plant.

Addictions, Chemical Dependency, Depression,
Desperation, Prayer, Sin, Trouble
Num. 13–14; Ps. 107; Mark 4:17; James 5:13

Date used __________ Place ____________________

Stephen W. Sorenson writes in *Discipleship Journal:*

For two years, because of severe tendinitis in both wrists, I could not pick up my young daughter, carry a log, or even open a twist-off pop bottle. To make matters worse, my wife and I, with help from family and friends, were building a major addition to our home when the tendinitis developed, so I couldn't even use a hammer. I wondered whether I would ever regain full use of my hands.

But our remodeling went on. We installed a second-story window on one blustery evening with the help of some Christian friends and a man named Willie, a retired military musician.

Afterward, before the window crew began eating dinner, I prayed a simple prayer. Willy listened carefully and watched how the rest of us interacted. Later, as he was leaving, he said, "People don't help each other like this anymore."

I replied, "Sure they do!"

Willy came back to our house, day after day. He dug up our septic tank, cut diseased trees, and simply spent time with us. I could sense he understood my pain and our need. One afternoon as he and I walked and talked in the woods, I discovered why.

For most of his life Willy had lived for his music, but a devastating ear problem developed, preventing him from listening to music of any kind. As a result, rather than being put off by my injury, Willy was drawn to me because of our common ground. And before we went separate ways, Willy became a Christian.

As I look back, I don't know if I would have taken time to talk with Willy had my wrists been well. Most likely I'd have been hammering nails or running a chain saw. So "all" I could do was listen and talk. But in God's plan that was enough.

Help, Evangelism

Date used __________ Place ____________________

Negligence 456

We often fail to consider the gradual, cumulative effect of sin in our lives.

In Saint Louis in 1984, an unemployed cleaning woman noticed a few bees buzzing around the attic of her home. Since there were only a few, she made no effort to deal with them. Over the summer the bees continued to fly in and out the attic vent while the woman remained unconcerned, unaware of the growing city of bees.

The whole attic became a hive, and the ceiling of the second-floor bedroom finally caved in under the weight of hundreds of pounds of honey and thousands of angry bees. While the woman escaped serious injury, she was unable to repair the damage of her accumulated neglect.

Sin, Problems

Date used __________ Place ____________________

New Life 457

The motor home has allowed us to put all the conveniences of home on wheels. A camper no longer needs to contend with sleeping in a sleeping bag, cooking over a fire, or hauling water from a stream. Now he can park a fully equipped home on a cement slab in the midst of a few pine trees and hook up to a water line, a sewer line, and electricity. Some motor homes have a satellite dish attached on top. No more bother with dirt, no more smoke from the fire, no more drudgery of walking to the stream. Now it is possible to go camping and never have to go outside.

We buy a motor home with the hope of seeing new places, of getting out into the world. Yet we deck it out with the same furnishings as in our living room. Thus nothing really changes. We may drive to a new place, set ourselves in new surroundings, but the newness goes unnoticed, for we've only carried along our old setting.

The adventure of new life in Christ begins when the comfortable patterns of the old life are left behind.

Habits, Change

Date used __________ Place ____________________

Patients who undergo organ transplants are routinely taken to the intensive care unit after surgery. There they are classified as being in critical but stable condition, even if the operation went well. The doctors and nurses keep a constant watch over them until they become strong enough to be transferred to a less intensive state of care.

New believers in Christ have undergone a serious organ transplant: they have received new hearts. They need careful follow-up and nurture if they are to make it. Leading people to new life in Christ is a cause for celebration. But let's remember they are in critical but stable condition.

Evangelism, New Believers

Date used __________ Place ____________________

In *General Patton's Principles for Life and Leadership,* Gen. George S. Patton Jr. says:

> Picking the right leader is the most important task of any commander. I line up the candidates and say, "Men, I want a trench dug behind warehouse ten. Make this trench eight feet long, three feet wide and six inches deep."
>
> While the candidates are checking their tools out at the warehouse, I watch them from a distance. They puzzle over why I want such a shallow trench. They argue over whether six inches is deep enough for a gun emplacement. Some complain that such a trench should be dug with power equipment. Others gripe that it is too hot or too cold to dig. If the men are above the rank of lieutenant, there will be complaints that they should not be doing such lowly labor. Finally, one man will order, "What difference does it make what [he] wants to do with this trench! Let's get it dug and get out of here."
>
> That man will get the promotion. Pick the man who can get the job done!

God too is looking for people to whom he can give authority and responsibility. Like Patton, he gives people jobs and watches to see how they respond. Most of all, God is looking for obedience and faithfulness.

Complaining, Faithfulness, Leadership
Matt. 26:17–19; 1 Cor. 16:15–16; 1 Tim. 3:10

Date used __________ Place ____________________

In the eleventh century, King Henry III of Bavaria grew tired of court life and the pressures of being a monarch. He made application to Prior Richard at a local monastery, asking to be accepted as a contemplative and spend the rest of his life in the monastery.

"Your Majesty," said Prior Richard, "do you understand that the pledge here is one of obedience? That will be hard because you have been a king."

"I understand," said Henry. "The rest of my life I will be obedient to you, as Christ leads you."

"Then I will tell you what to do," said Prior Richard. "Go back to your throne and serve faithfully in the place where God has put you."

When King Henry died, a statement was written: "The king learned to rule by being obedient."

When we tire of our roles and responsibilities, it helps to remember God has planted us in a certain place and told us to be a good accountant or teacher or mother or father. Christ expects us to be faithful where he puts us, and when he returns, we'll rule together with him.

Calling, Faithfulness

Date used __________ Place ____________________

Obedience 461

In *How Life Imitates the World Series,* Dave Bosewell tells a story about Earl Weaver, former manager of the Baltimore Orioles. Sports fans will enjoy how he handled star Reggie Jackson.

Weaver had a rule that no one could steal a base unless given the steal sign. This upset Jackson because he felt he knew the pitchers and catchers well enough to judge who he could and could not steal off of. So one game he decided to steal without a sign. He got a good jump off the pitcher and easily beat the throw to second base. As he shook the dirt off his uniform, Jackson smiled with delight, feeling he had vindicated his judgment to his manager.

Later Weaver took Jackson aside and explained why he hadn't given the steal sign. First, the next batter was Lee May, his best power hitter other than Jackson. When Jackson stole second, first base was left open, so the other team walked May intentionally, taking the bat out of his hands.

Second, the following batter hadn't been strong against that pitcher, so Weaver felt he had to send up a pinch hitter to try to drive in the men on base. That left Weaver without bench strength later in the game when he needed it.

The problem was, Jackson saw only his relationship to the pitcher and catcher. Weaver was watching the whole game.

We, too, see only so far, but God sees the bigger picture. When he sends us a signal, it's wise to obey, no matter what we may think *we* know.

Trust, God's Will

Date used __________ Place ____________________

462

In July 1976, Israeli commandos made a daring raid at an airport in Entebbe, Uganda, in which 103 Jewish hostages were freed. In less than 15 minutes, the soldiers had killed all seven of the kidnappers and set the captives free.

As successful as the rescue was, however, three of the hostages were killed during the raid. As the commandos entered the terminal, they shouted in Hebrew, "Get down! Crawl!" The Jewish hostages understood and lay down on the floor, while the guerrillas, who did not speak Hebrew, were left standing. Quickly the rescuers shot the upright kidnappers.

But two of the hostages hesitated—perhaps to see what was happening—and were also cut down. One young man was lying down and actually stood up when the commandos entered the airport. He, too, was shot with the bullets meant for the enemy. Had these three heeded the soldiers' command, they would have been freed with the rest of the captives.

Salvation is open to all, but we must heed Christ's command to repent and make him Lord. Otherwise, we will perish with the judgment meant for the Enemy.

Judgment, Salvation

Date used __________ Place ____________________

Obedience 463

In *Discipleship Journal* editor Susan Maycinik writes:

> The line between obedience and performance can be a blurry one. Yet it is an important distinction to grasp, because obedience leads to life, and performance to death. . . .
>
> Obedience is seeking God with your whole heart. Performance is having a quiet time because you'll feel guilty if you don't.
>
> Obedience is finding ways to let the Word of God dwell in you richly. Performance is quickly scanning a passage so you can check it off your Bible reading plan.
>
> Obedience is inviting guests to your home for dinner. Performance is feeling anxious about whether every detail of the meal will be perfect.
>
> Obedience is following God's prompting to start a small group. Performance is reluctance to let anyone else lead the group because they might not do it as well as you would.
>
> Obedience is doing your best. Performance is wanting to be the best.
>
> Obedience is saying yes to whatever God asks of you. Performance is saying yes to whatever people ask of you.
>
> Obedience is following the promptings of God's Spirit. Performance is following a list of man-made requirements.
>
> Obedience springs from fear of God. Performance springs from fear of failure.

Jesus promised that his yoke is easy, and his burden light.

Grace, Perfectionism, Performance, Works

Matt. 28:20; John 14:23–24; Rom. 8:1–17; Eph. 2:8–10; 1 John 5:3

Date used __________ Place ____________________

464

In *Discipleship Journal* author Elaine Creasman writes:

Pursuit of "good things" can hinder obedience. It has been said that "the good is the enemy of the best." I think of times my husband has asked me to do one thing for him during the day. When he gets home from work, I tell him all the good things I have done. But the question he always has for me is, "What about the thing I asked you to do?"

Many times I have answered, "I forgot," or "I didn't have time." Or I've dismissed his request as trivial.

God asks that same question of us: "What about the thing I asked you to do? . . ."

I'm sure Abraham could have thought of a lot of good things to do instead of taking Isaac to be sacrificed. But I see no excuses in Genesis 22. God commanded; Abraham obeyed.

Direction, Disobedience, Excuses, God's Leading, God's Will, Good Deeds, Obedience, Rebellion
Gen. 22:1–18; 1 Sam. 15:22–23; Isa. 1:19; Matt. 28:20; John 14:23–24; Heb. 5:8

Date used __________ Place ____________________

Obedience 465

According to the *Chicago Tribune,* in 1996 a professor at the University of Illinois found himself in an embarrassing situation. At that time Stuart Nagel was the most published professor at the university, with some sixty books to his credit. The subject of his writing was public policy, with an expertise in dispute-resolution theory. Nagel's car even bore a bumper sticker that said, "Mediate, Don't Litigate."

But in the spring of 1996 the professor who would eat and breathe conflict-resolution theory decided he had no choice but to take the University of Illinois to court. Nagel felt the university was trying to force him into early retirement, or worse, to terminate him without due process. His department head had put him under investigation, ostensibly over the quality of his classroom teaching. Nagel had sought a win-win resolution, but had failed to come to an agreement with the university. And so, with his interests at risk, the professor who abhors litigation went to court as a last resort.

We all know what he felt like. How difficult at times to keep from doing what we don't want to do. How hard at times to do what we want to do.

Conflict, Law, Peacemakers

Matt. 5:9, 23–26; Rom. 7:7–25; 12:18; 1 Cor. 6:1–8

Date used __________ Place ____________________

The appetite of Americans for Mexican food increased dramatically in the 1990s, to the point that in 1996 it was a $1.6 billion market. The market for salsa and refried beans and the like began to grow when small companies like El Paso Chile in Texas marketed an authentic-style Mexican food that even a native of Mexico City could love. Then several large American companies, such as Pillsbury, saw the potential in the market and began to buy out smaller companies and market Mexican-style food on a much larger scale. But what they labeled Mexican food was really a watered-down version of the original to suit American tastes.

"Heat must be carefully rationed at Old El Paso [the Pillsbury brand]," writes Glenn Collins in the *New York Times*. "'Forty percent of those on the East Coast want salsa as mild as it can be,' said Dr. Bernadette Piacek-Llanes, vice president of research and development for Pillsbury Specialty Brands. So Old El Paso, like Pace, has introduced mild, 'cool salsa' products."

Industry experts call these products gringo food, and it is clearly catching on. "About the only thing missing from the boom is Mexicans," writes Collins. "There are no Mexicans on Pillsbury's 10-member Old El Paso development team; its leader was born in India."

Bob Messenger, editor of the industry publication *Food Processing,* says that the "gringo-ization of Mexican food will continue. In 20 years, you won't even recognize what they'll be calling Mexican food."

In business there's nothing wrong with watering down a strong flavor, but the same impulse leads to disaster in our faith. Like the inauthentic gringo style of Mexican food, there is a gringo gospel that is simply not the real thing. The hot, offensive themes—such as the cross and the blood of Christ—are taken out, and a comfortable, people-pleasing substitute is found. The false gospel may be soothing to the taste, but it is powerless to save. The gospel will always be an offense to sinful humankind.

Atonement, Blood, Commitment, Compromise, Cross, Doctrine, Evangelism, False Gospel, Gospel, Hell, Judgment, Original Sin, Pleasing People, Resurrection, Substitutionary Death, Tolerance, Universalism, Wrath
John 6:41–66; Rom. 9–11; 1 Cor. 1:18–25; 15:1–57; Gal. 1:6–10; 5:1–11; 6:12–15; 2 Tim. 4:3–4

Date used __________ Place ____________________

467

During his reign, King Frederick William III of Prussia found himself in trouble. Wars had been costly, and in trying to build the nation, he was seriously short of finances. He couldn't disappoint his people, and to capitulate to the enemy was unthinkable.

After careful reflection, he decided to ask the women of Prussia to bring their gold and silver jewelry to be melted down for their country. For each ornament received, he determined to exchange a decoration of bronze or iron as a symbol of his gratitude. Each decoration would be inscribed, "I gave gold for iron, 1813."

The response was overwhelming. Even more important, these women prized their gifts from the king more highly than their former jewelry. The reason, of course, is clear. The decorations were proof that they had sacrificed for their king. Indeed, it became unfashionable to wear jewelry, and thus was established the Order of the Iron Cross. Members wore no ornaments except a cross of iron for all to see.

When Christians come to their King, they too exchange the flourishes of their former life for a cross.

Sacrifice, Cross

Date used __________ Place ____________________

Opportunity 468

Sometimes you can be tardy and get away with it; sometimes you can't.

According to the Associated Press, near midnight on the evening of June 30, 1997, United Airlines flight 728 from Chicago was bound for Harrisburg, Pennsylvania, and as happens it was behind schedule. Unfortunately the Harrisburg airport had informed the airlines that the lone airport runway would be closed from 11:30 P.M. to 6:30 A.M. for construction.

The pilot of flight 728 believed that he could land before the runway closed, but when he radioed the control tower he was refused permission to do so.

Well, it's a big country; you would think he could land say in Baltimore or Pittsburgh. But no, the plane was ordered to fly all the way back to Chicago so as not to disrupt other flight schedules. The airline put the 101 passengers up in hotels and gave them $25 travel certificates, and the next morning the 101 made the trip to Harrisburg one more time. Yes, they were angry.

A window of opportunity is just that. Never assume everything will be okay if you miss the cutoff time. Sometimes, as here, it just makes life harder; other times, we never get a second chance. So it is with the opportunity for salvation.

Assumptions, Authorities, Obedience, Rules,
Second Coming, Tardiness
Luke 4:19; Acts 17:30–31; 2 Cor. 6:1–2

Date used __________ Place ____________________

Original Sin 469

Movie director Ron Howard has been a repeat winner in the entertainment world. In his days as a child actor he played Opie on *The Andy Griffith Show,* and as a teen he starred in television's *Happy Days.* When he started directing movies, he had success with positive films like *Apollo 13, Parenthood, Splash, Cocoon, Backdraft,* and *Far and Away.*

But then in 1996 he went against the flow by choosing to direct a dark, troubling film called *Ransom,* starring Mel Gibson. The plot revolves around the efforts of the Mel Gibson character to rescue his kidnapped son.

According to Bernard Weinraub in the *New York Times,* Ron Howard chose this movie because he could identify with the Gibson character, a winning but flawed man.

"Ron seems to be a cheerful, easy-going guy," says Brian Grazer, Howard's friend and the movie's producer, "but inside is a very complex, very competitive person who has darkness and pain. He just doesn't show it to people. In his face he never shows it. And this movie was a creative way for him to express that. The complexity of the Mel Gibson character intersects with Ron personally. He's a winning character but flawed. Ron views himself that way. And what appealed to him about the movie is the idea of digging around psychologically into a person that he can relate to."

Ron Howard is honest enough to recognize that despite all his success there is a flaw within. Do you recognize that about yourself? The Bible calls that flaw sin, and every human being has it.

Adam, Confession, Redemption, Salvation, Sin, Success
Gen. 3; Rom. 3:9–20; 5:12–21; Eph. 2:1–10

Date used __________ Place ____________________

Author and Nobel laureate Elie Wiesel was a survivor of the Buchenwald concentration camp during World War II. In *All Rivers Run to the Sea,* he recalls how he became a U.S. citizen:

> I was working in New York City as a correspondent for a French newspaper when my travel permit expired. At the French consulate I was informed that the document could be validated only in France. I didn't have enough money to go back there, and I was anxiously wondering whether I would be deported from America. I went to the U.S. Immigration office, where an official smiled and said, "Why don't you become a U.S. Resident? Then later you can apply for citizenship." I stared at him. Could I actually become an American citizen?
>
> It is hard to put into words how much I owe that kindly immigration official, especially when I recall my annual visits to the Prefecture de Police in Paris, with its long lines and humiliating interrogations. The refugee's time is measured in visas, his biography in stamps on his documents. There is nothing romantic about the life of the exile.
>
> In later years, a high official asked whether I would like to have French nationality. Though I thanked him, I declined the offer. When I needed a passport, it was America that gave me one.

People go where they are welcome. In the church we must help seekers and sinners know we are glad they have come.

Acceptance, Evangelism, Kindness, Love, Mercy, Pharisaism, Welcome
Matt. 9:9–13; 11:19; Luke 15

Date used __________ Place ____________________

Outreach 471

According to *U.S. News & World Report:*

When it comes to the needy, former president Jimmy Carter enjoys exploring new ways of helping them. But even he admits that when it comes to dealing with society's problems, the church has some catching up to do.

"Most church members—including me—rarely reach outside to people who are different from us or less fortunate. Quite often my Sunday school class will say, 'Why don't we take up a collection and give a nice Thanksgiving meal to a poor family?' The next question is: 'Who knows a poor family?' Nobody does. We have to call the welfare office to get the name and address."

The first step in reaching out in the name of Jesus is to be friendly enough to find out the name of your neighbor. That especially means your disadvantaged neighbor.

Compassion, Evangelism, Justice, Mercy, The Poor
Isa. 58:6–12; Luke 4:18; 7:22; 14:12–24

Date used __________ Place ____________________

Outreach 472

In the book titled *Can a Busy Christian Develop Her Spiritual Life?* Jill Briscoe writes:

> Years ago, as I waited in line at a local shop, I heard the gossip. My neighbor's husband had left her. The night before he had packed his things into a van and driven out of her life.
>
> I knew my neighbor casually. When we did speak, which wasn't often, it was about the weather. Our subdivision was the type where people led their own lives and neighbors didn't really get to know one another.
>
> When I returned home, I struggled with what to do. Should I visit my neighbor, or pretend I knew nothing about her situation and go on with my day? In my mind I could see her sitting at her kitchen table, alone. She was in her fifties and the kids were grown.
>
> Finally, I got up the courage and walked over to her house. When she opened her door, I said, "I heard through the grapevine your husband left you last night. Can I do anything to help?"
>
> Immediately, she burst into tears and said, "Come in. Come in." I spent the entire morning with her—listening, putting my arm around her, and having coffee. But it was the start of a relationship.

Sometimes when we think of a needy world, we think of faraway places and masses of people in desperate circumstances. In reality, our needy world might be right next door.

Evangelism, Love, Ministry, Missions, Neighbors
Matt. 28:18–20; Luke 10:25–37

Date used __________ Place ____________________

Overcomers 473

On Sunday night, March 22, 1992, a twin-engine jetliner, USAir flight 405, waited in line to take off from New York's LaGuardia Airport. On board was Bart Simon, a Cleveland businessman. Outside, a snowstorm was blowing. After the plane sat in line for nearly thirty minutes, the control tower gave clearance for takeoff.

The Dutch-made Fokker F28 raced its engines and headed southeast down runway 13-31. The plane lifted into the air, but then the left wing dipped and scraped against the runway. The landing gear struck a set of navigational lights, and the plane touched back down to the left of the runway, splattering along in the mud for one hundred feet.

The plane then nosed briefly back up into the air, but the left wing hit antennas on the side of the runway, and the fuselage began to break apart. Finally the plane bounced into Flushing Bay.

Twenty-seven people were killed in the crash. But Bart Simon survived unharmed.

Surviving a plane crash is a traumatic experience. No one would blame Bart Simon if he chose never to fly again. No one would think twice if he decided the next day to drive home to Cleveland or to take a bus or train.

But on Monday, the day after the crash, Bart Simon climbed aboard another airplane and flew—safely—home to Cleveland.

Bart Simon is an overcomer.

Fear grounds many people. Fear paralyzes ministries, relationships, dreams, churches, careers. The only way to overcome is to do what we fear.

Fear, Perseverance, Tragedy
Phil. 1:6, 20; 1 Peter 3:14; Rev. 2:7; 12:11

Date used __________ Place ____________________

Elizabeth Mittelstaedt is the editor of *Lydia,* the largest Christian magazine in Europe, published in three languages—German, Romanian, and Hungarian. She and her husband, Ditmar, live near Frankfurt, Germany. In *Today's Christian Woman,* Elizabeth writes:

> Ten years ago, I spent five hours in a dentist's chair for what was supposed to be a routine dental procedure and was left with a severely damaged nerve in my jaw. As a result, shooting pain—worse than a severe toothache—pulsated constantly on the right side of my face.
>
> To rid myself of the excruciating pain, I traveled from one doctor to another for six months—to no avail. Nobody was able to prescribe something to ease my torment and despair.
>
> Finally, a doctor at the Mayo Clinic in Minnesota told me, "Mrs. Mittelstaedt, there's nothing more that can be done to repair the damage or relieve your pain. You'll have to live with it."
>
> When I returned home to Germany with this news, I felt discouraged and deeply depressed. Medical records show that many people who suffer with the same problem resort to suicide. I, too, felt death was the only escape, but as a Christian, I couldn't believe that was God's will for me.
>
> But the constant pain took its toll. I felt hopeless, with nothing left to hang on to. One day, during my morning walk, I crossed a small bridge near Frankfurt, looked down at the flowing river below, and heard a voice say to me, "Why don't you just jump?" But when I looked down at the water, I realized it was too shallow to drown in. Then the voice said, "Don't worry. It's stony down there. You'll hit your head and die anyway."
>
> At that moment, Matthew 4:5–7 came to my mind. I recalled how the devil had unsuccessfully tempted Jesus to jump from the highest point of the temple. So I said, "No, I am not going to jump. I am going to trust God."
>
> I began telling God what I was most afraid of—living in pain. Then I remembered that Jesus says we shouldn't worry about tomorrow—that he gives us strength for one day. I thought, *Somehow, I'll make it through the day.*
>
> As I looked out over our town and saw the beautiful steepled fairytale homes with flower-filled window boxes, white picket fences, and clean-swept sidewalks, I realized that behind this perfect facade were thousands of Europeans struggling with the aftermath of two World

Wars—broken marriages, depression, guilt, loneliness, and crushed hopes. I felt the Lord tell me, "Elizabeth, these women are suffering like you are today, and they want to give up. But their pain is different—it's emotional."

I no longer felt so alone in my pain. And suddenly I was filled with a desire to encourage those women. That morning, the vision for a Christian woman's magazine in Europe was born.

Almost a decade has passed since that day by the bridge. Today, *Lydia* is printed in three languages and reaches about one million readers. Its message is simple—hope and encouragement can be found through faith in Christ and his Word. When I receive letters from readers who say, "I didn't abort my baby, and I'm naming her Lydia after the magazine," or "Thank you—this magazine is my only friend," my heart is thrilled. It's been so healing for me.

Pain is still my companion—but it's no longer as overwhelming as it once was. When I searched God's Word for encouragement and comfort, I came upon Psalm 34:19: "Many are the afflictions of the righteous, but the Lord delivers him out of them all" (KJV). The words to the left of the comma describe my circumstances—and the words to the right give me real hope for the future. But I've learned that when we hang on to the comma in the middle—wait in faith on God's promise and offer our pain to him—it's never wasted.

Fear, Health, Perseverance, Suffering, Suicide
Ps. 34:19

Date used __________ Place ____________________

This article first appeared in *Today's Christian Woman* magazine, Jan/Feb 1995, published by Christianity Today, Inc., Carol Stream, Ill.

475

Alan Mairson wrote an article for *National Geographic* about beekeepers who raise and transport bees for a living. He told the story of Jeff and Christine Anderson and how their daughter overcame an allergy to bee stings.

To build up her immunity, doctors administered a series of injections to Rachel over a four-month period. But, in order to maintain immunity, she needed a shot or a bee sting every six weeks over several years.

So every six weeks Rachel's parents would go outside and catch a bee. Then, as Rachel recalls, "Mom would take hold of my arm and roll my sleeve up. Then my Dad would make the bee mad and stick it on me and count to ten before he took the stinger out. But it worked. Now when I accidentally get stung, it barely swells, it barely hurts."

In a world full of bees, a loving father must not shield his child from every sting. In fact for the child's own good the father must at times induce pain.

God the Father, Love of God, Temptation, Trials
Rom. 8:28; James 1:2–4; 1 Peter 1:5–9

Date used __________ Place ____________________

Pain 476

In his book *Broken in the Right Place,* Alan Nelson writes:

Somehow, pain, problems, and suffering do not fit into our concept of life and success.

My sons, with the help of their mom, have designated places for their belongings. Toys go in specific plastic tubs, clothes in the dresser and closet, and books in the book box. Even when the room is a mess, someone can quickly order it, primarily because everything has its place. But what do you do with an item which does not have an assigned spot? You stand in the middle of the room, holding it, perplexed, unsure of what to do with this foreign body. That is how most people handle their pain, discouragements and disillusionment. Their sense of direction halts. They stall as they search in vain for a place to put it, to make it fit into their orderly lives. . . .

Why in the world do bad things happen to good people? We can understand why they happen to bad people. . . . But somewhere we learn that good things should happen to good people, and of course, we're on the good people list. That's why we often do not deal well with obstacles and turmoil; we have no place to put them in our "good person" scheme of things.

Goodness, Suffering
2 Cor. 1:3–11; Phil. 1:29; Heb. 12:1–11

Date used __________ Place ____________________

Pain 477

In *Leadership* pastor and author Gordon MacDonald writes:

For the first time in my life, in my early thirties, I was experiencing physical pain, a spate of migraine headaches that came close to unbearable. I worried they were caused by a brain tumor and feared I would live with pain the rest of my life.

This may sound unbelievable, but I could almost set my calendar and watch to the onset of the migraines: They came during the month of May of every even-numbered year. They generally hit about one o'clock in the morning every other night for about three weeks, and then they stopped. I had four sequences of these.

I finally went to a headache specialist. "Ninety percent of my patients remind me of you," he said. "They are young men, heads of organizations or wanting to be heads of organizations. They're not at peace with themselves; they've got some people in their lives with whom they have unresolved relationships."

He had never met me and didn't know what I did for a living, but he described me perfectly. I knew exactly the unresolved relationships to which the doctor was referring. . . .

Down through history, some of the greatest moments of kingdom production have come during physical pain. . . . The question then becomes, "What does God want to teach me while I'm in the theater of pain?" Pain humbles us, forcing us to recognize our reliance on others and God. It reduces us to our true size.

It was during this dark moment that Gail and I, ten years into our marriage, first learned to pray together. It was one way I worked through my unresolved relationships. Over the next nine months, Gail and I pursued God together in prayer, in more than just a perfunctory way, and it changed our lives. I discovered the importance of saying to her, "I need you to pray for me," and that was something I had not done before. Years later, when Gail and I faced the blackest of my dark moments, the discipline of prayer we had learned during my physical pain was in place.

We don't know all that God is doing by allowing pain in our lives, but one good thing is certain: pain leads us to prayer.

Conflict, Marriage, Prayer, Relationships, Suffering, Trials, Weakness
Rom. 5:3–4; 2 Cor. 12:7–10; James 1:2–4

Date used __________ Place ____________________

Parenting 478

A recent Roper poll showed that parents may not be doing all they can to encourage their teens to remain sexually pure. Seventy-two percent of the teens who reported having sexual intercourse said they did it in the homes of their parents or their partner's parents. Six out of ten believe their parents know about their sexual behavior.

When parents say nothing about wrongdoing, in effect they condone wrongdoing.

Sex, Teenagers, Virginity
1 Thess. 4:3–8

Date used __________ Place ____________________

Parents 479

Michael Jordan's father, James Jordan, was murdered in the summer of 1993. Before that happened, Michael said this to columnist Bob Greene:

> My heroes are and were my parents. . . . It wasn't that the rest of the world would necessarily think that they were heroic. But they were the adults I saw constantly, and I admired what I saw.
>
> If you're lucky, you grow up in a house where you can learn what kind of person you should be from your parents. And on that count, I was very lucky. It may have been the luckiest thing that ever happened to me.

To Michael Jordan, good parents meant as much to him as his incomparable basketball skill.

Child Rearing, Example, Heroes
Eph. 6:4

Date used __________ Place ____________________

Joy Davidman in *Smoke on the Mountain,* writes:

Once there was a little old man. His hands trembled; when he ate he clattered the silverware distressingly, missed his mouth with the spoon as often as not, and dribbled a bit of his food on the tablecloth. Now he lived with his married son, having nowhere else to live, and his son's wife didn't like the arrangement.

"I can't have this," she said. "It interferes with my right to happiness." So she and her husband took the old man gently but firmly by the arm and led him to the corner of the kitchen. There they set him on a stool and gave him his food in an earthenware bowl. From then on he always ate in the corner, blinking at the table with wistful eyes.

One day his hands trembled rather more than usual, and the earthenware bowl fell and broke.

"If you are a pig," said the daughter-in-law, "you must eat out of a trough." So they made him a little wooden trough, and he got his meals in that.

These people had a four-year-old son of whom they were very fond. One evening the young man noticed his boy playing intently with some bits of wood and asked what he was doing.

"I'm making a trough," he said, smiling up for approval, "to feed you and Momma out of when I get big."

The man and his wife looked at each other for a while and didn't say anything. Then they cried a little. Then they went to the corner and took the old man by the arm and led him back to the table. They sat him in a comfortable chair and gave him his food on a plate, and from then on nobody ever scolded when he clattered or spilled or broke things.

One of Grimm's fairy tales, this anecdote has the crudity of the old, simple days. But perhaps crudity is what we need to illustrate the naked and crude point of the fifth commandment: honor your parents, lest your children dishonor you. Or, in other words, a society that destroys the family destroys itself.

Honor, Family

Date used __________ Place ____________________

In 1995 the Northwestern Wildcats football team had one of the most remarkable seasons in college football history. Prior to 1995 the Wildcats were the most notorious losers in the Big Ten, and for that matter in college football. They had set an NCAA record by losing thirty-four consecutive games between 1979 and 1982. They had not had a winning season in twenty-four years.

Then in 1995, under head coach Gary Barnett, the Wildcats finished the season 10–2, won the Big Ten Conference title, and went to the Rose Bowl ranked eighth in the nation.

Coach Gary Barnett earned all the credit he received, winning seventeen national coach-of-the-year awards.

In the spring of 1996 as the team prepared for the next season, Coach Barnett knew he had to fight the natural tendency to keep looking back on 1995. So he called a team meeting in the auditorium of the football center. In the *Chicago Tribune Magazine* Andrew Bagnato writes:

As the players found seats in the gently banked rows of plush chairs, Barnett mounted the stage and announced that he was going to hand out the awards that many of the Wildcats had earned in 1995. . . .

As Barnett called the players forward and handed them placards proclaiming their accomplishments, the 70-plus players in the room cheered and chanted their teammates' names. . . .

The players roared as Barnett waved the placard representing his 17 national coach-of-the-year awards. Then, as the applause subsided, Barnett walked to the side of the stage, stopping in front of a trash can marked "1995." He took an admiring glance at his placard, then dumped it in the can.

As silence descended on the auditorium, Barnett stepped to the side of the stage. . . . Then, one by one, the stars of the team dropped their placards on top of Barnett's. Soon, the trash can was overflowing with the laurels of the previous season.

Barnett had shouted a message to his assembled charges without uttering a word: What you did in 1995 was terrific, lads. But look at the calendar: it's 1996.

The only way to continue to achieve great things in the present and the future is to leave the past behind us.

Complacency, Discipleship, Future, Growth, Success
Phil. 3:7–16; Rev. 2:1–7; 3:14–22

Date used __________ Place ____________________

A common sight in America's Southwest desert is the century plant. It's unique. The century plant (*Agave Americana*) thrives in rocky, mountainous, desert sites. It has dramatic, splayed leaves that grow up to a foot wide. The plant can reach twelve feet in diameter.

But what makes the century plant unusual, as its name suggests, is its long reproduction cycle. For twenty or thirty years (no, not a literal one hundred years), the six-foot-tall plant stands the same height and puts out no flowers. Then one year, without warning, a new bud sprouts. The bud, which resembles a tree-trunk-size asparagus spear, shoots into the sky at a fantastic rate of seven inches per day and reaches an eventual height of twenty to forty feet. Then it crowns itself with several clumps of yellowish blossoms that last up to three weeks.

Like the century plant, many of the most glorious things that happen to us come only after a long wait.

Aging, Fruitfulness, Growth, Maturity
Gen. 21:1–7; Gal. 5:22–23; 6:9–10; Heb. 10:36

Date used __________ Place ____________________

Patience 483

In 1994 the British Broadcasting Corporation produced a radio program perfectly designed for the patience level of people in our fast-changing, fast-paced culture. The drama series, entitled "The Telephone Box," had three episodes. Each episode was one minute long. The entire story lasted three minutes.

Script writer Wally Daly said, "It is a real play and fulfills all the criteria, having a beginning, middle, and end."

All three episodes played on the same day, interspersed with music, because if there were a week between episodes, Daly explained, listeners would not remember what had happened.

Sometimes we want God to work in our lives at the same speed as "The Telephone Box." But God often works on a far different timetable.

Growth, Perseverance, Prayer, Sovereignty of God, Suffering, Time

Gal. 5:22–23; James 5:7–8

Date used __________ Place ____________________

According to a traditional Hebrew story, Abraham was sitting outside his tent one evening when he saw an old man, weary from age and journey, coming toward him. Abraham rushed out, greeted him, and then invited him into his tent. There he washed the old man's feet and gave him food and drink.

The old man immediately began eating without saying any prayer or blessing. So Abraham asked him, "Don't you worship God?"

The old traveler replied, "I worship fire only and reverence no other god."

When he heard this, Abraham became incensed, grabbed the old man by the shoulders, and threw him out of his tent into the cold night air.

When the old man had departed, God called to his friend Abraham and asked where the stranger was. Abraham replied, "I forced him out because he did not worship you."

God answered, "I have suffered him these eighty years although he dishonors me. Could you not endure him one night?"

Evangelism, Unbelievers

Date used __________ Place ____________________

Richard Dunagin writes:

At their school carnival our kids won four free goldfish (lucky us!), so out I went Saturday morning to find an aquarium.

The first few I priced ranged from forty to seventy dollars. Then I spotted it—right in the aisle: a discarded ten-gallon display tank, complete with gravel and filter—for a mere five bucks. Sold! Of course, it was nasty dirty, but the savings made the two hours of clean-up a breeze.

Those four new fish looked great in their new home, at least for the first day. But by Sunday one had died. Too bad, but three remained. Monday morning revealed a second casualty, and by Monday night a third goldfish had gone belly up.

We called in an expert member of our church who has a thirty-gallon tank. It didn't take him long to discover the problem: I had washed the tank with soap, an absolute no-no. My uninformed efforts had destroyed the very lives I was trying to protect.

Sometimes in our zeal to clean up our own lives or the lives of others, we unfortunately use "killer soaps"—condemnation, criticism, nagging, fits of temper. We think we're doing right, but our harsh, self-righteous treatment is more than others can bear.

Self-Righteousness, Criticism

Date used __________ Place ____________________

Some years ago a speedboat driver who had survived a racing accident described what had happened. He said he had been at near top speeds when his boat veered slightly and hit a wave at a dangerous angle. The combined force of his speed and the size and angle of the wave sent the boat spinning crazily into the air. He was thrown from his seat and propelled deeply into the water—so deep, in fact, that he had no idea which direction the surface was. He had to remain calm and wait for the buoyancy of his life vest to begin pulling him up. Once he discovered which way was up, he could swim for the surface.

Sometimes we find ourselves surrounded by confusing options, too deeply immersed in our problems to know which way is up. When this happens, we too can remain calm, waiting for God's gentle tug to pull us in the proper direction. Our "life vest" may be other Christians, Scripture, or some other leading from the Holy Spirit, but the key is recognizing our dependency upon God and trusting him.

Direction, God's Will

Date used __________ Place ____________________

Peacemakers 487

One of the indelible images from the Vietnam War is the photograph of a nine-year-old girl named Phan Thi Kim Phuc. During a battle between North and South Vietnamese troops, an American commander ordered South Vietnamese aircraft to drop napalm bombs on her tiny village. Two of her brothers were killed, and she was burned badly. Wearing no clothes, she fled up the road toward the cameraman. Because of the pain her arms are held out sideways, and her mouth is open in a cry of agony.

According to Elaine Sciolino in the *New York Times,* Ms. Kim Phuc suffered third-degree burns over 50 percent of her body, but she lived. She endured fourteen months of painful rehabilitation and scores of skin grafts. "It was so painful to have her wounds washed and dressed that she lost consciousness whenever she was touched."

Since then she has married, emigrated to Canada, and become a Christian who hopes someday to attend Bible college. Her burned skin lost sweat and oil glands, and she is still in much pain. Scars stretch up her arms to her chest and back. But despite her past and present suffering, in 1996 she accepted an invitation from several Vietnam veterans groups to join in Veterans Day ceremonies held at the Vietnam Veterans Memorial, where she laid a wreath and spoke words of forgiveness.

"I have suffered a lot from both physical and emotional pain," she told the audience of several thousand people, who greeted her with two standing ovations. "Sometimes I could not breathe. But God saved my life and gave me faith and hope. Even if I could talk face to face with the pilot who dropped the bombs, I would tell him, 'We cannot change history, but we should try to do good things for the present and for the future to promote peace.'"

Those who suffer the most can be the greatest peacemakers.

Forgiveness, Mercy, Suffering
Matt. 5:9; 18:21–35; Acts 7:54–60

Date used __________ Place ____________________

Perfection 488

According to the Associated Press, in 1997 the U.S. Treasury Department planned to put into circulation a new-look fifty-dollar bill with special features designed to thwart counterfeiters.

After printing an estimated thirty million copies of the new bills at a cost of $1.44 million, however, it was discovered that the bills had a flaw. There were small breaks in the fine concentric lines around the photo of Ulysses S. Grant.

That presented a dilemma to the Treasury Department. In the first year a new bill goes into circulation it is especially important that it have no flaws because persons unfamiliar with the bills may assume the defective bills are counterfeit.

Larry Felix, a spokesman for the Treasury's Bureau of Engraving and Printing, said, "Clearly if you're going to introduce notes for the first time, you're going to make sure the notes are as flawless as possible."

And so, the bills in question were put under seal at Federal Reserve district banks pending a decision whether to destroy them.

The more valuable something is, the more necessary that it be flawless. Human beings are infinitely more valuable than a fifty-dollar bill. Since we will live forever, since we are moral beings in a moral universe, since we are created in the image of a perfect and absolutely righteous God, God's standard for humanity can be nothing less than perfection.

Character, Flaws, Integrity, Judgment, Righteousness, Sin
Matt. 5:48; 12:36–37; Rom. 3:10–12, 23; 14:10–12

Date used __________ Place ____________________

Persecution 489

In 1995 Steve Kafka was voted into the Illinois High School gymnastics coaches Hall of Fame. Kafka coached the Glenbard East High School gymnastics team in Glen Ellyn to second-place finishes in 1987, 1988, and 1990. Then in 1995, after rebuilding a team at a different school, he took second one more time and finally in 1996 won the state championship.

To accomplish that, his gymnasts had to hit their routines in the state championship competition, when pressure is high and it's easy to fall. Actually the first time Kafka's team qualified for state, several Glenbard East gymnasts fell off the side horse, high bar, and parallel bars, and the team finished down in the standings.

But then coach Kafka got an idea. At the end of practice each day, he began conducting a practice meet, and he did two things to intentionally raise the pressure on the gymnasts. First, if anyone missed a routine, everyone had to do push-ups. Second, Kafka told the team to try and rattle each performer. And so while one gymnast performed on the side horse, his teammates would yell, threaten bodily harm, tell jokes, even throw rolled up socks at him.

"My gymnasts started to feel that competing in real meets was a breeze compared to practice," says Kafka. In the end, even a state championship—with TV cameras rolling and critical judges watching every move—was easy. Fighting through daily opposition taught Kafka's gymnasts focus and determination.

In the same way, persecution can lead true followers of Christ to a greater focus on Christ and a stronger determination to do his will without fail.

Character, Determination, Focus, Hardships
John 15:20; Heb. 12:1–13

Date used __________ Place ____________________

490

According to Michael Lewis in the *New York Times Magazine,* Senator John McCain of Arizona is much more than a politician. First and foremost he is a Vietnam War hero. As a Navy pilot, he was shot down by a North Vietnamese missile on October 26, 1967. Lewis writes:

> For nine days, McCain received no treatment for the injuries he sustained when he parachuted into a North Vietnamese mob: two broken arms, a shattered knee, a shattered shoulder and bayonet wounds in his ankle and his groin. He survived in captivity for the next five and a half years under constant, exquisite torture. . . . But McCain's capacity to suffer was the least of what the experience revealed about him. The truly astonishing part of the story . . . is that he did it . . . voluntarily.
>
> McCain belongs to a distinguished military family; his father and grandfather were both admirals, and his father was commanding the bombing of Hanoi at the time McCain's Navy fighter was shot down. The North Vietnamese planned for their famous P.O.W. to violate United States military policy, which dictated that prisoners return in the order they had arrived. His early release might demoralize American troops, they figured. Except that he wouldn't go along. For five and a half years, they tortured McCain. For five and a half years, he refused to go home.
>
> He had no choice in the matter, he later explained. To accept early release would have dishonored not only himself but his family. You just didn't do that.

There are times when the only way to escape suffering is unworthy of who you are. Those who are persecuted for their faith in Christ may face that choice. The only path worthy of a Christian is at all costs to stand with Christ for all to see.

Courage, Endurance, Hardship, Honor, Perseverance, Suffering

Matt. 13:21; John 15:18–16:4; Acts 7:54–60; 2 Cor. 11:16–33; Phil. 1:28–30; 2 Tim. 2:3; 3:12; Heb. 10:33; Rev. 2:10

Date used __________ Place ____________________

Persecution 491

In *The Calling* Brother Andrew writes:

We were planning to smuggle one million Bibles into China. Wanting to be sure that the believers in the country realized the immensity of the task and were willing to accept the risks, we sent Joseph, a Chinese team member, to meet with five key house-church leaders.

"Do you know how much space one million Bibles take up?" Joseph asked.

"We have already prepared storage places," they replied.

"Do you know what could happen to you," Joseph continued, "if you were caught with even a portion of these Bibles?"

"Joseph, all five of us have been in prison for the Lord," they replied. "All together, we've spent seventy-two years in jail for Jesus. We are willing to die if it means that a million brothers and sisters can have a copy of God's word."

With tears in his eyes, Joseph folded up his long list of questions and put it away.

Whether it is risking our life or risking our reputation, serving the gospel requires courage. God never said his work was safe.

Courage, Dedication, Evangelism, Gospel, Ministry, Pleasing People, Reputation, Sacrifice, Scripture
Rom. 1:16; Phil. 1:20; Heb. 12:1–4

Date used __________ Place ____________________

Victor Villasenor is a Hispanic writer who is a story in himself.

Raised in Southern California, says writer Jorge Casuso, Victor Villasenor was illiterate because of dyslexia until adulthood. Then a woman in Mexico taught him to read. Ironically, he decided he wanted to become a great writer and he asked God to help him.

While he worked for ten years as a laborer, digging ditches and cleaning houses, his mind was free to think and dream up characters and plots. At home he read voraciously, devouring more than five thousand books. He memorized favorite openings and analyzed paragraphs and sentences, taking them apart to see how they worked. And most important, he started writing. He wrote nine novels, sixty-five short stories, and ten plays. He sent them all to publishers. All were rejected. One publisher sent him a rejection letter that simply said, "You're kidding."

Incredibly he was encouraged by that. It meant that at least the publisher had read his submission. Then in 1972 after 260 rejections, Villasenor sold his first novel, which was called *Macho*. He then published a nonfiction work called *Jury: People vs. Juan Corona,* an award-winning screenplay called *Ballad of Gregorio Cortez,* and, the crowning work of his life, a two-part saga of his family called *Rain of Gold* that took twelve years to write.

With a lot of hard work on Villasenor's part, God answered his prayer.

Diligence, Failure, Overcomers, Work
Heb. 10:36

Date used ________ Place ________________

Perseverance 493

On opening day of the 1954 baseball season, the Milwaukee Braves visited the Cincinnati Reds. Two rookies began their major league careers with that game. The Reds won 9-8 as Jim Greengrass hit four doubles in his first big-league game. A sensational debut for a young player with a made-for-baseball name!

The rookie starting in left field for the Braves went 0 for 5. Not a very auspicious start for one Henry Aaron.

Failure, Spiritual Gifts

Date used __________ Place ____________________

Perseverance 494

During a Monday night football game between the Chicago Bears and the New York Giants, one of the announcers observed that Walter Payton, the Bears' running back, had accumulated over nine miles in career rushing yardage. The other announcer remarked, "Yeah, and that's with someone knocking him down every 4.6 yards!"

Walter Payton, the most successful running back ever, knows that everyone—even the best—gets knocked down. The key to success is to get up and run again just as hard.

Obstacles, Success

Date used __________ Place ____________________

Perseverance 495

John Killinger retells this story from *Atlantic Monthly* about the days of the great western cattle ranches:

A little burro sometimes would be harnessed to a wild steed. Bucking and raging, convulsing like drunken sailors, the two would be turned loose like Laurel and Hardy to proceed out onto the desert range. They could be seen disappearing over the horizon, the great steed dragging that little burro along and throwing him about like a bag of cream puffs. They might be gone for days, but eventually they would come back. The little burro would be seen first, trotting back across the horizon, leading the submissive steed in tow. Somewhere out there on the rim of the world, that steed would become exhausted from trying to get rid of the burro, and in that moment, the burro would take mastery and become the leader.

And that's the way it is with the kingdom and its heroes, isn't it? The battle goes to the determined, not to the outraged; to the committed, not to those who are merely dramatic.

Determination, Emotions

Date used __________ Place ____________________

On March 6, 1987, Eamon Coughlan, the Irish world record holder at 1500 meters, was running in a qualifying heat at the World Indoor Track Championships in Indianapolis. With two and a half laps left, he was tripped. He fell, but he got up and with great effort managed to catch the leaders. With only 20 yards left in the race, he was in third place—good enough to qualify for the finals.

He looked over his shoulder to the inside, and, seeing no one, he let up. But another runner, charging hard on the outside, passed Coughlan a yard before the finish, thus eliminating him from the finals. Coughlan's great comeback effort was rendered worthless by taking his eyes off the finish line.

It's tempting to let up when the sights around us look favorable. But we finish well in the Christian race only when we fix our eyes on the goal: Jesus Christ.

Focus, Zeal

Date used __________ Place ____________________

Perseverance 497

Even as a young amateur golfer Tiger Woods was known for mental toughness. In the *New York Times* Larry Dorman tells where some of that toughness came from:

> His father and mentor, Earl Woods, traces it to an incident that occurred in 1992 when Tiger was 16 and playing in the Junior Orange Bowl Tournament at Miami. The young man was, as Earl recalls it, "a little full of himself" and when things started going badly for him, he began to pout. Then he went into the tank, and stopped trying.
>
> Earl, a former Green Beret, chewed his son out. "I asked him who he thought he was," the elder Wood said. "I told him golf owed him nothing and that he had better not ever quit again." The way Earl remembers it, Tiger never said a word. And he has never quit again.

The best things in life don't come served on a platter to those who think they deserve it. They come to those who know they must persevere no matter who they are and no matter what happens.

Child Rearing, Expectations, Fathers, Persistence, Quitting, Self-Pity

Ps. 27:14; 1 Cor. 15:58; Gal. 6:9–10; Heb. 10:36

Date used __________ Place ____________________

Even the most talented people may not get it right the first time.

In a 1995 interview ex-Beatle Paul McCartney said he once wrote a song with the first line "Scrambled eggs, oh my baby how I love your legs."

Have you ever heard that song?

Not likely. McCartney tossed those words and wrote, "Yesterday, all my troubles seemed so far away."

Since then "Yesterday" has played on the radio more than six million times, more than any other record in history. "Yesterday" also happens to be McCartney's favorite song.

The difference between failure and success—between "Scrambled Eggs" and "Yesterday"—is persistence.

Ministry, Perseverance, Success, Writing
Acts 13:13; 1 Cor. 15:58; Gal. 6:9–10; Heb. 10:36

Date used __________ Place ____________________

Perspective 499

In 1984, 1988, and 1992 American speed skater Dan Jansen suffered a series of disappointments in his attempts to win Olympic gold. How did he keep coming back time and time again? He says he learned to keep things in perspective. In *Full Circle,* Jansen writes:

> When I was nine years old, I was competing at the youth national championships in Minnesota. I was in good position to win my first national title when, coming around a turn, I tripped on a rubber hose they had set up as a lane marker. That slip cost me the title by one point.
>
> I started crying. I was crying as Mom took off my skates and during the award ceremonies. I was still crying when we got in the car and when we pulled into our driveway six hours later.
>
> My father hadn't spoken a word to me all the way home. But as we got out of the car, he said quietly, "You know, Dan, there's more to life than skating around in a circle."

As bitter as any loss may be, when we know the Lord there is always much more to life than any disappointment we are now facing.

Disappointments, Loss, Priorities, Sports
Rom. 8:18; Phil. 3:7–11

Date used __________ Place ____________________

Perspective 500

Fraiser of Lisuland in northern Burma translated the Scriptures into the Lisu language and then left a young fellow with the task of teaching the people to read.

When he returned six months later, he found three students and the teacher seated around a table, with the Scriptures opened in front of the teacher. When the students each read, they left the Bible where it was. The man on the left read it sideways, the man on the right read it sideways but from the other side, and the man across from the teacher read it upside down. Since they always occupied the same chairs, that's how each had learned to read, and that's how each thought the language was written.

We, too, can be like that. When we learn something from only one perspective, we may think it's the only perspective. Sometimes it's good to change seats to assume a different perspective on the same truth.

Conviction, Truth

Date used __________ Place ____________________

Plans 501

On October 28, 1993, the U.S. Space Command watched as a two-ton chunk of Chinese satellite began to reenter the earth's atmosphere. The Space Command tracks more than seven thousand man-made objects orbiting near Earth, and according to their calculations this satellite would drop into the Pacific Ocean five hundred miles west of Baja, California. When it plunged into the atmosphere, however, it skipped south and took an unexpected detour, landing in the Pacific Ocean west of Peru.

Major Bob Butt explained that space debris traveling seventeen thousand miles per hour takes unpredictable twists and turns when it breaks into the thickening atmosphere. It's like dropping a penny into water. "Sometimes it goes straight down, and sometimes it turns end over end and changes direction."

This wasn't the first time the Chinese satellite had thwarted the predictions of scientists. It was launched October 8, 1993, carrying into space microgravity experiments. Ten days after launch, a capsule containing the experiments was to have separated and parachuted to earth for retrieval. But on October 18 when Chinese scientists radioed the reentry commands, the satellite went out of control, split in two, and stayed in orbit. The Chinese space agency predicted it would remain in orbit six more months. In fact it stayed in orbit only ten more days, coming down a few hours earlier than even the U.S. Space Agency thought.

Our lives are a lot like that Chinese satellite: unpredictable, defying our best laid plans, filled with surprises. That's why God tells us to approach our planning and praying with great humility.

God's Will, Humility, Prayer, Submission, Surprise
Prov. 16:9; 19:21; James 4:13–17

Date used __________ Place ____________________

According to *U.S. News and World Report,* medical studies have suggested that all cholesterol is not the same. There is "good cholesterol" and "bad cholesterol."

Good cholesterol consists of high-density lipoproteins, or HDLs. Bad cholesterol consists of low-density lipoproteins, or LDLs.

Bad cholesterol clogs arteries and leads to heart attacks.

"Good cholesterol," writes Rita Rubin, "seems to carry cholesterol out of the coronary-artery walls, thus preventing blockages. Studies show the rate of coronary heart disease falls as HDL levels rise."

Just as all cholesterol is not the same, the Bible says all pleasure is not the same. There is good pleasure and bad pleasure. Good pleasure is healthful, self-controlled, and obedient to God's commands. Bad pleasure is self-indulgent, addictive, and disobedient to God's commands.

Asceticism, Thanksgiving

Ps. 16:11; 103:5; 1 Tim. 4:3–5; 2 Tim. 3:4; Titus 3:3

Date used ________ Place ________________

People will go to amazing lengths to get "high." In 1994, says writer Gene Sloan in *USA Today,* undercover agents for the Arizona Department of Fish and Game arrested several people for toad licking—that's right, toad licking.

They had in their possession the Colorado River toad *(Bufo alvarius).* This toad, which is found from the Mexican border to the Grand Canyon, deters predators by secreting a milky white substance that includes a powerful drug classified as psychoactive under Arizona law. Drug aficionados get high by either licking the toads directly or drying the secretion and then smoking it.

One Arizona official warned that the drug is "poisonous and dangerous."

An addiction to pleasure is a sinful condition that can lead a person to do any number of vile—even deadly—things.

Addictions, Chemical Dependency, Prostitution
2 Tim. 3:4; Titus 3:3; 2 Peter 2:13

Date used __________ Place ____________________

Dr. George Sweeting wrote in Special Sermons for Special Days:

Several years ago our family visited Niagara Falls. It was spring, and ice was rushing down the river. As I viewed the large blocks of ice flowing toward the falls, I could see that there were carcasses of dead fish embedded in the ice. Gulls by the score were riding down the river feeding on the fish. As they came to the brink of the falls, their wings would go out, and they would escape from the falls.

I watched one gull which seemed to delay and wondered when it would leave. It was engrossed in the carcass of a fish, and when it finally came to the brink of the falls, out went its powerful wings. The bird flapped and flapped and even lifted the ice out of the water, and I thought it would escape. But it had delayed too long so that its claws had frozen into the ice. The weight of the ice was too great, and the gull plunged into the abyss.

The finest attractions of this world become deadly when we become overly attached to them. They may take us to our destruction if we cannot give them up. And as Sweeting observed, "Oh, the danger of delay!"

Repentance, Sin

Date used __________ Place ____________________

The Poor 505

On April 1, 1988, Dr. Gary Hamlin, an osteopath in Joplin, Missouri, opened a new medical practice where any patient who needed medical care received it. No one was turned over to a collection agency for non-payment. Medicare and Medicaid assignments were welcomed. Thirty-five to forty-five patients came to his clinic each day. To pay his overhead, Dr. Hamlin had to moonlight every other weekend in a local hospital.

In *The Christian Reader,* Dr. Hamlin explained what caused him to open such a practice.

"Luke 14:14 introduced me to the founding principle for the clinic. It was God's personal promise to me. 'And thou shalt be blessed; for they cannot recompense thee: for thou shalt be recompensed at the resurrection of the just.'"

Blessing, Giving
Luke 14:12–14

Date used ________ Place ________________

506

In *Christianity Today,* Philip Yancey writes about a time when the church he attended in Chicago faced something of a crisis.

> The pastor had left, attendance was flagging, a community outreach program now seemed threatened. The leadership suggested an all-night vigil of prayer.
>
> Several people raised questions. Was it safe, given our inner-city neighborhood? Should we hire guards or escorts for the parking lot? What if no one showed up? At length we discussed the logistics and the "practicality" of such an event. Nevertheless, the night of prayer was scheduled.
>
> To my surprise, the poorest members of the congregation, a group of senior citizens from a housing project, were the ones who responded most enthusiastically to the prayer vigil. I could not help wondering how many of their prayers had gone unanswered over the years—they lived in the projects, after all, amid crime, poverty, and suffering—yet they showed a childlike trust in the power of prayer. "How long do you want to stay—an hour or two?" we asked. "Oh, we'll stay all night," they replied.
>
> One black woman in her nineties, who walks with a cane and can barely see, explained . . . "You see, they's lots of things we can't do in this church. We ain't so educated, and we ain't got as much energy as some of you younger folks. But we can pray. We got time, and we got faith. Some of us don't sleep much anyway. We can pray all night if needs be."
>
> And so they did. Meanwhile, a bunch of yuppies in a downtown church learned anew a lesson of faith from the Gospels: Faith appears where least expected and falters where it should be thriving.

Faith, Prayer
Luke 6:20–26; 10:21; James 2:5

Date used __________ Place ____________________

Who wouldn't like to own a Jaguar XJS convertible? In many people's eyes, a snazzy Jaguar is something they dream for a lifetime about getting and for which they are willing to pay the steep price tag of fifty-six thousand dollars.

Marvin Jacobs, a San Francisco lawyer, bought his dream Jaguar, only to find that it didn't exactly make his life complete. *USA Today* reported in an article on state "lemon laws" that over the next three-and-a-half years Jacobs had to take his car to the shop a grand total of twenty-six times. Once the car even stalled on the Golden Gate Bridge during rush hour, causing a five-mile backup. When California's lemon law finally forced Jaguar to buy back the sour car, Jacobs said unloading it was "the best thing that ever happened to me in my entire adult life."

Material possessions—the things we so often dream of buying—can carry a much higher price tag than we anticipate.

Coveting, Materialism
Luke 12:15

Date used __________ Place ______________________

Leslie Hindman has served as president of the Midwest's premier auction firm. Each year she auctioned millions of dollars worth of decorative arts and home furnishings from the estates of the wealthy. This is a world of Van Gogh paintings and black lacquered desks that sell for tens of thousands of dollars. Nevertheless, her career has made material things one of the least of her priorities.

"I see people fighting about their stuff all the time," she says. "You realize life is not about possessions."

"A few experiences early in Hindman's career helped to cinch her disdain for material things," says writer Adrienne Fawcett in the *Chicago Tribune*. "Once, she was hired to hold an auction in the modest home of a suburban family whose mother recently had died. As Hindman held court, the siblings bid against each other for their mother's humble possessions, scarcely exchanging a word."

Another experience she will never get over was finding "a lifetime of diaries in the apartment of an elderly Oak Park woman who saved everything but had no children to whom to leave her things. Hindman tried to donate the diaries to historical societies, but none wanted them. . . . She saved them for a couple of years but finally threw them out. 'So,' she says emphatically, 'I save absolutely nothing.'"

After all is said and done, the true value of possessions is clearly seen.

Covetousness, Greed, Materialism, Things

Exod. 20:17; Matt. 19:16–30; Luke 12:15; James 5:1–6

Date used __________ Place ____________________

Power 509

On Wednesday, October 11, 1994, NASA's *Magellan* space explorer fell silent. The *Magellan* had circled Venus more than fifteen thousand times since arriving at the planet in 1990, but on this day NASA scientists intentionally changed the satellite's course and sent it veering into the planet where it burned to a crisp in the atmosphere.

Why would NASA send the *Magellan*—which cost nine hundred million dollars—plummeting into the planet? Because the *Magellan* was virtually out of power. One final experiment had drained its batteries to the point where it could no longer transmit data.

Without power, even the highest technology is worthless. Without the power of God, even the most committed Christian can bear no fruit.

Death, Endurance, Fruitfulness, Holy Spirit, Ministry
Zech. 4:6; John 15:1–8; Acts 1:8

Date used __________ Place ____________________

One New Year's Day, in the Tournament of Roses parade, a beautiful float suddenly sputtered and quit. It was out of gas. The whole parade was held up until someone could get a can of gas.

The amusing thing was this float represented the Standard Oil Company. With its vast oil resources, its truck was out of gas.

Often, Christians neglect their spiritual maintenance, and though they are "clothed with power" (Luke 24:49) find themselves out of gas.

Holy Spirit, Devotional Life

Date used __________ Place ____________________

511

In a seminary missions class, Herbert Jackson told how, as a new missionary, he was assigned a car that would not start without a push.

After pondering his problem, he devised a plan. He went to the school near his home, got permission to take some children out of class, and had them push his car off. As he made his rounds, he would either park on a hill or leave his car running. He used this ingenious procedure for two years.

Ill health forced the Jackson family to leave, and a new missionary came to that station. When Jackson proudly began to explain his arrangement for getting the car started, the new man began looking under the hood. Before the explanation was complete, the new missionary interrupted, "Why Dr. Jackson, I believe the only trouble is this loose cable." He gave the cable a twist, stepped into the car, pushed the switch, and to Jackson's astonishment, the engine roared to life.

For two years needless trouble had become routine. The power was there all the time. Only a loose connection kept Jackson from putting the power to work.

J. B. Phillips paraphrases Ephesians 1:19–20, "How tremendous is the power available to us who believe in God." When we make firm our connection with God, his life and power flow through us.

Prayer, Self-Reliance

Date used __________ Place ____________________

According to Eric Ferkenhoff in the *Chicago Tribune,* on Father's Day 1997 Ricardo Enamorado set out on a jet ski from Chicago's Wilson Avenue boat ramp and headed north along the shoreline of Lake Michigan. After traveling several miles north, at about 3 P.M. he turned around to head back south when the engine on the jet ski suddenly quit. Unable to restart it, he floated along nonchalantly, expecting help to come quickly on the busy waters off Chicago. Gradually, though, the wind and waves pushed Enamorado farther and farther from shore, and help did not come. By dusk he was frantic. Dressed only in cutoffs, tennis shoes, and a life preserver, he spent the night on the chilly waters of the lake.

The next day Coast Guard helicopters and a Chicago fire department chopper equipped with special radar began searching for the lost man. By the end of the day they still had not found him, and Enamorado, hungry and sunburned, spent another night on the dark waters of Lake Michigan.

Finally the next morning one of the search-and-rescue teams spotted a flash of light. Enamorado was signaling in the search team's direction with a mirror. The nearly two-day ordeal was over at last.

A loss of power can be more dangerous than we realize.

Goals, Holy Spirit, Motivation, Purpose, Zeal
Ezek. 37:1–14; Acts 1:4–8; Rom. 12:11;
Eph. 5:18; 6:10–18; 2 Tim. 1:7; 3:5

Date used __________ Place ____________________

Power of God 513

In *Who Needs God,* Harold Kushner writes:

The next time you go to the zoo, notice where the lines are longest and people take the most time in front of the cage. We tend to walk briskly past the deer and the antelope, with only a passing glance at their graceful beauty. If we have children, we may pause to enjoy the antics of the seals and the monkeys. But we find ourselves irresistibly drawn to the lions, the tigers, the elephants, the gorillas.

Why? I suspect that without realizing or understanding it, we are strangely reassured at seeing creatures bigger or stronger than ourselves. It gives us the message, at once humbling and comforting, that we are not the ultimate power.

Our souls are so starved for that sense of awe, that encounter with grandeur which helps to remind us of our real place in the universe, that if we can't get it in church, we will search for it and find it someplace else.

Awe, Creation, Pentecost, Reverence
Ps. 19:1–6; Rom. 1:18–23; 11:34–36; 1 Cor. 2:1–5

Date used __________ Place ____________________

Praise to God 514

In the *Pentecostal Evangel,* J. K. Gressett writes about a man named Samuel S. Scull who settled on a farm in the Arizona desert with his wife and children.

> One night a fierce desert storm struck with rain, hail, and high wind. At daybreak, feeling sick and fearing what he might find, Samuel went to survey their loss.
>
> The hail had beaten the garden and truck patch into the ground; the house was partially unroofed; the henhouse had blown away, and dead chickens were scattered about. Destruction and devastation were everywhere.
>
> While standing dazed, evaluating the mess and wondering about the future, he heard a stirring in the lumber pile that was the remains of the henhouse. A rooster was climbing up through the debris, and he didn't stop climbing until he had mounted the highest board in the pile. That old rooster was dripping wet, and most of his feathers were blown away. But as the sun came over the eastern horizon, he flapped his bony wings and proudly crowed.

That old, wet, bare rooster could still crow when he saw the morning sun. And like that rooster, our world may be falling apart, we may have lost everything, but if we trust in God, we'll be able to see the light of God's goodness, pick ourselves out of the rubble, and sing the Lord's praise.

Crisis, Perseverance, Thanksgiving, Trials
Acts 16:22–25; 1 Thess. 5:16–18

Date used __________ Place ____________________

Prayer 515

In *Contemporary Christian Music,* John Fischer writes:

I have a bad habit. When my children tell me about something they've learned for the first time, I often act as if I knew that. Even worse, sometimes I tell them how the same thing happened to me years ago.

When my wife hears something "new" from the kids, her mouth drops open and her eyes widen. It's as if she has never heard this kind of thing before. The kids' faces brighten, and they feel as if they have actually enlightened their mother.

I used to think my wife was just acting and sooner or later the kids would find out and feel lied to. Then I realized it isn't an act at all. Though she may already have experienced what they are trying to tell her, she's never experienced it through them. Their personal "revelations" are entirely new.

It's the same with God. As all-knowing and sovereign as he is, I'm sure he's still eager to hear our prayers because he has never heard it quite the way we say it. We are all unique. We have our own signature attached to all we do and say. Our lives, our experiences, and our faith expressed to him are never old.

God the Father, Mothers, Uniqueness
Matt. 6:8; 1 Peter 3:12

Date used __________ Place ____________________

Hyatt Moore of the Wycliffe Bible Translators writes:

On November 14, 1983, two American students named David and Ray teamed up to pray for the 40,000 Tira people in Africa. The large group had no Bible in their native tongue.

Two-and-a-half years later, other Christians, Jerry and Jan, joined them in praying daily for the Tira. Then, in March 1990, Jane and Marjeanne wrote to the Bibleless Peoples Prayer Project of Wycliffe Bible Translators, asking for the name of a Bibleless people to pray for. They too began praying. . . .

In August 1990, we heard that Avajani, a young Tira man, was beginning to translate the Bible. Great news! We wrote, telling him of those praying and how he was an answer to their prayers.

"I'm grateful," Avajani wrote back. "I have never known that there are teams praying for the Tira people. It is wonderful news to me. The same year and month when David and Ray started praying, I got saved. When Jerry and Jan began praying, I was accepted for theological studies . . . and now I have finished. Jane and Marjeanne can praise the Lord with me, too! In March 1990, a miracle happened. I met a man (a Wycliffe translator) who was able to arrange for me to study biblical translation principles and linguistics.

"God did another miracle. Many young Tira have become Christians."

Today, seven years after David and Ray began praying in faith, the Bible is being translated for 40,000 new readers.

Although we don't always see the effect of our prayers at the time, God hears and answers.

Bible, Faith, Missions
Mark 11:22–24; Heb. 11:1; 1 John 5:14–15

Date used __________ Place ____________________

Used by permission of *The Christian Reader.*

Prayer 517

Bill Gates, who is chief executive at Microsoft, is hooked up to the international computer network called Internet. Subscribers to the Internet can send through their computers electronic mail (called e-mail) to other users of the Internet. Bill Gates had an Internet address just like everyone. But then the *New Yorker* magazine published his Internet address. Anyone could send the computer genius a letter. In no time Bill Gates was swamped with five thousand messages. It was more than any human could handle. So Gates armed his computer with software that filters through his e-mail, allowing important messages through and sending other letters to electronic oblivion.

People are limited. They can handle only so much communication and offer only so much help.

God, on the other hand, never tires of s-mail (spirit mail). His ear is always open to our prayers. And he has unlimited capacity to help.

Compassion of God, Help, Trust
Matt. 7:7–11; 1 Peter 5:7

Date used __________ Place ____________________

In his sermon "The Disciple's Prayer," Haddon Robinson recalls:

When our children were small, we played a game. I'd take some coins in my fist. They'd sit on my lap and work to get my fingers open. According to the international rules of finger opening, once the finger was open, it couldn't be closed again. They would work at it, until they got the pennies in my hand. They would jump down and run away, filled with glee and delight. Just kids. Just a game.

Sometimes when we come to God, we come for the pennies in his hand.

"Lord, I need a passing grade. Help me to study."

"Lord, I need a job."

"Lord, my mother is ill."

We reach for the pennies. When God grants the request, we push the hand away.

More important than the pennies in God's hand is the hand of God himself. That's what prayer is about.

Devotion, God the Father, Love for God
Mark 12:30; Luke 11:1–4

Date used __________ Place ____________________

519

They tell us the 911 emergency system is the state of the art. All you need do is dial those numbers, and you will almost instantly be connected to a dispatcher. In front of the dispatcher will be a read-out that lists your telephone number, your address, and the name by which that telephone number is listed at that address. Also listening in are the police, the fire department, and the paramedics.

A caller might not be able to say what the problem is. Or perhaps a woman's husband has just suffered a heart attack, and she is so out of control that all she can do is hysterically scream into the telephone. But the dispatcher doesn't need her to say anything. He knows where the call is coming from. Help is already on the way.

There come times in our lives when in our desperation and pain we dial 911 prayers. Sometimes we're hysterical. Sometimes we don't know the words to speak. But God hears. He knows our name and our circumstance. Help is on the way; God has already begun to bring the remedy.

Crisis, Help

Date used __________ Place ____________________

Prayer 520

In 1996 the Chicago Bulls basketball team won their fourth world championship behind their leader Michael Jordan. Jordan's contract ended after the season, however, and fans in Chicago were uneasy about whether the Bulls could re-sign Jordan for the upcoming year. Would owner Jerry Reinsdorf be willing to pay the huge salary that everyone knew Jordan would request for a new contract?

On July 12, 1996, the Chicago media discovered the answer. The Bulls announced they had agreed to pay some $30 million.

Bob Verdi reported later in the *Chicago Tribune* that months prior to the negotiations, when snow was on the ground, Reinsdorf had joked with Jordan and his agent that when the season ended, if the negotiations took more than five minutes, they would be wasting their time. At a dinner with Jordan less than two weeks before negotiations began, Reinsdorf repeated his intention to wrap things up quickly. And when the time came to talk numbers, Reinsdorf paid Jordan's asking price without a qualm.

"I could have tried to talk Michael down from what he asked," said Reinsdorf. "But why? . . . Michael is unique. I can afford what he's getting, he deserves what he's getting, and if it's not the best business transaction I ever made, so what? This wasn't a business deal in the truest sense, anyway. Call them psychic dollars. When we couldn't give Michael what he deserved because of the salary cap, I told him there would be a day. Well, the day has come."

Like Michael Jordan asking for a big salary, we often come to God with large requests, and we wonder how he will feel about it. Jesus taught us that God's response to our prayers is guided in large measure by how he feels about us. God's sons and daughters are more special to him than Michael Jordan is to the owner of the Chicago Bulls. For God, prayer isn't some spiritual negotiation; prayer is love. God is giving "heart dollars."

Faith, Favor from God, Love of God

Ps. 37:4; Matt. 7:7–11; Mark 1:40–42; Rom. 8:31–32; Eph. 3:20

Date used __________ Place ____________________

In "Total Eclipse" Annie Dillard writes:

> The Ring Nebula, in the constellation Lyra, looks, through binoculars, like a smoke ring. It is a star in the process of exploding. Light from its explosion first reached the earth in 1054; it was a supernova then, and so bright it shone in the daytime. Now it is not so bright, but it is still exploding. It expands at the rate of seventy million miles a day. It is interesting to look through binoculars at something expanding seventy million miles a day. It does not budge. Its apparent size does not increase. Photographs of the Ring Nebula taken fifteen years ago seem identical to photographs of it taken yesterday.

Huge happenings are not always visible to the naked eye—especially in the spiritual realm. How often it is that this nebula resembles the process of prayer. Sometimes we pray and pray and seemingly see no change in the situation. But that's only true from our perspective. If we could see from heaven's standpoint, we would know all that God is doing and intending to do in our lives. We would see God working in hearts in ways we cannot know. We would see God orchestrating circumstances that we know nothing about. We would see a galaxy of details being set in place for the moment when God brings the answer to fulfillment.

Appearances, Change, Patience, Perseverance, Perspective
Dan. 10:12–14; Luke 12:5–13; 18:1–8

Date used __________ Place ____________________

In May 1996, ValuJet Flight 592 crashed into the Florida Everglades, killing 110 passengers. To determine the cause of the crash, the National Transportation Safety Board needed the plane's black box. That would not be easy to find. The crash had scattered plane debris across a large area of swamp. Dozens of searchers descended on the scene to sift through muck and water as much as eight feet deep in an attempt to find the black box.

Navy experts tried using special technology that detected submerged metal, without success.

Holding a rope that kept them spaced three feet apart, other searchers systematically poked through every square foot of the crash area. After fourteen days, they had found nothing.

For workers the physical conditions were nigh unbearable. The Florida sun beat upon them, and temperatures hovered in the 90s. Diesel fuel and caustic hydraulic fluid from the wrecked plane floated in the water, forcing searchers to wear several layers of protective rubber and latex despite the heat and humidity. Fourteen days of that had left many searchers dehydrated, but they had to find the black box.

Sergeant Felix Jimenez, of the Metro-Dade police, was one of the searchers. For fourteen days he had prayed for the bereaved families and for the safety of his fellow workers, but on the fifteenth day as he took a break, suddenly he realized he had failed to pray for one important thing: that God would help them find the black box. So he asked God for direction, resumed the search, and when he stuck his pole into the water, he hit something metallic. He pulled the object out of the muck. It was the black box.

Jimenez writes in *Guideposts,* "At the end of the day . . . I thought of the many days we had spent searching for the recorder, how we must have tromped over it many times, and I wondered why its retrieval had taken so long. Amid the low rustle of saw grass and the call of a great white heron, I seemed to hear the response: 'Why did it take you so long to ask?'"

Dependence
James 4:2

Date used __________ Place ____________________

Prayer 523

James David Ford, chaplain of the United States House of Representatives since 1979, told the following story about prayer to *Leadership* journal:

In the spring of 1976 I sailed the Atlantic Ocean with a couple of friends. In a thirty-one-foot vessel, we sailed from Plymouth, England, to New York—5,992 miles. During the trip, we hit a real hurricane—some of the waves were thirty-five feet high—and frankly, I was scared. My father had said, "Don't go. You have five children. Wait till they're grown."

The hurricane went into its third day, and I thought of my father's words about the children. I thought, *Why am I out here? Was this thing that I thought was courage and adventure really just foolhardy?*

The skies were black, and clouds were scudding by. I wanted to pray for God to stop the storm, but I felt guilty 'cause I'd voluntarily gotten into this. I didn't have to go across the ocean. . . .

Finally I came up with a marvelous prayer, seven words: "O God, I have had enough. Amen."

Within half an hour of that simple prayer, the sky in the west lifted like a screen in a theater, and there was blue sky.

Was my prayer tied to the opening of the sky? I don't worry about it.

One thing is certain: simple, sincere prayers are sufficient.

Deliverance, Desperation, Fear, Help, Rescue, Sincerity, Storms, Trials
Ps. 107:23–32; Matt. 6:7–8; Mark 4:35–41; James 4:2; 5:13–18

Date used __________ Place ____________________

In *How I Pray,* Billy Graham writes:

I heard about a young president of a company who instructed his secretary not to disturb him because he had an important appointment. The chairman of the board came in and said, "I want to see Mr. Jones." The secretary answered, "I'm terribly sorry, he cannot be disturbed; he has an important appointment."

The chairman became very angry. He banged open the door and saw the president of his corporation on his knees in prayer. The chairman softly closed the door and asked the secretary, "Is this usual?" And she said, "Yes, he does that every morning." To which the chairman of the board responded, "No wonder I come to him for advice."

To those who pray, God promises wisdom and help.

Spiritual Disciplines, Wisdom
James 1:5

Date used __________ Place ____________________

525

In a recent issue of *GLASS Window,* a contributor recalls that several years ago, *The British Weekly* published this provocative letter:

Dear Sir:

It seems ministers feel their sermons are very important and spend a great deal of time preparing them. I have been attending church quite regularly for thirty years, and I have probably heard 3,000 of them. To my consternation, I discovered I cannot remember a single sermon. I wonder if a minister's time might be more profitably spent on something else?

For weeks a storm of editorial responses ensued . . . finally ended by this letter:

Dear Sir:

I have been married for thirty years. During that time I have eaten 32,850 meals—mostly my wife's cooking. Suddenly I have discovered I cannot remember the menu of a single meal. And yet . . . I have the distinct impression that without them, I would have starved to death long ago.

Scripture, Church Attendance

Date used __________ Place ____________________

Prejudice 526

Charles Colson, in *BreakPoint,* tells a story from the childhood of a biologist named Benno Muller-Hill.

One day the boy's teacher set up a telescope to show students a planet and its moons. One by one the students looked through the telescope and said, yes, they could see the planet. Finally one student said, "I can't see anything."

The teacher angrily told him to adjust the lenses. Still the student saw nothing. Finally the teacher himself leaned over and looked. When he stood up, he had a strange expression on his face. He glanced at the end of the telescope and saw that the lens cap was still on.

Just as most of the students saw what they were told to see, many people see the world in the way "the world, the flesh, and the devil" tell them to see it.

Children, Dogmatism
Rom. 12:2; 1 John 2:15–17

Date used __________ Place ______________________

Pride 527

Pride is the dandelion of the soul. Its root goes deep; only a little left behind sprouts again. Its seeds lodge in the tiniest encouraging cracks. And it flourishes in good soil: The danger of pride is that it feeds on goodness.

Goodness, Humility

Date used __________ Place ____________________

Priorities 528

Daniel Okrent was the founding father of rotisserie baseball leagues back in the winter of 1979 and 1980. Since then the pastime has exploded, with more than two million people involved every year.

The basic idea of rotisserie baseball is that participants act like owners and general managers of a baseball team. Each spring they "draft" players from Major League baseball for their rotisserie team. The player's actual Major League statistics—such as a batter's hits or a pitcher's wins—are used in the rotisserie league to determine which team has the best record. During the season, rotisserie owners continue to make team moves, trading players and adjusting their lineups to see who can have the players with the best statistics.

Most rotisserie owners say they spend between five and fifteen hours a week on the game, watching ball games and sports reports and reading newspapers. Some rotisserie owners get carried away. When Cleveland Indians relief ace Steve Olin was killed in a boating accident during spring training, fanatic rotisserie players called the Cleveland Indians to ask who would replace him in the lineup.

One San Diego doctor called in his player move while in surgery.

Rotisserie inventor Daniel Okrent said he once received a letter from a Maryland woman who blamed her divorce on her husband's love affair with the game. Some have dubbed the wives of the game's fanatics "rotisserie widows."

Whether it is rotisserie baseball, bowling, bridge, or the things of God, where your interest is, there will your time and thoughts be also.

Commitment, Interests, Time

Matt. 6:21; Luke 14:15–35; Phil. 2:20–21

Date used __________ Place ____________________

Priorities 529

Film maker Walt Disney was ruthless in cutting anything that got in the way of a story's pacing. Ward Kimball, one of the animators for *Snow White,* recalls working 240 days on a 4-1/2 minute sequence in which the dwarfs made soup for Snow White and almost destroyed the kitchen in the process. Disney thought it was funny, but he decided the scene stopped the flow of the picture, so out it went.

When the film of our lives is shown, will it be as great as it might be? A lot will depend on the multitude of 'good' things we need to eliminate to make way for the great things God wants to do through us.

Sacrifice, Excellence

Date used __________ Place ____________________

530

Ben Patterson writes in *The Grand Essentials:*

I have a theory about old age. . . . I believe that when life has whittled us down, when joints have failed and skin has wrinkled and capillaries have clogged and hardened, what is left of us will be what we were all along, in our essence.

Exhibit A is a distant uncle. . . . All his life he did nothing but find new ways to get rich. . . . He spent his senescence very comfortably, drooling and babbling constantly about the money he had made. . . . When life whittled him down to his essence, all there was left was raw greed. This is what he had cultivated in a thousand little ways over a lifetime.

Exhibit B is my wife's grandmother. . . . When she died in her mid-eighties, she had already been senile for several years. What did this lady talk about? The best example I can think of was when we asked her to pray before dinner. She would reach out and hold the hands of those sitting beside her, a broad, beatific smile would spread across her face, her dim eyes would fill with tears as she looked up to heaven, and her chin would quaver as she poured out her love to Jesus. That was Edna in a nutshell. She loved Jesus and she loved people. She couldn't remember our names, but she couldn't keep her hands from patting us lovingly whenever we got near her.

When life whittled her down to her essence, all there was left was love: love for God and love for people.

Love, Aging

Date used __________ Place ____________________

Priorities 531

It was a 99° September day in San Antonio, when a 10-month-old baby girl was accidently locked inside a parked car by her aunt. Frantically the mother and aunt ran around the auto in near hysteria, while a neighbor attempted to unlock the car with a clothes hanger. Soon the infant was turning purple and had foam on her mouth.

It had become a life-or-death situation when Fred Arriola, a wrecker driver, arrived on the scene. He grabbed a hammer and smashed the back window of the car to set her free.

Was he heralded a hero? "The lady was mad at me because I broke the window," Arriola reported. "I just thought, *What's more important—the baby or the window?*"

Most questions of priority are not between something important and something trivial; rather, between the important and the most important.

Choices, Wisdom

Date used __________ Place ____________________

Priorities 532

Bill Cowher took over as coach of the Pittsburgh Steelers in 1992. He quickly showed himself to be a man with a future. The Steelers made the playoffs each of his first several seasons as coach and went to Super Bowl XXX in 1996. One thing that made Cowher an effective coach was that he focused on his priorities. In *Sports Illustrated* Tim Crothers writes:

> After almost every game, every practice, Pittsburgh Steelers head coach Bill Cowher drives straight home to his wife, Kaye, and their three daughters. He doesn't do ads for cars or frozen yogurt. He exists inside his two passions, family and football, exclusive of everything else.
>
> Cowher is so focused that one afternoon he was seated next to a woman at a civic luncheon and politely asked, "What is it you do?"
>
> The woman responded, "I'm the mayor of Pittsburgh."

Granted, it's a good idea to know who your mayor is, but Cowher shows us one essential truth: A person cannot focus on everything. A person with priorities must let some things go by the wayside. The more we focus on the Lord, the less we focus on the unimportant things of this world.

Devotion, Focus, Passion, World

Matt. 10:37–39; 2 Cor. 11:2–3; Phil. 3:7–16; Col. 3:1–3; Heb. 12:1–3

Date used __________ Place ____________________

Problems 533

One of the classic baseball television shots comes from the 1975 World Series, in which NBC captured Carlton Fisk, jumping up and down, waving his arms, trying to coax his hit to stay fair. It did—for a home run.

That colorful close-up would have been missed had the cameraman followed the ball with his camera, as was his responsibility. But the cameraman inside the Fenway Park scoreboard had one eye on a rat that was circling him. So instead of focusing the camera on the ball, he left it on Fisk.

Sometimes we encounter problems like that rat. We have no idea how they will be resolved, but because of them, we may see God work in a way we never would have without the problems.

Trust, Trials

Date used __________ Place ______________________

Promiscuity 534

In *The Door* Mike Yaconelli writes:

Author Susan Howatch made a fortune writing blockbuster novels like *Penmarric.* She had houses in several countries, drove a Porsche, and, after divorcing, had a number of "transient liaisons." But at age 30, she says, "God seized me by the scruff of the neck and shook me until my teeth rattled."

Now a Christian, she reflects: "I was promiscuous, but finally one morning I woke up and said, 'What am I trying to prove and to whom?' I knew exactly what—that even though my marriage broke up, I could still attract men. The fact that I could control men boosted my fractured ego."

Her conclusion: "Promiscuity is a sign that you're not aligned right with God or yourself."

Divorce, Ego, Self-Image, Sex
1 Thess. 4:3–7; 1 Peter 4:2–4

Date used __________ Place ____________________

Promises 535

Disregard for a moment your convictions about gambling, and take note of something special in this news story.

On Friday, March 29, 1984, Robert Cunningham ate a meal of linguine and clam sauce at his favorite restaurant, Sal's pizzeria, where he had been a regular customer for seven years. His waitress, Phyllis Penza, had worked at Sal's for nineteen years.

After his meal Cunningham made a good-natured offer to Penza. He said she could either have a tip or split his winnings if his number was drawn in the upcoming New York lotto. Penza chose to take a chance on the lottery, and she and Cunningham chose the numbers together.

On Saturday night, Cunningham won. The jackpot was six million dollars. Then he faced the moment of truth. Would he keep his promise? Would he give the waitress a "tip" of three million dollars?

Cunningham, a police sergeant, husband, father of four, and grandfather of three, said, "I won't back out. Besides, friendship means more than money."

Promises are to be kept no matter what the cost.

Friendship, Honesty, Money, Truth

Date used ________ Place ________________

Booker T. Washington describes meeting an ex-slave from Virginia in his book *Up from Slavery:*

I found that this man had made a contract with his master, two or three years previous to the Emancipation Proclamation, to the effect that the slave was to be permitted to buy himself, by paying so much per year for his body; and while he was paying for himself, he was to be permitted to labor where and for whom he pleased.

Finding that he could secure better wages in Ohio, he went there. When freedom came, he was still in debt to his master some 300 dollars. Notwithstanding that the Emancipation Proclamation freed him from any obligation to his master, this black man walked the greater portion of the distance back to where his old master lived in Virginia, and placed the last dollar, with interest, in his hands.

In talking to me about this, the man told me that he knew that he did not have to pay his debt, but that he had given his word to his master, and his word he had never broken. He felt that he could not enjoy his freedom till he had fulfilled his promise.

Debts, Money

Date used __________ Place ____________________

Promises of God 537

In 1979 Verna Bowman of Telford, Pennsylvania, gave birth to her fourth child, Geoff, and quickly learned from doctors the frightening news: the baby had defective kidneys. Writing in *Guideposts,* she tells that doctors ordered the child rushed to a children's hospital in Philadelphia, where he would receive kidney dialysis.

Still hospitalized herself, Verna prayed and prayed for her son, and as she did she soon felt God's nearness. Unbidden, the words of a Scripture text began to repeat in her heart: "This sickness is not unto death, but for the glory of God" (John 11:4). She wrote the words down.

Later her husband called to report on the baby's condition: "It's too soon to tell if he's going to make it," he said.

"He's going to make it," Verna replied, and she read him the verse that God had breathed into her heart. "I believe those words," she said.

"So do I, Verna," replied her husband. "So do I."

After three months of dialysis, Geoff's kidneys, though still defective, began to function on their own. Throughout his childhood Geoff took medication and tired easily. During that time Verna collected in her journal other Scriptures which encouraged her faith that her son would be all right.

When Geoff was thirteen, the doctors reported he would need a kidney transplant. Though unsettling at first, this news turned out to be the answer to her prayers. Verna herself provided the kidney, and the operation was a complete success. Geoff would be able to live a normal life.

Later Verna's daughter suggested they do something special with the Scriptures that had meant much to them during Geoff's long sickness. Verna often made quilts and her daughter was skilled at cross-stitch, so they decided to make a quilt that displayed twelve of the cherished promises from the Bible. Each Scripture was stitched onto white linen and bordered in a pattern of hunter green and burgundy. Three months later the quilt was completed and hung on the wall of their guest room. When others admired the quilt, it eventually was hung in their church as well as other churches in the area.

God's promises had made a great difference for Verna Bowman. When she chose to have these promises stitched onto a quilt, she made a fitting choice. As comforting as a quilt on a cold wintry night, so God's promises ward off soul-chilling fear. They warm the soul.

Faith, Fear, Revelation, Scriptures, Word of God

Ps. 145:13; 2 Peter 1:4

Date used __________ Place ____________________

Protection 538

To protect itself from aggressors, the horned lizard uses some unique defense mechanisms. In the *Smithsonian,* Susan Hazen-Hammond writes:

> When the creature is threatened by a large predator, it runs through an elaborate behavioral repertoire. First, the lizard will hiss and swell its body with air. If that doesn't work, the animal will flatten its body into a dorsal shield and tip it up toward the attacker. The predator may decide that this little animal might just be too difficult to swallow.
>
> When all else fails, however, the lizard's eyelids will suddenly swell shut. A hairlike stream of blood comes shooting out from a tiny opening near the animal's eyelids, to be shot point-blank at the aggressor. The blood must contain noxious compounds because it clearly repels the recipient. Then the eyelids shrink back to normal size, and the horny toad—its own cheeks streaked with blood—will look around with what at least one human observer saw as a triumphant expression.

Like the horned lizard, when we feel we have to defend ourselves, anything can happen. But when we're threatened, God wants us to entrust ourselves to him.

Anger, Defensiveness, Persecution, Suffering, Temper
1 Peter 2:19–23

Date used __________ Place ____________________

Protection 539

In October 1993, police sharpshooters in Rochester, New York, surrounded a car. In the backseat of the car was a man with a rifle. The police attempted to negotiate with the man. No answer. The police watched and waited. No movement. Finally the police discovered the truth: The armed man in the backseat was a mannequin.

When the authorities tracked down the owner of the car, he told them he keeps the mannequin in his car for protection. "You've got to do this," he said. "With the car-jackings, it helps if it looks like you've got a passenger."

These are dangerous times. Whom do you rely on for protection? A mannequin or the Mighty One?

Angels, Fear, Safety
Ps. 91; 121

Date used __________ Place ____________________

Providence 540

In 1937 Walt Disney released the first full-length animated movie: *Snow White and the Seven Dwarfs.* Producing an animated movie was a gargantuan task. Disney artists drew over one million pictures. Each picture flashed onto the screen for a mere one-twenty-fourth of a second.

As we watch the movie run at regular speed, it seems so simple. We have no idea all that goes into it.

Our lives are like that movie. God puts infinite thought, skill, and careful attention into every detail. Yet as our lives run at "regular speed," we have no idea how much God's providence fills every single second.

Help, Sovereignty of God

Ps. 139:13–18; Jonah 4:6; Matt. 10:29–31; Phil. 2:13

Date used __________ Place ____________________

541

Cliff Barrows has served as Billy Graham's lifelong associate and crusade song leader.

In 1945, before he met Billy Graham, Barrows and his fiancée, Billie, had scraped together enough funds for a simple wedding and two train tickets to a city with a resort hotel.

On arrival, however, they found the hotel shut down. Stranded in an unfamiliar city with little money, they thumbed a ride. A sympathetic driver took them to a grocery store owned by a woman he knew. The newlyweds spent their first night in a room above the store.

The next day, when the lady overheard Cliff playing Christian songs on his trombone, she arranged for them to spend the rest of their honeymoon at a friend's house. Several days later the host invited them to attend a youth rally where a young evangelist was speaking.

The song leader that night was sick, and Cliff was asked to take charge of the music for the service. The young evangelist, of course, was Billy Graham. The two have been partners ever since.

When things don't go the way you plan, God may have plans for you of his own.

God's Direction, Plans
Rom. 8:28; Phil. 2:13

Date used __________ Place ____________________

Providence 542

In *World Vision* magazine, John Robb wrote about an occasion when he saw God's perfect timing.

Robb was in Moscow to teach a seminar at the week-long Lausanne Soviet Congress on Evangelization. While there he met a man named Mirza who was a doctor from Azerbaijan. Azerbaijan is a Muslim region where there were only twenty known converts to Christ. Robb had an opportunity to tell Mirza about Jesus Christ and he wanted to give him some Christian literature. To Robb's dismay he found he had already given away all the Bibles he had brought, but he had one gospel tract left. Robb writes:

> [Mirza] showed up again the next day at my hotel room just as I was leaving for the airport. He expressed his appreciation for my friendship, saying that he hoped we could meet again.
>
> I thought, *Lord, what I'd give for a Russian New Testament right now.*
>
> Not ten seconds later there was a knock at the door. The Russian Gideons were there with a whole load of New Testaments. They had just received permission from the hotel management to place Bibles in every room! One of them held out a New Testament, as if to say, "Is this what you wanted?" I handed it to Mirza and we said goodbye.

God obviously had a purpose for Mirza. And when God is at work, there are no coincidences.

Divine Appointments, Evangelism, Sovereignty of God
Acts 8:26–39; 2 Cor. 2:12–16

Date used __________ Place ____________________

Provision 543

In *Pentecostal Evangel* pastor Dale Alan Robbins writes of an occasion early in his ministry when he and his wife were barely making ends meet:

When I arrived home, my wife Jerri saw the worry on my face. I had $3 in my wallet and there was one can of soup in the cupboard. After our meager supper, I quietly leafed through my Bible in the dim light. Tears streamed from my eyes. I wondered whether we were really called by God. I felt like giving up. Then I thought, *What alternative do I have? Who else but God do I have to turn to?*

I read the verse: "The effectual fervent prayer of a righteous man availeth much" (James 5:16). . . . Encouraged, yet still burdened, Jerri and I knelt at opposite ends of the little trailer to seek God. Into the night we prayed, until sleep finally overtook us.

I was awakened by a pounding at the door. From the window I could see the brilliant orange sunrise behind the city skyline. A fresh, white blanket of snow now covered the ground. Again, the knocking came.

"Who is it?" I asked.

A mystery voice replied, "I've got something for you."

Cautiously, I opened the door. There stood a short man with a grin on his face and two brown grocery bags in his arms. He quickly shoved the bags in the doorway, then turned, and walked away.

Jerri joined me. Stunned, we began to look through the bags. There were bread, meat, canned goods, and several cans of my favorite soup. They were the same items and brands we normally purchased. There was also a can of shaving cream. Who knew I had just used my last ounce of shaving cream? On the bottom of one sack was an envelope with cash. (Later I discovered it was the precise amount needed to fill our gas tank to get us to our next destination.)

On that wintry Saturday morning in Syracuse, my wife and I wept in our trailer and thanked God for hearing and answering our prayer. No one on the planet knew about our need; only our Lord God Almighty. And he dispatched a little grinning man to minister to us.

Earnestness, Money, Needs, Prayer, Seeking God, Supply

Gen. 22:14; Matt. 6:25–34; Phil. 4:19; Heb. 11:6; James 5:16–18

Date used __________ Place ____________________

In *Fresh Wind, Fresh Fire,* Jim Cymbala, author and pastor of the Brooklyn Tabernacle, tells the story of the first financial obstacle he faced upon coming to the tiny church:

When the first mortgage payment rolled around at the end of the month, the checking account showed something like $160 in hand. We were going to default right off the bat. How soon would it take to lose the building and be tossed out into the street? That Monday, my day off, I remember praying, "Lord, you have to help me. I don't know much—but I do know that we have to pay this mortgage."

I went to the church on Tuesday. Well, maybe someone will send some money out of the blue, I told myself, like what happened so often with George Mueller and his orphanage back in England—he just prayed, and a letter or a visitor would arrive to meet his need.

The mail came that day—and there was nothing but bills and fliers.

Now I was trapped. I went upstairs, sat at my little desk, put my head down, and began to cry. "God," I sobbed, "what can I do? We can't even pay the mortgage." That night was the midweek service, and I knew there wouldn't be more than three or four people attending. The offering would probably be less than ten dollars. How was I going to get through this?

I called out to the Lord for a full hour or so. Eventually, I dried my tears—and a new thought came. Wait a minute! Besides the mail slot in the front door, the church also has a post office box. I'll go across the street and see what's there. Surely God will answer my prayer!

With renewed confidence I walked across the street, crossed the post office lobby, and twirled the knob on the little box. I peered inside . . .

Nothing.

As I stepped back into the sunshine, trucks roared down Atlantic Avenue. If one had flattened me just then, I wouldn't have felt any lower. Was God abandoning us? Was I doing something that displeased him? I trudged wearily back across the street to the little building.

As I unlocked the door, I was met with another surprise. There on the foyer floor was something that hadn't been there just three minutes earlier: a simple white envelope. No address, no stamp—nothing. Just a white envelope.

With trembling hands I opened it to find . . . two $50 bills.

I began shouting all by myself in the empty church. "God, you came through! You came through!" We had $160 in the bank, and with this $100 we could make the mortgage payment. My soul let out a deep "Hallelujah!" What a lesson for a disheartened young pastor!

To this day I don't know where that money came from. I only know it was a sign to me that God was near—and faithful.

Money, Needs, Prayer, Providence, Supply
Matt. 6:25–34; 2 Cor. 12:8–10; Phil. 4:19; Heb. 13:5–6

Date used __________ Place ____________________

In the spring of 1995, revival broke out on many college campuses across America. One characteristic of this visitation from God was students dealing with sinful habits that they had previously let linger in their lives. Bonne Steffen interviewed several of the students for the *Christian Reader;* one student named Brian at Asbury College said:

I was a leader on campus. We had invited Wheaton students to come and share. At first, I was praying for other people, but then I began to think about my own struggles. I stood in line for three hours with one of my best friends all the time thinking, *How can I get up here and admit I'm less than perfect?* But I also realized that being on a Christian campus isn't protection from the world. I have really struggled with lust. I found I wasn't alone. It was an issue for a lot of others. Personally, I wanted the chain to be broken; I wanted that stuff out of my life. If it meant no magazines, no television, I was willing to eliminate them. A number of us signed a paper stating our desire for purity, which we put in a box and placed on the altar. I'm still accountable to other people. My deepest desire is to be pure in my heart and thoughts.

As this student shows, the desire for purity is the beginning of purity. Purity comes when we pursue it actively and forcefully.

Accountability, Confession, Lust, Repentance, Revival
Matt. 5:8, 27–30; 2 Cor. 7:1; James 5:16

Date used __________ Place ____________________

In his sermon, "A Purpose Runs through It," Bryan Wilkerson says:

One of the most beautiful movies of [recent years] was *A River Runs through It*, based upon the novel by the same title. The movie told the story of the Maclean family, who lived in Montana early in the twentieth century. The father of the family was a Presbyterian minister—stern but loving. His wife was supportive and nurturing. They had two sons: the oldest, first-born Norman, who tells the story, and a younger son, Paul. . . .

The real protagonist in the story is the river that runs through their part of Montana. That river becomes the focal point of their family life and the catalyst for everything significant that takes place in their individual lives. It was walking along the banks of that river on Sunday afternoons that the father forged a relationship with his young boys—turning over rocks, teaching them about the world, about life, and about the God who made it all. It was the river that the boys ran to after their studies were over, and sibling rivalry and brotherly affection flourished as they fished for trout together on that beautiful stream.

When it came time for these adolescent boys to prove their moxie, they took a death-defying ride down the rapids in a stolen boat. It was on the river that young Paul made a name for himself as the finest fly-fisherman in the territory. When Norman came back from college searching for himself and his roots, it was to the river that he went to fish, alongside his brother.

The Maclean family knew failure and success and laughter and fighting and change and disappointment, but always the river was there. It was the defining force and the spiritual center of that family. Montana would have been just a wilderness; their home, four walls and a roof; their individual lives just sound and fury—if not for the river running through it all.

I would like to suggest that there is a river that runs through the lives of Christian people, and that river is called the Purpose of God. . . .

For the remainder of the sermon Wilkerson deals with the tough questions that people in his congregation were facing after the death of a little girl in the church. As he explains difficult theological concepts, he repeatedly comes back to the image of the river, concluding with the following words:

"Christian, whatever has happened to you in the past, whatever your present circumstances may be, whatever the future might hold, know this: A river runs through it, and that river is called the Purpose of God."

Family, Fathers, God's Will, Goodness of God,
Providence, Roots, Sovereignty of God
Jer. 29:11; Rom. 8:28–30; Phil. 2:13

Date used __________ Place ____________________

Questions 547

In *The Hiding Place,* Corrie ten Boom writes about a question she asked her father.

> "Father, what is sex sin?"
>
> My father turned to look at me, as he always did when answering a question, but to my surprise he said nothing. At last he stood up, lifted his traveling case from the rack over our heads, and set it on the floor.
>
> "Will you carry it off the train, Corrie?" he said. I stood up and tugged at it. It was crammed with the watches and spare parts he had purchased that morning.
>
> "It's too heavy," I said.
>
> "Yes," he said. "And it would be a pretty poor father who would ask his little girl to carry such a load. It's the same way, Corrie, with knowledge. Some knowledge is too heavy for children. When you are older and stronger, you can bear it. For now you must trust me to carry it for you."
>
> And I was satisfied. More than satisfied—wonderfully at peace. There were answers to this and all my hard questions—but now I was content to leave them in my father's keeping.

And so it is that to find peace, we must leave many questions in our heavenly Father's keeping.

Knowledge, Mystery, Sex, Tragedy, Trials, Trust
Deut. 29:29; John 16:12

Date used __________ Place ____________________

According to writers Kent McDill and Melissa Isaacson, Don Calhoun worked for five dollars an hour at an office supply store in Bloomington, Illinois. He had attended two Chicago Bulls basketball games in his life, and now he was going to his third. When he strolled into Chicago Stadium, a woman who worked for the Bulls organization walked up to him and told him they were selecting him to take part in a promotional event during the game called the Million Dollar Shot.

The Shot came after a time-out in the third quarter. If Calhoun could shoot a basket standing seventy-nine feet away—that means he had to stand behind the free throw line on the opposite end of the court and throw the ball three quarters of the length of the court—he would win one million dollars.

Calhoun played basketball at the Bloomington YMCA but he had never tried a shot like this before. He took the basketball in his hands and looked over at Michael Jordan and the rest of the Bulls. He could see they were pulling for him.

Calhoun stepped to the line and let fly. As soon as the basketball left his hand, coach Phil Jackson said, "It's good." Indeed, the ball went through the basket in a swish. The stadium crowd went wild. Calhoun rushed into the arms of Michael Jordan, and the Bulls players crowded around slapping him on the back.

When Don Calhoun went home that night, he had only two dollars in his wallet, but he would receive fifty thousand dollars a year for the next twenty years of his life.

Sometimes one action, one decision, one moment can change everything for you. So it is when you choose to receive Christ into your life.

Born Again, Conversion, Gospel, Repentance, Salvation

John 1:12; 2 Cor. 5:17

Date used __________ Place ____________________

Recognition 549

Every young student knows of Isaac Newton's famed encounter with a falling apple. Newton discovered and introduced the laws of gravity in the 1600s, which revolutionized astronomical studies.

But few know that if it weren't for Edmund Halley, the world might never have learned from Newton.

It was Halley who challenged Newton to think through his original notions. Halley corrected Newton's mathematical errors and prepared geometrical figures to support his discoveries. Halley coaxed the hesitant Newton to write his great work, *Mathematical Principles of Natural Philosophy.* Halley edited and supervised the publication, and actually financed its printing even though Newton was wealthier and easily could have afforded the printing costs.

Historians call it one of the most selfless examples in the annals of science. Newton began almost immediately to reap the rewards of prominence; Halley received little credit.

He did use the principles to predict the orbit and return of the comet that would later bear his name, but only *after* his death did he receive any acclaim. And because the comet only returns every seventy-six years, the notice is rather infrequent. Halley remained a devoted scientist who didn't care who received the credit as long as the cause was being advanced.

Others have played Halley's role. John the Baptist said of Jesus, "He must become greater; I must become less." Barnabas was content to introduce others to greatness. Many pray to uphold the work of one Christian leader. Such selflessness advances the kingdom.

Selflessness, Body of Christ

Date used __________ Place ____________________

Reconciliation 550

In April 1969 more than one hundred black students at Cornell University took over the student union in a militant demonstration for civil rights. According to the Associated Press, they protested "the lack of Black studies programs and what they saw as the university's treatment of them as second-class citizens." Militants smuggled guns into the building and threatened violence.

Some of the most inflammatory rhetoric came from one black militant named Thomas W. Jones. He said that Cornell had only "hours to live," that he was ready to lay down his life, and that racist faculty and police would be "dealt with."

The takeover lasted thirty-four hours but ended peacefully. When the one hundred militants finally marched from the building, the same Thomas W. Jones was the last to leave. He walked out carrying a rifle and raising a clenched fist.

One month later James Perkins, the president of Cornell, was forced to step down.

But that isn't the end of the story.

Cornell dealt with the issues that concerned the militants. Thomas Jones earned his masters degree from Cornell one year later and helped Cornell organize a Black studies curriculum. He then went into business, working for TIAA-CREF, the world's largest pension fund, with $142 billion in assets. Jones eventually became president of the company. In 1993 Cornell appointed Jones to their board of trustees.

And in 1995 Thomas Jones made the grand gesture of reconciliation. On May 4 in a ceremony at Cornell, Jones endowed a five-thousand-dollar prize to reward efforts on campus to foster "interracial understanding and harmony." Jones named the annual prize after James Perkins, the former Cornell president forced to step down twenty-six years before.

Jones said Perkins had engineered one of the earliest college drives to enroll Blacks. "I simply feel the need to acknowledge," said Jones, "that he was an extremely decent man who had the courage to do the right thing in trying to help America solve its racial problems by improving educational access for minorities."

At the ceremony, Jones and Perkins sat side by side. Jones and Perkins, onetime foes, show that racial reconciliation is possible. And they show us something else: Racial reconciliation is beautiful.

Forgiveness, Prejudice, Race Relations
Gal. 3:26–28; Eph. 2:14

Date used __________ Place ____________________

Reconciliation 551

When we are in conflict with those near to us, God calls us to seek reconciliation as a first priority. Among the reasons is personal safety.

According to the Associated Press, in 1994, hospital emergency rooms in the United States treated 1.4 million victims of violence or suspected violence. Is this all about crime on the streets?

No. The Justice Department analyzed the data and reported in 1997 that roughly half of these victims were hurt by someone they knew. Seventeen percent of the victims, 243,000 people, were injured by a spouse, former spouse, or a current or former boyfriend or girlfriend. Eight percent of the victims were injured by a relative such as a parent or child. Twenty-three percent were hurt by friends or acquaintances. (These figures, which come from hospital emergency rooms, differ from those reported by the FBI's annual Uniform Crime Report, which reflects only offenses reported to police.)

God knows that hostile feelings between family and friends are literally dangerous. There is no telling how broken relationships will end.

Anger, Divorce, Family, Forgiveness, Peace,
Relationships, Ten Commandments, Violence
Exod. 20:12–17; Mal. 2:13–16; Matt. 5:21–26, 38–48;
18:15–35; Luke 6:27–37; James 3:8–18

Date used __________ Place ____________________

Reconciliation 552

In an interview with Will Norton Jr., best-selling novelist John Grisham recalls:

One of my best friends in college died when he was 25, just a few years after we had finished Mississippi State University. I was in law school, and he called me one day and wanted to get together. So we had lunch, and he told me he had terminal cancer.

I couldn't believe it. I asked him, "What do you do when you realize that you are about to die?"

He said, "It's real simple. You get things right with God, and you spend as much time with those you love as you can. Then you settle up with everybody else." Then he said, "You know, really, you ought to live every day like you have only a few more days to live."

That left an impression on me.

Few things impart more wisdom than to face up to the fact that we will all die sooner or later.

Conversion, Death, Family, Priorities, Repentance, Wisdom
Ps. 90:12; Eccles. 12:13–14; Heb. 9:27

Date used __________ Place ____________________

Johnny Cash once did an album called *American Recordings*. On the album cover is a picture of two dogs. One dog is black with a white stripe. The other dog is white with a black stripe. The two dogs are meant to say something about Johnny Cash.

In an interview with *Rolling Stone*, Cash explains what the two dogs mean. "Their names are Sin and Redemption. Sin is the black one with the white stripe; Redemption is the white one with the black stripe. That's kind of the theme of that album, and for me, too. When I was really bad, I was not all bad. When I was trying to be good, I could never be all good. There would be that black streak going through."

No one is all bad. No one is all good. We are all sinners who need to be redeemed. We all need Jesus.

Grace, Jesus Christ, Perfection, Salvation, Sin, Struggle, Works
Rom. 3:9–26; 7:7–25

Date used __________ Place ____________________

In the early nineties the plight of Keiko the orca whale, star of the movie *Free Willy,* stirred the concern of millions of people. Keiko's saga began when the media discovered that, like the whale in the movie, Keiko actually lived in an unhealthy environment.

Life magazine reported: "His tank at Mexico City's Reino Aventura theme park, full of chlorinated and artificially salted water, was barely large enough . . . for the 21-foot animal to turn around in. His muscles had turned flabby, and constant swimming in one direction had curled his dorsal fin. His water was far too warm—80 degrees—for his Nordic blood. An inadequate filtration system had him swimming in his own wastes, and he was breathing the world's smoggiest air. These hardships, along with an improper diet, had weakened his immune system. He was 1,300 pounds underweight, and warty eruptions, caused by the papillomavirus, marred his skin. In his frustration he had taken to gnawing at the edge of the pool—a habit that wore his teeth down to stubs."

Various activists crusaded to try to improve the whale's lot. After several years Dave Phillips at the Earth Island Institute formed the Free Willy Foundation, and millions of dollars began to pour in. The foundation built a new tank for Keiko at the Oregon Coast Aquarium in Newport, Oregon.

Life reported that Keiko's new home was "four times bigger than the one in Mexico. Filled with healthful 40-degree seawater from nearby Yaquina Bay, the new pool featured reversible currents to work against, waterjets to play among, even submerged rocks for navigation practice."

On January 7, 1996, Keiko was flown to his new home. Within a year Keiko had gained 1,000 pounds. The lesions on his skin were healing. And his fallen dorsal fin was on the rise.

The Free Willy-Keiko Foundation redeemed one very grateful whale. In the same way, God redeems us. Through Christ he rescued us from a hurtful situation that we had no power to escape and brought us into a healthful one.

Abundant Life, Deliverance, Healing,
Kingdom of God, Restoration, Salvation
John 10:10; Col. 1:13–14

Date used __________ Place ____________________

Rejection 555

Campbell Morgan was one of 150 young men who sought entrance to the Wesleyan ministry in 1888. He passed the doctrinal examinations, but then faced the trial sermon. In a cavernous auditorium that could seat more than 1,000 sat three ministers and 75 others who came to listen.

When Morgan stepped into the pulpit, the vast room and the searching, critical eyes caught him up short. Two weeks later Morgan's name appeared among the 105 rejected for the ministry that year.

Jill Morgan, his daughter-in-law, wrote in her book, *A Man of the Word*: "He wired to his father the one word, 'Rejected,' and sat down to write in his diary: 'Very dark everything seems. Still, He knoweth best.'

"Quickly came the reply: 'Rejected on earth. Accepted in Heaven. Dad.'"

Rejection is rarely permanent, as Morgan went on to prove. Even in this life, circumstances change, and ultimately, there is no rejection of those accepted by Christ.

Failure, Acceptance

Date used __________ Place ____________________

556

On December 20, 1995, an American Airlines jet crashed into a mountainside in Colombia, killing 159 passengers. Months later, airline officials determined that the cause of the crash was an error by the flight captain and a mix-up in computer coordinates.

According to Reuters, as flight 965 approached Cali airport from the north, the control tower radioed to the flight captain that he was to fly a straight path over the "Rozo" navigational radio beacon near the airport. The captain punched the letter "R" into the on-board computer, which he assumed would cause the autopilot to fly the plane toward the beacon. Unfortunately there was another radio beacon with a code name that began with the letter "R," the "Romeo" beacon, 132 miles to the left and behind the plane at the Bogota airport. The autopilot sent the plane to the wrong beacon—with disastrous results.

Accuracy and details are essential not only in navigation but also in religion. Punching in the letter "R" for any old religion will not do. The only way to have a relationship with God is through faith in Jesus Christ and the essential doctrines of orthodoxy.

Doctrine, Exclusiveness of the Gospel,
Orthodoxy, Truth, Universalism
John 14:6; Acts 4:12; Rom. 10:1–4; Gal. 1:6–9; 1 John 5:12

Date used __________ Place ____________________

Repentance 557

In his sermon "The Writing on the Wall," William Willimon tells the story of an aggravating funeral at a country church.

> The preacher pounded on the pulpit and looked over at the casket. He would say, "It's too late for Joe. He might have wanted to get his life together. He might have wanted to spend more time with his family. He might have wanted to do that, but he's dead now. It is too late for him, but it is not too late for you. There is still time for you. You still can decide. You still are alive. It is not too late for you. Today is the day of decision."
>
> Then the preacher told how a Greyhound bus had run into a funeral procession once on the way to the cemetery, and that could happen today. He said, "You should decide today. Today is the day to get your life together. Too late for old Joe, but it's not too late for you."
>
> I was so angry at that preacher. On the way home, I told my wife, "Have you ever seen anything as manipulative and as insensitive to that poor family? I found it disgusting."
>
> She said, "I've never heard anything like that. It was manipulative. It was disgusting. It was insensitive. Worst of all, it was also true."

Death, Decisions, Receiving Christ
2 Cor. 6:2

Date used __________ Place ____________________

Don Wyman's chain saw revved like a motorcycle and ripped through a three-foot-thick oak tree. The day was Tuesday, July 20, 1993, in a forest one hundred miles northeast of Pittsburgh, Pennsylvania, and Wyman, a mustached and burly mining company employee, was cutting up a fallen tree. It was about 4:00 P.M., and he was alone in the woods.

When he finished one cut, tragedy struck, say writers Pam Lambert and Tom Nugent. The tree snapped back in his direction and knocked him to the ground. The massive oak landed on his left shin, shattering bone and tearing flesh. Pinned to the ground, Wyman screamed in pain.

He tried to free himself. He still had his chain saw, but he couldn't reach enough of the tree to cut himself free. So he began digging around and beneath his leg, using the saw to chop the hard soil and then scooping the dirt with his hands. Every few minutes he paused and bellowed for help, to no avail.

Then he hit a large rock, too large to dig around or move. An hour had passed since the accident. *I'm going to bleed to death,* he thought.

He weighed his options. He could lie there, continue to call for help, and hope that by some slim chance a person would wander into earshot or that he could survive until his wife figured that something was wrong and sent someone looking for him. He could give up and bleed to death. Or he could do a very scary thing, a desperate measure in a desperate time. He had a pocket knife. Maybe he could muster the strength to amputate his own pinned leg and somehow get back to where someone could help him.

Wyman thought about it for a while, and then made his decision. He pulled the starter cord from his chain saw, wrapped it around his leg, and tied the cord to a wrench. Then he twirled the wrench until it cut off the flow of blood to his shin.

Somehow he amputated his own leg below the knee with his pocket knife.

Now, on one leg, he had to find help. He crawled 135 feet uphill over loose ground to his bulldozer. He climbed in, started the engine, and then drove the slow, grinding earthmover a quarter mile to his Chevy

S–10 truck, all the while clutching the wrench-and-starter-cord tourniquet. The truck had a manual transmission, but using a metal file to depress the clutch when he shifted, Wyman was able to drive to a farmer's home a mile-and-a-half away.

When dairy farmer John Huber saw the crazed looking man behind the wheel of the mud-splattered truck and cautiously approached to investigate, Wyman yelled, "I cut my leg off!" Wyman lifted what remained of his left leg as proof and shouted, "Help me! I'm bleeding to death."

Huber ran inside and phoned for emergency help. He then drove Wyman to a crossroads where they met an ambulance. Soon Wyman received the medical care that saved his life.

Don Wyman's leg was dear to him but as he lay bleeding to death beneath the oak tree, he recognized that keeping his leg might cost him his life. We too have things dear to us—sinful pleasures, lusts, and activities—that we do not want to give up. Losing them would be like amputating our own leg or gouging out an eye. Jesus said that we must be willing to repent of even the most precious sins if we want to inherit eternal life.

Choices, Courage, Priorities, Sin
Deut. 30:15–20; Matt. 5:29–30; 7:13–27

Date used __________ Place ____________________

559

When Michigan played Wisconsin in basketball early in the season in 1989, Michigan's Rumeal Robinson stepped to the foul line for two shots late in the fourth quarter. His team trailed by one point, so Rumeal could regain the lead for Michigan. He missed both shots, allowing Wisconsin to upset favored Michigan.

Rumeal felt awful about costing his team the game, but his sorrow didn't stop at the emotional level. After each practice for the rest of the season, Rumeal shot 100 extra foul shots.

Thus, Rumeal was ready when he stepped to the foul line to shoot two shots with three seconds left in overtime in the national championship game. Swish went the first shot, and swish went the second. Those shots won Michigan the national championship.

Rumeal's repentance had been genuine, and sorrow motivated him to work so that he would never make that mistake again. As Paul wrote, "Godly sorrow leads to repentance" (2 Cor. 7:10).

Failure, Work

Date used __________ Place ____________________

560

Paul Lee Tan's Encyclopedia of 7,700 Illustrations records:

The Romans sometimes compelled a captive to be joined face-to-face with a dead body, and to bear it about until the horrible effluvia destroyed the life of the living victim. Virgil describes this cruel punishment:

> "The living and the dead at his command
> were coupled face to face, and hand to hand;
> Till choked with stench, in loathed embraces tied,
> The lingering wretches pined away and died."

Without Christ, we are shackled to a dead corpse—our sinfulness. Only repentance frees us from certain death, for life and death cannot coexist indefinitely.

Sin, Life

Date used __________ Place ____________________

What causes ulcers? Stress, coffee, spicy food? Wrong, wrong, wrong, according to Daniel Haney of the Associated Press. For years that is what doctors presumed caused ulcers, but in the early 1980s two doctors—Barry Marshall and Robin Warren—discovered a bacterium in the lining of the digestive system that they suspected might be the real cause. The bacterium is called *Helicobacter pylori.*

The proof of Marshall and Warren's idea was slow in coming, but by the early 1990s—after some two thousand articles had appeared in medical journals on the subject of the bacterium—gastroenterologists agreed with them.

"It turns out that about half of all U.S. adults are infected with *H. pylori,*" writes Haney. "Most don't get ulcers. But when ulcers do occur, the bug is probably responsible for 80 percent or more. The only major exception is ulcers triggered by aspirin and some other pain killers."

Nevertheless, most people suffering stomach discomfort don't go first to a gastroenterologist; they go to their family practitioner or general internist. And news about the real cause of ulcers has been slow to reach them. Instead of prescribing an antibiotic that would cure the problem, many persist in prescribing acid-blocking drugs that may heal ulcers temporarily, but in time they often come back.

In a similar way, many people get only temporary relief for spiritual and emotional problems. If a person has a sin problem, no amount of self-help or technique will completely take away the pain or cure the disease. The antibiotic is repentance.

Pain, Self-Help, Sin, Technique, Therapy
Luke 5:27–32

Date used __________ Place ____________________

Reputation 562

Each week some three million people read the *National Enquirer.* But big supermarket sales don't necessarily add up to journalistic respect. The *Enquirer* will long be remembered for stories about space aliens and multi-headed humans. Mainstream journalists grumble because the tabloid pays big money to its sources for their tales. And, really, is Vanna White's new baby or the continuing saga of Oprah Winfrey's weight worthy of headlines?

But surprise, surprise, according to *New York Times* writer David Margolick, *The Enquirer* took the prize for reporting in its coverage of the O. J. Simpson case.

"As early as five years ago," wrote Margolick, "*The Enquirer* was on the case. And in a story made for the tabloids, it stands head and shoulders above them all when it comes to aggressiveness and accuracy. . . . With as many as 20 reporters on the case, *The Enquirer* has broken numerous stories."

In his article Margolick went on to list several facts that *The Enquirer* had been first to report. And then to emphasize his point, Margolick listed several erroneous stories that mainstream news agencies had reported but *The Enquirer* had not.

Christians are a bit like *The Enquirer*. God has chosen the "foolish" of the world to shame the "wise."

Election, Gospel, Grace, Ministry, Pride
1 Cor. 1:27–29; 15:8–10

Date used __________ Place ____________________

In *Guideposts* Joann C. Jones writes:

During my second year of nursing school our professor gave us a pop quiz. I breezed through the questions until I read the last one: "What is the first name of the woman who cleans the school?"

Surely this was some kind of joke. I had seen the cleaning woman several times, but how would I know her name? I handed in my paper, leaving the last question blank.

Before the class ended, one student asked if the last question would count toward our grade. "Absolutely," the professor said. "In your careers you will meet many people. All are significant. They deserve your attention and care, even if all you do is smile and say hello."

I've never forgotten that lesson. I also learned her name was Dorothy.

We have not begun to show the love of Christ to others until we have treated them with respect.

Dignity, Humility, Love, Significance, Worth
Rom. 12:16; Phil. 2:3; 1 Peter 2:17

Date used __________ Place ____________________

In *Moody* magazine, John H. Timmerman writes:

> In the back corner of my yard, partitioned by a rose bed and a 40-year-old lilac bush, rests a pile, 8 feet long, 4 feet wide, and 4 feet high—my compost pile. Old-fashioned chicken wire stapled to well-anchored stakes holds it in place. Into it I toss every bit of yard scrap and a heavy dose of kitchen scrap . . . a bit of lime now and then, a good dose of dog droppings, and an occasional handful of fertilizer.
>
> The compost pile burns hot, never smells, and each October yields about 70 bushels of fine black dirt, dark as midnight, moist and flaky, that I spread in the garden. . . . Gardeners call it "black gold." . . . It nurtures 80 roses and a half-dozen beds of perennials and annuals. . . .
>
> Could it be that what nourishes my plants nourishes me?

Timmerman compares his compost soil, which grows rich and fertile as it sits for months, to his life and the need of his soul for rest. Daily life hands us all kinds of things—good and bad—scraps, lime, and even "dog droppings." But as we take sabbath rest, these things are transformed. Godly rest can turn the difficulties of daily life into a rich resource for spiritual fruitfulness.

Fruitfulness, Sabbath, Stress
Exod. 20:8; Mark 6:31

Date used __________ Place ____________________

Restoration 565

In 1987 Donna Rice was involved in a scandal with presidential hopeful Gary Hart. She accompanied Hart, who was a married man, on a pleasure cruise to the Bahamas on a yacht called *Monkey Business.*

At the time, Donna Rice was a backslidden Christian, says Ramona Cramer Tucker in *Today's Christian Woman.* As a freshman in high school, Rice had received Christ at a Cliff Barrows crusade. Throughout high school her life revolved around choir, youth group, mission trips, and inviting friends to church.

When she went away to college, though, she gradually compromised to the point where she was far from God. Then, the Gary Hart scandal put her and her picture on the front page of newspapers and magazines across the country.

Her life fell apart. She resigned her job, and she was hounded by the press. She was offered millions to tell her story. As she wrestled with what to do, her mother and grandmother said something to Rice that would seem obvious: "Before you make any decisions, get your life straight with God."

But it wasn't obvious to Rice. She says, "I was stunned because I hadn't yet realized I could put the entire mess in his hands."

Then Rice's mother gave her a cassette tape from a former youth-group friend. "Donna, I imagine you're in a lot of pain right now," the friend said. "I just want you to know that God loves you and I love you."

Rice recalls, "When she began to share songs we used to sing together, I collapsed on the floor in my apartment and sobbed. I knew I—and no one else—was responsible for my choices. I cried out, 'God, it took falling on my rear in front of the whole world to get my attention. Help me to live my life your way!' God answered my plea by flooding me with his presence and forgiveness and by surrounding me with Christian fellowship."

Those who have slipped away from God can be restored. Never underestimate the role your words can play in leading someone to God.

Admonishment, Backsliding, Counsel, Evangelism, Exhortation, Intervention, Love, Repentance, Reproof

2 Cor. 5:10–11; Gal. 6:1–2; Heb. 3:12–13; James 5:19–20

Date used __________ Place ____________________

In the United States, businesses use millions of wood pallets each year to haul products. After a pallet has borne heavy, sometimes crushing weights and taken abuse from truck travel and forklifts, eventually it can no longer be used. Now cracked and smashed, or loose and floppy, pallets are something businesses must pay other companies up to five dollars per pallet to dispose of. Disposal companies burn the pallets, chew them into wood chips, or dump them in landfills.

One nonprofit company in New York had a better idea, writes Andrew Revkin in the *New York Times.* Big City Forest in South Bronx takes other companies' junk and turns it into treasure. The raw material of pallets is valuable hardwoods like rosewood, cherry, oak, mahogany, and maple. Big City Forest workers dismantle the pallets, salvage the usable wood, and recycle it into furniture and flooring. Recycled wood chips are worth only $30 a ton. But when used as flooring the value of the recycled wood is $1,200 a ton, and as furniture $6,000 a ton.

If that is what can be done with lifeless wood, how much more can people be restored to lives of value. Like Big City Forest, God is in the business of restoration. He takes people that seem worthless, people broken by the weight of sin, and transforms them into works of beauty and usefulness.

Discipleship, New Creation, Regeneration, Renewal, Worth
Ps. 23:3; Isa. 61:3; 2 Cor. 5:17

Date used __________ Place ____________________

567

Human ashes have been sprinkled into the sky from airplanes and spread over the ocean from ships. But according to the Associated Press, Brian Kelly had something more glorious in mind.

In July 1994 Kelly, who lived in suburban Detroit, suffered complications from surgery on his intestines. Knowing he was soon to die, Kelly told his family what he wanted done with his remains. His request was unusual, but his family granted it.

Kelly's boss, Mary McCavit, at Independence Professional Fireworks shop in Osseo, Michigan, rolled up Kelly's ashes in a twelve-inch-round fireworks shell. On Friday, August 12, at a convention of fireworks technicians near Pittsburgh, they shot that shell into the sky. It trailed two silvery comet tails as it ascended into the night sky, and then it exploded into red and green stars.

If you want to go out in a glorious display, you have to admit, that is pretty spectacular.

But that's nothing compared to the glory that God intends for the bodies of those who believe in Jesus Christ. The glory of our resurrection bodies will far surpass that four-second arc of light and color. Instead of a cannon report, there will be the awesome blare of the trumpet of God and the majestic voice of Jesus calling our bodies from the graves. In glorious resurrection bodies like that of Jesus Christ himself, we will ascend into the clouds and meet the King of Kings whose brightness is like the lightning shining from east to west. For ever and ever, Jesus said, we will "shine like the sun in the kingdom" of our Father.

Body, Death, Easter, Glory
Matt. 13:43; 1 Cor. 15:35–57; 1 John 3:2

Date used __________ Place ____________________

Resurrection 568

In *100 Meditations on Hope* Wayne A. Lamb writes:

In the midst of a storm, a little bird was clinging to the limb of a tree, seemingly calm and unafraid. As the wind tore at the limbs of the tree, the bird continued to look the storm in the face, as if to say, "Shake me off; I still have wings."

Because of Christ's resurrection, each Christian can look the experience of death in the face and confidently say, "Shake me off; I still have wings. I'll live anyway."

Death, Easter, Hope

Matt. 28:1–10; 1 Cor. 15; 2 Cor. 5:1–10; Phil. 1:21–23

Date used __________ Place ____________________

Poet Elizabeth Goldring developed blindness as an adult. According to writers Ron Kotulak and Jon Van, one day a doctor was testing her eyes with a laser device called a scanning laser ophthalmoscope when Goldring by chance noticed something important. As the laser scanned her eye, she could "see" certain images.

Further experiments were done by Robert Webb, the inventor of the laser device. Goldring found that the laser device was able to project on the retina of her eyes faces and words that she could see.

Based on these experiments, researchers believe many blind people have parts of their retinas that may be able to sense visual information projected directly onto their retinas by a laser.

After the experiments Goldring said, "That was the first time in several months that I had seen a word, and for a poet, that's an incredible feeling."

Just as Elizabeth Goldring could not see without the assistance of this laser device projecting words and images into her eyes, there are many truths we cannot see unless God reveals them to us by his Spirit. We are blind about spiritual things apart from revelation.

Spiritual Gifts, Word of Knowledge
Matt. 16:13–17; 1 Cor. 2:6–16

Date used __________ Place ____________________

Revenge 570

In Judith Viorst's children's book *I'll Fix Anthony,* the younger brother complains about the way his older brother Anthony treats him:

> My brother Anthony can read books now, but he won't read any books to me. He plays checkers with Bruce from his school. But when I want to play he says "Go away or I'll clobber you." I let him wear my Snoopy sweatshirt, but he never lets me borrow his sword. Mother says deep down in his heart Anthony loves me. Anthony says deep down in his heart he thinks I stink. Mother says deep deep down in his heart, where he doesn't even know it, Anthony loves me. Anthony says deep deep down in his heart he still thinks I stink. When I'm six, I'll fix Anthony. . . .
>
> When I'm six, I'll float, but Anthony will sink to the bottom. I'll dive off the board, but Anthony will change his mind. I'll breathe in and out when I should, but Anthony will only go glug, glug. . . . When I'm six my teeth will fall out, and I'll put them under the bed, and the tooth fairy will take them away and leave dimes. Anthony's teeth won't fall out. He'll wiggle and wiggle them, but they won't fall out. I might sell him one of my teeth, but I might not. . . .
>
> Anthony is chasing me out of the playroom. He says I stink. He says he is going to clobber me. I have to run now, but I won't have to run when I'm six. When I'm six, I'll fix Anthony.

Most of us know the feeling of Anthony's brother. The Bible calls it revenge.

Hatred, Forgiveness

Date used __________ Place ____________________

In 1946 Akio Morita and another man started a new company called Tokyo Telecommunications Engineering in a bombed-out department store in Tokyo, says writer Kevin Maney.

In 1955 Mr. Morita's company made the world's first portable transistor radio. An American company, Bulova, offered to buy the radios at a handsome profit, but the deal troubled Mr. Morita. Under the deal Bulova would sell the radios under their own name.

Morita wanted to establish his own company's brand name. So even though the deal would have brought his struggling company a much needed infusion of cash, Morita decided against the deal, telling the executives at Bulova, "I am now taking the first step for the next fifty years of my company."

Morita's company went on to become one of the greatest success stories in business. Besides the transistor radio, they built the first VCRs and the first compact disc players.

Incidentally, by the time he turned down the deal with Bulova, Morita had already changed the name of his company—to Sony.

In business the choice is often between present and future rewards—with the biggest rewards coming in the years ahead.

To enter the kingdom of God, we must forsake the enticing but small rewards this life offers to gain the reward of life eternal.

Faith, Priorities, Risk

Matt. 6:19–21; Rom. 8:18–25; 2 Cor. 4:16–18; Rev. 2:17; 3:5

Date used __________ Place ____________________

Rewards 572

Robert De Moor, in *The Banner,* writes:

The parable of the vineyard workers (Matt. 20) offends our sense of fairness. Why should everyone get equal pay for unequal work?

Back in Ontario when the apples ripened, Mom would sit all seven of us down, Dad included, with pans and paring knives until the mountain of fruit was reduced to neat rows of filled canning jars. She never bothered keeping track of how many we did, though the younger ones undoubtedly proved more of a nuisance than a help: cut fingers, squabbles over who got which pan, apple core fights. But when the job was done, the reward for everyone was the same: the largest chocolate dipped cone money could buy. A stickler might argue it wasn't quite fair since the older ones actually peeled apples. But I can't remember anyone complaining about it.

A family understands it operates under a different set of norms than a courtroom. In fact, when the store ran out of ice cream and my younger brother had to make do with a Popsicle, we felt sorry for him despite his lack of productivity (he'd eaten all the apples he'd peeled that day—both of them).

God wants all his children to enjoy the complete fullness of eternal life. No true child of God wants it any other way.

Family, Fairness

Date used __________ Place ____________________

Ray Stedman in *Talking to My Father,* writes:

An old missionary couple had been working in Africa for years, and they were returning to New York City to retire. They had no pension; their health was broken; they were defeated, discouraged, and afraid. They discovered they were booked on the same ship as President Teddy Roosevelt, who was returning from one of his big-game hunting expeditions.

No one paid attention to them. They watched the fanfare that accompanied the President's entourage, with passengers trying to catch a glimpse of the great man.

As the ship moved across the ocean, the old missionary said to his wife, "Something is wrong. Why should we have given our lives in faithful service for God in Africa all these many years and have no one care a thing about us? Here this man comes back from a hunting trip and everybody makes much over him, but nobody gives two hoots about us."

"Dear, you shouldn't feel that way," his wife said.

"I can't help it; it doesn't seem right."

When the ship docked in New York, a band was waiting to greet the President. The mayor and other dignitaries were there. The papers were full of the President's arrival, but no one noticed this missionary couple. They slipped off the ship and found a cheap flat on the East side, hoping the next day to see what they could do to make a living in the city.

That night the man's spirit broke. He said to his wife, "I can't take this; God is not treating us fairly."

His wife replied, "Why don't you go in the bedroom and tell that to the Lord?"

A short time later he came out from the bedroom, but now his face was completely different. His wife asked, "Dear, what happened?"

"The Lord settled it with me," he said. "I told him how bitter I was that the President should receive this tremendous homecoming, when *no one* met us as we returned home. And when I finished, it seemed as though the Lord put his hand on my shoulder and simply said, *'But you're not home yet!'*"

Yes, there *are* rewards for faithfulness, but not necessarily down here.

Faithfulness, Heaven

Date used __________ Place ____________________

Rewards 574

As Christmas 1996 approached, the Kingston Technology corporation of Orange County, California, informed its 523 employees they would soon receive an extra special Christmas bonus.

Having started in the owner's garage in 1987, Kingston Technology, like many high-tech companies, had experienced explosive growth, to the point where it now was the world's largest supplier of add-on memory boards for personal computers. And each year since the company had begun with just a handful of employees, the owners had followed a generous policy of giving 10 percent of the annual profits to the workers.

Well, in 1996 another company bought Kingston Technology for $1.5 billion. The arrangement called for Kingston's owners to retain control of their company, and they decided to carry on generosity as usual: they gave 10 percent of a billion or so dollars to their employees as a Christmas bonus! With the bonus computed on the basis of seniority and performance, that meant the average employee would receive $75,000, and the highest bonuses could reach $300,000.

This story had only one downside. When it hit the national news, Kingston Technology was besieged by a flurry of applications for employment, but alas they were not hiring.

The decision makers at Kingston Technology believe in giving lavish rewards to their workers. So does God. At the final judgment, the Christmas bonuses of this company will look like peanuts compared to the heavenly rewards God will shower upon those who have served him in this life. What's more, anyone who is willing is hired.

Heaven, Judgment Day, Treasures in Heaven

Matt. 6:19–21; 10:40–42; 25:14–30; Eph. 6:8; Rev. 22:12

Date used __________ Place ____________________

In December 1994 syndicated columnist Bob Greene told the inspiring story of Rob Mouw.

Rob played on the soccer team in his senior year at Wheaton Christian High School. In the final seconds of a big game against favored Waubonsie Valley, with his team behind by one goal, Rob was dribbling the ball in front of him, running at full speed toward the opponent's goal. Just before he shot the ball, though, he caught sight of the scoreboard. The clock read 00.00. But like any good athlete, Rob shot the ball anyway, and it went in for a goal. The referee signaled that the goal counted, and the game finished in a tie.

The Wheaton fans cheered. The Waubonsie Valley fans cried that time had run out.

Rob had a choice to make. He could say nothing and avoid a loss. After all, it was the referee's job to decide the calls, not his. Or Rob could do what was right.

Rob asked the referee whether the official time was kept on the scoreboard or the referee's stopwatch. The referee said the scoreboard time was official and then ran off the field. Rob went to his coaches and explained that just before his kick, he had seen zeros on the scoreboard clock. Since he hadn't heard a whistle, he kept playing. But his goal was late, and he didn't think it should count.

His coaches agreed, and so they went over to the opposing coaches, explained what had happened, and conceded victory to Waubonsie Valley.

Bob Greene ended his article with this quote from Rob Mouw: "Every time in your life you have an opportunity to do right, you should be thankful. For a person to know what right is, and then not to do it—that would be a sin. To have won the game—I mean, really, who cares? Doing the right thing is more important. It lets you have peace."

But that wasn't the end of the story, writes Kevin Dale Miller. "Sometime later Rob received a handwritten letter from a total stranger that said:

> Dear Rob, I read Bob Greene's wonderful column about you. I love sports and true sportsmen. My faith in our future was renewed and lifted by that column. Never lose your principles. Always stand for

> what's decent and right. That's what you told us all when you refused the victory!

The letter was signed by former President George Bush.

Doing what's right—it sometimes gets the attention and approval of the newspaper and even former presidents. It always gets the attention and approval of God.

Honesty, Integrity, Sportsmanship, Teenagers
2 Cor. 8:21; 13:8; 1 Tim. 4:12

Date used __________ Place ____________________

576

In the Antarctic summer of 1908–9, Sir Ernest Shackleton and three companions attempted to travel to the South Pole from their winter quarters. They set off with four ponies to help carry the load. Weeks later, their ponies dead, rations all but exhausted, they turned back toward their base, their goal not accomplished. Altogether, they trekked 127 days.

On the return journey, as Shackleton records in *The Heart of the Antarctic,* the time was spent talking about food—elaborate feasts, gourmet delights, sumptuous menus. As they staggered along, suffering from dysentery, not knowing whether they would survive, every waking hour was occupied with thoughts of eating.

Jesus, who also knew the ravages of food deprivation, said, "Blessed are those who hunger and thirst for *righteousness*." We can understand Shackleton's obsession with food, which offers a glimpse of the passion Jesus intends for our quest for righteousness.

Hunger, Scripture

Date used __________ Place ____________________

Righteousness 577

Good posture contributes to good health. That is what several studies and physicians suggest, says writer Brenda Kearns.

"Poor posture can cause headaches," says back specialist Laura Fleck, M.D. "The problem is your head," says Kearns. "It weighs 20 pounds, and when it's hanging forward, it strains the muscles that hold the neck vertebrae together."

Dr. Fleck also says that "many patients with low back pain have it because of poor posture." A spine out of proper alignment adversely affects the spinal disks and overworks back muscles.

Posture may have something to do with carpal tunnel syndrome. One study found that "women who practice good posture for most of their work day are four times less likely to get CTS."

Chiropractors have long claimed that poor posture affects a person's blood pressure and heart rate by adversely affecting the nerves that run from the spine to the rest of the body.

One of the visual words the Bible uses to describe a person of character is uprightness. Just as good physical posture contributes to health, so good spiritual posture—a righteous lifestyle—brings health to our spirit, soul, and body.

Character, Honesty, Integrity, Uprightness
Ps. 32:10; Isa. 48:22

Date used __________ Place ____________________

Author Ken R. Canfield, president of the National Center for Fathering, writes in *New Man:*

> Some 20 years ago, I was a "Big Brother" to a boy named Brian whose parents were divorced. Brian was caught in that time of his life when he was figuring out his identity as a young man and a son. My wife, Dee, and I were newlyweds with no children—yet. We came to know Brian's family, and his mother asked if I could spend some time with him.
>
> Brian and I spent many Saturdays together, and I'll never forget the way he watched me and listened closely to everything I said. We never did anything extravagant—usually just hung out together. Then one experience helped me realize that it's on God's heart to provide a male role model for the fatherless.
>
> One day I sat down and wrote Brian a short one-paragraph letter. It wasn't anything profound or heartwarming but said something like: "Dear Brian, I'm looking forward to getting together again with you this Saturday. I've enjoyed our time together, and I just want you to know that you're a great guy to be around. Your Big Brother, Ken."
>
> Nothing life-changing from my perspective. But the next time I visited Brian, I noticed my letter was proudly displayed on his wall and surrounded by posters of sports heroes. When I saw that, I realized the impact I could have in Brian's life.

Attention, Caring, Child Rearing, Encouragement, Example, Family, Fathers, Influence, Love, Men, Togetherness
1 Thess. 5:11; Heb. 3:13

Date used __________ Place ____________________

Role Models 579

In *Sports Spectrum* Harold Reynolds, ESPN baseball analyst and one-time all-star second baseman for the Seattle Mariners, writes:

> When I was growing up in Corvallis, Oregon, there was an NBA player named Gus Williams. Gus tied his shoes in back instead of in front like normal. I thought that was so cool. So I started tying my shoes in the back. I wanted to be like Gus. He wore number 10; I wore number 10. He wore one wrist band; I wore one wrist band.
>
> One day I was lying in bed and my stomach was killing me. I noticed that it wasn't my sports hero, Gus Williams, who came to my room to take care of me.
>
> It was my mother.
>
> That's when I began to understand the difference between heroes and role models. I stopped looking at athletic accomplishments to determine who I wanted to pattern my life after. Instead, I tried to emulate people with strong character who were doing things of lasting value.

Whom we look up to largely determines who we become. Choose your heroes well.

Character, Heroes, Mothers
1 Cor. 11:1; Phil. 3:17; 4:9

Date used __________ Place ____________________

Routine 580

In his book *Ordering Your Private World,* Gordon MacDonald tells how one of his college professors gave him a piece of priceless advice.

Here's how it happened. MacDonald read a paper to a special gathering of students and teachers at Denver Seminary expressing his views on a burning moral issue. To write that paper, MacDonald had cut two of his classes during the day, one of which was the missiology class of Dr. Raymond Buker.

Dr. Buker came up to MacDonald after the special meeting and said, "Gordon, the paper you read tonight was a good one but it wasn't a great one. Would you like to know why?"

MacDonald sensed this would hurt but said yes.

"The paper wasn't a great one," Dr. Buker said as he thumped his finger on MacDonald's chest, "because you sacrificed the routine to write it."

MacDonald writes:

> In pain I learned one of the most important lessons I ever needed to learn. Because my time as a Christian leader is generally my own to use as I please, it would be very easy to avoid routine, unspectacular duties and give myself only to the exciting things that come along. But most of life is lived in the routine, and Buker was right: The man or woman who learns to make peace with routine responsibilities and obligations will make the greatest contributions in the long run.

Correction, Responsibility, Self-Discipline
Luke 17:7–10

Date used __________ Place ____________________

Rumors 581

Imagine trying to put out a wind-blown forest fire with a squirt gun. That's what Gerber Products, the baby-food company, felt they were doing in 1997. Someone somewhere started a false rumor about the company that spread like wildfire.

According to John Schmeltzer in the *Chicago Tribune,* the rumor said Gerber had been involved in a class-action lawsuit and would give a $500 gift certificate to families with children to settle the suit. Supposedly all the parents had to do to get the money was send a claim form and copies of their children's birth certificates and social security numbers to a post-office box in Minneapolis by October 1, 1997.

Once the rumor caught fire, it began to spread along channels that gave it an appearance of legitimacy: notices were posted in hospitals and sent home with children by schoolteachers. One corporation even put the false notice in the envelope with their employees' paychecks.

Gerber Products tried to stomp out the bogus story, putting a notice on several internet web sites, tracking down sources of the rumor, and informing the media. Nevertheless, they received over 18,000 phone calls to their toll-free telephone number in the three-week period before October 1 from people requesting the bogus claim form.

According to Schmeltzer, the cost to Gerber Products of fighting this rumor was in the millions of dollars.

Passing along a rumor may seem harmless, but someone pays an undeserved price if we are not careful about the truth. Never take lightly the power of the tongue to do others harm.

Gossip, Speech, Tongue, Truth, Words
Rom. 1:29; 1 Tim. 5:13; James 3:1–12

Date used __________ Place ____________________

Gordon MacDonald writes:

One Saturday morning I sat in our kitchen obviously rattled and withdrawn, and my wife, Gail, was trying to discern what it was that was bothering me. Suddenly, she asked one question too many, and I broke into weeping. Even now, I remember the next two hours vividly because it seemed as if I would never be able to stop the flow of tears. . . .

For the previous two weeks I had minimized my sleep because of busyness; thus I was physically exhausted. I had allowed my schedule to become so packed that I had ignored any times of personal worship; thus I was spiritually empty. In what seemed to be a remarkable coincidence I had presided at two funerals of indigent men who had died on the city streets and whose lives and deaths seemed to me to be so terribly meaningless. The experiences had profoundly affected me. Additionally, I had been reading a then well-known author who was launching an attack on matters of personal belief important to me, and I was not responding well to his logic.

On that Saturday morning I was a dried-out man. My resources were nonexistent. Years and accumulated experience later, I would know better than to get backed into such a corner. But I didn't know that then. It was a difficult way to learn an important lesson about being empty.

Burnout, Emotions, Fatigue, Work
Mark 6:31

Date used __________ Place ____________________

Extended rest is an essential regimen for the physical recovery of those who run in a marathon. Many athletes, however, try to return to hard training too quickly, says writer Bob Condor in the *Chicago Tribune.*

Joe Henderson, a columnist for *Runner's World,* says, "Runners make the incorrect assumption that once the soreness in muscles is gone, then they are recovered. But thousands of microscopic tears in the muscles can take four to six weeks for complete healing."

Henderson recommends that marathon runners take a day off from regular training for every mile run in a competitive race.

Gregory Florez, president of First Fitness Inc., says, "There is also a risk of long-term damage to your joints if you don't force yourself to get enough rest."

Condor says, "Research reveals a biochemical phase of recovery. It takes time to balance fluids and hormones in the body after the extraordinary requirements of running 26.2 miles. . . .

"One study revealed faster recovery for muscle tissue by marathoners who did not exercise for a full 10 days after the race. But taking time from the running trail can be difficult for some people."

Runners aren't the only ones who don't want to get all the rest they need. With many things to do and goals to reach, taking a weekly day of rest for spiritual renewal can seem impossible. Nevertheless God instituted the Sabbath principle not just for the sake of our bodies but also for our soul and spirit.

Endurance, Healing, Renewal, Rest, Work
Exod. 16:22–30; 20:8–11; Matt. 11:28–29; Mark 6:31

Date used __________ Place ____________________

584

According to the Associated Press, the North Carolina state medical board suspended the license of a neurosurgeon in Wilmington, North Carolina, after an investigation turned up remarkably casual behavior on his part during brain surgery.

The investigation revealed that in the middle of one surgery, as a patient's brain was exposed, the neurosurgeon left the operating room for twenty-five minutes to go and have lunch. While he was having lunch, no other physician was present in the operating room to care for the patient.

In another case the neurosurgeon told a nurse to drill holes in a patient's head and work on the outer brain even though she was untrained for such procedures.

When a person regularly deals with awesome things, he or she can become too familiar and too casual with them. We must guard against that ever happening with the sacred things of God.

Overfamiliarity, Respect, Reverence
1 Sam. 2:12–17; 1 Peter 1:17–19

Date used __________ Place ____________________

585

Fred Craddock, in an address to ministers, caught the practical implications of consecration:

To give my life for Christ appears glorious. To pour myself out for others . . . to pay the ultimate price of martyrdom—I'll do it. I'm ready, Lord, to go out in a blaze of glory.

We think giving our all to the Lord is like taking a $1,000 bill and laying it on the table—"Here's my life, Lord. I'm giving it all."

But the reality for most of us is that he sends us to the bank and has us cash in the $1,000 for quarters. We go through life putting out 25 cents here and 50 cents there. Listen to the neighbor kid's troubles instead of saying, "Get lost." Go to a committee meeting. Give a cup of water to a shaky old man in a nursing home.

Usually giving our life to Christ isn't glorious. It's done in all those little acts of love, 25 cents at a time. It would be easy to go out in a flash of glory; it's harder to live the Christian life little by little over the long haul.

Consecration, Little Things

Date used __________ Place ____________________

In *Christian Living,* Lafcadio Hearn tells of a Japanese seashore village over a hundred years ago, where an earthquake startled the villagers one autumn evening. But, being accustomed to earthquakes, they soon went back to their activities. Above the village on a high plain, an old farmer was watching from his house. He looked at the sea, and the water appeared dark and acted strangely, moving against the wind, running away from the land. The old man knew what it meant. His one thought was to warn the people in the village.

He called to his grandson, "Bring me a torch! Make haste!" In the fields behind him lay his great crop of rice. Piled in stacks ready for the market, it was worth a fortune. The old man hurried out with his torch. In a moment the dry stalks were blazing. Then the big bell pealed from the temple below: Fire!

Back from the beach, away from the strange sea, up the steep side of the cliff, came the people of the village. They were coming to try to save the crops of their rich neighbor. "He's mad!" they said.

As they reached the plain, the old man shouted back at the top of his voice, "Look!" At the edge of the horizon they saw a long, lean, dim line—a line that thickened as they gazed. That line was the sea, rising like a high wall and coming more swiftly than a kite flies. Then came a shock, heavier than thunder. The great swell struck the shore with a weight that sent a shudder through the hills and tore their homes to matchsticks. It drew back, roaring. Then it struck again, and again, and yet again. Once more it struck and ebbed; then it returned to its place.

On the plain no word was spoken. Then the voice of the old man was heard, saying gently, "That is why I set fire to the rice." He stood among them almost as poor as the poorest, for his wealth was gone—but he had saved 400 lives by the sacrifice.

Love, Giving

Date used __________ Place ____________________

Joseph Ton was pastor of Second Baptist Church, Oradea, Rumania, until he was exiled by the Rumanian government in 1981. In *Pastoral Renewal,* he writes of his experience:

"Years ago I ran away from my country to study theology at Oxford. In 1972, when I was ready to go back to Rumania, I discussed my plans with some fellow students. They pointed out that I might be arrested at the border. One student asked, 'Joseph, what chances do you have of successfully implementing your plans?'"

Ton asked God about it, and God brought to mind Matthew 10:16—"I send you as sheep in the midst of wolves"—and seemed to say, "Tell me, what chance does a sheep surrounded by wolves have of surviving five minutes, let alone of converting the wolves? Joseph, that's how I send you: totally defenseless and without a reasonable hope of success. If you are willing to go like that, go. If you are not willing to be in that position, don't go."

Ton writes: "After our return, as I preached uninhibitedly, harassment and arrests came. One day during interrogation an officer threatened to kill me. Then I said, 'Sir, your supreme weapon is killing. My supreme weapon is dying. Sir, you know my sermons are all over the country on tapes now. If you kill me, I will be sprinkling them with my blood. Whoever listens to them after that will say, "I'd better listen. This man sealed it with his blood." They will speak ten times louder than before. So, go on and kill me. I win the supreme victory then.'"

The officer sent him home. "That gave me pause. For years I was a Christian who was cautious because I wanted to survive. I had accepted all the restrictions the authorities put on me because I wanted to live. Now I wanted to die, and they wouldn't oblige. Now I could do whatever I wanted in Rumania. For years I wanted to save my life, and I was losing it. Now that I wanted to lose it, I was winning it."

Martyrs, Fear

Date used __________ Place ____________________

In 1994 Northwest Airlines offered some unusual round-trip passages aboard one of their planes. Fifty-nine dollars bought a "Mystery Fare" ticket that provided a one-day trip to an unknown American city. Buyers didn't find out where they were heading until they arrived at the airport the day of the flight. Still, the airline had plenty of takers. In Indianapolis fifteen hundred people crowded the airline counter to buy the Mystery Fare tickets that were sold on a first-come, first-served basis.

Not surprisingly, when buyers learned their destination, not all were thrilled. One buyer who was hoping for New Orleans but found he had a ticket for Minneapolis walked through the airport terminal yelling, "I've got one ticket to the Mall of America. I'll trade for anything."

Mystery Fare tickets may be a fun surprise for a weekend vacation, but normally the last thing you want is a ticket to a mystery destination. And one time you never want a Mystery ticket is on the day of your death. You don't want to face eternity uncertain about whether you will go to heaven or hell.

Assurance, Eternal Life, Heaven, Hell, Judgment
John 1:12; 1 John 5:13

Date used __________ Place ____________________

Salvation 589

In 1973 Gary Kildall wrote the first popular operating system for personal computers, named CP/M. According to writer Phillip Fiorini, IBM approached Kildall in 1980 about developing the operating system for IBM PCs. But Kildall snubbed IBM officials at a crucial meeting, according to another author, Paul Carroll. The day IBM came calling, he chose to fly his new airplane. The frustrated IBM executives turned instead to Bill Gates, founder of a small software company called Microsoft, and his operating system named MS-DOS. Fourteen years later Bill Gates was worth more than eight billion dollars.

Of Kildall, who has since died, author Paul Carroll says, "He was a smart guy who didn't realize how big the operating system market would become."

In a similar way, people often don't realize how big God's kingdom will someday become. God comes calling with the offer of a lifetime, and we find other things to do.

Appointed Time, Excuses, Kingdom of God, Opportunity, Priorities
Luke 14:15–24; 2 Cor. 6:1–2

Date used __________ Place ____________________

The following drama was originally reported by Peter Michelmore in the October 1987 *Reader's Digest:*

Normally the flight from Nassau to Miami took Walter Wyatt Jr. only sixty-five minutes. But on December 5, 1986, he attempted it after thieves had looted the navigational equipment in his Beechcraft. With only a compass and a hand-held radio, Walter flew into skies blackened by storm clouds.

When his compass began to gyrate, Walter concluded he was headed in the wrong direction. He flew his plane below the clouds, hoping to spot something, but soon he knew he was lost. He put out a mayday call, which brought a Coast Guard Falcon search plane to lead him to an emergency landing strip only six miles away.

Suddenly Wyatt's right engine coughed its last and died. The fuel tank had run dry. Around 8 P.M. Wyatt could do little more than glide the plane into the water. Wyatt survived the crash, but his plane disappeared quickly, leaving him bobbing on the water in a leaky life vest.

With blood on his forehead, Wyatt floated on his back. Suddenly he felt a hard bump against his body. A shark had found him. Wyatt kicked the intruder and wondered if he would survive the night. He managed to stay afloat for the next ten hours.

In the morning, Wyatt saw no airplanes, but in the water a dorsal fin was headed for him. Twisting, he felt the hide of a shark brush against him. In a moment, two more bull sharks sliced through the water toward him. Again he kicked the sharks, and they veered away, but he was nearing exhaustion.

Then he heard the hum of a distant aircraft. When it was within a half mile, he waved his orange vest. The pilot dropped a smoke canister and radioed the cutter Cape York, which was twelve minutes away: "Get moving, cutter! There's a shark targeting this guy!"

As the Cape York pulled alongside Wyatt, a Jacob's ladder was dropped over the side. Wyatt climbed wearily out of the water and onto the ship, where he fell to his knees and kissed the deck.

He'd been saved. He didn't need encouragement or better techniques. Nothing less than outside intervention could have rescued him from sure death. How much we are like Walter Wyatt!

Christ, Self-Help

Date used __________ Place ____________________

Salvation 591

In January 1985, a large suitcase, unmarked and unclaimed, was discovered at the customs office at Los Angeles International Airport. When U.S. Customs agents opened the suitcase, they found the curled-up body of an unidentified young woman.

She had been dead for a few days, according to the county coroner. As the investigation continued, it was learned that the woman was the wife of a young Iranian living in the U.S. Unable to obtain a visa to enter the U.S. and join her husband, she took matters into her own hands and attempted to smuggle herself into America via an airplane's cargo bay. While her plan seemed to her simple though risky, officials were hard-pressed to understand how such an attempt could ever succeed. Even if she survived the journey in the cargo bay, she would remain an illegal alien, having entered through improper channels.

Some people believe they'll enter the kingdom of God on their own since they've been reasonably good citizens or church attenders. But entry plans of our own design prove not only foolish but fatal.

Good Works, Kingdom of God

Date used __________ Place ____________________

In 1818, Ignaz Phillip Semmelweis was born into a world of dying women. The finest hospitals lost one out of six young mothers to the scourge of "childbed fever."

A doctor's daily routine began in the dissecting room where he performed autopsies. From there he made his way to the hospital to examine expectant mothers without ever pausing to wash his hands. Dr. Semmelweis was the first man in history to associate such examinations with the resultant infection and death. His own practice was to wash with a chlorine solution, and after eleven years and the delivery of 8,537 babies, he lost only 184 mothers—about one in fifty.

He spent the vigor of his life lecturing and debating with his colleagues. Once he argued, "Puerperal fever is caused by decomposed material conveyed to a wound. . . . I have shown how it can be prevented. I have proved all that I have said. But while we talk, talk, talk, gentlemen, women are dying. I am not asking anything world shaking. I am asking you only to wash. . . . For God's sake, wash your hands."

But virtually no one believed him. Doctors and midwives had been delivering babies for thousands of years without washing, and no outspoken Hungarian was going to change them now! Semmelweis died insane at the age of 47, his wash basins discarded, his colleagues laughing in his face, and the death rattle of a thousand women ringing in his ears.

"Wash me!" was the anguished prayer of King David. "Wash!" was the message of John the Baptist. "Unless I wash you, you have no part with me," said the towel-draped Jesus to Peter. Without our being washed clean, we all die from the contamination of sin. For God's sake, wash!

Sin, Custom

Date used __________ Place ____________________

593

In 1981, a Minnesota radio station reported a story about a stolen car in California. Police were staging an intense search for the vehicle and the driver, even to the point of placing announcements on local radio stations to contact the thief.

On the front seat of the stolen car sat a box of crackers that, unknown to the thief, were laced with poison. The car owner had intended to use the crackers as rat bait. Now the police and the owner of the VW Bug were more interested in apprehending the thief to save his life than to recover the car.

So often when we run from God, we feel it is to escape his punishment. But what we are actually doing is eluding his rescue.

Fear of God, Running from God

Date used __________ Place ____________________

The name Norma McCorvey probably doesn't mean anything to you. But the pseudonym that Norma McCorvey used in the landmark Supreme Court case in which she was the plaintiff you will probably recognize—Jane Roe, of *Roe versus Wade,* the infamous decision in 1973 that legalized abortion on demand.

According to Kathleen Donnelly, in 1969 Norma McCorvey was working as a barker for a traveling carnival when she discovered she was pregnant. She asked a doctor to give her an abortion and was surprised to find it was against the law. She sought help elsewhere and was recruited as the plaintiff in *Roe versus Wade* by two attorneys seeking to overturn the law against abortion. Ironically, because the case took some four years to be finally decided, McCorvey never was able to abort the child and instead gave her baby up for adoption.

She remained anonymous for a decade or so, and then Norma McCorvey went public. Donnelly writes:

> Shaking, sick to her stomach and fortified by vodka and Valium—she told a Dallas television reporter she was Jane Roe of Roe v. Wade. . . . Next, she admitted she had lied about that pregnancy in the hope it would help her get an abortion: It was a casual affair that made her pregnant, not rape as she told her Roe lawyers. And, little by little, through occasional interviews, sporadic speaking engagements and a 1989 television movie, she revealed that before she gave birth to the Roe baby and gave her to adoptive parents, she had given birth to two other children. . . . Slowly, she began speaking of her long-term lesbian relationship. . . . [Her memoir *I Am Roe*] leaves little out: not her childhood of petty crime and reform school, or the affairs with lovers of both sexes, or the long nights spent drinking in Dallas dives, or the days of low-level drug-dealing that preceded Roe.

According to writer Jeff Hooten in *Citizen,* McCorvey soon went to work answering phones for a Dallas abortion clinic. Next door to the clinic the pro-life group Operation Rescue leased an office. After a time, Norma began to have a change of heart. One day she began referring callers to Operation Rescue. Hooten writes:

Her turning point came when a 7-year-old girl named Emily—the daughter of an Operation Rescue volunteer who greeted McCorvey each day with a hug—invited McCorvey to church. On July 22, [1995], McCorvey attended a Saturday night church service in Dallas. "Norma just kept praying, 'I want to undo all the evil I've done in this world,'" said Ronda Mackey, Emily's mother. "She was crying, and you knew it was so sincere."

In August of 1995 she announced she had become a Christian and was baptized in a swimming pool in front of ABC "World News Tonight" television cameras. For a short time she said she still supported abortions in the first trimester, but before long that conviction fell by the wayside. Says McCorvey, "I still feel very badly. I guess I always will . . . but I know I've been forgiven."

Norma McCorvey proves once again that our Lord Jesus came to seek and to save those who are lost.

Abortion, Conversion, Forgiveness, Mercy of God, Patience of God, Repentance, Sinners

Matt. 9:9–13; Mark 2:13–17; Luke 15:1–32; 1 Tim. 1:12–16; 2 Peter 3:9

Date used __________ Place ____________________

Sanctification 595

The Australian coat of arms pictures two creatures—the emu, a flightless bird, and the kangaroo. The animals were chosen because they share a characteristic that appealed to the Australian citizens. Both the emu and the kangaroo can move only forward, not back. The emu's three-toed foot causes it to fall if it tries to go backwards, and the kangaroo is prevented from moving in reverse by its large tail.

Those who truly choose to follow Jesus become like the emu and kangaroo, moving only forward, never back (Luke 9:62).

Vision, Progress

Date used __________ Place ____________________

Satan 596

Satan is a schemer who uses all sorts of tricks to lure people into sin. One of his tricks is illustrated by a Chicago-area drug user who became a police informant. As an informant this man's job was to induce other drug dealers to sell drugs to him or an undercover policeman, and this informant was unusually successful.

One of his most successful strategies for duping drug dealers, according to Ted Gregory in the *Chicago Tribune,* was to give them a challenge.

This informant says, "I'd tell them, 'Everybody says they can deliver, but you look a little young; or you look a little old; or you look like a nerd.' Let the people think that they're in control. . . ."

This informant succeeded in duping dealers because he understood their psychology. Satan also understands psychology, and he uses the same scheme. He dupes people into thinking they're in control. He challenges their egos. Only after sin takes its course do people find out that ultimately they are not in control—that they are suckers.

Control, Deception, Ego, Temptation
Matt. 4:1–11; 2 Cor. 2:11

Date used __________ Place ____________________

597

In thirty years of marriage James Dobson of Focus on the Family says he never considered committing adultery. But in *Focus on the Family* magazine he recalls one time when Satan tried his best to lure him into that trap:

> Shirley and I had been married just a few years when we had a minor fuss. It was no big deal, but we both were pretty agitated at the time. I got in the car and drove around for about an hour to cool off. On the way home, an attractive girl drove up beside me in her car and smiled, obviously flirting. Then she turned onto a side street. I knew she was inviting me to follow her. I didn't take the bait. I just went home and made up with Shirley. But I thought how vicious the devil had been to take advantage of the momentary conflict between us. That's why Scripture refers to him as "a roaring lion looking for someone to devour."

No one, not even the most prominent of Christian leaders, is immune from Satan's temptations. We need to be on our guard.

Adultery, Marriage, Sex, Temptation

Gen. 39:6–12; Exod. 20:14; 1 Cor. 10:12–13; 2 Tim. 2:22; 1 Peter 5:8

Date used __________ Place ____________________

Have you ever flown in an airplane and wondered why a full cup of coffee doesn't spill when the plane turns? That's right, no matter how steep is the banked turn—even if the wings are perpendicular to the ground—coffee won't spill, a magazine will drop straight to the floor, and stewardesses will walk upright down the aisle as if the plane were level. And unless you are looking out the window, you cannot tell which way the plane is turning. All because of inertia.

Pilots, too, are subject to inertia. When flying through clouds or fog, which prevent them from seeing the horizon, pilots cannot feel the plane's wings beginning to bank to the left or right. In fact in the early days of flight, pilots followed the myth of instinct: They believed they *could* feel the turn, and when their planes were accidently engulfed in fog or clouds, many banked unknowingly into a spiral dive that ended in a crash. That's why pilot William Langewiesche writes, "Instinct is *worse* than useless in the clouds."

To fly through clouds, pilots must rely on instruments like the artificial horizon. The artificial horizon is a gyroscopically steadied line that stays level with the earth's surface and unerringly indicates when the wings are banking left or right. The artificial horizon revolutionized flying, but when it was first invented, pilots resisted using it. The biggest problem flyers had was belief. They trusted their feelings more than their instruments.

In the Christian life God's Word acts as our primary flight instrument. Our feelings can mislead us, but God's Word tells us the truth.

Confusion, Faith, Feelings
Prov. 3:5–6; 2 Cor. 5:7

Date used __________ Place ____________________

In 1997 the Central American city of Managua, Nicaragua, adopted a program that most cities take for granted: The city named its streets and numbered its buildings.

Larry Rohter writes in the *New York Times* that for twenty-five years Managua, with a population of 1.5 million, had been without that basic necessity following a devastating 1972 earthquake, which relocated most residents. During that time people learned to make do, wandering down the wrong streets, asking strangers where to go, and making one wrong turn after another until they hopefully found their destination.

Illogical is a good word to describe the system, if you can call it that. "Formal addresses have come to be defined neither by numbers nor street names," writes Rohter, "but in relation to the nearest landmark, as in: 'From El Carmen Church, a block toward the National Stadium' or 'Across from Los Ranchos Restaurant.'

"That, in turn, has made it necessary to name the points of the compass in giving directions or addressing a letter, an issue that has been resolved in an equally baffling fashion. 'Toward the lake' has come to mean north, 'toward the mountain' means south, 'up' means east and 'down' means west.

"Furthermore, though some of the original guideposts still exist, many others have vanished, leaving all but pre-quake residents confused. A leading economic research institute, for instance, offers visitors the following address: 'From where the gate of El Retiro Hospital used to be, two blocks toward the lake, one block down.'"

Finding your way in Managua sounds a lot like trying to live without the clear guidance of God's Word. You're dependent on directions from others who may not know the right way. You live by trial and error. You wander and feel lost. How much better to have a map!

Absolutes, Culture Wars, Ethics, Lostness, Morality, Postmodernism, Ten Commandments, Truth, Values
Prov. 14:12; 2 Tim. 3:16–17

Date used __________ Place ____________________

Second Coming 600

You just know that some things are going to happen sooner or later.

That's the way it was with Michael Parfit, a writer for *Smithsonian* magazine. For a feature article on the mighty Mississippi River, Parfit rode in a twelve-foot rubber dinghy down the Mississippi from Memphis, Tennessee, to the Gulf of Mexico.

Parfit learned of the incredible power of this giant river. The Mississippi gathers its water from 41 percent of the continental U.S., catching water from Montana to New York. Half a trillion tons of water flow down the Mississippi every year, carrying downstream sixty-three thousand tons of soil a day.

A river this big is a threat to the surrounding countryside. That's why engineers have built levees to pinch the mighty giant and keep it from flooding the farmland and towns nearby. The levees on the lower Mississippi stand, on average, twenty-five feet high and run for 2,203 miles on both sides of the main river and its tributaries.

"As the wall was built over the years," writes Parfit, "people came to live under its protection. They tore down the forest and planted cotton, and the floodplain of the Mississippi became the expanse of farmland known as the Mississippi Delta."

More than eight million people live in the Delta. But at what risk? Parfit flew in a plane over the Mississippi Delta and saw plainly the river's tracks on the land, where it once had flooded the Delta.

"The levee . . . cages the giant, or appears to," writes Parfit. "And no one but birds and an occasional light-plane pilot notices the long sweep of the river's indelible script. What the river has written in the mud again and again is simple: 'Someday soon.'"

Someday soon will come another flood. That's what Parfit warned in February of 1993. Someday soon will come another devastating flood like the ones in 1882, 1927, and 1973.

"People in this valley get a sense everything is totally controlled," one engineer told Parfit. "That's a false sense of security. We haven't seen anything yet in this valley as to what this river can do. We're not in control of anything."

"The river," wrote Parfit in February 1993, "moves brown, swift, unpredictable, enormous, always murmuring 'Someday soon . . .'"

In February 1993 when his article was published, Parfit could not have imagined how right he would be. Only months after the publication of the article, in the summer of 1993, came one of the worst floods in the history of the Mississippi.

God's Word warns that *someday soon,* in a moment, in the twinkling of an eye, Christ will return to the earth, bringing the terrible wrath of God on all who have not prepared their lives for his coming. Nothing can stop him. The wise person gets ready.

Judgment, Wrath
Luke 17:24–37; Rev. 19:11–21

Date used __________ Place ____________________

Second Coming 601

Neil Howe and Bill Strauss wrote a book called *13th Gen: Abort, Retry, Ignore, Fail?* about America's thirteenth generation, the people born between 1961 and 1981. This generation (the thirteenth since America's founding fathers) has been the victim of bad luck and bad timing, according to the authors. The thirteenth generation was the first whose mothers took pills not to have children, the first to go through the divorce revolution, and the first to go to school when schools stopped teaching traditional curriculum. As a result they have a strange combination of optimism and pessimism about life.

"They're individually optimistic and collectively pessimistic," says Neil Howe. "I liken them to a group of skydivers hurtling to the ground with only one parachute among them, but each one expects he'll get it."

Is there good reason for such feelings?

The Bible is also marked by a striking combination of optimism and pessimism. Scripture is absolutely pessimistic about humankind's ability to solve the problems of this world. We are hurtling toward the end. But the Bible is absolutely optimistic about the future. Christ is coming again to establish the kingdom of God on the earth. For *everyone* who believes on him, there *is* a parachute.

Busters, Gospel, Hope, Optimism, World
1 Thess. 4:13–18

Date used __________ Place ____________________

Second Coming 602

In *Out of Africa,* Isak Dinesen tells this story about her Kenyan cook Kamante.

> One night, after midnight, [Kamante] suddenly walked into my bedroom with a hurricane-lamp in his hand, silent, as if on duty. . . . He spoke to me very solemnly, . . . "I think that you had better get up. I think that God is coming."
>
> When I heard this, I did get up, and asked why he thought so. He gravely led me into the dining-room which looked west, toward the hills. From the door-windows I now saw a strange phenomenon. There was a big grass-fire going on, out in the hills, and the grass was burning all the way from the hill-top to the plain; when seen from the house it was nearly a vertical line. It did indeed look as if some gigantic figure was moving and coming toward us. I stood for some time and looked at it, with Kamante watching by my side, then I began to explain the thing to him. . . . But the explanation did not seem to make much impression on him one way or the other; he clearly took his mission to have been fulfilled when he had called me.
>
> "Well yes," he said, "it may be so. But I thought that you had better get up in case it was God coming."

Just in case, be ready. Just in case, be awake. People have been wrong in the past about when he would come, but make no mistake, one day he *is* coming.

Readiness, Watching
Matt. 24:36–51

Date used __________ Place ____________________

Second Coming 603

In the 1987 NCAA Regional Finals, LSU was leading Indiana by eight points with only a few minutes left in the game. As is often the case with a team in the lead, LSU began playing a different ball game. The television announcer pointed out that the LSU players were beginning to watch the clock rather than wholeheartedly play the game. As a result of this shift in focus, Indiana closed the gap, won the game by one point, and eventually went on to become NCAA champions.

While Jesus called us to be aware of "the signs of the times," he clearly called us to expend our energies in faithful, active service. As we await Jesus' promised return, we are not so much to watch the clock as to be diligent servants during the time we have available.

Service, Signs of the Times

Date used __________ Place ____________________

Missionary Gregory Fisher writes:

"What will he say when he shouts?"

The question took me by surprise. I had already found that West African Bible College Students can ask some of the most penetrating questions about minute details of Scripture.

"Reverend, 1 Thessalonians 4:16 says that Christ will descend from heaven with a loud command. I would like to know what that command will be."

I wanted to leave the question unanswered, to tell him that we must not go past what Scripture has revealed, but my mind wandered to an encounter I had earlier in the day with a refugee from the Liberian civil war.

The man, a high school principal, told me how he was apprehended by a two-man death squad. After several hours of terror, as the men described how they would torture and kill him, he narrowly escaped. After hiding in the bush for two days, he was able to find his family and escape to a neighboring country. The escape cost him dearly: two of his children lost their lives. The stark cruelty unleashed on an unsuspecting, undeserving population had touched me deeply.

I also saw flashbacks of the beggars that I pass each morning on my way to the office. Every day I see how poverty destroys dignity, robs men of the best of what it means to be human, and sometimes substitutes the worst of what it means to be an animal. I am haunted by the vacant eyes of people who have lost all hope.

"Reverend, you have not given me an answer. What will he say?"

The question hadn't gone away. "'*Enough*,'" I said "He will shout, 'Enough!' when he returns."

A look of surprise opened the face of the student. "What do you mean, 'enough'?"

"Enough suffering. Enough starvation. Enough terror. Enough death. Enough indignity. Enough lives trapped in hopelessness. Enough sickness and disease. Enough time. *Enough!*"

Hope, Millennium

Date used __________ Place ____________________

Second Coming 605

During his 1960 presidential campaign, John F. Kennedy often closed his speeches with the story of Colonel Davenport, the Speaker of the Connecticut House of Representatives.

One day in 1789, the sky of Hartford darkened ominously, and some of the representatives, glancing out the windows, feared the end was at hand.

Quelling a clamor for immediate adjournment, Davenport rose and said, "The Day of Judgment is either approaching or it is not. If it is not, there is no cause for adjournment. If it is, I choose to be found doing my duty. Therefore, I wish that candles be brought."

Rather than fearing what is to come, we are to be faithful till Christ returns. Instead of fearing the dark, we're to be lights as we watch and wait.

Faithfulness, Service

Date used __________ Place ____________________

Secrets 606

In July 1994 Intel learned that its Pentium processing chip had a flaw. The chip would occasionally give wrong answers for division problems using large numbers. Intel believed this was a minor flaw, something they felt would affect the average user once every twenty-seven thousand years. So Intel decided not to make known the flaw and for months continued to promote and sell the flawed computer chip.

But by Thanksgiving word of the flaw began circulating among computer users. Intel finally acknowledged the problem but tried to downplay its significance. They refused to exchange the flawed chip except in special circumstances. Only when IBM decided to stop selling computers with a Pentium chip did Intel back down and agree to exchange the chip when anyone requested. The Pentium affair was a huge black eye on the image of the company, less because their chip had a flaw and more because they tried to cover it up.

We can point our fingers at Intel, but who of us has not done the same thing? Just as the problem with the Pentium chip eventually came out, so every secret sin in our lives will sooner or later come out. Cover-ups only aggravate the problem.

Confession, Judgment Day
Luke 12:2–3

Date used __________ Place ____________________

Secrets 607

On February 9, 1996, a railroad train running from Waldwick, New Jersey, to Hoboken ran through a red signal and smashed into the side of another train at a crossing. The crash killed the engineers of both trains and one passenger, and injured 158 other passengers.

One year later the National Transportation Safety Board announced the results of its investigation into the cause of the accident. The engineer of the train that ran the red signal was going blind. According to Matthew Wald in the *New York Times,* for nine years the engineer had progressively been going blind because of diabetes. He and his doctor both knew it. But he had kept his medical condition secret, no doubt for fear of losing his work, and the doctor, who reportedly knew that his patient was a railroad engineer, had not reported the man's condition to the railroad.

New Jersey requires that its engineers have a physical exam each year by the company's own occupational medicine specialist, but each year the engineer had "always answered no to the annual questions about whether he had diabetes, was taking any prescription medication or was under another doctor's care. He had had eye surgery twice, but apparently paid for it out of pocket rather than filing insurance claims," says Wald.

Unfortunately, the truth came out in a deadly way.

Some things we must not keep secret.

Community, Confession, Darkness, Denial, Healing, Honesty, Openness, Repentance, Transparency, Truth, Walking in the Light
2 Sam. 11–12; Eph. 5:13–14; James 5:16; 1 John 1:6–9

Date used __________ Place ____________________

608

During a hurricane in the Gulf of Mexico, a news report highlighted a rescue device used on the oil rigs. In case of fire or (in this case) hurricane, rig workers scramble into the bullet shaped "bus" and strap themselves into their seats. When the entry port is shut, the vehicle is released down a chute and projected away from the rig. The seat belts protect the occupants from the impact with the water. The capsule then bobs in the sea until the rescuers come to pick it up.

The device parallels the theological truth of Romans 8:1—"Therefore, there is now no condemnation for those who are *in* Christ Jesus." Justification does not mean our world always stops falling apart. The rig still may topple in the hurricane. But those in the right place, whether a rescue module or spiritually in Christ, are saved from the ultimate consequences of the storm. The storm will take its course. The welfare of the workers depends on whether they are *in* the rescue device.

Christ, Salvation

Date used __________ Place ____________________

Security 609

The 3-year-old felt secure in his father's arms as Dad stood in the middle of the pool. But Dad, for fun, began walking slowly toward the deep end, gently chanting, "Deeper and deeper and deeper," as the water rose higher and higher on the child. The lad's face registered increasing degrees of panic, and he held all the more tightly to his father, who, of course, easily touched the bottom.

Had the little boy been able to analyze his situation, he'd have realized there was no reason for increased anxiety. The water's depth in any part of the pool was over his head. Even in the shallowest part, had he not been held up, he'd have drowned. His safety anywhere in that pool depended on Dad.

At various points in our lives, all of us feel we're getting out of our depth—problems abound, a job is lost, someone dies. Our temptation is to panic, for we feel we've lost control. Yet, as with the child in the pool, the truth is we've never been in control over the most valuable things of life. We've always been held up by the grace of God, our Father, and that does not change. God is never out of his depth, and therefore we're as safe when we're "going deeper" as we have ever been.

Trust, Father God

Date used __________ Place ____________________

Security 610

In a sermon, Juan Carlos Ortiz spoke of a conversation with a circus trapeze artist. The performer admitted the net underneath was there to keep them from breaking their necks, but added, "The net also keeps us from falling. Imagine there is no net. We would be so nervous that we would be more likely to miss and fall. If there wasn't a net, we would not dare to do some of the things we do. But because there's a net, we dare to make two turns, and once I made three turns—thanks to the net!"

Ortiz makes this observation: "We have security in God. When we are sure in his arms, we dare to attempt big things for God. We dare to be holy. We dare to be obedient. We dare, because we know the eternal arms of God will hold us if we fall."

Faith, Obedience

Date used __________ Place ____________________

611

Glen Keane has done significant work as a Disney animator. He drew Ariel for *The Little Mermaid,* as well as the Beast and Aladdin in other Disney movies. He served as supervising animator for Disney's *Pocahontas.* One issue of *Premiere* magazine listed him as the one-hundredth most powerful person in Hollywood.

Keane came to work for Disney in 1974. "During that time, Keane was also increasingly open to questions of faith," writes Kevin Dale Miller in *Christian Reader.*

Raised a Catholic, he felt condemned by his sins and began looking for relief from his guilt.

Seeing his colleague Ron Husband reading a Bible one day during the lunch hour, Keane asked him what the Bible said about getting to heaven. Ron, who was also searching for answers, was studying John 3:16. He pointed it out to Keane and also gave him a Gideon's New Testament, which he had taken from a hotel room.

With the New Testament in hand, Keane walked down the street for lunch. On the way back, he read John 3:16 over and over. Slowly the truth and the implications of the verse sank in, and suddenly Keane found himself saying out loud, "I believe it! I believe it!"

"It was like suddenly I reached down and there was something there that wasn't before," Keane remembers. "There was a faith I could actually apply and believe with. From that moment on, I knew I was secure. I didn't need to fear judgment or hell or anything anymore."

Assurance, Belief, Conversion, Faith, Fear, Hell, Judgment
John 1:12; 3:16; Rom. 10:9–10

Date used __________ Place ____________________

Seeking God 612

Columnist Herb Caen writes in the *San Francisco Chronicle,* "Every morning in Africa, a gazelle wakes up. It knows it must run faster than the fastest lion or it will be killed. Every morning a lion wakes up. It knows it must outrun the slowest gazelle or it will starve to death. It doesn't matter whether you are a lion or a gazelle; when the sun comes up, you'd better be running."

Spurgeon writes likewise, "If you are not seeking the Lord, the Devil is seeking you. If you are not seeking the Lord, judgment is at your heels."

In the Christian life, it's not enough simply to wake up. We are called to run, to become more like Christ, to press ahead in godliness.

Godliness, Complacency

Date used __________ Place ______________________

Self-Absorption 613

Clifton Fadiman, in *The Little, Brown Book of Anecdotes,* tells a story about Vladimir Nabokov, the Russian-born novelist who achieved popular success with his novels *Lolita* (1955), *Pale Fire* (1962), and *Ada* (1969).

One summer in the 1940s, Nabokov and his family stayed with James Laughlin at Alta, Utah, where Nabokov took the opportunity to enlarge his collection of butterflies and moths. Fadiman relates:

Nabokov's fiction has never been praised for its compassion; he was single-minded if nothing else. One evening at dusk he returned from his day's excursion saying that during hot pursuit near Bear Gulch he had heard someone groaning most piteously down by the stream.

"Did you stop?" Laughlin asked him.

"No, I had to get the butterfly."

The next day the corpse of an aged prospector was discovered in what has been renamed, in Nabokov's honor, Dead Man's Gulch.

While people around us are dying, how often we chase butterflies!

Evangelism, Compassion

Date used __________ Place ____________________

Self-Centeredness 614

According to Alex Heard in the *New York Times Magazine,* for those who just can't get enough of themselves, a doll company in Denver, Colorado, has the perfect item: the My Twin Doll. For between $130 and $170 you can have a doll custom-made to be a mirror image of your adolescent self, right down to the hairstyle and wardrobe selections. Just send the company a photo, and soon you can go to sleep cuddling a doll-sized version of the one and only you.

Arrogance, Egotism, Pride, Self-Love
2 Tim. 3:2

Date used __________ Place ____________________

Self-Control 615

Some stories make very clear the importance of self-control.

In December 1993 a thirty-two-year-old man in Buenos Aires died of overeating. At death he weighed 660 pounds. Five days before he died, he ate an entire piglet for dinner, which put him in the hospital's intensive care ward. To carry him to the hospital, doctors had to call the town's fire brigade.

Any appetite that's out of control is dangerous, whether it is the appetite for food, sex, money, or power.

Addictions, Appetites, Depression, Gluttony, Greed
Rom. 16:18; Gal. 5:22–23

Date used __________ Place ____________________

According to the Reuters news service, on Wednesday, November 9, 1994, Goffrey Mayne of West Haven, Connecticut, pulled his car up to an intersection and thought he noticed a problem with his brakes. He shifted the car into park and got out of the car to check his wheels. With no one at the driver's seat, the car suddenly slipped into reverse and took off backward at high speed. The steering wheel spun, and the car began to circle round and round in the middle of the busy intersection.

The police and fire departments were called. The car kept circling at high speed, blocking morning rush hour traffic. Almost two hours passed with no end in sight. Finally the authorities devised a plan. They positioned tractor trailers to block traffic. Then they simultaneously drove three front-end payloaders—the type used for earth moving—into the out-of-control car. With the car pinned, firefighters broke the driver's side window, reached in, and turned off the ignition.

The car, as you would guess, suffered extensive damage.

Like a runaway car without a driver, people without self-control are a hazard to themselves and everyone around them. In the end, they are pinned only by painful necessity—debt, divorce, sickness, depression, unemployment, total rejection. How much easier it is to stay at the wheel and thereby save yourself the pain and expense.

Addictions, Discipline, Leadership
Gal. 5:23; 2 Tim. 1:7; 2 Peter 1:6

Date used __________ Place ____________________

Self-Control 617

Sandra had an unusual problem, and it would be the ruin of her family. She lived in Cincinnati, Ohio, with her husband, Alexander, and three children ages two, three, and five. When her husband could no longer bear with her problem, he moved out of the home. Two weeks later he called the police to report that his wife was neglecting the children. The police drove to Sandra's apartment and found deplorable conditions. The children's playroom was littered with broken glass and debris, and there were children's handprints in human feces.

Sandra's problem, said her husband, was a compulsion for surfing the Internet. She spent up to twelve hours a day at the computer.

Police Sergeant Paul Neudigate said, "She would lock the children in their room so as not to be bothered. The place was in complete shambles, but the computer area was clean—completely immaculate."

Police took custody of the children and charged Sandra with three counts of child endangerment.

In a world filled with interesting and pleasurable things, self-control is a survival skill.

Addictions, Balance, Interests, Moderation, Pleasure, Priorities
Prov. 25:16; Gal. 5:22–23; 2 Tim. 1:7

Date used __________ Place ____________________

In May 1996, 5-foot–7-inch, 118-pound Miss Venezuela won the Miss Universe contest. According to the *Chicago Tribune,* after her victory reporters asked her what she wanted to do first. "I'm going to do something," she said, "I haven't been able to do for three weeks—eat, eat, eat and sleep."

Apparently she kept her word. She quickly gained weight, to the point where pageant officials were complaining. One pageant official explained, "She has various swimsuit contracts, and they're not happy that she has gone a bit chubby."

She kept on gaining, though. According to *People Weekly,* by January 1997 a new personal trainer weighed her in at 155 pounds, and at one point she weighed 160 pounds. But with the help of her trainer within a few months she was back down to an ideal weight of 130 pounds.

Without ongoing self-discipline how quickly we can squander our accomplishments. Self-control must be a lifestyle, not an occasional event.

Discipleship, Discipline, Indulgence, Sinful Nature
Judges 16; 2 Sam. 11; Gal. 5:13, 23; Col. 3:23

Date used __________ Place ____________________

Selfish Ambition 619

According to the *New York Times,* in the summer of 1994, a Virginia state trooper, who was a member of the bomb squad, and his dog, Master Blaster, became local celebrities when they found bombs at malls in Hampton and Virginia Beach.

That bit of celebrity evidently went to the state trooper's head. A hidden camera later recorded him placing a bomb in a shed that he had been asked to search for explosives. He was arrested and later pled guilty to planting explosives at two malls, a courthouse, and a coliseum. He told investigators he had not intended to hurt anyone. The bombs—a cardboard tube filled with explosives, and pipes filled with gunpowder and nails—never exploded. He said he was simply trying to enhance his image.

Selfish ambition is one of the most powerful—and potentially destructive—motivations we can have. When we are in the grips of selfish ambition, we can rationalize almost anything.

Deception, Image, Reputation
Phil. 2:3; James 3:14–16

Date used __________ Place ____________________

Self-Righteousness 620

In September 1994 the Associated Press reported on a demonstration by Indian farmers in New Delhi, India. They were protesting the government of India's plans to import three million tons of Dutch dung to be used for farm fertilizer.

Why? asked Indian farmers. There is no shortage of cows in India. And dung from Indian cows would not be tainted by pesticides.

So in protest, about one hundred Indian farmers rolled six ox carts piled high with top-quality, home-grown dung right up to Parliament. Presumably they got the legislators' attention.

Our dung is better than their dung. That's a claim that resembles the pride of the self-righteous person: I am more righteous than they are.

Arrogance, Salvation
Luke 18:9–14; Rom. 3

Date used __________ Place ____________________

621

In the summer of 1993 Colin Powell, then Chairman of the Joint Chiefs of Staff, visited the American troops serving in Somalia. On one day he made a grueling twenty-three stops in twenty hours. "Meeting the troops," said Powell in a *Life* magazine profile, "that's what it's all about."

At one base Powell shook hands with four hundred GIs and posed with them for photographs. A picture accompanying the *Life* article shows one such scene. Surrounded by a sea of troops, Powell has his arms around two soldiers as one of them holds his own camera at arm's length to take the shot.

Why did Powell take time for this in the middle of his heavy schedule? Because he couldn't forget what happened on one visit to the Old Soldiers Home in Washington, D.C. As he went from room to room in the hospital, veterans proudly showed him their faded snapshots taken with their commanding officers. Powell says, "That picture they had taken forty years ago with their general was the high point of their lives."

The high point of a Christian's life is similar. Our relationship to our Lord is what gives us our strongest sense of worth and pride. And unlike a photo opportunity, our relationship with Christ lasts forever.

Jesus Christ, Pride, Self-Esteem
Rev. 22:4

Date used __________ Place ____________________

Self-Worth 622

At the Pan American Games, champion United States diver Greg Louganis was asked how he coped with the stress of international diving competition. He replied that he climbs to the board, takes a deep breath, and thinks, "Even if I blow this dive, my mother will still love me." Then he goes for excellence.

At the beginning of each day, how good it would be for each of us to take a deep breath, say, "Even if I blow it today, my God will still love me," and then, assured of grace, go into the day seeking a perfect 10!

Mother, Love

Date used __________ Place ____________________

Servanthood 623

Businessman Harvey Mackay, who authored the book *Swim with the Sharks,* wrote a newspaper column about the importance of leaders being willing to do any kind of work. As an example of being willing to do anything on the factory floor, Mackay mentioned Philip Pillsbury of the Pillsbury milling family. Mackay wrote:

> The tips of three of his fingers were missing. . . . [That's] the unmistakable mark of a journeyman grain miller, albeit a somewhat less-than-dexterous one. [Philip] Pillsbury had an international reputation as a connoisseur of fine foods and wines, but to the troops, his reputation as a man willing to do a hard, dirty job was the one that mattered . . . and you can be sure everyone was aware of it.

The best leaders see themselves as servants. The people that are greatest in the kingdom of God are those missing the tips of their fingers.

Example, Leadership, Work
Matt. 20:25–28; John 13:1–17

Date used __________ Place ______________________

In Elmer Bendiner's book, *The Fall of Fortresses,* he describes one bombing run over the German city of Kassel:

Our B-17 (*The Tondelayo*) was barraged by flack from Nazi anti-aircraft guns. That was not unusual, but on this particular occasion our gas tanks were hit. Later, as I reflected on the miracle of a twenty-millimeter shell piercing the fuel tank without touching off an explosion, our pilot, Bohn Fawkes, told me it was not quite that simple.

On the morning following the raid, Bohn had gone down to ask our crew chief for that shell as a souvenir of unbelievable luck. The crew chief told Bohn that not just one shell but eleven had been found in the gas tanks—eleven unexploded shells where only one was sufficient to blast us out of the sky. It was as if the sea had been parted for us. Even after thirty-five years, so awesome an event leaves me shaken, especially after I heard the rest of the story from Bohn.

He was told that the shells had been sent to the armorers to be defused. The armorers told him that Intelligence had picked them up. They could not say why at the time, but Bohn eventually sought out the answer.

Apparently when the armorers opened each of those shells, they found no explosive charge. They were as clean as a whistle and just as harmless. Empty? Not all of them.

One contained a carefully rolled piece of paper. On it was a scrawl in Czech. The Intelligence people scoured our base for a man who could read Czech. Eventually, they found one to decipher the note. It set us marveling. Translated, the note read: "This is all we can do for you now."

Perseverance, Small Things

Date used __________ Place ____________________

Servanthood 625

Bruce Thielemann, pastor of First Presbyterian Church in Pittsburgh, told of a conversation with an active layman, who mentioned, "You preachers talk a lot about giving, but when you get right down to it, it all comes down to basin theology."

Thielemann asked, "Basin theology? What's that?"

The layman replied, "Remember what Pilate did when he had the chance to acquit Jesus? He called for a basin and washed his hands of the whole thing. But Jesus, the night before his death, called for a basin and proceeded to wash the feet of the disciples. It all comes down to basin theology: Which one will you use?"

Love, Duty

Date used __________ Place ____________________

The folklore surrounding Poland's famous concert pianist and prime minister, Ignace Paderewski, includes this story:

A mother, wishing to encourage her young son's progress at the piano, bought tickets for a Paderewski performance. When the night arrived, they found their seats near the front of the concert hall and eyed the majestic Steinway waiting on stage.

Soon the mother found a friend to talk to, and the boy slipped away. When eight o'clock arrived, the spotlights came on, the audience quieted, and only then did they notice the boy up on the bench, innocently picking out "Twinkle, Twinkle, Little Star."

His mother gasped, but before she could retrieve her son, the master appeared on the stage and quickly moved to the keyboard.

"Don't quit—keep playing," he whispered to the boy. Leaning over, Paderewski reached down with his left hand and began filling in a bass part. Soon his right arm reached around the other side, encircling the child, to add a running obbligato. Together, the old master and the young novice held the crowd mesmerized.

In our lives, unpolished though we may be, it is the Master who surrounds us and whispers in our ear, time and again, "Don't quit—keep playing." And as we do, he augments and supplements until a work of amazing beauty is created.

Weakness, Perseverance

Date used __________ Place ____________________

Don McCullough writes in *Waking from the American Dream:*

During World War II, England needed to increase its production of coal. Winston Churchill called together labor leaders to enlist their support. At the end of his presentation he asked them to picture in their minds a parade which he knew would be held in Piccadilly Circus after the war. First, he said, would come the sailors who had kept the vital sea lanes open. Then would come the soldiers who had come home from Dunkirk and then gone on to defeat Rommel in Africa. Then would come the pilots who had driven the Luftwaffe from the sky.

Last of all, he said, would come a long line of sweat-stained, soot-streaked men in miner's caps. Someone would cry from the crowd, "And where were you during the critical days of our struggle?"

And from ten thousand throats would come the answer, "We were deep in the earth with our faces to the coal."

Not all the jobs in a church are prominent and glamorous. But the people with their "faces to the coal" play a vital role in helping the church accomplish its mission.

Humility, Body of Christ

Date used __________ Place ____________________

Ted Engstrom in *The Pursuit of Excellence* writes:

I was cleaning out a desk drawer when I found a flashlight I hadn't used in over a year. I flipped the switch but wasn't surprised when it gave no light. I unscrewed it and shook it to get the batteries out, but they wouldn't budge.

Finally, after some effort, they came loose. What a mess! Battery acid had corroded the entire inside of the flashlight. The batteries were new when I'd put them in, and I'd stored them in a safe, warm place. But there was one problem. Those batteries weren't made to be warm and comfortable. They were designed to be turned on—to be used.

It's the same with us. We weren't created to be warm, safe, and comfortable. You and I were made to be "turned on"—to put our love to work, to apply our patience in difficult, trying situations—to let our light shine.

Comforts, Security

Date used __________ Place ____________________

Shame 629

At 3 A.M. on April 5, 1956, newspaper columnist Victor Riesel walked out of Lindy's restaurant in mid-town Manhattan. In his columns Riesel had crusaded for some time against gangster infiltration and corruption of labor unions, and earlier that night he had done a radio broadcast in which he assailed the leadership of a Long Island union. Accompanied by a friend and his secretary, Riesel headed toward his car, which was parked on 51st Street.

Near a theater, according to Lawrence Van Gelder in the *New York Times,* a young man stepped from the shadows and threw liquid into Riesel's face. It was acid. The acid hit Riesel in the eyes and blinded him. One month later doctors told Riesel he would never see again.

Riesel later wrote, "There was no terror at the moment when I knew I had crossed the line into permanent darkness. There was only a sudden feeling of shame. I was afraid that people would treat me too gently or shy away from me as though from a freak. And suddenly, I wondered if I could go on writing and earning a living."

Even when it is undeserved, shame is one of the most painful of emotions. (Victor Riesel overcame his unwarranted feeling of shame. He continued to write a newspaper column that appeared in the New York *Daily Mirror* and was syndicated in as many as 350 newspapers until he retired in 1990.)

Courage, Disability, Overcomers
Isa. 61:7; Rom. 10:11; Heb. 12:2

Date used __________ Place ____________________

Sharing 630

In its January 25, 1988 issue, *Time* provided an insight on selfishness and its corollary, sharing. Speaking about the introduction of the videocassette recorder, the article said, "The company had made a crucial mistake. While at first Sony kept its Beta technology mostly to itself, JVC, the Japanese inventor of the VHS [format], shared its secret with a raft of other firms. As a result, the market was overwhelmed by the sheer volume of the VHS machines being produced."

This drastically undercut Sony's market share. The first year, Sony lost 40 percent of the market, and by 1987 it controlled only 10 percent. So now Sony has jumped on the VHS bandwagon. While it still continues to make Beta-format VHS's, Sony's switch to VHS, according to *Time,* will likely send Beta machines to "the consumer-electronics graveyard."

Even in a cut-throat business, sharing has its rewards.

Selfishness, Greed

Date used __________ Place ____________________

Signs of the Times 631

The May 1984 *National Geographic* showed through color photos and drawings the swift and terrible destruction that wiped out the Roman Cities of Pompeii and Herculaneum in 79 B.C.

The explosion of Mount Vesuvius was so sudden, the residents were killed while in their routine: men and women were at the market, the rich in their luxurious baths, slaves at toil. They died amid volcanic ash and superheated gasses. Even family pets suffered the same quick and final fate. It takes little imagination to picture the panic of that terrible day.

The saddest part is that these people did not have to die. Scientists confirm what ancient Roman writers record—weeks of rumblings and shakings preceded the actual explosion. Even an ominous plume of smoke was clearly visible from the mountain days before the eruption. If only they had been able to read and respond to Vesuvius's warning!

There are similar "rumblings" in our world: warfare, earthquakes, the nuclear threat, economic woes, breakdown of the family and moral standards. While not exactly new, these things do point to a coming day of Judgment (Matt. 24). People need not be caught unprepared. God warns and provides an escape to those who will heed the rumblings.

Warnings, Judgment

Date used __________ Place ____________________

In a book called *All Thumbs Guide to VCRs,* which is a repair guide for amateurs, author Gene Williams begins with a warning. He writes:

> Getting a jolt from the incoming 120 volts ac (120 Vac) is more than just unpleasant; it can be fatal. Studies have shown that it takes very little current to kill. Even a small amount of current can paralyze your muscles, and you won't be able to let go. Just a fraction more and your heart muscle can become paralyzed.

Williams knows that the naive amateur repairman doesn't have sufficient respect for the lethal power of electricity. The amateur knows that a shock hurts but he thinks he can always let go of the wire. It is the paralyzing power of even a small amount of electricity that makes it so dangerous.

So it is with sin. People dabble with sin because they don't fear its power to paralyze the muscles of the soul. Then it's too late. Even when people know a sinful behavior is hurting them and they want to quit, they can't let go. Sin is never safe!

Addictions, Correction, Restoration, Temptation
Matt. 19:16–24; Rom. 7:15–23; Gal. 6:1

Date used __________ Place ____________________

When people dabble in sin and seemingly get away with it, they gain a false sense of security. They're like swimmers in shark-infested waters.

In an article about the great white shark, which hunts off the coast of central California, writer Tom Cunneff says that sharks return year after year to particular areas and they put a dedicated effort into a single attack. A shark stalks its prey at a favorite location by swimming three to ten feet off the bottom in shallow water (30 to 110 feet), waiting up to three weeks before darting to the surface for an attack. Cunneff described one such attack.

> In December, James Robinson, a sea-urchin diver, was killed by a great white off San Miguel Island, near Santa Barbara. Robinson, 42, was doing what he had done hundreds of times before—treading water as he took off his diving gear and placed it aboard his boat. In an instant, though, the activity turned from the familiar to the fatal as the shark shot up from the depths for a swift kill. Two crew members stowing equipment on the boat whirled around when they heard Robinson scream. "A great white bit me," is all Robinson, his right leg nearly severed, could mutter once they pulled him onto the deck. He died a few hours later.

Just as this shark stalked its prey, so does Satan. If you choose to linger in the ocean of sin, you can be sure of this: There is a shark in the waters. And sooner or later . . .

Consequences, Occult, Reaping, Satan, Sowing
Judges 16; John 10:10; 1 Peter 5:8

Date used __________ Place ____________________

In generations past, smallpox was a much feared disease. It killed hundreds of millions of people and scarred and blinded many more. It was highly infectious, contracted by breathing the exhaled breath of an infected person.

At one time there was no cure for smallpox. During the Middle Ages, smallpox epidemics often raged across Asia, Africa, and Europe. In some wars more soldiers died from smallpox than from combat.

In 1796 an English physician named Edward Jenner developed the first smallpox vaccine, says writer Donald Henderson in the *World Book Encyclopedia,* and the vaccination soon spread around the world. Many countries required by law that citizens be inoculated.

The health effort was a great success. In the 1940s smallpox was completely eradicated in Europe and North America. In 1967 only thirty countries still suffered the ravages of smallpox. The World Health Organization began an aggressive program in Africa, Asia, and South America to completely eradicate smallpox from the earth. Vaccination teams traveled from village to village searching for smallpox cases. In 1970 only seventeen countries still suffered from the disease. In 1978 the World Health Organization announced that the world's last known case of naturally occurring smallpox was in Somalia in October 1977. In 1980 they formally announced that smallpox had been eliminated.

But stocks of the smallpox virus were stored in freezers at the Center for Disease Control and Prevention in Atlanta. In September 1994 a committee of the World Health Organization unanimously voted to destroy the last stock of the smallpox virus on June 30, 1995. In public health's greatest triumph, the smallpox virus would be completely eradicated from the earth, never again to torment humankind.

It's hard to imagine that such a deadly disease could be completely annihilated. It's also hard to imagine a world cleansed of the plagues of sin and death and evil. But God will one day judge the earth, and by the authority of Christ, sin and death and all that is evil will be thrown into the lake of fire. God will create a new heaven and a new earth wherein dwells only righteousness. There will be no more death or tears, for Christ will have won the final victory.

Consummation, Death, Earth, End Times, Jesus Christ
1 Cor. 15:24–28; Rev. 20, 21

Date used __________ Place ____________________

In 1982, "ABC Evening News" reported on an unusual work of modern art—a chair affixed to a shotgun. It was to be viewed by sitting in the chair and looking directly into the gunbarrel. The gun was loaded and set on a timer to fire at an undetermined moment within the next hundred years.

The amazing thing was that people waited in lines to sit and stare into the shell's path! They all knew that the gun could go off at point-blank range at any moment, but they were gambling that the fatal blast wouldn't happen during their minute in the chair.

Yes, it was foolhardy, yet many people who wouldn't dream of sitting in that chair live a lifetime gambling that they can get away with sin. Foolishly they ignore the risk until the inevitable self-destruction.

Repentance, Complacency

Date used __________ Place ____________________

A man living in a forested area found his home overrun with mice—too many to exterminate with traps. So he bought a few boxes of d-Con and distributed them around the house, including one under his bed. That night he couldn't believe his ears; below him was a feeding frenzy.

In the morning he checked the box and found it licked clean.

Just to make sure the plan worked, he bought and placed another box. Again, the mice went for the flavored poison like piranha.

But the tasty and popular nighttime snack did its deadly work. In the days that followed, all was quiet. Just because something is popular doesn't mean it's good for you. In fact, it can be deadly—like sin.

Popularity, World

Date used __________ Place ____________________

Time-lapse photography compresses a series of events into one picture. Such a photo appeared in an issue of *National Geographic.* Taken from a Rocky Mountain peak during a heavy thunderstorm, the picture captured the brilliant lightning display that had taken place throughout the storm's duration. The time-lapse technique created a fascinating, spaghetti-like web out of the individual bolts.

In such a way, our sin presents itself before the eyes of God. Where we see only isolated or individual acts, God sees the overall web of our sinning. What may seem insignificant—even sporadic—to us and passes with hardly a notice creates a much more dramatic display from God's panoramic viewpoint.

The psalmist was right when he wrote, "Who can discern his errors? Acquit me of hidden faults. Keep back your servant from presumptuous sins."

Faults, Holiness

Date used __________ Place ____________________

Thomas Costain's history, *The Three Edwards,* describes the life of Raynald III, a fourteenth-century duke in what is now Belgium.

Grossly overweight, Raynald was commonly called by his Latin nickname, Crassus, which means "fat."

After a violent quarrel, Raynald's younger brother Edward led a successful revolt against him. Edward captured Raynald but did not kill him. Instead, he built a room around Raynald in the Nieuwkerk castle and promised him he could regain his title and property as soon as he was able to leave the room.

This would not have been difficult for most people since the room had several windows and a door of near-normal size, and none was locked or barred. The problem was Raynald's size. To regain his freedom, he needed to lose weight. But Edward knew his older brother, and each day he sent a variety of delicious foods. Instead of dieting his way out of prison, Raynald grew fatter.

When Duke Edward was accused of cruelty, he had a ready answer: "My brother is not a prisoner. He may leave when he so wills."

Raynald stayed in that room for ten years and wasn't released until after Edward died in battle. By then his health was so ruined he died within a year . . . a prisoner of his own appetite.

Addiction, Appetites

Date used __________ Place ____________________

Mike Yaconelli writes in *The Wittenburg Door:*

I live in a small, rural community. There are lots of cattle ranches around here, and every once in a while a cow wanders off and gets lost. . . . Ask a rancher how a cow gets lost, and chances are he will reply, "Well, the cow starts nibbling on a tuft of green grass, and when it finishes, it looks ahead to the next tuft of green grass and starts nibbling on that one, and then it nibbles on a tuft of green grass right next to a hole in the fence. It then sees another tuft of green grass on the other side of the fence, so it nibbles on that one and then goes on to the next tuft. The next thing you know the cow has nibbled itself into being lost."

Americans are in the process of nibbling their way to lostness. . . . We keep moving from one tuft of activity to another, never noticing how far we have gone from home or how far away from the truth we have managed to end up.

Backsliding, Lostness

Date used __________ Place ____________________

In *A View from the Zoo,* Gary Richmond, a former zookeeper, has this to say:

> Raccoons go through a glandular change at about 24 months. After that they often attack their owners. Since a 30-pound raccoon can be equal to a 100-pound dog in a scrap, I felt compelled to mention the change coming to a pet raccoon owned by a young friend of mine, Julie. She listened politely as I explained the coming danger.
>
> I'll never forget her answer. "It will be different for me. . . ." And she smiled as she added, "Bandit wouldn't hurt me. He just wouldn't."
>
> Three months later Julie underwent plastic surgery for facial lacerations sustained when her adult raccoon attacked her for no apparent reason. Bandit was released into the wild.

Sin, too, often comes dressed in an adorable guise, and as we play with it, how easy it is to say, "It will be different for me." The results are predictable.

Warnings, Self-Deception

Date used __________ Place ____________________

In 1997 Timothy McVeigh was convicted of bombing the Federal Building in Oklahoma City, killing 168 people. During the trial one of McVeigh's old army friends testified in court and made a revealing observation about human nature.

According to Jo Thomas in the *New York Times,* the friend said, "I'd known Tim for quite a while. If you don't consider what happened in Oklahoma, Tim is a good person."

Most of us have a similar outlook on ourselves as we consider the prospect of standing before the Judge of all the earth someday. No, we likely have not been found guilty of murder, but we can downplay our sins and judge ourselves by what we have done right. We think, If this or that isn't taken into account, I'm a good person.

The problem for us is that these failings of ours are gravely serious in the sight of a holy God, whose standard is perfect righteousness. He does not overlook any sin. Without a Savior, every person faces eternal judgment.

Guilt, Judgment
Gen. 3; Rom. 3:10, 23

Date used __________ Place ____________________

The thirty-seven-year-old New York man was a small-time crook, the kind who would mug little old ladies for the cash in their purses. But on Sunday, July 21, 1996, this crook messed with the wrong little old lady. According to the *Chicago Tribune,* the mugger bumped into a ninety-four-year-old woman in Greenwich Village and snatched her wallet. The NYPD later picked him up, and as they drove him to the station, police lieutenant Robert McKenna told the suspect, "You just robbed the mother of the biggest mob chieftain in New York."

The ninety-four-year-old woman was Yolanda Gigante, and her son is Vincent Gigante, described by authorities as head of the Genovese mob, the nation's most powerful Mafia family.

The police lieutenant later said, "When the perp heard that, he just slumped down into the backseat of the radio car. He had a sort of stunned, resigned look on his face, sort of saying, 'How could I be so stupid?'"

Whenever we sin, we get ourselves into more trouble than we bargained for.

Consequences, Death, Satan, Sin, Sowing and Reaping, Temptation
John 8:34–44; 10:10; Rom. 6:23; 1 John 5:19

Date used __________ Place ____________________

Sinful Nature 643

"Pali, this bull has killed me." So said Jose Cubero, one of Spain's most brilliant matadors, before he lost consciousness and died.

Only 21 years old, he had been enjoying a spectacular career. However, in this 1985 bullfight, Jose made a tragic mistake. He thrust his sword a final time into a bleeding, delirious bull, which then collapsed. Considering the struggle finished, Jose turned to the crowd to acknowledge the applause.

The bull, however, was not dead. It rose and lunged at the unsuspecting matador, its horn piercing his back and puncturing his heart.

Just when we think them dead, sinful desires rise and pierce us from behind. We should never consider the sinful nature dead before we are.

Temptation, Vigilance

Date used __________ Place ____________________

According to the *Chicago Tribune,* on May 9, 1994, a group of fourth graders at Fuller school on the south side of Chicago accused their substitute teacher of sexually molesting them. By that afternoon the school board promised to bring in counselors for the children. By evening the story was all over the news broadcasts.

But the next day police investigators came and interviewed fourteen of the children, and authorities determined the charges were false. Apparently the children made their false accusation because the substitute teacher threatened to report their unruliness.

One radio announcer reported that one child had promised to give classmates a dollar if they would join in the lie.

Speaking to this problem, Jackie Gallagher, a spokeswoman for the teachers union, said, "[Sexual abuse charges] are one of the hazards of the profession—a new one. Kids get sharper. It is akin to putting glue on a teacher's chair twenty years ago."

The teachers union president said that exonerating the teacher doesn't always make everything better. "What usually happens," he said, "when a person is accused of this kind of thing, is they're exonerated by the board publicly but then later, quietly, they're let go."

Slander is a vicious crime that does lasting harm.

Lying, Reputation
Matt. 15:19

Date used __________ Place ____________________

On the afternoon of August 2, 1997, James Aliff, a thirty-nine-year-old unemployed construction worker, woke up and found himself in a tough spot: He was lying face down between the rails of a railroad bed.

According to the *Chicago Tribune* news service, "Police believe Aliff might have been drinking and passed out on the track. Aliff said he slipped on a rock while walking his dog and was knocked out."

Whatever the cause, when Aliff woke up, he quickly realized he was not alone. Passing over him was a 109-car freight train.

"I got a headache, let me tell you," he later said from his Oak Hill, Florida, hospital bed. "About every three or four seconds an axle would come along and crack me upside the head. It's a good thing I wasn't on my back, or that train would have torn my face off."

If you are asleep in a dangerous place, you never know what can come upon you. Stay alert, and stay out of danger.

Alertness, Danger, Drunkenness, Problems, Troubles, Vigilance
Col. 4:2; 1 Thess. 5:1–8; 1 Tim. 4:16; 1 Peter 5:8

Date used __________ Place ____________________

Ed Hinton writes in *Sports Illustrated* that champion race car driver Dale Earnhardt was known for being so calm before races that occasionally he would take a catnap just before the start. While other drivers would have a pulse rate of 100 to 120 before a race, his would be less than 60.

But on August 31, 1997, at the Southern 500 race in Darlington, South Carolina, Earnhardt unintentionally took catnapping to a dangerous new level. At the start of the race, Earnhardt fell asleep at the wheel—he went into a semiconscious state but kept on driving. When he reached the first turn, he hit the wall but kept on going. At the second turn he again hit the wall, harder this time. He continued slowly around the track for two laps, looking for his pit but unable to find it. Finally he pulled off the track. Later he would say he remembered nothing of this.

Sixteen doctors examined Earnhardt to find out what had happened. They found nothing definite but suggested three possible explanations. A small blood vessel may have spasmed and restricted blood to the brain. Or he may have had a temporary short-circuit of the brain because of a previous accident. The third option was vasodepressor syndrome, in which the pulse rate falls rather than rises under stress.

The doctors didn't think the problem would recur, and they cleared Earnhardt to continue racing.

Frightening but true, it is possible, for a while, to drive over one hundred miles an hour and yet be asleep. In the same way, we can be busily racing through life—our eyes seemingly open, our hands on the wheel, our foot to the floor—yet spiritually asleep. Sooner or later, though, the trouble begins.

Busyness, Complacency, Stress, Watchfulness
Mark 13:32–37; Luke 12:35–40; Eph. 5:14; Col. 4:2; 1 Thess. 5:4–7

Date used __________ Place ____________________

According to Matthew Wald in the *New York Times,* on Friday, January 17, 1997, David Riach and his mother Dorothy, both pilots, were flying a single-engine Piper Dakota over the northeastern United States. Their destination was Saranac Lake, New York. Twenty-five minutes after takeoff, however, Mr. Riach did not respond to a radio message from a flight controller in New York. The plane was apparently on automatic pilot. After the third attempt by the flight controllers, the pilot's mother radioed to the tower that he was not responding. A few minutes later, she radioed that her son was vomiting.

Then she, too, began to experience physical problems. She radioed that she was getting tired. A minute later she said she was very, very tired. Another minute later she said she felt nauseated. A few minutes later, in the final communication she had with controllers, she said she just wanted to get the airplane down.

For an hour and a half the airplane continued to fly on autopilot. Finally it ran out of gas and crashed in Alton, New Hampshire, with no survivors.

Authorities investigated and several days later reported that the cause of the accident was a triangular hole in the plane's muffler, which allowed carbon monoxide to be sucked into the plane's heating system. The chief investigator said that at the time of the crash the victims were unconscious but alive.

Sleep can be dangerous in the wrong place. One such place is in your spiritual life.

Alertness, Self-Control, Wakefulness, Watchfulness
Mark 13:32–37; Luke 12:35–40; Eph. 5:14; 1 Thess. 5:4–7

Date used ________ Place ________________

Small Things 648

One of the world's most remarkable artists could put his entire life's work on the tips of your fingers. His name is Nikolai Syadristy, and he is a microminiature sculptor.

What do microminiature sculptors create? Mr. Syadristy has poised three gold camels inside the eye of a needle—along with a pyramid and a palm tree, writes Howard Witt. He has inserted a flea-sized red rose inside a hollowed-out human hair, as if in a vase. On the flat edge of a cut human hair, he has balanced two tiny, working padlocks, complete with keys. He has copied a six-hundred-note musical score on a chrysanthemum leaf the size of a grain of rice.

Microminiature artists must overcome huge obstacles. One sneeze or cough, and months of work can disappear. Static electricity—the spark that comes when you walk on the rug in winter and touch something—is another challenge. "When I was working on the oasis scene," says Syadristy, "I lost two camels because of static electricity. An electrical surge is like a giant catastrophe for these miniatures."

To carve a chess set balanced on the head of a pin or an electric motor smaller than the belly of an ant, Syadristy must wear thick, Coke-bottle-like glasses and peer through a microscope.

There are only five other microminiature artists in the world.

How difficult it is to work with little things! It is through God's perfect control of far smaller details in creation—molecules and atoms and DNA—that he reveals his unimaginable power.

Power, Sovereignty of God
Matt. 10:29–30; Heb. 1:3

Date used __________ Place ____________________

Solitude 649

In his sermon "Finding God in a Busy World," John Killinger tells the story of a woman whose life was transformed by solitude.

Killinger had traveled to New York to preach, and one night he took a walk with one of his hosts on a promenade that overlooked Manhattan. The woman explained the significance of that place to her. She had gone through difficult times since moving to New York several years before. Her husband had left her. Her daughter had been difficult to raise. One night she had walked to this promenade in such pain and despair that she didn't know how she could go on. Says Killinger:

> She sat on one of the benches and looked across the bay at the city. She stared out at Liberty Island in the distance and she watched the tug boats as they moved in and out of the bay. She sat and she sat. The longer she sat, she said, the more her life seemed to be invested with a kind of quietness that came over her like a spirit.
>
> Down deep she began to feel peaceful again. She said she felt somehow that God was very near to her, as if she could almost reach out and touch God. Better yet, she didn't need to reach out. God was touching her. She felt whole and complete and healed as she sat there that evening. It became a turning point in her life.
>
> "Since then," she said, "whenever I feel under pressure at my job or from any personal problems, I come down here and sit on this very bench. I'm quiet; I feel it all over again, and everything is all right."

Solitude uniquely enables us to sense the presence of God.

Peace, Prayer, Presence of God, Problems,
Spiritual Disciplines, Stress, Trials
Ps. 46:10

Date used __________ Place ____________________

According to *New Man* magazine, writer, theologian, and onetime Harvard professor Henri Nouwen once broke away from his busy schedule to live for six months in a monastery. Here is why:

> I realized that I was caught in a web of strange paradoxes. While complaining about too many demands, I felt uneasy when none were made. While speaking about the burden of letter writing, an empty mailbox made me sad. While speaking nostalgically about an empty desk, I feared the day in which that would come true.
>
> In short, while desiring to be alone, I was frightened of being left alone. The more I became aware of these paradoxes, the more I started to see how much I had fallen in love with my own compulsions and illusions, and how much I needed to step back and wonder, "Is there a quiet stream underneath the fluctuating affirmations and rejections of my little world?"

That quiet stream of contentment, of course, is found only in the Lord. And periods of solitude with him can be crucial to finding it.

Busyness, Compulsion, Contentment, Loneliness, Peace, Rest, Sabbath, Security, Spiritual Disciplines, Work

Ps. 62:1–2; Matt. 11:28–30; Mark 1:35–37; 6:31; Phil. 4:7

Date used __________ Place ____________________

A certain very practical man, whom we'll call Bob, took absolutely nothing for granted.

Bob kept a large toolbox and first-aid kit in the trunk of his Volvo, just in case.

He had a Swiss Army knife and cell phone in his briefcase, just in case.

Bob had insurance on everything. Why, he had insurance on his insurance, just in case.

He carried an umbrella with him to work even when the weatherman said there was more chance that the Cubs would win the World Series than that it would rain, just in case.

He filled his safe-deposit box with solid-gold Krugerands, just in case.

He had enough pension-fund money and IRAs to live well and travel often, even if he lived to 125, just in case.

But in all his preparation there was one thing Bob gave scarce thought to: What would happen to his soul after he died? What could be more impractical? he thought. He did not read the Bible seriously for himself. He avoided church. "Most likely," he would joke with his friends, "we die like a dog, and then it's over."

Wouldn't you know it, when Bob was forty-nine, his car was broadsided in an intersection by a drunk driver, and Bob died instantly. To Bob's surprise, though, his soul did not extinguish like a candle.

God said to him, "How could you be so foolish! You prepared for everything but what matters most: where your soul will spend eternity. And now forever and ever you will have nothing—nothing but unremitting sorrow."

After several thousand years in hell, Bob admitted to himself, What a fool I was to focus all my attention on that brief life on earth and ignore the life that will never end.

So will it be for all who do not prepare to meet God.

Afterlife, Death, Hell, Judgment
Amos 4:12; Luke 12:13–21

Date used __________ Place ____________________

Sovereignty 652

In *Knowledge of the Holy,* A. W. Tozer attempts to reconcile the seemingly contradictory beliefs of God's sovereignty and man's free will:

An ocean liner leaves New York bound for Liverpool. Its destination has been determined by proper authorities. Nothing can change it. This is at least a faint picture of sovereignty.

On board the liner are scores of passengers. These are not in chains; neither are their activities determined for them by decree. They are completely free to move about as they will. They eat, sleep, play, lounge about on the deck, read, talk, altogether as they please; but all the while the great liner is carrying them steadily onward toward a predetermined port.

Both freedom and sovereignty are present here, and they do not contradict. So it is, I believe, with man's freedom and the sovereignty of God. The mighty liner of God's sovereign design keeps its steady course over the sea of history.

Choices, Free Will

Date used __________ Place ____________________

Sovereignty 653

During his days as guest lecturer at Calvin Seminary, R. B. Kuiper once used the following illustration of God's sovereignty and human responsibility:

I liken them to two ropes going through two holes in the ceiling and over a pulley above. If I wish to support myself by them, I must cling to them both. If I cling only to one and not the other, I go down.

I read the many teachings of the Bible regarding God's election, predestination, his chosen, and so on. I read also the many teachings regarding "whosoever will may come" and urging people to exercise their responsibility as human beings. These seeming contradictions cannot be reconciled by the puny human mind. With childlike faith, I cling to both ropes, fully confident that in eternity I will see that both strands of truth are, after all, of one piece.

Free Will, Responsibility

Date used __________ Place ____________________

Sowing and Reaping 654

Several years after inventing radar, Sir Robert Watson Watt was arrested in Canada for speeding. He'd been caught in a radar trap. He wrote this poem:

Pity Sir Robert Watson Watt,
strange target of his radar plot,
and this, with others I could mention,
a victim of his own invention.

Sin, Lawlessness

Date used __________ Place ____________________

Sowing and Reaping 655

Comedian and actor Chris Farley, of *Saturday Night Live* fame, was found dead in his downtown Chicago apartment on December 18, 1997. The Cook County medical examiner's office later reported that he died of an opiate and cocaine overdose. According to Mark Caro and Allan Johnson in the *Chicago Tribune,* Farley's problems with drugs were no secret, and his death at age thirty-three, though a shock, was no surprise to his friends. He had been in and out of various programs to clean up his life many times.

In Farley's obituary in the *New York Times,* James Barron quoted from a recent interview of Farley in *Playboy:* "I used to think that you could get to a level of success where the laws of the universe didn't apply," said Farley. "But they do. It's still life on life's terms, not on movie-star terms. I still have to work at relationships. I still have to work on my weight and some of my other demons. Once I thought that if I just had enough in the bank, if I had enough fame, that it would be all right. But I'm a human being like everyone else. I'm not exempt."

Sadly, his words proved to be prophetic.

Addiction, Consequences, Drugs, Laws, Money,
Self-Control, Spiritual Laws, Success
Gal. 6:7–8

Date used __________ Place ____________________

Spiritual Discernment 656

In his book *Enjoying God,* Lloyd Ogilvie writes:

One of the most astounding achievements in ophthalmological surgery is the implanting of a lens in a human eye.

After a friend of mine had this surgery in both eyes, and the bandages were removed, he exclaimed, "How wonderful to have new eyes! . . ."

Our hearts have eyes. . . . Before conversion, our "inner eyes" are clouded over with cataracts blocking our vision. We cannot see ourselves, others, and life in the clear light of truth. Nor can we behold God's true nature or see the beauty of the world that He's given us to enjoy. We are spiritually blinded. . . .

Conversion begins the healing of our heart-eyes by removing our spiritual cataracts. We understand what the cross means for our forgiveness, but we still do not perceive all that the Lord has planned for us and the power He has offered to us.

We need a supernatural lens implant in the eyes of our hearts. . . .

Paul calls this lens the "Spirit of wisdom and revelation." . . . The Spirit is the lens for the eyes of our hearts.

Blindness, Conversion, Heart, Holy Spirit
John 9; 2 Cor. 4:1–6; Eph. 1:15–23

Date used __________ Place ____________________

Spiritual Discernment 657

There is a haunting photo by Alain Keler in the October 1993 issue of *Life* magazine. It is of a boy playing a flute. The boy, named Jensen, is only ten years old, but he probably can play some very sad songs. For when you look at his eyes—or where his eyes should be beneath his long, dark bangs—you see only redness, empty sockets. Jensen lives in a charitable institution in Bogotá, Colombia.

Blindness is always tragic, but the cause of blindness in this case only multiplies the sorrow. In the caption next to the photo, Robert Sullivan explains that the boy was likely the victim of "organ nappers." Eye thieves.

When Jensen was ten months old, reports his mother, she took him to the hospital with acute diarrhea. The next day when she returned, bandages covered Jensen's eyes. Dried blood was spattered on his body. Horrified, she asked the doctor what had happened.

He answered harshly, "Can't you see your child is dying?" and dismissed her.

She rushed Jensen to another hospital in Bogotá. After examining him, the doctor gave chilling news: "They've stolen his eyes."

Jensen is somewhat fortunate. He is alive. The organ traffickers usually kill their victims, excise body parts, and broker them to those willing to pay for healthy kidney or cornea transplants.

Organ thieves in Bogotá, Colombia, are not the only ones stealing eyes. There is someone who steals a person's ability to see in an even more tragic way: Satan.

Blindness, Greed, Satan, Stealing
John 10:10; 2 Cor. 4:4; 1 John 2:11

Date used __________ Place ____________________

658

Chile is one of the astronomy capitals of the world, boasting three big-time observatories, including the Cerro Tololo observatory with its five telescopes.

Chile is the mecca of astronomers for several reasons. The sky is clear 85 percent of the time. The Cerro Tololo observatory is built 7,200 feet above sea level in the Andean foothills, where there is less air to distort a telescope's view. The region has a natural inversion layer that keeps the air at high altitude stable and the view better. Northern Chile is also directly under the Milky Way, so astronomers can peer into our galaxy for up to eight hours a night, in contrast to five hours at observatories in Hawaii, which is the astronomy capital of the northern hemisphere.

Certain places on earth offer a clearer view of the heavens, and certain spiritual disciplines offer a clearer view of spiritual things. Throughout the history of the church, believers have found that activities such as Bible memorization and meditation, fasting and prayer, solitude and study, celebration and worship, guidance and confession have helped them better see God and his truth.

Devotional Life, Prayer, Spirituality
Matt. 6:1–18; 1 Peter 2:2

Date used __________ Place ____________________

Lionel Poilane bakes the most famous bread in Paris—large, heavy, round loaves that people line up to buy. Poilane's bread is extraordinarily good because even in our technological age he uses old-fashioned ways. He bakes his bread in brick ovens over oak-wood fires using only the finest of stone-ground wheat. Rudolph Chelminski writes in *Smithsonian:*

> Poilane equips each unit with tools and receptacles that, to a large extent, are straight out of the 18th century. Next to each kneading-trough, for example, hangs a bucket for water, instead of the automated faucet common to most bakeries today.
>
> "I intentionally installed a medieval system," he explains as we amble from oven to oven. "In bakery school, students learn to push a button that delivers 60 liters of water at 40 degrees Celsius. I tried that, but then I realized that the push-button just stops them from thinking about what they're doing—it disengages man from his work. With the buckets, the baker has to think about the quality and quantity of each batch of dough. Sixty liters at 40 degrees isn't necessarily right, you see? In baking, everything is a question of variables—the temperature that day, the humidity, the quality of the flour, and the like. There are no absolute rules. A good baker has to be intuitive and adjust. That's why I like to call my buckets a form of retroactive progress."

The writer summarizes, "From the wicker baskets where lumps of warm dough lie in seductive repose, rising as yeast swells their volume, to the long-handled wooden spatulas on overhead racks to the brick and wrought iron of the ovens and the raging fires within them, everything about [his bakery reflects his] loathing for pointless automation and modern trappings." According to this master baker, technology cannot improve on the baking of fine bread.

Neither can technology improve on spirituality. Like the water bucket, long-handled wooden spatulas, wicker baskets, and oak-wood fires, the spiritual disciplines are ancient but effective. They cause us to be sensitive to God.

Basics, Devotional Life, Fundamentals, Prayer
Matt. 4:4; Acts 13:2–3; 1 Peter 2:2–3

Date used __________ Place ____________________

660

In *Honest to God,* Bill Hybels writes:

> Several years ago, I played on a park district football team. During the warm-up before our first game, I learned that I would play middle linebacker on the defensive unit. That was fine with me; my favorite professional athlete is Mike Singletary, All-Pro middle linebacker for the Chicago Bears.
>
> . . . When it was time for the defense to take the field, I stood in my middle-linebacker position, determined to play with the same intensity and effectiveness I'd so often seen in Mike. . . .
>
> The opposing offensive unit approached the line to run their first play. Mimicking Mike, I crouched low and stared intently at the quarterback, readying myself to explode into the middle of the action in typical Singletary style. The battle raged . . . and reality struck with a vengeance. Using a simple head fake, the quarterback sent me in the opposite direction of the play, and the offense gained fifteen yards.
>
> So went the rest of the game. By the fourth quarter I came to a brilliant conclusion: If I wanted to play football like Mike Singletary, I would have to do more than try to mimic his on-the-field actions. I would have to get behind the scenes, and practice like he practiced. I would have to lift weights and run laps like he did. I would have to memorize plays and study films as he did. If I wanted his success *on the field,* I would have to pursue his disciplines *off the field.* Discipline is no less important on the field of Christian living.

Devotional Life, Preparation, Success
1 Cor. 9:24–27; 1 Tim. 4:7

Date used __________ Place ____________________

National Geographic ran an article about the Alaskan bull moose. The males of the species battle for dominance during the fall breeding season, literally going head-to-head with antlers crunching together as they collide. Often the antlers, their only weapon, are broken, which ensures defeat.

The heftiest moose, with the largest and strongest antlers, triumphs. Therefore, the battle fought in the fall is really won during the summer, when the moose eat continually. The one that consumes the best diet for growing antlers and gaining weight will be the heavyweight in the fight. Those that eat inadequately sport weaker antlers and less bulk.

There is a lesson here for us. Spiritual battles await. Satan will choose a season to attack. Will we be victorious, or will we fall? Much depends on what we do now—before the wars begin. The bull-moose principle: Enduring faith, strength, and wisdom for trials are best developed before they're needed.

Devotional Life, Trials

Date used __________ Place ______________________

662

Awhile back on "The Merv Griffin Show," the guest was a body builder. During the interview, Merv asked, "Why do you develop those particular muscles?"

The body builder simply stepped forward and flexed a series of well-defined muscles from chest to calf. The audience applauded.

"What do you use all those muscles for?" Merv asked. Again, the muscular specimen flexed, and biceps and triceps sprouted to impressive proportions. "But what do you use those muscles for?" Merv persisted. The body builder was bewildered. He didn't have an answer other than to display his well-developed frame.

Our spiritual exercises—Bible study, prayer, reading Christian books, listening to Christian radio and tapes—are also for a purpose. They're meant to strengthen our ability to build God's kingdom, not simply to improve our pose before an admiring audience.

Service, Devotional Life

Date used __________ Place ____________________

Spiritual Disciplines 663

In the mid-1990s a system of exercise that had long been a staple of the dance community became popular in health clubs. It is called the Pilates method.

The system was developed by Joseph Pilates during World War II as a way to strengthen the bodies of immobilized patients. By using springs attached to beds, Pilates experimented with ways to strengthen muscles especially in the patients' midsection.

In the *Chicago Tribune* Bob Condor writes, "The Pilates system focuses on first building your 'power center'—the abdomen, buttocks and lower back—to make all body movements easier. 'If you don't have a strong torso, you will not be in full control of your arms and legs,' says Sean Gallagher, a physical therapist and athletic trainer who owns the Pilates Studio in New York. 'Everything we do starts with our center of gravity.'"

That certainly makes sense. It makes sense not only with our body, but in every area of our lives, including finances, relationships, work, and emotions. Our power center is our spiritual life. Those who are spiritually strong in the Lord find strength flowing into all areas of their lives. For that reason, nothing can benefit our lives more than the exercise of spiritual disciplines.

Devotional Life, Power, Spirit, Strength
Prov. 4:23

Date used __________ Place ____________________

In 1997 the Russian space station Mir became a byword for serial glitches. On June 25, 1997, it collided with a cargo ship, and the space station then suffered one problem after another, from computer failures to oxygen shortages.

The glitch on July 3, 1997, was with the eleven gyroscopes that kept the space station oriented toward the sun. According to the Associated Press, NASA reported that five gyroscopes in one of the ship's modules shut down apparently after communication problems with the control computer on Mir. The crew then shut off the remaining gyroscopes.

The purpose of the eleven gyroscopes was to keep the space station in the best position for its solar panels to soak up energy from the sun. To lose the gyroscopes, therefore, meant the loss of precious power.

Spiritual disciplines serve a purpose in our lives similar to these gyroscopes. We naturally tend to veer away from God and toward darkness. Spiritual disciplines keep us oriented toward the light, toward our power source.

Devotional Life, Light, Power, Prayer
Ps. 119:105; Matt. 4:4; 2 Cor. 3:18; 1 Peter 2:2–3

Date used __________ Place ____________________

In *Discipleship Journal* author Mark Galli writes about the motivation for spiritual disciplines:

> I love to play basketball. Just being on a court, dribbling, shooting, making moves, rebounding—to me it's a type of dance, an art.
>
> One afternoon during my college years, I was shooting hoops at my girlfriend's house. I was working on my Earl-the-Pearl (Monroe) move—dribble to the top of the key, fake right, spin left, accelerate to the basket for a lay-up. I practiced it fifteen or twenty times.
>
> A few weeks later, I overheard my girlfriend's father say to a friend: "Mark sure is a disciplined young man. You should see him practice basketball. He just never lets up."
>
> Me, disciplined? I wondered. Basketball workouts weren't discipline for me. I loved playing. I enjoyed perfecting those moves. Although I panted and sweated and wore myself out, I never had to "discipline" myself to practice. . . . I just loved the sport. Basketball was its own reward.

We should practice the spiritual disciplines for the intrinsic satisfaction they can give us. Jesus has taught us something that should be obvious but often is not: Knowing God is its own reward. The disciplines are merely the dribbling, the moves, the jump shots of the spiritual life.

You can no more enjoy God without the spiritual disciplines than you can enjoy basketball without dribbling or shooting. But the disciplines are not duties, laws, demands, or requirements. They are merely the conditions in which the joy of God is experienced.

Devotional Life, Joy, Prayer
Matt. 4:4; 1 Peter 2:2

Date used __________ Place ____________________

666

On January 16, 1995, Rachel Barton, of Winnetka, Illinois, commuted home on the train. Slung over her shoulder was her Amati violin, worth three hundred thousand dollars, on loan from a benefactor. Rachel is a violin prodigy who first appeared as a soloist with the Chicago Symphony at age eight.

The train stopped at the Elm Street station, and as Rachel exited, tragedy struck. Somehow she got caught in the door, according to Michael A. Lev in the *Chicago Tribune,* and the train started moving again: "Barton was dragged beneath the train for several hundred feet before a bystander heard her screams and notified a railroad official to stop the train. The huge wheels severed her left leg below the knee and seriously damaged the right leg."

Rescue workers and two passengers who used their belts as tourniquets saved Barton's life.

Two months and eight surgeries later, Rachel Barton held a press conference. Sitting in a wheel chair, beaming a beautiful smile, and wearing a glowing red dress, she talked of her plans to walk again, and to perform with the violin in the fall. She was already practicing on her violin several hours a day.

"In the years to come," she said, "I hope to be known for my music, not my injuries."

When we face traumatic pain and loss, we have a choice. We can focus on our past or our future, on our injuries or our gifts. Overcomers dream of the "music" they have yet to play.

Hope, Loss, Overcomers, Pain, Trauma
Phil. 1:20–22; 1 Peter 4:10–11

Date used __________ Place ____________________

In *Charisma,* John Wimber writes about a remarkable manifestation of a gift of the Spirit.

> I was once on an airplane when I turned and looked at the passenger across the aisle to see the word "adultery" written across his face in big letters. The letters, of course, were only perceptible to spiritual eyes. He caught me looking at him (gaping might be more descriptive) and said, "What do you want?" As he asked that, a woman's name came clearly into my mind. I leaned over the aisle and asked if the name meant anything to him. His face turned white, and he asked if he could talk to me.
>
> It was a large plane with a bar, so we went there to talk. On the way the Lord spoke to me again, saying, "Tell him to turn from this adulterous affair, or I am going to take him." When we got to the bar, I told him that God had told me he was committing adultery, the name of the woman, and that God would take him if he did not cease. He just melted on the spot and asked about what he should do. I led him through a prayer of repentance, and he received Christ.

Repentance, Secrets, Word of Knowledge
Luke 12:2–3; 1 Cor. 12; 14:25

Date used __________ Place ____________________

668

Of the thousands of professional baseball players who have stepped up to the plate over the game's history, until the morning of September 2, 1997, only seventy-three had had the distinct thrill of hitting a home run the first time at bat in their major league career. On this date Montreal Expos outfielder Brad Fullmer became the seventy-fourth, with a pinch-hit two-run shot off Boston Red Sox pitcher Brett Saberhagen.

Does such an auspicious beginning suggest great things to come for Brad Fullmer? Fullmer thinks so: "It has to be a good sign," he said.

Gary Gaetti would add weight to that argument. In 1981 as a Minnesota Twin he hit a homer his first time up and went on to hit 330 more by September 1997.

But after Gaetti and a handful of other fast starters, the numbers aren't very impressive. "Of the 73 players who preceded Fullmer," say Richard O'Brien and Hank Hersch in *Sports Illustrated,* "13 never hit another homer. Only two of the group's members have been enshrined in the Hall of Fame: Earl Averill and Hoyt Wilhelm, a pitcher."

When we take our first steps in serving the Lord, it's nice to start with a bang, but whether we do or don't says little about what we're really made of. That is proven over time.

Beginnings, Character, Ministry, Perseverance, Success
Mark 4:16–17; Eph. 4:11–12, 16; Phil. 1:6; Heb. 10:32–39

Date used __________ Place ____________________

Spiritual Perception 669

A former park ranger at Yellowstone National Park tells the story of a ranger leading a group of hikers to a fire lookout. The ranger was so intent on telling the hikers about the flowers and animals that he considered the messages on his two-way radio distracting, so he switched it off. Nearing the tower, the ranger was met by a nearly breathless lookout, who asked why he hadn't responded to the messages on his radio. A grizzly bear had been seen stalking the group, and the authorities were trying to warn them of the danger.

Any time we tune out the messages God has sent us, we put at peril not only ourselves, but also those around us. How important it is that we never turn off God's saving communication!

Prayer, Listening

Date used __________ Place ____________________

Spiritual Perception 670

In his novel *My Lovely Enemy,* Canadian Mennonite author Rudy Wiebe aptly pictures how different things look to the person with spiritual eyes:

> It could be like standing on your head in order to see the world clearer. . . . If one morning you began walking on your hands, the whole world would be hanging. The trees, these ugly brick and tile buildings wouldn't be fixed here so solid and reassuring; they'd be pendant. The more safe and reliable they seem now, the more helpless they'd be then.

Once we are given "eyes to see," we recognize what a frail and temporary world we live in. We see the spiritual world as the solid one.

World, Heaven

Date used __________ Place ____________________

Spiritual Perception 671

Tim Hansel in *When I Relax I Feel Guilty* writes:

An American Indian was in downtown New York, walking with his friend who lived in New York City. Suddenly he said, "I hear a cricket."

"Oh, you're crazy," his friend replied.

"No, I hear a cricket. I do! I'm sure of it."

"It's the noon hour. There are people bustling around, cars honking, taxis squealing, noises from the city. I'm sure you can't hear it."

"I'm sure I do." He listened attentively and then walked to the corner, across the street, and looked all around. Finally on the corner he found a shrub in a large cement planter. He dug beneath the leaves and found a cricket. His friend was astounded. But the Cherokee said, "No. My ears are no different from yours. It simply depends on what you are listening to. Here, let me show you." He reached into his pocket and pulled out a handful of change—a few quarters, some dimes, nickels, and pennies. And he dropped it on the concrete. Every head within a block turned. "You see what I mean?" he said as he began picking up his coins. "It all depends on what you are listening for."

Not only must Christians have "ears to hear" (Matt. 13:9), but they must learn what to listen for.

Money, Prayer

Date used __________ Place ____________________

Spiritual Perception 672

A Coloradan moved to Texas and built a house with a large picture window from which he could view hundreds of miles of rangeland. "The only problem is," he said, "there's nothing to see."

About the same time, a Texan moved to Colorado and built a house with a large picture window overlooking the Rockies. "The only problem is I can't see anything," he said. "The mountains are in the way."

People have a way of missing what's right before them. They go to a city and see lights and glitter, but miss the lonely people. They hear a person's critical comments, but miss the cry for love and friendship.

Sensitivity, Relationships

Date used __________ Place ____________________

Spiritual Perception 673

A Denver woman told her pastor of a recent experience that she felt was a sign of the times. She'd walked into a jewelry store looking for a necklace. "I'd like a gold cross," she said.

The man behind the counter looked over the stock in the display case and said, "Do you want a plain one, or one with a little man on it?"

Cross, Ignorance

Date used __________ Place ______________________

Spiritual Perception 674

Roger von Oech in his book *A Kick in the Seat of the Pants,* suggests:

> Take a look around where you're sitting and find five things that have blue in them. Go ahead and do it.
>
> With a "blue" mindset, you'll find that blue jumps out at you: a blue book on the table, a blue pillow on the couch, blue in the painting on the wall, and so on. . . . In like fashion, you've probably noticed that after you buy a new car, you promptly see that make of car everywhere. That's because people find what they are looking for.

At times in our lives, God seems strangely absent, but the problem is not that God has disappeared. We simply lack a "God" mindset. When we develop our sensitivity, we soon begin to see his work everywhere.

Faith, God's Presence

Date used __________ Place ____________________

Spiritual Perception 675

One morning in 1992, as scientist Sid Nagel of the University of Chicago stood at his kitchen counter getting breakfast, something caught his attention. What he saw was a dried coffee drop on his counter. Nothing unusual about that, but what caught his eye was the way the spot had dried. Rather than having a uniform color, the coffee spot had a dark concentration of minute coffee granules at the outer edges and a much lighter color toward the middle.

To Nagel that didn't make sense. It contradicted the physics principle that says materials suspended in liquid spread randomly and as uniformly as possible.

That night Nagel discussed his observation with another professor. After suggesting some theories, he too came to the conclusion that the dried coffee spot didn't make sense. The following Friday Nagel brought the problem to a weekly bag-lunch gathering of scientists, and the mystery of the coffee spot quickly became the buzz among the university's math, computer science, chemistry, and physics faculty. For months, though, no one could solve the puzzle.

Finally a group of scientists came up with this solution: "The liquid," writes William Mullen in the *Chicago Tribune,* "puddles out until it is stopped or 'pinned' by roughness on the surface it travels across. Evaporation along those edges becomes a capillary 'pull' that draws tiny coffee grains dispersed evenly in the liquid out to the edge. By the time evaporation is complete, virtually all the coffee particles are at the edge, thus creating the telltale dark rim."

The discovery could have practical application for paint manufacturers, electronic and computer engineers, and molecular biologists.

The ability to see the profound in the commonplace—to see a principle of physics in a coffee spot—is what makes for breakthroughs in understanding. A similar way of seeing helps us know God better. Either we can go through daily life oblivious to the activity of God around us, or we can pay attention to what God is trying to tell us in our circumstances. Those who are looking see the glory of God all around them. Those who pay attention find God's direction in even the mundane events of daily life.

Curiosity, Direction, God's Will, Hearing God, Insight, Learning, Observation, Questions, Wonder
1 Kings 19:9–13; Isa. 58; Jer. 14:1–7, 22; Amos 4; Jonah 4:5–11; Haggai 1:5–11; 1 Cor. 11:30–32

Date used __________ Place ____________________

According to the Associated Press, in the spring of 1994, Sweden's defense ministry determined that a Soviet submarine had violated Sweden's territorial waters. High-tech buoys around Stockholm had detected suspicious noises, and the military began a submarine hunt in the Baltic Sea that lasted several weeks.

This wasn't the first such alert. Ever since 1981, when a Soviet submarine ran aground near a southern naval base in Sweden, the Swedes had been wary of Soviet intrusions.

But the 1994 hunt didn't turn up any lurking submarines, and one year later the military made an embarrassing admission. The noises picked up by the high-tech buoys had been minks and other mammals splashing in the water in search of food. Minks are about the size of a cat and are plentiful in the islands that surround Stockholm.

When it comes to our enemies and our fears, imagination can easily get the best of us.

Demons, Satan, Vigilance
2 Cor. 10:2–5; Eph. 6:10–18

Date used __________ Place ____________________

Spiritual Warfare 677

In *The Christian Reader,* Robert Duran of Bethany Fellowship Missions writes of his return to one missions station.

Our horses carefully picked their way along the rock-strewn path. Finally, after two hours of travel by truck and eight hours on horses, we could discern the outlines of the small Huichole village in Mexico. We looked forward to seeing friends we had made in this remote village during three years of visits—most of all, Pastor Alfredo.

First to notice our arrival, the dogs and children loudly brought the news to all those indoors. Huicholes are patient and shy, but one woman, Maria Teresa, beckoned us to her door. Her husband, Santo, was sick and wanted to see us. Their low-walled, thatch-roofed house was built of stone with no windows. Santo lay on a bed made of blankets, which hardly raised him off the dirt floor. He greeted us weakly and was caught by a spasm of coughing.

The first time we had met, three years earlier, a villager had led us to Santo, one of their most feared witch doctors. Before we could introduce ourselves, he shook my hand and said, "Robert, I have been waiting for your visit."

Surprised, I asked, "How did you know my name?"

His reply was, "The guiding spirits left me yesterday. They told of your coming and that they could not stay while you were in the village."

Now, after many visits to the village, and to Santo's home, eighteen people had become followers of Jesus Christ.

Today Santo was happy to see us, and he wanted to talk. "Allow me to pray that I might receive Jesus Christ and follow him," we heard him say. Joyfully, we asked if he was willing to confess his sins and receive Christ as Savior. He nodded. Three times I began prayer, but Santo could not get the words out of his mouth. Finally, after we commanded demonic spirits to leave his body, Santo was able to pray.

Just three months later, Santo's wife told us that one morning, Santo had risen from his sleeping mat and asked for food. She made him tortillas and, as he ate, he told neighbors gathered in his house, "This is my last meal. Tonight Pastor Roberto's God is coming to take me to his house." That night he passed into eternity, a Christian saved and transformed by God's grace.

The kingdom of God is greater than the powers of darkness.

Demons, Exorcism, Occult

Matt. 16:18; Acts 16:16–18; 2 Cor. 10:3–5; Eph. 6:10–20; 1 John 4:4

Date used __________ Place ____________________

Used by permission of the *Christian Reader.*

678

In *World Vision* magazine John Robb writes:

Seven years ago, a giant tree stood on the banks of the Awash River, in an arid valley about two hours' drive southeast of Addis Ababa, Ethiopia. It had stood there for generations, seemingly eternal.

For years, the people who lived in the surrounding district had suffered through famines. . . . In their suffering, the people looked to the tree for help. Believing a spirit gave it divine powers, they worshipped the towering giant. Adults would kiss the great trunk when they passed by, and they spoke of the tree in hushed, reverential tones. Children said, "This tree saved us."

In 1989, World Vision began a development project there, including an irrigation system. . . . But even as they labored to build the system, the great tree stood like a forbidding sentinel of the old order, presiding over the community, enslaving the people through fear. For spirits need to be propitiated with animal sacrifices and strict observance of taboos.

When World Vision workers saw how the villagers worshipped the tree, they knew it was an idolatrous barrier to the entrance of Christ's kingdom and transformation of the community.

One morning as the staff prayed together, one of Jesus' promises struck them: "If you have faith, you can say to this tree, 'Be taken up and removed' . . . and it will obey you." In faith, they began to pray that God would bring down the menacing goliath.

Soon the whole community knew the Christians were praying about the tree. Six months later, the tree began to dry up, its leafy foliage disappeared, and finally it collapsed like a stricken giant into the river.

The people of the community were astonished, proclaiming, "Your God has done this! Your God has dried up the tree!" In the days and weeks afterwards, approximately 100 members of the community received Jesus Christ because they saw his power displayed in answer to the Christians' prayers.

Authority, Evangelism, Faith, Idolatry,
Impossibilities, Missions, Power, Prayer
1 Kings 18:17–40; Matt. 16:18–19; 19:26; 21:18–22;
Mark 9:23; 10:27; 11:12–26; Luke 10:17–18; 17:6; 18:27; Eph. 3:20

Date used __________ Place ____________________

Spiritual Warfare 679

The waters off Natal province in South Africa are shark-infested, writes Hugh Dellios in the *Chicago Tribune*. To maintain the tourist trade in the area, the Natal Shark Board has tried many different solutions. They have attempted using various odors as shark repellents, without success. They tried piping in sounds, such as that of the shark's archenemy the killer whale, without success. In earlier days they encircled bathing beaches with steel cages, or called in the navy to drop depth charges. Finally in the 1950s they stretched long nets around the circumference of the beach. That kept the sharks out but also accidentally caught and killed a large number of other marine life.

Now it appears the Natal Shark Board has a better solution. They have developed and patented what they call the Protective Ocean Device (POD). The POD puts out electrical impulses that irritate the shark's nose, which is sensitive to muscle movements in nearby fish and ultrasensitive to electrical currents. The new device, says writer Hugh Dellios, "will surround its owner with a low-level electric pulse that annoys the shark and persuades it that it isn't bearing down on a seal or other favorite taste-treat."

And so it is now possible with technology to drive away sharks.

Far more dangerous than a shark is our enemy Satan. But God has given us sure ways to repel his attacks: the Lord's name and Word, our righteousness and faith.

Name of Jesus, Prayer, Satan

Matt. 4:1–11; John 17:11–12; Eph. 6:10–18; James 4:7

Date used __________ Place ____________________

George Johnson writes in the *New York Times* that in October 1997 scientists at the University of California and the Space Telescope Science Institute released a "photograph" taken by the Hubble space telescope of a massive, unseeable star. Dubbed the Pistol Star, it stands near the center of our Milky Way Galaxy, burns as bright as 10 million suns, and is as large as the entire space inside of the Earth's orbit. Nevertheless neither the human eye nor telescopes can see it because it is shrouded by an impenetrable cloud of cosmic dust.

This raises the question: Where did the scientists get the photograph?

In reality, the picture is a computer-generated image based on measurements of infrared rays, which are not visible to the human eye but are detectable with scientific instruments. Computers convert these waves into colors, and, voilà, we see a picture of the biggest star in the galaxy.

Imagine, a colossal star blazing 10 million times brighter than the sun, but we can't see it without special equipment. Just as huge realities like this star are not perceptible without special equipment, so there are spiritual realities that a person cannot perceive without spiritual equipment. The fact that scientific instruments cannot detect the dimension of spirit does not mean that the spiritual world is not there, just that the instruments are limited.

Invisible Things, Naturalism, Perception,
Science, Sight, Spiritual Perception, Vision
Matt. 16:13–20; Mark 8:17–30; 1 Cor. 2:6–16; Eph. 1:17–18

Date used __________ Place ____________________

Spirituality 681

Our life in Christ can be compared to an aqueduct, the stone waterways that brought water from nearby mountains into parched cities in Italy and Spain, and that are still used in some countries today.

The objective foundation of our spiritual lives, the Word of God, is like the huge stone aqueduct itself. The subjective elements, our daily experience of Christ, is like the fresh water flowing through it.

Some Christians neglect the Word and seek only the subjective experience. But without the solid Word of God to contain and channel that experience, the experience itself drains away into error and is lost.

Other Christians boast well-engineered aqueducts based on extensive knowledge of the Bible, but they are bone dry. They bring no refreshment. Strong spiritual lives require both a strong knowledge of the Word of God and an intimate daily relationship with Christ.

Scripture, Devotional Life

Date used __________ Place ____________________

Stamina 682

A television documentary pointed out that the cheetah survives on the African plains by running down its prey. The big cat can sprint seventy miles per hour. But the cheetah cannot sustain that pace for long. Within its long, sleek body is a disproportionately small heart, which causes the cheetah to tire quickly. Unless the cheetah catches its prey in the first flurry, it must abandon the chase.

Sometimes Christians seem to have the cheetah's approach to ministry. We speed into projects with great energy. But lacking the heart for sustained effort, we fizzle before we finish. We vow to start faster and run harder, when what we need may be not more speed but more staying power—stamina that comes only from a bigger heart.

Perseverance, Heart

Date used __________ Place ____________________

Stature 683

The growth chart had slipped from the playroom wall because the tape on its corners had become dry and brittle. Five-year-old Jordan hung it up again, meticulously working to get it straight. Then he stood his sister against the wall to measure her height.

"Mommy! Mommy! Anneke is forty inches tall!" he shouted as he burst into the kitchen. "I measured her."

His mom replied, "That's impossible, Sweetheart. She's only 3 years old. Let's go see." They walked back into the playroom, where the mother's suspicions were confirmed. Despite his efforts to hang the chart straight, Jordan had failed to set it at the proper height. It was several inches low.

We easily make Jordan's mistake in gauging our spiritual growth or importance. Compared to a shortened scale, we may appear better than we are. Only when we stand against the Cross, that "Great leveler of men" as A. T. Robertson called it, can we not think of ourselves "more highly than we ought to think." Christ, himself, must be our standard.

Christlikeness, Pride

Date used __________ Place ____________________

Stealing 684

According to the Associated Press, in October 1994, agent Steven Sepulveda of the U.S. Secret Service reported that the biggest thief in calling-card history had been caught. The bandit stole more than one hundred thousand telephone calling-card numbers, sold them to computer hackers around the country, who in turn sold them to people overseas, who in turn made more than fifty million dollars worth of free phone calls to the United States.

The alleged thief, who was known as "Knightshadow" to computer hackers, worked as a switch engineer for MCI. He wrote a software program that diverted and held the calling-card numbers that ran through MCI's switching equipment. The Secret Service said this crime was by far the most sophisticated theft of numbers in history and was part of an international ring operating in Los Angeles, Chicago, and other U.S. cities.

Technology advances, but our sinful nature remains the same. Man continually invents new ways to sin, but God's hatred of sin remains the same.

Sinful Nature, Ten Commandments
Exod. 20:15; Rom. 1:28–32

Date used __________ Place ____________________

Stewardship 685

According to a January 15, 1989 article in the *Lexington Herald-Leader*, the family living in a home in West Palm Beach, Florida, told a film crew it was okay to use the front lawn as a set for an episode of the "B. L. Stryker" television series. They knew cars would be crashing violently in front of the house.

While the front yard was being blown up, the owner of the home was tipped off and called from New York demanding to know what was happening to his house. It seems the people who were living in the house were only tenants and had no right to allow the property to be destroyed as the cameras rolled.

Many times we live our lives under the mistaken impression that they belong to us. Paul tells us we were "bought with a price." We must live as those who know God will call us to account for the ways we have used this life entrusted to us.

Judgment, Lordship of Christ

Date used __________ Place ____________________

The Stradivari Society of Chicago performs an important role in the music world. The society entrusts expensive violins into the hands of world-class violin players who could never afford them on their own.

Top-flight violins made by seventeenth- and eighteenth-century masters like Antonio Stradivari produce an incomparably beautiful sound and now sell for millions of dollars each. Their value continues to climb, making such violins highly attractive to investors. But "great violins are not like great works of art," writes music critic John von Rhein. "They were never meant to be hung on a wall or locked up under glass. Any instrument will lose its tone if it isn't played regularly; conversely, an instrument gains in value the more it is used."

And so it is that those who own the world's greatest violins are looking for first-rate violin players to use them. The Stradivari Society brings them together, making sure that the instruments are preserved and cared for. One further requirement made by investors in such violins: the musician will give the patron at least two command performances a year.

Like the Stradivari Society, God also entrusts exquisite "violins" into the care of others. He gives us spiritual gifts of great value, which remain his property. He wants them used. He delights to hear beautiful music from our lives. And he wants us to play for him.

Faithfulness, Ministry, Spiritual Gifts

Matt. 25:14–30; Luke 12:48; Rom. 12:5–8; Eph. 4:8–16; 1 Peter 4:10–11

Date used __________ Place ____________________

Stress 687

Jay Kesler writes in *Campus Life:*

There are two ways of handling pressure. One is illustrated by a bathysphere, the miniature submarine used to explore the ocean in places so deep that the water pressure would crush a conventional submarine like an aluminum can. Bathyspheres compensate with plate steel several inches thick, which keeps the water out but also makes them heavy and hard to maneuver. Inside they're cramped.

When these craft descend to the ocean floor, however, they find they're not alone. When their lights are turned on and you look through the tiny, thick plate-glass windows, what do you see? Fish!

These fish cope with extreme pressure in an entirely different way. They don't build thick skins: they remain supple and free. They compensate for the outside pressure through equal and opposite pressure inside themselves.

Christians, likewise, don't have to be hard and thick skinned—as long as they appropriate God's power within to equal the pressure without.

Pressure, Power

Date used __________ Place ____________________

In *Broken in the Right Place,* Alan Nelson describes a scene from the book *A Layman Looks at the Lord's Prayer.*

> The author talks about watching a potter mold a lump of clay. On the shelves in his workshop stood gleaming goblets, beautiful vases, and exquisite bowls. The potter went to an odorous pit in the floor and took out a lump of clay. The smell was from rotting grass, which increased the quality of the material and made it stick better. The potter patted the lump of clay in his hands into a ball. Placing the lump onto the slab of stone with seasoned skill, the potter sat down on his wobbly little wooden stool. Already the master potter could envision the work of art this lump of earth would become. Whirling the wheel gently, the artist caressed the spinning mound. Prior to each touch, he dipped his hands into the two water basins flanking each side of the wheel. The clay responded to the pressure applied by his fingers. A beautiful goblet arose from the pile, responding to each pinch and impression.
>
> Suddenly the stone stopped, and the potter removed a piece of grit. His seasoned fingers detected the unpliable aggregate. The stone spun again, allowing him to smooth out the former lodging of the grit. Suddenly the stone stopped again. He removed another hard object from the goblet's side, leaving a mark in the vessel. The particles of grain within the cup resisted his hands. It would not respond to his wishes. Quickly the potter squashed the form back into a pile of clay. Instead of the beautiful goblet, the artisan formed the material into a crude, finger bowl. . . . When we resist the Master Potter's hand, we run the very real risk of becoming less than we could become.

Character, Discipleship, Growth, Repentance, Sovereignty of God
Isa. 64:8; Rom. 9:19–21; 2 Peter 1:5–9

Date used __________ Place ____________________

Stubbornness 689

According to the Reuters news agency, in the fall of 1994, Alberto Gauna, who lived in the northern province of Chaco in Argentina, became so depressed that he decided to take his own life. He took a .22 caliber gun, pointed it at his right temple, and pulled the trigger. The gun fired, but Alberto lived. So he pointed the gun at his forehead and pulled the trigger. The gun fired, but Alberto lived. So he pointed the gun once again at his right temple and pulled the trigger. Again Alberto lived. Again he fired. Again he lived.

With four bullets in his skull, he decided to shoot himself somewhere else. He pointed the gun at his stomach and pulled the trigger. The gun fired, but he remained conscious. So he shot himself again in the stomach, and still he lived!

Finally, thankfully, Alberto gave up. At the time the story was reported, he was in a hospital in serious condition.

Perseverance isn't always a virtue.

Depression, Ministry, Suicide
Rom. 1:28–32

Date used __________ Place ____________________

Stumbling 690

Every year for more than a decade, *The Parachutist,* which is the official publication of the United States Parachute Association, has published an article called their "fatality summary." In the article a writer analyzes the factors contributing to parachuting deaths in the previous year.

Parachutists are classified first as students, then after twenty jumps they receive their A license. After fifty jumps, they receive their B license. After one hundred jumps their C license. After two hundred jumps, their D license.

In the 1993 fatality summary Paul Sitter points to an alarming statistic. Fifty-nine percent of all parachuting fatalities were suffered by elite jumpers, those with a D license. A graph accompanying the article shows a dramatic upward spike for fatalities among those with two hundred to one thousand jumps. The line on the graph falls again for those with more than one thousand jumps.

The lesson is clear. Just because a person is mature doesn't mean he or she is invulnerable. Is it possible that some parachutists with between two hundred and one thousand jumps got overconfident?

Overconfidence, Pride, Temptation
1 Cor. 10:12; Gal. 6:1

Date used __________ Place ____________________

Stumbling Blocks 691

According to the Associated Press, on the evening of February 6, 1996, three friends drove the rural roads east of Tampa, Florida, with the intent of playing pranks. Tragically, their game was anything but funny. They pulled some twenty street signs out of the ground, including the stop sign at one fateful intersection.

The next day three eighteen-year-old buddies, who had just finished bowling, breezed through that intersection without stopping. Their car sailed into the path of an eight-ton truck, and they were all killed.

One year later the three perpetrators of the deadly prank were convicted of manslaughter. In June of 1997 they stood in orange jail jumpsuits and handcuffs before a judge in a Tampa courtroom, weeping and wiping their eyes, and were sentenced to fifteen years in prison.

It is a dangerous thing with tragic consequences for anyone to take down a signpost on the highway. It is no less dangerous for anyone to vandalize the signposts that God puts on the highway of life. When we honor God's commandments, we point the way to the signposts of life. If we dishonor God's commandments, we can unwittingly lead others to destruction.

Consequences, Example, False Teachers, Golden Rule, Immorality, Law, Lawlessness, Morality, Responsibility, Rules, Ten Commandments

Matt. 5:19; Luke 17:1–2; Rom. 14:13–15:4; 1 Cor. 8:9–13; 10:32; James 3:1; Jude 4; Rev. 2:20–21

Date used __________ Place ____________________

Stephen P. Beck writes:

Driving down a country road, I came to a very narrow bridge. In front of the bridge, a sign was posted: “Yield.” Seeing no oncoming cars, I continued across the bridge and to my destination.

On my way back, I came to the same one-lane bridge, now from the other direction. To my surprise, I saw another “Yield” sign posted.

Curious, I thought. *I'm sure there was one positioned on the other side.*

When I reached the other side of the bridge, I looked back. Sure enough, yield signs had been placed at both ends of the bridge. Drivers from both directions were requested to give the other the right of way. It was a reasonable and gracious way of preventing a head-on collision.

When the Bible commands Christians to “be subject to one another” (Eph. 5:21), it is simply a reasonable and gracious command to let the other have the right of way and avoid interpersonal head-on collisions.

Conflict, Meekness

Date used __________ Place ____________________

Success 693

In 1993 the alternative-rock group Pearl Jam enjoyed huge success with its second album, entitled "Vs." It sold 950,000 copies in its first five days, setting a new record. The previous record was 770,000 copies by Guns N' Roses's 1991 album "Use Your Illusion II."

Pearl Jam's lead vocalist Eddie Vedder made the cover of *Time* magazine.

You would assume all this success would make Eddie Vedder feel great about himself. Not so. "I'm being honest," said Eddie, "when I say that sometimes when I see a picture of the band or a picture of my face taking up a whole page of a magazine, I hate that guy."

Success does not guarantee a feeling of worth.

Meaning, Self-Image, Self-Respect, Significance
Rom. 8:31–39; Gal. 2:20; 1 John 3:1–3

Date used __________ Place ______________________

World War II brought unparalleled suffering and death to humankind. Experts estimate some fifty-five million people died, among them roughly six million Jews in concentration camps. Families and nations were shattered. Clearly this was a time of great, great evil.

But all was not evil. During the war, medical researchers intensified their efforts to fight disease and infection and as a result made great breakthroughs. Up until 1941, for example, doctors could not reverse the course of infection. "They could do little more than offer a consoling bedside manner as patients sank toward oblivion," writes Stevenson Swanson.

But the war caused England and America to search for a way to mass-produce penicillin, the original wonder drug. Although penicillin had been discovered by Alexander Fleming in 1928, for nearly a decade the medical community had done little with it. "It was dismissed as little more than an interesting microbiological phenomenon."

But as the probability of war increased in the late 1930s, all that changed. Research began in earnest in England for a way to mass-produce penicillin, which at that time could only be made in extremely small quantities.

In 1941 English researchers brought samples of penicillin to America, and a team of scientists began research into mass production in an agricultural lab in Peoria, Illinois. Within four months they found ways to increase the production of penicillin tenfold. The process was licensed to pharmaceutical companies, and production began in earnest.

"For all of 1943, penicillin production in the United States amounted to just 28 pounds," writes Swanson. "The cost of manufacturing 100,000 units was $20, or about $200,000 a pound. In two years, it fell to less than $2 per 100,000 units, and the country produced 14,000 pounds."

The discovery of the fermentation process for penicillin, the world's first antibiotic, triggered a rush by pharmaceutical companies to develop other antibiotics. Selman Waksman of Rutgers University soon discovered streptomycin, which treated tuberculosis. One antibiotic followed another until in the mid-1990s, well over one hundred antibiotics were available.

"Probably more than any other discovery in the history of medicine, the discovery of antibiotics has done the most to improve the lives of humans," said Dr. Gary Noskin, an infectious-disease specialist and professor of medicine at Northwestern University Medical School in Chicago.

Millions of people died in World War II, but out of the war came the drugs that have saved millions of lives and will go on saving lives. Dr. Russell Maulitz, a medical historian and professor at the Medical College of Philadelphia and Hahnemann University, says, "War is the perverse handmaiden of medical progress."

Just as good came from bad during World War II, so God is able to make great good come from the bad events of our lives.

Cross, Easter, Evil, Good from Bad, Trials, Trust
Gen. 50:20; Rom. 8:28

Date used __________ Place ____________________

Suffering 695

When Jewish psychiatrist Victor Frankl was arrested by the Nazis in World War II, he was stripped of everything—property, family, possessions. He had spent years researching and writing a book on the importance of finding meaning in life—concepts that later would be known as logotherapy. When he arrived in Auschwitz, the infamous death camp, even his manuscript, which he had hidden in the lining of his coat, was taken away.

"I had to undergo and overcome the loss of my spiritual child," Frankl writes. "Now it seemed as if nothing and no one would survive me; neither a physical nor a spiritual child of my own! I found myself confronted with the question of whether under such circumstances my life was ultimately void of any meaning."

He was still wrestling with that question a few days later when the Nazis forced the prisoners to give up their clothes.

"I had to surrender my clothes and in turn inherited the worn out rags of an inmate who had been sent to the gas chamber," says Frankl. "Instead of the many pages of my manuscript, I found in the pocket of the newly acquired coat a single page torn out of a Hebrew prayer book, which contained the main Jewish prayer, *Shema Yisrael* (Hear, O Israel! The Lord our God is one God. And you shall love the Lord your God with all your heart and with all your soul and with all your might.)

"How should I have interpreted such a 'coincidence' other than as a challenge to live my thoughts instead of merely putting them on paper?"

Later, as Frankl reflected on his ordeal, he wrote in his book *Man's Search for Meaning*, "There is nothing in the world that would so effectively help one to survive even the worst conditions, as the knowledge that there is a meaning in one's life. . . . He who has a *why* to live for can bear almost any *how*."

Meaning, Purpose

Date used ________ Place ________________

Support 696

Has any athlete had more fans than Michael Jordan? Probably not. Even so, Michael Jordan said something surprising about his need for emotional support to columnist Bob Greene. When Greene asked why he wanted his father to be in the stands during a game, Jordan replied, "When he's there, I know I have at least one fan."

Even the great Michael Jordan needs support. Loyal support. How much more do the rest of us need regular reminders that others are behind us—even when we aren't at our best.

Encouragement, Fathers, Loyalty

Rom. 12:10; 1 Thess. 5:14; Heb. 3:18

Date used __________ Place ____________________

When people are broken emotionally, they need others to support them until they can stand again.

Medical researchers have developed a bone-bonding compound that illustrates the help we can give others.

The chemical compound looks like toothpaste. Once injected into the body, it hardens in ten minutes. In twelve hours it reaches the compression strength of natural bone.

A study in the journal *Science* found the compound virtually identical to natural bone crystals. The compound so closely resembles real bone that the body does not reject it. Weeks after being injected into the body, the cement is replaced by real bone.

According to the Associated Press, clinical trials "show the material has allowed patients to discard casts early—or altogether—and to resume walking more quickly and with less pain."

In the same way, our encouragement enables others to overcome their pain and walk with the Lord.

Brokenness, Encouragement, Ministry, Weakness
Gal. 6:2; 1 Thess. 5:11

Date used __________ Place ____________________

Surrender 698

In *The Wonderful Spirit Filled Life,* Charles Stanley writes:

> In water-safety courses a cardinal rule is never to swim out to a drowning man and try to help him as long as he is thrashing about. To do so is to commit suicide. As long as a drowning man thinks he can help himself, he is dangerous to anyone who tries to help him. His tendency is to grab the one trying to aid him and take them both down in the process. The correct procedure is to stay just far enough away so that he can't grab you. Then you wait. And when he finally gives up, you make your move. At that point the one drowning is pliable. He won't work against you. He will let you help.

The same principle holds true in our relationship with the Holy Spirit. Until we give up, we aren't really in a position to be helped. We will work against him rather than with him.

Dependence, Holy Spirit
Gal. 2:20; Eph. 5:18

Date used __________ Place ____________________

Surrender 699

Bruce Larson, in *Believe and Belong,* tells how he helped people struggling to surrender their lives to Christ:

For many years I worked in New York City and counseled at my office any number of people who were wrestling with this yes-or-no decision. Often I would suggest they walk with me from my office down to the RCA Building on Fifth Avenue. In the entrance of that building is a gigantic statue of Atlas, a beautifully proportioned man who, with all his muscles straining, is holding the world upon his shoulders. There he is, the most powerfully built man in the world, and he can barely stand up under this burden. "Now that's one way to live," I would point out to my companion, "trying to carry the world on your shoulders. But now come across the street with me."

On the other side of Fifth Avenue is Saint Patrick's Cathedral, and there behind the high altar is a little shrine of the boy Jesus, perhaps eight or nine years old, and with no effort he is holding the world in one hand. My point was illustrated graphically.

We have a choice. We can carry the world on our shoulders, or we can say, "I give up, Lord; here's my life. I give you my world, the whole world."

Burdens, Rest

Date used __________ Place ____________________

Surrender 700

In an article about former *Today* show host Bryant Gumbel, Cheryl Lavin writes in the *Chicago Tribune Magazine:*

Gumbel loves golf. Loves golf. Belongs to four clubs. Plays 200 times a year, sometimes 54 holes a weekend. Owns 2,000 golf clubs. "It's the one thing that you do that is only about you. It's the thing I enjoy the most," he says.

Gumbel and Al Roker were discussing a poll in *Golf* magazine that asked, "Which would you rather give up, golf or sex?"

Without hesitating, Gumbel said sex. Roker was surprised. Gumbel said, "Maybe you've never had a great round of golf."

"Which would you rather give up?" is not always a hypothetical question. Sometimes God asks us to give up something enjoyable for something that is far, far more enjoyable. The more we see the true joys of the things of God, the easier any sacrifice becomes.

Accomplishment, Dedication, Devotion, Love, Obsession, Passion, Sacrifice, Sex

Matt. 5:29–30; 13:44–46; 16:24–26; 26:6–13; Phil. 3:7–11; 1 John 2:15–17

Date used __________ Place ____________________

Suspicion 701

Time magazine carried the following news item:

When the post office in Troy, Michigan, summoned Michael Achorn to pick up a 2-foot-long, 40-pound package, his wife, Margaret, cheerfully went to accept it. But as she drove it back to her office in Detroit, she began to worry. The box was from Montgomery Ward, but the sender, Edward Achorn, was unknown to Margaret and her husband, despite the identical last name.

What if the thing was a bomb? She telephoned postal authorities. . . .

The bomb squad soon arrived with eight squad cars and an armored truck. They took the suspected bomb in the armored truck to a remote tip of Belle Isle in the middle of the Detroit River. There they wrapped detonating cord around the package and, as they say in the bomb business, "opened it remotely."

When the debris settled, all that was left intact was the factory warranty for the contents: a $450 stereo AM-FM receiver and a tape deck console. Now the only mystery is who is Edward Achorn and why did he send Michael and Margaret such a nice Christmas present?

Our suspicion ruins many of the finest gifts of life.

Gifts, Skepticism

Date used __________ Place ____________________

Sympathy 702

When Edgar Guest, the American poet and writer, was a young man, his first child died. Writes Guest:

There came a tragic night when our first baby was taken from us. I was lonely and defeated. There didn't seem to be anything in life ahead of me that mattered very much.

I had to go to my neighbor's drugstore the next morning for something, and he motioned for me to step behind the counter with him. I followed him into his little office at the back of the store. He put both hands on my shoulders and said, "Eddie, I can't really express what I want to say, the sympathy I have in my heart for you. All I can say is that I'm sorry, and I want you to know that if you need anything at all, come to me. What is mine is yours."

[He was] just a neighbor across the way—a passing acquaintance. Jim Potter [the druggist] may long since have forgotten that moment when he gave me his hand and his sympathy, but I shall never forget it—never in all my life. To me it stands out like the silhouette of a lonely tree against a crimson sunset.

Grief, Kindness

Date used __________ Place ____________________

703

In 1947, a professor at the University of Chicago, Dr. Chandrasekhar, was scheduled to teach an advanced seminar in astrophysics. At the time he was living in Wisconsin, doing research at the Yerkes astronomical observatory. He planned to commute twice a week for the class, even though it would be held during the harsh winter months.

Registration for the seminar, however, fell far below expectations. Only two students signed up for the class. People expected Dr. Chandrasekhar to cancel, lest he waste his time. But for the sake of two students, he taught the class, commuting 100 miles round trip through back country roads in the dead of winter.

His students, Chen Ning Yang and Tsung-Dao Lee, did their homework. Ten years later, in 1957, they both won the Nobel prize for physics. So did Dr. Chandrasekhar in 1983.

For effective teachers, there is no such thing as a small class.

Small Things, Faithfulness

Date used __________ Place ____________________

Teamwork 704

A sea captain and his chief engineer were arguing over who was most important to the ship. To prove their point to each other, they decided to swap places. The chief engineer ascended to the bridge, and the captain went to the engine room.

Several hours later, the captain suddenly appeared on deck covered with oil and dirt. "Chief!" he yelled, waving aloft a monkey wrench. "You have to get down there: I can't make her go!"

"Of course you can't," replied the chief. "She's aground!"

On a team we don't excel each other; we depend on each other.

Body of Christ, Service

Date used __________ Place ____________________

Temporal 705

In the magazine industry, the August 1991 cover of *Vanity Fair* is one of the most well known in recent years. Movie star Demi Moore was on the cover. She was pregnant. Rarely do you see a pregnant movie star as cover girl for a fashionable magazine. But Demi's advanced pregnancy wasn't what shocked the country. Standing sideways, one arm wrapped under her stomach, the other wrapped across her bosom, Demi was stark naked.

At *Vanity Fair*'s tenth anniversary celebration in 1993, they paid tribute to "The Cover." In front of its New York headquarters, *Vanity Fair* unveiled a twenty-two-foot topiary of Demi Moore in her famous pregnant pose. She towers twenty-two feet in leafy-green glory.

Vanity Fair has provided the world an unforgettable illustration by picturing the beauty and fame of a human being in a living bush. Like the grass and the flowers of the field, it will wither and fall, while the word of the Lord will stand forever.

Bible, Death, Eternal, Pornography
Ps. 90:10, 12; 2 Cor. 4:16–18; 1 Peter 1:24–25

Date used __________ Place ____________________

Temporary Things 706

In a *Chicago Tribune* profile about the creator of the syndicated comic strip "Dilbert," Jane Meredith Adams writes:

> In an office just slightly bigger than a cubicle, Scott Adams transforms tales of idiotic bosses and meaningless empowerment teams into Dilbert, the chinless comic-strip hero to millions of cubicle-confined workers.
>
> Since Adams published his Internet address (scottadams@ aol.com), he has been deluged with questions from readers who wonder how he knows the exact level of ineptitude with which their company operates. It's because he has been there. Adams endured 17 years of cubicle employment—most recently as an applications engineer with Pacific Bell, a job he left last year after six years of "Dilbert" syndication.
>
> "I don't think I'll ever forget what it feels like to sit in a cubicle," says the cartoonist, "and realize you've been there for eight hours . . . and everything you did today will become unimportant in the next reorganization."

Scott Adams expresses a feeling we're all familiar with. We want what we do to last. Our work (and even our life) doesn't seem important if it is only temporary. The sure hope we have in God is that all we do for him has eternal significance.

Eternal Things, Futility, Future, Kingdom of God,
Ministry, Obedience, Significance, Will of God, Work, World
Eccles. 1:2–11; 12:13–14; Matt. 7:24–27;
1 Cor. 3:10–15; 15:58; 2 Cor. 4:18; 1 John 2:17

Date used __________ Place ____________________

Temptation 707

According to the *Chicago Tribune,* a Chicago area woman came home from work on Thursday, April 14, 1983, at 6 P.M., and when she walked into her apartment, she immediately became suspicious. Gasoline fumes filled the apartment. She thought maybe someone had been working there, so she called the landlady and the janitor. They said they had not let anyone in. With the gasoline fumes still strong, she called the police and fire department. The fire department came and inspected her apartment but found nothing.

Finally at 10:30 she prepared to go to bed. In her bedroom she noticed something unusual. There was a strange electric cord running to her bed and a bulge in the center of the mattress.

She again called the police. When the fire department took the mattress off of the box spring, they found a crude, homemade firebomb. Three one-gallon containers filled with gasoline were sitting on top of a hot plate connected to a timer that was set to go off at 3 A.M.

Subtle. Very subtle.

For that woman to be killed by that crude trap, she would have had to be utterly oblivious to everything in her world.

Surprisingly enough, Satan himself sometimes sets traps for us that are just this obvious. Although he can be the most cunning of deceivers, at times he tempts us in ways that are so obvious, so blatant, so brazen, only a fool would lie in that lumpy bed and turn out the lights.

The Bible tells us to run from temptation!

Satan, Self-Control, Spiritual Discernment
Matt. 4:3–11; James 1:14–15

Date used __________ Place ____________________

Temptation 708

In *Smithsonian* magazine, Michael Lipske wrote an article about carnivorous plants. The Venus Fly Trap is the most famous plant to feed on insects, but there are many others. The Pitcher Plant, for example, uses a sneaky method to attract its prey—a method that quickly reminds us of the methods of Satan.

Often this plant is brightly colored, mimicking flowers. Sometimes a trail of nectar-secreting glands starts at ground level and leads up the outside of the leaf, summoning ants from the ground to the trap above. Says Lipske:

> The hungry ant or other potential meal is lured to the mouth of the trumpet, so crowded with nectar glands it may be wet. But below this mother lode of sugar, the interior of the pitcher tube is waxy and slick. This is the start of the plant's slippery slope, where victims lose their footing and slide into the increasingly narrow tube. Down inside, the inner wall of the leaf is lined with glands that secrete digestive enzymes, which trickle down and collect in the bottom of the trap. The insect slips lower, to where the surrounding wall is lined with downward-pointing hairs that discourage exit. In some species, the bottom fluid contains an ingredient to stun the struggling captive. There may even be a wetting agent that helps soak and drown the victim.

Satan is the master deceiver. He sugarcoats the way to ruin with illicit pleasure. Once a person falls into the trap, Satan makes it extremely hard to escape. He stuns the victim. Then, alas, he digests the victim's soul.

Pleasure, Satan, Sin
1 Cor. 10:13; James 1:14–15

Date used __________ Place ____________________

709

In *The Christian Reader,* Lynn Austin writes:

The artificial lures fishermen use look so phony, it astonishes me that any fish would fall for them: shiny metallic and gaudy plastic, hot pink and neon colors in stripes and spots.

Satan knows what he can use to dazzle and distract me. After more than 10 years of introducing myself as "just a housewife," my enemy dangled before me the lure of a "real job" with a paycheck and prestige. To boost my flagging self-esteem, I snapped at the bait and signed a contract before prayerfully considering the consequences to our family life.

Within a few months, I knew I had made a mistake. Early morning meetings forced me to leave the house while my children were still asleep. Afternoon conferences that dragged on and on turned them into latchkey kids.

The demands of the job did not line up with my talents and interests. As the work pressures and the laundry piled up, I missed my daily quiet times with the Lord, my friends at Bible study, and my daughter's Mother's Day program at school.

When my contract expired a year later, I gratefully resigned. I had learned a hard lesson: not to be distracted by fancy lures that make me forget the things that really matter.

Contentment, Distractions, Family, Mothers
1 Cor. 10:13; 1 Tim. 6:6, 9; James 1:13–14

Date used __________ Place ____________________

Temptation 710

Writer and speaker Joni Eareckson Tada was paralyzed from the neck down in a diving accident. In her book *Secret Strength,* Joni wrote about facing temptation.

> I was in my late twenties, single, and with every prospect of remaining so. Sometimes lust or a bit of fantasizing would seem so inviting—and so easy to justify. After all, hadn't I already given up more than most Christians just by being disabled? Didn't my wheelchair entitle me to a little slack now and then?

Joni asks her readers:

> When God allows you to suffer, do you have the tendency to use your very trials as an excuse for sinning? Or do you feel that since you've given God a little extra lately by taking such abuse, He owes you a "day off"?

Joni Eareckson Tada teaches us that there is no excuse—not suffering, not great sacrifice, not even paralysis—for indulging impurity in our hearts.

Heart, Purity, Rationalization, Suffering
1 Cor. 10:13

Date used __________ Place ____________________

Temptation 711

Rick Green writes:

A former policeman with whom I stayed on a choir tour told me about being on duty during an ice storm. The ice was a half-inch thick on every tree in the area. He was called to a site where the ice and falling branches had caused a power line to come down; his duty was to keep people away from the area.

"There was a small tree near the fallen power line," he said, "the kind with a short trunk and lots of long thin branches. While that fallen power line was crackling and popping with electricity, it was throwing out sparks through the branches of that small tree. The sparks would reflect off the ice-covered branches sending out a rainbow of glimmering colors. I stood there and watched, and wondered how anything so beautiful could be so deadly."

I was reminded of the power of sin. We see something that seems beautiful, but when we reach out to touch, it becomes death to us.

Sin, Deception

Date used __________ Place ______________________

Temptation 712

Portia Nelson has written a piece titled: *Autobiography in Five Short Chapters.* It reads:

Chapter 1—I walk down the street. There is a deep hole in the sidewalk. I fall in. I am lost. . . . I am helpless. It isn't my fault. It takes forever to find a way out.

Chapter 2—I walk down the same street. There is a deep hole in the sidewalk. I pretend I don't see it. I fall in again. I can't believe I am in the same place, but it isn't my fault. It still takes a long time to get out.

Chapter 3—I walk down the same street. There is a deep hole in the sidewalk. I see it is there. I still fall in. . . . It's a habit. My eyes are open. I know where I am. It is my fault. I get out immediately.

Chapter 4—I walk down the same street. There is a deep hole in the sidewalk. I walk around it.

Chapter 5—I walk down another street.

Sin, Addiction

Date used __________ Place ____________________

Reports the *Denver Post:*

> Like many sheep ranchers in the West, Lexy Lowler has tried just about everything to stop crafty coyotes from killing her sheep. She has used odor sprays, electric fences, and "scare-coyotes." She has slept with her lambs during the summer and has placed battery-operated radios near them. She has corralled them at night, herded them at day. But the southern Montana rancher has lost scores of lambs—fifty last year alone.
>
> Then she discovered the llama—the aggressive, funny-looking, afraid-of-nothing llama. . . . "Llamas don't appear to be afraid of anything," she said. "When they see something, they put their head up and walk straight toward it. That is aggressive behavior as far as the coyote is concerned, and they won't have anything to do with that. . . . Coyotes are opportunists, and llamas take that opportunity away."

Apparently llamas know the truth of what James writes: "Resist the Devil, and he will flee from you" (4:7). The moment we sense his attack is the moment we should face it and deal with it for what it is.

Satan, Spiritual Warfare

Date used __________ Place ____________________

Temptation 714

During the Christmas season of 1996, a bizarre story came over the news about a hair-eating doll. The main feature of the doll in question, according to the Associated Press, was a mechanical mouth that chewed on plastic carrots and french fries. Unfortunately the doll couldn't tell the difference between plastic vegetables and children's hair. During the first five months the doll was on the market, the Consumer Product Safety Commission received thirty-five complaints from parents whose children had their hair caught in the mouth of the doll. One woman in Campbell, Ohio, had to cut off a shank of her daughter's hair after it became snarled in gears in the doll's throat.

Some things that appear quite harmless can entangle and hurt us. Most of us know what it's like to get involved innocently in a relationship or a pastime only to eventually find that we were caught up in something hurtful from which we could not break away. Temptation can come in an attractive package.

Addictions, Distractions, Entertainment, Habits, Money, Pastimes, Pleasure, Priorities, Snares, Time Management
Gen. 3:6; Matt. 4:3; 1 Cor. 15:33–34; 2 Cor. 11:14–15; 1 Tim. 6:9–10; Heb. 12:1

Date used __________ Place ____________________

Temptation 715

Playing for the Seattle Mariners in 1996, left-hander Terry Mulholland had one of the best pickoff moves in baseball. Over a period of five years, from opening day in 1992 until June 19, 1997, a total of only six runners were successful at stealing a base off Mulholland. Mulholland's pitching motion was so deceptive that a runner on first would think the pitch was going home, and he would start to lean toward second. At that instant, Mulholland would turn and throw to first, often catching runners in no-man's land for an embarrassing out.

Kansas City's speedy Bip Roberts knew that embarrassing feeling. Despite his base-stealing skill he too got picked off by Mulholland. Roberts said, "Sometimes, it seems as if he gives up a hit just so he can pick you off."

That statement perfectly describes the tempter. Sometimes people have the mistaken idea that Satan wants to give people pleasure. Satan no more wants to give us pleasure than a baseball pitcher wants to give up hits. Satan hates us and wants to inflict as much suffering into our lives as he possibly can. Satan offers the pleasure of sin only to inflict suffering later and to make that suffering permanent.

Pleasure, Satan, Sin, Sowing and Reaping
Matt. 4:1–11; John 10:10; Gal. 6:7–8; Heb. 11:25

Date used __________ Place ____________________

Temptation 716

Many are familiar with the promise of Romans 8:28 that "in all things God works for the good of those who love him." But have you ever wondered how anything good can come out of temptation? Why does God allow Satan to attack our faith, to shower us with doubts? One clue comes from the world of football.

Running back Rashaan Salaam won the Heisman trophy in 1995 for his outstanding rushing career in college. But in his rookie year with the Chicago Bears, the pros uncovered a weakness in Salaam's game: He was prone to fumble. Although he led the Bears in rushing during his rookie season, he coughed up the ball nine times.

The coaches devised a practice drill to try to correct the problem. They tied a long strap around a football. As Rashaan ran with that ball clutched against his chest, another Bear ran behind him yanking on the other end of the strap. Rashaan had to squeeze the ball with all his might to keep from losing it.

In many ways, that's what temptation does to us. The more the enemy of our souls tries to yank away our faith, the tighter we squeeze it to our heart. God allows temptation so that we will cling more fiercely to him.

Doubt, Faith, Perseverance, Testing
1 Cor. 10:13

Date used __________ Place ____________________

717

Dr. Paul Brand was speaking to a medical college in India on "Let your light so shine before men that they may behold your good works and glorify your Father." In front of the lectern was an oil lamp, with its cotton wick burning from the shallow dish of oil. As he preached, the lamp ran out of oil, the wick burned dry, and the smoke made him cough. He immediately used the opportunity.

"Some of us here are like this wick," he said. "We're trying to shine for the glory of God, but we stink. That's what happens when we use ourselves as the fuel of our witness rather than the Holy Spirit.

"Wicks can last indefinitely, burning brightly and without irritating smoke, if the fuel, the Holy Spirit, is in constant supply."

Holy Spirit, Good Works

Date used __________ Place ____________________

Testimony 718

On a wall near the main entrance to the Alamo in San Antonio, Texas, is a portrait with the following inscription:

> James Butler Bonham—no picture of him exists. This portrait is of his nephew, Major James Bonham, deceased, who greatly resembled his uncle. It is placed here by the family that people may know the appearance of the man who died for freedom.

No literal portrait of Jesus exists either. But the likeness of the Son who makes us free can be seen in the lives of his true followers.

Christlikeness, Witness

Date used __________ Place ____________________

Testimony 719

In *Sports Spectrum* Ken Walker tells how after a Monday night football game in 1990 several players did something for the first time that would later become a common sight. When the game ended between the San Francisco 49ers and the New York Giants, eight players from both sides gathered in a huddle in the center of the field at the 40-yard line nearer to the scoreboard. There they bowed their knees for all to see and prayed together in the name of Jesus Christ.

The brief prayer meetings caught on and gained their highest visibility several years later with Reggie White and his 1997 Super Bowl champion Green Bay Packers. One Packer, Eugene Robinson, explains the purpose of the players coming together to bow their knees: "We don't pray about who wins the game or any of that stuff. That's not what it's there for. We pray basically as an acknowledgment of who God is and that men will see that He exists."

The players have taken heat for their public stand. An article in *Sports Illustrated* advised the players to pray in private, and the NFL made noises for a while as though they would shut the practice down. But the players stood firm, some saying they were willing to be fined for the practice, and the prayer huddles went on.

One moment of truth for a believer is when he or she decides to publicly identify with Jesus Christ. Whether it be praying over a meal at a restaurant, carrying a Bible, wearing a pin, mentioning the Lord in conversation—it solidifies our commitment to Christ.

Acknowledging God, Boldness, Evangelism, Light,
Prayer, Salt, Taking a Stand, Witness
Matt. 5:13–16; Mark 8:38; Acts 4:29; 2 Cor. 3:12

Date used __________ Place ____________________

Testimony 720

In *Charles Kuralt's America* the author recalls a town meeting he once attended in Strafford, Vermont:

> What happens at a town meeting is pure democracy. Every citizen may have his or her say on every question. For a half-hour that day, for example, they debated the question of whether to go on paying $582.50 a year for outside health services deemed unsatisfactory by a farmer named Brown.
>
> The moderator, rail-fence-maker James Condict, said, "I'm going to ask for a standing vote. All those in favor . . ." and there it came, the Yankee expression that is the soul of the town meeting, "stand up and be counted."
>
> By a standing vote, Strafford agreed with farmer Brown.

To stand up and be counted is both pure democracy and pure commitment. Jesus calls his true followers to stand up and be counted as Christians.

Baptism, Boldness, Convictions, Courage, Witness
Mark 8:38; Phil. 1:20

Date used __________ Place ____________________

Testing 721

In the 1996 summer Olympics, sprinter Michael Johnson set records in the 200- and 400-meter races. To do so he had trained for some ten years to cut a mere second or two from his time. In *Slaying the Dragon* he writes:

> Success is found in much smaller portions than most people realize. A hundredth of a second here or sometimes a tenth there can determine the fastest man in the world. At times we live our lives on a paper-thin edge that barely separates greatness from mediocrity and success from failure.
>
> Life is often compared to a marathon, but I think it is more like being a sprinter: long stretches of hard work punctuated by brief moments in which we are given the opportunity to perform at our best.

The Christian life also resembles the life of a sprinter: long stretches of obedience and spiritual disciplines punctuated by great tests in which God gives us the opportunity to choose his eternal best.

Choices, Devotional Life, Discipleship, Discipline, Growth, Holiness, Obedience, Perfection, Preparation, Sanctification, Spiritual Disciplines

Gen. 22; Pss. 66:10–12; 81:7; Matt. 5:48; 28:20; 2 Cor. 7:1; 13:9; Phil. 3:7–15; Heb. 12:1–4; James 1:2–4; 1:12

Date used __________ Place ____________________

Mark Tidd of Webster, New York, describes an experience from his college days:

An old man showed up at the back door of the house we were renting. Opening the door a few inches, we saw his eyes were glassy and his furrowed face glistened with silver stubble. He clutched a wicker basket holding a few unappealing vegetables. He bid us good morning and offered his produce for sale. We were uneasy enough that we made a quick purchase to alleviate both our pity and our fear.

To our chagrin, he returned the next week, introducing himself as Mr. Roth, the man who lived in the shack down the road. As our fears subsided, we got close enough to realize it wasn't alcohol but cataracts that marbleized his eyes. On subsequent visits, he would shuffle in, wearing two mismatched right shoes, and pull out a harmonica. With glazed eyes set on a future glory, he'd puff out old gospel tunes between conversations about vegetables and religion.

On one visit, he exclaimed, "The Lord is so good! I came out of my shack this morning and found a bag full of shoes and clothing on my porch."

"That's wonderful, Mr. Roth!" we said. "We're happy for you."

"You know what's even more wonderful?" he asked. "Just yesterday I met some people that could really use them."

Giving, Generosity

Date used __________ Place ____________________

723

In the Chilean village of Chungungo water is nearly as valuable as precious metal. The region is arid and parched, forcing the village to truck in fresh water over dirt roads from miles away. Until recently the average person could afford a mere four gallons a day (compare that to the average American who uses ninety gallons a day), and buying even that meager amount soaked up 10 percent of household incomes. In Chungungo bathing was a luxury.

But then scientists experimented with an ingenious new system for obtaining water. The 330 residents of Chungungo now drink water—the freshest they have ever tasted—from high above, atop nearby El Tofo mountain. Under the direction of Dr. Robert Schemenauer, a Canadian cloud physicist, workers hung on eucalyptus poles a "wall" of finely woven propylene nets, each the size of eight queen-size bed sheets sown together. Seventy-five such nets sift the clouds that sweep in incessantly from the Pacific Ocean.

A close look at the plastic nets reveals propylene fibers meshed in tiny triangles. Like dew collects on grass, infinitesimally small water particles from fog collect on these fibers. Ten thousand such water particles must coalesce to produce one drop of water the size of a tear. Still, each water net collects forty gallons of water a day. The seventy-five nets on El Tofo sift a total of three thousand gallons daily from the drifting clouds and fog.

Sometimes our lives feel as dry and parched as the rocky soil around Chungungo, where only shrubs and cactus grow. What we need are spiritual water nets. Few things will flood the reservoirs of our soul like giving thanks to God.

Desert, Holy Spirit, Praise, Refreshment, Thirst
2 Chron. 5:13–14; Eph. 5:20; 1 Thess. 5:18

Date used __________ Place ____________________

Thanksgiving 724

A wine company advertisement in *Newsweek* magazine read, "The earth gives us wonderful grapes. The grapes give us wonderful wine. The wine wins us lots of new friends. Thank you, earth."

How easy it is to give credit and thanks to everything or everyone but the real source of all our blessings!

Creator, Idolatry, Worship
Rom. 1:21

Date used ________ Place ________________

In a sermon at Immanuel Presbyterian Church in Los Angeles, Gary Wilburn said:

In 1636, amid the darkness of the Thirty Years' War, a German pastor, Martin Rinkart, is said to have buried five thousand of his parishioners in one year, an average of fifteen a day. His parish was ravaged by war, death, and economic disaster.

In the heart of that darkness, with the cries of fear outside his window, he sat down and wrote this table grace for his children:

Now thank we all our God
With heart and hands and voices;
Who wondrous things hath done,
In whom his world rejoices.
Who, from our mother's arms,
Hath led us on our way
With countless gifts of love
And still is ours today.

Here was a man who knew thanksgiving comes from love of God, not from outward circumstances.

Contentment, Worship

Date used __________ Place ____________________

Thoughts 726

Dieters sometimes feel that just *thinking* about food adds inches to their waistline. Dr. Alan P. Xenakis, author of *Why Doesn't My Funny Bone Make Me Laugh?*, says dieters may be right. In certain people, thinking about food increases their insulin level, which makes them feel hungry. Thinking about food doesn't actually add pounds, but an increased appetite may!

Our thoughts stimulate other appetites as well, appetites that can lead to sin. To control our conduct, we first must control our thoughts.

Desires, Self-Control, Temptation
James 1:14–15

Date used __________ Place ____________________

Thoughts 727

An outbreak of cholera is nothing to take lightly, and in September 1996 Manila, the capital city of the Philippines, was in the grip of just such a plague. Three hundred people were suffering from acute symptoms of the disease, wrote Uli Schmetzer in the *Chicago Tribune,* and seven had already died.

The source of the problem was not a mystery. In the rainy season of August and September the streets and sewage canals of Manila become flooded and clogged. Flies and cockroaches proliferate, feed on the trash that floats on the surface, and become carriers of the cholera germs.

To combat the epidemic, Alfredo Lim, the mayor of Manila, had a novel idea. He put a bounty on flies and cockroaches: 1 peso (4 cents) for every ten flies brought dead or alive to health officials; 1.5 pesos (6 cents) for every ten cockroaches. Health officials targeted some of the poorest areas of the city, and on the first day of the program officials from the Department of Public Health went into the Paco district. Residents brought some two thousand insects in plastic bags and were paid on the spot.

"If we kill the flies at once," said Egmidio Espiritu, the chief of the health department, "we can stop the spread of these diseases."

Creepy little things can lead to big problems. Likewise, naughty little thoughts can someday result in serious, harmful sins. Work on cleaning up your thought life, and watch how your lifestyle changes.

Habits, Imagination, Rewards, Sin, Small Things, Words

Ps. 19:14; Matt. 6:24–34; Mark 7:20–23; Phil. 4:8; James 1:13–15

Date used __________ Place ____________________

Tongue 728

When the Green Bay Packers football team won the Super Bowl in 1997, many people thought back to the previous era of Packer greatness under legendary Green Bay coach Vince Lombardi. One of the players on those earlier world championship teams, offensive lineman Jerry Kramer, recalled this story:

> One day during the first year I played for him, he rode me unmercifully, pointing out how slow I was, how weak I was, how stupid I was. He convinced me. By the time I dragged myself into the locker room, I suspected I was the worst guard in league history. I sat in front of my locker, head down, contemplating quitting, when Lombardi came up behind me, mussed up my hair and said, "Son, one of these days you're gonna be the greatest guard in the league." Suddenly I was 10 feet tall, ready to do anything for him.

The tongue has awesome power to whittle other people down to nothing or to turn them into giants capable of great things.

Affirmation, Child Rearing, Confidence, Criticism, Discipleship, Encouragement, Leadership, Words
Prov. 12:18; 1 Thess. 5:11; Heb. 3:13

Date used __________ Place ____________________

Tradition 729

In the *New York Times Magazine* Robert Bryce writes:

> Autumn is prime time for the use of eyeblack in sports: baseball players in daytime playoff games and football players put dark stuff under their eyes, supposedly to reduce glare bouncing off their cheeks. One popular smear, called No Glare, contains crushed charcoal, paraffin, beeswax and petrolatum. Does it do anything? Dr. Oliver Schein, an ophthalmologist at Johns Hopkins School of Medicine, says, "Probably not." Even so, it's a tradition. The Pro Football Hall of Fame has a photo of the Washington Redskins fullback Andy Farkas using it way back in 1942. Bobby Valentine, when he managed the Texas Rangers, once wore eyeblack in the dugout. Boog Powell, the former Baltimore Orioles star, used it during his 17 years in the majors. "I don't remember it ever doing any good," he says. "But you looked cool."

We do well on occasion to examine our traditions to see whether we really know their purpose—and whether they accomplish that purpose.

Appearance, Ceremony, Effectiveness, Purpose, Religion, Ritual

Matt. 15:1–9; Mark 7:1–13; Col. 2:8

Date used __________ Place ____________________

Tradition 730

Until 1996 the Cleveland Browns football team had some of the most loyal fans in all of sports. For them Sunday was the main event of the week. Early on Sunday morning they came to Cleveland Stadium to enjoy tailgate parties and talk about their beloved Browns, and then in the afternoon they filed to the stadium to cheer and holler.

But all that changed in 1996. Owner Art Modell moved the team to Baltimore and changed its name to the Ravens, crushing the hearts of Cleveland fans.

Surprisingly, that didn't stop these fans from doing what they had done for years. On opening day, September 1, 1996, some fans showed up at Cleveland Stadium just as they had done for the last forty-six years and held tailgate parties. They wore Browns jerseys, waved Browns flags, and chanted, "Let's go, Brownies." Then shortly before 1 P.M. they refilled their cups and marched to the stadium gates. But the stadium was quiet and empty.

Traditions die hard, especially religious ones. An empty tradition is an end in itself, a habit without meaning. It is cheering fans without a team or a game, for God is gone.

Atheism, Habits, Religion, Ritual, Rules, Secularism
Ezek. 10; Mark 7:1–13; Col. 2:16–23

Date used __________ Place ____________________

Traditions 731

William Poteet wrote in *The Pentecostal Minister* how in 1903 the Russian czar noticed a sentry posted for no apparent reason on the Kremlin grounds. Upon inquiry, he discovered that in 1776 Catherine the Great found there the first flower of spring. “Post a sentry here,” she commanded, “so that no one tramples that flower under foot!”

Some traditions die hard.

Change, Innovation

Date used __________ Place ____________________

Trapped 732

According to the *Chicago Tribune*, in the early 1980s Ed Greer had a good white-collar job with Hughes Aircraft in El Segundo, California. Nevertheless he was miserable. He hated his work and he was feeling pressure from his wife and father. At one point he told a coworker, "Never become too good at something you hate. They'll make you do it the rest of your life."

Greer wasn't willing to do that, and on September 10, 1981, he disappeared. Without telling anyone his plans, he got on a plane and flew to Ft. Lauderdale, Florida. There he lived on the beaches and fixed boat engines. After a while he assumed someone else's name and moved to Houston, Texas, getting a regular job with a small oil exploration firm.

Meanwhile his wife divorced him in absentia. In an odd twist, Greer became somewhat of a fantasy hero to some yuppies who felt trapped in corporate America. Some said they wished they had the guts to do what he did. His former coworkers at Hughes Aircraft even began holding annual celebrations in his memory, with many wearing Ed Greer masks.

Finally in October of 1988, seven years after Greer abandoned his family and career, the FBI caught up to him.

In an interview, the forty-year-old Greer tried to explain his actions: "I felt trapped. I didn't like my life."

Many people can identify with him. Many feel trapped, under too much pressure, in circumstances they just don't like. Many wonder how to escape. But God has a different answer.

Career, Freedom, Fulfillment, Joy, Peace, Stress
John 16:33; Acts 16:22–34; 2 Cor. 1:3–11

Date used __________ Place ____________________

Treasures in Heaven 733

In a *Reader's Digest* article titled "You Can Make a Million," Randy Fitzgerald tells the story of how one immigrant couple amassed a fortune:

> Humberto and Georgina came to America from Cuba as penniless refugees in 1960. Humberto learned English in a Long Island, N.Y., high school; Georgina spent her early years in Los Angeles. They met when Georgina was a student at the University of Miami, and married in 1972. Both eventually landed jobs as reporters for a Fort Lauderdale, Fla., newspaper, a profession that rarely leads to great wealth. But a math teacher had taught Humberto the importance of compound interest, and early in the couple's marriage, they decided to save every possible dollar for investment.
>
> Their formula was simple though challenging. They bought only compact cars and paid their credit-card bills in full every month. They shopped at discount stores, clipped "cents off" coupons and took sack lunches to work. Some years the couple saved up to 66 percent of their income. In 1987 they began investing $1250 a month in five diversified-stock mutual funds. And that strategy over eight years produced the bonanza that gave them millionaire status. Last year they made more money from their investments than from their two salaries.

Storing up treasures like this sounds wonderful, doesn't it? But if this sounds good, imagine how great a treasure stored up in heaven will be. Jesus said the value of heavenly treasures far surpasses any treasure on earth. We should make the same effort and have the same focus as this couple did when we give our money to God.

Giving, Goals, Money, Rewards, Saving, Self-Control
Matt. 6:19–24

Date used __________ Place ____________________

Trials 734

In January 1993 the Galeras volcano, located in Colombia, South America, suddenly erupted. One week later a geologist, Dr. Fraser Goff, was sampling gas vents in a canyon west of the volcano summit. The guide who was with him jokingly said, "Do you want to look at some gold?"

Dr. Goff picked up some of the rocks and later cut them into thin slices. He found that there was real gold in the rocks, quite a bit of gold. The naked eye could see tiny gold nuggets in the slices.

This was the first time scientists had detected visible gold particles in an active volcano. More than a year later Dr. Goff announced that the Galeras volcano, which remained active, was spewing more than a pound of gold each day into the atmosphere and depositing forty-five pounds of gold a year into the rocks lining its crater. He explained that magma from inside the earth has many components, including gold, and estimated that there is a gold vein at the base of the volcano that is at least ten feet wide.

Just as the ultra high heat and pressure of a volcano can bring gold from below the surface of the earth, the pressure and fiery trials of our lives bring forth spiritual gold. If we draw close to God during difficult times, we find the gold of increasing faith, character, wisdom, and nearness to God.

Character, Faith, Stress
Rom. 5:2–5; James 1:2–4

Date used __________ Place ____________________

735

In *A View from the Zoo,* Gary Richmond tells about the birth of a giraffe:

The first thing to emerge are the baby giraffe's front hooves and head. A few minutes later the plucky newborn is hurled forth, falls ten feet, and lands on its back. Within seconds, he rolls to an upright position with his legs tucked under his body. From this position he considers the world for the first time and shakes off the last vestiges of the birthing fluid from his eyes and ears.

The mother giraffe lowers her head long enough to take a quick look. Then she positions herself directly over her calf. She waits for about a minute, and then she does the most unreasonable thing. She swings her long, pendulous leg outward and kicks her baby, so that it is sent sprawling head over heals.

When it doesn't get up, the violent process is repeated over and over again. The struggle to rise is momentous. As the baby calf grows tired, the mother kicks it again to stimulate its efforts. . . . Finally, the calf stands for the first time on its wobbly legs.

Then the mother giraffe does the most remarkable thing. She kicks it off its feet again. Why? She wants it to remember how it got up. In the wild, baby giraffes must be able to get up as quickly as possible to stay with the herd, where there is safety. Lions, hyenas, leopards, and wild hunting dogs all enjoy young giraffes, and they'd get it too, if the mother didn't teach her calf to get up quickly and get with it. . . .

I've thought about the birth of the giraffe many times. I can see its parallel in my own life. There have been many times when it seemed that I had just stood up after a trial, only to be knocked down again by the next. It was God helping me to remember how it was that I got up, urging me always to walk with him, in his shadow, under his care.

Discipline, Pain

Date used __________ Place ____________________

736

A man found a cocoon of the emperor moth and took it home to watch it emerge. One day a small opening appeared, and for several hours the moth struggled but couldn't seem to force its body past a certain point.

Deciding something was wrong, the man took scissors and snipped the remaining bit of cocoon. The moth emerged easily, its body large and swollen, the wings small and shriveled.

He expected that in a few hours the wings would spread out in their natural beauty, but they did not. Instead of developing into a creature free to fly, the moth spent its life dragging around a swollen body and shriveled wings.

The constricting cocoon and the struggle necessary to pass through the tiny opening are God's way of forcing fluid from the body into the wings. The "merciful" snip was, in reality, cruel. Sometimes the struggle is exactly what we need.

Struggles, Difficulties

Date used __________ Place ____________________

737

One of the healthiest things that can happen to a ponderosa forest is to have a forest fire every five to twenty years. Without a regular fire two things happen that can ultimately lead to destruction that lasts for hundreds of years.

First, "a healthy ponderosa forest is made of widely spaced, fire-resistant trees," writes Michael Parfit in *National Geographic*. "With overprotection young trees and competing species make a flammable understory so shaded that ponderosa seedlings can't grow." Thus new ponderosas stop springing up.

Second, dead wood, needles, and cones pile up in a thicker and thicker layer of combustible kindling on the forest floor. When a fire eventually does come to an overprotected forest—as it eventually must—the fire burns hotter and deeper. Instead of a healthy fire that burns quick and low over the floor of the forest, blackening the trunks of healthy trees but nothing more, the fire explodes in the crown of the trees. It also destroys the roots. The result is total destruction of every tree.

Such a fire ruins the forest ecosystem. The soil no longer absorbs rain, and it erodes.

As odd as it may seem, ponderosa forests need fire in order to be healthy and viable.

Christians also benefit from fiery trials, even though they are painful. They can burn away the temporal, worthless things that so easily pile up in our lives.

Affliction, Fire, Hardship, Pain, Troubles
Ps. 119:71; Rom. 5:2–5; Heb. 12:28–29; James 1:2–4

Date used __________ Place ____________________

Trivialities 738

A familiar Mother Goose rhyme goes:

Pussy cat, Pussy cat, where have you been?
I've been to London to visit the queen.
Pussy cat, Pussy cat, what did you there?
I frightened a little mouse under the chair.

Like that cat, Christians sometimes settle for petty involvements, trivial pursuits—chasing mice—when we have the opportunity to spend time with royalty, with the King! Instead of remaining content with minimum daily requirements, we can deepen our relationship with God and grow into maturity.

Maturity, Devotional Life

Date used __________ Place ____________________

739

Star NFL wide receiver Robert Brooks of the 1997 Super Bowl champion Green Bay Packers suffered a terrible season-ending knee injury after six games in 1996. Drew Baker writes in *Sports Spectrum* that Brooks (who started the Packer tradition of jumping into the stands after a touchdown) is a Christian, and as he sat in the locker room that day after the injury, he thought about what purpose God could have in this discouraging blow:

"God was telling me He needed to use me," says Brooks, "to show people that through Christ you can overcome anything—based on the way I was going to handle my injury. It was going to touch a lot of people's hearts and change a lot of people's lives in their everyday struggles. It wasn't a personal thing. I knew I was going to be okay. If I didn't play in the Super Bowl, that's fine, because it is more important that God is going to use me."

Before surgery, team chaplain Steve Newman visited Brooks's home and shared 2 Corinthians 1:3–4. This passage confirmed Brooks's postinjury conclusions: "It was the exact reason God was telling me He was using me. It took me to another spiritual level with God. If I hadn't known God was using me, I wouldn't have handled it as well."

Packer teammate and free safety Eugene Robinson, NFL leader in interceptions among active players, has observed the change in Brooks. He describes him as "real fired up. The Lord got hold of Robert."

To everyone's surprise, Robert Brooks recovered completely from his injury and played outstandingly the following season.

God's Will, Priorities, Purpose, Suffering, Trials, Trust
Rom. 8:28; 2 Cor. 1:3–7; Phil. 1:12–26; 2:12–13

Date used __________ Place ____________________

Trust 740

The relationship between a movie actor and a director can make or break a movie. A *USA Today* film critic writes, "In some directors' hands, an actor remains a lump of coal. In others, that same performer will metamorphose into a shining diamond onscreen."

She says Katharine Hepburn did her greatest films with director George Cukor. When Hepburn matched up with a different director, Stuart Millar, her movies suffered.

John Wayne did fifteen memorable movies with director John Ford, but the luster left when he worked with John Huston.

Cary Grant was at his best with director Howard Hawks but couldn't bear to watch his own performance in *Arsenic and Old Lace,* which he did with director Frank Capra.

What is the key to a consistently winning pair? Richard Brown, professor of cinema studies at New York's New School for Social Research, says, "It is only about one thing—trust. A director must trust that an actor has the character inside him or her and that it is within an actor's range. An actor must trust a director with his performance, his work and his image onscreen."

Trust is also at the heart of our relationship with the Divine Director, Jesus Christ. Christ has absolute confidence that by his Spirit he can make us into something glorious. The only question is, Do we trust him to bring out what is best in us?

Christlikeness, Discipleship, Growth
John 8:31–32; Rom. 8:28; James 1:2–4

Date used __________ Place ____________________

In *Living by God's Surprises,* Harold Myra writes:

My pastor, Bob Harvey, tells how early in his ministry a close friend died. In an effort to comfort the widow, also a close friend, Bob shared all his seminary textbook explanations of how and why God might have let this happen. But the woman rebuked him lovingly. "I don't need a God like that," she said. "I don't need to understand all this. What I need is a God who is bigger than my mind."

Counsel, Crisis, Death, God's Wisdom, Pain
Prov. 3:5–6; Rom. 8:28

Date used __________ Place ____________________

Trust 742

Not many people enjoy going to the doctor, but according to Reuters, in 1994, one London accountant took that to an extreme. The sixty-three-year-old man knew he needed bladder surgery but he could not overcome his fear of doctors and hospitals. So he self-reliantly did what had to be done: He tried to perform the surgery on himself. Tragically he got an infection from the self-surgery and later died. The coroner said, "Unfortunately, [his] drastic remedy went wrong. A simple operation would have solved the problem."

Just as this man didn't trust doctors or hospitals, many people don't trust God. In their self-reliance, they destroy themselves.

Fear, Independence, Salvation, Self-Reliance
Prov. 3:5–6; 28:26; Jer. 17:5–8

Date used __________ Place ____________________

743

Anyone who has lived or worked in a skyscraper knows tall buildings sway in the wind. There's no danger; the engineers know it will happen, but the sway is uncomfortable for people inside. When engineers and architects designed Citicorp Center in New York, they decided to do something about it.

At the top of the fifty-nine story building, they installed a machine called a tuned mass damper. The machine, writes Joe Morgenstern in *New Yorker* magazine, "was essentially a four-hundred-and-ten-ton block of concrete, attached to huge springs and floating on a film of oil. When the building swayed, the block's inertia worked to damp the movement and calm tenants' queasy stomachs."

When the winds of life gust around us, there is a stabilizing force in the heart of every believer that calms his or her fears. It is trust in God.

Faith, Fear, Stability, Trials, Trouble

Ps. 46:1–2; Prov. 3:5–6; Mark 4:35–41

Date used __________ Place ____________________

Trust 744

A television program preceding the 1988 Winter Olympics featured blind skiers being trained for slalom skiing, impossible as that sounds. Paired with sighted skiers, the blind skiers were taught on the flats how to make right and left turns.

When that was mastered, they were taken to the slalom slope, where their sighted partners skied beside them shouting, "Left!" and "Right!" As they obeyed the commands, they were able to negotiate the course and cross the finish line, depending solely on the sighted skiers' word. It was either complete trust or catastrophe.

What a vivid picture of the Christian life! In this world, we are in reality blind about what course to take. We must rely solely on the Word of the only One who is truly sighted—God himself. His Word gives us the direction we need to finish the course.

Direction, Scripture

Date used __________ Place ____________________

745

Sodium is an extremely active element found naturally only in combined form; it always links itself to another element. Chlorine, on the other hand, is the poisonous gas that gives bleach its offensive odor. When sodium and chlorine are combined, the result is sodium chloride—common table salt—the substance we use to preserve meat and bring out its flavor.

Love and truth can be like sodium and chlorine. Love without truth is flighty, sometimes blind, willing to combine with various doctrines. On the other hand, truth by itself can be offensive, sometimes even poisonous. Spoken without love, it can turn people away from the gospel.

When truth and love are combined in an individual or a church, however, then we have what Jesus called "the salt of the earth," and we're able to preserve and bring out the beauty of our faith.

Love, Saltiness

Date used __________ Place ____________________

746

The purple dinosaur named Barney is loved by millions of children. According to Reuters, on July 15, 1997, Barney had an accident. During filming of the *Barney & Friends* show, a cooling fan inside the sixty-pound dinosaur suit short-circuited and started to smoke. The actor playing Barney quickly got out of the suit but suffered smoke inhalation. He was taken to the hospital and soon released.

The story of the accident was carried on the news, and it upset many children. Scores of parents called the television station to say their children were afraid that Barney had been burned, or worse, that he was a fake.

A spokeswoman for the producers of the program said, "It can be really devastating to a three-year-old. They love Barney and they think that something terrible has happened to him, or that he's not real."

Fantasies like Barney can bring a person good feelings. But a fantasy is a fantasy, and sooner or later the truth comes out.

There are all sorts of fantasies. Those hostile to the God of the Bible must hold on to a great number of fantasies to justify their thinking and behavior. Sooner or later those fantasies are seen for what they really are.

Authenticity, Belief, Deception, Disillusionment, Doctrine, Error, Evolution, Fantasy, Illusion, Lies, Morality, Reality
Isa. 44:9–20; 1 Cor. 6:9; Eph. 4:22; 2 Tim. 3:13; Titus 3:3

Date used __________ Place ____________________

Truth 747

In *Discipleship Journal* author Mack Stiles tells the story of how he led a young man from Sweden named Andreas to Christ. One part of their conversation is especially instructive:

Andreas said, "I've been told if I decide to follow Jesus, He will meet my needs and my life will get very good."

This seemed to Andreas to be a point in Christianity's favor. But I faced a temptation—to make it sound better than it is.

"No, Andreas, no!" I said.

Andreas blinked his surprise.

"Actually, Andreas, you may accept Jesus and find that life goes very badly for you."

"What do you mean?" he asked.

"Well, you may find that your friends reject you, you could lose your job, your family might oppose your decision—there are a lot of bad things that may happen to you if you decide to follow Jesus. Andreas, when Jesus calls you, He calls you to go the way of the cross."

Andreas stared at me and asked the obvious: "Then why would I want to follow Jesus?"

Sadly, this is the question that stumps many Christians. For some reason we feel that unless we're meeting people's needs they won't follow Christ. Yet this is not the gospel.

I cocked my head and answered, "Andreas, because Jesus is true."

Those on the side of truth come to Jesus.

Cross, Evangelism, Gospel, Jesus, Persecution, Witnessing

Matt. 16:24–27; John 8:31–47; 14:6; 15:18–16:4; 18:37; Acts 14:22; Phil. 1:29; 1 Thess. 3:3; 2 Tim. 3:12; 1 Peter 2:21; Rev. 1:9

Date used __________ Place ____________________

When the new technology of high-definition television came on the scene, it had an immediate effect on how things were done in the studio. Low-tech television had such poor picture resolution that the visual details of a studio did not show up on the screen. Actors and newscasters wore thick pancake makeup to hide wrinkles, moles, and blemishes, but the makeup was invisible to the relatively crude camera. Fake books rested on shelves, and cardboard backdrops with painted wood grain stood as walls. Still, with low-tech television, the viewer was none the wiser. Says Jim Fenhagen, a set designer who works for the major networks, "With the old TV, you can get away with murder."

But high-definition television, using high-resolution digital technology, changed all that. The studio camera picks up everything from scratches on the desk to blemishes on the skin. That has forced a change in how things are done.

Like television personalities facing an unforgiving high-definition camera, when we come to God, we come to the one who sees us as we really are. We must be completely truthful with him.

Authenticity, Confession, Conviction, Faults, Guilt, Honesty, Hypocrisy, Scripture, Sin, Transparency, Vulnerability

John 16:8; Acts 5:1–11; 2 Tim. 3:16; Heb. 4:12–13

Date used __________ Place ____________________

The May 1987 edition of *National Geographic* included a feature about the arctic wolf. Author L. David Mech described how a seven-member pack had targeted several musk-oxen calves who were guarded by eleven adults. As the wolves approached their quarry, the musk-oxen bunched in an impenetrable semicircle, their deadly rear hooves facing out, and the calves remained safe during a long standoff with the enemy.

But then a single ox broke rank, and the herd scattered into nervous little groups. A skirmish ensued, and the adults finally fled in panic, leaving the calves to the mercy of the predators. Not a single calf survived.

Paul warned the Ephesian elders in Acts 20 that after his departure wolves would come, not sparing the flock. Wolves continue to attack the church today but cannot penetrate and destroy when unity is maintained. When believers break ranks, however, they provide easy prey.

Wolves, Satan

Date used __________ Place ____________________

750

In the late 1970s Hispanic writer Victor Villasenor decided it was time to write his big book. He envisioned a book that would inspire Hispanics, who he felt were desperately in need of heroes.

He heavily researched his family's story, traveling to Mexico, interviewing family members, corroborating stories, checking and rechecking details. The story, which he titled *Rain of Gold,* took him twelve years to write and filled 3,200 manuscript pages.

With a great sense of satisfaction and anticipation he sent the manuscript to his publisher. Sometime later he received shocking news. The publisher intended to publish his book as a fictional novel called *Rio Grande*. Villasenor was outraged.

The publisher had already given Villasenor seventy-five thousand dollars as an advance for the hardcover rights to the book. The book had the makings of a big seller. It was already set up as an alternative selection for the Book-of-the-Month Club.

Villasenor didn't care about all of that. He cared about giving his people a true story that would inspire them for hundreds of years to come. Says Villasenor, "Until a human being does it, we don't know if it's possible. And not knowing if it's possible kills us. That's why it has to be real people that did these things. It stretches human reality."

So Villasenor traveled to New York and shocked the publishing world by buying back the rights to the book. He then sold the book to a small university press for an advance of fifteen hundred dollars. That cost him big money and massive exposure, but it insured that the book would bear the original title *Rain of Gold* and be published as a true story rather than fiction.

Villasenor shows us that pursuing our vision of what is truly valuable is often done at a steep price.

Sacrifice, Truth, Vision
Matt. 16:23–26

Date used __________ Place ____________________

Helmut Thielicke in *How to Believe Again,* writes:

I once heard of a child who was raising a frightful cry because he had shoved his hand into the opening of a very expensive Chinese vase and then couldn't pull it out again. Parents and neighbors tugged with might and main on the child's arm, with the poor creature howling out loud all the while.

Finally there was nothing left to do but to break the beautiful, expensive vase. And then as the mournful heap of shards lay there, it became clear why the child had been so hopelessly stuck. His little fist grasped a paltry penny which he had spied in the bottom of the vase and which he, in his childish ignorance, would not let go.

Money, Greed

Date used __________ Place ____________________

752

Norman Cousins, after his experiences at UCLA medical school, notes a common misunderstanding about what is "real" and "unreal."

In Bob Benson's *He Speaks Softly,* Cousins is quoted:

The words "hard" and "soft" are generally used by medical students to describe the contrasting nature of courses. Courses like biochemistry, physics, pharmacology, anatomy, and pathology are anointed with the benediction of "hard," whereas subjects like medical ethics, philosophy, history, and patient-physician relationships tend to labor under the far less auspicious label "soft". . . . [But] a decade or two after graduation there tends to be an inversion. That which was supposed to be hard turns out to be soft, and vice versa. The knowledge base of medicine is constantly changing. . . . But the soft subjects—especially those that have to do with intangibles—turn out in the end to be of enduring value.

Ethics, Permanence

Date used __________ Place ____________________

J. Alistair Brown writes:

Walking through a park, I passed a massive oak tree. A vine had grown up along its trunk. The vine started small—nothing to bother about. But over the years the vine had gotten taller and taller. By the time I passed, the entire lower half of the tree was covered by the vine's creepers. The mass of tiny feelers was so thick that the tree looked as though it had innumerable birds' nests in it.

Now the tree was in danger. This huge, solid oak was quite literally being taken over; the life was being squeezed from it.

But the gardeners in that park had seen the danger. They had taken a saw and severed the trunk of the vine—one neat cut across the middle. The tangled mass of the vine's branches still clung to the oak, but the vine was now dead. That would gradually become plain as weeks passed and the creepers began to die and fall away from the tree.

How easy it is for sin, which begins so small and seemingly insignificant, to grow until it has a strangling grip on our lives.

But sin's power is severed by Christ, and gradually, as we yield daily to Christ, sin's grip dries up and falls away.

Sin, Surrender

Date used __________ Place ____________________

Vigilance 754

Dean Niferatos was riding the Number 22 CTA bus in Chicago. The bus brimmed with dozing office workers, restless punkers, and affluent shoppers. At the Clark and Webster stop, two men and a woman climbed in. The driver, a seasoned veteran, immediately bellowed, "Everybody watch your valuables. There are pickpockets on board."

Women clutched their purses tightly. Men put their hands on their wallets. All eyes fixed on the trio, who, looking insulted and harassed, didn't break stride as they promptly exited through the middle doors.

The Bible warns us to be vigilant, because evil is less likely to overtake us when we're watching.

Satan, Spiritual Warfare

Date used __________ Place ____________________

Steve Green, who sang six years with Bill and Gloria Gaither, tells about getting to know some of the work crews in the large auditoriums where their concerts were held.

The Gaithers prefer concerts-in-the-round, which means extra work for the "riggers," who walk the four-inch rafter beams—often a hundred feet above the concrete floor—to hang sound speakers and spotlights. For such work, understandably, they are very well paid.

"The fellows I talked to weren't bothered by the sight of looking down a hundred feet," says Green. "What they *didn't* like, they said, were jobs in buildings that had false ceilings —acoustical tile slung just a couple of feet below the rafters. They were still high in the air, and if they slipped, their weight would smash right through the flimsy tile. But their minds seemed to play tricks on them, lulling them into carelessness."

Satan's business is not so much in scaring us to death as persuading us that the danger of a spiritual fall is minimal. No wonder Peter advised us to "resist him, standing firm in the faith" (1 Peter 5:9).

Deception, Temptation

Date used __________ Place ____________________

According to United Press International, as the Vietnam war was nearing its end, a nightmare began for the family of private first class Alan Barton. Barton was killed by a land mine just outside his base in Vietnam. The army was unable to identify the remains. Meanwhile Barton was unaccounted for. Somehow the officers in charge did not see the relationship between those two events, and the army classified Barton as a deserter.

The family, of course, was devastated. Having your son labeled a deserter is a shame for any parents to endure but much more for this family—Barton's father was a twenty-year army veteran.

Alan Barton's mother did not believe her son had deserted. She insisted on his innocence. For thirteen years her son's unidentified remains lay in a military morgue in Hawaii as she fought to clear his name. Finally the army rechecked the morgue records, and this time they correctly identified Alan Barton's remains.

In February 1983 the army honored the soldier it had wronged. They gave Alan K. Barton a full military funeral. Soldiers sounded a twenty-one-gun salute, and a bugler played taps. Barton's mother wept into a tightly folded U.S. flag that moments before had draped her son's silver coffin.

In this world, even heroes may be wrongly incriminated. But just as this soldier's name was cleared and honored, so God promises to vindicate his servants. One day, either in this world or at the final judgment, the truth will come out. The twenty-one-gun salute will be given. The bugle will sound. The flag will be presented. And your name will be vindicated.

Name, Reputation, Slander
Ps. 135:14

Date used __________ Place ____________________

God has given certain creatures amazing capabilities. The chameleon, for example, shows uncanny accuracy in nabbing bugs with its tongue. Scientists have recently found out why, says Reuters. Chameleons have telephoto eyes.

According to Matthias Ott and Frank Schaeffel of the University Eye Hospital in Tübingen, Germany, the lizards have eyes that work like the telephoto lens on a camera. That requires a positive and negative lens. All other animals in the world have only a positive, convex lens. This is the first discovery of a creature that also has a negative, concave lens. The two lenses give the chameleons super-vision.

Being able to see in ways that others do not often makes the difference between success and failure.

Creation, Goals, Spiritual Discernment, Success
2 Kings 6:8–23; 1 Cor. 2:6–16; Eph. 1:17–18

Date used __________ Place ____________________

Vision 758

About 350 years ago a shipload of travelers landed on the northeast coast of America. The first year they established a town site. The next year they elected a town government. The third year the town government planned to build a road five miles westward into the wilderness.

In the fourth year the people tried to impeach their town government because they thought it was a waste of public funds to build a road five miles westward into a wilderness. Who needed to go there anyway?

Here were people who had the vision to see three thousand miles across an ocean and overcome great hardships to get there. But in just a few years they were not able to see even five miles out of town. They had lost their pioneering vision.

With a clear vision of what we can become in Christ, no ocean of difficulty is too great. Without it, we rarely move beyond our current boundaries.

Change, Complacency

Date used __________ Place ____________________

Vision 759

In the book *A Saviour for All Seasons,* William Barker relates the story of a bishop from the East Coast who many years ago paid a visit to a small, midwestern religious college. He stayed at the home of the college president, who also served as professor of physics and chemistry. After dinner, the bishop declared that the millennium couldn't be far off, because just about everything about nature had been discovered and all inventions conceived.

The young college president politely disagreed and said he felt there would be many more discoveries. When the angered bishop challenged the president to name just one such invention, the president replied he was certain that within fifty years men would be able to fly.

"Nonsense!" sputtered the outraged bishop. "Only angels are intended to fly."

The bishop's name was Wright, and he had two boys at home who would prove to have greater vision than their father. Their names: Orville and Wilbur.

Creativity, Skepticism

Date used __________ Place ____________________

Vision 760

When Apple Computer fell on difficult days a while back, Apple's young chairman, Steven Jobs, traveled from the Silicon Valley to New York City. His purpose was to convince Pepsico's John Sculley to move west and run his struggling company.

As the two men overlooked the Manhattan skyline from Sculley's penthouse office, the Pepsi executive started to decline Jobs's offer.

"Financially," Sculley said, "you'd have to give me a million-dollar salary, a million-dollar bonus, and a million-dollar severance."

Flabbergasted, Jobs gulped and agreed—if Sculley would move to California. But Sculley would commit only to being a consultant from New York. At that, Jobs issued a challenge to Sculley: "Do you want to spend the rest of your life selling sugared water, or do you want to change the world?"

In his autobiography *Odyssey*, Sculley admits Jobs's challenge "knocked the wind out of me." He said he'd become so caught up with his future at Pepsi, his pension, and whether his family could adapt to life in California that an opportunity to "change the world" nearly passed him by. Instead, he put his life in perspective and went to Apple.

Many people don't recognize a chance to change the world. Part of the Christian message is letting people know what a difference the gospel makes.

Evangelism, Service

Date used __________ Place ____________________

Warning 761

According to the *Chicago Tribune,* on May 17, 1987, an Iraqi F–1 Mirage aircraft fired two Exocet missiles at the Navy frigate *USS Stark,* which was patrolling in the Persian Gulf.

The *Stark* was equipped with radar systems to detect such missiles in the air. In the nerve center of the ship was the electronic warfare operator, a man who monitored these systems. If a missile was fired at the ship, he would be warned in two ways. An audible alarm would sound and a visual symbol would appear on the radar screen.

Nevertheless, without warning the Exocet missiles slammed into the side of the *USS Stark* just above the waterline, tearing a ten-foot hole in the ship and killing thirty-seven American sailors.

To learn what went wrong, the House Armed Services Committee launched an official investigation. After visiting the ship and talking to the crew, they reported that the tragedy had probably not resulted from equipment failure. Rather the cause was human error or omission on the part of several people. One was the electronic warfare operator in the ship's nerve center.

The report said, "The operator indicated that he had turned off the audible alarm feature because too many signals were being received that were setting off the alarm, requiring actions that distracted him from performing other signal analysis."

Then with the audible alarm off, according to the investigators, he may have been distracted at the time when the visual signals appeared on the radar screen.

Warning signals are usually an irritating interruption, but we turn them off at our peril.

End Times, Preaching, Second Coming
Matt. 24:42; 1 Thess. 5:1–8

Date used __________ Place ____________________

762

When New York's Citicorp tower was completed in 1977, it was the seventh tallest building in the world. Many structural engineers hailed the tower for its technical elegance and singular grace. The tower was notable for its sleek aluminum sides and provocative slash-topped design. The structural engineer who designed the steel superstructure was William J. LeMessurier, who not long after the building was completed was elected into the National Academy of Engineering, which is the highest honor his profession bestows.

But according to Joe Morgenstern in *New Yorker* magazine, one year after the building opened, LeMessurier came to a frightening realization. The Citicorp tower was flawed. Without LeMessurier's approval, during construction the joints in the steel superstructure had been bolted, which is a common and acceptable practice but does not make for as strong a joint as welding does. What made that a critical problem, though, was that in LeMessurier's calculations he had not taken into account the extra force of a nonperpendicular wind.

He now calculated that the joint most vulnerable to such winds was on the thirteenth floor. If that joint gave way, the whole building would come tumbling down. He talked with meteorologists and found that a wind strong enough to buckle that crucial joint came every sixteen years in New York.

LeMessurier weighed his options. If he blew the whistle on himself, he faced lawsuits, probable bankruptcy, and professional disgrace. He gave a fleeting thought to suicide but dismissed that as the coward's way out. He could keep silent and hope for the best. But lives were at stake.

So he did what he had to do. He informed all concerned. City and corporate leaders faced the problem in a professional manner, and plans were drawn to strengthen the joints by welding steel plates to them. Contingency plans were made to ensure people's safety during the work, and the welding began in August of 1978.

After the work was completed three months later, the building was strong enough to withstand a storm of the severity that hits New York only once every seven hundred years. In fact it was now one of the safest structures ever built.

The repairs cost millions of dollars. Nevertheless LeMessurier's career and reputation were not destroyed but enhanced. One engineer commended LeMessurier for being a man who had the courage to say, "I got a problem; I made the problem; let's fix the problem."

You may come to a point where you realize your life is like that flawed building. Although by all appearances you are strong and successful and together, you know you have points of weakness that make you vulnerable to collapse. What do you do?

You come clean, get help, and get fixed.

Accountability, Addictions, Appearance, Confession,
Failure, Reputation, Sexual Sin

2 Sam. 12:1–25; 1 Cor. 10:12–13; James 5:16; 1 John 1:9

Date used __________ Place ____________________

Weakness 763

In *Leadership,* Ben Patterson, dean of the chapel at Hope College and a former pastor, writes:

> In the spring of 1980 I was suffering great pain from what was diagnosed as two herniated discs in my lower back. The prescription was total bed rest. But since my bed was too soft, the treatment ended up being total floor rest. I was frustrated and humiliated. I couldn't preach, I couldn't lead meetings, I couldn't call on new prospects for the church. I couldn't do anything but pray.
>
> Not that I immediately grasped that last fact. It took two weeks for me to get so bored that I finally asked my wife for the church directory so I could at least do something, even if it was only pray for the people of my congregation. Note: it wasn't piety but boredom and frustration that drove me to pray. But pray I did, every day for every person in my church, two or three hours a day. After a while, the time became sweet.
>
> Toward the end of my convalescence, anticipating my return to work, I prayed, "Lord, this has been good, this praying. It's too bad I don't have time to do this when I'm working."
>
> And God spoke to me, very clearly. He said, "Stupid (that's right, that was his very word. He said it in a kind tone of voice, though). You have the same twenty-four hours each day when you're weak as when you're strong. The only difference is that when you're strong you think you're in charge. When you're weak you know you aren't."

Prayer is an admission of weakness and the single most important expression of true dependence on God.

Dependence, Ministry, Prayer
2 Cor. 12:8–10

Date used __________ Place ____________________

In the 1996 Masters golf tournament, Greg Norman, the White Shark, had one of the most devastating experiences an athlete of any sort can suffer. After three rounds he had a virtually insurmountable six-stroke lead. Eighteen more holes of even average golf would assure him of his Masters victory and possession of the coveted green jacket. But the bottom fell out for Greg Norman. On the fourth and final day of the tournament he shot a 78, and Nick Faldo shot 67 to come from six shots back and win by five strokes.

In the *New York Times* Larry Dorman writes:

> After the debacle, the golf star says he experienced "the most touching few days" of his life. People from all over the world contacted him with words of encouragement. The mail ran four times the volume of what Norman received when he won the British Open in 1993.
>
> "It's changed my total outlook on life and on people," Norman says of last April's defeat. "There's no need for me to be cynical anymore. My wife said to me, 'You know, maybe this is better than winning the green jacket. Maybe now you understand the importance of it all.' I never thought I could reach out and touch people like that. And the extraordinary thing is that I did it by losing."

When we are weak, some of the most beautiful things in life can happen to us.

Cynicism, Encouragement, Failure, Losing, Strength
Matt. 5:1–5; 2 Cor. 12:7–10

Date used __________ Place ____________________

765

John Templeton, who founded the Templeton Growth Fund, held his company's first annual business meeting forty years ago in the dining room of the home of a retired General Foods executive. The company had only one part-time employee and one shareholder.

Forty years later, the Templeton Funds have more than six hundred employees and thirty-six billion dollars in assets. If you had invested ten thousand dollars in the company forty years ago, you would now have three million dollars.

What has been John Templeton's basic stock market strategy? Gobble up stock market bargains. He buys the stock of good companies that for one reason or another other investors hate. In the 1930s he borrowed ten thousand dollars and bought the 104 stocks that traded for less than one dollar on the New York Stock Exchange. He made a killing.

Wherever you find success, you usually find someone who has discovered an effective principle or idea and worked it to perfection.

Money, Saving, Success
Prov. 8:12–21; 24:5

Date used __________ Place ____________________

766

In the *Christian Reader,* Ramon Williams writes that on April 28, 1996, a gunman walked into a crowded cafe in Port Arthur, Australia, and started shooting. Tony Kistan, a Salvation Army soldier from Sydney, and his wife Sarah were in the restaurant when the bullets began to fly. Courageously Tony stepped in front of his wife to shield her from the gunfire, and he was one of the first to fall. Thirty-four victims eventually died in the incident, including Tony Kistan. As he lay dying in his wife's arms, he spoke his last words, "I'm going to be with the Lord."

Those final words of faith were quoted by the Australian media and carried to the world. "At a press conference," writes Williams, "Tony's son Nesan, 24, explained why his father held this assurance and described his father's dedication to the gospel. Hardened journalists and photographers were seen wiping tears from their eyes. In life, Tony had been a man who witnessed for his Lord to strangers and friends alike, and now in death, he had witnessed to others through his simple last statement."

Being a witness for Christ in this evil world brings eternal purpose to even the most tragic and painful events.

Courage, Death, Faith, Heaven, Hope, Love, Paradise,
Protection, Purpose, Testimony
1 Cor. 13:7; 2 Cor. 5:1–9; Phil. 1:20–24

Date used __________ Place ____________________

767

To better understand the human body, in 1994, researchers made available a new computer tool called "The Visible Man." The Visible Man consists of almost two thousand computer images.

To produce the images, scientists at the University of Colorado Health Sciences Center took a man's body that had been willed to science and took CAT scans, X rays, and MRI images of it. Then they embedded the body in gelatin. They froze it, sliced it crosswise into 1,800 millimeter-thin sections, and digitally photographed each cross section.

Medical students can look at The Visible Man from any angle, call up an image of any cross section they desire, rotate the images, and put them back together again.

What The Visible Man does for the body, the Word of God does for the soul. God's Word pictures the inner person—our motives, priorities, thoughts, and sins.

Heart, Inner Healing, Inner Person, Judgment, Motives, Truth
John 17:17; 2 Tim. 3:16–17; Heb. 4:12–13

Date used __________ Place ____________________

768

Any of us more than twenty-five years old can probably remember where we were when we first heard of President Kennedy's assassination in 1963.

British novelist David Lodge, in the introduction to one of his books, tells where he was—in a theater watching the performance of a satirical revue he had helped write. In one sketch, a character demonstrated his nonchalance in an interview by holding a transistor radio to his ear. The actor playing the part always tuned in to a real broadcast.

Suddenly came the announcement that President Kennedy had been shot. The actor quickly switched it off, but it was too late. Reality had interrupted stage comedy.

For many believers, worship, prayer, and Scripture are a nonchalant charade. They don't expect anything significant to happen, but suddenly God's reality breaks through, and they're shocked.

Reality, Church

Date used __________ Place ____________________

769

"If a man will not work, he shall not eat." That may sound hard, but the wisdom of that Scripture is seen in the story of one New York man.

According to the Associated Press, this thirty-six-year-old resident of New York was quoted as saying, "I like to live decent. I like to be clean." Nothing wrong with that; the only problem was he didn't like to work. So he found other ways to satisfy his cultured tastes.

He would walk into a fine restaurant, order top cuisine and choice liquor, and then when the check arrived, shrug his shoulders and wait for the police. The sometimes homeless man actually wanted to end up in the slammer, where he would get three meals a day and a clean bed. He has pled guilty to stealing a restaurant meal thirty-one times. In 1994 he served ninety days at the Rikers Island jail for filching a meal from a café in Rockefeller Center.

New York taxpayers have paid more than a quarter of a million dollars over five years to feed, clothe, and house one lazy man.

Laziness, Responsibility, Stealing
Eph. 4:28; 2 Thess. 3:6–15

Date used __________ Place ____________________

No one imagined that Charles Dutton would have achieved anything, for he spent many years imprisoned for manslaughter. But when someone asked this now-successful Broadway star of *The Piano Lesson* how he managed to make such a remarkable transition, he replied, "Unlike the other prisoners, I never decorated my cell."

Dutton had resolved never to regard his cell as home. Christians, too, accomplish much in this world when they don't accommodate themselves to it, but instead are "longing for a better country—a heavenly one" (Heb. 11:16).

Heaven, Hope

Date used __________ Place ____________________

The World 771

According to the *Chicago Tribune,* on March 3, 1995, a thirty-eight-year-old man who was walking to his temporary job at a warehouse in Rosemont, Illinois, tried to get there by cutting across eight lanes of the Tri-State Tollway. After he crossed the four northbound lanes, however, the wind blew off his hat. The hat flew back across the northbound lanes, and he chased it. There a semi-trailer truck struck and killed him.

A person can lose everything by chasing after nothing.

Backsliding, Choices, Distractions, Eternal, Money, Priorities, Temporal, Values

Judges 16; Matt. 19:16–24; Heb. 12:1; 1 John 2:15–17

Date used __________ Place ____________________

In *A World of Ideas,* Bill Moyers quotes writer Jacob Needleman:

> I was an observer at the launch of Apollo 17 in 1975. It was a night launch, and there were hundreds of cynical reporters all over the lawn, drinking beer, wisecracking and waiting for this 35-story-high rocket.
>
> The countdown came and then the launch. The first thing you see is this extraordinary orange light, which is just at the limit of what you can bear to look at. Everything is illuminated with this light. Then comes this thing slowly rising up in total silence because it takes a few seconds for the sound to come across. You hear a "WHOOOOOSH! HHHHMMMM!" It enters right into you. You can practically hear jaws dropping. The sense of wonder fills everyone in the whole place as this thing goes up and up. The first stage ignites this beautiful blue flame. It becomes like a star, but you realize there are humans on it. And then there's total silence.
>
> People just get up quietly, helping each other up. They're kind. They open doors. They look at one another, speaking quietly and interestedly. These were suddenly moral people because the sense of wonder, the experience of wonder, had made them moral.

Those who have worshiped our wondrous God in spirit and in truth know the feeling. Worship is life changing.

Cynicism, Fear of God, Morals, Wonder
Exod. 20:20; Matt. 17:1–13; Rev. 1:12–18

Date used __________ Place ____________________

Worship 773

In *Touch and Live,* George Vandeman writes:

A young stranger to the Alps was making his first climb, accompanied by two stalwart guides. It was a steep, hazardous ascent. But he felt secure with one guide ahead and one following. For hours they climbed. And now, breathless, they reached for those rocks protruding through the snow above them—the summit.

The guide ahead wished to let the stranger have the first glorious view of heaven and earth, and moved aside to let him go first. Forgetting the gales that would blow across those summit rocks, the young man leaped to his feet. But the chief guide dragged him down. "On your knees, sir!" he shouted. "You are never safe here except on your knees."

Reverence, Humility

Date used __________ Place ____________________

In April 1996 Sotheby's auctioned the estate property of former first lady Jacqueline Kennedy Onassis. The prices that bidders were willing to pay exceeded by far what anyone at the auction house had expected. A rocking chair sold for two hundred times what Sotheby's estimated. A faux pearl necklace, once tugged on by the toddler John F. Kennedy Jr. in a now famous photo, had an estimated value of $500–$700 but sold for $211,500. A textbook of French verb conjugations brought $42,000. A humidor sold for half a million dollars.

Helyn Goldenberg of Sotheby's tried to explain the phenomenon: "This auction is merely a vehicle to get a piece of the magic, a piece of the dream. This is about a woman who was once the most admired woman in the world."

The greatness of the person increases the value of the property. In a similar way, God in his great glory brings indescribable value to his people.

Children of God, Creation, Dignity, Identity, Respect, Self-Respect
Rom. 8:28–30; Eph. 1:3–14; 1 John 3:1–2

Date used __________ Place ____________________

Worth 775

Alan G. Artner writes in the *Chicago Tribune* that in 1995 the Art Institute of Chicago owned a treasure that they knew nothing about. In the institute's permanent collection was a chalk drawing of an upraised hand in a position of blessing (or as we might view it today, in a position of waving hello). The drawing appeared to have suffered serious damage: highlights in lead white chalk had oxidized and turned black. The drawing came into the institute's permanent collection in 1943, when the widow of a University of Chicago paleontologist donated two thousand drawings. At that time scholars noticed nothing unusual about the drawing, and the appearance of damage deterred further interest. It went into storage with thousands of other drawings and copies by lesser artists.

But then in 1987 the Art Institute decided to reexamine and catalogue every work in its permanent collection. Again, institute scholars first assumed the drawing of the hand was a copy done by an assistant of the Renaissance master Raphael. When they showed it to Raphael scholar Konrad Oberhuber, however, they were in for the surprise of a lifetime. He believed the drawing came from Raphael himself.

So institute scholars flew the drawing to England to show to more experts and to compare it with other Raphael originals. The verdict: the chalk drawing was a bona fide work of the master Raphael, one of the greatest figures in art history.

The prized work needed restoration, however. The oxidized paint was chemically converted into a light grey. When the cardboard mount was removed, the institute found further evidence of authenticity: a watermark in the paper similar to ones used in Florence around the time of Raphael's death in 1520.

The chalk drawing became an invaluable part of the Art Institute's collection, the only original Raphael they owned and one of only twelve Raphael originals in North America.

The value of a picture depends on who created it. The same is true of a person. When we realize that we are fashioned by God—and not only fashioned by God but fashioned in his image—our worth skyrockets. As God's handiwork, our value exceeds all measure.

Creator, Dignity, Evolution, Self-Respect
Gen. 1:26–27; Ps. 139:14–16; Eph. 2:10; 1 John 3:1–3

Date used __________ Place ____________________

Worthiness 776

Cal Ripken Jr. is the Iron Man of baseball. On September 6, 1995, he broke the record held by Lou Gehrig of 2,130 consecutive games played. Of course, there were days when that consecutive streak was in danger. In a June 1993 game Ripken was involved in a bench-clearing brawl. In *Time* Steve Wulf writes:

> Ripken twisted his knee, and when he woke up the next morning, he couldn't put his weight on it. He told his wife, Kelly, he might not be able to play that night.
>
> According to Kelly, "Just before he left for the ball park, I said, 'Maybe you could just play one inning and then come out.' He snapped, 'No! Either I play the whole game or I don't play at all.' I told him, 'Just checking, dear.'"
>
> Ripken did play the full nine innings that night. In fact, he has played in 99.2 percent of every Orioles game since the streak began.

In any high pursuit, we face the temptation to lower our standards, to do just enough to get by. Cal Ripken Jr. had committed himself to walk worthy of the title Iron Man.

Commitment, Compromise, Determination, Overcoming, Perseverance, Standards, Walking Worthy
Eph. 4:1; Col. 1:27

Date used __________ Place ____________________

In a *Time* article prompted by the movie *Dante's Peak,* Jeffrey Kluger describes the physics behind the eruption of a volcano:

> Volcanologically active areas generally lie atop clashing tectonic plates, where fractures five or six miles below ground create chambers into which magma rises and pools. . . .
>
> Magma held in the chamber eventually makes its way toward the surface through channels in the overlying rock. As the ascending ooze climbs higher, the pressure on it is dramatically reduced, allowing gases trapped within to bubble out like carbonation in an opened bottle of soda. As this happens, the magma takes on a foamier consistency, increasing its speed and mobility. When this scalding froth rises high enough to make contact with subterranean water, the water flashes into steam, turning the whole hellish mix into a natural pressure cooker. Finally, the explosively pressurized magma blasts out of the earth in an eruption that can send rocks, ash and gases flying out at near supersonic speeds. . . .
>
> The first debris disgorged by a volcano is often a great gray mass of ash. The opaque cloud, made of pulverized rock and glass, falls like concrete snow on land and buildings miles away and may blot out the sun for days.
>
> After the ash, some volcanoes produce what is known as a pyroclastic flow, a ground-hugging cloud of superheated gas and rock that forces a cushion of air down the mountainside at up to 100 m.p.h., incinerating anything in its path. Other mountains spew that signature substance of the volcano: lava.

For decades Mount St. Helens in Washington was a disaster waiting to happen, with a great chamber of molten magma cooking beneath it. In 1980 Mount St. Helens exploded, killing sixty people. Kluger writes that Mount Rainier has a similar profile, with a huge chamber of magma boiling beneath it—and with little towns like Orting, Washington, in its shadow. According to government geologists, the question is not whether Mount Rainier will blow, only when—and will people be ready.

The same is true of God's wrath. We live in a window of mercy, but do not let the relative calm deceive you. Wrath is going to come suddenly upon the earth. Will you be ready?

Anger, Day of the Lord, Judgment, Prophecy, Second Coming, Tribulation
Rom. 1:18; 2:4–6; 2 Thess. 1:5–10; Rev. 14–16; 19:11–21

Date used __________ Place ____________________

Zeal 778

On August 7, 1994, a 5,200-horsepower locomotive pulled twenty-four cars from Chicago to Fort Wayne, Indiana, and back. On board the train were 846 passengers. The passengers weren't in a hurry to reach their destination, though, because their interest was not in travel per se but in the train. Most were members of the National Historical Railway Society.

Powering this train was a Class J, No. 611 steam locomotive. Steam locomotives may sound very old fashioned but they are very powerful. In fact some of the old steam locomotives were more powerful than three modern diesel locomotives.

The heart of their power, of course, is steam. Steam "is water turned to gas," writes Kate Eaton.

> You may think you see it above your whistling tea kettle or on your bathroom mirror, but that's not it. Steam is the clear vapor between the hot water and the visible mist. As it forms, at 212 degrees Fahrenheit, it expands to take up much more space than its liquid state. This explosive expansion, harnessed in a giant locomotive, is what powered 250-ton engines pulling 20 or more railcars through the Blue Ridge Mountains, across the Great Plains and over the deserts of the west. "It's a powerful force," said Robert Pinsky, of the Railway Society.

Just as steam gives power to a locomotive, so zeal gives power to a believer. The more we boil with zeal for Christ, the more power we have for service.

Complacency, Ministry, Passion, Service
John 2:17; Rom. 12:11

Date used __________ Place ____________________

Notes

(Referenced by illustration number not page number.)

1. Luaine Lee, "Great Scot," *Chicago Tribune,* 1 August 1993, sec. 5, p. 3.

2. Doug Cumming, *Atlanta Journal-Constitution.* As seen in *Reader's Digest,* September 1997, 141–142.

3. "Boy, 12, Commits Suicide before Beginning School," *Chicago Tribune,* 27 August 1996, sec. 1, p. 7.

4. Bill Powell, "Busted!" *Time,* 13 March 1995, 37–47.

"Losing His Barings," *People,* 13 March 1995, 50.

5. John Huffman, "Marketplace Christianity," *World Christian,* July/August 1994, 25.

6. "Mixed-up Bus Driver from Motor City Ends Day Nearer Mackinac," *Chicago Tribune,* 8 February 1995, sec. 1, p. 3.

7. "A Perfect Squelch," *Reader's Digest,* September 1990, 82.

8. Associated Press, "Cervical Cancer Risk Rises with Infidelity," *Chicago Tribune,* 7 August 1996, sec. 1, p. 6.

10. Otto Friedrich, "I Have Never Been a Quitter," *Time,* 2 May 1994, 47.

11. Frederick Buechner, *Wishful Thinking* (San Francisco: Harper & Row, 1993).

12. Eric Zorn, "In Traffic Disputes, Turn Away and Live," *Chicago Tribune,* 8 November 1994, sec. 2, p. 1.

13. "Philadelphia, New York Rank 1–2 in Survey of Hostile Communities," *Chicago Daily Herald,* 14 May 1994, sec. 1, p. 3.

14. Evan Thomas, "Inside the Mind of a Spy," *Newsweek,* June 1997, 34–35.

15. Shirley W. Belleranti, Scope , 1984; as seen in "Home Scuffed Home," *Christian Reader,* Sept/Oct 1995, 42.

16. Philip Elmer-Dewitt, "Fighting Noise with Antinoise," *Time,* 4 December 1989, 94.

18. Associated Press, "13 Years Later, Henderson Apologizes to Dallas Fans," *New York Times,* 6 January 1997, sec. C, p. 10.

19. T. Ray Rachels, "Blemishes," *Pentecostal Evangel,* 21 April 1996, 14.

20. Debbie Becker and Roscoe Nance, "Cyclist to Get Message Out," *USA Today,* 29 November 1994, sec. C, p. 2.

21. Rosie Mestel, "I'll Have the Cessna," *In Health,* Dec/Jan 1992, 14.

22. "Husband Pleads for Wife Who Ran Him Down," *Chicago Tribune,* 5 January 1995, sec. 1, p. 20.

24. Mary B. W. Tabor, "Determined Student Proves SAT Wrong," *New York Times,* 7 February 1997, sec. A, p. 1.

25. Gene E. Bradley with Wesley G. Pippert, "Miracle in the Desert," *New Man,* July/Aug 1997, 49, 51.

28. Canadian Press Photo, "An Act of Faith," *Chicago Tribune,* 17 December 1997, sec. 1, p. 11.

30. Richard Conniff, "Racing with the Wind," *National Geographic,* September 1997, 52–67.

31. Erma Landis, "Lite Fare," *Christian Reader,* March/April 1997, 11.

32. "New Horseradish Variety: Hazardous-Materials-Unit Hot," *Chicago Tribune,* 15 February 1995, sec. 1, p. 10.

37. Lynette Holloway, "Noxious Mold Chases Families From Homes," *New York Times,* 9 November 1997, p. 17.

38. "Researcher: Monday Funk All in the Mind," *Chicago Tribune,* 2 July 1997, sec. 1, p. 8.

39. V. Dion Haynes and Jim Mateja, "According to Security Experts, Few Celebrities Hire Trained Drivers," *Chicago Tribune,* 5 September 1997, sec. 1, p. 19.

40. Moira Hodgson, "Lethal Wild Mushrooms Deceive the Unwary," *New York Times,* 22 January 1997, sec. B, p. 6.

41. Bill McCartney, *From Ashes to Glory,* (Nashville: Thomas Nelson, 1995).

43. Philip Yancey, "A Bad Week in Hell," *Christianity Today,* 27 October 1997, 112.

44. "China May Sell Laser That Blinds," *Chicago Tribune,* 4 May 1995, sec. 1, p. 24.

47. Mike Harden, "Dictionary's Omissions the Definition of Baffling," *Chicago Tribune,* 23 August 1994, sec. 5, pp. 1, 5.

48. Alan Nelson, *Broken in the Right Place* (Nashville: Thomas Nelson, 1994), 65, 71, 72.

50. Kevin A. Miller, "You Can Say No (Without Feeling Guilty)," *Discipleship Journal,* March/April 1996, 49.

52. Jan Riggenbach, "Midwest Gardening," *Daily Herald,* 8 May 1994.

54. Kathleen Kroll Driscoll, *Rockland (Massachusetts) South Shore News*, as seen in *Reader's Digest* (November 1993), 145.

57. Julie V. Iovine, "Style over Substance," *Chicago Tribune,* 29 March 1997, sec. 4, p. 1.

58. Kevin Dale Miller, "Ordinary Heroes," *Christian Reader,* March/April 1996, 81; Rick Bragg, "She Opened World to Others; Her World Has Opened, Too," *New York Times,* 12 November 1996, sec. A, p. 1, sec. A, p. 10; *Guideposts*, Sept. 1996, 2–5.

59. Haman Cross Jr., "Daddy, I'm Pregnant," *New Man,* May 1997, 63; as adapted from *Urban Family.*

60. "Breathing Lessons," *People,* 15 January 1996, 26.

61. Devlin Donaldson, *Contemporary Christian Magazine;* as seen in *Christian Reader*, July/Aug 1996, 43.

62. Barnaby J. Feder, "Quaker Chief, Tied to Losses From Snapple, To Step Down," *New York Times,* 24 April 1997, sec. C, p. 1.

73. Reuters, "Runway Record," *Chicago Tribune,* 16 October 1997, sec. 1, p. 15.

74. Philip Yancey, "A Pilgrim's Progress," *Books & Culture,* Sept/Oct 1995, 10.

76. James Coates, "'Good Times' Virus Is Just a Bad On-Line Myth," *Chicago Tribune,* 21 May 1995, sec. 1, pp. 1, 17.

77. Jim Bradford, "Of Countries and Kingdoms," *Pentecostal Evangel,* 11 January 1998, 12–13.

78. Associated Press, "Here's the Dirt—Check Your Hands," *Chicago Tribune,* 17 September 1996, sec. 1, p. 11. Gordon Walek, *Daily Herald* (Chicago Suburban), 18 September 1996, sec. 3, p. 9.

79. B. Drummond Ayres Jr., "At 72, Bush Leaps Into Open Sky, Again," *New York Times,* 26 March 1997, sec. A, p. 10.

81. Bill Barnhart, "Market Report: In the Heat of Battle, Traders Rule," *Chicago Tribune,* 25 April 1994, sec. 4, p. 1.

84. Don Moser, "Offerings at The Wall," *Smithsonian,* June 1995, 55. Thomas B. Allen, *Offerings at the Wall* (Atlanta: Turner Publishing, 1995).

85. "Woman's Body Is Found in Kitchen—4 Years after Dying," *Chicago Tribune*, 27 October 1993.

86. John Ortberg, "What's Really Behind Our Fatigue?" *Leadership*, Spring 1997, 110.

87. *New York Times* News Service, "Friends Aren't a Cure for Common Cold, but They Help, Study Finds," *Chicago Tribune,* 25 June 1997, sec. 1, p. 9; *The Journal of the American Medical Association,* 25 June 1997.

88. Bill Jauss, "Catcher and Sox Both Seriously Hurt," *Chicago Tribune,* 20 July 1996, sec. 3, p. 10; Steve Rosenbloom, "Hit & Run," *Chicago Tribune,* 29 September 1996, sec. 3, p. 1.

89. "Dead Body Found under Bed in Hotel," *Chicago Tribune*, 13 March 1994, sec. 1, p. 23.

90. Erik Erikson, *Identity: Youth and Crisis* (New York: W.W. Norton, 1968), 17–18.

92. Jo Thomas, "Satisfaction in Job Well Done Is Only Reward for E-Mail Software Inventor," *New York Times,* 21 January 1997, sec. A, p. 6.

93. Dan Quayle, *Standing Firm* (Grand Rapids: Zondervan).

94. Anne Keegan, "Chicago Speak," *Chicago Tribune*, 24 February 1995, sec. 5, p. 1.

95. Carolyn P. Hagan, *Child;* as seen in *Reader's Digest,* November 1996, 113.

96. William Palmer, "Roots of Rage," *Chicago Tribune Magazine,* 28 September 1997, 20–21.

98. John Feinstein, *Inside Sports.*

99. Robert Johnson, "Born-Again Surgeon Is at One with God but Not with Peers," *Wall Street Journal*, 6 June 1994, sec. A, p. 1.

100. Jim Long, "Everything Changes," *Campus Life*, October 1994, 30.

101. Lloyd Ogilvie, *Enjoying God* (Dallas: Word, 1989), 21.

103. Jean Fleming, "Growing in the Good Times," *Discipleship Journal,* Sept/Oct 1996, 26.

104. Robert Coles, *The Moral Intelligence of Children,* (Random House, 1997).

105. Tribune News Services, "Health News," *Chicago Tribune,* 12 September 1996, sec. 1, p. 14; *New England Journal of Medicine,* 12 September 1996.

106. Ken Walker, "Ordinary Heroes," *Christian Reader,* Sept/Oct 1995, 62.

108. Mark Memmott, "Economists' Elder Statesman," *USA Today*, 26 September 1994, sec. B, p. 3.

109. Vivian Marino, "In Jewelry, Looks Can Be Deceiving," *Chicago Tribune*, 23 March 1995, sec. 6, p. 3.

110. Rosa Parks, *Quiet Strength* (Grand Rapids: Zondervan, 1995).

115. Neil McAleer, *The Mind-Boggling Universe* (Garden City, New York: Doubleday & Company, 1987).

116. Ron Kotulak and Jon Van, "Jupiter Might Be Key to Our Survival," *Chicago Tribune,* 28 September 1995, sec. 5, p. 4.

121. Tim Keller, "Preaching Hell in a Tolerant Age," *Leadership,* Fall 1997, 44.

122. "Skydiver Killed Saving a Novice," *Chicago Tribune,* 25 June 1997, sec. 1, p. 7; Reuters, "Skydiving Instructor Dies in Breaking Novice's Fall," *New York Times,* 25 June 1997, sec. A, p. 16.

123. Andrea Midgett, *Christianity Today,* 3 April 1995, 43.

125. Jeff Zeleny and Susan Kuczka, "Those Who Said No Shudder with Relief," *Chicago Tribune,* 30 March 1997, sec. 1, pp. 1, 15.

126. George de Lama, "Cool Customers," *Chicago Tribune*, 17 May 1994, sec. 5, p. 1.

131. Associated Press, "Man Dies While Running in Honor of Late Daughter," *Chicago Tribune,* 14 October 1997, sec. 1, p. 9.

132. John Wimber. *Living with Uncertainty*. (Anaheim, California: Vineyard Ministries International); as seen in *Christianity Today,* 7 October 1996, 50–51.

133. Nelson, *Broken in the Right Place*, 41–42.

134. Steve Jones, "Nichelle Nichols' Bold 'Trek' Following Her Own Star," *USA Today,* 28 November 1994, sec. D, p. 6.

135. Robert R. Jackson, "Portia Spider: Mistress of Deception," *National Geographic,* November 1996, 104–114.

137. Jeffrey Bils and Stacey Singer, "Gorilla Saves Tot in Brookfield Zoo Ape Pit," *Chicago Tribune,* 17 August 1996, sec. 1, p. 1.

139. John W. Yates, "Overcoming Discouragement," *Preaching Today*, no. 42.

140. "Lawnmower Traveler Spurns Trains and Planes," *Chicago Tribune*, 3 September 1994, sec. 1, p. 4.

141. Reuters, *America Online*, 13 December 1994.

142. William Oscar Johnson, "The Son Finally Rises," *Sports Illustrated*, 21 February 1994, 20–28.

144. Associated Press, "Ship's Crew Is Faulted in New Orleans Crash," *New York Times,* 19 December 1997, sec. A, p.18; Associated Press, "Hundreds Flee As Ship Rams Mall in New Orleans," *Chicago Tribune,* 15 December 1996, sec. 1, p. 3.

145. George O. Wood, "Life's Alternatives," *Pentecostal Evangel*, 26 March 1995, 6.

146. Andy Griffith, "Journey to Health," *Guideposts,* November 1996, 9.

147. Associated Press, "Overbearing Neighbor? Bank on It," *Chicago Tribune,* 26 June 1997, sec. 1, p. 12.

148. "Objecting to 'Acts of God,' Governor Balks at Bill," *New York Times,* 21 March 1997, sec. A, p.10.

149. Jane E. Brody, "Human Eye Is Reported to Set Clock for the Body," *New York Times*, 5 January 1995, sec. A, p. 8.

151. Johnson, "The Son Finally Rises," 20–28.

152. Per Ola and Emily d'Aulaire, "Now What Are They Doing at That Crazy St. John the Divine?" *Smithsonian*, December 1992, 32.

154. Tony Evans, *Returning to Your First Love* (Chicago: Moody Press, 1995), 128–129.

156. Peter Kendall, "Songbirds Dwindle; Imposters Thrive," *Chicago Tribune*, 1 April 1995, sec. 1, p. 1.

157. Jeff Gammage, "'Sponging' Investigated at Racetracks," *Chicago Tribune,* Sports, p. 16.

158. Jim Doherty, "For All Who Crave a Horn That Thrills, This Bud's for You," *Smithsonian,* September 1994, 96.

159. Richard Conniff, "Racing with the Wind," *National Geographic,* September 1997, 52–67.

160. "Demand for Killer Heroin Rises, Police Say," *Chicago Tribune,* 16 July 1996, sec. 1, p. 9; "The Night the Music Ended," *People,* 29 July 1996, 92–93.

161. Mickey Mantle with Jill Lieber, "Time in a Bottle," *Sports Illustrated,* 18 April 1994, 66–77.

162. Michael Kelly, *The New Yorker*.

164. "Author Penick Dies at 90," *Chicago Tribune*, 4 April 1995, sec. 4, p. 2.

165. Alex Tresniowski, "Oprah Buff," *People,* 9 September 1996, 80–81; Lisbeth Levine, "It's Not Who You Know . . . It's Who You Train," *Chicago Tribune,* 12 September 1996, sec. 5, pp. 1, 11. Newsmakers, "Oprah Hires an Ally in Battle of the Bulge," *Chicago Tribune,* 2 September 1996, sec. 1, p. 2.

166. "Uh, Oh. Pull Over—and Get a Thank-You," *Chicago Tribune,* 13 June 1993.

168. Reuters, *America Online,* 20 January 1995.

169. Reuters, *America Online,* 22 November 1994.

170. Graham R. Hodges, "The Lesson of the Cocklebur," *Leadership*, Fall 1988, 129.

177. Chris Edwardson, "Chris Edwardson, M.D., Discusses Evangelism in the Workplace," *Pentecostal Evangel,* 26 October 1997, 7.

178. Ira Berkow, "Born to Coach Basketball," *New York Times,* 21 April 1997, sec. C, p. 14.

179. *Today's Christian Woman;* as seen in *Christian Reader,* May/June 1996, 75–76.

180. "Captain Remembers Nuclear Horror on Soviet Submarine," *Chicago Tribune*, 20 August 1993, sec. 1, p. 4.

181. Roy Maynard, "Strong Arms," *World,* 13 December 1997, 13–14.

182. Mike Lupica, "Amazing Grace," *Esquire,* February 1995.

183. Associated Press, "Driver Ed Teacher Quits After Road Rage Lesson," *Chicago Tribune,* 16 October 1997, sec. 1, p. 11.

184. Don Shula & Ken Blanchard, *Everyone's a Coach* (New York: Harper Business, 1995; Grand Rapids: Zondervan Publishing House, 1995) 56–57.

187. "Biz Tips: Admit to Screwups?" *Chicago Tribune,* 17 April 1995, sec. 4, p. 3.

188. Ann Landers, "Freak Accidents Have Motorists Tongue-tied," *Chicago Tribune,* 24 August 1994, sec. 5, p. 3.

189. Larry Burkett, *Business by the Book* (Nashville: Nelson, 1990), 9–11.

191. "Summer Swan Song," *Life,* October 1993, 12–13.

198. Marshall Shelley, "My New View of God," *Leadership,* Fall 1996, 90.

199. Leon Jaroff, "Still Ticking," *Time,* 4 November 1996, 80.

200. Philip Yancey, "What Surprised Jesus," *Christianity Today,* 12 September 1994, 88.

202. Peter Gorner, "On the Record," *Chicago Tribune,* 20 July 1997, sec. 2, p. 3.

203. J. Allan Petersen, *Better Families;* as seen in *Leadership,* Summer 1996, 69.

204. "Penny for Your Thoughts, Dear Ex-Wife," *Chicago Tribune* online.

205. Jan Senn, "Carol Kent on Keeping Confident," *Today's Christian Woman,* Jan/Feb 1995, 68.

206. Gary J. Oliver, "The Cult of Success," *New Man,* September 1997, 74.

210. Matthew Mak, "Getting Over It: Fearful Drivers Get Help across Bridges," *USA Today,* 5 August 1992, sec. A, p. 6.

211. "Fatal Overreaction," *Time,* 14 August 1989, 33.

213. Associated Press, "Oops! Kidnap Note Aside, Couple Are OK," *Chicago Tribune,* 25 June 1997, sec. 1, p. 10.

214. John M. Broder, "Warning: A Batman Cape Won't Help You Fly," *New York Times,* 5 March 1997, sec. A, p. 1.

215. Richard Stevenson, "A Buried Message Loudly Heard," *New York Times,* 7 December 1996, 19, 21; Floyd Norris, "Greenspan Asks a Question and Global Markets Wobble," *New York Times,* 7 December 1996, 1, 20.

216. Paul Hoversten, "Lucid Quick to Get Feet Back on Ground," *USA Today,* 25 October 1996, 4A.

219. Tim Franklin, "Tyler, U.S.: Agony of da-feet," *Chicago Tribune,* 27 July 1996, sec. 3, p. 1.

220. Cindy Schreuder, "Science of the Seasons: Spring, the Miracle of Renewal," *Chicago Tribune,* 24 May 1995, sec. 1, p. 1.

221. Douglas H. Chadwick, "On the Edge of Earth and Sky," *National Geographic,* April 1995, 116.

222. Gordon MacDonald, *Restoring Your Spiritual Passion* (Nashville: Oliver-Nelson, 1986), 104–5.

227. Patti Davis, *Angels Don't Die* (HarperCollins); as seen in *Christian Reader,* Nov/Dec 1995, 60.

228. David Wallis, "A Question for: Jimmy Carter," *New York Times Magazine,* 26 October 1997, 19.

229. Jill Briscoe, *Running on Empty* (Wheaton: Harold Shaw, 1995), 101.

230. Christopher Thomas, "Old Foes Cross a Bridge to Forgiveness," *The Times of London,* 16 August 1995, sec. 1, p. 1.

231. Charles Swindoll, *The Grace Awakening* (Dallas: Word, 1990), 47–48.

233. Julie V. Iovine, "A New Cash Crop: The Farm as Theme Park," *New York Times,* 2 November 1997, 1.

234. "'Tis The Season—To Be Wasteful," *National Wildlife,* Dec/Jan 1997, 12.

235. "French Woman Marks 120th—Yes—Birthday," *Chicago Tribune,* 22 February 1995, sec. 1, p. 9.

236. Bill and Lynne Hybels, *Honest to God* (Grand Rapids: Zondervan, 1990), 39.

237. "Love Pays Off Big for Harvard Law School," *Chicago Tribune,* 3 October 1994, sec. 1, p. 14.

238. Stu Weber, "What It Takes to Reach Men," *Leadership,* Fall 1994, 128.

239. Carrie Dowling, "'The Baby's Here'—At 30,000 Feet," *USA Today,* 28 November 1994, sec. A, p. 3.

240. "The Shirt off My Back," *USA Today,* 20 May 1994.

243. Judith Miller, "He Gave Away $600 Million, and No One Knew," *New York Times,* 23 January 1997, sec. A, p. 1.

244. David W. Dunlap, "Zoo Gift Is Revoked Because Name on Plaque Is Too Small," *New York Times,* 15 May 1997, sec. A, p. 19.

245. Ron Barefield, "Bethesda Outreach Ministries: Making Missions Their Business," *Pentecostal Evangel,* 4 February 1996, 8–10.

246. Melissa Isaacson, "Getting assistant a ring would be Jordan's pleasure," *Chicago Tribune,* 1 June 1997, sec. 3, p. 8.

248. "Father Wants Defector Back from Korea," *Chicago Tribune,* 20 September 1982, sec. 1, p. 4.

250. Robert E. Wells, *Is a Blue Whale the Biggest Thing There Is?* (Morton Grove, Ill.: Albert Whitman & Company, 1993).

251. Stuart N. Robinson, "Letters," *Sports Illustrated,* 15 September 1997, 10.

254. Ramona Cramer Tucker, "Bodie Thoene: True Grit," *Today's Christian Woman,* Sept/Oct 1994, 61.

255. "Scorecard," *Sports Illustrated,* 27 June 1988, 9.

256. Frank W. Mann Jr., *Robins Reader,* as seen in *Reader's Digest,* May 1995, 209–10.

257. Martha Moore, "Shoe Firm Sets Pace, Wins Awards," *USA Today,* 24 June 1994, sec. B, pp. 1–2.

258. Tony Campolo, *World Vision,* Oct/Nov 1988.

260. Wendy Murray Zoba, "Bill Bright's Wonderful Plan for the World," *Christianity Today,* 14 July 1997, 24.

261. Spencer Reiss and Nina Archer Biddle, "The Strep-A Scare," *Newsweek,* 20 June 1994, 32–33.

262. Associated Press, "Fireworks Set Off Fire at Valley Forge Park," *New York Times,* 18 March 1997, sec. A, p. 10.

263. "It's a Frozen Tower of Pisa," *Chicago Tribune,* 19 April 1995, sec. 1, p. 3.

264. Paul Francisco, "Lite Fare," *The Christian Reader,* March/April 1993, 38.

265. "14 Hours And 9 Miles Later, Answer Is Still No," *Chicago Tribune* online, 28 July 1994.

266. William Langewiesche, "The Turn," *Atlantic Monthly,* December 1993, 115–22.

267. Swindoll, *The Grace Awakening,* 9.

271. Max Lucado, *In the Grip of Grace,* (Dallas: Word, 1996).

272. Stuart Briscoe, "Why Christ Had to Die," *Preaching Today,* #163, 4.

273. Luis Palau, "God's Ocean of Grace," *Pursuit,* vol. 4, no. 11.

274. Carey Goldberg, "Real-Space Meetings Fill In the Cyberspace Gaps," *New York Times,* 25 February 1997, sec. A, p. 8; "Bill Gates: Richest American Ever," *Fortune,* 4 August 1997, 38–39.

281. Gary Thomas, "The Freedom of Surrender," *Discipleship Journal,* Sep/Oct 1996, 52.

282. Marya Smith, "First Person: Deposition Reader," *Chicago Tribune Magazine,* 13 June 1993, 33.

283. Barbara Kantrowitz et al., "The Fugitive," *Time,* 27 September 1993, 54–60.

285. "The Best and Worst of Everything," *Parade,* 28 December 1997, 6–7.

286. Mitchell May, "Assumed-Identity Crisis," *Chicago Tribune,* 17 August 1997, sec. 2, p. 5.

288. Associated Press, *Chicago Tribune,* 1 September 1996, sec. 1, p. 6.

289. Jon Van, "'Jackhammer' Used in Clearing Arteries," *Chicago Tribune,* 10 November 1993, sec. 1, p. 7.

290. Scorecard, "The Razor's Edge," *Sports Illustrated,* 4 November 1996, 22.

291. "Secretive Censor Defacing Books," *Chicago Tribune,* 22 May 1994, sec. 1, p. 8.

292. George O. Wood, "Psalm 103: Deep Healing," *Pentecostal Evangel,* 26 October 1997, 6.

293. John Wimber, *Living with Uncertainty,* (Anaheim, California: Vineyard Ministries International); as seen in *Christianity Today,* 7 October 1996, 50–51.

294. Ken Jones, *When You're All Out of Noodles* (Nashville: Thomas Nelson, 1993).

295. Paul Hoversten, "Jupiter's Winds: 10,000-Mile-Deep 'Giant Flywheel,'" *USA Today,* 22 May 1996, sec. A, p. 3.

296. Dave Dravecky with Ken Gire, *When You Can't Come Back* (Grand Rapids: Zondervan, 1992).

297. Max Lucado, *Six Hours One Friday* (Sisters, Ore.: Multnomah, 1989), 43–44.

299. Leith Anderson, "Next Life in the House of the Lord," *Preaching Today* (Christianity Today, Inc.), tape #157.

300. Joni Eareckson Tada, *Preaching Today* (Christianity Today, Inc.), tape #157.

301. Quotables, *Chicago Tribune,* 23 September 1996, sec. 1, p. 17; "Stranded U.S. Astronaut at Last May Be Retrieved," *Chicago Tribune,* 16 September 1996, sec. 1, p. 7.

302. John von Rhein, "Alarms Go Off with CSO Ending Its Centenary Season," *Chicago Tribune,* 20 October 1991, sec. 5, p. 5.

305. Lisa Belcher-Hamilton, "The Gospel According to Fred: A Visit with Mr. Rogers," *The Christian Century,* 13 April 1994, 382.

306. Charles Swindoll, *Flying Closer to the Flame* (Dallas: Word, 1993), 71–73.

307. Ogilvie, *Enjoying God,* 50.

309. Paul Grabill and Eric Harrah, "One of the Nation's Largest Abortion Providers Discusses His Decision to Follow Jesus," *Pentecostal Evangel,* 18 January 1998, 8.

310. John L. Eliot, "Earth Almanac," *National Geographic,* August 1996, 136.

312. "Black Cadet Commissioned 123 Years Later," *Chicago Tribune,* 23 September 1997, sec. 1, p. 6.

313. Salman Rushdie, *Imaginary Homelands,* (Viking Penguin).

314. Paul Quinnett, *Pavlov's Trout* (Keokee), as seen in *Reader's Digest,* May 1995, 210.

316. David Neff, "Why Hope Is a Virtue," *Christianity Today*, 3 April 1995, 24.

317. "Male Despair Tied to Atherosclerosis," *Chicago Tribune,* 26 August 1997, sec. 1, p. 8.

318. Ronald Pinkerton, *Guideposts*, September 1988.

319. James W. Arnold, *St. Anthony Messenger,* as seen in *Reader's Digest,* April 1995, 25.

321. Richard Jerome and Elizabeth McNeil, "Stringed Victory," *People,* 28 April 1997, 111–114.

322. Tracey Bailey, "Lesson of a Lifetime," *Guideposts,* April 1997, 14–17.

323. "Judges Deflate Texas Steer's Championship," *Chicago Tribune,* 7 June 1992, sec. 1, p. 24.

325. Jim Corley, "Getting Past the Showroom," *Christian Reader,* Jan/Feb 1998, 52.

326. "Quotable," *Chicago Tribune,* 11 July 1997, sec. 1, p. 21.

327. *Christianity Today,* 25 April 1994, 44.

328. *Sports Illustrated Presents* (special commemorative edition), February 1997, 72.

329. Peter Kendall, "Exterminator's lethal brew leaves expensive residue," *Chicago Tribune*, 3 July 1997, sec. 1, p. 1.

330. Michiko Kakutani, "The Making of a Myth Who Rode Into the Sunset," *New York Times,* 25 February 1997, sec. B, p. 6.

331. Cal Ripken Jr. and Mike Bryan, *The Only Way I Know* (New York: Viking, 1997).

332. Nancy V. Raine, "Returns of the Day," *New York Times Magazine,* 2 October 1994, 34.

333. *New England Journal of Medicine,* 2 March 1995, 614.

336. Emory Thomas Jr. *Wall Street Journal,* 21 March 1995, 1; as seen in *Reader's Digest,* January 1996, 89.

337. "Even Blindfolded, Moms Show Touch for Newborns," *Chicago Tribune*.

338. John Noble Wilford, "Hubble Detects Stars That Belong to No Galaxy," *New York Times,* 15 January 1997, sec. A, p. 9.

339. Philip Hersh, "Solid Gold," *Chicago Tribune*, 9 November 1994, sec. 5, p. 1. Dave Kindred, "What Was Meant to Be," *Sporting News,* 28 February 1994, 10–11.

340. Andy Woodland, "He Loves Doing 'Paarat' for You," *Christian Reader,* May/June 1997, 44.

341. Tom Friend, "This Time, Dad Can't Stop Joe from Quitting," *Chicago Tribune*, 19 April 1995, sec. 4, p. 3.

342. Paul Thigpen, "Where's the Joy," *Discipleship Journal,* May/June 1996, 21.

345. Al Hinman, *Your Health;* as seen in *Ladies' Home Journal,* May 1996, 45.

346. "Supreme Court Turns Deaf Ear to 1,600 Appeals," *Chicago Tribune*, 4 October 1994, sec. 1, p. 3.

347. "Why We Pray," *Life,* March 1994, 59.

349. "The Best and Worst of Everything," *Parade,* 28 December 1997, 7.

350. Associated Press, "Lab-Made Virus Destroys Cells Infected by HIV," *Chicago Tribune,* 5 September 1997, sec. 1, p. 3.

351. Charles Krauthammer, "Slippery When Upset," *Chicago Tribune*, 5 May 1995, sec. 1, p. 21.

352. Ron Grossman, "The Big Fellow," *Chicago Tribune*, 24 August 1994, sec. 5, pp. 1–2.

354. Seth Mydans, "Singapore, Where Ruin Is the Reward for Error," *New York Times,* 12 December 1996, sec. A, p. 11.

355. "In California City, Acts of Kindness Are Becoming Contagious," *Chicago Tribune*, 29 October 1993.

356. Phillip Keller, *Pleasures Forevermore* (Eugene, Ore.: Harvest House, 1992), 47–49.

357. Jon Van, "Study Finds Doctors Respond Well to Sweet Treatment," *Chicago Tribune*, 22 February 1995, sec. 1, p. 4.

358. Steve Sjogren, *Conspiracy of Kindness* (Ann Arbor, Michigan: Servant Publications, 1993), 15–17.

359. Jim Bakker, *I Was Wrong* (Nashville: Thomas Nelson, 1997).

360. Jill Briscoe, *Running on Empty* (Wheaton: Harold Shaw, 1995), 20.

361. James Coates, "Orbiting On-line: The Evolution of the Internet," *Chicago Tribune*, 26 March 1995, sec. 7, p. 4.

362. "Mississippi Senate Votes to Ban Slavery," *Chicago Tribune*, 17 February 1995, sec. 1, p. 11.

364. Philip Yancey, "As Casey Stengel Said . . ." *Christianity Today*.

365. Ron Mehl, *The Cure for a Troubled Heart* (Questar Publishers, 1996).

366. T. H. Watkins, *National Geographic,* September 1996, 85.

369. Stephen Lee, "Tougher Buoys of Summer," *Chicago Tribune,* 12 July 1996, sec. 2, p. 1.

370. Gary Fields, "Oil-spill Research Ship Hits Fragile Reef, Leaks Fuel," *USA Today,* 12–14 August 1994, sec. A, p. 1.

371. Scott Turow, *Presumed Innocent* (New York: Farrar, Straus, and Giroux, 1987), 3.

375. Alix M. Freedman and Suein L. Hwang, "How Seven Individuals With Diverse Motives

Halted Tobacco's Wars," *Wall Street Journal,* 11 July 1997, sec. A, p. 1.

376. Holcomb B. Noble, "W. Lain Guthrie, 84, Jet Pilot Who Refused To Dump Fuel," *New York Times,* 28 March 1997, sec. A, p. 17.

377. Leith Anderson, "The Trouble with Legalism," *Moody,* October 1994, 15.

378. Robert Frank, "As UPS Tries to Deliver More to Its Customers, Labor Problems Grow," *Wall Street Journal,* 23 May 1994, sec. A, p. 1.

379. Jon Van & Ron Kotulak, "Forced Exercise May Do More Harm Than Good," *Chicago Tribune,* 30 October 1997, sec. 5, p. 3.

380. Lynn Austin, "Satan's Tackle Box," *The Christian Reader,* July/Aug 1994, 55–56. Abridged from *Moody.*

383. "French Woman Marks 120th—Yes—Birthday," *Chicago Tribune,* 22 February 1995, sec. 1, p. 9.

385. Dan Schaeffer, "We're No Longer Home Alone," *Moody,* Nov/Dec 1997, 59.

388. Associated Press, "For Man Who Fell Into River, Lo, an Angel," *New York Times,* 25 December 1996, sec. A, p. 10.

389. Fred Mitchell, "Payton Searching for Missing Super Bowl Ring," *Chicago Tribune,* 2 July 1996, sec. 4, p. 3.

391. As abridged in *The Christian Reader,* May/June 1995, 34.

392. Gordon Wilson, "When Love Meets a Brick Wall," *World Vision,* June/July 1994, 12–13.

393. Bruce Thielemann, "Legions of the Unjazzed," *Preaching Today,* no. 36.

394. Paul Pearsall, *The Ten Laws of Lasting Love* (New York: Simon & Schuster, 1993), as seen in *Reader's Digest,* March 1995, 148–49.

395. Philip Yancey, "The Riddle of Bill Clinton's Faith," *Christianity Today,* 25 April 1994, 29. Chuck Colson, "How to Confront a President," *Christianity Today,* 25 April 1994, 64.

401. Associated Press, "Popularity of 1996 Film Fills Shelters with Unwanted Dalmatians in 1997," *Chicago Tribune,* 10 September 1997, sec. 1, p. 11.

402. Rita Price, *Columbus Dispatch,* as seen in *Reader's Digest,* January 1996, 88.

403. Melissa Hendricks, *Johns Hopkins Magazine;* as seen in *Reader's Digest,* November 1996, 112–113.

404. Dave Goetz, *Leadership,* Spring 1996, 26.

408. Stephen Franklin, "Lessons from a Labor-Management War," *Chicago Tribune,* 15 May 1994, sec. 7, p. 1.

409. Ogilvie, *Enjoying God,* 19–20.

414. "A Secret Song," *Time,* 13 February 1989, 41.

415. Don Van Natta Jr. and Elaine Sciolino, "Body, and Tombstone of Lies, Are Removed," *New York Times,* 12 December 1997, sec. A, pp. 1, 16.

417. "Bride Gives Groom a Lifesaver in Form of a Transplanted Kidney," *Chicago Tribune,* 10 November 1994, sec. 1, p. 6. "Bride-to-be Promises Hand, Heart—and Kidney to Fiancé," *Chicago Tribune,* 10 October 1994, sec. 1, p. 2.

418. James Dobson, *Focus on the Family Newsletter,* February 1995.

421. Ruth Ryan, *Covering Home,* (Word, 1995); as seen in *Reader's Digest,* September 1995, 87.

422. Skip Gray, "The Way of the Cross," *Discipleship Journal,* July/Aug 1997, 49.

425. Joe Martin, "Mister Boffo," *Universal Press Syndicate,* 1997; *Chicago Tribune,* 9 February 1997, sec. 9, p. 1.

426. Tom Junod, "Arms and the Man," *Sports Illustrated,* 14 June 1993, 72, 74.

427. Jim Williams, *Reader's Digest,* August 1997, 112.

428. Ron Kotulak and Jon Van, "Flying Jets with Brain Power," *Chicago Tribune,* 12 February 1995, sec. 5, p. 3.

429. Reuters, "Chinese Doctors Take Pin from Brain after 40 Years," *America Online,* 29 October 1994.

430. Phyllis Berman, "Harry's a Great Storyteller," *Forbes,* 27 February 1995, 116.

431. Jim Doherty, "For All Who Crave a Horn That Thrills, This Bud's for You," *Smithsonian,* September 1994, 102.

432. "Self-taught Chef Has Star Quality," *Chicago Tribune,* 6 March 1995, sec. 1, p. 2.

435. Patrick O'Driscoll, "Rural Areas Rustle Up Rules for City Slickers," *USA Today,* 8 August 1997, sec. A, p. 4.

436. Jim Mateja, "10 That Made a Difference," *Chicago Tribune,* 16 June 1996, sec. 12, pp. 1, 5–6.

437. Victor Lee, "Lee'd Stories," *Sports Spectrum,* October 1997, 5.

438. Ian Hall with Joyce Wells Booze, "They Named Him Samuel," *Pentecostal Evangel,* 11 February 1996, 18–19.

439. Paul Sullivan, "Yanks, Fan Grab Opener from Orioles," *Chicago Tribune,* 10 October 1996, sec. 4, pp. 1, 5.

440. Tim Stafford, "The Making of a Revolution," *Christianity Today,* 8 December 1997, 17–18.

442. "Health Deduction for Self-Employed OKd," *Chicago Tribune,* 4 April 1995, sec. 1, p. 3.

443. Ron Kotulak and Jon Van, "A Cliché Proven," *Chicago Tribune,* 15 August 1993, sec. 5, p. 4.

448. Associated Press, "Mentally Disabled Man Gambles Away a Social Security Windfall," *Chicago Tribune,* 25 August 1997, sec. 1, p. 3.

449. Wendy Murray Zoba, "Bill Bright's Wonderful Plan for the World," *Christianity Today,* 14 July 1997, 24.

451. Brian Burrell, *Words We Live By* (S&S Trade: 1997).

454. Howard Witt, "Armenia Turns to Time Bomb for Fuel," *Chicago Tribune,* 22 November 1993, sec. 1, p. 1.

459. Porter B. Williamson, *General Patton's Principles for Life and Leadership* (Tucson: Management & Systems Consultants, Inc., 1988).

463. Susan Maycinik, "Obedience or Performance?," *Discipleship Journal,* March/April 1996, 8.

464. Elaine Creasman, "A Holy Jealousy," *Discipleship Journal,* May/June 1996, 66.

465. Rogers Worthington, "Expert can't mediate his own dispute," *Chicago Tribune,* 8 July 1996, sec. 1, p. 1.

466. Glenn Collins, "The Americanization of Salsa," *New York Times,* 9 January 1997, sec. C, pp. 1, 4.

468. Associated Press, "Passengers Get to Airport—the Long Way," *Chicago Tribune,* 3 July 1997, sec. 1, p. 8.

469. Bernard Weinraub, "Casting Ron Howard Against Type," *New York Times,* 12 November 1996, sec. B, pp. 1, 4.

470. Elie Wiesel, *All Rivers Run to the Sea* (Knopf); as seen in *Reader's Digest,* June 1997, 156–157.

471. Jimmy Carter, *U.S. News & World Report;* as seen in *Christian Reader,* July/Aug 1997, 29.

472. Jill Briscoe, *Can a Busy Christian Develop Her Spiritual Life?* (Minneapolis: Bethany House Publishers, 1995).

473. "Crash Probe Focuses on Ice Buildup," *Chicago Tribune,* 25 March 1992.

474. Elizabeth Mittelstaedt, "Afterwords," *Today's Christian Woman,* Jan/Feb 1995, 72.

475. Alan Mairson, "America's Beekeepers," *National Geographic,* May 1993, 82–83.

476. Nelson, *Broken in the Right Place,* 43.

477. Gordon MacDonald, "Pastor's Progress," *Leadership,* Summer 1997, 81–82.

478. "Half of Sexually Active Teens Tell Survey: Wish I'd Waited," *Chicago Tribune,* 18 May 1994.

479. Bob Greene, "I Know I Have at Least One Fan," *Chicago Tribune,* 15 August 1993, sec. 5, p. 1.

481. Andrew Bagnato, "Good Guys Finish First (Sometimes)," *Chicago Tribune Magazine,* 1 September 1996, 15.

482. LeAnn Spencer, "Botanic Garden Viewing Century Plant's Growth as the Stalk of the Town," *Chicago Tribune,* 11 April 1995, sec. 1, p. 1.

483. "Got a Minute? That's All an Episode Takes," *Chicago Tribune,* 18 August 1994, sec. 1, p. 19.

487. Elaine Sciolino, "A Painful Road from Vietnam to Forgiveness," *New York Times,* 12 November 1996, sec. A, pp. 1, 8.

488. Associated Press, "30 Million New $50 Bills Are Withheld," *Chicago Tribune,* 25 September 1997, sec. 1, p. 22.

490. Michael Lewis, "The Subversive," *New York Times Magazine,* 25 May 1997, 36–37.

491. Brother Andrew with Verne Becker, *The Calling* (Moorings); as seen in *Christian Reader,* July/Aug 1996, 107.

492. Jorge Casuso, "Epic in the Making," *Chicago Tribune,* 5 December 1991, sec. 5, p. 1.

497. Larry Dorman, "Woods's Clubs Not Magic Wands," *New York Times,* 22 October 1996, sec. B, p. 16.

498. "New Beatles Lyrics? Not Egg-zactly," *Chicago Tribune,* 10 March 1995, sec. 1, p. 2.

499. Dan Jansen, *Full Circle* (New York: Villard Books, 1994).

501. "Satellite 'Skips' down to Earth," *Chicago Tribune,* 29 October 1993, sec. 1, p. 19.

502. Rita Rubin, "Cholesterol, Round 2," *U.S. News & World Report,* 28 June 1993, 61.

503. Gene Sloan, "Arizona Says People Step One Toad over the Line," *USA Today,* 4 August 1994, sec. A, p. 1.

505. "Ordinary Heroes," *The Christian Reader,* Jan/Feb 1993, 82.

506. Yancey, "What Surprised Jesus," 88.

507. Blair Walker, "Laws Serve Lemon-Aid to Car Buyers," *USA Today,* 23 May 1994.

508. Adrienne W. Fawcett, "The House That Hindman Built," *Chicago Tribune,* 16 June 1996, sec. 15, pp. 1, 6.

509. "$900-million Venus Probe Plunges to Its End," *Chicago Tribune,* 13 October 1994, sec. 1, p. 27.

512. Eric Ferkenhoff, "Jet-Skier Rescued after Lake Ordeal," *Chicago Tribune,* 18 June 1997, sec. 2, p. 2.

513. Harold Kushner, *Who Needs God* (New York: Summit, 1989).

514. J. K. Gressett, "Take Courage," *Pentecostal Evangel,* 30 April 1989, 6.

515. John Fischer, *Contemporary Christian Music,* August 1992.

516. Hyatt Moore, "Praying a Bible into Existence," *The Christian Reader,* Jan/Feb 1993, 46.

517. James Overstreet, "When E-mail Turns to J(unk)-Mail," *USA Today,* 26 September 1994, sec. B, p. 7.

518. Haddon Robinson, "The Disciple's Prayer," *Preaching Today,* no. 117.

520. Bob Verdi, "Paying for Air," *Chicago Tribune,* 13 July 1996, sec. 1, p. 1.

521. Annie Dillard, "Total Eclipse," *The Annie Dillard Reader* (New York: Harper Collins, 1994), 11–12.

522. Felix Jimenez, "Search for the Black Box," *Guideposts,* January 1997, 14–17.

523. James David Ford, "Pastoring a House Divided," *Leadership,* Fall 1996, 112.

524. Billy Graham, *How I Pray,* (Ballantine Books, 1994).

526. Charles Colson, "The Blind Leading the Blind," *BreakPoint,* April 1994.

528. Ken O'Brien, "Would You Trade?" *Chicago Tribune*, 15 May 1994, sec. 18, pp. 1, 4.

532. Tim Crothers, *Sports Illustrated;* as seen in *Reader's Digest*, December 1995, 99–100.

534. Mike Yaconelli, *The Door;* as seen in *Christian Reader,* Sept/Oct 1996, 36.

535. "Waitress Takes Tip That's Worth Millions," *Chicago Tribune*, 4 April 1984, sec. 1, p. 6.

537. Verna Bowman, "Quilt of Many Promises," *Guideposts,* May 1997, 6–9.

538. Susan Hazen-Hammond, "'Horny Toads' Enjoy a Special Place in Western Hearts," *Smithsonian,* December 1994, 90.

539. "Sign of the Times," *Chicago Tribune*, 8 October 1993.

540. "From Film to Art," *USA Today,* 28 November 1994, sec. D, p. 1.

541. James Dobson, *When God Doesn't Make Sense* (Wheaton: Tyndale House, 1994).

542. John Robb and Brenda Spoelstra, "A Miracle in Moscow," *World Vision,* Aug/Sept 1991, 13.

543. Dale Alan Robbins, "When All Else Fails, It's Time to Pray," *Pentecostal Evangel,* 19 May 1996, 20–21.

544. Jim Cymbala with Dean Merrill, *Fresh Wind, Fresh Fire* (Grand Rapids: Zondervan, 1997), 16–17.

545. Bonne Steffen, "Cross-country Revival," *Christian Reader,* Sept/Oct 1995, 80.

546. Bryan Wilkerson, "A Purpose Runs through It," *Preaching Today*, no. 133.

547. Corrie ten Boom, *The Hiding Place* (Grand Rapids: Chosen, 1988).

548. Melissa Isaacson, "Fan Hits 1 in Million—and Bulls Win, Too," *Chicago Tribune*, 15 April 1993, sec. 4, p. 1. Kent McDill, "Shot Heard 'Round the World," *Suburban Chicago Daily Herald*, 15 April 1993, sec. 3, p. 5.

550. "Ex-Cornell Militant Names Prize after Old Foe," *Chicago Tribune*, 5 May 1995, sec. 1, p. 12.

551. Associated Press, "Nearly Half of Those Hurt by Violence Knew Assailant," *Chicago Tribune,* 25 August 1997, sec. 1, p. 4.

552. Will Norton Jr., "The Write Stuff," *Aspire,* November 1995, 55.

553. Jancee Dunn, *Rolling Stone,* 30 June 1994, 35.

554. "Almost Home," *Life,* March 1996, 52. "Update: Free Willy," *Life,* January 1997, 16.

556. Reuters, *Chicago Tribune,* 24 August 1996, sec. 1, p. 20; Dan McGraw, "Human Error and a Human Tragedy," *U.S. News & World Report,* 8 January 1996, 38.

557. William Willimon, "The Writing on the Wall," *Preaching Today*, no. 129.

558. "Injured Woodsman Pinned under Tree, Amputates Leg," *Chicago Tribune*, 22 July 1993, sec. 1, p. 9. Pam Lambert and Tom Nugent, *People,* 9 August 1993, 42.

561. Daniel Q. Haney, "The Ulcer Bug," *Daily Herald,* 8 April 1996, Suburban Living, p. 1.

562. David Margolick, "Best O.J. Reporting from—Would You Believe—The National Enquirer?" *Chicago Tribune Online,* 27 October 1994.

563. Joann C. Jones, *Guideposts;* as seen in *Reader's Digest,* August 1996, 147–148.

564. John H. Timmerman, "Black Gold: Nurturing the Heart," *Moody,* September 1994, 14.

565. Ramona Cramer Tucker, "Enough Is Enough," *Today's Christian Woman,* Sept/ Oct 1996, 129.

566. Andrew C. Revkin, "Taking Lowly Pallets and Finding Treasure," *New York Times,* 5 March 1997, sec. A, p. 13.

567. "Pyrotechnician Says Farewell by Rocket's Red Glare," *Chicago Tribune,* 14 August 1994, sec. 1, p. 6.

568. Wayne A. Lamb, *100 Meditations on Hope;* as seen in *Christianity Today.*

569. Ron Kotulak and Jon Van, "Discoveries: Laser Provides Unexpected Sight," *Chicago Tribune*, 30 April 1995, sec. 5, p. 5.

571. Kevin Maney, "Sony's Legend Stepping Down," *USA Today*, 28 November 1994, sec. B, p. 2.

574. Carey Goldberg, "Windfall Sets Off a Blizzard of Bonuses for a Company," *New York Times,* 25 December 1996, sec. A, p. 9.

575. Bob Greene, "A Young Athlete's Greatest Move," *Chicago Tribune,* 18 December 1994, Tempo section, p. 1. Kevin Dale Miller, "Ordinary Heroes," *The Christian Reader,* May/June 1995, 35.

577. Brenda Kearns, "The Simple Posture Trick That Can Save Your Life," *Woman's World,* 23 September, 1997, 20.

578. Ken R. Canfield, "A Child Is Crying for You," *New Man,* May 1997, 98.

579. Harold Reynolds with Roxanne Robbins, "I Couldn't Have Hand-Picked a Better Family," *Sports Spectrum,* September 1997.

580. Gordon MacDonald, *Ordering Your Private World* (Nashville: Oliver-Nelson, 1985), 106–7.

581. John Schmeltzer, "Gerber Tries to Control Rumor Rerun," *Chicago Tribune,* 27 September 1997, sec. 2, p. 1.

582. MacDonald, *Restoring Your Spiritual Passion,* 51–52.

583. Bob Condor, "At Ease," *Chicago Tribune,* 23 October 1997, sec. 5, p. 6.

584. Ann Landers, "This Surgeon Was Definitely Out to Lunch," *Chicago Tribune,* 12 February 1995, sec. 5, p. 3.

588. "'Mystery Fare' Leaves Some Sad, Some Glad," *Chicago Tribune,* 28 August 1994, sec. 1, p. 4.

589. Phillip Fiorini, "Computer Programming Pioneer Kildall Dies at 52," *USA Today,* 14 July 1994, sec. B, p. 2.

594. Kathleen Donnelly, "Norma McCorvey Has Regrets, but Being the Plaintiff in Roe V. Wade Isn't One of Them," *Knight-Ridder/Tribune News Service,* 22 June 1994; Jeff Hooten, *Citizen,* February 1997. As seen in *Knight-Ridder/Tribune News Service,* 20 January 1997.

596. Ted Gregory, "The Informer," *Chicago Tribune,* 5 May 1995, sec. 5, p. 1.

597. James Dobson, *Focus on the Family;* as seen in *Christian Reader,* Sept/Oct 1996, 36.

598. William Langewiesche, "The Turn," *Atlantic Monthly,* December 1993, 115–22.

599. Larry Rohter, "For the Mailmen Lost in a Maze, Amazing News," *New York Times,* 15 November 1996, sec. A, p. 6.

600. Michael Parfit, "And What Words Shall Describe the Mississippi, Great Father of Rivers?" *Smithsonian,* February 1993, 36.

601. Cheryl Lavin, "Fast Track," *Chicago Tribune Magazine,* 13 June 1993, 10.

602. Isak Dinesen, *Out of Africa* (New York: Ingram, 1988).

606. Janice Castro, "When the Chips Are Down," *Time,* 26 December 1994, 126.

608. Matthew L. Wald, "Engineer in '96 Rail Crash Hid His Failing Sight From Railroad," *New York Times,* 26 March 1997, sec. A, p. 15.

611. Kevin Dale Miller, "The Man Who Brought Pocahontas to Life," *Christian Reader,* July/Aug 1995, 41.

614. Alex Heard, "Your Twinn," *New York Times Magazine,* 21 December 1997, 21.

615. "660-pound Man Dies after Eating Piglet," *Chicago Tribune,* 17 December 1993.

616. "Stuck in Reverse, Driverless Car Snarls Traffic for 2 Hours," *Chicago Tribune,* 10 November 1994, sec. 1, p. 9.

617. Associated Press, "Internet Surfer Loses Kids over Her Obsession," *Chicago Tribune,* 17 June 1997, sec. 1, p. 13.

618. Newsmakers, "Slim Fast or Else, Miss Universe Told," *Chicago Tribune,* 20 August 1996, sec. 1, p. 2; *People,* 10 February 1997, 48–49; *People,* 29 December 1997, 160.

619. "State Trooper Guilty of Planting Bombs," *New York Times,* 6 January 1995, sec. A, p. 12.

620. "Praise for Indian Dung," *Chicago Tribune,* 8 September 1994, sec. 1, p. 4.

621. Sue Allison Massimiano and Claudia Glenn Dowling, "The Demobilization of Colin Powell," *Life,* July 1993, 43.

623. Harvey Mackay, "Avoid Contagious Business Flaw," *Chicago Tribune,* 6 December 1993, sec. 4, p. 10.

629. Lawrence Van Gelder, "Victor Riesel, 81, Columnist Blinded by Acid Attack, Dies," *New York Times,* 5 January 1995, sec. A, p. 17.

632. Gene B. Williams, *All Thumbs Guide to VCRs* (Blue Ridge Summit, Pa.: Tab Books, 1993), 1.

633. Tom Cunneff, "The Great White's Ways," *Sports Illustrated,* 15 May 1995, 8.

634. "Last Stores of Smallpox Virus Doomed," *Chicago Tribune,* 10 September 1994, sec. 1, p. 16. Donald A. Henderson, "Smallpox," *The World Book Encyclopedia* (1985).

641. Jo Thomas, "Friend Says McVeigh Wanted Bombing to Start an 'Uprising,'" *New York Times,* 13 May 1997, sec. A, p. 1.

642. *Chicago Tribune,* "Here's One for the 'Stupid Criminals' File," 23 July 1996, sec. 1, p. 7.

644. Jacquelyn Heard and William Recktenwald, "Teachers Union Springs to the Defense of Exonerated Substitute," *Chicago Tribune,* 18 May 1994, sec. 2, p. 5. *Chicago Tribune Magazine,* 1 January 1995, 16.

645. Mitchell May, "Turn of Events: Bed of Rails," *Chicago Tribune,* 10 August 1997, sec. 2, p. 6.

646. Ed Hinton, "Asleep at the Wheel," *Sports Illustrated,* 15 September 1997, 88–89.

647. Matthew L. Wald, "Fumes Knocked Out 2 Before Plane Crash," *New York Times,* 22 January 1997, sec. A, p. 16.

648. Howard Witt, "Art's Miniature Man," *Chicago Tribune,* 1 August 1993, sec. 5, p. 1.

649. John Killinger, "Finding God in a Busy World," *Preaching Today,* no. 132.

650. Henri Nouwen, *New Man;* as seen in *Christian Reader,* Nov/Dec 1996, 43–44.

655. James Barron, "Chris Farley, 33, a Versatile Comedian-Actor," *New York Times,* 19 December 1997, sec. A, p. 21; Mark Caro and Allan Johnson, "For Farley, Comedy Was His Life," *Chicago Tribune,* 21 December 1997, sec. 1, pp. 1, 20; Steve Mills, "Drug Overdose Killed Comedian Farley," *Chicago Tribune,* 3 January 1998, sec. 1, p. 1.

656. Ogilvie, *Enjoying God*, 53–54.

657. Robert Sullivan, *Life,* October 1993, 10.

658. Gary Marx, "Space Race," *Chicago Tribune,* 15 August 1993, sec. 5, pp. 1, 6.

659. Rudolph Chelminski, "Any Way You Slice It, a Poilane Loaf Is Real French Bread," *Smithsonian,* January 1995, 54, 56.

660. Hybels, *Honest to God*, 26–27.

663. Bob Condor, "A Gentler Workout," *Chicago Tribune,* 14 September 1995, sec. 5, p. 4.

664. Associated Press, "Gyroscopes Shut Down on Hobbled Mir," *Chicago Tribune,* 4 July 1997, sec. 1, p. 8.

665. Mark Galli, "Spiritual Disciplines: From Duty to Delight," *Discipleship Journal,* Nov/Dec 1993.

666. Michael A. Lev, "Injured Violinist Has a Special Kind of Pluck," *Chicago Tribune*, 22 March 1995, sec. 1, p. 1.

667. John Wimber, "John Wimber Calls It Power Evangelism," *Charisma,* September 1985, 38.

668. Richard O'Brien and Hank Hersch, "Scorecard," *Sports Illustrated,* 15 September 1997, 20.

675. William Mullen, "Right under Your Coffee, Serious Science Occurring," *Chicago Tribune,* 23 October 1997, sec. 1, p. 1.

676. "You Can Tell It's a Mink by Its Tiny Periscope," *Chicago Tribune*, 9 February 1995, sec. 1, p. 23.

677. Robert Duran, *The Christian Reader* (Jan/Feb 1993), 47.

678. John Robb with Larry Wilson, "In God's Kingdom . . . Prayer Is Social Action," *World Vision,* Feb/March 1997, 3–4.

679. Hugh Dellios, "Swimming Without the Sharks," *Chicago Tribune,* 6 July 1996, sec. 1, pp. 1, 12.

680. George Johnson, "Casting an Eye on Sights Unseen," *New York Times,* 12 October 1997, sec. 4, p. 5.

684. "MCI Worker Is Charged in Huge Phonecard Theft," *Chicago Tribune,* 4 October 1994.

685. John von Rhein, "Pulling Strings," *Chicago Tribune,* 13 June 1996, sec. 5, pp. 1, 4.

688. Nelson, *Broken in the Right Place*, 84–85.

689. Reuters, "Man Shoots Self Four Times in Head but Lives," *America Online*, 1 November 1994.

690. Paul Sitter, "Worst in a Decade," *The Parachutist,* July 1994, 21.

691. Associated Press, "3 Teens Get 15 Years for Removing Stop Sign in Fatal Prank," *Chicago Tribune,* sec. 1, p. 16.

693. "Pearl Jam Soars" and "Quotables," *Chicago Tribune*, 30 October 1993, sec. 1, pp. 21–22.

694. Stevenson Swanson, "From Death, Life," *Chicago Tribune*, 23 April 1995, sec. 5, pp. 1, 6.

696. Bob Greene, "I Know I Have at Least One Fan," *Chicago Tribune*, 15 August 1993, sec. 5, p. 1.

697. "Bone-bonding Compound Hastens Fracture Repair," *Chicago Tribune*, 24 March 1995, sec. 1, p. 15.

698. Charles Stanley, *The Wonderful Spirit Filled Life* (Nashville: Thomas Nelson, 1992), 48–49.

700. Cheryl Lavin, "The Prime Time of Bryant Gumbel," *Chicago Tribune Magazine,* 28 September 1997, 15.

705. "There Goes the Neighborhood," *Life,* November 1993, 24.

706. Jane Meredith Adams, "The Man Behind Dilbert" *Chicago Tribune,* 5 February 1996, Tempo, 1.

707. "Mattress Too Lumpy for Comfort—She Finds a Bomb under It," *Chicago Tribune,* 16 April 1983, sec. 1, p. 5.

708. Michael Lipske, "Forget Hollywood: These Bloodthirsty Beauties Are for Real," *Smithsonian,* December 1992, 49–59.

709. Lynn Austin, "Satan's Tackle Box," *The Christian Reader,* July/Aug 1994, 55–56. Abridged from *Moody.*

710. Joni Eareckson Tada, *Secret Strength* (Portland: Multnomah Press, 1988), 29–30.

714. Associated Press, "Agency Reports More Cases of Hair-Eating Doll," *New York Times,* 31 December 1996, sec. A, p. 9.

715. "Quotable," *Chicago Tribune,* 18 September 1996, sec. 4, p. 3; *Chicago Tribune,* 19 June 1997, sec. 4, p. 4.

716. *Chicago Tribune,* 29 August 1996, sec. 4, p. 10.

719. Ken Walker, "Time to Bow or Bow Out?" *Sports Spectrum,* September 1997, 22–25.

720. Charles Kuralt, *Charles Kuralt's America,* (New York: G. P. Putnam's Sons, 1995).

721. Michael Johnson, *Slaying the Dragon* (Harper Collins, 1996).

723. "Drinking the Sky," *Life,* November 1993, 80–84.

724. *Newsweek,* 20 June 1994.

726. Alan P. Xenakis, *Why Doesn't My Funny Bone Make Me Laugh?* (New York: Villard, 1993).

727. Uli Schmetzer, "Wanted Dead or Alive: Manila's Flies, Roaches," *Chicago Tribune,* 17 September 1996, sec. 1, p. 6.

728. Jerry Kramer, "Winning Wasn't Everything," *New York Times,* 24 January 1997, sec. A, p. 17.

729. Robert Bryce, "Sun-B-Gone," *New York Times Magazine,* 5 October 1997, 21.

730. "Two-Minute Drill," *Chicago Tribune,* 2 September 1996, sec. 3, p. 4.

732. "'Trapped' Yuppie Tells Why He Dropped Out," *Chicago Tribune,* 5 February 1989, sec. 1, p. 10.

733. Randy Fitzgerald, "You Can Make a Million," *Reader's Digest,* July 1996, 28.

734. Sandra Blakeslee, "A Fiery Volcano in Colombia Is Said to Be Spewing Gold," *New York Times,* 28 October 1994, sec. 1, p. 1.

737. Michael Parfit, "The Essential Element of Fire," *National Geographic,* September 1996, 118–123.

739. Drew Baker, "Alternate Routes," *Sports Spectrum,* October 1997, 12–13.

740. Susan Wloszczyna, "Actor-director Alchemy Brings Out the Best in Both," *USA Today,* 1 August 1994, sec. D, p. 4.

741. Harold Myra, *Living by God's Surprises* (Dallas: Word, 1988), 84.

742. Reuters, "This Just In," *America Online,* 11 December 1994.

743. Joe Morgenstern, "The Fifty-Nine-Story Crisis," *New Yorker,* 29 May 1995, 47.

746. Reuters, "Actor Is Hurt by Short-Circuit in 'Barney' Suit," *Chicago Tribune,* 17 July 1997, sec. 1, p. 12.

747. J. Mack Stiles, "Ready to Answer," *Discipleship Journal,* March/April 1997, 42–43.

748. Joel Brinkley, "It's All in the Details," *New York Times,* 3 March 1997, sec. C, pp. 1, 8.

750. Jorge Casuso, "Epic in the Making," *Chicago Tribune,* 5 December 1991, sec. 5, p. 1.

756. "Final Salute for Cleared 'Deserter,'" *Chicago Tribune,* 2 February 1983.

757. "Unique Lens Explains Chameleons' Super-vision," *Chicago Tribune,* 23 February 1995, sec. 1, p. 16.

761. James O'Shea, "Report Cites Mistakes by Ship, Plane," *Chicago Tribune,* 14 June 1987, sec. 1, p. 1.

762. Morgenstern, "The Fifty-Nine-Story Crisis," 45–53.

763. Ben Patterson, "Heart & Soul," *Leadership,* Fall 1996, 130.

764. Larry Dorman, "Support from around the World Overwhelms Norman," *New York Times,* 18 April 1996, sec. B, pp. 11, 14; as seen in *Reader's Digest,* September 1996, 106.

765. John Waggoner, "Templeton Celebrates, Looks to Future," *USA Today,* 1 August 1994, sec. B, p. 4.

766. Ramon Williams, "News Clips: Powerful Last Words," *Christian Reader,* July/Aug 1996, 81.

767. Anita Manning, "Anatomy of a Research Tool," *USA Today,* 29 November 1994, sec. D, p. 1.

769. "'Serial Eater' Dines in High Style on His Way to Slammer," *Chicago Tribune,* 22 May 1994, sec. 1, p. 21.

771. "Worker Chasing Hat Killed on Tollway," *Chicago Tribune,* 4 March 1995, sec. 1, p. 5.

772. Bill Moyers, *A World of Ideas* (New York: Doubleday, 1989).

774. Steve Kloehn, "Fame Has Price, and Many Are Willing to Pay It," *Chicago Tribune,* 26 April 1996, sec. 1, pp. 1, 24.

775. Alan G. Artner, "Sleuthing Uncovers Hand of a Master," *Chicago Tribune,* 17 May 1996, sec. 1, p. 1.

776. Steve Wulf, "Iron Bird," *Time,* 11 September 1995, 68–74.

777. Jeffrey Kluger, "Volcanoes with an Attitude," *Time,* 24 February 1997, 58–59.

778. Kate Eaton, "All Aboard!" *Chicago Tribune,* 4 September 1994, sec. 17, pp. 1, 5.

Subject Index

(Referenced by illustration number not page number.)

Scripture Index

(Referenced by illustration number not page number.)

1 Corinthians

2 Corinthians

Galatians

Ephesians